The Retreat of Reason

The Retreat of Reason

A Dilemma in the Philosophy of Life

INGMAR PERSSON

CLARENDON PRESS · OXFORD

OXFORD
UNIVERSITY PRESS

Great Clarendon Street, Oxford OX2 6DP

Oxford University Press is a department of the University of Oxford.
It furthers the University's objective of excellence in research, scholarship,
and education by publishing worldwide in

Oxford New York

Auckland Cape Town Dar es Salaam Hong Kong Karachi
Kuala Lumpur Madrid Melbourne Mexico City Nairobi
New Delhi Shanghai Taipei Toronto

With offices in

Argentina Austria Brazil Chile Czech Republic France Greece
Guatemala Hungary Italy Japan Poland Portugal Singapore
South Korea Switzerland Thailand Turkey Ukraine Vietnam

Oxford is a registered trade mark of Oxford University Press
in the UK and in certain other countries

Published in the United States
by Oxford University Press Inc., New York

British Library Cataloguing in Publication Data

Data available

Library of Congress Cataloging in Publication Data

Persson, Ingmar.
The retreat of reason : a dilemma in the philosophy of life / Ingmar Persson.
Includes bibliographical references and index.
1. Life. 2. Thought and thinking. 3. Reason. I. Title.
BD435.P47 2006 128—dc22 2005020151

Typeset by Newgen Imaging Systems (P) Ltd., Chennai, India
Printed in Great Britain
on acid-free paper by
Ashford Color Press Limited, Gosport, Hampshire

ISBN 0–19–927690–0 978–0–19–927690–5

1 3 5 7 9 10 8 6 4 2

CONTENTS

ACKNOWLEDGEMENTS

I suppose I would not have done philosophy as seriously if I had not thought that it could have implications for how one should live. For me philosophy would be less fascinating if it presented purely intellectual challenges or puzzles. I hope this book reflects this personality trait. Still, the way I live unfortunately reflects the conclusions of the book less than I would have liked.

Although this book project has been the focal point of my philosophical efforts for twenty years, I have failed to achieve the insight and clarity I desired. Perhaps I am able to make some further progress but not, I think, unless I get the weight of this material off my mind.

Since this book has been long in the making, it is difficult to remember everyone who has helped me along the way. But I would like to mention Roger Crisp, Jonathan Dancy, Fred Feldman, Nils Holtug, Ted Honderich, Ray Martin, Jeff McMahan, Kasper Lippert-Rasmussen, Janet Radcliffe Richards, Julian Savulescu, Peter Singer, Paul Snowdon, Galen Strawson, Larry Temkin, Michael Zimmerman and former colleagues at the Department of Philosophy, Lund University. My greatest philosophical debt is however clearly to Derek Parfit. His seminal book *Reasons and Persons* is an obvious source of inspiration. Derek also read a draft of the whole book at a midway stage and generously discussed it at great length with me. I would also like to thank two readers of OUP for valuable comments. A special thanks to my editor at the Press, Peter Momtchiloff, without whose encouragement this book would certainly not have been published now or in the near future.

Chapters 19 and 21 contain my paper "Self-doubt: Why We are Not Identical to Things of Any Kind", *Ratio* 17, December 2004. In chapter 20, there is a long argument which originally occurred in my "The Involvement of Our Identity in Experiential Memory", *Canadian Journal of Philosophy* 27, December 1997.

Gothenburg University, May, 2005   I. P.

INTRODUCTION

Some are wise, some are otherwise.
(quoted by J. S. Mill from
a newspaper)

To the general public, a philosopher seems to be, roughly, a person who seeks insight into the nature of reality, and tries to live in accordance with this insight. Philosophical *wisdom* could be taken to consist in the achievement of this aim. In ancient times, philosophers seem more or less to have corresponded to this conception (the conception may have been modelled on their example). In broad outline, they sketched a view of the world, to the effect that it was all motion, all unified or divided into two kinds of dimension, was constituted by atoms, was governed by fate, beyond knowledge, etc., and promptly proceeded to expound, against the background of this world-view of theirs, how one rationally should live. Some later philosophers, such as Spinoza and Schopenhauer, clearly conform to this pattern.[1]

In the practice of contemporary philosophers, there remains little of this ambition to let *a practical philosophy of life*, that is, of how to live, emerge out of a theoretical understanding of general features of reality. Fundamental practical principles, for example, of utility or justice, are rather left standing on their own, without any metaphysical underpinning. Theoretical inquiries, on the other hand, are rarely rounded off by an attempt to assess what impact their outcome should have on one's way of life. Often such practical conclusions are not called for, since today philosophy is so diversified and specialized that an answer to many philosophical questions will not have any implications for the business of living. An understanding of the distinction between the analytic and the synthetic, of conditionals, of their role in the analysis of causation, of the relation between intention and desire, of the relation of proper names to definite descriptions, etc., surely harbours no notable practical implications.

All the same, there are some 'big' philosophical problems the solutions to which are not in this way practically neutral or innocent. Now, it is definitive of philosophy that it is

---

[1] Cf. what John Cottingham has recently called the "synoptic" conception of ethics "as an integral part of a comprehensive philosophical system including both a scientific account of the physical world and a theory of human fulfilment" (1998: 14).

possible, within its boundaries, not only to try to solve these problems, but also to broach the question of the practical import of the solutions. Other scientific disciplines, for example theoretical physics, may deal with equally general problems (to some extent the same ones, for example about the nature of space and time). But philosophy is unique in encompassing both the theoretical and the practical dimension.

The very size and complexity of these fundamental problems of course constitute a formidable obstacle to letting an exploration of them issue in an appraisal of their practical import. This exploration itself is bound to consume so much time and energy that little may be left over for a 'derivation' of any practical precepts. Although this is a thick book, it is not nearly as thick as it would be if I were to do anything like full justice to the topics raised. So, the provisional character of the conclusions at which I arrive must be stressed. There could be no final word on how one should live in the light of philosophical truth or aware-ness of the general structure of the world, as knowledge and reflection constantly progress.

A further, more theoretical, reason for why there are few attempts to merge the theoretical and practical may be found in the widespread belief that an 'ought' cannot be derived from an 'is'. As will transpire, I share some of the intuitions behind this dictum, in particular the intuition that no recognition of any facts could logically constrain one to adopt any conative or affective attitude to them. But, first, it could force one to *give up* some attitudes on pain of being irrational since, as we shall see in Part I, some attitudes comprise factual assumptions. Second, I cannot see why philosophy must confine itself to logical truths or inferences (as the logical positivists once prescribed). Philosophers could well avail themselves of empirical generalizations, whether recognized by common sense or by psychology. Such generalizations may support claims to the effect that human persons are so constituted that, given exposure to such and such facts, their conative or affective responses will be thus and so. It is legitimate for a philosophical inquiry to appeal to such generalizations since, I believe, the whole of human society and science relies on such contingent foundations.

To get down to a more specific level, the present essay is engaged in the enterprise of fusing the theoretical and the practical in seeking a general understanding of our nature as persons existing through time and intentionally shaping our existence, with a view to finding out what attitudes to our nature this understanding makes rational or gives us most reason to adopt. This exploration of the practical implications of philosophical the-ories might be called a (practical) philosophy of life. Its leading question is: 'In the light of philosophical truth, or the most general facts of reality, what do I have most reason to aim or strive for in my life?'

The Dilemma between Fulfilment and Rationality

In ancient Greece it was apparently often assumed that living rationally, in accordance with the philosophical truth about nature, would be to lead the happiest or most fulfilling or satisfying life. If so, the above life-philosophical question would have a single, unequi-vocal answer: 'In the rational way which is also the most satisfying'. As Martha Nussbaum has pointed out (1994: e.g. ch. 1), the ancient Greek philosophers frequently compared philosophy to medicine: just as it is the physician's aim to restore patients to bodily health by the application of medical precepts, so philosophers should help patients to attain mental health and a fulfilling life by the application of reason and arguments. Among other things, she quotes an Epicurean definition of philosophy to this effect: "Philosophy is an activity that secures the flourishing [eudaimon] life by arguments and reasoning".[2] For instance, the Epicureans famously tried to show that the fear of death, which casts a long shadow over life, is irrational.

The present work, however, argues not merely that being rational, or living in the light of philosophical truth and reason, counteracts our aim for happiness in its actual form (whatever that precisely is), but that it counteracts it, *even if the latter aim be fully rationally constrained*. At least some ancient philosophers, like the Epicureans, seem to have had in mind in particular the aim for *one's own* happiness. But suppose that rationality obliges us to strive as much for the happiness of others (some may have assumed, falsely, that striving for our own happiness harmonizes with this striving). Then my claim is that making ourselves rational will not simultaneously turn us into efficient instruments to achieve this rationalized aim for happiness. This is so because many of our most entrenched attitudes will be seen to be irrational, and so the attempt to re-model ourselves according to the requirements of rationality will inevitably draw a lot of time and energy from the pursuit of the rationalized happiness aim. Thus, our irrationality is so deep and pervasive that the aim of removing it will conflict even with a rationally ironed out fulfilment aim.

This conflict raises the question of whether we have most reason to aim for satisfaction or for rationality—a question that may appear curious. For, on the one hand, it may seem evident that we have most reason to aim to be rational or to have only reason- or truth-based attitudes. On the other hand, it is a familiar idea that what we have most reason to do, or what is the rational thing to do, is that which maximizes satisfaction, especially in our own life.

The examination of the rationality of attitudes in Part II dissolves this air of paradox by distinguishing between rational attitudes in the sense, roughly, of attitudes being based on an adequate representation of everything there is reason to believe true, and attitudes that it is rational to have *given* this body of beliefs *and* certain intrinsic aims or desires, for example, an aim for fulfilment. These species of rationality will be called, respectively, the *cognitive* and the *relative* rationality of attitudes. Relative to a leading aim for fulfilment, it is rational to forbear from having cognitively rational attitudes that interfere with this aim. It is only relative to a master-aim to lead a rational life that, necessarily, it is rational to have any cognitively rational or truth-based attitude and no other.

In Part I I defend the claim that desires and emotions can be appraised as cognitively (ir)rational in the sense of being (in)compatible with what there is reason to think true, by showing that, apart from distinctive non-propositional ingredients, they necessarily have propositional contents of certain types. Because of this combination of features, they might be called 'para-cognitive' attitudes. The propositional content is also a precondition for the possession of these attitudes being assessable in terms of relative rationality.

---

[2] 1994: 15; cf. Long and Sedley (1987: 156).

It may be that these propositional underpinnings of para-cognitive attitudes are contradicted by the picture of reality that emerges as the result of philosophical reflection or scientific research. This is actually rather likely in view of the fact that our most fundamental or ubiquitous attitudes seem either to be, or to be close relatives to, elements of an instinctual make-up shared with higher non-human animals. These attitudes will consequently be geared to the beliefs of creatures with an outlook much more restricted than our present one, and it would surely not be surprising if at least some of these beliefs were revealed to be false or untenable by our current, more scientific world-view. If so, these attitudes are cognitively irrational or illusion-based.

Nonetheless, it may be rational to continue to uphold these attitudes, relative to an aim for happiness, for example, an aim to lead the happiest life, if giving them up would be disturbing enough. Although most of us have the aim to be happy, I shall, however, argue that at least some of us also have as an intrinsic and ultimate aim, one that has been held to be especially appropriate for philosophers, namely the aim to live the (cognitively) rational life in accordance with truth and reason, to scrap beliefs we discover to be false or unfounded, and para-cognitive attitudes based on them. Given the latter aim, it will of course be irrational to stick to cognitively irrational attitudes. So we may be embroiled in a conflict: there may be ways of thinking and attitudes of ours such that it is both rational and irrational for us to retain them, relative to different aims of ours.

Those who possess a dominant intrinsic desire to exhibit only patterns of thought and attitudes that are cognitively rational will be named *rationalists*. Their opponents are *satisfactionalists*. We shall first come across the latter in the shape of *prudentialists*, who are equipped with the dominant, intrinsic aim that *their own* lives—viewed temporally neutrally if they are rational—be as fulfilling as possible.[3] For rationalists, it is (relatively) rational to try to extinguish even the most deeply ingrained attitudes that do not meet the desideratum of cognitive rationality, while this enterprise is (relatively) irrational for prudentialists if this makes their lives less fulfilling.

Now, we are neither pure rationalists nor pure prudentialists, but we have, to different degrees, a streak of both dispositions in us. Therefore we face in the philosophy of how to live a *conflict* or *dilemma* because, typically, we want *both* to think and react in fashions that have a solid basis in fact *and* to lead lives that are as happy or fulfilling as possible. It is not hard to understand why we should have been equipped with a desire to seek truth and form para-cognitive attitudes in conformity with it: clearly, in many situations, having this trait enhances our chances of survival. Generally, desires that have survival value—such as desires to acquire material possessions and to make some sort of impression upon our fellow beings—presuppose that we know our current situation in the world and will keep track of how our actions will change it. To the extent we thought we lacked such knowledge, we would desire to have it and to have it impregnate our attitudes. It is equally obvious that we desire felt satisfaction or pleasure. One way to

---

[3] Prudentialism is a version of what Derek Parfit terms the *self-interest theory*, a version according to which its aim, that one's life go, for oneself, as well as possible, is analysed rather along the lines of what he calls *preference-hedonism* (1984: app. I).

gauge the importance of this desire is by noting that in most human cultures there is a practice of taking certain drugs to have pleasant, but delusory, experiences (albeit drugs can also be taken in an inquisitive spirit).

Granted that we seek pleasurable satisfaction, it might, however, be questioned whether we seek to *maximize* it, for example, seek to maximize the satisfaction of our lives. Is not our aim rather the more modest one of leading lives that are 'satisfying enough', on the lines of the 'satisficing' model advocated, for example, by Michael Slote (1989)? I agree that it is reasonable to adopt the satisficing model as regards *local* aims which compete with each other. Here the attempt to maximize the satisfaction one obtains from one aim may make one lose too much as regards other aims. But this reason for restraint does not apply to the overarching, global aim of life satisfaction. Thus, I cannot see any reason for aiming at less than maximization here (cf. Schmidtz, 1995: ch. 2).

For some, then, there is most reason to do what promotes the rational life, for others to do what promotes the most satisfying life. Those who adopt the former stance exemplify a form of *idealism*, in the sense that theirs is an aim that runs contrary to the prudentialist aim that one's own life be as satisfying as possible. Idealism can consist in the pursuit of other aims than rationality (e.g. artistic or athletic ones), but it is particularly apposite to consider the rationalist aim of living in the light of philosophical truth in the context of a quest for philosophical truth. Further, as will surface, this truth can significantly modify the satisfactionalist aim. But even a rationally modified satisfactionalism will turn out to be at odds with the aim to gain para-cognitive attitudes that are perfectly cognitively rational, though this clash compels these satisfactionalists to abandon their aim as little as rationalists are compelled to abandon their aim because it makes them more miserable than fulfilled. In compliance with one's individuality or personality, one may autonomously choose one lifestyle or the other. That is, there is room for an *individualism*, for one's individuality to express itself, in one's reply to the question of how one should live in the light of philosophical truth.

As implied, we shall first see this individualism at play in the intra-personal realm of *prudence*, in which the effects of one's actions only upon oneself are considered. Then we shall trace how it seeps into the inter-personal realm of *morality*, where this restriction is lifted, and consequences for other beings are taken into account. (But no full picture of morality is attempted.) I shall contend that, for the inter-personal domain, cognitive rationality lays down a demand of *personal neutrality* which rules out, first and foremost, one's being specially concerned about someone because that being is oneself. This requirement of course distances the aim to be rational from the prudentialist aim to maximize one's own satisfaction, but it might be thought to make the former aim an ally of the more rational satisfactionalist aim of maximizing the satisfaction of *all alike*. It will, however, be seen that this is not so, for, as the requirement of personal neutrality is based on the rational insignificance of personal identity, it permits individualism to extend beyond the intra-personal zone and invade the inter-personal one. It permits the pursuit of ideals, like rationalism, when this runs counter not only to the maximization of one's own fulfilment, but also to the maximization of the fulfilment of others.

An Objectivist or Subjectivist Framework?

I might be asked, however, whether there is not reason, for all, to rank highest either the rationalist or the satisfactionalist aim. If so, in the event of a conflict, we would all have reason to pursue the highest ranking one. In Part II, however, I argue that what is a reason for one depends on one's *desires*, in the end one's (ultimately) intrinsic desires. That is, I favour an *internalist* (or desire-based) account of reasons as opposed to an *externalist* one. Furthermore, I contend that *all* such desires provide reasons, that there is no *objective* requirement that such reasons have to meet to provide reasons.

In broad outline, the argument is this. Beliefs are designed to fit the facts of the world. This gives sense to the claim that there is something we are required to believe: the facts. Desires have the opposite direction of fit: they are formed to change the world so that *it* fits their content. For your desires to have this function, you are required to desire that which you can bring about. But that is all that is required by the direction of their fit. If you can bring it about that *p*, and can refrain from this, then it is unclear, in view of the fit of desire, what it could mean to say that you are required to desire one alternative rather than the other. For whatever you desire, there can be the requisite fit. On the other hand, if you cannot possibly bring it about that *p*, you are required not to desire to bring it about that *p*, since the requisite fit is ruled out. So, although you cannot be required to *have* any desire, there are desires you can be required *not* to have. In contrast, the fit of beliefs requires you to have beliefs that fit the facts rather than ones that do not.

Certainly, this does not amount to a conclusive proof that there is nothing that you are positively required to desire; it is well-nigh impossible to prove such a negative existential claim. But, due to the unclarity surrounding such requirements which, I conjecture, flows from their not being called for by the direction of fit of desires, these requirements, even if they exist, can probably never be so solidly established that they will possess enough authority to seriously challenge intrinsic desires widely shared, like the desires for truth and happiness. (They could exclude only desires that nobody will actually have, like Derek Parfit's Future-Tuesday-Indifference, to be discussed in Part III.) It is most likely that, according such requirements, both truth and happiness would come out as non-hierarchically ordered objectives, both of which we are required or permitted to desire. Otherwise, these requirements could scarcely earn credibility for, in the absence of considerations of fit, it seems that they have to earn their credibility by conforming to intrinsic desires that we already hold. Therefore, in relation to our fundamental para-cognitive attitudes, these requirements will have to be *compliant*, never *commanding*.

It follows that, with respect to our dilemma of rationalism and satisfactionalism, no appeal to objectivism will resolve it. Now, since I am at a loss to construe objectivism, and little would be gained for my purposes by assuming its truth, I shall proceed on the basis of the more parsimonious subjectivist assumption that there are no objective constraints on reason-grounding intrinsic desires. In any event, however, when the rationalist and a satisfactionalist life-style diverge, there is no reason valid for all, independently of the orientation of their intrinsic desires, to pursue one lifestyle rather than the other.

This subjectivism also defines (intrinsic) *value* in terms of what satisfies (ultimately intrinsic) desires. Accordingly, all values will in some sense be values *for* some subject (of desires). But we shall also be in need of a narrower notion of a value *for* a subject, in terms of which the fulfilment of those of one's desires that are in some sense *self-regarding*, but not, for example, those that are other-regarding, is good for oneself. I shall say that a desire is 'self-regarding' if the content of it contains an in a certain way ineliminable reference to the subject having the desire. In this sense, the prudentialist aim is self-regarding, since it is to the effect that *oneself* reap maximal fulfilment.

To say that one's desires are fulfilled does not imply that one *experiences* any fulfilment. Of course, if one desires to obtain certain experiences, for example of pleasure and pain (these experiences will be scrutinized in the first two chapters), one must necessarily have experiences of these kinds for one's desire to be fulfilled. Typically, when such desires are fulfilled, one will also be aware of this fact, and this will affect one's desire, so that it gives way to an experience of satisfaction or pleasure.

As opposed to this *experiential* kind of fulfilment, there is *a purely factual* notion of fulfilment consisting simply in that there is in fact something matching the object of a desire, and not entailing that the subject is aware of this fact. As it is doubtful whether we spontaneously desire a life that scores high with respect to factual fulfilment, I shall in speaking of the prudentialist aim of leading the maximally fulfilling life understand fulfilment in the experiential sense. (In practice, this may make little difference since, as will transpire, prudentialists will strive to have, as far as possible, desires that are experientially fulfilled whenever they are factually fulfilled.)

Psychological hedonism implies that all one's self-regarding (ultimately) intrinsic desires are to the effect that one obtain or avoid certain experiences, experiences that feature qualities of pleasure and pain, respectively. I argue in Part I that psychological hedonism is false and that there are self-regarding intrinsic desires for other things than one's own experiences, and consequently for other things than one's own hedonic experiences. There are also non-self-regarding intrinsic desires. To refute psychological hedonism may seem to be like shooting a dead duck, but it is worth doing since, as we shall see, its falsity supports the claim that it is not in any sense irrational to reject the aim of satisfactionalism, whether in the prudential or in the personally neutral shape, in favour of some ideal, like rationalism. For if one intrinsically desires other things than one's own pleasure, one may desire this more strongly than pleasure. Then one's master-aim may not be to make one's life as full of pleasure or (felt) satisfaction as possible, and we have seen that there is no objectivist, externalist norm requiring it to be so. Thus, to have as one's master-aim the rationalist aim that one's attitudes be as cognitively rational as possible is rationally permissible.

Ideals, like the rationalist aim, may or may not be self-regarding (as will emerge in Part IV, if they are self-regarding, they will have to be derivable from desires that do not refer to the subjects themselves if they are to be rationally defensible). But even a purely factual fulfilment of non-self-regarding desires is of value for subjects, in the broader, subjectivist sense. We may call this *impersonal* value in contrast to the *personal* value of something satisfying a self-regarding desire. Personal values are thus values *for* subjects in a double sense. Pleasure is one thing of personal value for us, but not the only thing, since it is not the only thing we intrinsically desire to have.

Suppose that the rationalist desire to be cognitively rational rather than a prudentialist desire to lead the most fulfilling life is now one's dominant aim. Then what is now best for one may not be what is inter-temporally most fulfilling for one. There will be a clash if the rationalist aim demands the eradication of cognitively irrational attitudes whose eradication will decrease inter-temporal fulfilment, owing to the fact that they are so deeply rooted in our constitution. Parts III, IV, and V explore three such clashes between rationalism and a satisfactionalism that is gradually tightened up rationally.

Temporal Biases

Part III discusses whether *the temporal location* of things with value for us is of rational importance. Being persons, we are conscious of ourselves as subjects of experience and desire existing not only at the present time, but also in the past and the future and, consequently, of things being (in the broad sense) good and bad for us not only in the present, but also in the past and future. Now it is a well-known fact that, in appraising values located at different times, we display various biases, for example, we are spontaneously inclined to be *biased towards the near future* and to prefer a closer, smaller good to a more distant, greater good. Yet prima facie it seems cognitively irrational to regard such differences purely in timing as evaluatively significant. This impression is indeed borne out, but not by there being any underlying belief about temporal facts that philosophical analysis reveals to be cognitively irrational. The cause of the irrationality is instead that these facts induce us to represent things in distorted ways.

It follows that rationalists are obliged to rid themselves of the bias towards the near. It might seem that rational (as opposed to naïve) prudentialists would have to agree because they must be temporally neutral as regards their self-interest, as this bias is likely to make one's life on the whole worse by exaggerating the importance of some parts of one's life at the expense of other parts. Nonetheless, there is a conflict between rationalism and prudentialism for, as this bias is so deep-seated, it will not be relatively rational for prudentialists to embark upon the project of obliterating it completely.

Moreover, the bias towards the near is not the only temporal bias under which we labour: there is also *a bias towards the future* which upgrades the future in relation to the past. Since this bias cannot induce us to act contrary to the goal of a temporally neutral maximization of our own fulfilment, (rational) prudentialists have less of a reason to wish to be liberated from it. Rationalists are, however, obliged to extinguish it in order to attain the full temporal neutrality which is cognitively rational. This is likely to be a life-long occupation which is detrimental to the aim of the inter-temporal maximization of one's own satisfaction. Therefore, as regards temporal attitudes, there is, given our actual psychology, a clash between what is the (relatively) rational course for rationalists and for (rational) prudentialists. Still, the rationalists' pursuit of temporal neutrality as an ideal in the sense of something to be pursued even when it runs counter to the inter-temporal maximization of their own fulfilment is no less rationally permitted than this prudentialist pursuit. There is, then, in the intra-personal domain of prudence, no master-aim that all of us have most reason to adopt.

The Bias towards Oneself

A second region of strife, discussed in Part IV, is intimately related to the first one. When confronting the problem of the extent to which one's future good or satisfaction merits one's present concern, one will come up against not only the relevance of the fact of its temporal location, but also the relevance of the fact that it is *one's own*. Spontaneously, one is strongly disposed to be *biased towards oneself*, that is, one is more anxious to see to it that a desire be fulfilled if it is *one's own* rather than somebody else's. In this part I shall contend that an analysis of the concept of our identity through time reveals this difference to be without rational importance and, hence, this bias to be cognitively irrational. The bias towards oneself will, however, be seen to be based not directly on the thought that this fact of identity obtains, but on the exaggerated vividness of the representation of one's own future experiential states with which this thought is associated.

If so, the prudentialist aim of seeking to maximize the fulfilment of certain desires because they are one's own is cognitively irrational. Rational satisfactionalists will have to be personally neutral as well as temporally neutral. But, obviously, satisfactionalists cannot take on board personal neutrality and still remain prudentialists as they can take on board temporal neutrality. This change will instead turn them into *inter-personal* or *personally neutral* satisfactionalists whose aim is to maximize the fulfilment of *everyone's* desires. As regards personal partiality, there is then a head-on opposition between prudentialism and rationalism, while their opposition as regards temporal partiality is merely a result of the contingent fact that this partiality is so deeply rooted in our nature that it is counter-productive for prudentialists to try to dispose of it completely.

In the inter-personal sphere of morality, rationalism and personally (and temporally) neutral satisfactionalism are related to each other roughly as, in the intra-personal sphere of prudence, rationalism is related to (temporally neutral) prudentialism. Rationalists are committed to try to eradicate the bias towards oneself, however ravaging the psychological scars will be. In contrast, it will probably not be (relatively) rational for personally neutral satisfactionalists to try to completely wipe out this bias, since this elimination project may disturb their personality to the extent that they become less efficient in contributing to their goal. Still, it will probably be rational for them to 'trim' this bias. So there is a conflict between the rationalist and the satisfactionalist pursuit even if the latter is cognitively rationally constrained to the extent of incorporating not only temporal, but also personal, neutrality.

Again, this does not imply that we have more reason to choose one pursuit rather than the other. For rationalists, striving to have personally neutral attitudes is a legitimate ideal. As it is rationally permissible to be a rationalist idealist in the intra-personal domain of prudence, it is permissible to be so in the inter-personal sphere of morality. This follows from my analysis of personal identity in the first half of Part IV which reveals it to be rationally insignificant. Since the distinction between ourselves and others is rationally insignificant, we may in the moral domain handle the life and desires of another (relevantly alike) individual as in the prudential domain we may rationally handle our own life and desires. For instance, as we may contravene the inter-temporal maximization of our own fulfilment in the name of some ideal, we may contravene the inter-temporal fulfilment maximization of another. In itself, the fact that it is another rather than oneself is irrelevant.

Hence, we see that the conflict between prudentialism and rationalism in the realm of prudence spills over into the moral realm. Individualism, having gained a foothold in prudence, can march into the moral domain as well, since personal identity is rationally unimportant. The fact that inter-personal maximization is not rationally required in the moral sphere or, alternatively expressed, that idealism is admissible, shows that a *moral individualism* is true. There is, in neither of these spheres, any aim that we all have most reason to adopt as there presumably would be if the aims of rationalism and satisfactionalism had coincided.

In the final chapters of Part IV, I shall say something about the resources we have to resolve the conflicts moral individualism allows. These resources have to do with the fact that we are mutually dependent upon each other and that we would not have survived as a species if our individual variations had been too great for co-operation to be possible. Such pressures may incline us to set aside our possible ideals in our dealings with others and promote their leading the sort of lives they at the present time autonomously choose, whether they be rationalists or satisfactionalists. But I do not try to establish that a consensus will result; the point is only that the cognitively rational requirement of personal neutrality does not imply that there is a single kind of life—not even if it is indeterminately specified as the kind of life they autonomously choose to lead—that we have most reason to have others leading. Our autonomy encompasses not only our own life, but extends to our handling of the lives of others. If, contrary to fact, the most fulfilling life were also cognitively rational, so that this life would be, for each of us, the one we ourselves had most reason to lead, it would also be the one we had most reason to have others leading.

Responsibility and Desert

Part V reviews a final conflict, regarding our attitudes with respect to *responsibility and desert*. A main contention is that, although our talk of responsibility to a considerable degree is compatible with determinism, it contravenes this doctrine by encapsulating claims of desert. A precondition for such claims being true of us is, I maintain, that we are self-determined in a sense that contradicts both indetermination and determination by causes external to our responsibility and control. It may appear that such an assumption of self-determination requires extravagant postulates about a self who can act as a 'first cause'. But I argue that it is of a more negative character, requiring merely an *absence* of causal speculation. This *epistemic* notion of self-determination is presupposed when desert-related emotions such as anger and gratitude, pride and shame, admiration and contempt, envy, remorse, and feelings of guilt are felt. I also hypothesize that assessments of desert can be construed as outgrowths of such emotions, in particular, anger and gratitude.

But the notion of desert, so construed, is nothing that rationalists, who must relentlessly pursue causal inquiry, will employ, irrespective of whether determinism reigns in the realm of mind and action or there are gaps of indeterminism in it. It follows that rationalists are rationally constrained to give up thinking in terms of desert and exhibiting desert-related emotions. But it is evident that these emotions, like the biases towards the future and the near and towards ourselves, are engraved in the depth of our being, that it is hard to the point of being well-nigh impossible to erase them. Consequently, the stage is set for another collision between rationalism and satisfactionalism even if the latter aim be rationally cleansed.

We are, however, now brought to query whether satisfactionalism, thus cleansed, will in the inter-personal realm amount to an inter-personal (and inter-temporal) *maximization* of satisfaction or whether some distributive pattern must also be imposed. For the notion of desert is linked to that of *justice*: it is just to receive what one deserves, other things being equal. But it should not be taken for granted, as utilitarians traditionally appear to have done, that a rejection of desert means a rejection of justice. This is not so if there is a formal principle of justice laying down that a state is just if and only if individuals fare equally well, unless there are reasons, like deserts, making it just that they fare unequally well. If all such reasons for inequality lack application, the conclusion that follows is not that justice must be rejected, too, but that there is justice if and only if all fare equally well.

It is not part of the objective of this book to work out how egalitarian considerations should shape the goal of inter-personal maximization, to answer, for example, questions about when one inequality is worse than another and how to weigh sums of fulfilment against degrees of inequality in the distribution of it. The point is just to bring out that, if an egalitarian maximization to the effect of all being as equally well off as possible on as high a level as possible, unless they autonomously choose otherwise, is the result of rationalizing the goal of satisfactionalism, there will still be a tension between this goal and a rationalism which demands discarding all desert-related emotions along with the concept of desert. For the self-absorption and psychological disruption that the attempt at this removal involves will hinder the effective implementation of the goal of egalitarian maximization. So, in all likelihood, it is relatively rational for egalitarian maximizers to keep something of the desert-equipment, whereas it is rational for those who pursue rationalism as an ideal to try to weed it out completely.

The Two Meanings of 'Retreat of Reason'

Consider a person who succeeds in complying with the requirements of cognitive rationality, that is, a person who is not subject to temporal and personal biases and desert-related emotions. Such a person will be most like some sages and 'world-renouncers' depicted in religious literature, perhaps especially of the East. It is suitable to speak of such a person as having entered a retreat, namely *a retreat of reason*. This provides one of the senses of the title of this book. But although this is the rational life, without cognitively irrational attitudes, we are not rationally required to adopt it. We are (relatively) rationally required to strive for this sort of life given that we are in the grip of a dominant rationalist desire, but not, for example, if our main aim is that of satisfactionalism, even if this aim be rationally regimented—and there is nothing making us rationally required to have one leading aim rather than the other.

Given even a master-aim of rationally purified satisfactionalism, it will not be rational to fully internalize the requirements of temporal and personal neutrality and to dispose of the concept of desert and related emotions. There is a point at which it will be rational relative to this aim to, so to speak, let reason retreat or withdraw, to restrain the quest for knowledge and/or cease to dwell upon truths with a mind to having them impregnate one's para-cognitive attitudes. This constitutes the other sense of 'the retreat of reason', namely that of reason retreating (from the ruling position in one's personality). The extent of this withdrawal of reason will vary in relation to how rationally regimented satisfactionalism is—for example whether it be prudentialist and incorporates only temporal neutrality, or it incorporates personal neutrality and a rational conception of justice, as well—but the withdrawal will never shrink to nothing.

The chief objective of the present essay is to display that rationalism diverges from satisfactionalism or the pursuit of fulfilment or happiness, even if the latter pursuit is rationally regimented, and to contend that, despite this conflict, neither aim is irrational. A consequence of this dilemma is that, in the intra-personal sphere of prudence, there is no kind of life that everyone has best reason to have. Nor is there, in the inter-personal sphere of morality, any kind of life that we all have best reason to see others have (such as, the kind of life that contains as much satisfaction as possible, compatibly with as equal a distribution between lives as possible). To be rational in the inter-personal or moral domain is not necessarily to be a philanthropist, a do-gooder, who aims to do what is best and just for others; it may take the idealist shape of a more intellectual, philosophical life, also aimed at making one's para-cognitive attitudes concord with truth.

My presentation of this dilemma shows that it arises even if one affirms a view of the world that is completely 'naturalistic' in the sense that everything in the world can be described by empirical science, so that, for instance, there are no non-empirical selves to which we are identical and which (non-deterministically) direct our actions, and no values irreducible to natural phenomena such as para-cognitive attitudes. As already remarked, I do not think that naturalism with respect to value is necessary for the dilemma to arise. For, even if there were some objective requirements of practical rationality, it is most unlikely that they would rank the aims of rationalism and satisfactionalism relative to each other. More likely, they would sanction, in a non-hierarchical fashion, both of these aims, as well as any other widespread aims—or suffer a fatal loss of authority or credibility.

We would not be in this predicament if a life in harmony with philosophical truth and reason did not necessitate a major attitudinal reform. It is seemingly often taken for granted that the cognitive groundings of our fundamental para-cognitive attitudes must be more or less sound. Then it could scarcely be so hard for us to make rationally required adjustments that it could wreak havoc on our rational satisfactionalist aims. But I believe that this comfort—offered by various forms of ethical intuitionism—is denied us: philosophical explorations can reveal our most deep-rooted attitudes to be radically misguided. The persistence of the self through time and its self-determination do not meet the standards the justifiability of these attitudes calls for. The cognitive irrationality of our para-cognitive attitudes is so profound and large-scale that eradicating it will be at odds with even a completely rationalized satisfactionalist aim. Hence, if reason does not retreat from controlling our attitudes, it will force us to retreat from these attitudes.

PART I

The Nature of Para-cognitive Attitudes

1

PAIN AS A
SENSORY QUALITY

IN this part my chief objective is to explore the nature and rationality of what I shall call *para-cognitive attitudes*, namely desires and emotions. I shall, however, start by examining *sensations* of pain and pleasure or, in other words, *bodily* pains and pleasures. The reason for this is that I agree with David Hume's statement: "Bodily pains and pleasures are the source of many passions, both when felt and consider'd by the mind" (1739–40/1978: 276). More precisely, I hold there to be sensory qualities of pleasure and pain the exemplification of which forms the object of a fundamental class of our intrinsic or underived para-cognitive attitudes (cf. Audi, 2001: 86).

The doctrine of *psychological hedonism* affirms that *all* intrinsic desires and emotions take as their objects the instantiation of these qualities of pleasure and pain, that pleasure is the *only* thing sought for its own sake and pain the *only* thing shunned for its own sake. In assessing this doctrine, it is vital to distinguish the pleasure which is the *object* of a desire from the pleasure which is *consequential* upon the desire's (believed) satisfaction (and would be so even if the object of the desire is not pleasure) and which may be the object of a *higher-order* desire. For if one confuses the idea that pleasure is always consequential upon the (believed) fulfilment of one's desires, with the idea that pleasure can be the object of desire, one may slide to the hedonist thesis that the object of desire must ultimately be pleasure, that other things we obviously desire are only means to pleasure. Once such confusions are cleared up, all credibility of psychological hedonism evaporates, or so I shall argue in Chapter 3.

This finding is of importance in the present context, for if psychological hedonism were true, then, as regards one's own life, there might be no rational alternative to prudentialism. For suppose that the only thing we desire for its own sake was exemplifications of pleasure; then, with respect to one's own life, the only rational course might well be to desire that it contain as much pleasure as possible, whether this be bodily pleasure or the emotional pleasure of happiness and fulfilment. On the other hand, if there are other things or qualities we desire for their own sakes, prudentialism will be the supremely rational course only if there is a reason why we should not desire any of these things more than pleasure, should not be ready to undergo a loss of pleasure for their sakes (and I shall contend that there is no such reason).

The Sensory Quality View of Pain

Sensations of pain will be discussed first because the view I shall take on the nature of hedonic sensations is less controversial here than in the case of pleasure. I shall term this view *the sensory quality view*, SQ. This is the tenet that a sensation of pain is a sensation with a special intrinsic property of painfulness, just as a sensation of warmth or sphericality is a sensation exemplifying a property of warmth or sphericality. SQ has been advocated by many contemporary philosophers, including R. M. Hare (1969) and Roger Trigg (1970).

A sentence like 'A subject, *A*, is feeling—or has a sensation of—something hot' could describe either how something feels to *A* or how something that *A* is feeling is *really* like (or a combination of both). Read in the former way, it is a report of the *content* of *A*'s feeling or of what she is *immediately* feeling.[1] In contrast, the sentence 'A has a sensation of pain' will unequivocally be understood as describing the content of *A*'s sensation, for we do not even pre-reflectively adopt the view that the quality of painfulness can inhere in a physical thing as we adopt the view that the quality of heat can (though it may not in fact) inhere in it.

The reason that we are not tempted to think that pain inheres in *external* objects as we are tempted to think that heat does is not entirely clear. I suggest that it has do with the fact that the quality of being painful does not 'mesh' with spatial qualities in the way thermal qualities do. An object that is tactually felt to have spatial qualities *must* have some thermal quality as well, but it need not possess any hedonic quality like painfulness. (The latter quality is instead 'supervenient' upon the former ones in a sense I will soon try to explicate.) The reason is not, I believe, that, even when pain is caused by contact with some external object, we always feel it *in our own bodies*, since this seems true of heat as well. For instance, the sensation of heat may continue, even though the contact with its source is broken, no less than a sensation of pain.

Another difference between sensations of pain and of heat is this. When one feels a pain somewhere in one's body, for example in the ears, one is not inclined to think that one's ears really exemplify the property of being painful as one is inclined to think that they are really warm when one feels them to be so. This is probably due to the fact that other subjects can often tactually feel one's ears to be warm by touching them—as, indeed, one can oneself do—when one inwardly feels them to be so.

This shows that sensations of pain in a body are tied to a perception of that body that is unique to one subject, to wit, the subject whose body the body in question is said to be. I have elsewhere (1985*a*: ch. 4.5) contended that every conscious being perceives its own body in a unique way, 'from the inside' (this form of perception will assume great

---

[1] I discuss immediate perception in (1985*a*: ch. 1.2).

significance in Part IV). In the content of this perception, the body is given as a three-dimensionally solid thing. I now claim that one's pains are located in this phenomenal 3-D solid. Since no other subject feels one's body from the inside as a 3-D solid, no other subject experiences one's pains that are located in it.

As a rule, how one's body is felt to be in this unique perception is not at odds with how it appears to outer senses and how it really is according to the realism of common sense. This may obscure the true location of pains. But in some cases, such as the cases of amputees who suffer from so-called phantom limbs, there is a discrepancy that is revealing. With respect to pain felt in a phantom limb, Ronald Melzack writes:

> the pain may resemble, in both quality and location, the pain that was present before the amputation . . . Thus, a patient who was suffering from a wood sliver jammed under a finger nail, and at the same time lost his hand in an accident, subsequently reported a painful sliver under the finger nail of his phantom hand. (1973: 55–6)

The phantom limb experience consists in having a perception of one's body from the inside the content of which presents this body as having a limb that, in fact, it has now lost. The phantom limb pain is located in the sensory content of this missing part. Since "the pain may resemble, in both quality and location, the pain that was present before the amputation", it is reasonable to conclude that it has all the while been located in the content of this unique perception of a body from the inside.

It lies outside the scope of the present essay to inquire whether, despite such possibilities of illusion, the 3-D immediately perceived could normally *be* one's physical body or whether it always is something that merely in a Lockean fashion represents this body. But I have tried (1985*a*: ch. 5.2) to specify the conditions under which something immediately perceived is part of physical reality. In the present connection, it is pertinent to point out that these conditions must be such that, even if the 3-D immediately perceived is physical in nature, it does not follow that everything located in it—including pains—is physical.

So, when one is feeling a pain somewhere in one's body, the property of painfulness is exemplified in that region as immediately perceived from the inside. This property is simple and unanalysable. Like other simple, sensory features one can only get to know painfulness fully by immediately perceiving instances of it: "It is however as impossible to describe the quality of pain as it is to describe any other unanalysable quality like redness" (Trigg, 1970: 26). Nonetheless, even if one cannot verbally spell out what the property of painfulness is intrinsically like, what it is like in itself, one can characterize the relations that instances of it typically bear to other property-exemplifications.

The Supervenience of Painfulness

Of necessity, it is never the case that a sensation is just painful: a pain must also be cutting, or stinging, burning, throbbing, ripping, etc. A sensation's possessing the quality of painfulness is dependent upon its possessing some quality of the latter kind in a way that its possessing a quality of the latter range is not dependent upon its being painful. Suppose that you have a sensation of heat that is painful, that is, a sensation that is painfully hot; then you can imagine what it would be like to have this sensation just as it is in every other way, except that it is not painful. In contrast, you can form no intelligible notion of what it would be like to feel a sensation which would be exactly like this one, in respect of painfulness and all, except that it lacked the quality of heat. When a quality in this asymmetric fashion is dependent upon another, I shall say that the exemplification of the former property is, to use a fashionable term, *supervenient* on the exemplification of the other feature. I define this relation as follows:

(S) A quality F (e.g. of painfulness) is a supervenient quality of a sensation if, and only if, (1) F is an intrinsic quality of the sensation, (2) it is a logically necessary truth that if a sensation is endowed with F then it has some other intrinsic quality, G, but (3) it is logically possible that the sensation be just as it is, with G, save that it lacks F.

Contrast this relation of supervenience with a case of symmetrical dependence. A sensation of heat must also have certain spatial features, a certain (even if diffuse) tactile size and form. Here, however, the converse also holds: a sensation that has a certain tactile form and size must also possess some thermal feature: the geometrical pattern felt must be 'covered' by some thermal quality (or in the case of a pattern seen, some colour). One cannot remove the quality of heat, without replacing it by any other thermal quality, and still have an imaginable sensation. Hence, the dependence between spatial and thermal qualities of sensations does not qualify as supervenience because it does not satisfy condition (3). It is bilateral in a way the relation of supervenience must not be.

Supervenience as here defined should not be confused with other conceptions of it found in the literature. These other conceptions of supervenience involve the idea that if F is supervenient on G then it is nomologically or at least contingently necessary that if anything has G then it has F as well.[2] I do not dispute the usefulness of such an explication of the notion of supervenience, but it is unsuitable for my purposes because I want to use the notion to give phenomenological descriptions of the content of immediate perception. It may be that there is a nomological relationship underlying, for example the heat of a sensation and its painfulness, but if so, this is nothing immediately perceived. That is, my phenomenological conception of supervenience does not *demand* the presence of such a connection, though it is compatible with it.

The property of painfulness is analogous to the property of being dazzling. A light cannot be just dazzling; it must have other features like being of a certain colour, but it can be conceived to possess these features without being dazzling. Suppose that you perceive a dazzling white light; you can then imagine what it would be like to perceive this white light without it being dazzling, but you cannot remove its whiteness, leaving the impression in every other respect—including its being dazzling—intact. A light must necessarily have some colour.

---

[2] See e.g. Blackburn (1988), Hare (1989), and Kim (1984, 1985).

A light becomes dazzling by reaching a certain intensity, and there must be some underlying quality that has this intensity. Similarly, I propose, a sensation acquires the property of being painful by reaching a certain intensity—usually the intensity that is correlated with the stimulus beginning to do harm to the body. In the case of every painful sensation, it seems to me possible to conceive of a qualitatively similar sensation of a lower intensity, a sensation that as a result lacks the quality of painfulness.

Feeling and Being Aware of Feeling

The fact that a sensation possesses this supervenient feature of painfulness leads to its having characteristic effects. A sensation of pain exercises an influence on attention that is roughly proportionate to the intensity of its painfulness: the more intensely painful it is, the stronger its hold on attention, all other things being equal.[3] If a pain is very mild, or pretty mild, but monotonous, and one perceives other things that may attract one's attention, one may 'forget' about the pain, that is, not think about, or attend to, it at all. But a pain from which one is distracted is still being felt; it does not stop to return when attention is again directed at it.

This is often enough denied. For instance, D. M. Armstrong declares:

> An 'unfelt bodily sensation', I suggest, is *a permanent but unfulfilled possibility of feeling a certain sort of sensation*. To say that I have a headache, but that I am not feeling it, is to say that something is engaging my attention, and that if it were to stop engaging my attention, I would feel a headache. But it does not imply that there is a headache going on in any more substantial sense than this. (1962: 51; cf. Trigg, 1970: e.g. 95)

To begin with, let me draw attention to the question-begging manner in which Armstrong (and, following him, Trigg) presents the issue. As is apparent from the quotation just given, Armstrong speaks of "unfelt bodily sensations" when the correct phrase would be 'unnoticed (or unattended) bodily sensations'. Without further ado a sensation to which the subject does not attend is identified with a sensation that is not felt. Thus, Armstrong writes:

> We may pay little attention to our sensations, we may scarcely feel them, but we cannot dispense with feeling them altogether. If we do not *feel* a sensation at all, then we do not *have* that sensation. (1962: 49)

To be sure, it sounds paradoxical to speak of a sensation that one has but does not feel. However, what is at stake is whether it is possible to have or feel a sensation to which one does not *attend* at all, and I fail to see anything paradoxical in affirming this. Armstrong loads the dice in his favour by conflating these two claims.

To see how implausible Armstrong's doctrine that an unnoticed pain is a pain that the subject does not feel, but only would feel if its attention were not engaged by other

---

[3] As opposed to Trigg (1970: 46), I take this to be a contingent rather than a logical truth.

things, consider another immediately perceived item that exercises less attraction on attention than pain. Suppose that I do not attend to a sound because it has been going on monotonously for quite some time. Then it is normally the case that, if the sound abruptly stops, my attention straightaway turns to the fact of its absence. (Indeed, the stopping of the sound will make me realize not merely that I am not now hearing it, but that I have just *stopped* hearing it—which implies that I did hear it the moment before.) On the other hand, imagine that I plug my ears not to hear the sound: if it then stops, this fact will not capture my attention. Consequently, in the former case the sound must stand in some relation to my mind in which it does not stand to my mind in the latter case. It is natural to hold that this relation is hearing: I hear the sound (albeit I do not attend to it) only in the former case. It is the fact that I suddenly cease to hear the sound that alerts my attention. On Armstrong's view, however, what is the case is not that, up to a moment ago, I actually heard the sound, but that I *would* hear it were certain counter-factual conditions to obtain (i.e. were my attention not engaged by other things). This makes one wonder how the fact that this conditional ceases to be true of me could have the power to affect my attention when the fact that many similar conditionals (e.g. that I would hear the sound if my ears were not plugged) cease to be true of me does not affect my attention. An instance of hearing that is conditional on the former conditions is no more actual or real than an instance that is dependent on the latter circumstances.

If this does not convince the reader of the absurdity of Armstrong's view, I must refer to another work of mine (1985a: ch. 3.1) where I argue at greater length that there is a sensory order distinct in kind from the conceptual one of thinking, attending, etc. From this it follows not merely that it is false that, if one feels a sensation (or more generally, immediately perceives something), one must necessarily notice and (to some extent) attend to it. It also follows that the converse, the incorrigibility thesis—namely, that if one *thinks* that one is feeling a certain type of sensation (immediately perceives something of a certain kind), one *is* feeling a sensation of that type (*does* immediately perceive something of that kind)—is untenable.

Trigg embraces the incorrigibility thesis with respect to pains: "If I think that I am feeling pain, then I am feeling pain" (1970: 86). Discussing "the well-known case of someone flinching under a dentist's drill, apparently in pain, when the drill has not yet touched him", he claims that if the patient

> insisted he had felt pain, we are in no position to contradict him on the grounds that there was no apparent physical cause. Ultimately only he can tell us whether he was in pain or not. (1970: 8–9)

Considering a similar case, Armstrong is strongly tempted to adopt the same attitude as Trigg, but he adds that he is ready to accept "error, within limits" (1962: 55).

It seems to me obvious that Armstrong's concession is necessary if the view is to have any semblance of cogency. It is surely a patent fact that certain factors—desires and emotions, preconceptions, carelessness, weariness, etc.—can cause us to misclassify our sensations. Take for instance a case discussed by Armstrong: you have been told by your doctor that a pain you have felt in the vicinity of your heart is a symptom of a serious heart condition. Now imagine that you feel a stab of a similar sort in the same region; then, in your upset state of mind, you might well take the new pain to be exactly similar to the old one in both quality and location. If prolonged attention to the pain is possible, you will in all probability rectify your mistake. Trigg will, however, have to say that this misdescribes the case: if your opinion on the nature of the pain changes, then the pain itself changes. That is certainly counter-intuitive.

If one grants Armstrong's concession, however, one will have to admit that thinking that one is feeling a certain sensation does not constitute feeling that sensation, that the latter is distinct from the former and that the relations between them have a contingent character. It is simply that, *as a matter of fact*, people are not fallible to the extent that they are capable of making very gross mistakes about their sensations. This is something that I could happily accept.

Reactions to Pain

Sensations of pain have other typical effects than those on attending and thinking, effects that are more conspicuous, for they consist in certain bodily reactions. Some of these are not under direct voluntary control: one starts to sweat, one's heart begins to beat more quickly, one's blood vessels contract, one's blood pressure rises, one turns pale and weak. Other bodily responses consist in patterns of behaviour that can be intentionally executed as basic actions (though they may not be so executed when they occur as responses to pain):[4] one tries to withdraw from the source of the pain (if it is external), one may tend to protect or keep still the limb injured, one may rub it, one's body grows tense, one grimaces, one clenches one's teeth and fists, one digs the finger nails into the palms of one's hands, one screams or groans.

Some of these potentially intentional forms of behaviour are obviously designed to eliminate or minimize both the sensation of pain and the bodily harm of which it is normally a sign, for example the withdrawal from the source of the pain and the keeping still of the limb injured. Others may seem to be designed to fit neither of these ends, but they may all the same have at least the function of mitigating the sensation of pain. There is experimental evidence indicating that, if the stimulation of other receptors increases, the sensitivity of the ones that originally caused one to feel pain decreases: that, for example, "vibration decreases the perceived intensity of mild or moderate levels of pain" (Melzack, 1973: 110). Applications of new painful stimuli are known to have an even greater power to lessen sensitivity to a pain already felt (Melzack, 1973: 183). Therefore, it is not improbable that by boosting the sensory input overall, behaviour patterns such as rubbing the bodily part injured, flexing the muscles, digging the nails into the palms, and screaming have the function of reducing the intensity of a pain felt. In any event, it is beyond question that sensations of pain elicit some behavioural responses that can be

---

[4] A basic action is an act that one performs without performing it by performing any other action: for instance, one may cause the shadow of one's arm to move by moving one's arm, but the latter action is normally done without one's doing it by means of anything else. For further details and references, see Persson (1981: e.g. ch. 2.4).

said to be *negative* responses to these sensations in the sense that they are designed to eliminate or alleviate them.

These bodily reactions, including the non-voluntary ones, are, however, not only caused by *sensations* of pain; they are also caused by *thoughts* to the effect that one is now feeling pain, regardless of whether these thoughts are true or false. Trigg's example of a person flinching under the dentist's drill, in spite of the fact that it has not touched him, is not unrealistic. If one takes a traditional empiricist tack and is willing to grant that thoughts of the form 'I am feeling pain at present' can be coded in 'images' or sensuous representations that so to speak are copies of, or isomorphic with, sense-impressions, it is not hard to understand how such thoughts can have effects similar to the ones of actual sensations. Given that the states of feeling pain and thinking that one is feeling pain can be as like each other in intrinsic respects as you please, and differ essentially only in respect of their causal ancestry—the latter typically being caused by the former[5]—it is not surprising that their effects can be similar, for these are determined by intrinsic features of the causes.

Not only thoughts to the effect that one *is* feeling pain *at present* have the power to call forth these bodily reactions, but also thoughts to the effect that one *will* feel pain—on the proviso that one does not believe that one will not then be averse to the pain felt. (In Part IV this future-oriented concern will be closely examined.) From an evolutionary point of view it is easy to comprehend why it is that we are equipped with this future-oriented concern. It is reasonable to hypothesize that the capacity to conceptually register sensations and other items immediately perceived has not been rubbed out in the struggle for survival because it enhances the chances of survival. But the increase as regards chances of survival would be slight if only thoughts to the effect that one is feeling pain at present, and not also thoughts to the effect that one will feel pain in the future, made an impact on behaviour.[6]

Plainly, a great deal of these evolutionary advantages would be lost if sensations of pain did not exercise a strong influence on attention. For suppose that it was frequently the case that one's thoughts dealt with other topics than with one's current pains; then, on the assumption that both sensations and thoughts have the capacity to give rise to bodily changes, their respective effects may counteract and cancel out each other. The upshot could be a harmful paralysis. As indicated, it is possible not to attend to a pain currently felt if it is mild, if there are other things that strongly attract one's attention or if one is well-versed in the art of voluntarily directing one's attention. It is a fact of everyday experience that, if for any of these reasons, attention is averted from a pain, the bodily reactions characteristic of pain will tend to subside. However, the fact that it is possible not to attend a present pain does not contradict the generalization that pains exercise a pull on attention in proportion to their intensity. And, given that thoughts have the power to produce behaviour, we should expect this generalization to hold.

---

[5] I enlarge on this topic in (1985a: ch. 3.2).

[6] Since I have elsewhere (1985a: 61–70) defended a sort of epiphenomenalism, I would like to point out that what is said in the text about the evolutionary advantage of being able to enter certain mental states is compatible with the thesis that the mental does not causally influence the physical. This is so if, as I have suggested, statements about what mental episodes cause are read as elliptical statements about what the neural states, with which they are nomologically correlated, cause.

The fact that it is possible not to attend to a pain shows that it is not necessarily the case that pains make one *suffer*. To suffer from a pain is to have one's attention held captivated by it and, as a result, to react negatively to it—that is, to want to be rid of it. If one suffers from a pain, one must *dislike* it, for this is to react negatively to it. But since the latter expression is often used in a dispositional sense—meaning roughly that one would react negatively to something were one to perceive and attend to it—it is possible to dislike a pain without at the moment suffering from it.

Rejection of the Reaction View of Pain

According to the theory I have outlined above it is just a contingent fact that subjects dislike sensations of pain, that they suffer from and desire to be rid of sensations with this particular sensory quality when they experience them. Some philosophers would, however, insist that it is instead a conceptual or necessary truth that pains are disliked. This claim can take different forms.

In one form it does not contradict the central tenet of SQ, namely that sensations of pain have a special, intrinsic quality. The claim is merely that the possession of this quality is not sufficient for the sensation to be classifiable as one of pain: it must also evoke a negative reaction like dislike. Although Hare and Trigg argue that 'a sensation of pain' in one of its uses connotes a sensation with a special intrinsic quality, they also believe that there is another use in which the term means a sensation with this quality that is also the object of dislike; Trigg even contends that the latter use is the primary one (1970: 64–5).

There is not much to quarrel about here. The heart of the matter is whether or not there is a special, intrinsic quality that sensations of pain must have. It matters little whether, in everyday parlance, the phrase 'a sensation of pain' expresses nothing but a sensation's having this quality. If it does not, one could coin a term that expresses just this. For my own part, I am, however, inclined to think that this is precisely what the term conveys. Certainly, since it is almost universally true that subjects dislike sensations having this property, it will normally be inferred that they dislike what they are feeling when it is reported that they are feeling pain. But this inference can be blocked by the consistent addition 'but they do not mind what they are feeling'. In other words, the implication that the sensation is disliked is 'cancellable' and 'conversational', not something *entailed by* the original statement.[7]

Another form of the denial of SQ is more contentious, since it denies its central tenet. Its claim is that whether or not a sensation is a pain does not at all depend on its intrinsic features: a sensation is a pain if and only if it calls forth a certain reaction of avoidance and dislike. This is *the reaction view* (of pain), R.

Armstrong is an R-theorist:

> To have a pain in a certain place, we now say, is to feel a disturbance of our normal bodily state at that place; together with an immediate and interested dislike of that feeling; and a concern for the place where the disturbance feels to be. (1962: 106)

---

[7] I here appeal to a well-known distinction drawn by H. P. Grice (1967).

Dislike of a sensation is immediate if one dislikes it for its own sake, and it is interested if one particularly dislikes that *oneself* has to experience the sensation. Since Armstrong speaks of feeling "a disturbance", he does not unequivocally eschew all reference to a sensory quality characteristic of pains. But the concluding claim of his book seems sufficient to remove any doubt: "Bodily sensations involve impressions of thermal and spatial properties only" (1962: 128). The programme of Armstrong's book is to reduce the number of 'secondary' qualities as far as possible.

Another champion of R is Kurt Baier:

> *Whatever* he feels on the occasions when he naturally manifests pain, he will learn to call 'pain'. And since he learns the words on the occasions when he feels something which he wants to stop, reduce in intensity, of whose return he is afraid etc., the very meaning of 'a pain' will be 'something which I dislike', 'something which I do not enjoy'.[8]

R is a real rival to SQ, but before marshalling arguments against it I shall take a brief critical look at the learning argument that Baier employs to support R. (By the way, this is also the argument on the strength of which Trigg claims that the use of 'a pain' that alludes to dislike is primary.) Let us grant that, if it is to be possible to teach children the meaning of 'a sensation of pain', there must be some observable circumstances—like an effect of the sensation, such as behaviour, or a cause of it, such as injury—that indicates when they feel it. It still does not follow that any reference to these circumstances must be part of *the meaning* of 'a sensation of pain'. A description like 'the type of sensation that is an effect of cause C and that causes behaviour B' can be used *to fix the reference or denotation* of 'a sensation of pain' without determining its meaning or connotation.[9]

Having disposed of this argument in favour of R, I now turn to arguments against it.

(1) That a sensation is disliked is not *sufficient* for it to be a sensation of pain. As both Hare (1969: 31) and Trigg (1970: 22) point out, there are sensations which one dislikes having, but which are not painful. We react negatively to some tickles and itches, to the sensations produced by electric shocks and by scraping the nails against a blackboard, to some sensations of cold (e.g. ones caused by a drop of icy water dripping down one's back) and of heat (e.g. ones caused by one's having worn wellingtons for a long time on a hot day), to the sensations produced by suffocation and to odious smells and tastes. All these sensations are unpleasant, but, *pace* R, they are not strictly speaking painful.

I do not think this criticism can be met by specifying the behaviour reactions to pains in greater detail, for there is a great variety in respect of responses to pains: how one reacts to a headache is very different from how one reacts to being pricked by a pin. Consequently, if a formula were to include all patterns of behaviour that could be evoked by sensations of pain, but exclude all patterns that are called forth by other sorts of sensation, it would have to be extremely complex—so complex that it could not plausibly be held to be part of the meaning of 'a sensation of pain'.

(2) Nor is it *necessary* that a sensation be disliked for it to be painful. As Hare emphasizes, "the 'threshold' of dislike of pain is usually somewhat above the threshold of the pain

---

[8] (1958: 275); cf. also Rem B. Edwards (1979: 28, 35).   [9] To utilize Saul Kripke's famous distinction (1980).

itself" (1969: 34–5). For instance, if one presses a pin gently against the skin, it seems that there is a phase in which the resulting sensation is recognized as painful, but so mildly painful that one does not mind having it. The R-theorist could, however, retort that the negative response is not altogether absent here: it is rather that it is very weak, because the pain is so mild. This is a retort that is hard to refute.

Fortunately, there is another kind of phenomenon that buttresses the same conclusion, namely so-called asymbolia for pain. To all appearances, this is a condition of failing to respond negatively even to intense pains. Trigg quotes from the case study of a man with a serious head injury who lacked the ability to respond appropriately to various stimuli: "When the patient was suddenly pricked, even very strongly, he failed to withdraw the part injured" (1970: 70). Notwithstanding this fact: "During the examination the patient never failed to report on every single sensation and to describe correctly whether it was painful or whether it was innocuous" (1970: 70). The last mentioned fact, in conjunction with the fact that the patient was well aware of the abnormality of his attitude to pain and tried to devise explanations of it, indicates that his head injury had not damaged his capacity to understand the meaning of 'a sensation of pain'. So, it is reasonable to join Trigg in taking the man's reports of pains at face value and to conclude that he really felt pain, though he did not react negatively to it (cf. Tye, 2003: 56).

(3) Suppose, however, that both (1) and (2) are wrong and that there is a negative behaviour response, B, such that subjects (tend to) exhibit B when and only when they experience sensations of pain. Nonetheless, there would be reason, I claim, to regard the descriptions 'a sensation that expresses itself in B' and 'a sensation of pain' as not logically, but only materially, equivalent. For it makes sense to explain why B was displayed in response to a sensation by pointing out that the sensation was painful. For instance, it is perfectly natural to explain why I eventually withdrew from a source of heat by pointing out that the sensations of heat that I received eventually turned painful.

Phenomenological scrutiny bears out that in situations of this kind the sensations induced change character and that this change is the cause of the subject's sudden withdrawal from an object in whose vicinity the subject has been for some time. If R had been correct, such explanations would be vacuous; they would have the force of 'I withdrew from the object because the sensations I received from it turned into ones of a kind that makes one withdraw from an object that is their cause'. According to R, what causes my withdrawal must simply be that the sensations of heat reach a certain intensity. But this is implausible. If my sensations of heat have steadily increased in respect of intensity, why do I want them to cease when they reach a certain intensity? Plainly, because they are then turning painful. R is unacceptable because it makes this statement boil down to a tautology.

On the strength of these reasons I conclude that R cannot be sustained. There is a sensory quality of painfulness that is supervenient on other intrinsic qualities of sensations of pain. As a matter of empirical fact, that sensations have this supervenient quality makes subjects dislike them.

Some concede that there is such sensory quality of painfulness, but still reject the view that its relation to dislike and negative behavioural responses is purely empirical or contingent. Timothy Sprigge maintains that "pleasure and pain are distinct qualities of experience which necessarily tend to influence behaviour in certain ways" (1988: 148; cf. also Platts, 1980: e.g. 81). He can hold this view because he explicitly rejects a thesis about causality normally attributed to Hume, namely, that the causal relations in which a thing stands to other things is a contingent matter which is not included in what the thing is in itself (1988: 141).

Although I cannot argue it fully here, I cannot but think that the belief that there are qualities of the kind that Sprigge takes pleasure and pain to be is a belief in something incoherent. It seems to be a belief that there are qualities such that (*a*) they are intrinsic qualities of something, but that (*b*) they nonetheless incorporate something of the relations that this thing has to external things. But this appears to be a straight contradiction. Certainly, it is possible to identify or refer to an intrinsic feature of a thing in terms of the relations instances of it has to other things, and, given this identification, it will of course be a matter of necessity—*de dicto*—that instances of it bear these relations. But to be interesting Sprigge's thesis must be about terms that rigidly designate or express the essence of the features in question, and then his position seems incoherent.

2

PLEASURE AS A SENSORY QUALITY

WHILE SQ at present is the standard view with respect to pain, R is among contemporary philosophers the orthodox view on the nature of pleasure.[1] The general claim of R with respect to pleasure is formulated by Trigg as follows:

> Just as the unpleasantness of a pain must be distinguished from a pain-quality, so the pleasantness of a sensation must not be thought to be a property of the sensation. If there is no pleasure-quality, all that pleasant sensations have in common is their pleasantness. In other words, we like them. If we did not like a sensation, we would not call it 'pleasant', and if we did like it, it must be pleasant. (1970: 114)

Certainly, there are writers who go against the prevailing opinion by acknowledging the existence of sensations of pleasure, but not much effort is spent on elucidating their nature,[2] and the extent to which they are involved in situations in which there is pleasure is underestimated.[3]

I shall here develop a version of SQ to the effect that there are sensations of pleasure in the sense that they are sensations that are equipped with an intrinsic, supervenient feature of being pleasant or pleasurable and that this is what causes them to be universally liked. I also hold—though this linguistic thesis is less important—that, when we ordinarily describe something as a sensation of pleasure, what we claim is strictly speaking that the sensation has this supervenient feature; that the sensation is liked by subjects—that is, that they desire it to go on for its own sake—is merely implied in a loose, cancellable manner.

---

[1] The literature in which R with respect to pleasure is defended includes—apart from the works cited in Ch. 1 which hold the same view of pain—the following: Ryle (1954: ch. 4); David Perry (1967); Gosling (1969); Trigg (1970: ch. 4); Fuchs (1974); Brandt (1979: 35–42); and Telfer (1980: 12–18).

[2] See Hospers (1961: 112), Davis (1981: esp. 307–8); and Sumner (1996: 106–8).

[3] See Alston (1967b) in which an R-account is developed for situations in which I take sensations with a quality of pleasantness to occur.

A Sensory Quality View of Pleasure

There are certain facts that apparently lend credibility to taking the feeling of pleasure as a reaction to some sort of sensation rather than as a sensation with this quality, though in reality it is erroneous to take them to undercut SQ. These facts are best brought out by means of an illustration. (It should not be inferred, however, that whenever we feel a sensation of pleasure, the situation has the structure to be illustrated; this is not true of an orgasm, for instance.)

If I come into contact with an object that is burning hot, I do not first feel the heat and then the pain; I am feeling the heat and the pain simultaneously. In terms of my version of SQ, I express this by saying that the quality of painfulness is supervenient on the quality of heat. Compare a situation in which I am feeling something to be pleasantly warm: here I am normally feeling the warmth somewhat before I am feeling any pleasure. If I am chilly and sit down in the sun, I will feel the warmth of the sun almost at once, but it is not until the warmth has so to speak pervaded me that I will feel the warmth as pleasant. What happens seems to be this. When I am cold, my muscles and blood vessels are contracted. As the warmth permeates me, my muscles relax and my blood vessels dilate. I suggest that pleasure is felt when this relaxation and dilatation is felt, that the quality of pleasure is supervenient on exemplifications of these qualities rather than on those of warmth.

Similarly, blows are felt as painful straightaway, but caresses and massage have to be felt for some time before they become pleasant. The reason is again, I hypothesize, that these forms of treatment have to produce a bodily effect of relaxation in order for any pleasure to be felt. The quality of pleasure is supervenient on this relaxation as given in sensation. Since it is not unreasonable to regard this relaxation and dilatation as a 'reaction' to the warmth and the treatments mentioned, it is not unreasonable to regard the feeling of pleasure as a reaction to the sensations of warmth and of touch. But this is another type of reaction than the one of liking or desiring to prolong of which R speaks, so SQ has not been undermined.

Presumably, not any degree of relaxation and dilatation is felt as pleasurable. One can be too hot and then the contact with something cool is pleasant, although this contact surely causes vasoconstriction. A reasonable surmise is that relaxation of muscles and vasodilatation is felt as pleasurable only when it serves or enhances bodily functioning.[4] But further specification of these matters must be left to neurophysiological expertise.

If this is on the right track, pleasure is associated with felt states beneficial to the organism, just as pain is the correlate of states harmful to it. (Of course, this is precisely what should be predicted, given the tendencies to seek and prolong sensations of pleasure and to avoid and cut short sensations of pain.) But it does not follow that we should revive the traditional opposition between pleasure and pain, for, as was noted in the foregoing chapter, there are other sensations than those of pain that are disliked for their own sakes: itches, tickles, sensations of scraping one's nails against a blackboard, of

---

[4] One of the few contemporary adversaries of R, Dent, suggests that "a very common feature associated with being pleased" is "an increase in vitality, an upsurge of a sense of well-being, a certain quickening of one's life" (1984: 41).

having an electric shock or a drop of icy water under one's collar, etc. It is clearly implausible to maintain that there is only a difference of degree between these other disliked qualities and that of painfulness, that the former represent a lower degree of the latter, since, for example, the sensation of having an electric shock can be much more intense than that of a pain. So, there is not *one* negative counterpart to the positive sensorily felt quality of pleasure, but a whole range of them, a whole range of sensorily felt qualities disliked for their own sakes.

There is, I think, nothing surprising about this lack of symmetry, for there are many ways of disturbing proper bodily functioning, and it may be important for survival that several of these are registered in different sensory qualities which are linked to different protective measures. In contrast, the return to normal functioning, which causes the cessation of these measures, could be signalled by a single quality.

Not only tactile impressions of temperature and pressure can occasion sensations of pleasure and their negative counterparts (excepting sensations of pain which exclusively belong to the sense of touch). Sensations of smell and taste can also be accompanied by such sensations. I think that the underlying mechanism here is the same as the one sketched above. The experience of certain smells and tastes causes certain muscles of one's throat and stomach to relax, so as to prepare them for the reception of food and drink. Pleasure is felt in connection with the feeling of this process of relaxation rather than in connection with the feeling of the smell or taste itself. Analogously, other smells and tastes cause these muscles to contract, in the manner of the initial phases of vomiting, and a quality of nausea intrinsically disliked is supervenient on these contractions as presented in sensation.

There seems to be some experimental backing for this hypothesis. The psychologist P. T. Young describes an experiment in which subjects were confronted with an unpleasant and disgusting smell, namely the smell of the rotten flesh of a rat. He summarizes the outcome of the experiment as follows: it "showed an *increase*, during disgust, in gastrointestinal tone". On the basis of this, he proposes that one should "define *disgust* as a pattern of response associated with anti-peristalsis" (1961: 395).

This enables us to deflect an objection Trigg launches at SQ:

> It is very apparent that sexual pleasure has little in common with, say, the pleasures of eating. Both provide sensations which we usually like, but the sensations are completely dissimilar. To assimilate a pleasant taste to sexual pleasure on the grounds that they both come under the umbrella concept of 'sensation of pleasure' is clearly ridiculous. Equally implausible would be any attempt to suggest that different tastes had the same quality, and could be classified as being in some way the same sensation, merely because they were pleasant. (1970: 110–11)

It should be plain that my version of SQ does not harbour the ludicrous corollary that two pleasant tastes (or smells) share a common quality of taste (or smell). What they have in common is that they produce the same type of changes in, roughly, the region of the throat and stomach. Furthermore, it is the sensations of these changes, and not the sensation of the taste (or smell) itself, that are supposed to have a quality in common with sexual pleasure. As an orgasm obviously seems to involve processes of relaxation, I fail to see that such a view "is clearly ridiculous".

Beauty and Ugliness

Are pleasant and unpleasant sights and sounds analogous to pleasant and unpleasant smells and tastes? To answer this question we have to take note of a difference between seeing and hearing, on the one hand, and smelling and tasting (and tactile feeling) on the other. What is immediately seen or heard is normally not seen or heard as being located in the subject's body, but in the external world. In contrast, a smell is always experienced in the nostrils and a taste in the mouth. The fact that smells and tastes are experienced in connection with the body makes it impossible to draw a clear borderline between the sensation of a smell or a taste and the sensation of bodily changes that result directly from it. There is a single continuous sensation that expands through the body and that could come to exemplify the quality of pleasure and its negative counterparts.

In contrast the body does not play the same intimate role in seeing and hearing: what is seen or heard is usually not seen or heard in the body, and it is therefore possible to draw a distinction between what is seen or heard and what is felt in or with the body. This does not mean that visual and auditory impressions cannot produce bodily effects, but it means, I suggest, that they have become intrinsically more articulated and diversified than olfactory and gustatory impressions which, owing to their bodily link, so readily give rise to bodily effects.

Here we find the reason why there are qualities supervenient on properties immediately seen and heard, but not on those immediately smelled and tasted. We have in the foregoing chapter encountered one such property, namely, the property of being dazzling. Two more important features of this kind are the features of *beauty* and *ugliness*.[5] The quality of beauty is exemplified by a sight or a sound, I suggest, when the stimulation causing it is just right for the sense modality involved, while the quality of ugliness appears when there is something wrong with this stimulation. That these qualities are instanced in what is seen or heard (rather than in one's body as felt from inside) is evidenced by the fact that one does not experience beauty and ugliness *after* first perceiving the sight or sound. The property of dazzlingness is also instantiated as the result of an unfitting stimulation of the sense-organ involved, but—in contrast to the case of ugliness— it is here unfitting to the degree that something like pain is felt in the sense-organ.

Perhaps the difference between seeing and hearing, on the one hand, and smelling and tasting, on the other, is most clearly seen if one compares what it is like to see something dazzling (or to hear a sound that is piercing) to the corresponding phenomena of smell and taste, for example, tasting something that is extremely spicy. In the latter case there is no gustatory quality of 'too much', but only something like sensations of burning heat. However, to see a dazzling light (or to hear a piercing sound) is not just to have painful or unpleasant sensations in the eyes (ears). This is evidence that there are no qualities

---

[5] For further discussion of beauty, see Persson (1992a).

supervenient on olfactory and gustatory ones, like the quality of being dazzling is supervenient on the visual ones.

The qualities of beauty and ugliness are similar to those of pleasure and its negative counterparts in that they arouse liking and dislike respectively. (That this is so is probably beneficial at the stage during which the capacities to see and hear are still under development.) Nonetheless, the quality of beauty is not identical to that of pleasure; nor is the quality of ugliness identical to any of the sensory qualities disliked in themselves. Beauty and ugliness are something seen or heard, while pleasure and its negative counterparts are something felt. It is hard to believe that qualities supervenient on what is seen or heard could be identical to qualities supervenient on something felt. The upshot of all this is that we have to recognize at least two positive sensory qualities, namely pleasure and beauty, and add ugliness to the longer list of negative ones. I am by no means claiming to have given a complete list of the qualities that are liked and disliked in themselves, but completeness is not essential for my purposes.

Let me say one thing in response to critics who are tempted to complain that the list is too long. I think that philosophers have in general underestimated the number of sensory qualities. For instance, they have been wont to talk as if things immediately seen just have colour and a few spatial properties like shape and size, while in fact they can be dim, clear, dazzling, radiant, shiny, and dull, to give a random sample of further possible properties (many of which may go unnamed in everyday language).

Rebuttal of Objections to the Sensory Quality View

Incomplete though this list may be, it enables us to show that the fact that a sense-impression is liked in itself is not sufficient for it to be one of pleasure, just as the fact that a sensation is disliked in itself is not sufficient for it to be a pain. For the quality of beauty is also liked for its own sake. Likewise, it seems sensible to think that the liking of a sensation is not necessary for it to be one of pleasure. It seems plausible to hold that there are sensations of pleasure of such a low intensity that the subject does not bother whether or not they go on. It is also arguable that in the case of pleasure there is something corresponding to asymbolia for pain. Buddhist saints claim to have overcome all desire, including the desire for pleasure. If such individuals still experience sensations of pleasure occasionally—for instance, when becoming warm after having been cold—they will experience them without the concomitant of any desire that they go on.

However, the most important point is this: even if it were the case that a sensation was of pleasure if and only if it was liked in itself, this would only be a material equivalence, not a logical one, for the fact that a sensation is one of pleasure *explains* why it is liked in itself, just as the fact that it is painful could explain why it is disliked in itself. This has, however, been denied by Trigg:

> The reason we normally dislike a pricking pain is that it is a pain, and not that it is a
> pricking sensation. If it is maintained that sensations of warmth and coolness have a

> special quality because they are pleasures, this suggests that we like that quality, and not the warmth or the coolness. It suggests that I like to feel a cool hand on my hot brow because it is a sensation of pleasure, and not because I like the feeling of coolness. I like to feel a hot-water bottle when I am chilled because I like feeling pleasure, and not the warmth. It is, however, clear that in these cases it is the warmth and the coolness which we appreciate and nothing else. (1970: 108–9)

Surely, it is clear that it is *not* the warmth and the coolness in themselves that one here likes. One might experience the same degree of coolness when one is not overheated, and the same degree of warmth when one is not chilled, without liking them. It is the fact that the circumstances are such that they are felt as *pleasantly* cool and warm, respectively, that makes one like them. In other words, the coolness and the warmth are liked because they cause one's blood vessels to contract or to dilate to a state that is better for bodily functioning and that is correlated with a sensation of pleasure. To be sure, it would be misleading to say that we like just the pleasure and not the coolness (or warmth), for the pleasure is exemplified by the very same sensations as the coolness (or warmth), albeit it is strictly speaking not supervenient on this quality. Yet this sensation is liked for the reason that it exemplifies pleasure.

In a spirit similar to Trigg's, Alan Fuchs argues that "the completely identical phenomenological situation can be both pleasant and unpleasant to the same person at different times" (1974: 495–6). His example is a scratch that is "extremely pleasant" to start with, but which eventually gets "downright irritating", in spite of the fact that the sensation remains unchanged. Fuchs diagnoses his example along the lines prescribed by R: what happens is that my attitude to the sensation changes from liking to dislike. This shift is due not to the fact that the sensation has changed in quality, but to the fact that it has *not* changed.

Two comments are in order. First, it is not realistic to think that the sensation would undergo no change, for as the scratch continues, the skin is bound to get irritated and sore. Secondly, it is true that one can begin to dislike something because it goes on without any change. This happens when one gets *bored* with something. But being bored with a sensation (a rare phenomenon, it appears) is evidently different from finding it "irritating", as for instance an itch may be irritating, just as being interested in a sensation (e.g. because it is strange) is evidently different from finding it pleasant. (Being bored and being interested will be discussed more fully in the next chapter.)

A further objection to the view that there are sensations with a quality of pleasantness is that this cannot be true because, while sensations have bodily location, a feeling of pleasure has not. This objection is suggested by Gilbert Ryle's remark "We can tell the doctor where it hurts . . . but we cannot tell him, nor does he ask, where it pleases us" (1954: 58; cf. D. Perry, 1967: 83). This is a tendentious formulation in that it employs the verb 'pleases' which commonly designates an *emotion* (an emotion being, as will be seen in Chapter 5, something having propositional content: one is pleased *that* something is the case) rather than, say, 'is feeling pleasure'. It is quite clear that we have sensations of pleasure which can be bodily localized. Itches, for instance, have bodily location, and it is a commonplace that when one succeeds in scratching the place where it itches, the itch often gives way to a feeling of pleasure. Plainly, this feeling or sensation of pleasure is located roughly where the itch was located.

Let me consider just one further objection, this time by David Perry:

> one could not concentrate on one's pleasure to the extent that one no longer heeded the thing he enjoyed . . . Not only does pleasure require that one be alive to that which gives pleasure; pleasure does not compete with its object for one's attention. Pleasure does not distract one from its object . . . An organic sensation, on the other hand, might well distract and hinder a person's activity. (1967: 96)

Perry recognizes two forms of pleasure: enjoyment and the emotion of being pleased.[6] Since whenever one experiences enjoyment or is pleased, there must be something which one enjoys or about which one is pleased, he asserts that pleasure necessarily has an object. Of these two we are at present concerned with enjoyment rather than with being pleased (emotions will be the topic of Chapters 5 and 6) and with the question of whether enjoyment can compete with its object for one's attention.

Imagine that I am drinking a wine the taste of which I thoroughly enjoy; then it does seem to me that my enjoying the wine would interfere with my paying that close attention I would pay to its taste were I a connoisseur trying to rank it in relation to other wines. Conversely, if I were attending closely to its properties of taste, I would be unable to enjoy its taste to the same degree. So, enjoyment does appear to compete with its object for one's attention. Naturally, as long as I am enjoying the taste of the wine, I must be 'alive' to its taste in the sense that I must be feeling it, but, as was concluded in the foregoing chapter, there can be feeling accompanied by little or no attention.

According to my view, enjoyment in the sense in which one usually enjoys a sensation—the sense in which enjoyment is opposed to suffering and *not* the sense in which it is opposed to boredom (this distinction will be examined in the next chapter)—consists in having a sensation in which the quality of pleasure is exemplified and which, due to this exemplification, causes one to (continue to) attend to it and to desire to prolong it for its own sake. This desire is, strictly, a desire to keep the quality of pleasure exemplified for its own sake, but in practice this will be achieved by prolonging the whole sensation. Since enjoying a sensation involves attending to it primarily in respect of its being the bearer of the quality of pleasure, enjoyment implies that other aspects of the sensation are the object only of peripheral attention.[7]

This concludes my review of the most important objections to my version of SQ with respect to pleasure that I have been able to extract from the literature. Since I regard

---

[6] Contrast Fred Feldman (1997: 462 ff.) who seems to claim that all pleasure is of the propositional form of being pleased.

[7] The view of sensations of pleasure and pain defended in this and the preceding chapter should not be conflated with the claim that being *good* and being *bad* are intrinsic properties of sensations, that the latter are properties the sensing of which makes one have intrinsic desires that the sensations go on and cease, respectively. For the latter claim, see Sprigge (1988: 155); Goldstein (1989); and Tye (2003: 57–60). As will transpire in Part II, esp. Ch. 10, I regard the value of something as being definable in terms of desires towards it. Thus, pleasure is good in itself in virtue of being desired for its own sake.

myself as having met all of them, I conclude that the form of SQ here presented is vindicated and that R, the doctrine that the fact that a sensation is of pleasure consists in its being liked for its own sake, has been refuted.

A Broadening of Hedonism

A number of recent criticisms of psychological hedonism are premised on the assumption that there are no sensations with an intrinsic quality of being pleasurable. It follows from my argument that these criticisms are misguided: there is such a quality which is *one* thing that we like or desire for its own sake. So, hedonism surmounts this hurdle. But pleasure is not the only thing intrinsically liked: there is at least one other sensory quality that is liked in itself—namely, the quality of beauty—and, alongside pain, a whole range of sensory qualities—including that of ugliness—that are disliked in themselves. Consequently, psychological hedonism stands in need of a corresponding broadening.

Let us refer to the upshot of this broadening as *extended hedonism* (or *sensualism*). It is to the effect that the only things liked and disliked for their own sakes are sensations with certain intrinsic qualities. These qualities may be lumped together under the label of 'hedonic' qualities. In the next chapter, we will, however, see that this broadening is not nearly enough, for there are things intrinsically liked and disliked other than sensory qualities.

3

BEYOND HEDONISM

PSYCHOLOGICAL hedonism implies that there is a *homogeneity* as regards the objects desired and avoided for their own sakes, since it takes all of them to have the sensory qualities of being pleasurable and painful, respectively. We shall see that this homogeneity is of relevance to the rationality of the strategy of maximizing felt fulfilment, both inter-temporally and inter-personally. In Chapters 1 and 2 we secured a precondition necessary for the success of the hedonist enterprise when we concluded that the requisite qualities of pleasure and pain exist. If there had been no such qualities but, say, 'an experience of pleasure' had just meant the same as 'an experience liked or desired for its own sake', there would be no implication that the experiences desired for their own sakes have any intrinsic quality in common. (Hedonism would then be indistinguishable from what I later in this chapter will call experientialism.) On the other hand, it has also been concluded that there are other sensory qualities than pain and pleasure liked and disliked for their own sakes. So, a tenable hedonism would have to be an *extended hedonism* (or *sensualism*).

Psychological hedonism is normally given an egoistic or self-regarding slant: its claim is that everyone intrinsically seeks only states of affairs consisting in that *they themselves* feel pleasure and shuns only states consisting in that *they themselves* feel pain. In Chapter 10 I shall define the notion of a *self-regarding* desire as a desire that (1) has a *self-referential* content to the effect that something be true of *oneself* and that (2) is not ultimately derived from any desire whose content is not self-referential. Now, assuming to begin with that our intrinsic desires are self-regarding, are they always to the effect that we ourselves experience pleasure (or beauty or any other kind of hedonic or sensory quality) and escape pain (or any other kind of hedonic or sensory quality)?

Two Kinds of Enjoyment: Sensual and Interest Enjoyment

It is plain that people like or enjoy such things as, say, doing philosophy and playing golf. Hedonists will have to construe the enjoyment of these activities as parallel to the case of enjoying the taste of a wine considered in the last chapter. They will have to claim that just as experiencing the taste of a wine can induce one to feel sensations of pleasure, so doing philosophy and playing golf can produce such sensations, and that that is why these activities are pursued. Likewise, if philosophy and golf are not liked or enjoyed, this is because engaging in them fails to produce sensations of pleasure and perhaps gives rise to sensations of pain or of some other negative sensory quality instead.

I shall contend that such construals are mistaken and that, therefore, extended hedonism is false: other things than sensations are liked and disliked, sought and shunned, for their own sakes. Perhaps many will take this conclusion to be too obvious to be worth arguing for. I do not really dissent, but, as indicated, the point has bearing on the plausibility of the satisfactionalist goal of fulfilment-maximization (and, so, on the possibility of pursuing rationalism as an ideal). Hence, it is worth while to explain in some detail why other states of affairs than hedonic or sensory ones are desired as ends.

Reflections along the following lines undercut extended hedonism. Human and non-human beings have innumerable capacities: they have a capacity to gain knowledge about the facts of the world, a capacity to move their own bodies in countless ways, to run, swim, jump, etc., and by means of moving their bodies they can manipulate surrounding objects, turn them into tools, food, and other useful things. I suggest that these capacities are generally coupled with desires to exercise them for their own sakes, that these capacities are normally correlated with inclinations to pursue as ends the activities for which there is a capacity. If these capacities did not go with such desires, there would be a great risk that they would never be adequately exercised. Suppose that it turned out that no pleasurable sensations could foreseeably be won and that no painful ones could foreseeably be warded off by the exercise of a certain capacity; then it would never be exercised, given the truth of hedonism. Therefore, it is to be suspected that in a well-adjusted creature, the capacities with which it is endowed are coupled with desires to exercise them for their own sakes.

Notice that the object of such a desire is to exercise an activity and not (merely) to have the *sensation or experience* of exercising it, though it is by means of the latter that we ascertain that we succeed in engaging in the activities. The object of the desire is to explore our own capacities or the world surrounding us. Thus, the desire presupposes that the experiences we receive are veridical experiences of an independent reality. It is in this sense truth-related. I shall refer—in rough compliance with everyday usage, I presume—to such intrinsic desires as *interests*: we generally take an interest in or are interested in pursuing those activities for which we have capacities or abilities.

In outline, the pattern of distribution among humans of the theoretical and practical capacities indicated, and the correlated interests, appears to be as follows. There is a set of basic capacities-cum-interests that virtually every human being possesses to some degree, but individuals differ both in respect of the degree to which they are equipped with these capacities-cum-interests and in respect of the more specialized forms they assume. All have some ability to move their own bodies, and take an interest in so doing, but a few have this capacity-cum-interest to the extent required to be top athletes. All have the power-cum-interest to manipulate objects in their environment, but only a few to the degree necessary to be good craftsmen or artists. All have some capacity-cum-interest in acquiring knowledge of the world, but in many cases this is largely limited to parts of the world closest to them, while fewer have the set necessary to gain the more extensive general knowledge of the world obtained in scientific disciplines.

Now consider one of these interests, for instance, the interest taken in gaining know-ledge for its own sake, that is, *curiosity*. This trait is found not only in human beings. If, for instance, a rat is put in a cage, it soon begins to explore its new environment, even though it is not hungry, thirsty, etc., and so cannot reasonably be thought to be driven by a desire to receive the pleasurable sensations associated with the satiation of these needs. But it is in humans that the interest in collecting information about oneself and one's environ-ment achieves its most sophisticated manifestations, in the scientific exploration of the universe. It is important not to commit the mistake of thinking that when one is motivated by curiosity, one is driven by a desire to obtain sensations of pleasure (or any other sensations).

One reason why this mistake is easily committed is that when one engages in activities in which one takes a strong interest, one will *enjoy* what one is doing, and in the foregoing chapter it was pointed out that in one of its uses 'enjoyment' designates a phenomenon that involves sensations of pleasure as objects of desire. What is contrarily opposed to the latter form of enjoyment is *suffering*, while the present form of enjoyment is opposed to a lack of interest which (if the uninterested thing cannot be avoided) manifests itself in *boredom*. Enjoying philosophy is to be contrasted with being bored by it, while enjoying a massage naturally stands in opposition to being made to suffer by it. In view of these dif-ferent contraries, it would be rash to assume that enjoyment in both forms amounts to the same. There is, I want to argue, both the hedonist mistake of tending to assimilate the enjoyment of pursuing an activity in which one takes an interest to sensual enjoyment and the opposite anti-hedonist fallacy of tailoring the latter on the model of the former.

The object of both forms of enjoyment is always something which one experiences or is aware of.[1] (Note that this is not to say that the object of enjoyment is always some experience or other; an experience must not be confused with that *of* which it is an experi-ence: the latter may, but need not, be something which exists independently of the experience.) For instance, if one enjoys playing tennis, what one enjoys is this activity as one experiences or is aware of engaging in it. The awareness in question is awareness of a concrete particular, basically an event or state, not awareness of a fact, not awareness *that* something is the case which is what is at stake in being pleased that something is the case (cf. Wayne Davis's distinction between epistemic and non-epistemic awareness, 1982: 242–4). When one enjoys what one experiences, one (intrinsically) wants to go on experiencing it and, hence, if what one experiences is an activity, one wants to continue (attentively) engaging in it.[2]

---

[1] The thesis that the object of enjoyment can always be construed as something experienced is advanced by Davis (1982: 245–6) and Sircello (1989: 23–8).

[2] This is essentially Ryle's idea expressed in the following passage: "To say that a person has been enjoying digging is . . . to say that he dug with his whole heart in his task, i.e. that he dug, wanting to dig and not wanting to do anything else (or nothing) instead" (1949: 108).

This desire need not exist prior to the commencement of the experience; as Richard Warner emphasizes, the experience enjoyed *causes* the desire to come—or to remain—in existence (1980: 517; see also Warner, 1987: ch. 4). But the experience not only sustains this desire that it be prolonged, it also satisfies it (though I have claimed that in the case of interests this is so only on the assumption that the experience is veridical). Warner suggests that what is typical of something being enjoyed is precisely that it "causes a desire which it simultaneously satisfies" (1980: 517).[3] That is, one's enjoying something would then basically consist in one's experiencing or being aware of this thing—say, the intricacies of a philosophical argument—and this sustaining a desire to go on experiencing or being aware of it, which is satisfied by the continuation of one's experience or awareness.

However, this generation-cum-satisfaction of a desire appears not to be sufficient for enjoyment if it occurs in the absence of all feelings of pleasure. Suppose that one has some desire to go on having the experience that one at present is having, that this desire is satisfied to a degree sufficient for it to persist as a desire that the experience go on longer still, but not sufficient for any satisfaction to be *felt* (in the next chapter I argue that this is possible); then one may be described as taking an interest in the experience, but hardly as enjoying it. In agreement with this, Davis (1982) insists that enjoyment involves one's *feeling* pleasure as the result of one's desire being continuously gratified, that enjoying something includes the emotion of being pleased that one gets what one intrinsically desires.[4]

If this is right, we arrive at the following trio of distinct states: (*a*) enjoying an experience which consists in having the desire, that it go on, fulfilled to the degree that one feels satisfaction; (*b*) having an experience which merely sustains one's interest, that is, which continuously generates desires concerning the continuation of the experience, which it successively satisfies, but not to the degree that satisfaction is felt; and (*c*) being bored by an experience which consists in its failing to generate desires concerning its continuation. In the middle category, when one has an experience which merely sustains one's interest, one may feel some mild frustration if the experience is interrupted. There is then a contrast with the middle case between sensual enjoyment and suffering, namely the case of having a perfectly neutral or indifferent experience. One would not feel any frustration if this experience were interrupted.

Between boredom and suffering there is the difference that boredom consists in the *absence* of any desire to go on with something with which one has to go on rather than, as in the case of suffering, having a desire *not* to have an experience that one is having. True, being bored is a state in which one wants not to be; one is averse to go on with activities that do not evoke one's interest. So if one fails to achieve discontinuation, one is bound to be frustrated. But this is to say that one's being bored may *make* one frustrated, unhappy, etc., not that this state *consists* in any of these emotions.

---

[3] Cf. also Sircello (1989: 18 ff.). Sircello criticizes Warner for specifying the content of the desire as that something occur rather than that it continue (1989: 220). On this rather fine point, I am inclined to side with Sircello.

[4] Warner (1987: 131–2) tries to capture the experiential aspect of enjoyment by insisting that the desire involved be *felt*. But it seems to me that to feel a desire is something like to feel a tension which is normally not pleasurable.

One is bored with something experienced if one's awareness of it fails to discover aspects of it which makes one want to know what it will offer next if awareness is prolonged. On the other hand, when one is occupied with something experienced in which one takes an interest, one's desire to go on with it, paying close attention to it, is kindled by one's successively noticing new aspects of it. So, the object of interest must possess a certain richness of aspects, though it need not be exciting enough to make one feel that pleasure or satisfaction which is distinctive of (interest) enjoyment.

This pleasure, being *the upshot* of one's taking one's desire (to engage in some experienced activity) to be fulfilled, cannot of course provide *the object(ive)* of the desire—as a pleasurable sensation forms the object of desire in sensual enjoyment. But its presence, along with the linguistic fact that the verb 'enjoy' is employed in both cases, may mislead one into conflating the two types of enjoyment I am in the process of distinguishing, construing either both or neither hedonistically. For instance, the writers discussed do not separate these two forms of enjoyment.[5]

In the case of sensual enjoyment, one's desire to continue to experience the thing enjoyed is not kept alive by one's constantly noticing new aspects of it. That which one sensually enjoys may be very simple, for example feeling a sensation of warmth. Here one's desire to prolong the experience is instead sustained by the quality of pleasantness instantiated in the sensations experienced. As in the case in which one is allowed to pursue an interest, one will here experience the emotion of being pleased or satisfied if one succeeds in keeping the activity going. In the contrary opposite of sensual enjoyment, suffering from an activity that involves the having of sensations, there is frustration and displeasure because one is having sensations with qualities one dislikes for their own sakes. It is not just—as it would be were one simply bored by a sensation—that one's being conscious of the sensations fails to generate a desire to continue to have them; instead the sensations possess a quality like painfulness that induces one to desire to be rid of them for their own sakes.

I take it, then, as established that it is a mistake to construe the interest we take in the exercise of our repertoire of basic theoretical and practical capacities as being hedonically or sensually grounded (just as it is a mistake to view the enjoyment occasioned by the having of some sensations as resulting from an interest taken in them). It is not the case that that in which one takes an interest is necessarily equipped with any sensory quality of, for example pleasantness, which stimulates one's interest (nor is it the case that indulging in the interest always produces effects that possess such a quality, for example that indulging in curiosity results in knowledge the application of which helps one to secure pleasure). Thus, not all of our self-regarding intrinsic desires are to the effect that we experience pleasure (or some other sensory quality) or avoid pain (or some other sensory quality). In other words, extended hedonism is false. We have intrinsic desires to explore—that is, we take an interest in—what we perceptually experience of ourselves and our environment.

---

[5] A speaker of Swedish should be less prone to this confusion, since the distinction is in this language marked by the use of different verbs, 'njuta' in the case of sensual enjoyment and 'finna nöje i' in the case of taking enjoyment in the pursuit of an interest.

Some circumstances that obscure the falsity of even extended hedonism have also been exposed in the process of arriving at this conclusion. There is the ambiguity of 'enjoyment', between 'interest enjoyment' and 'sensual enjoyment', which I have tried to elucidate. It is only the latter which is enjoyment of something that involves having sensations with qualities like pleasure which are intrinsically desired. But since interest enjoyment may bring along pleasure *consequent* upon the realization that the intrinsic desire to engage in some activity has been fulfilled, the risk increases that this form of enjoyment is misconstrued in analogy with sensual enjoyment, that is, as encompassing an intrinsic desire for pleasure.

The picture is further complicated by the fact that we are likely to possess a *higher-order* desire to experience the pleasure of having our lower-order desires fulfilled. This may create the impression that we have lower-order desires *in order to* enable us to experience desire fulfilment, as means to this sort of pleasure. Of course, this position does not entail the hedonist claim that pleasure is the *only* thing intrinsically desired, since it does not exclude the existence of intrinsic lower-order desires for other things than pleasure. But it does entail that pleasure is the *superior* object of desire because it is the end for which other things are desired. It is, however, not reasonable to contend that this is the explanation why we in fact have acquired the lower-order desires we possess, for obviously many of these were acquired long before the higher-order desire for fulfilment. Rather, the claim must be that we should review our lower-order desires, dispose of those which are not readily satisfiable, and replace them with ones that are, so that felt satisfaction be maximized.

This is the master-aim of what I call prudentialist satisfactionalists: to see to it that one leads the life that contains as much felt fulfilment as possible. But why should we have a dominant, intrinsic desire to the effect that we maximize our pleasure, including the pleasurable experience of desire-fulfilment? Suppose we have intrinsic lower-order desires for other things than pleasure, for example a rationalist desire to know the truth and live in accordance with it. We are then informed that there are other desires, for example, for pleasure, the having of which would maximize our pleasure, including the desire-fulfilment of our lives. This is certainly *a* reason to acquire these desires instead, for we do intrinsically desire pleasure. But it is not necessarily a compelling reason, since our desire to be cognitively rational may be stronger, and so far we have been given no reason why it should not be so. If so, it would not be irrational to eschew the pleasure-boosting change.

Obviously, this reasoning presupposes that we intrinsically desire other things than pleasure, so it would be undercut if the homogeneity with respect to the objects of intrinsic desire that hedonism assumes were true, that is, if these objects all exemplified the quality of pleasure. There would then be no reason to object to the satisfactionalist fulfilment-maximizing policy of which prudentialism is a form. But to an extent that will be clearer in the next section, we have intrinsic desires for other things than pleasure; so, this argument for satisfactionalism being rationally required fails.

The Falsity of 'Experientialism'

It is important not to make the mistake of thinking that, although the considerations adduced refute extended psychological hedonism, they do not refute a psychological *experientialism* to the effect that the only thing intrinsically desired by us is *to have experiences* of one kind or another. For, as we have seen, in interest enjoyment we do not desire to have certain experiences for their own sakes; we desire to have these experiences on the assumption that they are veridical.[6] Interests are desires to explore ourselves and our environment rather than merely to have experience as of exploring them; our interests are reality-oriented. However, the falsity of experientialism is shown also by the existence of certain 'social' desires the content of which is that one be surrounded by other conscious beings who perceive and understand one and whose uptake is friendly and generous, that is, desires to the effect that others have certain experiences of oneself.

It would be wrong-headed to contend that such desires are not intrinsic, but are derived from desires to the effect that others *behave* in a friendly manner towards one, *treat* one well in various ways, for the reason that this is something one can experience oneself, whereas one cannot experience how others *experience* oneself. The following thought-experiment shows the untenability of such an interpretation. Suppose that epiphenomenalism is true (I think the coherence of epiphenomenalism must be admitted, even if it is considered to be false). That is, suppose that (*a*) there are mental properties, for example experiential states, distinct in kind from any physical properties; and that (*b*) the exemplification of mental properties makes no difference to the physical world. Now imagine two worlds:

(W_1) In this world animate beings are equipped with nervous systems some states of which are correlated with the instantiation of mental features.

(W_2) In this world animate beings are endowed with something analogous to the nervous systems just mentioned; these nervous systems make the beings respond in physical, observable ways exactly as do their duplicates in W_1 on the same physical, observable stimuli, but the states of these nervous systems are never correlated with the exemplification of any mental features; you are yourself the only being of the kind that exists in W_1.

We firmly believe our world to be like W_1, but suppose a philosophical sceptic comes along and provides you with cogent reasons to believe that your world is instead like W_2. Then you would probably find yourself hoping or wishing that your world be like W_1. You would be relieved and glad if you were presented with evidence warranting the belief that your world is really like W_1. You would react like this because you would feel intolerably lonely in a world like W_2. In other words, you have a desire to be surrounded

---

[6] Cf. Robert Audi's "axiological experientialism" which grants that the reality which makes experiences veridical has "inherent" value (2001: 98–100; cf. 1997: 254–9).

by other beings with minds or consciousness on which you could leave certain 'imprints'. This desire cannot be derived from desires that others behave in certain ways, for in that case what ultimately matters would be present in W_2, too.

Hence, I conclude that we have desires that others experience us in certain ways that do not boil down to desires that we experientially engage in exchanges with them. Perhaps this is particularly obvious in the common desire that others remember one—preferably in a complimentary way—after one is dead and gone (cf. Sidgwick, 1907/1981: 52–3). So, *pace* experientialism, some of our self-regarding intrinsic desires concern other things than that we have experiences of something or other. (These desires are self-regarding, since they concern that others have experiences of *oneself*.)

I shall not now pursue the question of whether we have *non-self-regarding* desires of, for instance, the same orientation, that others have experiences, although these have nothing to do with *us*. In passing, let me just note that it seems reasonable to conjecture that some of our social desires are genuinely *other-regarding*, are to the effect, for example that others be understood and remembered (such desires may manifest themselves in art criticism and the writing of biographies) or that they be well off, although this is in no way related to oneself. That is, however, chiefly a topic for Part IV.

From the starting-point of traditional psychological hedonism—that the only objects of intrinsic desires are to the effect that oneself experience pleasure and avoid pain—we have successively widened the scope of intrinsic desires. First to match an extended hedonism (or sensualism), which allows as objects of intrinsic desire sense-experiences with other qualities than pleasure and pain. Then we provided room for interests to explore our own capacities and the world surrounding us. Now, in this section we have seen that even such a doctrine to the effect that all our intrinsic desires have to do with ourselves having an experience of something or other is too restricted and that our self-regarding intrinsic desires range beyond our own minds and experiences to the minds and experiences of others. Finally, we noted that there is then not much plausibility in the view that we cannot have non-self-regarding desires concerning the experiences of others. To this we may add the possibility of having non-self-regarding intrinsic desires concerning non-experiential matters, such as, say, the continued existence of the earth in a state in which it is no longer inhabited by conscious life. (These will later be called impersonal values.)

But even if the claim that we intrinsically desire nothing but to experience something or other is false, it still seems true that the *primary* objects of our intrinsic desires are made up by matters of which we ourselves have experiences, that is, intrinsic desires to this effect are the first ones we acquire. This may be because such desires require minimal intellectual equipment. Thus, infants and a lot of non-human animals are capable of having them. Furthermore, throughout our lives certain experiential matters retain a primacy in the sense of a hold on attention which makes it well-nigh impossible to concentrate on abstract matters when present experience is intrusive, that is, when a pain is acute or when an overheard conversation is loud. As will transpire in later parts, this is of crucial importance for the main theme of this book.

The homogenization project of psychological hedonism is then so far from being successful that it seems that we can put virtually no restrictions on the objects of our intrinsic desires. To repeat, this is essential for this work. If traditional psychological hedonism were true (that we intrinsically desire states of affairs only in proportion to how much pleasure they offer us), this would remove one avenue of objection against the satisfactionalist goal of maximizing different forms of pleasure being rationally required. There would then be no possibility of appeal to other objects of intrinsic desire that may be more fervently desired.

Suppose instead, as I have argued, that we intrinsically desire other things than pleasure. Then the question arises whether it would be irrational to desire these things, for example philosophizing, more than pleasure and thus stick to them even if they were to lead to a smaller total of pleasure. Perhaps there are reasons for making such claims; for the moment the point is just that the question arises only if the hedonist homogenization project fails, and there is a plurality of intrinsically desired objects.

It should, however, be stressed that even if pleasure is not the sole goal, it does not follow that satisfactionalism, whose master-aim is to maximize the pleasure of desire-satisfaction and other pleasures, is irrational. Since there *are* felt states with an intrinsic quality of pleasure (the feeling of fulfilment being one of them), pleasure is a possible object of intrinsic desire. Some may be disposed to desire pleasure more strongly than anything else. As a result, they may form a higher-order desire to the effect that their lower-order desires be such that they will enable them to experience a maximum of pleasurable fulfilment. There is, so far, as little of an argument showing such a higher-order desire to be irrational as there is showing it to be rationally required. So, the stage is set for a drama in which forms of satisfactionalism, like prudentialism, will be one of the protagonists. But it will not be the only protagonist: the drama to be enacted is not a monologue of satisfactionalism, but a dialogue between it and other voices, in particular that of rationalism.

4

AN ANALYSIS OF DESIRE

I HAVE made rather frequent use of the notion of wanting or desiring something. It is now time to dissect this notion, in particular to bring out its connections to rationality. Setting aside the employment of the verb 'want' in which it is synonymous with 'need' or 'lack', I shall assume that there are no important differences of meaning between it and the verb 'desire'. Given the ambiguity mentioned, I shall use 'desire' rather than 'want' as the noun designating the state I have in mind, although I sense that the noun carries connotations different from the corresponding verb.[1] (For those who do not regard this noun as sufficiently broad for my purposes, a possible alternative would be the semi-technical term 'attitude of wanting (desiring)'.)

I shall carry out an investigation into the notion of desire that will issue in a definition of an important kind of desire that I will term 'decisive' desire. The reason for the name is that it is a desire that takes shape when a decision is made. In other words, I think it is the phenomenon which is ordinarily called an intention. As I conceive a decisive desire, it is a tendency to act or behave in some fashion.

A way to bring out that the connection between desiring and acting is conceptual rather than contingent is the following. Desires have different degrees of intensity or strength. Now consider two competing desires—that is, two desires that cannot both be fulfilled at the same time—one of which is stronger than the other. Surely, it is not just a contingent truth that, if any of these desires manifests itself in behaviour, it is the strongest one. The desire that expresses itself in behaviour *must* be the strongest one, because we principally determine the strength of desires by checking which ones win out and manifest themselves in behaviour in situations of conflict.

To what extent are there ways of ascertaining the strength of a desire that are independent of behaviour? It might be suggested that the intensity of a desire is also reflected in the intensity of certain feelings that precede the behaviour. This proposal first founders on the fact that, as I shall argue in due course, desiring does not always involve any feelings. Secondly, when it does involve feelings then, I shall suggest, these feelings are sensations of incipient behaviour, of slight muscular tensions, etc. and, hence, the feelings are not

---

[1] Cf. Davis (1986).

entirely independent of behaviour. Thus I conclude that, since it is an essential feature of desires that they admit of degrees, and this feature cannot be made sense of independently of behaviour, the notion of desire cannot be understood independently of behaviour. A desire is basically a tendency to act, though we will see that it also tends to affect thought processes.

I shall here assume that to act is to cause a state of affairs to materialize or to become a fact (cf. Persson, 1981: ch. 2.1). Consequently, if a desire is a tendency to act, it is a tendency to cause a state of affairs—that is, something that can be cast in a propositional form or in a that-clause—to become a fact. Of course, in everyday language the content of desire is seldom rendered in this form. Sometimes, however, the transposition is an easy matter. To want one's friends to remember one after one is dead and gone is presumably to be recast as to want to cause (it to be a fact) that one's friends remember one after one is dead and gone. It is less clear how a desire to move one's finger should be recast. But if to perform an action is to cause something to become a fact, the action of moving a finger is naturally construed as causing this finger to move. Thus, I suggest that wanting to move one's finger should be interpreted as wanting to cause (it to be a fact) that one's finger moves, rather than as, say, wanting to cause (it to be a fact) that one moves one's finger. However, these niceties matter less in the present context than they would do had the purpose been that of analysing the concept of (intentional) action.[2] Here I just need a convenient standard rendition of the content of desire. It will be the infinitive construction 'to cause (bring about, etc.)...' completed by a propositional variable, p, q, etc.

Intelligent and Non-intelligent Desires

A fundamental distinction I would like to draw is between *non-intelligent* desire and *intelligent* desire. The former can be instinctive or innate, but it can also be acquired, by an intelligent desire becoming, through habit, non-intelligent. An example of a non-intelligent desire, which is also instinctive, is the desire to flinch or withdraw from a source of pain.[3] This desire is sparked off by a sensation of pain to which some attention is paid, at least momentarily (providing we are dealing with a creature capable of attention). It consists in a tendency to act in a manner that is so to speak designed by nature to put an end to the sensation. The behaviour displayed is not indulged in because it is viewed by the agent at the time of acting as an effective means of stopping the pain. It occurs automatically or on reflex when the pain is felt (and registered in thought).

Contrast this with what it would be like to act on an intelligent desire in response to a sensation of pain. Suppose that the action that will make the pain disappear is the pushing of a certain button. In order for this action to be performed, it does not suffice that I am aware of the pain. I must also *think* that if I press the button then I will (probably or

---

[2] Therefore, they are discussed in greater detail in Persson (1981: ch. 5.2).

[3] Certainly learning—e.g. that pain is associated with bodily damage—can add to the aversion to pain, as insisted e.g. by Hall (1989), though it seems to me that he exaggerates the role of learning.

possibly) get rid of the pain, for no instinct of mine gears the pressing of buttons to the relief of pains. I perform the action of causing the button to be pressed *because I take* it to be the action of pressing a certain button which, in my opinion, is an effective means of eliminating the pain felt. That I think of the action thus plays an essential part in the causal genesis of the action. An intelligent desire to cause that some bodily change, p, takes place is a tendency to cause to materialize a state of affairs because one conceives of it as (probably, possibly) p. If nothing goes awry, an intelligent desire manifests itself in an action that is *intentional*; this happens when the states of affairs caused to materialize actually are as the agent conceives them. Hence, what distinguishes intentional from non-intentional actions is that one's correct conception of one's action plays an essential role in the origin of the intentional action.[4]

So, if one is to have an intelligent desire to cause that one's finger moves, one must have a conception or idea of what it is to cause one's finger to move, while this is not necessary for one to have a non-intelligent desire to the same effect. It is likely that we acquire this conception by moving our fingers as the result of non-intelligent desires, that is, on reflex. Having non-intelligent desires and acting on reflex is then primary in relation to having intelligent desires and acting intentionally. But it is also the case that comparatively simple actions that were once executed as the upshot of intelligent desires and, hence, intentionally, by regular practice, can be performed out of non-intelligent desires and on reflex or out of habit. As opposed to instinctive desires, these *acquired* non-intelligent desires are *secondary* in relation to intelligent desires. Had we not been endowed with the ability to learn, by repeated practice, to do unthinkingly what we earlier could do only with detailed attention, we would never have been able to master fairly complicated activities such as typing or driving a car.

One difference between non-intelligent and intelligent desires that p be the case is, then, that in the latter case one must have a conception of what it is to cause p. This necessitates another difference: one cannot think that the state of affairs that one is or will be causing is (probably, possibly) p, unless one thinks that one *can* (probably, possibly) cause—that is, that one (probably, possibly) has the ability and opportunity to cause—p to become the case. Hence, a necessary condition for one's having an intelligent desire for p is that one thinks that it is at least possible (relative to one's present body of beliefs) that one can cause it to become a fact that p. In the case of a pain felt, it is the awareness of the pain that causes one to think about how one can get rid of the pain and to conclude, immediately or after a period of thinking, that one can accomplish this, say, by pushing a certain button.

Imagine, however, that this conclusion is erroneous and that by actually pushing the button one becomes absolutely convinced that one cannot remove the pain by this means; then one will cease to have the intelligent desire to push the button, and one will consequently cease to press it intentionally (in order to stop the pain). Should one also become convinced that one can do nothing at all to eliminate the pain, one can no longer possess an *intelligent* desire to be rid of the pain. But one can still have a non-intelligent or,

---

[4] This analysis of intelligent desire and intentional action is elaborated in Persson (1981: chs. 5 and 6).

more specifically, instinctive desire to rid oneself of it, a desire that issues in more or less refined bits of behaviour designed by nature to remove pains.

It is because intelligent desires essentially involve a thought or belief to the effect that one can accomplish something that they are assessable as rational or irrational. They are (ir)rational if these beliefs are (ir)rational. Instinctive desires lack this essential propositional ingredient and are therefore not assessable in these terms.

Wanting and Wishing

The state of being absolutely certain that one cannot eliminate a pain, but nevertheless having a non-intelligent desire to be rid of it is the state of *wishing* to be rid of the pain or wishing that one could rid oneself of the pain.[5] I do not present this distinction between intelligently desiring and wishing as a pure description of everyday use. Occasionally, this distinction surfaces in everyday parlance. For instance, the reason we find it more natural to speak of wishing the past to be different, wishing that we had acted differently in the past, than to speak of wanting these things is presumably that we are absolutely convinced that we have no power to change the past. But I would admit that this distinction is sometimes blurred, and would be prepared to see my distinction as trimming ordinary usage, as encapsulating a stipulative element.

So when one is conscious of a sensation of pain, what happens in conative respects could be the following. This consciousness triggers off certain innate patterns of behaviour designed to remove the pain. If they fail to abolish it, one is caused to think about how the pain is to be eliminated (we saw already in Chapter 1 that pain can affect thought processes). Given that this thinking issues in some strategy about how this is to be accomplished, the consciousness of the pain then tends to cause behaviour which one takes to put this strategy into practice. That is, one has an intelligent desire to eliminate the pain (by a certain means). If this behaviour also fails to remove the pain, one may *hope* that there be another means of ridding oneself of the pain. Hoping this is having a non-intelligent desire to *ascertain* that there is such a means, which is elicited by the thought that there might be. But if one becomes convinced that this cannot be achieved, this conviction, by virtue of encapsulating the idea of the pain, may still tend to cause behaviour designed by nature rather than by oneself to put an end to the pain. Then one merely wishes to be rid of the pain or wishes that one could rid oneself of the pain. Thus, instinctive desire is the source from which intelligent desire, wishing and hoping flows, given different cognitive constraints.

It might be thought that I cannot hold wishes and hopes to be rational and irrational, since I take them to be non-intelligent desires. However, as a matter of conceptual necessity, they involve also beliefs, for example a wish to be rid of a pain one is feeling involves the belief that one cannot stop this pain. (The desire is non-intelligent because

---

[5] For references to discussions of the distinction between wanting and wishing, see Persson (1981: ch. 5 n. 15) and Davis (1986: n. 2).

the belief leaves no room for intelligent action.) So, wishes and hopes can be (ir)rational because the beliefs they involve are (ir)rational. This ground for (ir)rationality will be further elucidated in the next two chapters when emotions are discussed.

Wanting for its own Sake and Wanting for the Sake of Something Else

To explain the distinction between non-intelligent and intelligent desires, I have focused mainly on desiring bodily movements to occur, that is, changes that you can cause to occur in basic actions, without doing anything else in order to achieve this. Of course, a desire to rid oneself of a pain is not of this sort; it has to be fulfilled by doing something else, such as withdrawing a hand. In contrast to the latter objective, this objective is also desired *for its own sake* or *as an end (in itself)*. A state of affairs, that is, the exemplification of some property (by something), is desired in this way if it is desired even if considered in isolation and apart from its relations to any other states of affairs which it does not entail. I shall refer to such desires as *intrinsic* desires. (I am here thinking of desires whose intrinsicality is *ultimate* as opposed to acquired or derivative, to allude to a distinction I explain in Chapter 10.)

As indicated above, a desire such as the one to eliminate a pain can manifest itself in other ways than in an action that one thinks will eliminate the pain. If one has not discovered any means to accomplish this end, it may manifest itself in one's casting about to find such a means which is acceptable, that is, to which one is not more averse, either for its own sake or because of its other consequences. Although perhaps not in this particular instance—but, say, in that of getting a pleasure—a desire for an end can also express itself in one's looking for a situation in which one can attain it while sacrificing the attainment of as few as possible of one's other ends. Thus, it is an oversimplification to declare that an intelligent desire to cause p is nothing but a tendency to cause what, in one's view, is p.

When I want to withdraw my hand, the thought that I am capable of withdrawing my hand, by itself, hardly tends to cause what I think is exercising this capacity. For this to be caused, the withdrawal realistically needs to be linked to some state of affairs, like that of being free of pain, that supplies a *reason* for it. I might then be said to have a *derivative* desire to withdraw my hand.

Thus, I can be said to desire the state of affairs consisting in my hand's withdrawing, p, because I desire a situation, s, composed of other states of affairs—such as my being painfree—beside that of p, states of affairs which I think will probably obtain on the assumption that p will obtain (but not in the absence of this assumption, other things being the same). An advantage of this way of putting it is that the strength of my desire for p can then be determined as the strength of my desire for s multiplied by the probability of s given p.[6] So, I desire that my hand withdraws, because I desire the situation that my hand withdraws and that my pain ceases (a situation that I judge probable to obtain if my hand

---

[6] This idea is expounded more formally by Frank Jackson (1984: esp. 7–12).

withdraws), and the strength of the former desire equals the strength of the latter desire multiplied by the probability I assign to the obtaining of the situation mentioned, given that my hand withdraws. Here my desire that my hand withdraws is derived from my desire for a complex of which this state of affairs is a component (and the desire for this complex derives from desires for other components of it, such as the state of affairs consisting in that my pain ceases).

Unfortunately, this account of derivative desires can seem to generate counter-intuitive consequences. Consider a cashier who (intentionally) hands over money to a robber because he thinks that the robber will otherwise carry out his threat to kill him. Some philosophers have claimed that the cashier does not here want to hand over the cash to the robber, but is *forced* to do so.[7] If the clerk had wanted to hand over the money, why force him to do it? Nonetheless, the cashier would seem to want the situation consisting in his handing over the money and staying alive, which he judges likely to obtain if he hands over the money. At any rate, he wants this situation *more* than—or *prefers* this situation to—the situation of his not handing over the money and not surviving, which he judges probable to obtain on the assumption that he does not hand over the money. Perhaps the construction of wanting more or preferring is more suitable than that of wanting *simpliciter*, because the alternative situation is desired to some degree. Let us, however, ignore this distinction and read 'wanting' as covering 'wanting more (preferring)', for after all something is wanted more than its alternative when the alternative is not wanted at all. In the present context, we can afford to put aside the distinction between desiring and preferring, since it is no less counter-intuitive to describe the clerk as preferring to give the robber the money.

I believe, however, that a convincing case can be made out for portraying the cashier as wanting to hand over the money. To be sure, he is forced or coerced to act in this manner, but what is subjected to coercion here—in contrast to the case of purely physical coercion (e.g. when the cashier's hand is in the grip of a stronger hand)—is his will or faculty of forming (derived) desires. The clerk is forced to (derivatively) *want* to hand over the cash. That is why we speak of his *will* as not being free, of him as not acting of his own free will.

We do not speak of the bank clerk as wanting to give the money to the robber, for this would imply that he wants what is *normally* made likely to obtain by a cashier giving bank money to a robber. But what the cashier wants is something entirely different, namely what *in these particular circumstances* is made probable by him giving money to a robber. He wants to give money to a robber when this, and only this, in the current circumstances makes probable his staying alive. The circumstances must be abnormal or extraordinary in some way if the cashier is aptly to be said to be *forced* or *coerced* to (want to) perform the action of giving money to the hold-up man.

Notice that not only threats but also offers can 'force' one to want something. Suppose that somebody offers to pay me a million dollars if (and only if) I eat a worm. Now I

---

[7] For references, see Persson (1981: 111). Cf. also Richard Swinburne (1985), who maintains that one does not desire to do something when one is disposed to do it because of its "extrinsic" consequences; and Staude (1986). More recently, G. F. Schueler has argued for a narrower sense of desire (1995: 29 ff.).

certainly do not desire the conjunction of states of affairs that normally is likely to obtain given that I eat a worm. But I do desire the conjunction of states of affairs that probably comes to be if I eat a worm in this particular situation where the offer has been announced. So, I can be described as being forced (to want) to eat the worm in order to earn the million dollars. However, there is a difference between facing a threat and an offer: while the cashier can be described as being forced to hand over the money to the robber (full stop), I am more naturally described as being forced to eat the worm *in order to* earn the million dollars. More importantly, whereas the cashier can properly be portrayed as acting under duress, and not of his own free will, when he complies with robber's demand, I can scarcely be characterized in the same terms when I succumb to the offer and eat the worm. I believe that this difference has to do with what makes us characterize me as being presented with an *offer*, but the cashier as being presented with a *threat*, namely the fact that the 'interference' is *welcomed* by me in the former case, but *regretted* by the cashier. I shall return to this topic in Chapter 33.

To summarize, when one is described as wanting p, this usually conveys that one wants some situation, s, that is normally probable given p. Suppose now that one is instead averse to (i.e. desires the absence of) s, but that at a particular time, t, the circumstances are peculiar in that p brings along q which one desires more than one is averse to p. (In other words, one's desire for the situation $s^\star$ which is normally probable given q is stronger than one's aversion towards s, assuming equal probabilities given q and p respectively.) Then it would be misleading to say that, at t, one desires p, for that would suggest that one desires s; instead one is portrayed as being forced to bring about, p in order to accomplish q. It would be impeccable, however, to depict one as wanting p and q at t (say, the cashier as wanting to hand over the money *and* save his life) for one desires the situation that normally obtains, given p and q.

Decisive Desiring

I have characterized an intelligent desire for p as a tendency, primarily, to cause what one thinks is that p, but also to reflect upon means of achieving this. This is, I believe, an apt characterization of a desire in the context of deliberation when it competes with other desires. But consider the desire that comes out of this process victoriously: not only as stronger than its rivals, but as so strong that further deliberation about alternatives and consequences is deemed pointless. I shall call such a desire 'decisive' because I see it as taking shape when the deliberator ends deliberation by deciding. As it is plausible to say also that a decision creates an *intention*, I believe this to be the same thing as a decisive desire. But if anyone thinks that an intention is something over and above any desire, I need not insist on this point.

To desire decisively to cause p now is to be in a state which not just *tends* to cause now what one thinks is that p, but which causes—or at least begins to cause—this. Nor is it necessarily a tendency to indulge in means–end thinking, for in order to desire p

decisively one must already have convinced oneself that there are acceptable means to it.[8] True, one need not have specified them, as long as one knows them to be acceptable (and available), but the space for means–end thinking is nevertheless restricted. Decisively desiring that p excludes further consideration of alternatives to it; in this sense, it is having *settled* upon a course of action.[9] So to desire p decisively is rather like desiring a whole sequence of events including p—from some basic actions that are in the situation necessary and sufficient means to causing p, to intrinsically desired consequences of p at this time—so much more (or on so much stronger grounds) than one desires any alternative sequence at the time that further deliberation ceases. That one intentionally brings about p is logically sufficient for ascribing to one a decisive desire to (try to) bring about p (but of course not necessary: only trying to bring it about is necessary for this ascription).[10]

Since a decision (and an intention) to bring about p is expressed by a sentence of the form 'I *shall* bring about p', the same goes for a decisive desire. But 'I shall bring about p' does not express *the content* of decisively desiring (deciding, intending) as 'A will bring about p' expresses the content of a predictive belief. The present analysis of desiring does not provide it with any propositional content of its own in the same sense as a belief has such content. As a tendency to bring about what, in one's view, is (or might be) p, it presupposes that one thinks that one can (possibly) bring it about that p, but of course that is not a propositional content distinctive of desiring (one can entertain it without having a desire). So, to obtain a complete indicative sentence one must import a 'shall'-operator which expresses the attitude of desiring rather than its content. This observation will be of some importance in the discussion of practical reasoning in Chapter 8.

Cognitivism and Conativism about Motivation

Let me now put forward a definition of decisively desiring (or intending) something at the current time which sums up the main thrust of the discussion so far.

(D) *A* decisively desires to (try to) cause p now = *A* is in a state such that his thinking that he can (possibly) now bring about p (and thereby a certain complex 'situation') causes something to become a fact that he thinks (possibly) is that p.

This definition simplifies matters a bit, by concentrating on what is true of decisively desiring irrespective of whether 'p' stands for something that can be brought about in a basic action or something more distant (thus, it leaves out that the

---

[8] Cf. a claim, made e.g. by Schueler (1995: 22–3) about intending. If one is uncertain about the means to p—about one's ability to apply them or their efficiency—one only has a decisive desire to *try* to bring about p.

[9] As Alfred Mele puts it (1992: 142). Cf. also Michael Bratman (1987: 16–17). Both of these writers hold that intentions are something over and above desires in the sense that they have "an executive feature that is not reducible to relative motivational strength" (Mele, 1992: 167). My inclination is to think that the relation between desire and intention is analogous to the relation between (tentative) belief and conviction—a conviction that p being a belief that p on grounds strong enough to bring to an end further consideration of whether or not p is the case.

[10] Again, for my account of the relation between desire and intentional action, see (1981: chs. 5 and 6).

state may also cause *A* to specify means to *p* he believes there to be). As will transpire, (D) will also have to be expanded to cater for cases of having a decisive desire for a future time.

Needless to say, a decisive desire is an intelligent desire. If the desire were a non-intelligent and instinctive one, the tendency would be designed by nature rather than by the subject himself to issue in its becoming a fact that *p*. Then there need not be a thought in the modality of what one can bring about. A thought to the effect, for example that one is feeling pain (or perhaps in a creature that lacks all capacity for classifying its sensory data, simply a sensation of pain) would suffice. (D) highlights intelligent desires because they are the desires for which we can have reasons.

(D) portrays desires as states that move or cause one to act. This is required for desires to be something that genuinely motivates. In the case of intelligent desires, part of what moves one to act is the thought that one can bring about some state of affairs. This makes a desire a motivational state directed towards the attainment of a goal one has set oneself. But according to (D), thinking is not the full motivating cause. (D) asserts that *A*'s thinking that he can bring about *p* is sufficient to motivate him only given that he is in a certain 'state'. This state is meant to be something non-cognitive.

The inclusion of such a state is moot. It is affirmed by *conativists* (of motivation), but opposed by *cognitivists* who maintain that motivating factors can be purely cognitive, like thoughts and beliefs. Cognitivists can agree with conativists that intentionally bringing about *p* entails (decisively) desiring to bring about *p*. But, if so, they will deny that the ascription of a desire incorporates the attribution of a separate motivational factor alongside the cognitive ones. That is, they will reject (D)'s reference to a non-cognitive motivational state as necessary, by interpreting a desire as the tendency of purely cognitive factors to influence behaviour.[11]

Cognitivists may also object to (D) because it depicts thoughts as *causal* factors. They may hold that, whether or not it constitutes a basis for an ascription of desires, the influence thoughts exercise over action is non-causal. The best support for a causal interpretation consists in an appeal to simplicity, I think: if one is able to break down the phenomena of desire and intentional action into components, for example, propositional thoughts and bodily movements, which *could* intelligibly be causally related—and I have tried to accomplish this in (1981)—then considerations of simplicity recommend that they be regarded as *being* thus related, since that would make the domain of desire and action continuous with the rest of nature where causality presumably reigns.[12]

Now, given the correctness of this interpretation, can conativism be defended? Strictly speaking, we should distinguish between a conceptual and an empirical issue. The conceptual one concerns whether the (ordinary) concept of desire contains a reference to some non-cognitive factor which, in conjunction with cognitive ones, causally influences behaviour. The empirical one concerns whether there is in fact such a factor, that is,

---

[11] As will be seen in Ch. 9, these cognitivists include Thomas Nagel (1970), Don Locke (1974), John McDowell (1978, 1981), and T. M. Scanlon (1998: ch. 1).   [12] For a recent defence of causalism, see Mele (2003: ch. 2).

whether a concept with such reference applies to reality. If the reply to the first question is yes, but the reply to the second one no, our attributions of desire are erroneous, and the concept of desire must be revised for them to be true. I shall argue for a positive answer to the conceptual question and assume that there is no reason not to give the same answer to the empirical question.

A belief p is a disposition that usually actualizes itself, among other things, in one's occurrently thinking p in situations in which the question of the truth of p arises.[13] Now a belief cannot have any effect on behaviour unless it manifests itself in occurrent thought. Suppose I go shopping and that parsley is among the many items I need to buy. However, as I walk around in the shop it momentarily slips my mind that I need to buy parsley; so I do not buy it. It would not be correct, I believe, to describe me as losing this belief (that I need parsley), later having to acquire it anew. It is rather that possession of a belief is compatible with its content occasionally failing to show up in episodic thinking at relevant moments. But, and this is one thing the example is designed to illustrate, when a belief fails to surface in occurrent thinking, the subject will not act on it.[14] This is why the *definiens* of (D) speaks of (episodic) thinking rather than believing.

In other words, in (D) I have sought to characterize what it is to have an *occurrent* desire. But we are also said to possess desires, although our minds are occupied with other matters. I can be said to have a desire to continue working on this manuscript at times when all thoughts of it are far from my mind, and indeed even when I am asleep or unconscious. Such desires are *dormant*. In my opinion this distinction just reflects the distinction between episodically thinking that something is the case and dispositionally believing it to be the case. That is to say, to have an (intelligent) desire for p which is dormant involves having a belief that one can bring about p instead of an episodic thought to this effect.[15] It should be added that, when I spoke above of a decisive desire, I was talking about the strongest desire in one's set of *occurrent* desires with conflicting contents.

So, since our (occurrent) attitudes and actions are determined by what we episodically think of, or attend to, the outcome of the competition for attention is important. As that which we are capable of attending to at any moment is just a tiny fraction of what we dispositionally believe and of what is perceptually present, this competition is very hard. The attentive selection made is likely to be biased. It will appear that this is the main source of the attitudinal irrationalities to be explored in this book.

There is, however, a further point of the parsley example—other than displaying the causal role of episodic thought—which is the main one in the present context. The

---

[13] I discuss the relation between thinking and believing in (1981: ch. 3.1). Among other things, I make the point, also made by Mele (2003: 31), that a belief must at some time have been manifested in episodic thought. As Mele notes (2003: 32–3), this point carries over to dispositional desires in the definition of which belief figures.

[14] It should be noticed that this does not imply that one cannot act on 'unconscious' thoughts in every sense. For although a thought is conscious in the sense that it is episodically represented, this representation may be so brief that one may not notice or be conscious of having it. Such episodes can influence one's behaviour.

[15] Note that what in Brandt's terminology corresponds to my notion of occurrent desire is "effective desire"; his "ocurrent desires" are rather counterparts to my dormant desires, since actual thinking about the state of affairs desired is not here required (1979: 25–8).

example allows one to infer something about the strength of my desire to get parsley, namely that it is rather weak. If it had been strong as, say, a heavy smoker's desire for tobacco, the thought of parsley would certainly not have slipped my mind. Should it momentarily have left my mind because I was distracted by, say, the sight of a beautiful woman walking by, it would be bound to recur soon. In other words, an effect of desiring parsley, if one cannot get it straightaway, is to keep one episodically think- ing of parsley, for example to see to it that one's belief that one needs it is regularly manifested in occurrent thought. But then, contrary to cognitivism, a desire for parsley cannot boil down to the causal power of an (occurrent) thought of parsley, for, once it has disappeared, this thought cannot cause later instances of the same thought. Rather, the desire must be a state that can persist in the absence of any thought of its objective in order to facilitate associations from distracting thoughts back to this objective.

Dispositional belief states cannot themselves cause their manifestations in episodic thought, for at any time we are in countless such states, and only very few of them are represented in episodic thought. Something other than these states themselves must then determine this selection. What is currently perceived and episodically thought are presumably among the factors contributing to this selection. But we are now considering a case in which current perceptions and thoughts are *distracting* me from the thought of parsley. What could lead me back to it? I claim that a desire seems precisely to be something that facilitates associations from such distractions back to the thought of parsley. The stronger the desire, the easier it is to make the association, that is, the more tenuous can the link between the episode which ignites the association and the objective of desire be. But for a desire to do this work, it must obviously be something over and above such cognitive and sensory episodes.

A desire is thus a non-conceptual and non-sensory state that, among other things, tends to facilitate the appearance of its objective in occurrent thought, if it is not already there. This is a further effect on thought-processes, alongside the one of making one indulge in means-end reasoning mentioned earlier. In this case, too, if the desire is intense, one may find it hard to think about anything else, whereas if it is weak, this is a matter that easily slips one's mind.

My argument has been to the effect that to understand how a desire can tend to keep its objective manifested in mental episodes, it must be construed as something over and above what is manifested in such episodes, for it is at work in the absence of any suitable mental episodes, precisely in order to promote their reappearance. Now, if a desire is a state below the surface of consciousness that tends to cause itself to be, so to speak, regularly afloat, it is reasonable to think that once it is afloat, in the shape of the occurrence of suitable episodic thoughts, the state will in conjunction with these thoughts tend to produce behaviour. For it seems that the state is designed to produce the thoughts because they are necessary to produce the behaviour. As the temporal consciousness of a creature expands, a state that is designed to have the function of tending to produce a certain pattern of behaviour immediately is likely to develop also the function of keeping itself in existence until the time is ripe for producing this behaviour.[16]

We may summarize the upshot of this reasoning in a definition as follows:

(D*) At t, A has a dormant decisive desire (to cause) p at a future time, $t+ =$. At t, A is in a state such that, if it persists at $t+$, it will tend to cause A's belief that he can bring about p (and thereby a certain situation) to manifest itself in episodic thought at $t+$, and by this means to cause what A thinks is p at $t+$.

The conativist conception of a desire is also supported by the consideration that, in view of the great differences between human individuals, it appears natural to suppose that not every subject capable of entertaining some thought would behave similarly (though no two subjects are in fact likely to have exactly the same thoughts and, if it were to occur, it is likely to pass unnoticed). As we saw when discussing physical pain in Chapter 1, the phenomenon of asymbolia for pain shows that not even in the case of this sensation, every individual who feels it tries to get rid of it. On the conativist conception, desires gesture towards something that can account for this behavioural difference: some individuals are, and some are not, in a state which in conjunction with this experience produces a certain type of behaviour.

So, to conclude, it seems the best bet to put one's money on the conativist conceptual claim that the concept of desire postulates a state—presumably neural in character—which does not receive mental expression of a conceptual or sensory character. (I will shortly try to strengthen the support of this claim by arguing that desiring does not necessarily involve feeling anything.) This is how I think the state alluded to in (D) and (D*) should be interpreted.[17]

It seems that an allegiance to determinism underlies this postulation of an intrinsically unknown explanatory state which our ordinary concept of desire encapsulates. So, it is *conceivable* that this postulate is untenable, for example that there is in fact nothing causing the recurrence of thoughts of objects desired. However, there is as yet no reason to believe this rather than that neurophysiological research will bear out the truth of the postulate. This confirmation would not only underwrite the legitimacy of talk of desires as separate explanatory factors, but would also in some respects supersede it, since the explanations couched in neurophysiological terms would specify what the postulated

---

[16] Compare Scanlon's claim: "A person has a desire in the directed-attention sense that P if the thought of P keeps occurring to him or her in a favorable light" (1998: 39). One important difference between this account and mine is that, whereas Scanlon, consistently with cognitivism about motivation, identifies a desire with the tendency of certain thoughts to occur, I take it to be a distinct state that tends to cause the occurrence of these thoughts (and appropriate behaviour). What more plausible cause of this insistent occurrence of thoughts than a desire could there be? Scanlon's account has also been rightly criticized by Mele as being "overly intellectualized" (2003: 78) because it involves taking the subject as seeing the considerations that keep cropping up "as reasons for acting in a certain way" (1998: 40). Surely, subjects can have desires, even intelligent ones, though they lack the concept of a reason.

[17] Thus Mark Platts makes a mistake when he thinks that the state to which a dispositional conception of desire (which he terms "the classical misconception") refers to must intrinsically be "mental" or "an 'introspectible something' (a feeling)" (1991: 34). The concept of desire has been designed to refer to a *non-introspectible* factor that, alongside mental episodes (and abilities), helps to produce behaviour.

factors are intrinsically like, whereas talk of desires identifies them in a rather vacuous extrinsic or relational fashion, as 'something that in conjunction with certain thoughts tends to cause certain behaviour'.

Desire and Feeling

I shall end this discussion of the concept of desire by commenting on the relation between desiring and feeling. Noel Fleming writes that a desire is

> any affective state that might lead someone who had it or was in it to do something...
> To have a desire is to be subject to perturbation, to be disposed to feel moved, however slightly or greatly, for the sake of or in connection with what we know or believe about the fate of what we desire. Desiring as opposed to merely wishing presumably requires being disposed to act; but being disposed to act is not enough, and being disposed to feel is necessary. (1981: 213–14)

Two important claims are here advanced: (1) to be in an affective state, to feel something is a necessary condition for having a desire; and (2) this affective state is among the factors that tend to move one to act. These two claims are summed up by Fleming in the following statement: "To have desires is to be affected in a way that tends to set in motion" (1981: 220). I shall argue that both (1) and (2) are false: it is not the case that desiring is necessarily accompanied by feeling, and, even when this is so, the feelings are not among the factors that spark off the tendency to act.

Something that can confer on (1) a semblance of plausibility is that a lot of desires involve tendencies to move one's body, and such tendencies can result in incipient bodily movements—for example muscular contractions—that are felt. Thus, if I have a desire to raise my arm to draw somebody's attention to me, but this desire is almost immediately defeated by another desire (to pass unnoticed) that seizes me, the first desire may still have had time to manifest itself in some slight, but noticeable, muscular contractions in my arm. I think this might be what we refer to when we say things like 'I felt a desire to raise my arm'.

As long as one has cases like this mind, it is tempting to agree with Kurt Baier that desire "involves a felt impulse toward doing something" (1958: 111). But consider a desire to remain lying down relaxing: there is certainly no "felt impulse toward doing something" here, nor any other feelings, save those springing from the state of lying down. Remember also that not all desires involve desires to move one's body. Think of somebody who wants to call something to mind or to visualize something and straightaway proceeds to do so. If the feelings that could most plausibly be held to be essential for desiring are feelings of incipient bodily movements, we should not expect any feelings here.

So (1) is in all probability false. However, what is even more important is the falsity of (2). Even when they are present, these feelings are not among the conditions that trigger off those behavioural tendencies in which desires consist; they are part of the effect rather than of the cause. To be sure, there are desires that are prompted by something felt. This is true of the tendency to withdraw from a source of pain. It is also true of desires that originate in a state of bodily need that makes itself felt in bodily sensation, like the desire to eat which is sparked off by pangs of hunger. Perhaps the word 'desire' is particularly at home in cases like this, and so the use of it may lead some to take these cases as models for all cases of desiring and wanting. But this would of course be a gross error, as should be evident by now.

There is another way to tie the state of desiring to some state of feeling. Desires are either fulfilled or not fulfilled (apart from those that simply cease to exist through the incentive vanishing from one's mind, for example because of forgetfulness, loss of consciousness, etc.). If (in the opinion of the subject) they are fulfilled, there will be feelings of fulfilment or satisfaction, while if (in the subject's view) they are not, there will be feelings of discontent and frustration. Therefore, it may be concluded, even though the state of desiring itself does not necessarily encapsulate any feelings (let alone any feelings that prompt behaviour), it is nevertheless true that desires are normally bound up with feelings.

My reply to this is that it is not always true that subjects feel (dis)satisfaction upon realizing that their desires have been (dis)satisfied. Consider a desire or preference which is very weak: when taking a walk, I form a weak desire or preference to walk along the other pavement, but a moment later I notice that the traffic is so heavy that I am prevented from crossing the street. Surely it is unreasonable to insist that I must here feel frustration to some degree. The feeling of frustration probably reflects a state of bodily tension that results from a behavioural tendency not being allowed to follow its path. But if this tendency is weak, is it not sensible to surmise that the tension can be too slight to make itself felt? What reason is there to insist that it must be strong enough to make itself felt?

Moreover, it is even less plausible to hold that one must feel fulfilled upon realizing that a desire has been fulfilled (even disregarding the possibility that the desire can be based on false beliefs). Consider, for instance, a rather weak desire that is fulfilled without any impediment, as a matter of course, like a desire to continue walking when one is walking. The reason why it seems so far-fetched to claim that one will feel satisfaction as this desire is translated into behaviour is, I suggest, that, since this tendency smoothly runs along its course without being hemmed in by anything, no tension is building up, and the (pleasurable) feeling of fulfilment is the feeling of the relaxation of such a tension. In order for satisfaction to be felt, it is necessary that both the desire not be too weak and its gratification not be instantaneous.

Consequently, it is not true that whenever there is desiring, there are feelings—typically, feelings occur when the desire is fairly strong. However, even if this generalization had been true in the actual world, it would still have been just a contingent truth. For it is conceivable that there be creatures equipped with efferent pathways just like actual beings, but lacking the afferent connections indispensable for the feeling of their own bodies from inside. These creatures would have none of the feelings here in question. All the same, they could have desires. With their efferent pathways intact, it would be possible for their thoughts to have bodily effects. No doubt it would be difficult for them to move their bodies in a controlled and precise manner, as this is dependent upon feedback in the shape of bodily sensations. But it seems that, by relying on vision, these beings could learn to perform at least simple bodily movements at will (they might lack limbs that allow them to perform more precise movements). This suffices for their being in possession of (intelligent) desires.[18]

Therefore, the concept of desire is independent of that of feeling and emotion: we can conceive of individuals who have desires, but no feelings or emotions.[19] It should be noted, however, that it is not a corollary of this that, *if* a subject of desire is capable of having feelings and emotions, it is a purely contingent matter what states of feeling go with what states of desiring. It is not a contingent matter that somebody who desires to bring about *p* will *hope* to succeed in bringing this about rather than *fear* it and that this subject will be *pleased* or *glad* rather than *displeased* or *sad* upon being notified of success. (The ground of the non-contingency of these propositions will emerge in the next two chapters when emotions are subjected to analysis.) Yet it is a contingent matter that something rather than nothing be felt.

[18] There seem to be actual cases that (in relevant respects) match this description: "the disembodied lady" as reported by Sacks (1985: ch. 3).

[19] Hence it follows, as I conclude (1981: 123–8), that theorists are in error when they contend that the concept of desire is a theoretical construct that receives its sense by being embedded in a set of laws or lawlike propositions which link it to the concepts of feelings and emotions.

5

THE CONCEPT OF EMOTION

THE topic of this essay is the rationality of attitudes where the term 'attitudes' covers desires and emotions. In the present chapter I shall put forward an account of the nature of emotions according to which they can be assessed in respect of rationality. Like (intelligent) desires, they have this property because they comprise propositional thinking. But, as in the case of desires, there is more to emotions than propositional thinking; that is why I have called desires and emotions *para-cognitive* attitudes. So my second task will be to spell out what this surplus is, and how it differs from the surplus encompassed in desiring. This will lead onto a broader exploration of the relationship between desire and emotion. First, however, I shall try to vindicate the idea that emotions can be appraised as rational, can be supported by reasons, because they involve propositional thinking or thinking that something is the case.

Emotions resemble desires in that they have *objects* or *contents*: just as when there is desire, there is something that is desired, so whenever there is an emotion, there is something at which this emotion is directed. For instance, when one is afraid, there is something *of* which one is afraid, for example the person or dog next door; when one experiences hope, there is something *for* which one hopes, for example the protection of the black rhinoceros; when one is angry, there is something *with* which one is angry, for example the friend who betrayed one; when one is pleased or glad, there is something *about* which one is pleased or glad, for example, that one spotted a rare bird; and so on.

As can be seen from these examples, emotional objects may belong to different ontological categories: a concrete thing, an event, or a fact. It seems to me, however, that emotional objects can always be rephrased in a propositional form, that the object of an emotion can always be rendered as a—putative—fact. Thus, if I fear my neighbour, I must take something to be true of him—for example, that he is an arsonist and might set the house on fire—in virtue of which I fear him. That is, my fear of my neighbour is a fear that he is an arsonist and might burn down the house. Analogously, one's hoping for the protection of the rhinoceros is a hope that it will be successfully protected. This being so, I shall speak of the (propositional) *content* of an emotion rather than of its object, since the latter may suggest a concrete thing. Note that there need not be anything *real* towards which an emotion is oriented: it is true that I cannot be described as fearing *my neighbour* if I do not in fact have one, but even if this person is a figment of my imagination, my fear is real. I could be described as being afraid because, as I believe, I have a neighbour who is dangerous.

It is a familiar claim that emotions differ from sensations in respect of this feature of essentially having content.[1] This is a feature upon which we rely when we distinguish pain as a sensation, physical pain, from emotional or mental pain. When I am pained by a bereavement or a humiliation, the pain is of the latter kind, for there is some believed fact that pains me or gives me pain. In contrast, when I am just feeling a sensation of pain, say, a stab of pain in the chest, there is nothing that pains or gives me pain in the present sense. Certainly, there is a cause of my sensation, but this is presumably not logically necessary, and in any event I need in no sense be aware of this cause. But clearly, I cannot be pained by a bereavement, unless I am aware of this bereavement or think that I have suffered this sort of bereavement. The content of my emotional pain is the content of a thought of mine; it is capable of giving me pain because it is something I think is the case. When I am just feeling physical pain, none of this is true: there is no propositional content that gives me pain by being the content of some thought of mine. The same is true of physical pleasure: when I stretch my legs after sitting long in a cramped posture, there need be nothing that gives me pleasure by being thought of by me. As opposed to this, when I am pleased that something is the case, for example, that I have spotted a rare bird, this qualifies as an emotional or mental pleasure because there is of necessity some state of affairs—that I have spotted a rare bird—which, by being the content of a thought of mine, gives me pleasure.

So one cannot be glad, sad, etc. that *p* without thinking, believing, or knowing *p*, but in order to have these emotions, it is not necessary to think, believe, or know that one is having an emotion the content of which is *p*. A conflation of these two statements leads to the view that one cannot have an emotion without knowing or being conscious of having it. As I regard this view as implausible, I should like to stress that it is not entailed by the thesis that emotions are essentially content-oriented.

Sometimes it is, however, disputed that emotions necessarily have contents (or objects). For instance, Gosling maintains that it is just an accident of language that 'feels pleased' cannot occur on its own, that one has to be described as being pleased at, about, or with something (1969: 153). But if there were a state in which one could be described as feeling pleased without this state's being directed at anything, this would merely show that 'feels pleased' sometimes designates a *mood* rather than an emotion. Indeed, there *are* states of this kind: one can be in a pleasant or good mood, one can be happy or in a state of euphoria. Like sensations, moods differ from emotions in not having propositional contents (cf. for example, Trigg, 1970: 5–6). We should also be aware of the possibility that sometimes when a state of feeling apparently has no content, it really has some very indefinite content, for example that something or other good will happen sometime (cf. Davis, 1988: 459–60).

---

[1] It has been expressed, e.g. by Kenny: "The most important difference between a sensation and an emotion is that emotions, unlike sensations, are essentially directed to objects" (1963: 60).

Moods are more intimately related to emotions than are sensations. For instance, it does not appear to be a contingent truth that if one is in a happy mood then one is more disposed to experience the emotion of being happy about this or that than one is when one is not in a happy mood. We would not describe a creature as being in a happy or joyous mood if we knew it to be incapable of experiencing the emotion of happiness or joy. Obviously, nothing of the sort characterizes the relation between physical pain/pleasure and its emotional counterpart: it is not true in general, let alone of necessity, that feeling physical pain/pleasure makes a being more prone to feel pained or pleased by some state of affairs. None of this entails, however, that to be in a mood is nothing but to be disposed or to tend to have the corresponding emotion. If this was true, to be in a mood would be similar to having a certain kind of *temperament* (for example, to be a happy or cheerful sort of person), only more short-lived. But this is manifestly not true, for moods are *felt* just as emotions are. It is more plausible to hold that a mood involves whatever the corresponding emotion involves, apart from the thought the content of which provides the emotion with its content. I shall revert to the question of what this 'surplus' could consist in after dissecting the emotional reaction.

I believe that my distinction between emotions and moods exists in everyday parlance, though perhaps in a somewhat fuzzy form. But for my purposes the claim that emotions necessarily have contents could be read as a stipulation. I want to focus on a certain class of states of mind that have propositional contents: the states of mind to which we refer when we speak of being afraid *of* something, being angry *with* something, etc. Even if in ordinary discourse the term 'emotion' does not designate exactly this class, it approximates to it nearly enough for the term to be a natural choice as a label for this class. The reason why I want to highlight this class is that I am interested in some states of mind that can be appraised in respect of rationality. Now, if a state of mind necessarily has content, and if it has content in virtue of involving an episode of propositional thinking the content of which is the content of the state, then, since propositional thoughts can be assessed in respect of rationality, the whole can be so assessed, at least in a derivative sense.[2]

Emotions Not Merely Judgements

However, one writer, Robert Solomon, who is out to explode "the myth" that "the emotions are irrational forces beyond our control" (1976: 239; cf. also e.g. pp. xvi–xvii and ch. 6), goes to the extreme of *equating* emotion with judgement, more specifically an evaluative one: an "emotion is an evaluative (or 'normative') judgment" (1976: 186). Solomon seems to reach this position because of his view that only what we *do* can be assessed as reasonable or unreasonable. So in order to make good his claim that emotions can be so assessed he is committed to hold that "our passions are our own *doings*, and thus our responsibility" (1976: 25). Since judgements are described as being *made*, and

---

[2] This is as much as Hume concedes when he declares that "passions can be contrary to reason only so far as they are *accompany'd* with some judgment or opinion" (1739–40/1978: 416).

emotions apparently involve them, the step to the conclusion that emotions or passions *are* some sort of judgements is only a short one.

But it is patently false that only what we do and are responsible for can be appraised in respect of rationality. Our thoughts or beliefs that something is the case can obviously be rational or irrational, yet they are not actions for which we are held responsible. For example, my thought that I am feeling pain when I am in fact feeling pain is irresistibly caused by my sensation of pain; being in these circumstances, I cannot help thinking this thought. Nonetheless thoughts can be rational and reasonable. Therefore, emotions can be so too without being things done for which we are responsible.

In spite of this, Solomon could be right in construing emotions as evaluative judgements. But weighty considerations militate against such a view. Intuitively, it seems undeniable that, in the words of William Alston, an "evaluation can be either emotional or unemotional" (1967a: 485).[3] Suppose that it is maintained, say, that to be in a state of fear is to judge that something poses a threat; then to feel strong fear, to be terrified, would be to judge that something presents a very grave threat. It is, however, at least logically possible to be calm, detached, and show no signs of bodily or behavioural disturbance or perturbation when one makes an (evaluative) judgement (whatever its intrinsic characteristics). In contrast, it is not even logically possible to be very fearful or terrified while showing no signs of being disturbed; certain patterns of behaviour or bodily changes are characteristic of fear. Wayne Davis provides a long list of what this "involuntary arousal" comprises, dividing the items into three kinds:

> *Visceral*: rapid heartbeat, even pounding; perspiration, most commonly sweaty palms and armpits; abdominal distress, most commonly a knotted stomach, but in more extreme cases diarrhea, frequent urination, and sometimes even loss of control over bodily functions; increased respiration rate, or sudden inspiration; and pallor, which results from constriction of blood vessels in the skin. '*Cortical*' (i.e. psychological): restless sleep, even insomnia; and channelled and disorderly cognition, indicated by a lessened ability to concentrate, deliberate, and draw rational conclusions, and by a restricted range of perception, attention, and memory. *Motor*: muscular tension, even trembling or shaking; and last but not least, impulsive or reflexive action, performed without deliberation, and difficult to control, such as facial expressions, postural adjustments (e.g. cowering), vocalizations (e.g. screaming), and even fleeing or freezing. (1988: 462–3)

Impressive as this list may be, I do not claim that it is exhaustive (there is, for instance, also dryness of mouth and throat), but it is more than sufficient for present purposes.

All of these symptoms need not be present whenever fear is experienced—not, for example, if the fear is weak and ephemeral—but most of them are certainly present whenever a normal person is in a state of strong fear or terror. It is, however, perfectly conceivable that a person judges that something poses a grave threat, and yet displays

---

[3] For a criticism of Solomon, see Stephen R. Leighton (1985). However, I think Leighton goes too far in his critique of the judgemental approach in contending (1985: 139) that (*a*) what kind of emotion is in question is determined by the feelings involved rather than by the judgement; and that (*b*) the feeling may outlive the judgement and still be an emotion (rather than a mood).

none of these reactions: that is, a person can be fearless in the face of grave danger. Consequently, to be in a state of (strong) fear is not just to make an evaluative judgement; it is also to exhibit a certain pattern of behaviour or bodily changes. But if it is conceded that to experience a strong emotion includes displaying fairly pronounced bodily reactions, it should also be conceded that experiencing a less intensive emotion includes displaying bodily reactions, albeit of a less pronounced character. It is reasonable to agree with William Lyons (1980: 125), that the strength of such bodily reactions is our criterion for the strength or intensity of an emotion.[4]

It is true that sometimes when we apply emotion terms, it is not asserted that any bodily reactions are present. For instance, a doctor might tell the patient, 'I fear that you will have to undergo surgery', without having the bodily reactions typical of fear. But this observation does not weaken the case I am making, for we immediately recognize such uses as a non-literal, polite turn of phrase. The doctor is not really reporting an emotion, but is rather just expressing sympathy with the patient by talking as though she were sharing the patient's fear. I suggest that we take as a criterion for the reporting use of emotion terms that they are in order only if some of bodily changes listed occur (cf. Shaffer, 1983: 167–8).

To sum up the result of the discussion so far: in order for A to (occurrently) have an emotion it is necessary that (1) she is (episodically) thinking some propositional thought and that (2) she exhibits some pattern of bodily changes. In the absence of (1) the emotion could have no content, since the content of the emotion is constituted by the content of thinking, while the deduction of (2) would result in an unemotional state of thinking or judging. It is plausible to hypothesize that the thoughts and the patterns of bodily change do not just appear in conjunction, but that the former *cause* the latter, for it is that of which we think that *makes* us afraid, glad, angry, etc. I shall not here attempt to defend this proposal to analyse in causal terms the notion of emotions having contents or objects, since it is today the prevalent view.[5] It should be noted, however, that it is not the content or object that is the cause, but episodes of thinking with this content.

Emotion and Desire

I shall now try to say something more specific about the two elements involved in emotions. Let me start with (2), the pattern of behaviour and bodily changes. In some cases, it seems clear that this pattern includes components that support the ascription of some desire. For example, if I fear my neighbour's dog (say, fear that it might bite me), I will

---

[4] Contrast Davis (1988) who, distinguishing the propositional fear that *p* from the experiential state of fear, maintains that only the latter incorporates involuntary arousal. I agree of course that one can have a fear that *p* without being in a state of fear, but regard it as more natural to hold that there is merely a difference in degree between the two, that is, that the former, too, involves, an "involuntary arousal", though to a lesser extent. Similarly, I believe the difference between being in a state of fear and one of anxiety to be one of degree, whereas Davis takes the former to encompass a new element of unhappiness (1988: 471 ff.). In the former case, the involuntary arousal may be so intense that it is felt as unpleasant.

[5] See, e.g. Lyons (1980), J. R. S. Wilson (1972), and Gordon (1987). When I speak of a thought 'causing' a bodily change, I do not wish to exclude that there can be overdetermination, i.e. another sufficient cause of the bodily change which does not include the thought.

tend to flee or at least stay away from this dog. Similarly, if I am angry with somebody, I will desire or tend to attack this person. Presumably inspired by such reflections, some writers have concluded that the emotional reaction *always* includes—or even is constituted by—some desire. Thus, we find the psychologist Magda Arnold concluding that "the emotional *quale* consist/s/precisely in…unreasoning involuntary attraction or repulsion" (1960: 172) and that "we can now define emotion as *the felt tendency toward anything intuitively appraised as good (beneficial), or away from anything intuitively appraised as bad (harmful)*" (1960: 182).[6]

This characterization of the conative tendency putatively involved seems, however, too narrow to fit even all cases of fear which admittedly includes such a tendency. If a philanderer fears that he has been infected with HIV, there cannot, literally, be any tendency "*away from*" the state of affairs feared.

Lyons's way of specifying the desire involved in fear is broader: "a want to avoid or be rid of the danger" (1980: 64). Yet it is evident that one can fear that one carries HIV while being utterly convinced that one can do nothing to get rid of the virus or to avoid its harmful effects—indeed, this insight is likely to aggravate one's fear. Hence, the "want to avoid or be rid of the danger" cannot be intelligent here. But could a non-intelligent desire to avoid or be rid of the thing feared manifest itself here when the usual strategies of withdrawing, fleeing, hiding, etc. from the thing feared look so out of place? I think it could here take the form of a tendency to avoid or be rid of *consciousness* (on one's own part) of the fact feared, for example, that one carries HIV. So the subject afflicted by this fear will tend to: avoid being tested, avert attention from evidence either raising the probability that he is infected or proving the lethal outcome of the infection, prevent himself from thinking of the possibility of being infected, persuade himself that cures will soon be discovered, etc. All this could be part of an intelligent or calculated strategy to keep oneself in an untroubled state of mind. But it seems clear that these tendencies also occur prior to and independently of such calculation, as an instinctive way to avoid or rid oneself of the thing feared: instinctively one flees in one's mind when a real flight is evidently impossible.

I find it most reasonable to hold that a non-intelligent desire to somehow protect oneself against the state of affairs feared is encapsulated in the emotion of fear. But I would like to argue that there is an antithetical relationship between fear and *intelligent* desire: to the extent that one views it to be within one's power of intentional action to see to it whether or not p materializes, one cannot fear the materialization of p. It is absurd to fear something that one is convinced is fully within one's control. (As Gordon (1987: 79–84) puts it, the uncertainty of whether or not p must be non-deliberative.) The mountaineer is afraid of falling only because he knows that, despite his skill, he might fall. Had he been convinced that it was within his capacity to prevent every possible fall, he could not possibly be afraid that he might fall.

That a climber can be described as being afraid of climbing a certain mountain might seem to contradict this. However, what he is afraid of here is not that he will climb the

---

[6] Other theorists that give pride of place to conation include Joel Marks (1982 and 1986*b*).

mountain—which is something that is up to him—but that he will fall *if* he climbs it (cf. Davis, 1988: 460). And again, he can be afraid of this only to the extent that he thinks it beyond his power to exclude every possibility of this happening (or every possibility of a fall leading to that in virtue of which he fears the fall, presumably death or serious injury). Of course, a mountaineer can normally do something to decrease the risk of falling, and when this is so, his fear of falling will be channelled into intelligent behaviour to this effect. But fear does not *require* the endorsement of any such possibility of preventive action: a climber, trapped on a ledge that he thinks might give away any moment, will be in the grip of a fear of falling, though he realizes that there is *nothing* he can do to make this event (or its fateful consequences) less likely.

It is also plausible to regard the emotion of anger as involving some non-intelligent or, more precisely, instinctive desire, a desire to lash out at the being that has made one angry. But to the extent that this desire becomes intelligent, is channelled into reasoning about means to harm this being and about the degree to which it should be harmed in order to make up for the harm that one has suffered oneself or to deter it from further mischief, anger has been replaced by something else lacking its instinctive nature.

So, some emotions encompass instinctive (and so non-intelligent) desires, that is, they encompass behavioural tendencies designed by nature to bear on the content of the emotions in question (cf. Dent, 1984: 79–80). Nonetheless, it would be erroneous to join Arnold in her general claim that *all* emotions involve such desires. (Since Arnold speaks of "unreasoning involuntary attraction or repulsion", I assume that she has something like my non-intelligent desires in mind.) While admitting that some emotions, like fear and anger, comprise desires (1980: 51–2), Lyons maintains that emotions such as sorrow, grief, wonder, awe, surprise, and despair do not include any desires (1980: 37, 52, 58, 96–7, 150–1). To this list one could add joy (cf. Alston, 1967a: 481) or gladness, being pleased, relief and disappointment.

In contrast, Arnold believes that, for example, joy and sorrow "urge us to remain where we are" (1960: 148). She thinks that joy urges us to this "because we have what we want and nothing else is needed" (1960: 148). However, the situation of having achieved what one wanted need not be one of desiring that the situation remains as it is; it could simply be one of a desire going out of existence through being satisfied. Imagine that I am overjoyed, delighted, pleased, or glad because I take myself to have discovered the solution to a problem that has greatly bothered me or to have scored a goal. Then it makes no sense to ascribe to me a desire 'to remain where I am', that is, I take it, that this remains the case, for nothing could obliterate it. Surely, it is simply that my desire (to solve a problem, to score a goal) has ceased to exist through being fulfilled.

It is natural to take the bodily changes involved in such emotions as joy, gladness, satisfaction, or delight to consist in the pleasurable relaxation that could result when a tendency to act is thought to overcome obstacles in its path and is being successfully completed. So, one is glad or pleased because some of one's desires are thought to be fulfilled or to be capable of fulfilment (without other equally strong desires being frustrated). A relief that p (e.g. that one has made a narrow escape) is the cessation of a fear that not-p (that one will not escape) and of the entailed wish that p. But to say that one's having *had* a certain desire or wish is necessary for the having of an emotion is altogether different from saying that the having of an emotion partly consists in the having of a desire.

Like joy, the negative counterparts of sorrow, sadness, grief, despair, etc. involve the cessation of desire rather than desire itself, but, although these states are alike in respect of the absence of the tension characteristic of unfulfilled desire, they are very different. For in the case of these negative emotions the desire does not cease through being fulfilled, but by being crushed by insurmountable obstacles. Consequently, while there are feelings of vigour and expansiveness in the positive emotions, owing to the desire having victoriously reached its goal, there are feelings of lack of vigour, hollowness, and quiescence in the negative emotions, because the desire has been definitely defeated. It is instructive to examine the change from fear to sorrow or despair, for example, from fearing that a friend has died to feeling sorrow or despair because (it is definitely established that) (s)he has died. In the former case, there is resistance to the possibility of the friend's death, for example some tendencies to shrink back from evidence indicating that (s)he is dead, whereas in the latter case, all such tendencies have been quashed by the realization that the friend's death is an undeniable and irrevocable fact. A feeling of powerlessness and hollowness results.

We must, however, not overlook the psychological possibility of a desire surviving, in the shape of a wish, despite the fact that the subject becomes utterly convinced that it cannot be fulfilled. This is the case when one *regrets* that p instead of being sad that p. In contrast, disappointment at p's being the case entails that the hope that not-p, and so the wish to discover this to be a fact, has died through the realization that p is the case. Similarly, hopelessness and despair entail the death of the wish that things be different. It is a fact about the human psyche that a firm conviction that p not always crushes every non-intelligent desire for not-p. Naturally, there is on the positive side no counterpart to the distinction between frustration, or a desire persisting without any prospect of fulfilment, and sadness, or a desire being crushed by this prospect: there is just the desire dissolving to become satisfaction.

I conclude, then, that some, but not all, emotional reactions include desires, that is, tendencies to behave in ways that are designed to have a bearing on the content of the emotion in question. These desires are non-intelligent and, like the rest of the patterns of bodily changes making up emotional reactions, they are to all appearances innate. One thing that could lead one to the mistaken view that all emotional reactions include desires is that the propositional object of an emotion must be about something about which one is concerned and so *would* have desires or wishes towards under appropriate conditions. One cannot feel anger, fear, gladness, pride, or even surprise about something to which one is totally indifferent. But this explanatory claim must be kept apart from the claim that a desire is part of the *explanandum*, the emotional reaction.[7] Furthermore, it

---

[7] Cf. Robert C. Roberts's distinction between "basic" and "consequent" concern (2003: 144). He makes the point I have just made by affirming that consequent concern is present only in the case of some emotions, whereas the basic concern is a necessary condition.

may be doubted that this type of explanation is much more informative than maintaining that someone has an emotion about something because it is something about which she is disposed to have such an emotion.

What then characterizes all the varying patterns of somatic change composing different emotional reactions? My suggestion is that they are of a kind *normally felt* in proprioception or bodily sense. Surely, it is typical of emotions that they are felt, so if a pattern of bodily processes is to make up an emotional reaction, it must be of a sort that is normally felt.

The reason why I claim that these somatic patterns are *normally* felt rather than they must *necessarily* be felt is the following. Suppose that the afferent pathways of A are cut so that he cannot proprioceptively feel the pounding of his heart and the other ingredients in the involuntary arousal normally felt. Despite this, could not A properly be described as fearing that *p* if he displays the involuntary arousal characteristic of fear as a result of thinking *p*? Davis replies affirmatively (1988: 471), and this reply is not implausible. If so, it cannot be claimed that 'A fears that *p*' entails 'A is feeling fear that *p*'.[8] Nonetheless, it is plainly not a contingent fact that in the case of all emotions, E, we find it natural to talk about 'feeling E'. Surely, this is because normally when one has an emotion things feel a certain way to one. Thus, I claim that an emotional response is a set of automatic bodily responses of a kind that is normally felt by the subject (in proprioception).

Lyons, however, maintains that the subject of an emotion "may feel nothing because she is so absorbed" (1980: 58) by the content of the emotion. But this claim rests on an assumption that I take myself to have refuted in Chapter 1, namely that "you cannot have unfelt feelings, that is feelings of which one is unaware" (1980: 117, cf. 6). It is even unnecessary to grant, as does Goldie (2000: 64), that *in one sense* feeling an emotion is being reflectively aware of the feeling. Having a feeling and being aware of having it are distinct phenomena.

Emotion and Evaluation

Let us now take a closer look at the other component of an emotion, that is (1) (on p. 65), the propositional thought that I have denominated the cause of the felt pattern of bodily changes. It has been argued that such a cause must have some special features in virtue of which it arouses this pattern. Arnold writes:

> we find that at the base of every emotion there is some kind of perception or aware-ness of an object, a person or a situation, which in some cases becomes emotional, in other cases remains (in the words of William James) a "cold perception". Therefore, it stands to reason that the perception that arouses an emotion must be somehow different from the mere perception as such, which does not arouse an emotion (1960: 93).

---

[8] Roberts denies this implication because he believes that to feel afraid, angry, etc. is to be aware that one is afraid, angry, etc. (2003: ch. 4.2). But, surely, feeling afraid, etc. do not require more of self-consciousness than being afraid, etc. require.

From her definition of emotion quoted above, it should be apparent in what she takes this difference to consist. An emotion is called forth because I appraise the object perceived or known "as desirable or undesirable, valuable or harmful for me":

> To arouse an emotion, the object must be appraised as affecting me in some way, affecting me personally as an individual with my particular experience and my particular aims (1960: 171).

In a similar vein, Lyons claims that an evaluation must intercede when an emotion is evoked:

> the sort of attitude essential to emotion . . . must be evaluative, for only such an attitude is sufficient explanation for why we are physiologically stirred up (1980: 58).

So long as one is merely in the "cognitive" (1980: 59) state of acquiring knowledge or (true) beliefs about a situation, there is no "reason to get worked up" (1980: 58) about it. Like Arnold, Lyons declares that the causally potent evaluation must be "passionate and partial", that is, must relate "to ourselves, or to our quasi-selves, our friends or loved ones" (1980: 35).

Against the Arnold–Lyons view that all emotions involve evaluations as causal factors, I would first like to object that there are emotions for which this seems palpably false. Consider the emotion of surprise (astonishment, wonder, amazement): it is surely not plausible to hold that in order to be surprised that p, I must judge it to be good or bad that p. All that is necessary in the way of judgement to be surprised that p is that prior to discovering that p, I held it to be very probable or certain that not-p. (Something that is necessary, though not in the way of judgement, might be an interest in whether or not p.)

Moreover, infants and non-human animals, who presumably are incapable of making value-judgements, are apparently subject to emotions like anger and fear. Dent, in defending the contention that "passions . . . do depend upon their subject holding certain things to be good or bad" (1984: 54), tries to meet this objection by distinguishing a "frustration–aggression" reaction (1984: 58), that is independent of evaluation, from proper anger and by contending that "the notion of fear covers two different patterns of response" (1984: 60), one of which does not rest on evaluation. But it is hard to see how this procedure could be deemed to be anything but *ad hoc*.

My second point cuts deeper. To evaluate something as good or bad must either be (*a*) to judge that it is equipped with some *objective* feature, that is, some feature that is independent of para-cognitive attitudes like desires and emotions; or (*b*) to imply that it is somehow the object of such attitudes. If (*a*) is true, it is mysterious why an evaluation of something should be thought to cause bodily responses if other 'cognitive' states or beliefs about how something is objectively like are supposed to be causally impotent in this respect, for the former is here of the same kind as the latter. Arnold, however, seems to come down in favour of (*b*) when she equates evaluatively appraising something as appraising it as "affecting me personally", and possibly this holds for Lyons, too, though he is harder to pin down (cf. Gaus, 1990: 70). So, suppose (*b*) is opted for.

Take, for example, the variant of (*b*) that I shall adopt in Part II which defines the notion of something having intrinsic value for you in terms of it fulfilling an intrinsic

desire that you have at least dispositionally. The claim, for example, that if you hope that
p will be the case, you must take it to be good for you that *p*, then boils down to that you
must take *p* to satisfy some desire or wish of yours. But your making this judgement
seems redundant: the crucial point is surely that you *in fact* have some desire or
wish that *p* will satisfy, not whether you judge this to be the case. If this desire is there,
your thinking that *p* might be the case will naturally induce hope in you that *p*, since
hoping that *p* appears to be something like occurrently desiring to find out that *p* is the
case as the result of thinking that it might be. Thus, when a propositional thought elicits
an emotion, it is, as I remarked in the foregoing section, entirely reasonable—even if not
very informative—to assume that there is an underlying dispositional desire directed at
the thought. But this is different from claiming that a reference to desire, by way of a
desire-based evaluation, needs to occur when an emotion is felt. This seems wholly
superfluous; so, we cannot by reference to such evaluations mark off the propositional
contents that do not remain "cold" but "become emotional".

The Essence of Emotion

The outcome of the investigation into emotion so far can be summarized by saying that
there is an emotion if and only if there are two sorts of states or events, one of which
is the cause of the other. More precisely,

(E) *A* is having a type of emotion (such as anger, fear, joy) that *p* iff: *A* is thinking that *p* is
(probably, possibly) the case, and this directly (i.e. not via any other mental event)
causes a certain normally felt pattern of changes in *A*'s body.

The reason why I describe *A* as thinking, rather than believing, *p* is the by now familiar
one that if a normally felt pattern of somatic changes is to be caused—and the emotion is
to be had in the occurrent sense—a belief must be manifested in episodic thought. This
comes out in the fact that one could find emotional relief by seeking distraction. If I am
sad or disappointed because, say, I have not got the job for which I applied, I may get out
of my melancholic state of mind by going to the cinema or doing something else that
keeps my mind occupied and prevents me from episodically thinking of the fact that
I failed to get the job. This means would not be an effective, albeit temporary, remedy if
the felt pattern was causally sustained by my belief that I did not get the position, for I do
not lose this belief. It is effective in extinguishing or subduing this pattern because it is
causally sustained by my episodic thinking of my failure.[9]

Now (E) is compatible with the following three significantly different views of what an
emotion *is* or consists in: (*a*) a complex event consisting in the propositional cause and the
normally felt somatic pattern that is its effect; (*b*) this pattern itself, when it has a propositional cause; and (*c*) the propositional thinking itself, when it causes this sort of pattern.

---

[9] Cf. the stress Roberts lays on the vividness of the representations involved when he describes his construals as "cross-
ings of percepts, images, thoughts, and concepts" (1988: 191; cf. 2003: 77).

The difference between these three views is easily overlooked. For example, when Lyons expounds his "causal-evaluative theory of emotions", he slides between them. Aside from the fact that he insists on the presence of an evaluation and does not demand that the belief be episodically actualized, the quotations $(a^\star)$, $(b^\star)$, and $(c^\star)$ match, respectively, (a), (b), and (c) above: $(a^\star)$ "emotions are complex items involving beliefs, evaluations, wants and physiological reactions to these" (1980: 181); $(b^\star)$ "X is to be deemed an emotional state if and only if it is a physiologically abnormal state caused by the subject of that state's evaluation of his or her situation" or an "emotion is...a bodily state caused by an attitude, in this case an evaluative attitude" (1980: 57–8); and $(c^\star)$ "the concept of emotion as occurrent state amounted to an evaluation which caused unusual physiological changes in the subject of the evaluation" (1980: 207; cf. 52).[10]

When the alternatives (a)–(c) are explicitly distinguished, the question arises which one is preferable. Since the differences between the options are rather subtle, this question is not easy to answer. To my mind, a couple of considerations put (b) in the most favourable light. As already indicated, it appears to be a conceptual truth that an emotion is something *felt*. Bodily sensations and the somatic processes of which they are sensations are something felt, but a propositional thought is not. This is an indication that an emotion is neither identical to a thought—that is, (c)—nor to a complex of which a thought is a component, that is (a). Furthermore, it is natural to speak of an emotion as occurring *as a response* to a thought—for example, it is the thought that the snake at my feet is highly poisonous that *makes* me afraid. I have already quoted Arnold to the effect that "the perception which *arouses an emotion* must somehow be different from the mere perception of an object as such, which does not *arouse an emotion*" (italics added).

This suggests another advantage of (b): if this alternative is correct, the common intuition that to be subject to an emotion is to be in some sense *passive* is easily vindicated. It is natural to say that something is passive to the extent that it is being acted upon by some cause, the cause being that which is active. Now, if an emotion is a normally felt pattern of somatic changes which has a certain type of cause, it is a state or an event that is passive in this sense of being an effect or something caused.[11] An emotion is essentially passive because it is essentially an event that is caused in a certain way. In contrast, a desire is an active state, for it is a state that *causes* certain patterns of behaviour which are somehow connected to something in some way represented by the state. When desires are identified by being assigned a certain content, they are identified by reference to what they (tend to) cause, while emotions, when their content is specified, get their causes specified. I think that we identify emotions by reference to their causes—that is, conceive

---

[10] Correspondingly, an intentional action could be viewed either as the complex event of certain mental states causing some result, as this result itself when it has this cause or as these mental states themselves when they have this effect. For further discussion and references, see Persson (1981: 16–18).

[11] Gordon, too, views the passivity of emotions as amounting to their essentially being states that are caused in a certain way (1987: 113–15). He also points out that it is fallacious to infer from this either that (a) the subject is acted upon by *the emotions* (in fact it is thoughts that act upon the subject) or that (b) the subject can not do anything to produce or prevent emotions in himself (1987: 115–21). However, Gordon differs from me in taking an emotion to be an underlying cause of what I call the felt bodily pattern (1987: e.g. 93–4, 105–6).

them as passive states—because they consist in a great number of felt bodily reactions that occur together since they have a common cause (more of this in a moment).

Despite the essential passivity of emotions, it makes sense to divide them into 'active' and 'passive' depending on whether or not the patterns caused include desires relating to their contents (cf. Dent, 1984: 64–5), for, as we have seen, not all emotions do. Active emotions would then number anger and fear, while passive emotions would encompass joy and sadness. This division is not inconsistent with the essential passivity of emotions, for, although the state of desiring is by nature active, it is a state one is generally caused to be in (though this is not logically necessary, as in the case of emotions); and when a desire is imputed as a part of the ascription of some emotion, the subject is implied to be in a state of desiring as the result of the operation of a certain propositional cause.

A Comparison with William James's View

The conception of emotions summed up by (E) may not appear all that different from the classical one that William James expresses when he affirms that

> bodily changes follow directly the perception of the exciting fact, and that our feeling of the same changes as they occur IS the emotion. (1890/1950: ii. 449)

One difference is that, whereas I have conceded that, on occasion, these "bodily changes" need not be felt, James apparently *identifies* the emotion with the feelings themselves. So, if the feelings were to occur in the absence of the counterpart bodily changes, we could still have an emotion. Antonio Damasio supports this possibility by speculating about there being "neural devices that help us feel 'as if' we were having an emotional state, as if the body were being activated and modified" (1994: 155). So far as I can find, everyday experience provides little, if any, evidence for the postulation of such neural devices enabling us to feel emotions in the absence of somatic changes (as opposed to in the presence of very slight changes). But if this regularly occurred, we could describe the emotional reaction disjunctively: bodily changes or sensations of them or (most commonly) both. For present purposes, nothing hangs upon these details.

A more important difference between James and me is that, whereas James believes that an emotion can have "a purely bodily cause" (1890/1950: 449), I have insisted that the cause of an emotion is perforce a propositional thought. This difference is crucial, for it enables me to fend off criticism to which James's theory is vulnerable. As has been pointed out (e.g. by Alston, 1967a: 482–3, and Lyons, 1980: 7–8), on an account such as James's, we would be forced to say that an emotion was present if a felt pattern of bodily changes typical of, say, fear, was caused to occur by an injection of some drug like adrenalin. This is clearly counter-intuitive: an injection can certainly make one afraid, but not in this way. Obviously, my view escapes this criticism, since I have claimed it to be logically necessary that, if an emotion is to be present, the cause of the normally felt pattern must be a propositional thought.

In fact, the link between the felt pattern and its propositional cause is even tighter. Not any old instance of a felt pattern of bodily change which happens to have a cause of this sort is an emotion: it must be a set of changes which are identified by reference to their common propositional cause because this is what standardly holds the changes together. Suppose that I feel hunger because I have been thinking that I shall soon have a delicious meal; then it does not follow that I am the subject of an emotion because a bodily change I am feeling happens to have a propositional cause. The reason is that we are familiar with this sort of change occurring in the absence of such causes. Therefore, it is not a type of change identified in terms of a propositional cause. In contrast, an emotion is a pattern or set of normally felt somatic changes that are lumped together under a single concept because it has a common propositional cause which is standard for that pattern.

We recognize different types of (basic) emotions, like joy, sorrow, fear, anger, pride, etc. because these patterns make up qualitatively different, recurrent kinds of pattern. If there had not been this differentiation of the physiological effects of thought, there would be room for nothing but general locutions such as 'having an emotion that p' or 'reacting emotionally to p'.

This does not imply, however, that the distinction between two emotions always rests on intrinsic differences in the felt bodily patterns. That would be implausible, since the kinds of emotion named by everyday vocabulary are numerous. And, as Lyons points out,

> the wealth of experimental evidence about the physiological aspects of emotions has yet to confirm the possibility of distinguishing emotions by reference to physiological changes alone. (1980: 15; cf. Roberts, 2003: 153–4)

My approach is, however, not wedded to the success of this enterprise of differentiating between emotions solely on a physiological basis. I am free to hold that sometimes the difference between two kinds of emotion is a difference as regards their propositional causes. Two emotions may be related as species to genus in the sense that the content of one is a specification of the content of the other. Clearly, the difference between joy and *Schadenfreude* is precisely this: the latter is joy because of somebody else's misfortune. The same is probably true of sadness and pity or compassion (=sadness because of another's misfortune), sadness and grief (=sadness because of bereavement), anger and indignation (=moral anger), and regret and remorse (=moral regret). Surely, the place to look for the difference between these is not in how they feel, but in what contents they take. (We should also be alive to the possibility that one emotion may be a mixture of two other emotions.)

Nevertheless, it is clear that there are a fair number of emotions that are not related as species to genus. Examples are: joy, sadness, fear, hope, anger, gratitude, pride, shame, and surprise. Each of these involves its own characteristic pattern of felt bodily processes. These emotions are in all probability distinguishable on the basis of physiological aspects.[12]

---

[12] Cf. Gaus's claim that "at least with regard to the fundamental emotions, types of emotional states are characterized by unique feelings" (1990: 64). Gaus agrees that the feeling or affective response "is grounded in (that is, justified and caused by) certain beliefs" (1990: 64), but differs from me in denying that the content of this response (and of the emotion) can be construed in terms of the content of the grounding or causing belief (1990: §5).

The discussion of what lies behind the classification of emotions into types will be resumed in the next chapter. In the present context, the point is only to stress that it should not be expected that this classification rests solely on differences in respect of felt patterns of physiological changes.

Emotions and Rationality

The fact that emotions are conceptualized in terms of their propositional cause also holds the key to why there can be reasons for them or why they can be classified as rational and irrational. It has been argued—for example, by Lyons (1980: 8)—that, while emotions can be thus classified or assessed, this is not true of felt patterns of bodily changes. The reply to this is that emotions can be said to be rational and irrational because it is logically necessary that they are causally sustained by episodes of thinking that can be assessed in this way. This is what I call the cognitive (ir)rationality of emotions.

In contrast, it would seem that moods cannot be assessed in respect of rationality, if I have been right in holding that they do not have content—moods being just felt bodily patterns. But, although it seems to me true that moods *in themselves* cannot be cognitively rational or irrational, I think a case can be made out for saying that the circumstances can be such that *given them* it can be (ir)rational to *be* in a particular mood. As already indicated, there seem to be conceptual links between moods and emotions, for example between the mood of being anxious or fearful and the emotion of fear. If one is anxious, one is necessarily disposed to be afraid of this or that. Moreover, one can in practice not remain in the state of being anxious without actualizing this disposition by being afraid of something, for the felt pattern of bodily processes in which the mood consists is likely to subside if it is not nurtured by propositional causes. Normally, a mood of anxiety is also created in the first place by the subject's being afraid of this or that. It is not just a contingent truth, I suggest, that a mood consists in felt physiological changes that, in this way, *can* be causally initiated and sustained (and hence undermined) by episodes of propositional thinking of the subject (who must accordingly be capable of undergoing these episodes). In the light of this, consider a subject whose circumstances are such that it is more rational for it to think thoughts that make it feel secure and confident than ones that make it frightened. Then it might be said to be unreasonable of this subject to be in a fearful mood, for this mood would necessarily be undermined if it were thinking thoughts that are rational. *Given its happy circumstances*, the mood of this subject is unreasonable.

In any event, the main aim of this chapter is to single out emotions as a class of reactions that can be assessed in respect of rationality in virtue of having propositional content—just as the main aim of the foregoing chapter was to single out intelligent desires as being similarly assessable. Furthermore, just as in the foregoing chapter intelligent desires were distinguished from non-intelligent desires which may be caused by feeling or perceiving instead of propositional thinking, so we must distinguish emotions from some similar felt bodily reactions which are caused by perceiving instead of propositional thinking. For instance, to be startled by something is very similar to fearing something, but it is caused by a mere perception, for example of a loud sound, and in my terminology this disqualifies it from being an emotion (contrast Pugmire, 1998: 37–8). Something, for example a scary mask, that startles when it suddenly appears may continue to sustain fear-like symptoms when it continues to be perceived. Indeed, even vividly imagining this thing may induce these symptoms (though it could hardly startle one). Analogously, irritation, though it may be an emotion akin to anger, may also be caused by a mere perception, for example of a monotonous sound or an itch. However, one is unlikely to be so persistent in imagining such a sound that one could thereby cause oneself irritation! In contrast, sexual excitement or arousal, amusement and laughter, and disgust are as likely to be caused by vivid imaginings as by perceptions.

In spite of their being obviously emotion-like, none of these reactions qualifies as an emotion in my terminology for the reason that their causes are not propositional thoughts, thoughts that something is the case. (The kind of enjoyment, suffering, and boredom which we considered in Chapter 3 are disqualified for the same reason.) They are feelings, all right, but not emotions. It may be objected that it is arbitrary to exclude them from the class of emotions.[13] Now, I do not claim to have cut nature at the joints. I readily grant that there is a continuum from sensation to what I call emotion and that distinctions in this continuum can be drawn somewhat differently for different purposes. My purpose is to single out a class of phenomena that can be appraised as (ir)rational and that, I think, necessitates the involvement of assent to a proposition.

In a thorough study of the emotions, Robert C. Roberts, however, summarizes his position on these matters by saying that even if

> many or most emotions in fact involve judgments over their propositional content, the judgment is neither necessary nor sufficient for the emotion. It is better to think of emotions as a kind of appearance or impression that is, in the normal case, supported by judgment. (2003: 106)

Roberts thinks his view is supported by irrational phobias, like fear of spiders or heights (2003: 89–91). Here subjects feel fear, though they do not really believe they are threatened. Roberts compares these phobias to perceptual illusions, like the bent stick illusion: "The fear is no less an impression of a threat than the illusion is the impression of a bent stick" (2003: 92). But I do not think that Roberts succeeds in showing the consistency of this parallel with the fact that phobias are after all thought of as irrational, whereas perceptual illusions are not (2003: 91–3). So far as I can see, the charge of irrationality requires the presence of judgement or of thinking that something is the case. As Roberts himself acknowledges (2003: 306–7), when there is evidently no requirement of belief, as in the case of amusement—you can be as much amused by jokes that you do not believe to be true—there is no question of irrationality.

My hypothesis is that, for example the perceptual appearance of spiders induces the phobic subjects to think that spiders are dangerous against their better judgement. (We shall discuss such irrational thinking at greater length in Part II in connection with

---

[13] This is a charge that is pressed by John Deigh (1994).

weakness of will.) Desensitization training aims to break this irrational association between appearance and judgement by exposing the subjects first to small spiders—which are hardest to think of as dangerous—and successively to bigger ones.

Roberts calls the perceptual entities which are central to his theory of emotions, and which may or may not be propositional and assented to, "construals". His main thesis is that "emotions are concern-based construals" (2003: 64). Concerns are "desires and aversions, along with the attachments and interests from which many of our desires and aversions derive" (2003: 142). It is clear that our "construals" can be based on our concerns in the sense that they may be caused by them. For instance, in the case of a well-known ambiguous drawing, the subject's libido may make him "construe" it as a drawing of a young woman rather than of an old woman. As Roberts of course realizes, a construal's being based on a concern in this causal sense is not enough to turn the construal into an emotion, since there need not be any emotion in the construal of the drawing. So, he requires that the concern somehow be "taken up" by the construal (2003: 145). But it is unclear to me how a conative entity can be taken up by and become part of a perceptual entity (for instance, to appeal to a notion that will be discussed in Part II, they have different directions of fit, as Roberts himself points out, 2003: 147). Therefore, I do not see how Roberts's theory, despite all its sophistication, escapes the fundamental objection to Solomon's judgement theory: that it reduces emotions to something which does not seem emotional. It seems to me that Roberts's talk of construals being based on concerns mixes a plausible idea—that when a thought evokes an emotion there is something like an underlying concern which could do something to explain it—with an obscure one.

This concludes my general exposition of the concept of an emotion. In the last decades of philosophizing about emotions there has been a tendency to downplay feelings, declaring them not to be an essential part of emotion.[14] The tendency has been to identify emotions either with evaluative judgements or cognitive–conative sets. In opposition to this trend, I have contended that emotions are automatic physiological processes felt in proprioception—which have a cause in episodic propositional thinking that is characteristic of their kind (a similar position is adopted by Shaffer, 1983). The reaction caused often, but not always, includes non-intelligent desires.

As opposed to one of Ronald de Sousa's "central theses", namely "that emotions are not reducible to any of the other things to which they have at some time or other been assimilated" (1987: 23; cf. also Rosenthal, 1983: 186–8), my account is reductive. However, what de Sousa is particularly out to show is that emotions are not reducible to desires and beliefs (1987: 165), while, to repeat, it is felt bodily changes that is the centrepiece of my analysis.

---

[14] The most recent manifestation of this trend is Roberts's rich *Emotions* (2003). But there are challenges to this trend, see Deigh (1994) and Pugmire who declares "Feeling is what matters most about emotions, their core force" (1998: 135), though what he means by "feeling" is probably something different from what I do. Similarly, Goldie takes emotions to involve "feeling towards" which is claimed to be something other than feeling bodily changes because the latter lacks the requisite intentionality (2000: e.g. 58). Goldie pays little, if any, attention to the idea that bodily feelings can acquire intentionality by having standard propositional causes. Instead, he claims rather mysteriously that "feeling towards" is an instance of "thinking of with feeling" where "feeling is essentially related to the content, so that there could not be some other psychological episode, say belief or thinking of, with the same content but with no feeling" (2000: 72). This content may also be inexpressible in words (2000: 61).

Another argument against reductive analyses, put forward by David Rosenthal (1983: 187–8), is that they cannot make sense of our classification of emotions into different types. I hope to undermine this charge by providing precisely such a classification in the next chapter. The main motivation for this classification is, however, to facilitate the discussion of desert and responsibility in Part V.

6

A TYPOLOGY OF EMOTION

In this chapter I shall put forward a classification of emotions. (It could be set beside Roberts's more extensive analysis (2003: ch. 3) which unfortunately was published too late for me to be able to benefit much from it.) As I said at the end of the last chapter, my classification is designed to serve the discussion of the rationality of desert- and responsibility-related emotions in Part V. I do not deny that there might be other purposes for which other ways of dividing emotions are more useful.

As pointed out in Chapter 5, emotions can differ to the extent of being given different names in everyday language without their consisting in different kinds of felt patterns. This happens when an emotion is a species of another emotion in the sense that the content of the former is a specification of the content of the latter, as in the case of indignation and anger, etc. It also happens when two emotions are distinguished on grounds of differences in their strength or intensity, that is, differences in respect of the strength or intensity of the felt pattern. In this way, *fear* differs from *terror, horror*, and *dread, anger* from *fury* and *rage*, *indignation* from *outrage*, *surprise* from *astonishment*, *puzzlement* from *amazement*, *gladness* (or *joy*) from *delight*, *admiration* from *reverence*, and so on. Assuming a contrast between differences in degree and differences in kind, I shall not count these differences as differences of kind in the felt patterns of bodily changes. So, along with cases in which one emotion is a species of another, cases in which emotions differ merely with respect to intensity will not here be counted as different *kinds* of emotion in the relevant, basic way.

Although emotions are to be classified as being of distinct kinds if and only if they consist in different kinds of felt somatic pattern, it would be unwise to try to elucidate this classification by scrutinizing merely these felt patterns. For it is notoriously tricky to describe bodily sensations (and, for that matter, sensations and sense-impressions in general), and without any proper equipment for measuring the physiological processes of which the sensations are sensations, these processes cannot be precisely recorded, either. Fortunately, it is logically necessary that if a felt pattern is to constitute an emotion, it must by caused by a propositional thought which is typical for that kind of pattern. As a consequence, it is reasonable to expect that a marked difference as regards the effect—that is, the felt pattern—reflects a difference in the cause. Conversely, differences in the structure of the contents that emotions take should provide clues to differences in the resulting felt patterns. Since differences in the former respect are easier to describe, I shall approach the latter via the former.

Factive and Epistemic Emotions

Compare

    (1) *A* is *glad* that *p* (e.g. that he has won on the Pools)

to

    (2) *A hopes* that *p*.

(1) is true only if *A* is *convinced* or *certain* that *p*. Moreover, (1) entails that it is true that *p*. In fact, it can plausibly be argued that this statement entails that *A* *knows* that *p* (see Gordon, 1987: 40–3). Needless to say, this does not mean that gladness is only possible if there is knowledge; it merely means that the content of gladness is properly expressed in the manner of (1) only if there is knowledge. Somebody who is of the opinion that not-*p* would have to say something like '*A* is glad because he is convinced that *p*'. If *A*'s attitude to the truth of *p* is weaker, the correct report could be '*A* is glad because he thinks it is probable or possible that *p*'.

    A lot of positive emotions behave in these respects like being glad: being happy, pleased, overjoyed, delighted, and relieved. But not the emotion of hope. *A*'s hoping that *p* does not entail that *p* is the case and, more significantly, it is incompatible with his being certain that *p*. It requires *A* to think that there is some probability that *p*, that given his body of evidence it is not excluded that *p*. But this (subjective) probability must not amount to certainty; that not-*p* must be assigned some probability. Gordon calls emotions like hope *epistemic* and ones like gladness *factive* (1987: 25 ff.).

    Of course, this distinction cuts across negative emotions as well. Consider the following pair:

    (3) *A* is *sorry* that *p*,

and

    (4) *A fears* that *p*.

Like (1), (3) entails that *A* knows that *p*. In this respect to be sorry is like a lot of other negative emotions: to be sad, unhappy, disappointed, displeased, to regret, and to grieve. All of these are factive emotions, while fearing (worrying, dreading, or being anxious about) *p* is an epistemic emotion like hope.

    Since believing that *p* is probable to some degree less than 1 goes with believing not-*p* to be probable to the remaining degree, there is a complementarity between hope and fear. Suppose that *A* believes there to be a 0.5 probability that he has won on the Pools and a 0.5 probability that he has not; then he is exposed to feeling both hope that he has won and fear that he has not. However, he cannot be in the grip of both hope and fear at the very same moment. Which emotion he is feeling at a certain moment is due to which alternative he is episodically thinking about at that time: if he dwells on the possibility of his having won, hope will be called forth, while if the other possibility occupies his mind, he will experience fear. Thus, a person in this sort of situation is subject to a characteristic vacillation between hope and fear. Which alternative one most frequently dwells upon in such situations is determined by one's temperament (whether one is an 'optimist' or a 'pessimist'), one's present mood, or external circumstances.

There is, however, an asymmetry between fear and hope. Consider the distinction between hoping and *longing*. When life feels miserable, I may be longing for death, but I cannot hope for death (i.e. hope that I shall die), for I am *certain* of my mortality. I can hope for an *early* death (that I shall soon die), for this is something that may be merely epistemically possible, but this makes it inappropriate to long for an early death. In short, if it is true that I long for death—that is, long for my dying to occur—then it must be true that I *know* that this state will occur (I may even know when it will occur). If I had been uncertain in this matter, I would have to hope for death.

As opposed to this, it is obviously possible to fear death, even though one knows one is to die. The fact that a prisoner in a death row knows that he will be executed in a few hours does not prevent him from fearing death. This fear of death feels like the fear that one may die at any moment, which is a fear of something that one regards as merely possible. It is, however, not an epistemic fear, but a factive fear properly expressed by: 'The fact that the prisoner will soon die makes him afraid.' (This is probably an understatement; the prisoner is more likely to dread his imminent death.)

This factive fear is the negative counterpart of longing. In other words, fear seems to be the negative counterpart of both hope and longing. Does this mean that 'fear' designates two kinds of emotion or that 'hope' and 'longing' designate the same emotion? My suggestion is that in the more basic sense, in which different kinds of emotion imply different kinds of felt bodily reaction, there is just one positive and one negative emotion, but there is obviously a difference as regards the propositional content or cause.

To hope for something and to long for it both involve *wishing* it. As we saw in Chapter 4, a wish is a non-intelligent desire for something that the subject is convinced that it cannot cause to materialize. The difference between hope and longing lies in the thought causing the wish and consequently in the precise content of the wish. A hope that *p* seems to be a wish to ascertain that *p* is the case caused by the thought that it might be. It thus presupposes that the subject sees it as uncertain whether or not *p* will be (has been or is) the case. In contrast, a subject longing for it to be the case that *p* must take itself to be certain that *p* will occur (and perhaps even certain about when it will occur). Longing is a wish, caused by this conviction that *p* will be the case, that *p* be the case sooner, that time so to speak be 'speeded up', so that the gap between the present and the realization of this state of affairs is sooner closed.

Note that to say that hoping and longing consist in wishing does not imply that they are desires rather than emotions, for they possess the essential passivity of emotions: they are felt, bodily states—though primarily or exclusively of a conative nature—*caused* by the having of certain propositional thoughts.

Fearing that *p* also involves having a wish (that *p* not be the case). It may be objected that the applicability of 'fear' extends further down the phylogenetic ladder than the applicability of 'wishing' (and of 'hope' and 'longing'). But it should be remembered that a wish is a non-intelligent desire, and when such a desire activates behaviour which does not succeed in achieving its aim of eliminating the danger, the animal is in a situation similar to that of an animal which thinks that it cannot eliminate the danger, even though it is incapable of entertaining this kind of thought.

If factive fear that *p* were strictly parallel to longing, it would involve a wish that time be 'slowed down' so that *p* materializes later. But surely, when one fears that *p* what one wishes for is in the first instance that *p* *never* materializes; one wishes to avoid it *altogether*. That is, whether one is subject to factive fear, and believes that *p* will be realized, or epistemic fear, and believes that it may not be realized, one will tend to have the same wish, that *p* not be the case. This may be the reason why we speak of 'fear' in both cases.

As mentioned in the foregoing chapter, fear includes more than a wish, namely, physiological changes, like a quickened heart-beat, cold sweat, pallor, trembling, etc. I think these changes are present in both forms of fear, though it may be that the respective effects inherit some differences from the difference in respect of the epistemic modality of the causing thought.

The noted vacillation between hoping that *p* and fearing that not-*p* then involves swinging between a wish that *p* be the case caused by the thought that it might be and a wish that not-*p* not be the case caused by the thought that it might well be. In contrast, there is of course no complementarity between longing and factive fear, since longing does not presuppose epistemic uncertainty.

To anticipate a point of some importance for Chapter 16, longing of the sort that involves *impatience* is essentially directed at the future, to a state of affairs that is held to materialize in the future. Of course, it makes no sense to wish that time be speeded up so that some past event happens sooner. Instead, one might grieve over the inexorable 'passage' of time which removes the event further and further from the present. Similarly, it would be curious to fear factively that something happened in the past. As long as something has not happened, one may have an absurd hope that it will not happen, even though one firmly believes that it will. But when one knows that it has happened, there is only room for the wish that it had not, that is, for *regret* that it did happen (or for desireless emotions such as sadness and despair).

Positive and Negative Emotions

In expounding the distinction between factive and epistemic emotions, I have called upon another distinction that cuts right across it, namely the distinction between *positive* and *negative* emotions. As examples of positive emotions I have enumerated to hope, long, to be glad, pleased, happy, overjoyed, delighted, and relieved. Others will be added to the list later on: to be proud or grateful and to admire. Among the negative emotions we find: to be afraid, worried, sad, displeased, unhappy, horrified, terrified, disappointed, ashamed, angry, jealous, envious, to regret, despair, and have contempt. In fact, with the exception of surprise (astonishment), puzzlement (amazement), and wonder (awe), it is arguable that every emotion named in everyday language is classifiable as either positive or negative.[1] Consequently, the ground of this distinction merits attention.

Gordon suggests that whether an emotion is positive or negative turns on whether it involves a *wish* that the content be true or that it be false (1987: 29–32). In the case of positive factive emotions this wish is assumed to coexist with a conviction that it is fulfilled. Thus he writes:

> we may say that the *positive* factive emotions arise from wish-*satisfaction*—a state in which one simultaneously *wishes it to be the case* that p and *believes that it is* the case that p. (1987: 53)

Similarly, negative factive emotions allegedly arise from wish-*frustration*, wishing something not to be the case when one believes (often correctly) that it is the case.

In view of the earlier criticism of the idea that all emotions involve desires, we should regard Gordon's proposal with suspicion. I do not think it is true, for instance, that despair involves having a wish or desire that things be otherwise. Despair is felt when hope is crushed or, more precisely, when not only a firm conviction is established, but it quashes the wish that things be otherwise. Despair or hopelessness seems to involve feelings of hollowness and powerlessness which occur precisely as the result of a wish being definitely defeated. Certainly, it is possible to retain a wish that p were not the case, in the face of a conviction that it *is* the case. As remarked, this appears to be what *regretting* that p is the case consists in. But this regret is clearly different from, say, being subject to despair of its being the case that p.

The criticism can, however, be made more telling in the case of positive factive emotions, for while it makes perfectly good sense to be absolutely certain that p and still wish that p were not the case (this is what happens when regret is experienced), it makes doubtful sense to wish that p is the case when one is absolutely certain that it *is* the case. Surely, the wish here gives way to a feeling of satisfaction. Of course, in some cases a certainty that p generates a desire to see to it that p *remains* the case, but this is not always so. Suppose I wish to spot a certain rare bird, say, a hook-billed kite, and I become utterly convinced that I now have succeeded in spotting one. Then it is surely not the case either that I go on wishing to spot this bird or that this wish is transformed into a wish that it remains the case that I have spotted one, for once this has become the case, it will remain so forever.

It might be objected that I would not be subject to a positive emotion when spotting the kite if beforehand I had not had a wish to spot this kind of bird. I think this is false, too (in addition, it is hardly what Gordon—see (1987: e.g. 52)—has in mind). Consider factive emotions in the production of which, I admit, an antecedent wish or desire does figure. One cannot be *pleased* or *satisfied* that p unless one has had an (occurrent) desire for p and

---

[1] For this reason, Ortony et al., 1988: 32, deny that surprise is an emotion, but that seems to me counter-intuitive.

one realizes that p has come to be. This emotion consists in the feelings of relaxation and increased vigour or heightened vitality that can result from realizing that a desire has been fulfilled. The feelings of gladness, joy, and delight appear no different. But in their case it seems not required that there has been a pre-existing, occurrent desire or wish that the objects of gladness, joy, etc. be the case. Hence, the most reasonable conclusion seems to be that these feelings of relaxation, vigour, etc. can have another source than desire fulfilment. (As indicated in the foregoing chapter, I agree, however, that one must be *disposed* to have wishes regarding, or be concerned about, these objects.)

On the negative side, to be displeased or frustrated requires the presence of a pre-existent desire that to some extent survives the conviction that it has not been fulfilled, for it is the feeling of tension that results from awareness that a desire has been obstructed in its path. (In this respect, they resemble regret.) If the obstacle is overwhelming enough to crush the desire, a state of despair ensues. Thus, this state presupposes a pre-existing occurrent desire. Although sadness, sorrow, and grief as regards p consist in similar feelings of lack of vigour and energy like despair, I think it is not implied that the source of the feeling lies in the extinction of an unfulfilled occurrent wish for not-p. Rather, it is simply a feeling of being powerless, so that one is incapable of wishing this in face of one's current conviction that p is the case.

If, however, it is false that all emotions that can be classified as either positive or negative are so classifiable because they involve occurent wishes or desires, what could be the ground of this distinction? A suggestion that lies close at hand is that an emotion that is positive is so because it involves feelings that have the sensory quality of being pleasurable, while a negative emotion is one that involves feelings having a sensory quality that is intrinsically disliked, like that of being painful. This idea is not popular nowadays, but its merits may be undervalued. It is plausible to hold that moods can be divided into positive and negative ones, just like emotions. But moods lack content; so the division cannot depend on desires having a related content. The current proposal is that it instead has to do with what the felt pattern is intrinsically like.

Unfortunately, this is not unproblematic. Although it certainly feels pleasant to be glad and unpleasant to be sad, it is sometimes unclear that admittedly positive and negative emotions encapsulate such feelings. Above I expressed my inclination to hold the view that hope involves nothing but the wish that something thought to be epistemically possible, but beyond one's power, be found out to be the case. If hoping is nothing but having a wish, then it is hard to see how it could involve much of pleasurable sensations. It seems far more plausible to think that the positive character of hope has to do with there being a chance of something being as one wishes it to be. Consider also the negative counterpart of hope, fear. Although feeling fear is for the most part unpleasant, it seems that feeling slight fear—mere 'tickles' of fear—can be pleasant.

This adds up to the following conception of the distinction between positive and negative emotions. An emotion with the content that p is positive just in case it consists in a felt pattern of bodily changes that is intrinsically desired and/or it involves a wish that p be the case, while it is negative just in case it consists in a felt pattern intrinsically disliked and/or it involves a wish that p not be the case. Sometimes it is a defect of a *definiens* that it includes a conjunction or a disjunction. This is so when it is not possible to detect any reason why the particular limbs in question are brought together in the *definiens*. But in the present case the limbs obviously have a common feature in the reference to desires.

It should be kept in mind, however, that even if an emotion is positive in itself, for the sake of the felt pattern it encompasses, it may possess 'extrinsic' features on account of which it is negative. This is true of *Schadenfreude*. It is in itself positive or desirable because it is a species of joy, but one's being in this state is likely to have bad consequences for others, since it implies that one has malicious standing wishes or desires, to the effect that someone else be harmed. Precisely the opposite is true of pity and compassion which I take to be the negative counterparts of *Schadenfreude*. Here one is sad or sorry because of the way something has gone for another, just as in the other case one is glad or delighted that this is so. 'Pity' and 'compassion' designate a negative emotion such that having it is likely to lead to positive action because it is linked with a benevolent concern for the weal and woe of another.

Agent-Oriented Emotions

I have discussed some factive emotions the possible contents of which are virtually unrestricted. Individuals can be glad or sad about something they have themselves done or something they have passively undergone, about something done or undergone by others, about something that will happen in the future or has happened in the past, and so on. The contents of epistemic emotions like hope and (one kind of) fear are similarly unrestricted, though an epistemic constraint is here in operation. Accordingly, I shall call these factive and epistemic emotions—as well as specifications of them, like compassion and *Schadenfreude*—*plain* emotions.

Within the class of factive emotions, I shall now distinguish two broad groups of emotions, each of which has characteristic restrictions on their contents. The first of these groups will be called *agent-oriented* emotions. *Anger* is the agent-oriented emotion most often discussed. The emotion of anger is necessarily elicited by the thought that that with which one is angry has caused some effect which is negative or which one wishes had not occurred. Anger consists in a set of bodily responses that include a tendency to behave aggressively towards this cause or agent. Thus, imagine that Cain inflicts pain on Abel by hitting him with a stick. This would make Abel angry with Cain only if he sees Cain as having *caused* him the pain.

It might be objected that if Cain beats Abel with a stick, the (movement of the) stick is also a cause of the pain felt by Abel, so why is Abel not angry with the stick as well as—or instead of—with Abel? A possible reply is that that with which one is angry must be an agent in the qualified sense of being capable of acting *intentionally*. It has been suggested that the target of anger is "(roughly) another's ill will" (Gordon, 1987: 64) or an agent who has "culpably offended" (Roberts, 2003: 204). In terms of our example, Abel would then be angry with Cain because he sees him—and him alone—as having *intentionally* caused him the pain.

This idea is, however, hard to reconcile with the fact that persons often get angry not only with infants and non-human animals, but also with inanimate objects: for example, with their cars when they will not start. To effect a reconciliation here one would have to contend that anger in these cases is made feasible by one's, at least momentarily, taking these inanimate things to be agents capable of having the intention to cause harm to other beings (see Gordon, 1987: 56). But it appears to me as an altogether too fanciful hypothesis to ascribe, even momentarily, to the person kicking a car in anger an animistic conception of the car as an entity motivated by evil intentions.

The solution that I favour is instead this. Abel is angry with Cain rather than with the stick because he sees Cain as causing the movement of the stick. He is not angry with the stick because he sees it as not being, as I shall put it, a *blank* cause of the pain, but as a cause he fits into a causal network as an effect. In contrast, he is angry with Cain because there is nothing external to Cain which he sees as causing him to act in the manner he does—that is, he sees Cain as a blank or original cause of the pain he is feeling. In other words, one is angry with something only if one sees it as an in this epistemic sense blank cause of something one wishes to be without, like a pain felt. So the man who kicks a car in anger does so because he is for the moment not (episodically) aware of anything external to the car causing it to behave as it does. Had it straightaway occurred to him that the car's failure to start is the effect of, for example, someone's sabotage, the anger would have been directed at this agent rather than at the car. The idea that individuals be in this way temporarily oblivious to the external causes of inanimate things' behaviour is clearly less extravagant than is the idea that they temporarily subscribe to positive conceptions that are palpably false, like animistic ones.

This account can be buttressed by an evolutionary explanation of why anger—or more precisely, the tendency to behave aggressively, to hit back, etc.—should be geared to what is seen by the subject as a blank cause in the present sense of *not* seeing its activity as being caused by the activity of something external (rather than in the sense of positively seeing its activity as being uncaused by the activity of all other things). The reaction of taking vengeance, of for example doing something designed to cause pain to somebody who is believed to have inflicted pain on oneself, probably has survival value because it is liable to deter (potential) aggressors from causing harm in the future. Now, it could have this value only if it is directed at proper targets. Proper targets are entities with consciousness and, more particularly, a capacity to feel pain, since the behaviour one automatically tends to engage in when one is in anger is designed to cause pain. But tracing an effect, such as a pain one is feeling, to its causal conditions in the mind of another is a rather sophisticated feat. If the performance of this feat had been necessary for being angry, only a few non-human animals would be capable of it (and would thereby be the beneficiaries of its advantages).

It is a far less advanced feat to view perceivable events as being causally connected. Consequently, we should expect there to be a large group of animals with the ability to trace effects (upon themselves) to causes in the physical activities of other beings, but without the ability to see these activities as the outcomes of the mental states of the other beings (mental states which must not be seen as the results of factors external to these beings). All of these animals will see the disappearance of a causal chain into a consciousness as the end of it; they will view the bodily movements immediately resulting from mental states as blank causes, that is, they will neither see them as being causally determined nor as undetermined. Hence, if their anger reactions are triggered by the idea of something as a blank cause, the targets of their reactions will include entities with consciousnesses that guide their behaviour. Certainly, in some cases the target will be improper, as in the case of the man kicking his car. But this is often so for the reason that human beings have invented machines the causes of whose activities are almost as little open to view as the causes of the behaviour of conscious beings. In a natural environment, anger directed at blank causes will in a majority of cases be oriented towards conscious beings. Admittedly, the precision is not so great as it could have been if the triggering thought had been to the effect that the agent was a conscious being, but this is outweighed by the fact that anger with the first kind of causal source could be much more widely spread among organisms.

Of course, an adult human being is normally capable of tracing the behaviour of other conscious beings to the causal antecedents in their minds. Indeed, in our reflective moments we are even aware of the fact that, at least in many cases, these mental states are the upshot of causal factors outside these conscious beings, that now react in a certain way because of their earlier lives. But that this is so is not anything that is perceivable: we do not *perceive* the mind of another and hence not its reactions to something external to it. That is why, in our more unreflective frames of mind, we may be oblivious to the fact that an activity which is caused by the mental states of another could have a further cause, and may instead view this agent as a blank cause. The possibility of being angry with an agent rests on this unawareness. This is the important point for, as will be seen in Part V, it accounts for the naturalness of viewing the target of anger as *deserving* punishment, since attributing desert to something involves taking it to be a blank cause.[2]

The positive counterpart of anger is, "perhaps surprisingly" (Ortony et al., 1988: 151), *gratitude*, which is felt to what is seen as a blank cause of something which is positive or which one is glad about. As anger comprises a tendency to behave in ways that are designed to cause pain to another, gratitude comprises a tendency to behave in ways that are designed to cause pleasure to another. Note that gratitude seems a privilege of more developed animals (it seems that, say, birds can get angry, but it is more doubtful whether they can be grateful). This parallels our findings in the case of hope and fear. It is also noteworthy that the more intense emotions of terror/dread and rage/fury have no (labelled) counterpart on the positive side. The explanation of this fact is presumably that the reactions of fleeing and fighting back have greater survival value than their positive counterparts.

In view of these considerations, it should not be surprising that there is something peculiar about anger and gratitude being directed at oneself. There is, for instance, no need to deter oneself from inflicting further pain on oneself by inflicting pain on oneself: the pain

---

[2] In presupposing the notion of a blank cause, anger differs from the similar emotion of *irritation* or *annoyance*. A buzzing sound or an itching or tickling sensation may make you irritated or annoyed, but you can only be angry with the insect producing it, not with the sound or sensation.

already inflicted on oneself should be a sufficient deterrent. Here *regret*, or a wish that things had been different, is a more natural reaction. *Remorse* is regretting that one has responsibly brought about something one wishes that one had not brought about because it contravenes a *moral* norm.[3]

Feelings of guilt are appropriate whenever remorse is, but the converse does not seem to hold. These feelings are induced by the belief that one is blameworthy by *owing* somebody something. The reason why one owes somebody something may be that one has acted wrongly (but, it may seem, not necessarily morally wrongly, or wrongly to others[4]). This is not always so, however.[5] Suppose a friend has done you a favour and you know that you ought to return the favour now because the friend is in a fix. If you akratically postpone returning the favour, the thought of your suffering friend is likely to make you feel guilty, but you are unlikely to feel remorse as long as the opportunity for action is still as good. It is odd to wish that you had acted rather than decide to act when the opportunity is still there. Furthermore, you may feel guilty because of a wrongful action done not by yourself, but by some agent so intimately related to you that you identify with that agent. Thus, Germans born after 1945 may feel guilty about the Nazi atrocities, but could scarcely feel any remorse in this regard.[6]

Indignation is a species of anger that is directed at someone who is regarded as having acting wrongly not merely from one's personal point of view, but from the point of view of morality (cf. Gordon, 1987: 56–7). *Resentment* is likewise a species of anger, but it is more long-term: if one is powerless to prevent someone repeatedly acting in a way that makes one angry with him, one will grow to resent him on account of his actions (cf. Ben-Ze'ev, 2000: 396). Therefore, resentment requires greater mental capacities than anger to be felt, and it will probably be felt only towards responsible agents. In this it is like indignation, but unlike the latter, it does not imply a condemnation of the target as having acted immorally (contrast Rawls, 1971: 488). As pointed out by Rawls (1971: 445–6, 483) and Gibbard (1990: 139, 295–300), remorse and feelings of guilt are as a rule experienced by subjects at whom indignation, resentment, or anger could be properly

---

[3] Cf. Gabriele Taylor (1985: 98). She also stresses that regret, but not remorse, may be felt because of events for which one regards oneself as in no sense responsible, like the passing of the summer.

[4] Cf. Wallace (1994: 238–40). If so, it follows that one may feel guilt without feeling remorse, simply because one does not take one's wrongful action to be morally wrong.

[5] Apart from the fact that Allan Gibbard mistakenly associates feelings of guilt with the idea of acting morally wrongly rather than owing somebody something, he puts the cart before the horse when he defines moral wrongness by reference to feelings of guilt—and resentment (1990: 45). Surely, it should rather be the other way around: the feeling of guilt is the feeling that is occasioned by the thought that one has perpetrated a wrongful act against somebody. Gibbard comes closest to facing this objection when he discusses whether the feeling of guilt involves the thought of one's being at fault (1990: 148–50). He claims that the feeling does not involve this thought because there is such a thing as feeling guilt senselessly. To this it could be retorted that feeling guilt senselessly does rest on a thought that one is at fault, but a thought that one recognizes to be irrational, a thought that one cannot help having, although one realizes that it is at odds with one's evidence (see the Nazi example in the next footnote).

[6] It follows that I cannot agree with Bernard Williams that what he terms "agent-regret" is "psychologically and structurally a manifestation of guilt" (1993: 93). Also, I differ from him in denying that guilt can rationally and properly occur even when one is not responsible, though if agent-regret is properly *regret*, it can rationally be felt in these circumstances. (Thus, I think it is irrational for young Germans to feel guilty about Nazi crimes, but quite proper for them to deeply regret them.) Williams thinks that branding the guilt felt in these circumstances as irrational "carries no useful message" (1993: 93).

oriented. *Bitterness* is an emotion that their victims could experience, since it is an emotion that one will have if one thinks one has been wrongly treated or, more generally, has received less than one deserves.

Jealousy appears to manifest itself in a mixture of anger, fear, or sorrow.[7] It arises in a three-party context (Farrell, 1980: 530): when one is jealous, one typically regards oneself as running the risk of being deprived by some third party of some personal favour—like affection, attention, or esteem—that a second party bestows on oneself. Jealousy occurs because the loss of this favour is seen by one as diminishing one's personal worth. This is the core of this emotion. It is the possibility of the loss of the favour, and the consequent loss of personal worth, that induces fear and the certain fact of their occurrence that induces sorrow. The strength of this fear or sorrow, and thus of jealousy, is a measure of how important it is for one's self-esteem to be favourably received by the other. The anger is normally directed not only at the third party whom one sees as threatening to rob one of the favour of the second party, but also at the second party, since it, too, is regarded as partly responsible for the favour being in the process of shifting its objective. The presence of anger is evidenced by the fact that jealousy often issues in violent acts, crimes of passion. It is this element of anger which makes me place jealousy in this section, despite the fact that it is not a straightforward agent-oriented emotion.

Jealousy is often confused with *envy*. The latter is, however, frustration because one sees oneself undeservedly worse off in some respect than another. This respect might be a personal favour of some other being but, in contrast to the case of jealousy, not the favour of some *particular* being to whom one has some sort of valued connection: the favour of any being as good will do (cf. Ben-Ze'ev, 2000: 282, 290). Thus, envy leads to competition over the same particular goods only if there is scarcity. There is also a connection between jealousy and envy for the reason that, if another possesses a desirable asset, there will often seem to one to be a risk that, in virtue of that asset, the other will rob one of the favour and esteem of individuals important to one. Thus, Salieri might be envious of Mozart in so far as he sees him as possessing qualities of a kind that Salieri himself wishes to possess, namely, outstanding musical gifts. But he is jealous of Mozart to the extent that he thinks that, owing to these gifts, Mozart will or might rob him of the reputation and esteem particular individuals would otherwise reserve for him.

If one is frustrated by the thought of another's possession of some good even though it is something one could not have oneself or the possession of which would not make one better off (because one has already got something better), one *begrudges* that individual. Rawls (1971: 533) characterizes begrudging and being jealous as the "reverse" of envy. He then rightly sees envy as presupposing the envious subject's being worse off (1971: 532). But begrudging does not presuppose the superiority of the subject: I can begrudge people that their health is just as good as mine. Begrudging appears to me to be the desire to deprive others even though one does not think that one is worse off than

---

[7] Roberts (2003: 258) mentions these three emotions, while some other writers, like Farrell (1980) and Neu (1980), mention only anger and fear. As Roberts stresses, bringing out the connection between jealousy and these emotions is not enough to pinpoint it.

they and that deprivation would make oneself better off (except relatively, by making them worse off).

By taking up emotions like being envious and begrudging I have, however, reached emotions that with greater justification should be put in the next category to be introduced. This overlap between my categories indicates that my categorization is rough-and-ready, but it can still serve its purpose of summing up classes of emotions that are relevant to the discussion of responsibility in Part V.

Comparative Emotions

The second class of factive emotions on the contents of which it is possible to impose substantial restrictions is *comparative* emotions.[8] The most discussed member of this category is *pride*. I shall follow this practice of spending most energy on pride.

Hume sometimes expresses himself as though pride and self-satisfaction were the very same emotion (1739–40/1978: 320). This is wrong already for the reason that, as I shall soon argue, pride is not necessarily directed at oneself: one can be proud of other things than oneself. So what is true is, at most, that to be proud of oneself is to be satisfied or pleased with oneself. This is also false, but it is instructive to see why.

I can be proud of myself because my ancestors are noblemen or because of the ample gifts—intelligence, beauty, etc.—with which nature has endowed me. But it would take an odd view of the world for me to be pleased or satisfied with myself for these reasons. For saying that I am pleased or satisfied with myself because I possess these properties seems to imply that it is the result of a desire of mine to bring it about that I am equipped with these features. (As indicated above, the emotion of being pleased or feeling satisfied necessarily results from the realization that a desire of one's has been satisfied.) But one would have to be mad to ascribe such a feat to oneself.

Superficially it might seem that the same thought can cause both self-satisfaction and pride, for example the thought that one has won a marathon race. But this thought leads to self-satisfaction only if it is taken as showing something like one's having *exercised* one's powers well—this being something that can intelligibly be assumed to be due to one's will. The victory can be a source of pride even if it is taken as demonstrating one to possess certain powers or abilities which are such that no sensible being could take itself as being capable of equipping itself with them.

The properties of oneself on account of which one is proud of oneself need not, then, be such that one sees them as resulting from one's own will or efforts, but they must not be such that one sees them as resulting from the activity of causes external to oneself. In this respect, pride resembles agent-oriented emotions: the features in question must be 'blankly' ascribed to oneself. One can be proud of oneself because of one's beauty and intelligence only if one's causal investigation stops short at one's possession of them. If

---

[8] The present distinction between agent-oriented and comparative emotions has been arrived at independently of, and does not coincide with, Jon Elster's distinction between emotions of interaction and emotions of comparison (1999: 141).

one sees one's beauty and intelligence as the upshot of hereditary factors that might have bestowed these properties on another, one's pride is undercut.

There is another difference between pride of oneself and being pleased with oneself. I can be pleased with myself in some respect, for example in respect of my ability to type, without being proud of myself in this respect. This is so, if my ability to type is sufficient for my purposes, but in no way superior or remarkable. As Hume puts it, the quality of ourselves that supplies the ground for pride must be "peculiar to ourselves, or at least common to us with a few persons" (1739–40/1978: 291). I would rather put it like this: when one is proud of oneself because of some feature F, one must find oneself superior in respect of F to the members of some reference class of importance to one, and thereby deserving of praise, which presupposes that *being F* is blankly ascribed. Since the superiority makes one deserving of *praise*, it goes without saying that F must be a feature thought to have positive value.

Needless to say, it is this element of comparison that provides the rationale for the label 'comparative emotion' (contrast Roberts, 2003: 275, who denies that pride is essentially comparative). The comparison issues in an (alleged) superiority making one deserving of praise that gives the felt pattern of pride its distinctive character of comprising a 'swelling' of the self and a desire to draw attention to oneself. Presumably, it is also this entailed conception of oneself as superior that makes some moralists condemn pride (of oneself) as a vice.

The opposite of pride is *shame*. Consequently, the state of being ashamed of oneself is nurtured by the thought that one is deserving of blame because one is inferior in respect of some valuable property, one's instantiation of which is seen as a blank occurrence. Shame consists in feelings of contraction and in a wish to hide away.

Admiration is another comparative emotion which, like pride, is directed at somebody who is held to be superior to oneself in some respect that makes for praiseworthiness. It differs from envy in that one holds the admired object to deserve its superiority. As Roberts points out (2003: 265), we commonly say that we admire such things as sunsets and natural scenery. But, unless we do not mean simply that we enjoy or take pleasure in these things, these attitudes require that we put down natural beauty to some agent that it makes sense to praise.

Initially, it might be tempting to think that pride and admiration differ in that while the former is essentially directed at oneself, the latter is essentially directed at some responsible agent other than oneself. Hume, for instance, claims that the object of pride is always "self, or that succession of related ideas and impressions, of which we have an intimate memory and consciousness" (1739–40/1978: 277). Recently this thesis has been reaffirmed by Gabriele Taylor: "pride is always self-directed" (1985: 35 n.). I cannot here enter into the details of Hume's and Taylor's views, but I think it is fair to say that they cannot be sustained unless the following is true: whenever a subject is proud, that *of* which the subject is proud can always be (re)described as itself. Thus, if a man is said to be proud of his wife because she is a woman of great intelligence, sensibility, and beauty, this can be rephrased as his being proud of *himself* because he has a wife who is a woman of great intelligence etc. This is so because to be proud of his wife, he must see her (alleged) superiority as reflecting on himself, showing him to have superior qualities as well.

No doubt there are men who fit this description, but hopefully there are also men who are proud of their wives, but who do not wish the attention and admiration their wives receive to be redirected onto themselves—and even such men who are ashamed of themselves and think themselves not worthy of their wives. In some cases, it may be even more bizarre to construe instances of pride as at bottom self-directed. It is a commonplace that, when talking to foreigners, people often express pride of some of their compatriots because of their feats and achievements. It seems wrong to hold that, at bottom, people are here expressing pride of themselves because they belong to the same nation as some eminent person.

A more plausible interpretation is that people can be proud on behalf of others because they have the ability to 'identify' with them, the ability to imagine, from the inside, what it is like to be them and, consequently, to be concerned that their desires be fulfilled (e.g. to imagine being in the shoes of a player of the national team and receiving cheers). This is the same sort of attitude as we adopt to future stages of ourselves when we anticipate how things will be like for them (hence, the appropriateness of speaking of an "extended self", as does, e.g. Ben-Ze'ev, 2000: 516). As we will see in Chapter 23, it is a mark of the imagination involved in (experiential) anticipation that it is not voluntary, but automatically elicited. It seems reasonable to think that the same must be true of the imaginative identification in pride. Given my hypothesis that, like anger, pride rests on a belief—or rather an absence of beliefs—about causal origin, it appears natural to conjecture that when one is proud of another, one must believe there to be some connection with respect to origin of the other to oneself.

Thus, the fact that national bonds sometimes—especially in the presence of foreigners—allow people to be proud of their compatriots (as Gabriele Taylor recognizes, 1985: 30) would then have to do with their belief in a common origin which is more likely than other origins—for example, the present foreigners'—to culminate in greatness. (One need not believe that it has culminated in greatness in oneself, so one need not be proud of oneself.) Analogously, when a man is proud of his beloved wife, his love of her could enable him to identify with her imaginatively, to see things from her perspective and endorse her aims as she herself is presumed to endorse them; but for him to feel proud of her he must believe that the origin of her having the properties that he is proud that she has somehow has to do with himself, though not necessarily to the extent that he has reason to be proud of himself, too.

So, although I agree that there has to be belief in some link to oneself as regards the origin of the individual of which one is proud, I claim that there are instances of pride that are irreducibly pride of something other than oneself and that this is so because persons have the capacity to identify imaginatively with other beings (but not, of course, with inanimate things; so therefore pride of, for example, one's material possessions is always pride of oneself). This conclusion is amplified in Part IV when I argue that some of the psychological relations to which I have appealed in my account of pride—for instance, imagination from the inside and the concern consequent upon it—is not, contrary to what some have assumed, essentially directed to the self. If this is so, any alleged essential self-directedness of pride could not be anything more than a linguistic accident to be remedied, for example, by the coining of a new term like 'other-pride' (by analogy with 'self-pity').

In contrast, it is incontestable that admiration must be directed at another. A person admired is thought of as superior to oneself: it is of the essence of admiration that the person admired is somebody to whom one looks up and can aspire to emulate. However, this does not seem to explain the difference between admiration and pride, for the latter could also be oriented towards somebody judged superior to oneself. But in fact the characterization of admiration given suggests wherein the *differentiae* is to be found: one can look up to, and aspire to emulate, somebody only if one 'sets oneself apart' from this person, that is, only if one does not imaginatively identify with this person in the sense that being proud of somebody requires identification with him or her. Thus, whether one is proud of or admires another depends upon whether or not one's connection with him or her is such as to permit imaginative identification. (When superiority is vast, reverence takes the place of admiration.)

Contempt is the negative counterpart of admiration: it results from regarding somebody, with whom one does not identify, as inferior to oneself in some respect of some blankly ascribed feature, and so deserving to be blamed or badly treated. But there is a noteworthy difference between admiration and contempt: the latter is not necessarily other-directed, for there is such a thing as *self*-contempt. How could that be? The reason is that one could dislike oneself as one was at some time other than the present to such a degree that one is no longer able to identify with this person. It is then no longer possible to be *ashamed* on behalf of this person, for shame, being the opposite of pride, demands identification. So one will feel contempt for this being, contempt being an emotion that presupposes the absence of identification. But to admire oneself for what one was in the past, one would have to regard one's past self as superior, and under these circumstances one has no reason to give up identification with one's past self. Consequently, one will end up being proud of one's past self rather than admiring it.

Akin to shame is the emotion of *embarrassment*; it is so like that it is tempting to view embarrassment as a mild "particular form" of shame (Williams, 1993: 89). Underlying embarrassment is the thought that somebody with whom one identifies is deserving of laughter and ridicule, and this response might seem to be a milder form of what one deserves in shame. But the inferiority in embarrassment stems from something *external* to one, such as one's being *observed* in special circumstances rather than from one's then possessing any inherent features as in shame. Thus, one can be embarrassed by being caught in the act of undressing, though the fact that one undresses is nothing to be ashamed of: everybody undresses, so it is nothing that makes one inferior. It is just the fact that one happens to be observed while doing so that makes one inferior. Therefore, although embarrassment and shame have in common the relation of inferiority, they are best regarded as differing not only in intensity. Embarrassment has to do with being inferior due to circumstances one happens to be in.

Some Leftovers

I have distinguished agent-oriented and comparative emotions from plain ones with an ulterior purpose in mind: the discussion of responsibility and causal origin in Part V has a special bearing on the rationality of the former two. Nonetheless, this tripartition could have a point even were one to classify emotions for no other purpose than to understand their nature. But I am willing to concede that, from this perspective, my tripartition would leave something to be desired. For instance, although remorse is probably a species of regret, the former comes out as agent-oriented and the latter as plain. Moreover, because of its link to anger, jealousy must be counted as an agent-oriented emotion rather than as comparative. But envy is more of a comparative emotion, yet these emotions are so similar that they are often confused. However, this need not worry me as long as my typology does not miss any fundamental emotion to which reference is relevant in the discussion of responsibility in Part V.

Of course, I do not claim to have surveyed every kind of emotion, for there is an indefinite number of them. Feeling lonely, locked up, confident, on top of the world, and so on may all be different kinds of emotion, caused by beliefs to the effect that one is lonely, in a situation like that of being locked up, etc. Presumably, though, they are merely specifications of such emotions as sadness, fear, hope, joy, etc.

In my review, some para-cognitive attitudes are missing, although they are often cited as prime examples of emotion, namely, love and hate.[9] The reason for this omission is that they straddle the distinction between desire and emotion. To love, or like, *doing* something is to desire to do it, just as to hate, or dislike, doing something is to want to avoid doing it.[10] Loving, or liking, *somebody*, because of certain features of hers, is an emotional state by the passivity criterion of being a state which is identified by its cause, but it is a conative state of loving or liking to engage with her in various activities related to the desire-arousing features.

Loving somebody differs from merely liking her in that it typically includes what in Part IV I shall call *concern* for (the well-being of) her, that is, desires to the effect that the desires of her be satisfied for their own sakes. Liking can be purely instrumental: if one likes someone because she is good at something, one will desire to engage in this activity with her, and one may desire that her desires be fulfilled only to the extent that this is necessary to make the engagement in this activity profitable. Similarly, dislike of somebody

---

[9] For instance, in the tripartition of emotions that Ortony et al. (1988) present, they constitute the third category, emotions that focus on objects, alongside emotions that focus on events—which roughly correspond to my plain emotions—and emotions that focus on agents—which roughly correspond to my agent-oriented and comparative emotions.

[10] Contrast Gaus who asserts that liking and disliking are emotions (1990: 65) and who even goes as far as to claim that "the overwhelming majority of emotions, if not all, can be described—not fully, but partly—as a type of liking or disliking of something" (1990: 69). The latter claim—with which Ben-Ze'ev chimes in (2000: 94)—must be false if, as argued in the foregoing chapter, it is false that all emotions involve desiring or wishing. Contrast this claim to Dent's view that "love . . . underpins all our other emotional responses" (1984: 82)—even hate (p. 84)! As his discussion of hate shows, this claim does not mean that love is *an ingredient of* all other emotional responses, but rather that they *arise from* it. This is in line with my concession in the foregoing chapter that something like concern dispositionally understood can feature in the explanation of an emotion.

need be nothing more than a desire to stay away from her and, if one dislikes her on the ground of some aspect of her behaviour, a desire that she be hindered from indulging in this form of conduct. In contrast, hate also involves malevolence, that is, a desire that life in general for this individual be made difficult.

Loving and hating somebody differ from the agent-oriented emotions of anger and gratitude in that, while one may be angry with or grateful to somebody, because of a single fact noticed about her, love or hate are normally sustained by multiple grounds that are proverbially hard to sort out. It seems typical of hatred of somebody that it grows out of being angry with this person for several things, over time, in circumstances in which one is unable to avenge oneself. There may be a transition from anger, via resentment of various aspects of a person, to hate of the whole person. In opposition to this, love does not primarily grow out of gratitude, though it may partly do so. To love somebody is to be *attracted* to her, while to hate is not exactly to be *repelled* by someone or finding her *unattractive*. The opposite of love is rather both hate and something like repulsion or disgust than simply hate. Love and hate will be further discussed, largely by implication, in Part IV when I examine their constituents (that is, in the case of love, liking, and concern).

PART II

Reason and Value

7

INTRODUCTION: SUBJECTIVISM AND OBJECTIVISM

THE notions of the *evaluative* and the practically *normative* are so intimately related that they are sometimes used interchangeably. If it is of *value* that *p*, there is, normatively, a *reason* to (want to) bring about that of which *p* is a consequence, and conversely. In Chapter 10 I shall defend a theory of values according to which they are necessarily related to desires, as that which fulfil certain desires. Accordingly, I view reasons for desiring as also being desire-dependent. Even so, the notions of values and reasons, as that which, respectively, fulfil and direct desires, are distinct.[1]

On the theory here advocated, all values will be (normally implicitly) values *for* subjects (with desires) in a sense, since (like reasons) they will be relative to desires. But I want to show also how, with the help of a notion of a self-regarding desire, a distinction between values that are *personal* or *for* subjects, in a narrower sense, and values that are *impersonal* can be drawn within the framework of this theory. This is the sense in which the prudentialist maximizing aim is self-regarding.

This theory of value is *subjective* in the sense that value will be construed as something that stands in a certain relation (of fulfilment) to a subjective state, namely, a desire. Subjectivists about value claim that a necessary and sufficient condition of something being of value (and generating reasons) is that it is the object of some attitude formed

---

[1] I reject Scanlon's "buck-passing" account according to which "to call something valuable is to say that it has other properties that provide reasons for behaving in certain ways with regard to it" (1998: 96). First, it is awkward at least for some intrinsic values. When we call pleasure intrinsically valuable, we do not seem to be saying that it has some properties that provide reasons for pursuing it. The tautology 'Pleasure is pleasure' does not seem to provide a reason for pursuing pleasure, and pleasure seems to have no other properties that provide us with reasons. Secondly, something can have value for beings too simple-minded to be in possession of reasons. It could be replied that this assertion means that the valuable thing has properties that provide *us* with reasons to see to it that the beings get the thing. But, apart from the fact that this is strained, it seems to me sometimes to be precisely the fact that the thing is valuable for them (e.g., feels, smells or tastes good to them) that is our reason. It could also be replied that this assertion means that the simple-minded creatures *would* have certain reasons had they been in possession of the capacity to have reasons. But, aside from the fact that this suggestion is vulnerable to the first objection, it needs to be qualified, since, conceivably, the change consisting in their acquiring this capacity could be accompanied with other relevant changes, like the loss of their liking of pleasure.

under some empirical or evaluatively neutral conditions. *Objectivists* will insist, at least, that this is not a sufficient condition for something's being of value (and generating reasons). They may add that we must impose on the relevant desire some objective constraint, with respect to which the desire can be judged proper, fitting, etc. Or they may deny even that a relation to a desire or some other attitude is a necessary condition for something being of value.

There are then two forms of objectivism: objectivists can either deny both the necessity and the sufficiency of the subjective condition or deny just its sufficiency.[2] These alternatives express *externalist* and *internalist* objectivism, respectively. (Subjectivism, by insisting on the necessity of the subjective condition, is necessarily internalist.) "The objective list theory" discussed by Parfit (1984: 4, 499–502) is objectivism of the externalist sort. It lists certain things—for example knowledge, beauty, love, the development of one's talents—as good and other things—for example being deceived, ugliness—as bad, irrespective of whether they attract or repel. But Parfit also considers another theory that adds a constraint to the effect that the items on the list be desired. This theory claims that "what is good or bad for someone is to have knowledge, to be engaged in rational activity, to experience mutual love, and to be aware of beauty, while strongly wanting just these things" (1984: 502). With this addition, we obtain a version of internalist objectivism.[3]

In the next chapter I shall try to undermine externalism by arguing that practical reasons are desire-dependent. I shall then, in Chapter 9, proceed to explain why internalism should take a subjectivist form. This is not because I regard myself as being able to refute (internalist) objectivism—in fact it is extremely difficult to establish a negative existential claim to the effect that there are no objective constraints—but I shall present a reason for thinking it wrong to look for any objective reasons and values. It springs from the fact that desires have a 'direction of fit' opposite to that of beliefs,[4] and the direction of fit of an attitude determines the normative requirements governing its formation. Furthermore, to show that objectivists have not had anything very illuminating to say on the nature of objective reasons and values, I shall criticize some important suggestions made. This dearth makes it unrealistic to think that we could devise an objectivist account convincing enough to challenge widespread attitudes of the sort making up the main topic of this book. So, when I have distinguished, as I will do below, *intersubjectivist* values, which I have no scruples to endorse, from objectivist values, the absence of the latter from this work will make little difference.

As indicated, although they are interrelated, we should in the practical sphere distinguish the normative, dealing with reasons for the formation of attitudes of desire and the

---

[2] Wayne Sumner (1996: 38–9) rejects the last possibility and, thus, internalist objectivism. The position that the subjective condition could be sufficient, but not necessary, for the presence of value is neither objectivist nor subjectivist. If intelligible at all, it is a doctrine of mongrel values, some being subjective, others objective.

[3] Parfit, like Sumner, takes himself to be discussing theories of self-interest or well-being, i.e. goodness for somebody in the narrower sense. Parfit's idea is developed along Aristotelian lines by Stephen Darwall (2002: ch. 4).

[4] The term 'direction of fit' appears to have been coined by Mark Platts (1979: 256–7), but the idea of contrasting beliefs and desires in this fashion is older, going back at least to Anscombe (1957). See also e.g. Searle (1983) and Humberstone (1992). For Platts (1991: 48–9), characterizing a desire as having a fit opposite that of a belief is the best one can do to specify its nature, although he is forced to admit that this characterization is metaphorical (because he denies that it can be cashed out by construing a desire as a disposition to act).

performing of consequent actions, from the evaluative, having to do with the objects of these attitudes. In the theoretical sphere the normative rules of belief are shaped to preserve the truth of the content believed; that is, they are based on that to which there is to be a fit. Since beliefs are designed to fit truth, the formation of beliefs will comply with truth-preserving rules, that is, truth is the master notion and belief the servant one. If desires are not designed to fit anything, the normative rules governing their formation cannot have the function of preserving what they are designed to fit. They must rather flow, I suggest in Chapter 9, from the nature of desire itself which in this case is the master notion to which there is to be a fit: desires are to make the world fit their content. This yields a requirement *not* to have desires that one cannot fulfil, but no requirement to *have* any one of the desires one can fulfil. In the case of both belief and desire, however, the normative requirements are extracted from the respective directions of fit of these attitudes. Norms positively to have certain desires cannot be extracted in this fashion and are therefore not relied on in this work.

Objectivity and Subjectivity

My use of the pair 'objective–subjective' is related to certain other well-known uses of it. For instance, when the state of affairs of a physical thing's being equipped with some secondary quality, like colour, is claimed to be subjective, what is often meant is that it is equivalent to, or at least entailed by, some state of affairs about how some subjects would perceptually respond to the thing, for example how it would look to them under certain conditions. Generally, a fact consisting in a quality being attributed to a physical thing is subjective just if it is entailed by a fact about what subjective or mental states some subjects would be in with respect to the thing. Objectivists about the quality attributed dispute this and maintain that the attribution of it to the thing is not thus reducible to subjective states of affairs. However, the term 'subjective' as employed by me in this investigation is a specification of this more general concept, since the mental states in question are specified as *para-cognitive* attitudes, in particular desires. An alternative label would be 'desire-relativism', for the present approach construes reasons and values as relative to desires.

Para-cognitive attitudes, like desires and emotions, are higher-order mental responses that rest on lower-order mental states, namely, cognitive reactions. They will thus be subjective even *in relation to the world as represented by the latter*. In contrast, when an observer perceives a physical object as having a secondary quality, this will typically be due to the *physical* properties of the object and to the observer's sensory receptors, and not at all to how things are conceived or represented by the observer. So, perceptual responses are so to speak ground-level mental states that present the basic subjective world. Some— including myself (1985a: ch. 3)—would claim that this perceptual world is the basis for a second level of subjective reactions, namely of conceptual or cognitive responses which classify and interpret the perceptual or sensory content. But, however that may be, para-cognitive attitudes constitute a still higher layer of subjective responses, for, as is apparent from the analysis in Chapters 4–6, they are responses which involve thoughts or cognitions.

In other words, there are distinguishable layers of subjective or mental responses, and para-cognitive attitudes can be described as being subjective relatively to cognitive responses, since they are responses to how things are presented or represented in the latter responses. When I speak of 'subjectivity', I use the term in this narrower sense. It follows that the objectivity of values can be put in question without imperilling the objectivity of facts in general.[5] For in my usage it will be uncontroversial that secondary qualities are objective features of physical things, since our perceptions of the world as being endowed with them are independent of our cognitive states.

Objectivity and Intersubjectivity

Objectivity should not be confused with intersubjectivity, as I have already indicated. Suppose that more or less every human subject responds to some event, for example somebody's slipping on a banana peel, by laughing at it; then it may be an intersubjective fact that this event is funny or amusing. However, it is not an objective fact if to say that something is amusing is to say that it generally tends to evoke the attitude of amusement, for this fact involves a reference to some para-cognitive attitude. An intersubjective fact, on the other hand, involves a reference to some attitude that is *shared* (by some collective). Some writers claim that values are objective when, in my terminology, all they mean is that they are intersubjective.[6]

Whereas I attempt to make do without any appeal to objective values, it is part of the argument of this book that there are values that are intersubjectively shared among human beings, and other beings whose conative constitution is like ours, that is, that there are states of affairs towards which all these beings will adopt the same desires under specified conditions (for example of being equally well informed about them and representing this information equally vividly). Matters of numerical identity belong to such states of affairs, as I will claim in later parts. These claims about there being intersubjective values for human beings are just *empirical* claims about what they would desire under certain conditions.

If, in addition, these values turned out to be objectively valid, this would make no difference for the purposes of this book. It would be another matter were objective values securely established in a domain in which there is nothing approaching intersubjective values, in which people disagree about what is most valuable or desirable, as I hold that they do with respect to living the rational life and living the most fulfilling life. Here it would make a difference if one evaluation could be shown to be objectively invalid. But, against the background of what was said above about direction of fit, it seems very

---

[5] Cf. the criticism of J. L. Mackie by McDowell (1983).

[6] When Michael Smith speaks of "the objectivity of moral judgements" he appears to have intersubjectivity in mind for he writes that " 'objective' here simply signifies the possibility of a convergence in moral views" (1994: 6). Nor does the view Nagel (1986) designates as objectivist seem to me to rule out intersubjectivism; see my review of the book (1988a). Cf. also E. J. Bond, who claims reasons and values to be objective merely in the sense that they are there to be *found out* or *discovered* (1983: e.g. 61, 97); they are there prior to awareness of them. This is true of real reasons in my terminology.

unlikely that objective values can be set out so forcefully that they can settle such disagreements by disposing of one contender. Consequently, for the main theme of this book, the objectivity of values is no crucial issue: they are either redundant, if they coincide with human intersubjective values, or too shakily grounded to undermine widely spread evaluations from which they diverge.

Imagine that there are no objective values. Then it is reasonable to hold that para-cognitive attitudes which are based on vividly represented, adequate beliefs (about empirical or non-evaluative matters) are unassailable. For they cannot be criticized on the ground that they rest on any irrational or false theoretical beliefs. Nor can they go against values, since the notion of value will have to be definable in relation to attitudes that rest on just this kind of theoretical scaffolding. But it is at least logically possible that two persons who are fully and accurately informed about all relevant facts have conflicting para-cognitive attitudes about something, for example how to live. Hence, if there are no objective values, nothing can show one of them to be wrong, for there is no form of crit-icism of these attitudes that is autonomous of, and extends beyond, an epistemological criticism of the factual beliefs at their basis.

Given the great individual variation in human personalities, even objectivists must acknowledge that it would be implausible to claim that the same sort of life would be best for all. But they may claim that there is a limit to the variation: some ways of life are too deviant to be accepted as valuable. As David Brink puts it:

> We can imagine lives in which people satisfy their dominant desires and meet their self-imposed goals, which we are nonetheless not prepared to regard as especially valuable. (1988: 226)

Examples of 'deviant' desires would be desires to kill or torture, to count grains of sand on some beach, to eat one's own excrement, etc. Surely, it might be protested, even though some subjects may succeed in deriving great quantities of fulfilment from acting on desires of this sort, we would not consider their lives valuable.

To begin with, it should be admitted, on any plausible view, that if these lives are felt to be, by the subjects who lead them, very fulfilling, there is *something* valuable about them, namely, that they are felt to be fulfilling. The claim must be that there is also something objectionable about them because the fulfilment flows from desires having so base objects. But on subjectivism nothing is valuable *full stop* or *absolutely*; everything that is valuable is valuable *relative to* some desire or attitude of somebody, and in this sense valu-able *for* some subject. Now subjectivists are committed to the view that, *to these eccentrics themselves*, their lives are in every respect valuable (on the—unrealistic—assumption that the desires mentioned are what I shall call in Chapter 10 ultimately intrinsic). However, subjectivists are plainly not committed to the judgement that, *relative to their own desires*, these eccentric lives are in every respect valuable (though, as we saw, it is reasonable to concede that in some respect these lives are valuable). But, since it is presumably this relativity to oneself that is implicit if one asserts these lives to be valuable full stop, sub-jectivists are not wedded to this judgement.

This may not ease the qualms of everyone: critics of subjectivism may want to claim that there is an absolute sense in which lives dominated by immoral, trivial, or disgusting desires, however replete with felt satisfaction they may be, are so bad in some respect that they are bad overall, for anyone. But if there are such absolute or objective values, the beings who lead the lives indicated must be blind or insensitive to them. This opens up the theoretical possibility of ourselves being similarly maladjusted to values. But are we really prepared to admit that there is even a theoretical possibility that we are mistaken about such things as pleasure, knowledge, and beauty being of value? This strikes me as repugnant. If we are objectivists, however, we must admit this as a possibility, even if it be a faint one. But I cannot see that this is any easier to swallow than the claim that the—surely highly hypothetical—lives considered cannot be condemned as worthless, all told, for each and everyone.

It is, however, to be expected that there are substantial uniformities in what humans fundamentally want under similar cognitive conditions. Otherwise the coexistence and co-operation essential for their survival would be impossible. There are also reasons of survival explaining why the convergence will not be around desires to do harmful or trivial things like hurting oneself and fellow beings or counting grains of sand. (Where the interests of humans diverge—something that is also of survival value—a certain interest is usually shared by a group, like an interest in poetry or pottery.)

To take an example that will loom large in Part IV, for evolutionary reasons it is to be expected that virtually all persons will be concerned about their future well-being. It has, however, been observed that if someone were now to lack such a prudential desire then, on subjectivism, this person would not now have any reason to do anything that would secure his future well-being. For instance, Robert Audi remarks that such a person "would not even have a reason to step out of the way of an advancing brush fire" (2001: 124; cf. Parfit, 1997, 2001). If this is thought to be odd, it should be noticed that the situation may be analogous with respect to theoretical reason and fundamental, general beliefs upon which the common-sense picture of the world (and its development in science) rest.

Consider the spontaneous tendency to make inductive extrapolations, what in Chapter 13 I shall call *the mechanism of spontaneous induction*. According to it, it is the case that if we have observed a number of Xs having feature F, we spontaneously imagine that the next X we shall observe will also have F. Given that one exhibits this tendency, the circumstance that one perceives that a fire is advancing will provide one with a reason to believe that one will soon be painfully burnt. Yet, it seems we have no reason to believe in the general principle behind this piece of inductive reasoning. We can support, or question, particular applications of this principle, such as the one exemplified, by other particular applications of the principle. But it seems we can give no (non-question-begging) reason to believe that the principle of induction itself will hold in the future as it has done in the past.

The same may hold of our spontaneous inclinations to believe that our putative memory-images in general faithfully represent the past and to believe that the environment really is as we perceive it to be (and to believe that some of the other bodies we perceive have minds). Particular instances of these beliefs can be supported or questioned by other specific memory-claims or reality-claims, but there appears to be no (non-question-begging) reason to believe that our memory or perceptual representations are in general veridical. On the other hand, there is no reason to doubt the reliability of these spontaneous belief-tendencies. So, we can permissibly let them carry us along. Our lack of positive reasons both for and against would have been more troublesome if we had not found ourselves subject to these belief-tendencies, but had had to reason ourselves into endorsing them. This situation is, however, nothing we need to fear, for there are strong evolutionary reasons why these tendencies will be universally shared.

My suggestion is, then, that there is a parallel between the practical and the theoretical case to the effect that reasons do not take us all the way, but leave some fundamental desires and beliefs without their support. Thus, as we have no reason to believe in induction, memory, or perception, we have no reason to be concerned about our future welfare. There is only an evolutionary reason explaining why this concern will be universal. Since we have no general reason to resist this concern, though we may have reason to resist it in specific cases, we can as a rule permissibly give in to it. Then we shall have reasons to put into effect particular means that will ensure our future well-being. The fact that we have no justificatory reason to be concerned about our future need not worry us—in fact, this seems less worrisome than that we have no justificatory reason for some of our basic empirical beliefs (because beliefs are designed to fit the facts). Moreover, it would be peculiar, though probably not incoherent, if we had reasons to be concerned about ourselves in the future (or about others), but not to make the inductive extrapolations necessary for these reasons to come into operation.

Against this background, it seems no coincidence that David Hume, who is famous for doubting inductive reasoning, also made the following, equally famous, provocative pronouncement about practical reason:

> 'Tis not contrary to reason to prefer the destruction of the whole world to the scratching of my finger. 'Tis not contrary to reason for me to chuse my total ruin, to prevent the least uneasiness of an *Indian* or person wholly unknown to me. 'Tis as little contrary to reason to prefer even my own acknowledg'd lesser good to my greater. (1739–40/1978: 416)

Hume's point here may well be that these preferences are not *logically* absurd, that there is no body of truths relative to which the formation of these preferences can be logically ruled out.[7] If so, I do not wish to quarrel with him. I would like to insist, however, that though it is *conceivable* that beings who perfectly understand the issues form such preferences, *we* shall *in fact* not do so, just as we shall not fail to imagine spontaneously that the next X will be F when all the observed Xs have been F. We shall in fact not prefer a calamity happening to ourselves to "the least uneasiness" occurring to another (simply for the reason that this being is distinct from ourselves), nor shall we prefer our getting a lesser good to a greater one. As in the case of spontaneous induction, such aberrations are logically possible, though there is an evolutionary reason why they are not the norm (in contrast to reasons justifying them). In my opinion, this general, contingent fact is the basis for maintaining, for example, that for all beings with our conative constitution,

---

[7] I have, however, argued (1997a) that the standard interpretation of Hume's view on reasons is mistaken.

numerical distinctions are of no rational significance, so that it is not rational to make a huge sacrifice in order to provide someone else with a trivial good, and that it is rational to prefer to have a greater rather than a smaller quantity of the same kind of good.

Objectivism and Realism

What I have termed objectivism about value is sometimes—see, for example, Quinn (1978)—labelled *realism* about value (especially moral value and properties), but other writers reserve the term 'realism' for a different purpose. For instance, Geoffrey Sayre-McCord stipulates that

> realism involves embracing just two theses: (1) the claims in question, when literally construed, are literally true or false (cognitivism), and (2) some are literally true. (1988*b*: 5)

A great deal hangs on the phrases "literally construed" and "literally true", but Sayre-McCord himself stresses that, according to this definition, there are only two ways of being an anti-realist: one may either construe the relevant sentences in a non-descriptivist or non-cognitivist fashion or hold that, though they make truth-claims, they are all false. He cheerfully accepts that—descriptivist—subjectivism and intersubjectivism are both forms of realism because on these views the sentences under scrutiny make truth-claims about the subjective states of single individuals or groups of individuals, some claims of which are presumably true (1988*a*: 14 ff.).

In a similar spirit, though a bit more hesitantly, Brink (1988: 21) takes realism to be neutral between subjectivism and objectivism about value. Brink construes realism with respect to value as asserting that (1) there are evaluative facts or truths, and that (2) these facts or truths are independent of the evidence for them (1988: 17; cf. A. Miller, 2003: 4). (Brink speaks of moral rather than evaluative realism, but since he regards moral realism as a special case of a general, metaphysical realism, I do not think he would object to my application of his conception of realism.) It is obvious that, if this is upheld as a sufficient condition for realism, certain forms of subjectivism would qualify as realism. For if *p*'s being of value for one consists in one's desiring it under certain value-free conditions, then there are evaluative facts, and these facts are of a kind that is not reducible to or construable in terms of one's thinking, believing, or having evidence that they obtain.

However, Brink himself emphasizes that his explanation of realism should not be seen as stating a sufficient condition. Moreover, his reason for saying that it fails to formulate a sufficient condition seems to be precisely that, if it had been sufficient, certain subjectivist views that make (moral) value dependent on desire would have to be classified as realist (1988: 18). But if Brink feels the urge to strengthen his account of realism so as to exclude these views (in fact, he omits doing so only because he can think of no satisfactory supplement), one wonders if he is really consistent in declaring that realism should be so conceived that it is neutral between subjectivism and objectivism.

A drawback of Sayre-McCord's and Brink's conception of realism is that, while it makes descriptive forms of subjectivism come out as forms of realism, it turns non-descriptive forms of subjectivism—such as R. M. Hare's prescriptivism—into versions of anti-realism. But in the most salient respect these views agree on what there is: the evaluative character of something consists in nothing but its relation to desires formed in certain circumstances. In other words, they take the same stance on the issue of the reality/irreality of value; therefore, it seems reasonable to lump them together as forms of anti-realism or irrealism. What they disagree about is a matter of *linguistic analysis*: whether value-judgements are to be construed as *statements about* or *expressions of* attitudes or desires. But that is not a disagreement about what there is in the world.

This speaks in favour of requiring of value realism that it take values to be irreducible to attitudes, that is, not to be entailed by the presence of attitudes. Realism would then imply objectivism. But I am attracted to the idea of adding a further constraint on realism that will turn into a certain kind of objectivism. This constraint is that objectivism about the normative and evaluative is realist only if it sees them as irreducible to what is neither normative nor evaluative, but natural or empirical. G. E. Moore famously espoused an objectivism which was realist in this non-naturalist sense.

Characterized vaguely enough to be neutral between descriptivism and non-descriptivism, subjectivism about value is the idea that what is valuable is fully determined by what is desired, or received with some positive emotion, under certain purely empirical or value-free circumstances. Objectivism denies at least that this is sufficient to determine what is of value. The question whether subjectivism should assume a descriptive or non-descriptive form is subordinate to this question.

Is McDowell's Theory of Value Objectivist?

As an example of a professedly realist theory of value concerning which doubts can be entertained whether it is a version of objectivism, rather than of intersubjectivism, consider the influential theory outlined by John McDowell in a number of papers. McDowell suggests (e.g. 1985) a parallel between secondary qualities and values: just as to judge that a thing has some secondary quality SQ is to judge that it possesses some feature F in virtue of which it is perceived by certain percipients as having SQ, so to say that it is of value is to say that it is equipped with some feature G in virtue of which it elicits certain attitudes in certain subjects. Evidently, this theory is internalist, since nothing can be of value unless it calls forth the appropriate attitudes in the circumstances specified: "Values are not brutely there—not there independently of our sensibility—any more than colours are" (1985: 120).

It might, however, be argued that McDowell's theory does not qualify as an objectivist one in my terminology, for if an object evokes some attitude, then it would seem that there logically must be something about it—like the property G—in virtue of which it evokes the attitude in question. Otherwise, how could it be claimed that it was this particular object that evoked the attitude? If this is correct, it follows that, given that certain subjects respond with a suitable attitude to some object, it can be inferred that this object is of value, on McDowell's account. In other words, a subjective condition is sufficient for the presence of value.

To be sure, there should be a way of designating the causally operative feature, G, such that the statement that the thing has this property, thus designated, is objective. (A designation that expresses what this property is like in itself, irrespective of its effect on our sensibilities and attitudes, will fit the bill.) But, with respect to the justifiability of attitudes, this is immaterial if the judgement that the thing possesses that feature (thus designated) cannot serve as a basis for a criticism of the resulting attitudes as proper or improper, but the causing of the attitudes is instead sufficient for inferring that the object has whatever feature is necessary to make it valuable.

Perhaps McDowell wants to imply that there is such a justificatorily relevant way of designating the causally operative property in the case of values when he professes to discern "a crucial disanalogy between values and secondary qualities" (1985: 118) to the effect that

> a virtue (say) is conceived to be not merely such as to elicit the appropriate 'attitude' (as a colour is merely such as to cause the appropriate experiences), but rather such as to *merit* it. (1985: 118)

He also declares that some things have properties which "validate" our attitudinal responses (1985: 119).

Now whether or not this position qualifies as truly objectivist depends on how McDowell construes the property-identifications that allegedly could validate the attitudes induced. Suppose that his view is that the ascriptions incorporating these identifications can be seen to validate our attitudes, though the identifications do not allude to our attitudes; then—but only then—could McDowell be an objectivist in my sense. (More precisely, he would then be likely to be a realist objectivist in the sense suggested in the last section because his notion of meriting is presumably irreducible.) For under these circumstances no subjective condition can be sufficient for the presence of value, since these property-identifications would not be subjective, and the truth of ascriptions of them would be necessary for something's being of value.

But McDowell may seem to repudiate this view of the matter when he asserts that the explanatory ascriptions must be "constructed" from the same "point of view" as the one from which our attitudes are adopted and that we deprive ourselves of access to them if we take up any perspective "external" to this point of view (1985: 119–20). Perhaps then McDowell means that the explanations in question validate or make sense of particular responses by way of appealing to a wider range of attitudes. It is well known that a particular response will appear more comprehensible if it can be classified as an instance of a widespread pattern of attitudes (a pattern that one's own attitudes also exemplify). But, of course, these explanations cannot then validate this larger setting of attitudes. So on this interpretation McDowell would espouse an intersubjectivist rather than a genuinely objectivist position; that is, he would see values as being created by agreements in attitude.

I will not probe McDowell's account any further at this point, but I will return to it in Chapter 9. Here I have just used it to illustrate the distinction between objectivism and intersubjectivism. It is sometimes held that common sense assumes the truth of objectivism, and tends to 'objectify' (or rather 'reify') values. I find this doubtful, but I believe that spontaneously we are inclined towards intersubjectivism in the sense that, in the absence of evidence to the contrary, we tend to assume that our fellow beings share our attitudes: that they find funny, tasty, etc. what we ourselves find funny, tasty, and so on. This is why one often says that something is thus and so when all one's evidence supports is that it is—or appears—thus and so *for oneself*. But the alleged tendency to objectification (reification) has been held to amount to more than this propensity to extrapolate from one's own case; it has been taken to encapsulate also a tendency to 'project' our attitudes—or some property generated by our attitudes—on to the objects that evoke them (see Mackie, 1980: 71). For my own part, however, I find no introspective corroboration for the postulation of such a mechanism of projection.

The purpose of this chapter has been to distinguish between subjective, objective, realist, and intersubjective conceptions of values and reasons. The theory I will develop is subjectivist, and stays clear of any objectivist or realist constraints, but it is compatible with there being intersubjective values. However, as I have also stressed, it is unlikely that it would matter much for the purposes of this book if any objective values were established, since they will probably be in agreement with intersubjective convergences of attitude.

In more detail, the argument of this part will proceed as follows. In Chapter 8 I argue that reasons for action and desire are conveniently put in a conditional form where the consequent state of affairs must be capable of calling forth an (in the end) intrinsic desire. This is my formulation of internalism with respect to reasons for action and desire. In Chapter 9 I try to rebut the charge that it does not suffice that the consequent have this capacity to evoke desire, but that it is necessary that this state of affairs be objectively valuable in a sense implying that the desire is fitting, justified, required, etc. After rejecting this (presumably realist) objectivism, I move on in Chapter 10 to give a subjectivist explication of the notion of value, which distinguishes impersonal value from that sort of personal value that crops up in the prudentialist aim. In Chapter 11 I spell out some relations between having reasons and being rational. I conclude by considering, in Chapters 12 and 13, how the view of practical rationality delineated copes with the irrationality of weakness of will. A subjectivist view which construes norms of practical rationality as 'constitutive' of desire—so that one cannot consciously or deliberately infringe these norms—seemingly leaves very little room for this kind of irrationality. It will be seen that this kind of irrationality is due to dispositional beliefs receiving distorted or biased representation in episodic consciousness. It is worth dwelling on this matter, since this is the notion of attitudinal irrationality that will be put to work in Parts III, IV, and V.

8

THE STRUCTURE OF
REASONS: INTERNALISM

I SHALL distinguish between three kinds of reason or, better, three different contexts in which we speak about 'a reason' or 'reasons'.[1] First, consider the reasons there *really are* for, or against, desiring or believing something. These are *truths* that count in favour of, or against, desiring or believing something. Secondly, we can 'appropriate' these reasons and make them *our* reasons for desiring or believing. We do this by acquiring belief in them. So, our reasons are the *contents* of our states of believing, not these states themselves. Since our beliefs may be false, our reasons need not be among the reasons there really are (contrast Broome, 1999: 410). I call these reasons which are—true or false—contents of our beliefs *apparent* reasons, as opposed to *real* reasons which are truths counting in favour of, or against, something.[2]

Finally, if we desire or believe something because of our reasons for desiring or believing it, the fact that we have those reasons is *the reason*—or explanation—*why* we have this desire or belief. Reasons in this third, *explanatory* sense are *facts*, for example to the effect that we have certain beliefs, and not contents of beliefs, as our reasons are. For, I believe (*pace* Dancy, 2000: ch. 6.3), it takes facts to explain other facts, for example the fact that one has a certain desire. The contents of our beliefs can be truths, and so imply facts, but in reporting them as *our* (apparent) reasons, we leave it open whether they are real reasons. On the other hand, a mere appeal to the reasons there really are in favour of some attitude cannot explain its occurrence. The truth that there is gold in the mountains cannot explain why one greedy prospector set out for the mountains, while another one did not. But the fact that the first, but not the second, prospector has acquired belief in this truth can. So it is facts to the effect that we have certain beliefs rather than the facts that may make those beliefs true that explain our attitudes and actions.

---

[1] Baier proposes another tripartite classification of reasons depending on whether they occur in deliberation, justification, or explanation (1958: ch. 6.2.). His main contrast, though, is between justification and explanation, and this appears to have set a standard of distinguishing between just justificatory or normative reasons and motivating ones.

[2] Cf. Persson (1981: ch. 1) where apparent reasons are called 'phenomenal'. Later, these reasons, as contents represented in *episodic* thought, will be distinguished from dispositional reasons that are contents of dormant beliefs.

Of these three appeals to reasons, it is only the first two that are of primary interest here. The third, explanatory sense has a broad range of application including entities which cannot *have* any reasons: for instance, there is a reason or explanation why a rock is falling to the ground, though it cannot, of course, have any reason for doing so. Although apparent and explanatory reasons are very different, they are often confused under the label of 'motivating reasons'. Because the term 'motivate' is unfortunately ambiguous, both our (apparent) reasons for acting and the (explanatory) reasons why we act may be said to motivate us. Those contents believed that in our eyes count in favour of our doing an action motivate us to do it. But the fact that we believe those contents may also be said to motivate us to do the action; that is why an explanation of our action will refer to them. The confusion is further helped under way by the fact that 'a belief' can designate either the content believed, which can be an apparent reason, or the state of believing something, which can be an explanatory reason.

Yet these two types of reason are very different. Our (apparent) reasons for doing something may be opposed by reasons *against* doing it. They may *grow stronger* as we deliberate, and finally they may *make* us act. None of this is true of explanatory reasons. It is important to underline that it is things believed rather than our believing in them that are our apparent reasons. For when we make a real reason our reason, *the very same thing* that is the real reason becomes our reason. That which really tells in favour of something now tells in favour of this thing in our minds, by our having acquired belief in it. So, our reasons are *propositions*, that is, the kind of entity that completes 'that'-clauses and that has truth-value, propositions that we believe in or think true.[3] But it is the fact that we believe in those propositions that explains facts to the effect that we have certain para-cognitive attitudes or execute certain acts. In other words, the (explanatory) reason *why* you did the action may be the fact that you *had* a certain (apparent) reason for doing it.

It follows from this that those who have maintained that reasons are not *causes* of our attitudes and actions are doubtless correct to the extent that they are talking about real and apparent reasons. For real reasons cannot causally affect us, unless we believe in them, and then it is not they, as abstract objects of belief, that causally affect us, but the fact that we believe in them that does so. Hence, it is compatible with this admission that real and apparent reasons are not causes of that for which they are reasons to claim that the having of certain reasons, the thinking of certain thoughts, the contents of which are reasons, could be such causes. If so, we could be giving causal explanations when we claim that the reason why subjects acted in certain ways was that they had certain (apparent) reasons. (Call this variety of reason-why explanations (apparent) *reason-explanations*.) So, it

---

[3] Cf. e.g. Persson (1981: 90), Bond (1983: 16, 21 ff.), and Darwall (1983: 31–2). In contrast, Dancy argues that it is states of affairs that are real reasons, propositions, even true ones, being "too thin or insubstantial" (2000: 116) for the purpose. But if, as Dancy grants, real reasons can be identical with apparent reasons, which are thought-contents with which we reason, they must be abstract. At the same time, if propositions are true, there is a "contact with the realities" that Dancy wants (2000: 115), in the form usually called 'correspondence'. Moreover, it seems, contrary to Dancy (2000: 117), that apparent reasons must be "representational", for how could we otherwise account for the intensionality or non-substitutivity of their contexts?

would be a fallacy to infer from the admission that real and apparent reasons cannot be causes that reason-explanations cannot be causal.[4]

It should be noted, however, that detailing someone's reasons is not necessarily trying to explain anything in terms of them. For the fact that you had apparent reasons for doing something does not imply that you acted for those reasons. Specifying those reasons is just reporting or describing what in your eyes counted in favour of, and perhaps even justified, a possible course of action. In deliberating, you are in search of real reasons, that is, truths that support something, just as we are when we try to advise you or try to justify your behaviour afterwards. All these undertakings can be called *normative* as their aim is to determine whether some action *should be* done or *should have been* done. In contrast, citing someone's apparent reasons is a purely *descriptive* task in which we try to establish what someone thinks or believes about some matter rather than what is true about it, whether or not this is done with a view to explaining something.

The Conditional Form of Reasons

Real and apparent reasons for action, then, are propositions, but not any proposition could be a reason for doing something. Evidently, the reason-proposition must somehow *be about* that, for example an action, for which it is a reason. Equally obviously, it must also be about something else—something that is connected with this action and that is adduced as a reason for or in support of it. I believe that the *conditional form* is especially suitable to express this connection and thus the form of reasons for actions. I claim that a reason for one to bring about p (or cause it to become a fact) is always formulable as a conditional statement: if (and/or only if) one brings about p, q is brought about (by one).[5] (I shall soon take up the question what further constraints q must satisfy for this conditional to be a *reason* for one to bring about p and argue that it must be such that, if one is aware of q, one must *desire* that q be the case.)

I cannot here pursue the matter of how 'if-then' constructions are to be understood (but see Persson, 1981: ch. 4.1). Suffice it to say that I do not take them to be equivalent to material implications, but regard them as asserting the consequent to be deducible from the antecedent in conjunction with certain background assumptions. Thus, I think that someone who sincerely asserts that if p then q presupposes a body of truths such that with the addition of p to it (which addition must not produce a contradiction), q follows logically.

On this construal, the conditional form turns out to be very flexible. It can express a lot of different relations, causal and circumstantial as well as conceptual. When 'If p then q' expresses a causal statement, background material in the shape of causal laws

---

[4] Similarly, it is a mistake to argue, as does Jean Hampton, that "a reason-based explanation is not a normal efficient cause explanation, because it posits the reason as that 'for the sake of which' a person acted" (1998: 160). By "the reason" is meant the agent's apparent reason which is not supposed to be a cause.

[5] I here assume what I have argued for elsewhere (1981), that acting can be understood as causing something to become a fact.

are indispensable to make q inferable; when it expresses a circumstantial connection, other facts about the situation, for example conventions regulating it, supply the background; and when it formulates an entailment-relation, q follows from p itself.

A Parallel between Practical and Theoretical Reasons

Reasons are considerations for or against the adoption of propositional attitudes. If these attitudes are purely cognitive, like believing or thinking some proposition true, the reasons are often called 'theoretical'. If the attitudes are para-cognitive, consisting in a cognitive attitude plus some non-cognitive element, as in the case of desiring or having an emotion, the reasons are usually called practical. (True, actions are not para-cognitive attitudes, but then a reason for acting is, I think, strictly speaking, a reason for *trying* to act, and trying is, at least in this sort of case, an intention, that is, a decisive desire, in the process of being executed, perhaps not successfully. Thus, reasons for action are at bottom reasons for a para-cognitive attitude.) A merit of employing conditionals as the standard formula of practical reasons is that this formula can also be used to bring out the structure of theoretical reasons—thus making possible a close comparison between practical and theoretical reasons.

Now, it is plain that if I have an (apparent) reason for thinking q (true), I cannot just be thinking (it true that) if p then q. Clearly, I must also think p (true). The conditional provides a mere link between p and q. If there is not endorsement of the truth of p, there is nothing that so to speak can be channelled along this link. But thinking q for a reason consists precisely in having one's endorsement of the truth of q transferred or derived from one's endorsement of the truth of other propositions, since the truth of if p then q and p is seen by one as guaranteeing the truth of q. So if I, who think if p then q, am to have an (apparent) reason for thinking q, I must also be thinking p.

It follows from this account that the truth of the thoughts if p then q and p could be a reason for one to think q only if one is in a position to become convinced of the truth of p *prior to*, and thus *independently of*, becoming convinced of the truth of q. For otherwise one's endorsement of the truth of q cannot *result* from the endorsement of the truth of p, and this is essential for it to be the case that one thinks q because of a reason one possesses which has to do with p. Thus, p or p & q cannot be reasons for thinking p.

Of course, this does not imply that the direction of reasoning is always the same as the chronological or causal order of that about which one reasons. To illustrate, the fact that I see something is usually preceded and caused by my retinae being stimulated. But even if I am in possession of this causal truth, I will scarcely think that I see something for the reason that my retinae are stimulated. On the contrary, I will rather conclude that my retinae must be stimulated because I see something. The reason for this is that, normally, I have no avenue to what is going on in my visual receptors, except via inference from facts about my seeing something (and background physiological knowledge).

To return to reasons for desire and action, I have advocated the view that for it to be true that one has an apparent reason for causing p to become a fact one must have a thought that could be expressed in the standard formula '(Only) if I cause p, q will be caused'. The glance at theoretical reasons should make it apparent that something is missing here: a counterpart to the thinking that p is the case, that is, something that is to be transferred or derived along the conditional link in the process of reasoning. I shall argue that this missing element is a *desire* on the subject's part that q be the case. In the case of reasons for desire and action, it is a desire that is transferred or derived in the process of reasoning, a desire that, if strong enough, will issue in action. That is to say, a necessary condition for one's thinking that (only) if one brings about p then q will be brought about, to be (one of) one's apparent reason(s) for bringing about p is that one desires q to be the case. If one is *averse* to its being the case that q, this thought is an apparent reason for one *not* to bring it about that p, while if one is indifferent to whether or not q becomes the case, this thought is for one neither a reason for nor against the action of causing it to become a fact that p.

How Desires Enter into Reasons

A couple of differences between reasons for action and theoretical reasons are now noticeable. With respect to reasons for action I have put forward the following two theses: (*a*) One's reasons are propositions of a conditional form that are either truths or contents of one's thought, and (*b*) propositions about some action become reasons for one to perform it by having a bearing on one's desires, by one's desiring something that is a consequence of doing the action (and which is thus expressible by the consequent of the conditional). Now add to these theses a claim about desires made in Chapter 4: (*c*) desires are tendencies to act and not, like thoughts, states that represent a distinctive sort of content.[6] This leads up to a further thesis about action-reasons: (*d*) although a reference to one's desires is part and parcel of *the characterization* of some—conditional— proposition as a reason for one, nothing of it is *part of one's reason itself*.[7] A desire has no specific content which could be a part of an apparent reason (such contents being, as we have seen, what form these reasons).

In contrast, the theoretical counterpart to the desire—for example the thinking true of the antecedent of a conditional—essentially possesses a propositional content of its own. If, as I argued in Chapter 4, a thought cannot be causally operative unless it receives mental representation, such a representation must pop up for a piece of mental reason- ing or inference to occur. But, as regards a desire, there is no distinctive content that needs

---

[6] Two examples of writers who take desires to be states having a special content (though they do not deny that desires are behavioural tendencies) are Davidson and Hare. Davidson regards constructions of the form 'It is desirable that . . .' as expressing the content (1980: 86), while Hare favours the imperative form 'Let me bring it about that . . .' (1971: 84 ff.). But in my view both of these locutions have other functions.

[7] Cf. Garrett Cullity and Berys Gaut: "The claim is not that a reference to desires enters the *content* of one's reasons, but that desires are *conditions for the presence* of those reasons" (1997b: 8). Contrast Schueler (1995: 72–5). Furthermore, my internalism offers a *formal* constraint that things which are reasons logically must meet; contrary to what Schueler believes (1995: 54 ff.), it does not attempt to offer deliberators substantive information about what things are reasons for them.

to receive representation for the desire to play a part in a practical reason(ing), the presence of which explains an action.

Thus, we must carefully keep apart providing a full reason-explanation of why one acted as one did and fully spelling out the content of one's apparent reasons. For one thing, what is stated in an explanation in terms of one's apparent reasons is that one *is thinking* certain things, but one's apparent reasons, and what one represents to oneself, are *the content* of these thoughts. It is logically impossible that one represents to oneself, in episodic thinking, one's being in all the cognitive states that one in fact is in, that of every thought that one is thinking at a time, one is currently thinking that one is thinking it (see Chapter 30). Consequently, some of one's current desires, being initiated by thoughts not monitored, are also outside the scope of one's present episodic representations. But these desires must be cited in a complete (reason-) *explanation* of one's reasoned actions, for they are a part of what it is to *have* a reason. Furthermore, the citation of a desire also encapsulates a reference to a non-representational explanatory factor, as I argued in Chapter 4; but even apart from this, it adds an element which need not be mentally represented by the subject. Hence, we must draw a sharp distinction between what is part of a subject's apparent reasons and what is part of an explanation in terms of the having of those reasons: the latter includes the former, but not vice versa.

Practical Reasoning Not Inferential

From this difference between a thought and a desire—that the thought, but not the desire, has a content of its own which must be represented to take effect—a further difference between theoretical and practical reasoning springs: the former, but not the latter, is an *inferential* process. That is, when one thinks q for the reason that if p then q and p, one can be described as having *inferred* q from if p then q and p. But when one desires to bring about p for the reason that only if one brings about p then q, where the latter is something desired, there is no content that can be inferred. As we saw in Chapter 4, a desire is not a mental episode with a distinctive content which can be inferred in an instance of practical reasoning.

Moreover, one will not desire (to bring about) p for this reason if one has a stronger intrinsic aversion to p or links it to some other state of affairs than q to which one is more averse than one is attracted to q. So, to desire p for this reason, one may have to weigh or balance the desire for q against contrary desires and find it the strongest. (If it is not the strongest, one will only have an insufficient reason for desiring p.) But clearly, to arrive at a desire for p through such a weighing is not to *infer* it (cf. Searle, 2001: 253–4).

Nor can this obstacle be overcome by simply stipulating that the desire for q be the strongest one in the competition, as for instance, Robert Audi tries to do when he writes that "practical reasoning, like any reasoning, requires an inferential passage from one or more premises to a conclusion" (1989: 110). Provided it is granted that a piece of reasoning is genuinely practical only if it results in the making of a decision, I deny that practical reasoning can be inferential.

This claim can be buttressed by an examination of a somewhat modified version of what Audi refers to as a "basic schema for practical reasoning" (1989: 99). More precisely, it is the instantiation that he calls the "optimality pattern" (1989: 147):

(1) I want to bring about q more than anything else.

(2) If I bring about p, I have a better chance of bringing about q than if I do anything else.

(3) Conclusion: I should bring about p.

Here the conclusion has the semblance of following from the premises and of being genuinely practical in the sense of being expressive of a decision. However, I believe this appearance to be deceptive, due to an ambiguity in (3).

On one reading, (3) is equivalent to the judgement 'I ought to bring about p' which I take to be tantamount to a statement like:

(3′) I have more reason to bring about p than anything incompatible with it.

But this makes the reasoning theoretical. For drawing the conclusion (3′) is not to decide, but to form a *belief* about the thrust of one's reasons. This might be called a judgement of *rational normativity*. It might also be objected that this inference is not valid: it might be that I ought not to want q or believe (2), though I do; and then (3′) is false (cf. Broome, 1999: 410). However, although this may be so, this is hardly anything that I can consistently believe when inferring (3′): I must then take it that I have this desire and belief on the strength of the reasons there are. Consequently, it would seem possible to secure the validity of the inference by plugging in premises to this effect (though this is nothing I need to insist upon).

It is however possible to interpret (3) instead as the making of a decision:

(3″) I *shall* bring about p.

This sense of 'should' might be called *expressive*. (Or, if you prefer, *expressively normative* if you consider this 'shall'/'should' to be the same as that in second-person cases like 'Thou shalt/should not kill', where it expresses what is often called norms.) But on this reading (3) is evidently not deducible from (1) and (2): surely, an endorsement of (1) and (2) cannot *logically* constrain one to make the decision expressed by (3″) or any other decision.[8]

It may be asked why, since if (1) and (2) are true, I will normally decide to bring about p. As we saw in Chapter 4, to decide to bring about something that is desired "more than anything else", one must believe that one has at one's disposal in the circumstances sufficient means—stretching all the way back to some basic action that one can execute without any means—to accomplish it. Furthermore, one must continue to desire this

---

[8] If (3) is disambiguated in the way here sketched, a problem that bothers Audi disappears, namely the problem that the reasoning embodied in (1)–(3) need not be practical, but may be theoretical as well (1989: 101–5). This is due to the fact that (3) vacillates between (3′), which makes the reasoning theoretical, and (3″) which is required for a practical reading.

thing in the light of these means and their other consequences, and desire it sufficiently strongly to prevent one from engaging in further deliberative activities like looking for alternative means. Now, let us assume that bringing about p is a means of the sort described and that the further conditions for deciding are guaranteed by (1). Why, then, can one not infer (3″), which expresses a decision, from (1) and (2)?

The reason for this is that, as soon as one registers one's motivational state by making the statement (1), one's cognitive state alters, by the addition of a new propositional thought, and this may, logically, affect one's state of desire, so that one no longer wants q (as much). Whether or not this is likely is neither here nor there; it is a logical possibility and that is all that matters.

So, the upshot is: either the reasoning is theoretical, and then it may be inferential, or it is practical, by issuing in a decision, but then it is not inferential. Suppose, however, that (1) is replaced by

(1′) I shall bring about q.

This is an improvement to the extent that the first premise now refrains from *reporting* my desire that q, as a statement of a piece of theoretical reasoning of mine avoids reporting my beliefs and instead states their content (as indeed premise (2) does).[9] Now, given the additions suggested in connection with the inference to (3′), it seems that (3′) becomes inferable from (1′) in conjunction with (2). For (1′), not being a propositional thought, cannot affect one's desires; so the objection just raised is evaded.

If so, it seems that we after all have an inference that is genuinely practical. But no, for in this context (3″) does not express the making of a decision (contrast Broome, 1999: 407). True, it constitutes an inferential transformation of the intention formed by the decision that (1′) might express. But effecting such a transformation is not making a decision: for example, having decided to make a phone call at noon, I do not make a decision to make it now when I realize that it is noon now, though I acquire the intention to phone now. If I continually update my intention, as I register the passage of time ('I shall do it in ten minutes, in nine minutes . . .), I do not execute a series of decisions. Deciding requires bringing to an end deliberation that I have not reopened in this sort of case. Similarly, when the specification of means in (2) makes me move from (1′)—which, as remarked in Chapter 4, as an intention presupposes that there are acceptable means—to the intention expressed by (3″). The content of my intention is inferentially transformed in light of new factual information, but this is not practical in the sense of issuing in the making of a decision. A decision is made only when one desire so strongly comes out of the process of weighing desires against each other that it puts an end to this process. This a desire can never achieve by being inferred.

---

[9] Cf. Schueler's distinction between practical reasoning that reveals one's desires and reports of them that form premises or parts of its content (1995: 96–108). Still, it has been one of my claims that desires do not have any specific content—expressible by sentences of the form 'I shall . . .' or any other form—as a belief that p has a specific content expressible by 'p'.

The Direction of Derivation

There are other noteworthy differences between practical and theoretical reasoning: for instance, a striking asymmetry between the 'direction' of the derivation of desire (or intention) in practical reasoning and the direction of the derivation of belief in theoretical reasoning. In the latter case, it flows unproblematically from a sufficient antecedent to its consequent: if I think that if p then q and that p, I have a reason for thinking that q, and may proceed to infer that q. But it would be peculiar to make the general claim that, if I think that if I bring about p then q is brought about and desire to bring about p, I have a reason to desire to bring about q and may proceed to derive this desire. For if, say, I think that eating sweets will make me put on weight, and I desire to eat sweets, it is certainly not the case that I am given a reason to want to put on weight and am required to derive a desire to do so. Surely, if, *per impossibile*, it turns out that I can eat sweets without putting on weight, I have no reason to be frustrated (I will instead be relieved).

Yet, if p is sufficient for q, q is necessary for p, and reasoning to necessary means is often held to be a paradigm of practical reasoning: if I want to eat sweets and believe that a necessary means to this is taking sweets out of my pocket, I have a reason to want to take them out and may form a desire to do so (in the absence of countervailing reasons). It follows that a necessary *means* is not just any old necessary *condition*.

It might be said that a means is *a cause* of the end. Since my increase in weight is an effect instead of a cause of my intake of sweets, it cannot be a means to it. But although causal means are causes, not all means are causal: for instance, I may break a record by means of taking a very long leap. However, the central point for present purposes is not that this causal requirement is not a necessary condition, but that it is not sufficient for something to be a means I employ. When I move my finger, a cause of the finger-movement may be certain neuro-muscular happenings. Nonetheless, I do not, and cannot, (intentionally) move my finger *by means of* (intentionally) causing those happenings.

The reason is, I suggest, that I ascertain that I am moving my finger *prior to, and thus independently of*, establishing that I am causing those neuro-muscular happenings. I perceive that I am moving the finger, but if I know at all that the neuro-muscular events occur, I have to infer it from the fact that I have moved my finger and scientific knowledge which correlates this movement with the occurrence of these events. Things would stand differently if I could directly monitor the micro-process as they occur in the interior of my body. Then they would be, for me, *epistemically prior* in relation to the finger-movement, and this would enable me to use the causing of them as a means to the movement. If, under these circumstances, I wanted to move my finger, I would have reason to want to cause those events, and to feel frustrated, if I notice that I fail to do so, since this would be a sign that I shall fail to attain my end of moving the finger. In actual circumstances, however, I have no reason for frustration if, after moving my finger, I am informed that, by a miracle, I did this without the occurrence of the neuro-muscular events. Thus, an agent must be able to manipulate a means to an end, or to tell whether it has been applied, prior to knowing whether the end is attained.

As regards theoretical reason, in order for the thought if p then q and p to be a reason for me to think q, establishing p must have, for me, epistemic priority to establishing q. I must be in a position to ascertain p prior to and independently of q, if my reason is to be that *because of which* I think q. The inference is from the epistemically prior to the posterior. In the practical case, we have now seen, the derivation runs in the *reverse direction*, from the epistemically posterior to the prior: one transfers one's desire from q to a necessary condition for it, p, only if p has epistemic priority for one. This is required for one to see p as a (necessary) *means*, as something one brings about 'on one's way' to accomplishing q. A means is so to speak a 'landmark' or 'rail' by which one steers on one's way towards the end, something that for one can be a sign that the end is in the making. Obviously, if one could come to think that one has brought about p only by inferring it from the fact that q has been brought about, or only after one has observed q to have been brought about, one could not see p thus.

Hence, I claim that the derivation or transference of desire in practical reasoning runs from the epistemically posterior to the prior and not, as the transference of thought and belief in the theoretical case, from the epistemically prior to the posterior. It is not hard to understand why conative derivation should take this direction, given the direction of fit of desires. One's desire to cause q cannot make the world fit its content, that is, issue in one's causing what (one thinks) is q, unless it causes what one sees as necessary preliminaries to making the world fit this content.

This leads onto the further point that in order for there to be a reason to desire a means, it is not enough that it be a necessary means for the end. It must be sufficient in the circumstances for it. For it is useless to bring about a necessary means which is part of no sufficient condition for the end: this will not contribute to making the world fit the content of one's desire.

It should be noticed that this point supports the claim that practical reasoning is not a matter of inference, for inference hinges simply on the necessity of that which is inferred. In contrast, means to which desire is transferable need not be necessary at all: there is reasoning to means that are the *best* ones of several alternatives—as the discussion of Audi's optimality pattern in the preceding section implies. But for the sake of simplicity, I shall henceforth have in mind means that as well as being sufficient in the circumstances are necessary.

When one discovers such a first step or means, p, which is necessary and in the circumstances sufficient, all that follows is that one has *some* reason to desire (to bring about) p. This reason need not be sufficient to make one desire p. The weighing of desires that we have already touched upon comes into play here. One may have an intrinsic aversion to the means, and it may have other consequences which repel one. If so, one's reason for desiring p may not be strong enough to call forth a desire to this effect. On the other hand, this reason can be supported by other reasons, that is, p may have other consequences that attract one. Or one may have an intrinsic desire for p with the help of which one comes to desire p all things considered. One will then desire to cause p partly in order to cause q, that is, one will be disposed to bring about what one thinks is p partly to be 'on one's way' to bringing about what one thinks is q.

In contrast, if causing p is for one epistemically posterior to causing q, there is no reason why a disposition to cause what one thinks is q should spawn a disposition to cause what one thinks is p, for the latter disposition is not due to come into operation until one has accomplished what one desired, namely q. This derivation makes no sense in the case of an attitude—desire—whose direction of fit is to make the world match its content, whereas it makes prefect sense in the theoretical case where the reasoning concerns an attitude—belief—whose content is believed to fit the world. For in the latter instance, one reasons from something—epistemically prior—whose fit has been established to something—epistemically posterior—whose fit is still to be established.

This also creates a possibility which arguably has no practical counterpart, namely the possibility of being in possession of *conclusive* reasons, for example when one is *convinced* of the truth of if p then q and p. If this reason is real, there *cannot* be any stronger real reason for believing not-q. In contrast, if the reasoning is from the posterior to the prior, new discoveries can always be made that—without undermining the truth of earlier reasons—upset the balance of reasons.

In formulating reason-constituting conditionals, I adopt the convention of letting the epistemically prior condition figure in the antecedent and the posterior condition in the consequent. Thus, this could express that bringing about p is a necessary means to q: 'Only if I bring about p will q be brought about'. However, I shall assume that when agents subscribe to this conditional, they also believe that they can bring about p and that doing so will be sufficient in the circumstances for accomplishing q. Given the second assumption, this conditional will imply 'If I bring about p in the present circumstances, q will be brought about'. The latter provides a reason to bring about p only to the extent that p is regarded as a necessary, or the best, means to q. Hence, without further assumptions, neither conditional is perfectly suited to express the reason-giving relationship.

A Defence of Internalism

When discussing the desire-dependence of reasons for action, I have so far concentrated on apparent reasons. The dependence must take a weaker, hypothetical form in the case of one's real reasons, since one may be unaware of these. As these reasons are propositions that need not form objects of thought for the subjects to whom they are reasons, it would be too strong to demand that the subjects *actually* have desires directed towards them. The most that can be claimed is that the fact that, only if one brings about p then q is brought about, could constitute a reason for one to bring about p just in case one *would* desire q were one to think of q.

To my mind this desire-dependence or internalism of reasons for action seems just as natural as the corresponding belief or thinking-true dependence of theoretical reasons, that is, the thesis that one's believing if p then q cannot compose an apparent reason for one to believe q unless one (independently) believes p and that it cannot compose real reason for one unless one can be (independently) brought to believe p (say, by p being presented by sense-perception). If p were a proposition that we could not psychologically be brought to believe (at least not independently of q), then it seems obvious that it could not be a reason for us to believe q. In this sense it seems hard to deny that there is a psychological dimension to 'reasons', as there is to 'explanation'.

Therefore, it is not surprising to find that some writers, who have objected to the thesis that reasons for action are desire-dependent, appear to want to quarrel only with the stronger version of this doctrine, the doctrine that ties reasons for action to *actual* desires of the subject.[10] Perhaps they only mean to object to theorists who have in this way over-stated the desire-dependence of action-reasons—possibly because of a predominant interest in 'motivating' (apparent or explanatory) reasons. However, I shall take the desire-dependence of reasons for action and desire that defines *internalism* to amount to this: if there are (decisive) real reasons for one to bring it about that p (to the effect that (only) if one brings about p, then q, r, etc. result), and one is aware of them (i.e. they are apparent reasons, too) and, as a result, is able to rightly hold that one ought to bring about p, then, necessarily, one (decisively) desires to bring about p (because one desires to bring about q, r, etc.).[11] *Externalism* denies the necessity of this claim.[12]

I shall now argue for this claim.[13] On internalism, if the real reasons for me to bring about p (a basic action in my repertoire) are sufficiently stronger than the reasons not to do so, then, if I am aware of these reasons, that is, if they are contents of thoughts of mine, I must necessarily decide to bring about p. In other words, when presented with these reasons, it is not logically possible for me to ask sincerely 'Why shall I bring about p?'

But here we must be careful not to confuse 'shall' with 'should' in what was above called the rationally normative use, according to which 'I should (or ought to) bring about p' means roughly the same as 'I have sufficiently strong reasons to bring about p'. In this sense, my question would be asking for sufficiently strong reasons to bring about p, when I have just been given sufficiently strong reasons to bring about p. Of course, this question is sensible neither on internalism nor on externalism.

Rather, we should take 'shall' as having the expressive(ly normative) sense. According to this sense, the question expresses a state of indecision in which one is not sufficiently motivated to make the decision expressed by 'I shall bring about p'. On internalism, this question is absurd, for if it is true that I have apparent reasons to bring about p that are sufficiently strong, I am necessarily ready to decide that I shall bring about p. Here, if one

---

[10] See Bond (1983: e.g. the passage from p. 36 quoted in ch. 7), and Nagel (1986: 139, 151).

[11] This formulation allows internalism to take both the *cognitive* form in which the 'ought' judgement states a *truth* about one's reasons and the *non-cognitive* form in which it expresses a non-truth functional attitude as a decision. For instance, John Ibberson (1986: 70, 85–6) takes the latter view when he declares that, in normative contexts, to call some-thing a reason is to prescribe that, other things being equal, it be acted upon. The connection is here to the desires of the speaker who may not be identical to the subject said to have the reasons. More recently, another non-cognitivist account has been developed by Gibbard (1990). However, I incline towards cognitivist internalism on linguistic or grammatical grounds to the effect that constructions lacking truth-value, e.g. imperatives, do not possess a syntactic richness matching that of normative or evaluative sentences. For example, non-cognitivist analyses of such sentences of conditional form, in the third person and past tense would seem to be contrived. But this is a controversy I shall not pursue any further.

[12] The terms 'internalism' and 'externalism' became popular in the wake of Bernard Williams's 'Internal and External Reasons' (reprinted in Williams, 1981), in which he defends internalism.

[13] In my argument I have in mind in particular the strong case Parfit makes for externalism in an unpublished manu-script. As this is a work in progress, I shall not quote from it.

is in a position to claim truly that one has sufficiently strong reasons to bring about p, then, necessarily, one is ready to decide to bring it about.

In contrast, on externalism, there is no absurdity in asking in this sense 'Why shall I bring about p?' when I have just been given reasons to bring it about that are sufficiently strong, for being in a position to claim these reasons is compatible with remaining in a state of indecision. Thus, it is compatible with asking for something other than reasons that could put an end to this state of indecision, and one wonders what this could be. It seems rather that there could not possibly be this slack, that asking for reasons for and against bringing it about that p is asking for something that could not merely put one in a position of concluding that one should, or ought (not) to, bring it about, but also, necessarily, in the position of deciding one way or the other. It seems hardly a contingent fact that reasons for and against bringing it about that p are what, if strong enough, would make me decide one way or the other, that what answers the question 'Why should I (or ought I to) bring about p?' must also be capable of answering the decision-question 'Why shall I bring about p?' If so, externalism commits the fault of driving a wedge between two questions between which there is no space.

To put the point more precisely, it is helpful to distinguish between two situations of becoming aware of real reasons for bringing it about that p.

(1) In the first situation, I am aware of the *content* of the reasons I have to bring about p, and not (just) the fact that I have such (real) reasons. If so, then, on internalism, I am necessarily motivated to bring about p, since, definitionally, my reasons are tied to my desires. If these apparent reasons are stronger than any competing ones, I am more strongly motivated to bring about p than any alternative state of affairs. Hence, internalism rules out, in this situation, my sincerely asking 'Why (shall I) bring about p?' in a sense implying that I am undecided about whether to bring about p. This is in line with the situation in the theoretical realm where I certainly cannot ask 'Why (shall I) believe that p?' in this sense when my apparent reasons for believing this are sufficiently stronger than the reasons for any alternative.

(Note, however, that this does not imply that the sentence 'I have sufficient reason (or ought) to bring it about that p, so I shall do it' is a logical truth, as it is likely to be on non-cognitive internalism. For once I am self-consciously aware of my current apparent reasons as my reasons, as having the requisite relation to my desires, I have a new propositional thought that could conceivably affect the balance of my reasons. However, even though this reaction is conceivable, it is unlikely to occur in a well-adjusted being, as explained below.)

On externalism, there could, however, be room to ask 'Why (shall I) bring about p?' in the expressive(ly normative) sense implying that I am undecided, for it does not make it logically necessary that my having apparent reasons makes me motivated. This would then have to be a request for something other than externalist reasons, something that could motivate one to make a decision. But what could plausibly fill this gap?

As we shall see in the next chapter, it is not possible to escape this consequence by maintaining that, though reasons are not definitionally tied to desires, we are *required* to have certain desires in accordance with them in the sense that we can be required to believe what is evidently true. It is arguably absurd to ask 'Why shall I believe that this appears red to me?' when something clearly appears red to me (although the latter does not entail that one has any belief: see Persson, 1985a: ch. 3). For this seems to be something I am required to believe if I am to qualify as having any beliefs involving the concept of red. But there cannot be anything that I am similarly required to desire, for the reason that beliefs and desires have opposite directions of fit. Beliefs fulfil their function if and only if their contents fit the world, and are given up if their contents are disclosed not to do so. But desires fulfil their function if and only if they make the world fit their objectives, and must be given up when this fit is or cannot be achieved. Hence, there is nothing that it is absurd not to desire in the same non-contingent sense in which it is absurd not to believe what is evidently true according to one's senses. All one is required to desire to attain the relevant fit is some state of affairs which one can bring about and can refrain from bringing about, but this does not require one to desire anything specifically.

Certainly, externalists could affirm that, *as a matter of fact*, we always intrinsically desire the things we realize we have a sufficient reason to desire intrinsically. For instance, we intrinsically desire not to feel physical pain, and we also have a reason to have this intrinsic desire, owing to the nature of pain. But, according to the analysis of pain given in Chapter 1, it is conceivable that, as the result of some mutation, we lose this intrinsic aversion to pain. Then, on externalism, it seems we would still have a reason to be intrinsically averse to pain. But that is distinctly odd.

Externalists might reply that 'pain' must here have a richer meaning which includes an intrinsic aversion to the sensation designated by the term. If so, externalists do not face the absurdity of having to admit that we have a reason to be intrinsically averse to the sensorily pain-like sensations to which we are no longer intrinsically averse. This move requires, however, that we are prepared to regard the aversion allegedly entailed by the concept of pain as beyond the pale of reasons—as, indeed, Parfit seems to be (1984: 123). Internalists will say that we have reason to apply means to fulfil this non-rational desire. But externalists will add that we have reason to have an intrinsic desire with the same object as the non-rational desire, namely, that a sensation with a certain sensory quality stop. This reason-based desire must, of course, be *distinct* from the non-rational desire with the same object. But this duplication of desires appears superfluous, since the first non-rational desire seems enough to fill the function of moving us to put an end to our pain. The acquisition of such a desire fills a function when we consider pains that we shall feel in the future (or the pains of others), but not in the case of pains we are currently feeling. Thus, it is a feature that may make externalism attractive as regards future pains, which makes it awkward in the case of one's current pains.[14]

Furthermore, externalists owe us an explanation of why beings have a reason to avoid pain for its own sake when and only when they have a non-rational, intrinsic aversion to pain, though their reasons—as opposed to internalist ones—are logically independent of

---

[14] Ruth Chang also argues that desires to continue to have, or to avoid, hedonic sensations provide reasons (2004: 75–9). However, she adopts the "hybrid" view that reasons can also be provided by facts external to the attitudes of subjects. But this hybrid view seems to me unstable, since if you concede that external facts can provide reasons, they could also be what makes the fact that someone wants something provide a reason for her.

desires. Therefore, I conclude that in the quite possibly simplest and clearest case of an intrinsic desire, the desire not to feel a pain that one is feeling, externalism faces difficulties. This case rather supports the internalist view that we cannot have any reasons for intrinsic desires, *qua* their being intrinsic.

(2) Imagine next that I know only *that* I have sufficient real reasons for bringing about *p*; I am not aware of the contents of those reasons, which it will take further enquiries to get to know. In terms of my internalism, this roughly means: I know that there are facts such that, were I to be conscious of them, I *would* be motivated to bring about *p*. This certainly does not *entail* that I *am* motivated to bring about *p*. It is logically possible that I am unmotivated and give vent to this by saying something like 'Why bring about *p*, why bother to do so?' However, there is an evolutionary explanation of why we should be motivated to seek and spell out real reasons we take there to be, if we understand them as internalists understand them: they will guide us to satisfy our (intrinsic) desires as fully as possible. And, as we have seen, when we have spelt out our reasons then, on internalism, we shall necessarily be accordingly motivated. Certainly, it is logically possible that, owing to acedia or spiritual weariness, we never get around to seek or spell out the reasons we know there to be. But we can rest assured that, being creatures which have survived for a long time, this must be the exception.

Externalists, by contrast, cannot avail themselves of this explanation of why in general we shall seek and spell out reasons we know there to be, since they hold that the existence of our reasons is not conceptually related to our desires. Of course, they could postulate a desire to seek and spell out the externalist reasons we take there to be. But it seems hard to explain, for example in evolutionary terms, why we should have this desire. To be sure, if these reasons in fact turn out to be for things it promotes our survival to desire, like the absence of pain, it would be intelligible why we desire to find out what we have externalist reason to desire. But this suggests that it is a mere coincidence that we take an interest in finding out what these reasons are. This makes externalism appear less palatable than internalism.

It should be noted that these arguments hit not merely externalism proper, but also what one might call forms of *ideal* internalism. This brand of internalism states that not any old fact that induces an (intrinsic) desire, if attention is drawn to it, is a real reason (for the subject in question); the fact is qualified as a reason only if the subject from which the desire is called forth satisfies further conditions C, for example to the effect of being impartial.[15] This sort of internalism is exposed to the reasoning above for one could ask 'Why (shall I) act on the considerations that I would act on in C, for example when I am deprived of certain pieces of information and certain desires that I in fact possess?' Like externalists, ideal internalists could claim that, as a matter of fact, we have a desire to act on the considerations we would act on in C, but, again, it is not obvious why we should have such a desire.

---

[15]   For an example of what I have termed ideal internalism, see Darwall (1983). On his view (see esp. ch. 15), "principles that ground reasons" are ones that one would choose for all to act on were one not merely behind a Rawlsian veil of ignorance, but also equipped only with desires that are common to all rational subjects.

Misconstruals of the Purport of Internalism

It seems that resistance to the desire-dependence of action-reasons can often be traced to misunderstandings of this view. First, some philosophers appear to believe that this view is logically tied to a conception of desires to which it may be historically tied: a Humean conception of desires as "passions", that is, a kind of non-representational mental episodes that urge or impel agents to act. In the words of McDowell the internalist doctrine relies on an

> inexplicit adherence to a quasi-hydraulic conception of how reason explanations account for action. The will is pictured as the source of the forces that issue in the behaviour such explanations explain. (1981: 155)

He goes on to argue that if "it strikes an agent that his reason for acting as he does consists entirely in his conception of the circumstances in which he acts" (1978: 18), then it smacks of falsification to insist on the citation of a desire in the explanation of the action. Certainly, it would be to falsify the facts to insist that a desire was a part of *the agent's (apparent) reasons* or in any other way a part of what "strikes" or episodically occurs to him. But, in my version, the desire-dependence of reasons does not imply that desires are necessarily part of the agent's reason or of what episodically occurs to him. It claims that to describe certain thoughts—that make up the *whole content* of the agent's reasons—*as reasons* (for the agent) is to say that they are related to the agent's desires, that they have at least the potential of arousing his desires when his attention is drawn to them. And a desire, as I conceive it, is not a mental episode, but a non-experiential, postulated entity that alongside thoughts gives rise to behaviour.[16]

Of course, this entity must be mentioned in an *explanation* which refers to the agent's reasons. But we have seen that we must carefully keep apart the explanatory concept of a reason—'the reason *why*'—and the concept of an apparent reason—'*somebody's* reason': the latter is constituted by propositions entertained by the agent, while the former cites facts to the effect that the agent endorses these propositions as true and has certain desires linked to them. McDowell, however, appears oblivious to this distinction for he moves freely between the claim that a desire does not function as an independent component in the agent's reason (1978: 15) and the claim that it does not so function in the explanation of his action (1978: 16). This may have helped to mislead him into assuming that internalism is committed to a Humean outlook on desires.[17]

But aside from this misconception of desires along Humean lines, the error of thinking that, if reasons for action are desire-dependent, desires must form a part of the agent's reason or be included in that of which the agent is conscious when acting, may be pernicious in another way. It may take the form of believing that if one part of one's reason is

---

[16] This is also my response to Scanlon's claim that "we should not take 'desires' to be a special source of motivation, independent of our seeing things as reasons" (1998: 40). He regards it as "trivially true that whenever a person is moved to act he or she has an 'urge' to act that way". Possibly, this "urge" qualifies as a desire as conceived by me.

[17] That the denial of internalism may be the result of linking it to a Humean conception of desire is also suggested by Michael Smith (1987; 1994: ch. 4).

the thought 'Only if I bring it about that p, q will result', then, if reasons are desire-dependent, another part of it must be the thought 'I desire q'. Hence, if one causes p for this reason, one does so thinking that it is a way of fulfilling a desire one has. So, apparently, internalism as regards reasons for action is wedded to the claim that all agents, who act for reasons, act with a view to satisfying their own desires.

This is a gross misunderstanding of the purport of internalism. What this account claims is that q be desired by one and not that one be conscious of this fact. One can bring about p for the reason that, as one sees it, only if one brings about p then q, without being aware that one desires that q and so without thinking that the realization of p will fulfil a desire one has (see e.g. Darwall, 1983: 37). Suppose, however, that one does transcend to the meta-level of monitoring one's present desires and thus *is* aware of this desire and consequently sees the bringing about of p as a way of satisfying it. Then internalists claim that if these are one's reasons for being moved one to action, a *second-order* desire to fulfil one's present desires must be ascribable to one, and this may be a reason why one acted of which one is not conscious. In fact, there is, as was remarked above, an obstacle in principle to one's being aware of all the desires that one has when acting, since one cannot be aware of all one's present thoughts. For one cannot in thinking a thought think that one has this very thought, and some of the thoughts of which one is unconscious may be causally operative.

It is of great importance to realize that internalism with respect to reasons for action is not linked up with the thesis that we always act in order to fulfil our own desires; that sort of claim will be a main objective of criticism in Part IV.[18]

Thirdly, there is the misapprehension that insisting on the presence of a desire leads to shallow explanations. Writing of a masochist, David McNaughton claims that

> According to that thesis we have fully explained someone's choosing to be flogged when we have explained that he believes it will cause him great pain and that is what he desires. This is surely mistaken; more is required to have fully explained his action. We need to appreciate the masochist's view of the whipping, to discover the light in which it can be seen as attractive. (1988: 112)

However, internalism does not exclude the information on which McNaughton insists. Internalism is not confined to the rather fatuous explanation 'The masochist underwent a whipping because he thought it would cause him pain and he wants to feel pain.' It is perfectly consistent with this theory to go on explaining why the masochist desires to feel pain, by bringing out what he sees as attractive about it. Explicitly or implicitly, this form of explanation will appeal to desires for that which forms the attractive aspect, desires from which the desire to feel pain is derived.

It seems that McNaughton here takes for granted something that Scanlon refers to as "the standard desire model", according to which "desires are not conclusions of practical reasoning but starting points for it. They are states which simply occur or not" (1998: 43). But, as I have repeatedly stressed, (intelligent) desires are para-cognitive attitudes—in

---

[18] For further discussion of this matter, see Persson (1990). Cf. also Pettit's and Smith's (1990) distinction between background and foreground desire (though I take exception to their claim that a desire is "a sort of state which closely parallels belief" (p. 591)).

Scanlon's terminology, "judgment-sensitive attitudes" (1998: 20)—for which reasons and reason-explanations can be provided.

Reasons for Emotions

The practical reasons on which I have so far concentrated are, basically, reasons for desiring since, as indicated, reasons for acting and intending are reducible to such reasons. But practical reasons also comprise reasons for having emotions. For it is of course possible, as was pointed out in Chapter 5, to have emotions for reasons, for example, I can be sad or fear that I am getting certain spots on the skin for the reason that these spots are an infallible sign that I am suffering from a terminal illness. These reasons are, however, not necessarily reasons for desire, since, as argued in Chapter 6, sadness does not comprise having any desire or wish. Nonetheless, desires or wishes—for example, not to suffer from the illness—may be part of the reasons for emotions.

Reasons for emotions can also be put in conditional form: for example, my reason for being sad about, or fearing, the spots can be expressed as 'I am suffering from this terminal illness only if my skin gets such-and-such spots', where the consequent about the illness evokes the emotion in question. Of course, the antecedent does not necessarily concern the possibility of my performing some action, since this possibility is not essential for having the emotions of, for example, sadness and fear, as it is essential for having an intelligent desire.

In the case of emotions, the current of derivation is also from the epistemically posterior to the prior. This is because their direction of fit is the same as that of desires: in first fearing that p and then, upon becoming convinced that p, becoming sad that p, I first fear that the world will fit the proposition p and then am sad because it does. If the spots are among the first noticeable symptoms of the disease, I will derive a separate fear of the spots from my fear of getting the disease, but this is not so if the spots make their appearance late in the course of the illness, at a point when I am already certain that I am afflicted by it.

This implies that the derivation of one emotion from another of the same kind is restricted to epistemic emotions, like fear and hope, as opposed to factive ones, like sadness and gladness (to hark back to a distinction espoused in Chapter 6). For me to be sad that I have contracted the disease, I must be convinced of my having the disease. But this conviction, in conjunction with my belief that the spots are a sure sign of the disease, provides me with no reason to be derivatively sad that I have the spots, upon discovering them, for this makes my conviction that I am infected no firmer. In contrast, my fear of the disease may give me reason derivatively to fear finding the spots on my skin, since this may make it more probable that I have the disease. However, both epistemic and factive emotions can be derived from desires or wishes, when the appropriate epistemic conditions obtain (probability and certainty, respectively). In principle, this derivation is parallel to the derivation of desires.

To bring out the crucial dimension of epistemic priority, I have proposed to adopt the convention of formulating conditionals so that the epistemically prior state of affairs always appears in the antecedent and the posterior in the consequent. Thus, in terms of the last example, if there is a biconditional relationship between the spots and the illness, and the spots are in the position of epistemic priority, the conditional should be formulated as 'I have the disease if and only if I have the spots' rather than as 'I have the spots if and only if I have the disease'.

9

AN OBJECTIVE
REQUIREMENT?

ONE of the chief suggestions emerging from the foregoing chapter is that a real reason for one to (want to) bring about p is a truth of the form that only if one brings about p then q results, in which one desires q or would desire q were it brought to one's attention. This is a formulation of internalism or the desire-dependence of real reasons (from which follows internalism with respect to apparent reasons). However, this leaves room for an objective constraint on the desires on which real reasons are conceptually dependent. It might be claimed that not any conditional truth about an action the consequent of which elicits a desire is a real reason for executing the action. This is so only if the consequent is such that it can be judged *fitting, required*, etc. to desire it. Now, it is reasonable to say that it is fitting or required to desire a state of affairs if and only if it is *objectively valuable*—*objectively* valuable because the feature of the state of affairs that makes it fitting to desire it is independent of desire.

Real reasons, it is reasonable to continue, must ultimately be grounded in states of affairs that are objectively valuable in themselves, and the norms of practical reasoning are designed to preserve this objective value (as the norms of theoretical reasoning are designed to preserve truth). This is a picture of the normative and the evaluative that may be presented by internalist objectivism.

An Analogy with Foundationalism

To try to get a grip on this notion of objective value, let us compare it to the correspondence-theoretic notion of truth and internalist objectivism to *foundationalism* in epistemology (this can be done without endorsing the truth of the correspondence theory or foundationalism). For one to have in one's mind a real reason supporting one's thought that q, it is not enough that in awareness of the fact if p then q, one thinks it true that p if presented with this proposition; this thought must also *be* true. So the fact p should be presented in such a way to one that p is thought true only if it is in fact true. This can be done by providing (conclusive) reasons for p in its turn, by presenting one with propositions to the effect that if *r* then *p* and *r*. But, evidently, this type of justification cannot go on *ad infinitum*; nor can some reason be left unjustified, for this lack of justification would spread and infect the whole chain of reasons forged by one.

It is at this juncture foundationalism enters the scene. It suggests that the way out of this regress lies in the fact that some thoughts can be justified by reference to something of a different kind than thoughts, something that in its turn does not cry out for justification. This is sense-experience: some thoughts are the result of having sense-experiences to which they correspond, and thus are true of in the correspondence-theoretic sense. When the thought that I see something blue, for example, occurs to me because of my experience of seeing something of this colour, I can be certain of its truth because it consists in a correspondence with the experience that directly causes it. We may say that I here perceive *that* something is blue (this locution implies truth). Thoughts that are thus justified by reference to sensory experience could be termed *basic* thoughts. According to foundationalism, they generate the justificatory power of the whole system of reasons that might be erected.

In analogy with this, internalist objectivism may claim that to justify or give real reasons for a desire for *p*, it is not enough to point to a fact that only if *p* is brought about then *q* results to somebody who has a desire for *q*. One must also show that it is fitting or required to desire *q*. This may be achieved by producing a real reason, the consequent of which is the object of desire, from which the desire for *q* can be derived. But, evidently, this type of justification cannot go on without an end; some state of affairs must be desired for its own sake or as an end (in itself), and not because of any reasons. That is, it must be an objective of *intrinsic* desire. (In the present context, I assume that intrinsic desires are *ultimately* intrinsic, that is, that they have not started their life as being based on apparent reasons. For this distinction, see the next chapter.)

Intrinsic desires cannot, however, be left unjustified, objectivists may continue, for then the whole system of reasons one has rooted in them will be drained of its justificatory power. But since, *ex hypothesi*, they are not justified by reference to other desires, their basis—like that of basic thoughts—must be sought in something of a different kind. As basic thoughts can be justified (we have imagined) by appeal to sense-experience, so, internalist objectivists may suggest, (ultimately) intrinsic desires can be justified in terms of something showing them to be fitting or required. Such intrinsic desires are the conative counterparts to perceivings-that.

Before attempting to assess the merits of this internalist objectivism, let me under-score that I construe the intrinsicality of desires more narrowly than it traditionally may have been. I propose to employ the phrase 'desiring something for its own sake (or as an end)' or, alternatively, 'intrinsically desiring something' in contradistinction to 'desiring something for an (apparent) reason' rather than in contradistinction to the traditional contrast 'desiring something as a means'.[1] Consider a case in which you desire an

---

[1] This implies that Joseph Raz is wrong when he claims: "There is always a reason for any desire" (1999: 56). Raz makes the denial of this claim seem more implausible than it is by not distinguishing having no reason for a desire from having reasons against it, e.g. when he writes: "We cannot want what we see no reason to want any more than we can believe what we think is untrue or contrary to the evidence" (1999: 53).

experience because it is pleasurable. As we saw in Chapter 2, this is desiring to have the experience because of one of its intrinsic properties that is supervenient on some of its other intrinsic properties. In this situation, it seems wrong to say that you desire to have the experience as a *means* to experience pleasure because that would suggest that there is an external relation between the experience and pleasure, whereas the experience in fact includes the pleasure. Nonetheless, it is true that you desire to have the experience for the reason that it constitutes something pleasurable; it is pleasure and no other intrinsic feature of the experience that is strictly the object of your intrinsic desire.[2] This narrow use tailors intrinsic desires for the role of stopping points of reasoning.

I want now to present a reason for thinking that there are no states of affairs such that it is fitting or required to form intrinsic desires with them as objectives. I shall do this by pursuing a parallel—already broached in the foregoing chapter—to basic thoughts in which we are required to invest belief in the light of matching sense-experience.

As I pointed out, there is a reason for asserting that it is not logically possible for me to wonder, for example, 'Why shall (or should) I think it true that I see something blue?' when I see something blue. Instead I must tend to respond to awareness of this sort of experience by thinking it true that I see something blue. This is because of the direction of fit of thoughts or beliefs: they are states formed to be true, to fit the facts. Therefore, to qualify as an instance of thinking-true or believing, the thought that I see something blue must be formed to fit the facts, but then it will be formed to fit what I see when I see something blue. Forming a belief that fits the facts in this simple situation is necessary for being granted the capacity to form it.[3]

The crux is, however, as we have seen, that it is something of a commonplace that beliefs and desires have opposite directions of fit. While beliefs are formed in order that *they* (i.e. their contents) fit the facts, and are abandoned if they fail in this respect, desires are rather states to make *the world* fit them (their objectives), and the fact that there is no fit is no reason to give them up; instead they often cease to exist when there is a fit. So the direction of fit of desires is opposite to that of belief.

This means that there is not an argument parallel to the one I just ran for basic thoughts which supports the conclusion that there are propositions fit or required to be intrinsically desired.[4] We cannot claim, for example, that there are (true) propositions such that, if they are the content of our thought, we are required to respond by intrinsically desiring that they fit the facts if our desire is to have the fit required of desires, for no such fit with the facts is required of desires. We cannot logically rule out that something is a desire because its content lacks the requisite fit as in the above situation we could logically rule out that something is a belief on this ground, for, in contrast to beliefs, the content of desires is not required to fit anything. While the direction of fit of beliefs requires something like truth—the rationale of having beliefs would be undercut if there

---

[2] Like Scott MacDonald (1991) I recognize at least two other ways alongside a proper means-end relationship in which something can be "subordinated" to an end: it can in some sense constitute the end and contribute as a part to it.

[3] So, in contrast to what Hampton seems to suggest, one does not here comply with "a norm ('one ought to believe what is true')" (1998: 48), that one could consciously disobey.

[4] By making this appeal to opposite directions of fit, I part ways with Audi, who also pursues a parallel between practical reason and foundationalism (2001: pt. II).

was nothing like truth—the direction of fit of desires does not do so: the rationale of having desires would not be undercut if it were established that there were nothing by reference to which their content could be judged as fitting and which we are therefore required to desire.

However, while we are not positively required to *have* any intrinsic desires, there are desires that we are required *not* to have. If we cannot bring about *p*, we are required not to desire intelligently to bring about *p*. This is because desires are had to make the world fit their content. But if we cannot bring it about *p*, we cannot make the world fit the content of our desire for *p*. The crucial point is, however, that, if we can bring it about that *p*, and can abstain from it, there is nothing constraining us to desire intrinsically one thing rather than the other. It cannot be that we are required to desire intrinsically one alternative if our desire is to fill its function, is to have its assigned fit, as it can be in the case of basic beliefs.

Of course, I have not disproved the existence of objective values conceived as something that we are required to desire intrinsically. I have merely supplied a reason for why we should not expect to find such a conception readily at hand as we do in the case of belief (in the form of truth). Thereby, the onus of proof is placed on objectivists (*pace* Nagel, 1986: 143): they must put forward such conceptions, and their adversaries have to refute them only when they are put forward. In the absence of readily available proposals, the adversaries have nothing to argue against, for it is not a manageable task to show that there is no *conceivable* way to construe such values.

Direction of Fit and Rules of Reasoning

Because beliefs are designed to fit the facts, or be true, it is possible to define rules of theoretical reasoning or belief formation objectively in terms of truth-preservation—a valid inference as one whose conclusion is true if its premises are—and yet obtain rules that determine what to believe or think true. Take, for instance, the *modus ponens* inference. It must be true that *q* if it is true that if *p* then *q* and *p*. Since believing or thinking true is designed to fit the facts, one logically cannot believe or think if *p* then *q* and *p* but not-*q*. We might say that rules of theoretical reasoning defined in terms of truth-preservation are internal to or constitutive of what it is to believe.

It might be objected that the thoughts 'if *p* then *q*' and '*p*' are distinct events from the thought 'not-*q*', so their co-occurrence with the latter must be logically possible. But in order for the thought that if *p* then *q* to be ascribable to one, it is not enough that a token of the sentence type 'if *p* then *q*' occurs in one's mind. It must also occur *with the meaning it ordinarily has*. And it cannot have this meaning if this thought occurs in conjunction with the thoughts *p* and not-*q*. It can have this meaning only if, when it occurs in conjunction with the former thought, it is accompanied by *q* rather than not-*q*, if either.[5]

---

[5] A related line of argument is found in Edgley (1969: 78 ff.).

Thus, since beliefs are to fit truth, logical rules that are defined in terms of the preservation of truth-value will constrain the formation of belief. This constraint can be called 'normative' in the sense that it is not just a description of how subjects in fact think, for it will stand even if they do not follow it. It is, however, not normative in the sense that it can be *consciously* violated: one can break the laws of logic only as long as one is unaware of this fact, for instance because one does not bring together 'if p then q' and 'p' in a conjunctive fashion. (In contrast, one can knowingly defy a piece of expressive normativity, e.g. a command or regulation.)

If desires are not designed to fit anything external, there is no hope that rules of practical reasoning defined objectively—in terms of some states of affairs fit to be desired or objectively valuable—will also be rules internal to or constitutive of desiring. It will be possible to ask 'Why desire p?' when 'p is objectively valuable' has been derived from, say, 'q is objectively valuable' and 'Only if p is caused will q result', simply for the reason that it is possible to ask 'Why (intrinsically) desire q?'

Of course, we could define 'objectively valuable' so that it applies to a specific group of states of affairs only on the contingent condition that they are (or will be) desired. But it is hard to take seriously the idea that rules of practical reasoning are to be defined as preserving objective value in this sense. For these rules will be an artificial construct, since they attempt to span two sets of rules that we have seen must be distinct, namely rules for the preservation of some objective feature and rules constitutive of desiring.

It is reasonable to believe that in the practical sphere, as in the theoretical one, it is by reference to that against which the fit is to be made, the master-notion—desire and truth, respectively—that the normative rules of reasoning are to be defined. Reasons of symmetry make us expect that the practical rules will also govern that which is to fit desires, as the rules of theoretical reason (in the way indicated) govern the servant or subordinate notion of belief. It seems apt to say that those facts which are found to fit the objects of desires (conforming to the rules of practical rationality) are *valuable*. If the notion of value is in this way defined in terms of the fulfilment of desire, as the subjective theory of value to be developed in the next chapter proposes, that which the rules of practical reasoning guide us to desire will be values.

It can now be explained how such rules are internal to or constitutive of desiring, as rules of theoretical reasoning are internal to or constitutive of believing or thinking true. In Chapter 4, I characterized a desire for q as an internal state that, in conjunction with certain thoughts, tends to bring about what the agent thinks is q.[6] Now, granted the absence of defeating circumstances (such as, say, an independent aversion towards p), if one is in such a state and thinks that only if p is brought about will q result, one *cannot* be in a state of tending to bring about what one thinks is not-p. For then one's desire that q cannot have the requisite fit: to make the world fit its content. One must rather be in the state of tending to bring about what one thinks is that p, if one is in either state. This is

---

[6] In passing, let me remark that this analysis of desire squares with the direction of fit assigned to desires: clearly, a tendency to bring about what one thinks is q is not designed to fit what is the case, but rather to affect the facts so that they fit its objective.

necessary for the ascription of the conditional thought (as here laid out) in the context of one's being in the state of bringing about what one thinks is q.

This account allows one to answer one objection that an account that defines practical rules of reasoning internally without reference to objective value or suchlike is likely to incur. The objection is to the effect that such an account disposes of genuine rational normativity by reducing it to psychological laws (e.g. of desiring). It should be apparent that this objection is mistaken: for just as little as such a 'law' of believing as *modus ponens* is the 'law' of derivative desiring merely an empirical generalization about how we all reason in fact. It is a logical truth which makes up a standard of *right* reasoning or derivation of desire. Thus, it is genuinely normative.

It is normative in the same sense as are the rules governing the formation of belief which are defined in terms of the truth-preservation of belief-contents. In both cases, it is a sense that does not admit of conscious violation. Hence, the reference to something objectively external to the propositional attitudes in question is not necessary for normativity. Instead, the normativity regulating the derivations of a particular attitude flows from the direction of fit of this attitude.

This connects with a difference between theoretical and practical reasoning noted in the foregoing chapter: the former is an inferential process, a matter of inferring one propositional content from another (that guarantees its truth), while the latter is not, for what is arrived at, a desire, does not have a distinctive content which can be inferred. Still it does have content, albeit one 'borrowed' from the beliefs that it involves. If desires did not have any thought-content, they could not be the subject of reasoning, that is, the formation of desires could not be a norm-governed activity.

It may be objected that conceding this normativity makes a chink appear in the armour of subjectivism, a chink through which objectivism can invade. For it may seem to undercut any *principled* objection subjectivists can have to norms to the effect that it is fitting or right to desire some things (cf. Parfit, 1997: 129; 2001: 37). I think this objection can be met. Like the inferential norms of theoretical reasoning, the practical norms here conceded have a *hypothetical* form laying down that *if* one state of affairs is desired (believed), then some other state of affairs must be desired (believed). They do not *categorically* require one to desire any state of affairs, whatever one's other desires are. In the theoretical domain, it is at this point of making contact with something external to the attitude that the appeal to truth enters, but we have seen that this has no counterpart in the practical domain. The direction of fit of desires is singularly unfit to permit the extraction of any categorical requirement.[7]

I conclude, then, that internalism without any objectivist element is the correct account of practical reasons. This internalism has been extracted out of a commonly recognized feature, namely the direction of fit of desires which is opposite to that of

---

[7] Contrast Hampton, who believes there to be an "Instrumental Norm: 'Act so as to perform the most effective means to a desired end'" (1998: 144) and that hypothetical imperatives therefore have a normative authority identical to that of categorical imperatives (1998: e.g. 161–6). On my view, there cannot be this parity, since the hypothetical imperative expresses something that is constitutive of desiring, which a categorical imperative cannot do because of the direction of fit of desires.

beliefs. But of course by such a procedure one cannot rule out rival accounts being developed on the basis of different assumptions.[8] Still, it should be enough to make intelligible the difficulty I, for one, have in forming a plausible conception of something that transcends the bounds of this internalism, and so why I prefer to make do without reliance on any such conception. If my argument has been anywhere near the truth, such a procedure should not be doomed, since the direction of fit of desires ensures that the absence of an objective standard of correctness will at least not have the same devastating effect as the removal of truth in the theoretical domain. Moreover, if there were to be such an objective standard after all, my argument throws doubt on the possibility of establishing it so securely that it can be used to disqualify the sort of widespread conative patterns whose rationality I shall discuss.

The Possibility of Justifying Intrinsic Desires

On the subjectivism at which I have arrived, our reasons for desiring are anchored in our intrinsic desires, but these cannot be justified in terms of any reasons which specify some objectively valuable states of affairs. Hence, if our intrinsic desires had had another orientation, our intrinsic values and the whole edifice of reasons we have built on them would be different. Imagine someone intrinsically desiring that p envisaging the possibility of instead having an intrinsic desire that not-p; he would then have to countenance the fact that not-p would instead have been intrinsically desirable (for him), with wide-ranging repercussions for what his reasons would be. Thus, it seems that the whole system of reasons rests on an insecure or shaky foundation. Now, Mark Platts has argued that it seems

> a brute fact about human motivation and human desires that if this agent, at the point of action, considers this other possibility in his own terms, then he will cease to be motivated by his desire that p. (1980: 79)

Platts's suggestion is that, if we were not to believe in the existence of states of affairs that are objectively valuable, we would cease to have desires. Certainly, it is reasonable to think that, if we reached the belief that there is nothing to which our basic beliefs correspond, we would fail to see the point of forming such beliefs. But I do not think the same holds for desires because their direction of fit is the opposite one: if desires are not designed to fit anything, why should realizing that there is indeed nothing external to which they fit lead us to give them up?

A qualification should also be inserted into the statement that, on subjectivism, we cannot have any reasons for intrinsic desires: strictly speaking, it is only true that we

---

[8] Not to mention somebody, like J. David Velleman (1996b) who, also from observations on the direction of fit of an attitude and what is constitutive of it, develops such a different account of practical reason that it would lead too far afield (into the nature of action) to comment on it here. Besides, it is revised in (2000: ch. 1).

cannot have any reasons for desires, *qua* or *in so far as* they are (ultimately) intrinsic.[9] It should not be overlooked that if, on a certain occasion, I desire *q*, say, not to feel pain, solely for its own sake—that is, without having any apparent reasons for being averse to it—there could still be *real* reasons for and against desiring *q*. A reason for wanting not to feel pain might be that, if pain is felt, it will be difficult to concentrate on the pursuit of some interest, such as doing philosophy, and a reason for wanting the pain might be that, it will inure oneself against the hardships life inevitably brings along or that it might prevent one from being overcome by boredom.

Taking such reasons into account, it may turn out that, *overall or all things considered*, I should desire to have the pain. Of course, it has not been shown that I was wrong in having an *intrinsic* desire not to feel the pain, but as long as I did not consider any reasons for and against desiring not to feel it, my intrinsic aversion to the pain constituted my entire conative response to it. It is this response—that I desire not to feel the pain *simply for its own sake*—that my attention to relevant reasons forces me to revise. Henceforth, I desire to feel the pain all things considered, though I retain my intrinsic aversion to it (this is on the proviso that the derived desire for it is stronger than the intrinsic aversion).

This shows that, even given objectivism, practical reasoning cannot aspire to be footed on that rock-bottom ground that foundationalism attempts to lay for theoretical reasoning. If a basic thought has been justified by appeal to sense-experience, it will in conjunction with a suitable true conditional constitute a reason that no upshot of any further investigation can undermine or outweigh. This inspires the hope of building an epistemic edifice pervaded by this certainty.

In contrast, even if an intrinsic desire for *q* could have been shown to be required by reference to some objective standard, it could still be that one is wrong in desiring *q* all things considered, in the light of what real reasons there are for and against desiring it. One must then concede that, contrary to what one has earlier thought, its consequence *q* does not supply one with a reason for derivatively desiring *p*. The postulation of objective requirements would not remove this 'defeasibility' of practical reasons.

In other words, every end (in itself) is provisional. What is desired, on a particular occasion, simply for its own sake would perhaps not be desired overall, if its consequences were considered. (If so, this provides one with a reason to see to it that one loses this intrinsic desire.) Thus, subjectivism leaves room, contrary to what some believe, for something that can properly be called a rational criticism of ends.

Suppose, however, that one's intrinsic desire for *q* stands up as a desire all things considered, so that the fact that only if *p* then *q* provides one with a reason to desire *p*. Then one may still discover that *p* is also a means to some state of affairs 'side-ordered' with *q* which one has a stronger desire to avoid all things considered. This discovery would not divest one of one's reason to bring about *p*. It would instead draw one's attention to the existence of a stronger, competing reason against bringing it about.

---

[9] This should be distinguished from the question whether we can have reasons for *seeing to it* that we have (ultimately) intrinsic desires, just as reasons for believing something must be distinguished from reasons for seeing to it that we have a belief to this effect. I am not denying that we can have reasons for seeing to it that we (not) have certain intrinsic desires.

Thus, one's reason for desiring *p* would not be *conclusive*. A reason for desire and action can never acquire this status. This follows from the direction of fit of desire and the consequent direction of practical reasoning from the epistemically posterior to the prior. There is always the risk that further prying into the consequences will throw up reasons that upset the current balance. We simply stop looking for reasons when we find them strong enough and it seems to us that further search will not change this, for example because of increasing epistemic uncertainty.

So, the existence of an objective standard by reference to which our intrinsic desires can be justified, as intrinsic, would not mean that derived desires rest on a rock-bottom ground of conclusive reasons, as derived beliefs are conceived as ideally doing on traditional foundationalism. Nonetheless, such standards would permit us to justify our intrinsic desires, as such, which is impossible on subjectivism (since on it reasons are desire-dependent, giving reasons for a desire amounts to displaying it as derivative). Does this make objectivism superior in one respect? I do not think so because it achieves this at the expense of introducing postulates that cannot be justified. Suppose we justify our intrinsic desire not to feel pain by claiming that there is a desire-independent reason to have an intrinsic desire not to feel it; then a justification for the latter claim could be demanded.

The reply might be that this claim is a necessary truth, like logical or mathematical truths. But I think that the view that it is a necessary truth, for example that those who feel pain have a reason to be intrinsically averse to what they are feeling, could be sustained only if there were some necessary connection between feeling such sensation and being intrinsically averse to it. For it is plausible to claim that it is a necessary truth that those who think *p* and that it entails *q* have a reason to think *q* only because there is an underlying necessary truth to the effect that if *p* then *q* and *p*, then *q*. Similarly, if someone were to claim that it is a necessary truth that those who possess the concept of red have a reason to think that what they see is red when they see something red, they would have to offer a rationale like the following: someone who does not apply the concept of red to what is seen under these circumstances cannot be said to possess it.

But, barring the trivial possibility that was rejected in Chapter 1, namely, that describing a sensation as one of pain entails that the subject is intrinsically averse to it, it seems that no necessary connection can be made out between feeling a pain and being intrinsically averse to what one is then feeling. For instance, it cannot reasonably be maintained that somebody who does not react to pains with intrinsic aversion must necessarily be incapable of aversion. As we have seen, the direction of fit of desires is not such that we can deduce any requirement to have desires out of it. But if it is just a contingent fact that subjects are intrinsically averse to pains, the alleged necessary truth must be that there is a reason for subjects to be intrinsically averse to pain when and only when they are in fact intrinsically averse to it. For, as we observed in the foregoing chapter, it is not plausible to hold there to be such a reason in possible worlds in which subjects are not intrinsically averse to pains. But, as we also observed in that chapter, it is not plausible to think that there is a reason to duplicate this aversion.

So, if objectivists promise us a practical justification for our intrinsic desires, it is a false promise. As the simple case of physical pain illustrates, it is hard to see how the idea of there being such reasons can be made good. Subjectivists supply no such promises of justification; they have to content themselves with presenting explanatory reasons of why we have the (ultimately) intrinsic desires they ascribe to us (e.g. an evolutionary explanation of why we have an intrinsic aversion to pain).

Desiring as Perceiving: A First Attempt

To substantiate these general considerations, let us look at some difficulties into which some attempts to construe desires as counterparts to perception can get enmeshed. For instance, Dennis W. Stampe has proposed:

> Desire is a kind of perception. One who wants it to be the case that p perceives something that makes it seem to that person as if it would be good were it to be the case that p, and seem so in a way that is characteristic of perception. To desire something is to be in a kind of perceptual state, in which that thing seems good. (1987: 359)[10]

Stampe puts forward this suggestion to account for what he calls "the authority of desire", namely the alleged fact that the "fact that I want something, in and of itself, is ordinarily a reason for me to act accordingly" (1987: 342). The way the perceptual analogy is supposed to explain this authority is as follows (1987: 362 ff.). Perceptual states are the source of the rationality of beliefs in the sense that its looking, sounding, feeling, etc. to me as if p is the case provides me with a reason for believing that p *is* the case (this reason may of course be outweighed by other reasons). Similarly for desire, if having a desire is being in a state of something's appearing to one as if it would be a good thing: it would provide one with a reason for believing that it would in fact be good—at least for oneself (1987: 375)—if this were the case.

It is, however, unclear how such a perceptual state could supply one with a reason to act (as opposed to a reason to believe) that motivates to action. Stampe's perceptual analogy leaves out the motivational aspect of a desire, that desiring p is to tend to bring about what is ideally, if one's thought is true, that p (cf. 1987: 354). Stampe can, of course, add this aspect to his conception of a desire as a perceptual state, thereby obtaining a construal of a desire for p as a state of its seeming to one a good thing that p which disposes one to bring about p in a world in which one's beliefs are true.[11] But this raises the question: how does its seeming to one to be an—objectively—good thing that p explain and justify one's being disposed to act thus?

Stampe not only fails to unwrap his objective conception of goodness to the point where it yields an answer to this question; he also declines to clarify how instances of the property of goodness can be causally potent in producing perceptual experiences of it. His account clearly requires this, for he speaks of the sensitivity involved in desire as being activated, ideally, "by and only by the apparent goodness of a state of affairs" (1987: 360).

---

[10] Related to this is de Sousa's claim that "emotions are best regarded as a kind of perception, the objects of which are what I call *axiological properties*" (1987: 45). Roberts also takes the view that emotions are perceptions (1988, 2003).

[11] Elsewhere (1986: 168), Stampe seems inclined to take precisely this step.

In another paper Stampe argues that he can do without this notion of goodness and that it can be replaced by the notion of *need* (1986: 167–9). If this proposal is to have any plausibility, however, the notion of need must be broadened far beyond the sphere of bodily needs, and this creates difficulties. For the concept of need is a relative one: one needs something *for* something else, for example, those things for which one has bodily needs are things needed in order to survive or maintain normal bodily functioning. But if the concept is to be broadened, a reasonable suggestion would seem to be that the objectives for which one needs some things are set by one's *values* or *desires*, and this either re-introduces values or closes a circle. Furthermore, the concept will still be unsuitable to capture intrinsic desires. For instance, when I want to feel pleasure, it is surely not the case that it seems to me that I need pleasure (for something).

So, the perceptual analogy does not advance understanding of what it is introduced to illuminate, the so-called authority of desire. But not only that, it also sits ill with certain widely recognized features of desires. It is more or less common ground that desires are like beliefs in that one can reason one's way to them; desires can be formed as the upshot of practical reasoning. Linked with this is the fact that desires can be classified as reasonable/rational or unreasonable/irrational. None of this is true of perceptual states. Stampe is forced to resort to strained moves to explain away this glaring difference between desires and perceptual states, such as the move of denying that "intermediate desires" arise in deliberation (1987: 369–71).

But, if we reject the perceptual analogy, what are we to say about the so-called authority of desire, the alleged fact that my (now) wanting *p* provides me with a reason for (now) bringing it about that *p*? (It is another question whether my future desires supply me with reasons for now acting so as to fulfil them.) I do not think that this desire of mine normally provides *me* with any reason for acting accordingly, although it may, of course, be the explanatory reason of why I act thus. (Similarly, my having certain perceptions may be the explanatory reason of why I think that things are as represented by them, but they are not *my* reasons for thinking thus.) One's reasons are, as Stampe remarks (1987: 337), things from which one can reason, propositions that one takes or assumes to be facts. But when I desire to bring it about that *p*, I need not represent my desire to myself, although I could, of course, ascend to this meta-level (see Persson, 1990, and Pettit and Smith, 1990).

It is instead among the reasons, if any, that I have for desiring *p* that we shall standardly find my reasons for causing it to be a fact that *p*. If the desire is intrinsic, I do not typically perform the corresponding action for any reason, but for its own sake.

Desiring as Perceiving: Further Attempts

McDowell has also advocated the idea that we should think of the "exercises of our affective or conative natures either as themselves in some way percipient, or at least as expanding our sensitivity to how things are" (1981: 143). If so, desires would seem to have a fit similar to that of (other) cognitive states. McDowell condemns as a piece of "the eighteenth-century philosophy of mind" the idea that desires are factors that are needed over and above the (allegedly) inert cognitive states to explain the occurrence of actions.[12] According to his view of the matter, "a conception of a set of circumstances can suffice on its own to explain an action" (1978: 19). Discussing the difference between an ordinarily prudent person and one who is indifferent to his own future, he writes:

> It is not that the two people share a certain neutral conception of the facts, but differ in that one, but not the other, has an independent desire as well, which combines with that neutral conception of the facts to cast a favourable light on his acting in a certain way. The desire is ascribable to the prudent person simply in recognition of the fact that his conception of the likely effects of his action on his own future by itself casts a favourable light on his acting as he does. So the admitted difference in respect of desire should be explicable, like the difference in respect of action, in terms of a more fundamental difference in respect of how they conceive the facts. (1978: 17)

Speaking of virtue, he proposes that we take the

> special view of the virtuous person's conception of the circumstances, according to which it cannot be shared by someone who sees no reason to act as the virtuous person does. (1978: 16)

McDowell here presents himself as a spokesman of what was called, in Chapter 4, the cognitivist theory of motivation. His version of that theory has it that there are some thoughts or conceptions—among them the ones of prudential and virtuous persons—such that the fact that they are present is by itself sufficient to explain acting in accordance with them (given suitable abilities to act). For they are sufficient to animate anyone who has them in mind to (try to) perform certain actions. The cognitivist theory is opposed to the conativist theory of motivation, the thesis of which is not only that the citation of a desire is necessary to complete a reason-explanation (or, alternatively, that a desire is involved in the execution of an intentional action), but, crucially, that this citation encapsulates a reference to a non-cognitive explanatory factor (a claim which does not imply that this factor is a mental episode or an introspectible item). The concept of desire that I defined in Chapter 4 belongs to this category, for 'the state' to which it refers is intended to be a non-cognitive factor which in conjunction with certain thoughts of the subject tends to have certain effects. This conception thus implies that thoughts by themselves are not sufficient conditions for motivational effects (but nevertheless it is not, contrary to McDowell's insinuation, a Humean or eighteenth-century one).

Motivational cognitivists such as Thomas Nagel (1970: e.g. ch. 5), Don Locke (1974: 176), Jonathan Dancy (1993: chs. 1–3; and 2000: ch. 4), T. M. Scanlon (1998: ch. 1) and McDowell do not repudiate the claim that acting intentionally or for a reason encompasses the presence of a desire. Rather, they concede that ascribing a desire to somebody is consequential upon, or follows from, it being the case that this individual has been moved to act by some thought or conception. They reject only the conativist claim that a desire is an explanatory factor alongside cognitive ones.

---

[12] On the strength of other reasons, Stanley Benn also rejects the "Humean" separation of the conative from the cognitive (1988: e.g. 28). For a recent criticism of McDowell on these matters, see Blackburn (1998: 92–104).

On this conativist claim, a desire is something which tends to give rise to certain effects. I have suggested that it is this that accounts for the direction of fit characteristic of desires. Now, although it may seem incontrovertible that one and the same mental state cannot possess both directions of fit, an attempt has nevertheless been made to show that this is possible. McNaughton argues:

> To be aware of a moral requirement is . . . to have a conception of the situation as demanding a response. Yet to conceive of a situation as demanding a response, as requiring one to do something, is to be in a state whose direction of fit is: the world must fit this state . . . But the agent's conception of the situation is purely cognitive. That is, the agent has a belief that he is morally required to act and so his state must have the direction of fit: this state must fit the world. (1988: 109)

However, "to conceive of a situation as demanding a response", as demanding the world to fit *something conceived*, is not to have a conception "whose direction of fit is: the world must fit this state", that is, must fit *the conception had*. Although what is conceived has one direction of fit, the conceiving of it may have another. For instance, when one conceives of something as an order, what one conceives of, the order, has one direction of fit, but one's conceiving of it has another. Thus, McNaughton has not shown that there is a single thing that has both directions of fit.[13]

Desires are, I have contended, something over and above cognitive states; they are states having the opposite direction of fit of being designed to change the world to fit their content. This fit can be explained by their being states which are identified in terms of their causal power, of what they tend to effect. Such an explanation first leads one to question McDowell's view of desires as something "expanding our sensitivity to how things are". It appears to be a central doctrine of his that our attitudes are not reactions to isolable cognitive representations that could be possessed by a creature which failed to react to them as we do (1981: 144–5). In the same vein, McNaughton claims that "*only someone who shares our human tastes and sensibilities* can be aware of things in the way that we are" (1988: 114). But it is not clear why we should grant that desires reveal aspects of reality that would otherwise remain hidden when this expansion, being something cognitive, cannot by itself account for the crucial aspect of the reverse, non-cognitive fit of desires.

On the other hand, if this aspect can be accounted for by a reference to causal effects on behaviour, why assume that, if there is a difference in this regard between subjects, there must be some cognitive difference between them? In other words, why assume the cognitivist view that "a conception of a set of circumstances can suffice on its own to explain an action"? This seems particularly dubious if I was right in Chapter 4 to claim that we need to refer to desires to explain why cognitive dispositions acquire the representation in episodic consciousness which is necessary for motivational effects.

Secondly, there is a resurrection of the old problem about how this non-cognitive surplus could be justified. As just mentioned, McDowell seems to hold that there are some thoughts or propositions such that everyone who is conscious of them will respond

---

[13] For a more recent attempt to cross "the cognitive-conative divide", see Helm (2001).

similarly to them. Still, this would just be a contingent truth: it is logically possible that there be creatures in which the very same thoughts tend to produce different patterns of behaviour. So, there is room to ask which, if any, of these possible responses are the proper or fitting ones, and we are just as far as ever from getting an answer to this question (cf. the fruitless attempt to understand the notion of "merit" in Chapter 7). Subjectivists are happy to concede that, if a state of affairs is intrinsically desired by every one of us, then it is of intersubjective value (relative to our desires). The crucial question arises when we envisage other imaginable beings with intrinsic desires of a different orientation. If it is maintained that what they desire is not of value (even relative to their desires), subjectivists will protest and demand a rationale for disqualifying these imaginable desires as a ground for value (for their holders). It is this rationale that objectivists still owe us.

Nonetheless, there seem to be some things to which more or less all of us display the same desires (physical pain is a case in point). This provides a basis for a measure of human intersubjectivism. (In the following parts of the book I shall attempt to spell out some elements of this intersubjectivism.) To the extent that such an intersubjectivism is forthcoming, it is of little *practical* importance that objectivists have not fulfilled the promise of supplying a standard by reference to which converging (intrinsic) desires can be assessed as fitting or unfitting.

Of course, I have not proved that objectivists *cannot* fulfil this promise—in fact, I do not see how this could possibly be proved. All I have done is to employ the widely recognized difference in direction of fit between beliefs and desires to suggest why the objectivist approach is misconceived. It is, however, not essential to the main objective of this book—which is to set forth certain dilemmas as regards satisfactionalism and rationalism—that all kinds of objectivism are false: not the kinds that would preserve these dilemmas. To be sure, if the truth were to lie in a version of objectivism that repudiates either the value of rationality or satisfaction, my enterprise would be jeopardized. But since objective values are so controversial, they surely could not present themselves so authoritatively to us that fundamental value disputes can be resolved by appeal to them.

When an investigation can be conducted in the setting of either one of two competing theories, it is advisable to conduct it in the setting of the more parsimonious one—which in this case is subjectivism. To enact my dilemma in the more contentious framework of objectivism might create the misunderstanding that, if this view has to go by the board, the dilemma will be undercut. As will transpire in Part IV, there is a tendency to assume that subjectivism inexorably leads to the acceptance of the satisfactionalist goal of fulfilment-maximization, especially in the prudentialist form. By letting my drama of satisfactionalism versus rationalism unfold on the stage of subjectivism, I demonstrate the falsity of that assumption and, thereby, strengthen the foothold of the dilemma.

10

THE DESIRE RELATIVITY
OF VALUE

IT might be useful to sum up how the argument of this part has gone so far. In Chapter 8 I advanced the thesis that the practical reasons we have are propositions of a conditional form, propositions that either must be thought true by us (apparent reasons) or in fact be true (real reasons). Moreover, the consequents of these propositions—which, at least in my formulation, are from an epistemic point of view posterior—must either in fact be desired (apparent reasons) or be desired if we were to be aware of them (real reasons). Since the process of deliberation, of exploring reasons for and against, cannot go on indefinitely, some states of affairs must be the object of intrinsic desires, must be desired simply for their own sakes and independently of apparent reasons. Such states of affairs, which are intrinsically desired by deliberators at particular times, provide the starting (or stopping) point of their practical reasoning at that time.

Here objectivists might protest that any old states of affairs forming the objects of intrinsic desires will not supply the moorings of practical reasoning. If the known fact that only if one causes p then q will be caused is to be a *real* reason for one to cause p, it is not enough if one intrinsically desires q : q must also be of *value*, though this may not be necessary in the case of apparent reasons. (Compare this to the theoretical case: in order for one to have a real reason to believe q, one's beliefs if p then q and p must be true, but this is not necessary for one's having an apparent reason.) The fact that one intrinsically desires q cannot establish that q is of value, objectivists maintain. This can be established only if one desires what one is objectively required to desire.

However, as I argued in Chapter 9, desires have a direction of fit which is opposite to that of beliefs, namely, that of making the world fit their objectives. So, while we might be required to believe what is evidently true (to meet the standard of having the belief in question), we are only required *not* to (intelligently) desire that which we cannot bring about (obviously, we cannot be required to bring about all that we can bring about, since this is often both p and not-p). This leads on to the suggestion that, whereas the truth of the belief p is due to its fit with the fact p, its being valuable (that it is a fact) that p must rather be due to its fitting, or fulfilling, a desire for p. Both the truth of a belief and the value of a fact would then consist in a fit to the master-notion (of a fact and a desire respectively), but the direction of fit is reversed. Thus, we land in a subjectivist definition of value in terms of what fits (ultimately) intrinsic desire.

On subjectivism (at least of the kind espoused here), the notion of value is a *relative* one: every value is relative to some desire or other attitude. To characterize a fact as valuable is not to characterize it as it is in itself; it is to say that it bears a certain relation—of fulfilling—to something else, a desire. A claim that something has value *simpliciter* must be read as elliptical. Its truth-value is indeterminate, as long as the reference-class is not specified, for example, because the speaker thinks it is extensive enough not to bother to specify it. This relativity could be expressed by saying that, according to subjectivism, all values are values *for some subject (of desire)*, since desires are necessarily states of some subject. But, as we shall see, this relativist formulation is liable to mislead because it can be used for a narrower notion.

A well-known objection to the subjectivist strategy is that desires might be based on misconceptions of their objects. If this is true of a desire for *p*, it might be that you will regret having this desire when it is fulfilled. But then it seems wrong-headed to hold that the fulfilment of this desire is of value to you. The remedy I suggest consists in singling out a species of intrinsic desire that cannot involve any mistakes in this regard—*ultimately intrinsic desire*.

A Subjectivist Definition of Value

Let us distinguish what a property *explicitly* entails from what it *implicitly* entails. A property, being *F*, explicitly entails that, and only that, which one logically must think, or be conscious of, when one thinks or is conscious of *F* being instantiated, while being *F* implicitly entails what it entails, though not explicitly. For instance, if one thinks that something is a triangle, one must logically think that it has three angles and sides—so this is an explicit entailment of the property of being a triangle. On the other hand, since it probably makes sense to ascribe this thought to somebody who is not aware of the fact that the sum of a triangle's angles is 180 degrees, this is implicitly entailed by being a triangle.

Now you have an *ultimately* intrinsic desire, for example, to feel pleasure, just in case you have this desire only because of what you know that its object, pleasure, explicitly entails, what you must know to know what it is to feel pleasure. Since this desire is based only on this, its object could not be misconceived if it is really to be a desire that pleasure be felt (nor can one when one wants something in this way forget what one wants it for—a slip mentioned by Audi, 2001: 126). Such desires are 'incorrigible'.[1] To know what it is

---

[1] Richard Fumerton suggests that "it seems possible that I might want something *X* for its own sake when imagining its occurrence, even though I would feel quite differently were I to find out that *X* has actually occurred" (1990: 138). Accordingly, he distinguishes between contemplative and cognitive desiring or valuing. But if what one imagines occurring is exactly the same as what one later observes occurring, I cannot see how one's attitudes could possibly differ in the two cases. What frequently happens, of course, is that when one imagines an event, one gets something wrong and that this mistake is rectified when one observes it occurring. But this is a sort of situation that I believe to be impossible as regards ultimately intrinsic desires; so I ignore Fumerton's distinction.

to *F* in many cases (like that of feeling pleasure) presupposes that you have been aware of yourself *F*-ing, though it may be enough to have been aware of yourself exemplifying some similar property (e.g. to know what it is to run, it may be enough that you have been aware of yourself walking). But, definitionally, the object of an ultimately intrinsic desire is something that is desired only because of what it explicitly entails.

As we have seen, an experience which is pleasurable will have other intrinsic properties (upon which pleasure supervenes). If, as is likely, you do not have an ultimately intrinsic desire for the exemplification of these properties, which together with pleasure make up *G*, you do not have this sort of desire for the *whole* thing *G*, but desire it *for the reason* that it has pleasure as one of its intrinsic properties. Since this desire is reason-based, it is not intrinsic in my terminology. It is, however, probably what Audi means by intrinsic desires when he claims that such desires can be rational or well-grounded as well as ill-grounded (2001: 87–8). For there cannot be any ground or reason for the ultimately intrinsic desire for pleasure (that pleasure is pleasure is no reason). There is some justification for Audi's usage, when the relevant reason refers to intrinsic or non-relational properties of the object of desire. But such desires will not qualify as ultimately intrinsic in the sense here defined; since they are reason-based, they are derivative, though the reason consists in the predication of a property internal to their object. It may be that in the course of time the apparent reason sinks into oblivion and, thus, that your desire for *G* is no longer reason-based. Then it has transformed into an *acquired* or *derivatively* intrinsic desire for *G*.

This transformation from a reason-based or derivative desire to a (derivatively) intrinsic one does not demand an internal relation, as the one between a part and a whole, to come into operation. The external relation of a means to an end serves as well. Imagine that for a long time one has desired *p* for the reason that, as one sees it, it has *q* as a causal, conventional, or in some other way contingently external consequence. Eventually, one may have become so accustomed to striving for *p* that one no longer considers what it leads to. One's desire for *p* has then turned into an intrinsic desire, for it is no longer based on any apparent reasons. But it is a derivatively intrinsic desire (a "non-instrumental" desire in Audi's terminology, 2001: 82), not an ultimately intrinsic desire. Perhaps this phenomenon occurs, for instance, in the case of a miser's desire for money. (It is very hard to ascertain whether or not such a transformation has occurred, though.) Were one now to discover that one's intrinsic desire has this origin and that it is false that *p* has *q* as one of its consequences, one would regard one's derivatively intrinsic desire for *p* as wrong, and it may lose its hold.

Return now to ultimately intrinsic desires and imagine that somebody points out to you that the objective of one of your ultimately intrinsic desires, *p*, has some logical or contingent consequence, *q*, of which you have not been aware and towards which you have an intense aversion. Could this show that you were wrong in having an ultimately intrinsic desire for *p*? Clearly not, for an aversion towards *p* because it has *q* as a hitherto overlooked consequence could not contradict an ultimately intrinsic desire for *p*: *q* cannot be explicitly entailed by *p*, since you were not aware of the entailment. As a result of becoming aware of this consequence, you could only draw the conclusion that you should not desire *p* *all things considered*. No consequence of *p* of which one could be unaware and could need to be informed of could undercut one's ultimately intrinsic desire for *p*.

An ultimately intrinsic desire is a desire to the effect that a certain property (e.g. being pleasurable) be exemplified or that a property (e.g. being painful) not be exemplified. Like all intelligent desires such desires involve beliefs, for example to the effect that some property is (not) exemplified and that one could bring about a change in this regard. These beliefs could conceivably be false, but that is irrelevant. For what we are interested in are beliefs whose falsity would make us doubt the value of the fulfilling fact, were a desire fulfilled, not falsehoods that make it impossible to fulfil the desire.

The proposal I have in mind is to define what is of value for us in terms of what fulfils our ultimately intrinsic desires (for short, 'intrinsic desires'), for they cannot be infected by relevant cognitive mistakes. As indicated, I do not think we should say that having an acquired or derivatively intrinsic desire satisfied is necessarily of value for one. Imagine that for a long time I desire to take a certain pill because I believe it will do me good, whereas it in fact has bad effects. In the course of time, it slips my mind that I desire the pill for a reason. Surely, it would not be of any value for me to have this desire satisfied and be exposed to the bad effects. (Let us assume that I do not realize that this desire has been satisfied, so that I do not obtain any pleasure from this source.)

To make my proposal to define value in terms of the fulfilment of (ultimately) intrinsic desires more precise, note that corresponding to the distinction between intrinsic and derived *desires*, there is a distinction between intrinsic and extrinsic (or, as they are commonly, but misleadingly, called, instrumental) *values*. (Actually, the adjective 'intrinsic' masks an underlying linguistic difference: while things are desired or valued for their own sakes, or as ends (in themselves) rather than in themselves, they have value in themselves rather than for their own sakes.) It is, of course, intrinsic value that I propose to define as that which fulfils an intrinsic desire.

The term 'intrinsic value' has, however, been used—for instance, by G. E. Moore—in a stronger sense than mine, to designate that something has a value that is independent of *all* matters extrinsic to it. This use is adopted by Christine Korsgaard when she claims that, if things have intrinsic goodness or goodness "*in* themselves, they are thought to have their goodness in any and all circumstances—to carry it with them, so to speak" (1983: 171). This rules out the subjectivist idea that intrinsic goodness can be *relative to something*, for example, desires, because the goodness of *p* consists in its standing in the relation of satisfying to some desire, for of course this goodness will not hold "independently of all conditions and relations" (1983: 187). (Perhaps this is also why Audi (2001: 123–4) thinks that "instrumentalists" about practical reason are "at best unlikely" to appeal to intrinsic goodness.)

So, one might think that this goodness is 'extrinsic', since this is Korsgaard's contrast to intrinsic goodness. She characterizes extrinsic goodness as "the value a thing gets from some other source"; in other words, things that are extrinsically good "derive their value from some other source" (1983: 170). This naturally suggests that the "other source" *is valuable or good*, that the goodness of *p* is extrinsic if and only if it derives from *p*'s standing in some relation to some other facts that are *good*. But the value of the things that subjectivists want to designate as intrinsic is not conceived as being derivative from the value of something else. In particular, their idea is not that its value derives from the value of the desire fulfilled, but rather that a value (that is not present beforehand in either relatum) is *created* when a desire is fulfilled.

In contrast, on the view Korsgaard attributes to Kant, a desire or an instance of willing, provided it is rational, appears to have intrinsic value, a value that is "conferred upon" the object desired (1983: e.g. 182–3).[2] But this theory is different from the subjectivist one I am developing—and, I think, less plausible. For on the Kant–Korsgaard approach, it seems not to be *the materialization* of *p* that *satisfies* a desire which is of value, but rather *the proposition p as an object of desire*, for it appears to be upon this which the act of desiring or willing must confer value, since it is the objective of willing. But then we seem to face the odd consequence that it is evaluatively unimportant whether the object of a desire materializes.

Never mind, the main point I am out to make is that, on the given characterization, extrinsic value is not a proper contrast to intrinsic value, as conceived by Moore and Korsgaard, for whereas extrinsic value will here mean derivative value (i.e. a value that derives from the value of something else), their intrinsic value must be *neither* derivative *nor* relative (in the subjectivist sense). Consequently, this terminology leaves no term for values that are relative, but not derivative.

Against this background, it is not surprising that some ambiguity or wavering in Korsgaard's conception of the extrinsic goodness can be detected. Just after the characterization of intrinsic value quoted above, she writes that extrinsic goodness "is derived from or dependent upon the circumstances" (1983: 171). This covers both the possibility that goodness is relative and that it is derivative for, of course, the notion of something's goodness being *dependent upon the circumstances* is much broader than that of its goodness being *derived from another source*, which suggests that this source is *good*. The objection to her characterization is, then, that it lumps together two quite different ideas: that (1) the goodness is *extrinsic* or derivative from something external (that possesses goodness) and that (2) it is a *relative* notion. I propose to keep these ideas apart by using 'intrinsic' in opposition to 'extrinsic', and 'absolute' in opposition to 'relative'.

My concern is then with intrinsic value within the framework of a subjectivist theory, according to which all value is relative. The definition of it I would like to put forward is as follows:

(IV) It is intrinsically valuable for *A* that *p* becomes (or remains) the case if and only if *A* has an ultimately intrinsic (intelligent or non-intelligent) desire that *p* becomes (or remains) the case or would have such an intrinsic desire to this effect were *A* to think of *p* (as something she might be able to bring about if the desire is intelligent).

The reference to what *A* would intrinsically desire if . . . is essential because a state of affairs can be of intrinsic value for one even though one has never thought of it or has once thought of it, but has now forgotten all about it. Note, however, that *p* is of intrinsic value for one *at present* only if one would *at once* start to desire it were one to be conscious of it. If it takes training or habituation to develop a desire for *p*, it could only be of *future* value for one.

---

[2] Recently, Korsgaard has admitted that in her earlier papers she "made it sound too much as if value were some metaphysical substance that gets transferred from us to our ends via the act of choice" (1998: 63). But, apparently, she still holds on to the view that value which is "conferred" by willing is extrinsic. For another discussion of this view of hers, see Rabinowicz and Rønnow-Rasmussen (1999: 36–9).

Given (IV), we can lay down that q has derivative value for you if there is a state of affairs, p, such that p has intrinsic value for you, and it is a fact that if you bring about q, then p results, and no state of affairs having a greater negative intrinsic value for you also results. The derivative value of q can be either extrinsic as it is when p is external to q or non-extrinsic as it is when p is internal to q (e.g. when the value of feeling something pleasantly cool is derived from that of feeling something pleasant). The more common form of derivative value is extrinsic: for example, when q is a causal means to p, and q's value is instrumental.

I intend the last subjunctive clause of (IV) to be read as presupposing that A has the *capacity* to think certain thoughts—hence, she must be a conscious being (though she need not be a being capable of propositional thinking to have non-intelligent desires). So it follows from (IV) that something can now be of value, can be good or bad, only for an entity that is now endowed with consciousness. If, however, a being has the potential to develop a capacity of consciousness, things may be good or bad for it in the future. In my view, this is sufficient for it to be possible now to act wrongly to the being by doing something that will have bad consequences for it at a future time at which it has developed consciousness (or, indeed, to deprive it of consciousness of good things).

What if it is doubted whether the possession of consciousness is necessary for being a subject for whom something may have current value? It may be asked why the satisfaction of a striving which is not, owing to the absence of consciousness, a desire—for example, a plant's striving towards the sunlight—cannot constitute a valuable state of affairs for it. The reply is, I think, that it cannot because the context 'the plant strives to . . .' is *extensional* in the sense that materially equivalent descriptions can be substituted in it, whereas the context 'it is valuable for X that . . .' is not. In the former context, one may substitute for 'to be in the sunlight' a description of what happens on a micro-level when a plant is in sunlight (processes such as photosynthesis). But a substitution of any materially equivalent description will not do when a (conscious) being desires to be in the sun or when this state is said to be valuable for it. For instance, when what is valuable for me is that the smell I am perceiving is pleasant, it does not follow that it is valuable for me that certain chemicals stimulate some of my sense-receptors (I would not be worse off if, *per impossibile*, the latter had not happened when I perceived the smell).

Alternative Subjectivist Conceptions

This way of defining value by reference to desires could profitably be contrasted with an idea that Henry Sidgwick found "intelligible and admissible" (though there is an alternative conception that he judges to be "more in accordance with common sense"):

> a man's future good on the whole is what he would now desire and seek on the whole if all the consequences of all the different lines of conduct open to him were accurately foreseen and adequately realised in imagination at the present point of time.[3]

---

[3] (1907/1981: 111–12). Sidgwick's idea is taken up by Rawls (1971: § 64).

Such a proposal—of hypothesizing omniscience—might seem to offer the promise of an alternative route around the difficulty of desires having faulty doxastic bases. There is, however, a seemingly devastating objection to it. A lot of the intrinsic desires we have presuppose that we are not omniscient. We are *curious* about an endless number of subject matters, ranging from fundamental truths about the universe to trivial daily affairs. Given curiosity or an intrinsic desire to acquire knowledge about something, it is of value to become more knowledgeable about it. As things stand, we are curious about what the future has in store for us, but this curiosity would, of course, not survive "if all the consequences of all the different lines of conduct open to" us "were accurately foreseen". Consequently, the Sidgwickian proposal is unacceptable because it rules out the value of a number of states of affairs that appear to be of value for us as we in fact are (albeit not for us in an omniscient state).

This observation shows that practical deliberation is threatened not only by the Scylla of knowing too little, but also by the Charybdis of knowing too much. It is frequently remarked that we are generally forced to make up our minds about what to do under circumstances of regrettable ignorance. The fact that something intrinsically desired may always, when its consequences are inspected, turn out to be undesirable overall is one thing that makes it hard to be confident about what to aim for in a particular situation. Moreover, when this is settled, there remains the difficult problem of determining what is the most effective way of accomplishing this aim. Apart from this, there is the uncertainty stemming from the fact that even the most well-tried means occasionally fail (e.g. the car that has taken one to a certain destination countless times suddenly breaks down). In short, when we decide on what to do, we often have to do so almost blindly: a course of action that seems to be very rewarding could in fact turn out to cause misery and premature death.

So it would appear to be desirable to know more about the consequences of the different lines of conduct open to us. In deliberating about whether to embark on some research-project whose completion will take several years, I would like some guarantee that I will not die or fall seriously ill before its completion and that the conclusions at which I shall arrive will be worthwhile. But it would seem that in practice I cannot get such a guarantee without knowing in considerable detail what will happen—including what results I shall reach—if I embark on the project, and of course this is bound to still the curiosity or desire to know that is the prime motivating force behind engaging in research. Therefore it seems that one is here caught in an insoluble dilemma of either having to accept a risk of making erroneous assessments or draining one's future of an important source of value.

Of course, it is not true that omniscience will drain one's future of *all* value or satisfaction: for instance, it will not deprive one of the value of experiencing sensory pleasure, for anticipating a pleasure will normally not make one cease desiring it. Quite the contrary, anticipation of a pleasure is itself pleasant, and so it adds to the amount of value. Yet, a significant subset of the things we value consists in states of affairs fulfilling desires that presuppose ignorance, and for these the dilemma sketched arises.

There is, however, an idea, at first blush easy to confuse with Sidgwick's, that escapes the objection just delineated. Peter Railton suggests that in order to find out what is good or valuable for *A*, we should consider an idealization of him, *A*+, "who has complete and vivid knowledge of himself and his environment, and whose rationality is in no way defective" (1986: 174). We find out what is of value for *A* by asking *A*+ "what he would want his non-idealized self *A* to want—or more generally, to seek—were to find himself in the actual conditions and circumstances of *A*".[4]

Suppose, however, that *A* has an, in practice, ineradicable, false belief to the effect that, in an afterlife of infinite duration, he will be harshly punished if in the present life he engages in a certain very enjoyable activity that is compatible with other enjoyable activities and that is harmless to others. Because of this belief, he concludes that it is best for him to abstain from this activity and, as a result, leads a much duller life—without getting any reward in the non-existent afterlife. It seems clear that this conclusion is false and that what is best for *A* is that he indulge in the enjoyable activity. This is also the conclusion he would reach were it not for his false belief.

But it may well be that this is not what his fully rational self, *A*+, would advise him(self) to (want to) do in *A*'s actual, deluded circumstances. For it may well be that, if *A* were to engage in the activity, he would experience so much anxiety, because of his belief in later punishment, that this would destroy the enjoyment obtainable from the activity. If so, *A*+ would presumably advise *A* to abstain from this activity. We have, however, seen that this is not what is best for *A*. It is rather what is best for *A* *given* his false, ineradicable belief. But *A* is not asking what is best for him given any false beliefs he might have; he is asking simply what is best for him.

The source of the difficulty lies in the fact that, while any false, ineradicable beliefs that *A* might have will present themselves as such to *A*+, they will not, of course, present themselves as such to *A*. But these cognitive defects affect how *A*'s life goes. Now, *A*+ can take these cognitive defects into account as factors determining what is best for *A*. His conclusion will then concern what is best for *A* *given* these shortcomings, but we have seen that this is not what *A* is after in asking what is best for him. Or *A*+ can abstract from these shortcomings and ask what advice he should give to *A* could *A* be freed of all false beliefs, and all their attitudinal effects such as fear of an afterlife punishment. However, it is hard to see what relevant differences there would be between *A* under these circumstances and *A*+. In other words, Railton's model now appears to collapse into Sidgwick's: what is good for *A* would be a matter of what the fully rational, omniscient *A* would want for himself in his ideal state.

Personal and Impersonal Values

The way out of these quandaries lies, I think, in the sort of 'evaluative foundationalism' that I have outlined, according to which all value flows from intrinsic value that is

---

[4] 1986: 174. For similar proposals, see e.g. Smith (1994: 110–12) and Rosati (1996).

founded on incorrigible, ultimately intrinsic desires, that is, desires whose objects are desired only because of what they explicitly entail. To develop this subjectivist theory further, I want to show how it draws a distinction I have already alluded to, namely, the distinction between *personal* values, on the one hand, and *impersonal* values, on the other. The former may be said to be values *for* somebody, but we have already seen that this locution can be used to express the relativity of subjectivism—which is defined by (IV) above—and the notion I am now after is a narrower one, one in which one can distinguish between values that are values for somebody and values that are not *within* the framework of this subjectivist value theory. We need this narrower notion to characterize the prudentialist aim to lead the most fulfilling life, that is, the life that is (intertemporally) best *for oneself*.

It is not plausible to hold that the fulfilment of any intrinsic desires one may have—for example, a desire that everyone be equally well off or that there be life on earth forever—is personally good for oneself. Hence, we need some restriction on the intrinsic desires whose fulfilment is personally good for one. It lies close at hand to think that this has to do with the desires being *self-regarding*. The prudentialist aim should come out as self-regarding in this sense.

In Chapter 3 I anticipated a definition of the notion of such a desire as a desire that (1) has a self-referential content to the effect that something be true of *oneself* and that (2) is not ultimately derived from a desire whose content is not self-referential. Among my self-referential desires, we might find a desire to the effect that one of my kidneys be transplanted to a sick relative of mine. This desire is self-referential because its content is that something be true of *me*. Imagine, however, that this desire ultimately derives from a desire of mine that is not self-referential, for example, a desire for saving lives when this can be done without too great a risk to other lives, and that the reference to myself enters in the belief-premises of the derivation, for example, in a belief that I can now save the life of this relative of mine without too great a risk to my own or any other life, by letting one of my kidneys be transplanted. Then my desire to have my kidney transplanted is not self-regarding, on my proposal. Intuitively, this seems to me right.[5]

A self-regarding desire must not be confused with an *egoistic* or *selfish* desire (though the latter must be self-regarding). Suppose instead that my desire that *this* relative of mine be well is due to my concern about people closely genetically related to *me* and a belief that this person is appropriately related to me. Then my desire to have my kidney transplanted to this relative would be self-regarding, but it would hardly be egoistic or selfish. The latter sort of desire is to the effect that one's own self-regarding desires be fulfilled *rather than* the self-regarding desires of others. Thus, an egoistic desire presupposes a certain outcome of a conflict between the fulfilment of one's own self-regarding desires and those of others.

---

[5] In a discussion of C. D. Broad's idea that other-regarding desires can be self-referential, Blackburn remarks that "it is plausible to suppose that in a very weak sense" all such desires must be self-referential because "a thing has to bear some relation to an agent in order to figure in her decision-making" (1998: 154). Granted, the outcome of decision-making will have to be self-referential, and so there must be self-reference *somewhere* in the premises. But I cannot see why the desires (rather than certain beliefs) that function as the ultimate starting-points must be self-referential. Thus, there is room for desires that are not self-regarding in my usage but, e.g., other-regarding.

The prudentialist aim, however, is likely to be egoistic as well as self-regarding. It is self-regarding because it is basically an aim or desire that, inter-temporally, *one's own* fulfilment be as great as possible. But it seems likely that one's aim of leading a life that contains as much fulfilment of one's own desires as possible will be best advanced by one's having self-regarding desires which will sometimes conflict with the fulfilment of the self-regarding desires of others, and which one will then be prepared to fulfil. (As will soon be seen, prudentialists will especially have desires to the effect that they themselves have certain experiences.) Thus, prudentialism will tend towards egoism, though it is logically compatible with one's having, and fulfilling, both self-regarding desires concerning the desire-fulfilment of others and genuinely other-regarding desires.

The Fulfilment of Self-regarding Desires and Personal Value

The contents of many of the self-regarding desires of prudentialists, and indeed of humans generally, are likely to be to the effect that they themselves have some *experience* or other. Typically, these desires cannot be fulfilled without one's *realizing* that they are fulfilled. For instance, my desire now to see a beautiful sight or to read a book that amuses me cannot be fulfilled without my being aware of it. Such desire fulfilment is *experiential*: when p's becoming the case fulfils your desire for p in this sense, it causes a change in you with respect to p, for example, it causes you to cease desiring p and instead to *experience* pleasure that p has come to obtain because you are aware that p has become a fact. We may say that it satisfies not merely your desire, but *you*, as your feelings indicate.

There is, however, also another concept of desire fulfilment that is *purely factual*: it consists simply in p's becoming the case at a time t when you desire that p become the case at t. Fulfilment in this sense does not require consciousness on your part of p's being the case, and there need be no causal effect on your desire; it need not give way to a feeling of satisfaction, but may remain intact. My desire that something I have written be read by somebody this very minute may be fulfilled in this sense without being experientially fulfilled.

Note that, as conceived here, experiential fulfilment of a desire *entails* a factual fulfilment of it: it is fulfilment that subjects feel or experience because, as they are aware, some desires of theirs *have* been fulfilled, and not because they *falsely believe* that they have been fulfilled. The latter may be termed *illusory* fulfilment.

In Chapter 3 I concluded that not only psychological hedonism, but also the wider thesis of experientialism—that is, the thesis that the object of every (ultimately) intrinsic desire had by anyone is that they themselves have some experience or other (especially experiences that one thinks one will like when one has them)—is untenable. I appealed to the fact that we have various social desires and, as a consequence, may desire such things as that our names be remembered as long as humanity exists or that traces of our deeds persist forever (though nobody is around to observe them). It is hardly feasible to construe such desires as being derivative from desires that we will have some experiences after our deaths. Nor are they desires that we can realistically hope will ever be experientially fulfilled, as opposed to my desire that I am now being read. So, we must acknowledge the existence of intrinsic desires for other things than our own experiences that may be merely factually fulfilled, and not just temporarily, but permanently.

I assume that it will be granted that a subjectivist view should take the experiential fulfilment of self-regarding intrinsic desires to be personally good for the subject. But is this true of the purely factual fulfilment of self-regarding desires, too? (If so, there are at least two good things about a situation in which there is experiential fulfilment, for over and above the fact that the desire in question is fulfilled, the desire to experience the feeling of satisfaction is also fulfilled.) I think the answer is 'yes': for instance, I think it is good for me if my desire that I not be slandered behind my back, whose fulfilment I cannot consistently hope to ascertain, is (factually) fulfilled. (But it will not matter much for what follows if this point is conceded.)

It should be kept in mind, though, that in many cases in which one forms a self-regarding desire in the belief that it may be experientially fulfilled, it is not nearly as good for one that it is merely factually fulfilled. Imagine that my desire that I be read by somebody who really understands me is fulfilled merely in the factual way. Then I miss not just the pleasure consequent upon my knowledge of this fact. The frustration or sorrow that I may feel because of the absence of this knowledge will also detract from the value of the situation, so that, all in all, it may be negative. This may efface the fact that factual fulfilment does count or is of value.

Suppose that the alternatives are: having my desire to be read and understood actually satisfied, while not believing that it is, and having this desire actually frustrated, while believing that it is satisfied; what would I prefer? A priori, no preference is more likely than the other. If I am inclined to acquire the belief that this desire is satisfied, and am unwilling to put this belief to the test, this is evidence that I prefer the latter alternative. If I require very strong reasons to acquire this belief, being anxious to be deceived, this makes it likely that I prefer the first alternative. It is a mistake to think that, if subjects desire states of affairs specified like this one, 'to be read', they must prefer that these states of affairs really obtain to their falsely believing that they obtain.[6]

It might be thought that this mistake is clearly revealed to be a mistake by the following case: I want to sign another insurance policy, not because I believe that I shall really need it, but to alleviate my neurotic sense of insecurity. To alleviate this feeling, a firm belief that I have signed the policy is enough. So, acquiring this belief is the important thing; actually signing the policy is only a means to this. But suppose I happen to sign the policy without realizing it; it might then be doubted that my desire has really been satisfied. However, if it has not been satisfied, its content must have been inaccurately specified: perhaps its proper content is 'to sign an insurance policy in circumstances in which there is awareness of what is going on'. This leads onto another topic: that the content of a desire may be partly implicit.

Consider my desire to travel by train tomorrow: is the mere fact that I will travel by train tomorrow sufficient to fulfil it? Not if the desire is, to borrow Parfit's phrase,

---

[6] A mistake that Blackburn might tempt one to make (1998: 140–1).

implicitly conditional on its own persistence (1984: 151),[7] that is, not if it is a necessary condition of my now having this desire that (*a*) I believe I will still desire to travel by train tomorrow. If, as appears likely, it is conditional in this fashion, it is also necessary for its fulfilment that this desire persists tomorrow. So, if made (more) explicit, the content of the desire is: to travel by train tomorrow if I then still want it.

But even this is probably not enough: suppose that I am sound asleep or unconscious tomorrow when I am dumped on a departing train (this is compatible with my still possessing the desire to travel in a dispositional sense). This situation brings out a further possible condition for the persistence of my desire (already touched upon in the insurance example): (*b*) my belief that I shall be able to *experience* a possible train journey tomorrow, and so experience the fulfilment of my desire. If this is a further condition, my desire will not be fulfilled, unless this belief is true. My desire to travel by train is then at bottom a desire to travel by train tomorrow if I still want to then and will be able to experience the journey. Experiential fulfilment of my desire is then requisite to constitute a state that is of value for me. On the other hand, supposing my desire is not implicitly conditional on (*b*), a purely factual fulfilment will do to create a state of value for me. This is the case if I want the train trip simply as a convenient means to be elsewhere tomorrow.

Of course, it is unlikely that my desire to travel by train is conditional neither upon (*a*) nor (*b*), but other self-regarding desires may realistically be thought to have this double unconditionality, for example, a desire of mine that my name be remembered after my death. Such a desire cannot reasonably be held on the proviso that one keeps it and experiences its fulfilment.

I shall say of a desire not conditional on (*b*) that it is not *(implicitly) conditional on its yielding experiential fulfilment*. (A desire cannot have this conditionality without being conditional upon (*a*), but the reverse is possible.) My desire to sign the insurance policy possesses this (implicit) conditionality on experiential fulfilment. The experiential fulfilment of this desire is a means to alleviate my neurotic insecurity (a more than sufficient means, since illusory fulfilment would do the trick). But on the account here proposed, the mere factual fulfilment of self-regarding, intrinsic desires unconditional upon their yielding experiential fulfilment is of personal value for the subject. This is so, both if they are conditional upon their own persistence and this condition is met, and if they are free of this conditionality.

Impersonal Values, Ideals, and Higher and Lower Values

Let us now turn to desires whose contents are not self-referential. Suppose I desire that a certain sport event be televised tomorrow. In all likelihood, this desire is derived from a self-referential desire of mine to watch—that is, that I watch—the event on TV tomorrow, a desire that is probably conditional on my belief that tomorrow I shall (still) desire to watch

---

[7] Cf. also "desires that presuppose their own existence" in Gordon (1986).

the event on TV and, of course, that I shall then be able to do so. If so, it will surely be of no value for me to fulfil my desire that the event be on TV, if the desire to watch the event cannot be fulfilled; it is the (experiential) fulfilment of the latter desire that is of value for me.

It would not be a realistic interpretation in this case, but other non-self-referential desires are not reasonably construed as being derivative from self-referential desires. Suppose, for instance, that I desire that in the future no species of mammals or birds on earth be extinct due to human interference. As it is not reasonable to construe this desire as being derivative from any self-referential desire of mine, there is no risk of the value of its fulfilment deriving from that of the fulfilment of such a desire. Moreover, it is scarcely implicitly conditional on factors corresponding to (a) and (b) above, since in all probability it concerns what will happen long after my death.

It seems, however, to be absurd to hold that it is good, or makes things good, *for me* if, by the end of humanity, thousands of years after my death, my desire is factually fulfilled by its turning out then that humans have exterminated no species of mammal or bird. The reason for this, on my analysis, is that the desire is not self-regarding and that the fulfilment of it is not experiential. If a non-self-regarding of mine, for example, that there be peace in the Middle East this year, is *experientially* fulfilled, then this is personally good for me. But this is because it would satisfy my self-regarding desire to experience fulfilment. So the sense in which personal values are 'for' subjects can be explicated in terms of the self-regarding content of the relevant desires; there is no need for a separate clause requiring that the fulfilment be experiential.

Naturally, to subjectivists like myself, those values that are impersonal will still be values for some subject in the sense that they are values *from the point of view of, or relative to, a desire of some subject*. But they are not *personal* values for some subject. To prevent confusion, we should not say, for example, that there be peace in the Middle East is of value *for me*. I suggest we should rather say that it is of *impersonal*, as opposed to *personal*, value for me, and reserve the unqualified locution 'value for me' for the latter case in which there is double relativity.

I find it plausible to hold that many humans have non-self-regarding desires (or wishes)—of ecological, moral, political, artistic, etc., import—whose purely factual fulfilment is of impersonal value (for them). Since these desires are not conditional upon their own experiential fulfilment, we do not continue to have them because of the fulfilment they may allow us to experience. Rather, it is just their objectives for what they are in themselves that provide us with a reason to try to keep desiring them. In contrast to desires that are conditional upon their experiential fulfilment, we see having desires for these objectives as something having value apart from the felt satisfaction with which these desires could supply us.[8]

Instead of being derived from self-referential desires, these non-self-regarding desires may generate such desires—to the effect that we contribute to their realization—desires

---

[8] This distinction shows the falsity of Darwall's claim that as soon as "we are aware that something has value only *for us* we cannot draw the craftperson's distinction between the way she regards pick up sticks (which she may intrinsically like) and the way she regards her craft" (1983: 165), i.e., as something that gives meaning to her life and is not a mere vehicle of pleasure.

whose factual fulfilment is also of value, though impersonally so, since the desires are not self-*regarding*. Thus, unless it is experiential, the fulfilment of a merely self-referential desire will not be of personal value for the subject. However, it should be borne in mind that, though derivable, such contributory desires can already be held as intrinsic. To this extent, they are self-regarding, and their fulfilment may be of personal value.

Whether or not self-regarding, desires that are conditional neither on their experiential fulfilment nor on their own persistence can be held though they are at odds with maximizing one's inter-temporal fulfilment. I shall call such desires *ideals*, and they will play a prominent role in Part IV. We will see that there are ideals that cannot be criticized as cognitively irrational. Rationalism is such an ideal: one can desire that lives be led in the light of philosophical truth, and that oneself contribute to this goal as far as possible, even if one should cease desiring this, and the lifelong fulfilment of this desire will go against one's leading a maximally fulfilling life. It is this which gives rise to the conflict between rationalism and prudentialism.

Thus, Brink is wrong when he writes that subjectivism "would seem to counsel the cultivation of desires that are most easily satisfiable and the extirpation of desires with more risky objects" (1988: 227). I have maintained that agents necessarily act in accordance with those occurrent desires of theirs that are strongest at the time of action—that, factual errors aside, they will do what will in fact maximize the fulfilment of their *present* desires or what will be best relative to their *present* (intrinsic) desires. But this is different from the prudentialist aim of making one's *whole life or existence* as fulfilling as possible, that is, of living in the way which, *through time*, makes the sum of fulfilment of one's intrinsic desires as great as possible. These aims may coincide if one's dominant present desire is the prudentialist one but, of course, this is no counsel subjectivism entails. As I have just indicated, subjectivism leaves room for ideals or more generally for desiring that states of affairs obtain at—future or hypothetical—times at which one envisages not desiring them and, consequently, at which their materialization will not be of (personal or impersonal) value for one.[9]

According to subjectivism, the answer to the life-philosophical question 'As far as philosophical truth goes, how should I live, that is, how have I most reason to live?' will depend upon what one's current intrinsic desires are and what will maximally fulfil them. In other words, subjectivism is committed to a version of what Parfit calls "the Present-aim Theory" (in the next chapter, I argue that we should settle for what is in effect what Parfit calls the "deliberative" version of this theory (1984: 94, 118), without wanting to get bogged down by exegetical matters). This is, however, a purely formal constraint which does not impose any restriction on the substantive content of one's current intrinsic desires.[10]

Prudentialism is one possible specification of this content, and I shall conclude by saying a few more words about it. I have taken it to be the aim of leading a life that

---

[9] Gordon (1986: 106–7, 112–13) appears to stress this point.

[10] See Parfit (1984: secs. 34–5). I argue (1990) that Parfit does not unequivocally treat the Present-aim Theory as a formal theory in this sense.

contains a maximum of pleasurable desire fulfilment. This need not be taken to mean the greatest *quantity* of pleasurable desire fulfilment, where this quantity is obtained by multiplying the intensity and duration of the fulfilment. One instance of pleasurable desire fulfilment may be greater for you than another by being of a *higher quality*. This is so when you prefer the enjoyment of listening to Mozart for a short period to the enjoyment of listening to muzak for a much longer period, though you estimate that the latter contains a greater quantity of enjoyment. For even if the enjoyment of Mozart may be more intense, it need not be so much more intense that this can outweigh the much longer duration of listening to muzak. (Note, however, that you would not prefer listening to Mozart if it gave you no enjoyment at all.) Likewise, a brief instance of excruciating pain may be worse for qualitative reasons than days of very mild pain, though it is quantitatively smaller.[11]

I think the aim of a inter-temporal maximum of pleasurable desire fulfilment will make prudentialists strive to have, as far as possible, lower-order desires for pleasurable experiences and desires that are implicitly conditional upon yielding such experiences. But they may have, and act upon, other sorts of desire if this is compatible with their goal. They may have desires not conditional upon their experiential fulfilment, such as not to be backstabbed by friends, and even desires not conditional on their persistence, for example, desires concerning how they will be remembered after death. These things may be (personally) good for them, though not as weighty goods as pleasurable experiences. They may even be equipped with desires that are not self-regarding, for example, a desire that the population on earth will not grow fifty years from now, though their purely factual fulfilment is scarcely something that is better *for them*.

It seems to me, however, that having the experience-related desires that prudentialists will tend to have will promote not merely their goal of inter-temporally maximizing their experiential fulfilment, but also the goal of inter-temporally maximizing their factual fulfilment. The reason for this is that the experiential fulfilment of a desire entails, in addition to the purely factual fulfilment of it, the factual fulfilment of the hedonist or satisfactionalist desire to experience fulfilment. Thus, experiential fulfilment normally means a 'double dose' of factual fulfilment. Consequently, there might in practice be little difference between the prudentialist goal of maximizing experiential fulfilment and the goal of maximizing factual fulfilment.

---

[11] I show (2004*b*) how the distinction between higher and lower qualities of fulfilment can be used to meet problems for maximization theories like the repugnant conclusion.

11

THE RATIONALITY OF PARA-COGNITIVE ATTITUDES

THE notion of it being rational for one to (want to) bring about something, *p*, is ambiguous. There is the exclusive sense in which it means that one is rationally *required* to (want to) bring about *p*. The implication is then that it would be *irrational not* to (want to) bring about *p*. But there is also a non-exclusive sense in which it is equivalent to its being *rationally permissible* or *not irrational* to (want to) bring about *p*. This does not exclude that it is also permitted not to (want to) bring about *p*.

Rationality is an epistemic notion which is relative to the subject's background knowledge or beliefs. This means that the notion of what it is rational for one to do is more intimately related to what one has apparent reasons to do than what one has real reasons to do. The exclusive sense is tantamount to it being the case that, were one to think rationally, one would have decisive apparent reasons to (want to) bring about *p*. The non-exclusive sense is tantamount to it being the case that, were one to think rationally, one would not have decisive apparent reasons to omit to (want to) bring about *p*. Real reasons for acting and desiring, if strong enough, make one rationally required to act and desire in accordance with them if, by thinking rationally, one would appropriate them, that is, turn them into apparent reasons.

It follows from the account of reasons here presented that ultimately intrinsic desires cannot, as such, be rationally required, because there is nothing objective—nothing external to or different in kind from desires—that can serve as such requirements. If you rationally think that you can bring about *p* (and can refrain from it), there is nothing that can make you rationally required to intrinsically want to bring about *p* rather than not-*p*, for the requisite fit is possible whichever you desire. There is nothing comparable to sense-experience that can make you rationally required to have one basic thought, for example, that you see something blue, rather than another one.

However, an ultimately intrinsic desire can be *ir*rational or rationally illegitimate.[1] Suppose that it is irrational to think that one can cause *q*; that were one rational, one

---

[1] *Pace* Hume who seems to assume that reason can oppose passion only by producing a contrary desire (1739–40/1978: 414–15).

would see the impossibility of this, for example that one can travel backwards in time or move about independently of one's body and all other material bodies. Then an intrinsic (or indeed any intelligent) desire to bring about q would be irrational. That is, there is a rational requirement *not* to desire that q be the case (which of course should not be confused with desiring not-q), since this desire cannot make the world fit its object.

Hume insists that here " 'tis not the passion, properly speaking, which is unreasonable, but the judgment" (1739-40/1978: 416). It is indeed true that the irrationality of desires is derivative from the irrationality of the propositional thoughts they encapsulate. But since they *encapsulate* such thoughts, since the ascription of desires conceptually involves reference to propositional thoughts or judgements, I see no objection to characterizing desires themselves as irrational when these thoughts are irrational. Because of its source in cognition, I think it is appropriate to term this (ir)rationality *cognitive*, though it is (ir)rationality of a para-cognitive attitude.

But, according to the account of reasons here propounded, one can be rationally required to desire something only *relative* to or *given* some of one's other desires. In the end, these desires cannot be ones that one has because one is rationally required to have them. They will have to be ultimately intrinsic desires, which can only be rationally legitimate. The rational requirement derives from the direction of fit of these desires and appropriate conditional beliefs that are rationally held.

As regards the relation between the two forms of rationality of desires that we have distinguished, cognitive and relative rationality, it should be noted that it may be relatively irrational for one to have desires that are cognitively rational, just as it may be relatively rational to have desires that are cognitively irrational. As will transpire, this can be true of satisfactionalists.

Let us now review the conditions under which one can be rationally required to desire p by other desires one has, that is, the conditions under which, were one to think rationally, one would have decisive apparent reasons to desire p. As has emerged from the foregoing chapters, this is a complex matter. To begin with, that one rationally thinks that only if one brings about p then q will be brought about and that one has an intrinsic desire for q is certainly not enough to make one relatively required to desire p. This is so because one may have an intrinsic aversion to p, or to some of its other consequences, which is stronger than one's desire for q. In effect, this means that to find out what one is rationally required to want, one needs to survey all one's current rational(ly permissible) intrinsic desires and ask what would maximize their fulfilment.

This may be a crucial difference between theoretical and practical rationality: practical rationality has a holistic character that theoretical rationality does not possess, at least on model of foundationalism (which is a possible or intelligible model of theoretical rationality; I do not assert it to be the correct one). A means–end relationship to a single intrinsic desire cannot make one rationally required to have any desire, as the deducibility of a thought from a basic thought supported by sense-experience can make one rationally required to have it. It is only if this desire, in relation to other intrinsic desires with which one is equipped, is sufficiently strong to form a decisive desire that there is such a requirement.

The two main points of this discussion of the rationality of desire are the following. (*a*) Both cognitive and the relative rationality of desires depend on theoretical rationality, for example, of thinking rationally about one's power of acting and about some conditional relationships, such as the means–end relation. (*b*) One can be rationally required to want something only in the relative sense, that is, only relatively to other desires one has. In the end, the latter will have to be ultimately intrinsic desires which, as such, are at best non-exclusively rational in the cognitive sense. I have defended (*b*) in preceding chapters, but should now like to defend (*a*) against a rival view.

Parfit supposes that he smokes only because he has the irrational belief that smoking will protect his health. To the question "Does the irrationality of my belief make my desire to smoke irrational?" he replies "Not in any useful sense. Given my belief that smoking will achieve my aim, my desire to smoke is rational" (2001: 28). In his view, "our desires are rational if they depend upon beliefs whose truth would give us reasons to have these desires" (2001: 25). Parfit is here talking about non-normative beliefs. As regards normative beliefs, he claims "desires are rational when and because the normative beliefs on which they depend are rational" (2001: 32).

But imagine that your irrational non-normative belief is such that it cannot be true because it is logically impossible. Imagine, for instance, that you believe that the only way you can prevent yourself from dying from the incurable disease you now have is by travelling backwards in time and ensuring that you do not contract it. If, in response to this belief, you want to travel backwards in time to avoid the disease, it would seem that your desire is irrational. For it is a desire to do something that no rational person believes could be done. Parfit's account would, however, rather seem to imply that your desire is rational. For if your belief were true, it would seem that you would have a reason for your desire, since the normative belief on which this desire depends—to the effect that one has reason to protect one's health—may well be rational.

It may be replied that Parfit could escape this objection by making an exception for irrational beliefs in what is logically impossible. But I think such a revision would not go far enough. I believe we should distinguish between whether *the derivation* of a propositional attitude, like a desire or belief, is rational and whether *the attitude derived* is rational. In Parfit's example the derivation of the desire to smoke is indeed perfectly rational. But that is not sufficient for the desire derived to be rational. This also requires that the premises from which the derivation is made are rational. For the derived desire incorporates them—Parfit's desire to smoke is more precisely a desire to smoke *in order to protect his health*—and so inherits their (ir)rationality.

The requirement about the rationality of the premises holds also for the derivation of beliefs. Suppose I rationally believe *p* if and only if *q* and irrationally believe *p*. If the rationality of the derivation of a belief was sufficient for the derived belief to be rational, my derived belief that *q* would be rational. But with the help of this belief and the belief that *p* if and only if *q*, I could rationally derive *p* and so rationally believe *p*. Thus, by means of an irrational belief that *p*, I could arrive at a rational belief that *p*! This shows that the fact that the derivation of a belief is rational is not sufficient for the derived belief to be rational. In addition, we should require that the premises be rationally held. I claim that the same goes for the practical case in which a desire is derived: for this desire to be rational, the beliefs and desires that form the starting-point of the derivation must be rational, as well as the derivation itself.

I conclude, then, that (a) is true as well as (b). With this in mind, we may define cognitive rationality and a requirement of relative rationality for desires along the following lines:

(RD) (1) A's ultimately intrinsic desire for q is cognitively rational iff: this desire is among the ones A would have were she to form her ultimately intrinsic desires solely on the basis of the thoughts she would have were she thinking rationally; and

(2) A is rationally required to desire p iff: were A to think rationally, she would find herself with ultimately intrinsic desires to which she would believe p stands in such a relationship that she has decisive apparent reasons to want p, that is, she has beliefs to the effect that p fulfils these desires better than any alternative.

Thus, when one is rationally required to have some desire, this is always given some other, in the end ultimately intrinsic, desire one possesses, though this desire is not always made explicit. I shall adopt the convention that when these presupposed desires are made explicit, and thus the relativity of the rationality is made explicit, they need not be intrinsic desires satisfying (1). Otherwise we would not be capable of talking about what one is rationally required to desire given the prudentialist aim, since its bias towards oneself is not cognitively rational, as will transpire in Part IV.

Velleman's Criticism of Brandt

It is illuminating to compare and contrast (1) of (RD) with Brandt's similar sounding proposal that an intrinsic desire is rational "if it would survive or be produced by careful 'cognitive psychotherapy' " (1979: 113)—that is, repeated exposure to all available relevant information represented in an "ideally vivid way" (1979: 113; cf. 11, 149).[2] A crucial difference between this proposal and mine is that Brandt counts an intrinsic desire as rational if it *survives* cognitive psychotherapy. As Brandt himself notes, this brings along a "surprising" corollary: actual desires which "resist extinction by inhibition and anything else, since they have been so firmly learned at an early age . . . qualify as rational" (1979: 113) simply in virtue of their recalcitrance. Critics—like David Velleman (1988)[3]—have not been slow to fasten on this no doubt counter-intuitive corollary. It is in order to escape this complaint that (1) of (RD) is phrased in terms of what desires would be formed, that is produced, under the conditions stated, were the subject to form her

---

[2] Brandt's conception of an intrinsic desire is broader than mine of an ultimately intrinsic desire: a lot of the desires he classifies as intrinsic, I view as at least originally derivative, and their resistance to cognitive psychotherapy consists in their being sustained by intransigent conditional beliefs linking the objectives to other desired objectives. For this point, as well as other good criticisms of Brandt, see Fumerton (1990: 145–50).

[3] A lot of Velleman's objections to Brandt turn on this aspect of his proposal and the fact that Brandt wants to explicate the notion of goodness in terms of rational desire; therefore, my account evades them.

desires afresh. It is to be understood that the (episodic) thoughts referred to be present before the mind sufficiently long to take full effect.

Another objection of Velleman's concerns that the facts of which one would think were one to undergo cognitive psychotherapy

> would have to be represented in a particular medium, and there is more than one medium available. I can state the facts, I can picture them, I can diagram or map them, and their motivational impact may well depend on their medium of representation. (1988: 365)

Velleman is alive to the possibility that Brandt may have considered this point and attempted to cater for it by demanding that the facts be represented in an ideally vivid way. He also reports that Brandt has told him that "being an empiricist at heart, he regards sensory images as the most vivid mode of representation" (1988: 367 n.). But Velleman disputes that a vivid picture is more vivid than a vivid description and affirms that the difference is "in kind of vividness, not in degree" (1988: 367).

However, if one understands vividness as I have proposed—namely, in terms of richness of informational content—there can be no doubt that in general sensory images are more vivid representations of (immediately) perceptible states and events (not facts, as Velleman puts it) than linguistic descriptions. Velleman tries to back up his view by speculating that

> Perhaps all representations tinge their subject matter with some extraneous colour, because they must employ a verbal or visual or, in any case, symbolic medium, with purely fortuitous connotations, in representing what is in itself neither verbal nor visual nor in any way symbolic. (1988: 370)

But if one employs the medium of visual images to represent something visual, for example colours, it is plainly not true that one puts a visual medium, "with purely fortuitous connotations", to use in representing something that is not visual. The fact that an image of a colour normally is derived from a visual impression of the corresponding colour from which the concept of the colour is also derived makes it implausible to claim that its connotations are "purely fortuitous" or that representation in terms of it adds an extraneous tinge. There is reason to hold neither that a representation of a colour in a vivid image adds anything extraneous nor that there is anything that it necessarily leaves out.

It might be conceded that even if sensory images provide an ideal way of representing what is directly perceptible, there is no such way of representing more abstract or perceptually less accessible states and events. Here some conventional medium, like language, is needed, and we will have a choice of styles, some of which may differ in their motivational impacts. But if two styles of describing the same event apparently differ in their motivational effects, we should ask whether they really convey the very same facts: perhaps, for example, the metaphors of one description call to mind resemblances to external matters which the other description fails to evoke. If so, there is a difference in respect of facts conveyed, and this difference could in principle be made more explicit. It is only if two styles of description would produce different motivational effects which could not be put down a difference in their propositional content that we would not know which to recommend to someone exercising cognitive psychotherapy. But that this is the case is nothing that Velleman has shown.

Moreover, if it should turn out to be the case that different media or styles of representation would differ in their motivational effects without this being due to differences in the propositional or factual content that they somehow convey, this is something that will affect and render indeterminate not only subjectivist explications of practical rationality like Brandt's and mine, but any reasonable explications of the notion, even objectivist ones. For it is hard to deny that some clause about the exposure to information should enter into such explications.

Rational Thinking

If a definition like (RD) is along the right track, practical rationality rests upon theoretical rationality, for the notion of rational thinking crops up in (RD). Theoretical rationality and epistemology is so vast a field that nothing approximating to justice can here be done to it, but a few remarks on the rationality of thinking-true or believing may be in order. An explication of this notion has to strike a balance between being too 'intersubjective' or 'impersonal' and too 'subjective' or 'personal'.

Brandt seems to me to fall into the trap of construing theoretical rationality too intersubjectively. On the view offered by him, a desire is rationally held only if it is produced by or survives exposure to all *available* relevant information. Information available is then explained to consist in:

> the propositions accepted by the science of the agent's day, plus factual propositions justified by publicly accessible evidence (including testimony of others about themselves) and the principles of logic. (1979: 13)

Brandt is unperturbed by the fact that this conception will enable us to criticize people as being irrational in having certain beliefs, "although they may not themselves be aware of the known facts which make them so" (1979: 13). However, it strikes me as wrongheaded to accuse you of being irrational in thinking *p* if you have no reason to suspect that there are any known truths that undermine the probability of *p* (cf. Gibbard, 1990: 18–19). It is another matter that, although you are not irrational in believing *p*, given your inferior epistemic situation, *the belief* that *p* can be declared to be irrational—meaning by this that it is irrational relative to the best epistemic situation known.

One would be going too far in the subjective or personal direction were one to suggest that what is rational to think is what is best supported by the reasons that in some sense one has in one's mind, for one is often aware of the incompleteness of these reasons. It is important to recognize that in many situations one is aware not so much of (putative) facts bearing on the matter at issue—that is, of reasons—as of *means* of acquiring such facts or reasons. Excepting private matters, the body of (alleged) facts about any topic that one has present before one's mind—or, for that matter, dispositionally stored in it— is very modest compared to the body one knows one can lay one's hands on by going to a library, for instance. It appears irrational to form a belief on the basis of one's present information when one knows or reasonably believes that one could come into possession of a much more comprehensive body of information that might well significantly alter the relevant probabilities.[4]

A proposal that avoids both the objections of being too impersonal and of being too personal, I believe, would be this:

(RT) *A*'s episodically thinking (true) *p* is rational if:

A's thinking *p* is determined by the weight of all the apparent reasons bearing on whether or not *p* that she has, and these make up all the relevant reasons that she has reasons in her mind—in an apparent or dispositional form—to think could be assembled by her.

Imagine that *A* thinks that the relevant reasons initially stored in her mind are inadequate and that there are further relevant (real) reasons to be acquired. She acquires all these reasons and endorses *p* in proportion to the support provided by these (now apparent) reasons—that is, by a body of reasons that, so far she can see, is so comprehensive that no further addition attainable by her will alter its bearing on the topic at hand. This is the situation I have in mind in designing (RT), and it is the one in terms of which the notion of rational thinking cropping up in (RD) could be defined.

There is another type of situation somewhat similar to this: *A* thinks that beyond the reasons in her mind there are further relevant (real) reasons to be acquired, but she does not bother to acquire these reasons because she is convinced that they will in any case favour *p*. Nevertheless, *A* thinks *p* because of this conviction about the thrust of the (unknown) real reasons. This situation is clearly possible, but would her thinking *p* be rational if it rested on such a ground? My inclination is to say that it would be rational only if the conviction about the thrust of the unknown reasons is rational, but to leave it at that would, of course, be blatantly circular.

It might be suggested that we could escape the circularity by applying the same recipe again: that the conviction that the unknown reasons will warrant that the belief *p* is rational if *A* holds this conviction because she has gathered all the pertinent reasons that she has reason to think would make a difference to the issue and these support the conviction. In fact, I believe this to be the correct way out, but I shall not insist on this. I rest content with pointing out that (RT) is devised with the first situation in mind and that it states only a sufficient condition of rational thinking.

There is another set of complications which centres around the notion of the further real reasons that could be assembled or acquired by *A*. It is a well-known fact that it is sometimes inadvisable to try to acquire some pieces of information which one could acquire if one tried hard enough. In deliberating, you often reach a point at which it seems clear that trying to collect further pieces of information, though possible, is likely to frustrate important desires. Suppose, for instance, that *A* has a dominant, rational

---

[4] In passing, Brandt mentions a " 'subjective' " conception of rationality (1979: 72); it is not clear to me whether this conception coincides with the one I propose or the one I find too subjective.

desire to make a lot of money at once. A normally reliable friend tips her off that a certain horse will win a race. If A bets a small sum on the horse, and the horse wins, she will get the money needed in time. A believes that she can get hold of further information that will either confirm or undermine the friend's tip, but she is also aware that acquiring this information will take so long that it will be too late to bet on the horse. In such a case A might be said to be irrational if she tries to collect the further information. But if she acts rationally in not trying to extend her evidence, and if her evidence supports the belief that the horse will win, it would seem that she must be rational in having this belief. This is so, despite A's knowing herself to be in a position to gain further relevant information that may make it improbable that the horse will win.

It is possible to respond to this objection by appealing to an analogue to the above distinction between cognitive and relative rationality: between thinking a *thought* that is cognitively rational and being relatively rational in *thinking* a thought *given* the possession of some desire. In the end this will be ultimately intrinsic desires, so let us take this as our example in defining relative theoretical rationality, as opposed to the cognitive rationality defined by (RT):

(RT*) A's thinking *p* is (relatively) rational given her ultimately intrinsic desires if:
A's thinking *p* is determined by the weight of all the apparent reasons bearing on whether or not *p* that she has, and these make up all the relevant reasons she has reason in her mind to think could be assembled by her compatibly with maximally fulfilling her ultimately intrinsic desires.

(RT) and (RT*) will converge upon what it is rational think on one condition, namely, that within the set of A's ultimately intrinsic desires the desire to be as well-informed as possible is dominant to the degree of outweighing the conjunction of other in the situation conflicting ultimately intrinsic desires of hers. A will then seek out all the reasons she has reason to think that she can get hold of, and she will be relatively rational in thinking thoughts that are cognitively rational.

Of course, in practice nobody has a desire as general as the desire to be as well-informed as possible. There are always some matters in which one takes an interest and about which one in particular likes to be well-informed, while one is indifferent to others. I shall here be especially concerned with the desire to be well-informed about those general aspects of the universe that form the subject matter of philosophy—and, more specifically, those that have a bearing on the formation of para-cognitive attitudes. I shall refer to the desire to be as well-informed as possible about these aspects, and to shape one's attitudes in the light of this information, as *the rationalist desire*, and to persons (whether actual or imaginary) for whom it is the supreme or strongest desire as *rationalists*.

In the next three parts of the book, I shall investigate the cognitive rationality of certain para-cognitive attitudes, for example of temporal and personal partiality: is it rational(ly legitimate) to prefer one thing that is personally good to another simply because it is closer to the present or to prefer that one person obtain some such thing rather than somebody else simply because the first person is oneself? My reply will be that this is not cognitively rational, that is, that these are not preferences one would have were one to form them on the basis of one's cognitively rational thoughts. It does not follow from this, however, that one is rationally required to give up these preferences *whatever* the orientation of one's intrinsic desires. Given certain orientations, it may be (relatively) rational to have desires that are cognitively irrational.

This is certainly not so for rationalists: they are obliged to scrap desires that are cognitively irrational. But, although many of us are equipped with the rationalist desire, we also have other intrinsic desires some of which may be stronger. For instance, there is also the satisfactionalist (intrinsic) desire whose objective is to produce pleasure and the feeling of desire-fulfilment. The form of this that is to the effect that one's own life contain as much (experiential) fulfilment as possible is the *prudentialist* (fulfilment-maximizing) desire and subjects who are dominated by it are *prudentialists*.

As already pointed out, it is important not to confuse the—somewhat indeterminate—objective of the prudentialist desire, that one lead *a life* in which the fulfilment of one's (intrinsic) desires be as great as possible, or that one's fulfilment be *inter-temporally* maximized, with the state of affairs consisting in one's *present* desires being maximally fulfilled, for one's strongest present desire may not be this prudentialist desire, but, for example, the rationalist desire.

A main theme of this essay is the extent to which the rationalist desire and the satisfactionalist desire diverge, even if the latter is rendered cognitively rational. We shall first explore how rationalism diverges from the prudentialist form of this aim, that is, the extent to which living so as to maximize the (experiential) fulfilment of one's own life diverges from living attitudinally tuned to a true philosophical picture of the universe. While rationalists are rationally required to reject all cognitively irrational attitudes, prudentialists, on the contrary, are rationally required to keep those of these attitudes the loss of which will make their own life less fulfilling, and as we shall see there are a number of these. If, as I think is the case, there is something of both a rationalist and a prudentialist in many of us, we face a dilemma.[5]

Summary of Kinds of Reason

It may be helpful to end this chapter with a list of the types of (practical and theoretical) reason that have been distinguished so far:

(1) Real reasons which are constituted by what is actually the case,

(2) The reasons that one can *actually* acquire (*a*) if one tries as hard as one can to make one's reasons as comprehensive as possible or (*b*) if one tries as hard as one

---

[5] It follows that what is rational for one need not be rational for another. Sometimes when this subject-relativity is apparently denied, the denial is just that—apparent. For instance, Nicholas Rescher argues: "The universalized aspect of rationality turns on its being advisable by person-indifferent and objectively cogent standards for *anyone in those circumstances* to do the 'rationally appropriate' things at issue. The standards of rational cogency are general in the sense that what is rational for one person is also rational for anyone else in his shoes" (1988: 158). However, on the very same page he has already warned us that "we here construe 'circumstances' very broadly, including not only the outer and situational, but also the inner conditions that relate to a person's physical and psychological make-up". This seems to trivialize the universality or non-relativity of rationality.

can compatibly with maximizing the fulfilment of one's present ultimately intrinsic desires,

(3) The reasons that, on the basis of good or bad reasons, one *thinks* one can acquire on the proviso of either (*a*) or (*b*) of (2),

(4) Apparent reasons which are represented by episodic thoughts,

and

(5) Dispositional reasons that are dispositionally stored in the mind.

The distinction between (4) and (5) which has just been hinted at will assume greater significance in the next two chapters.

Some appear to have thought that the notions of rationally desiring and thinking should be defined in the terms of the reasons spelt out in (2). But I have argued that, with the supporting reasons spelt out along the lines (4) and (5), (3) is a preferable alternative— (3*a*) in the case of the notion of a cognitively rational thought or desire, and (3*b*) in the case of the notion of a thought or desire that it is relatively rational for one to have given the orientation of one's ultimately intrinsic aims.

12

WEAKNESS OF WILL

As I argued in Chapter 8, it is a merit of internalism that it leaves no room for any embarrassing indecision concerning doing (or wanting to do) what one has most apparent reason to (want to) do. However, it might seem to have the countervailing demerit of making impossible a phenomenon that common sense takes to occur, namely the phenomenon of weakness of will. Let us see what precise form this difficulty takes for the internalist position here advocated.

This view entails that if A at t has in her mind, in some sense, reasons such that she is in a position to truly claim that she ought or should—that is, has decisively stronger reasons—to bring about p rather than not-p at t, then necessarily, if A intentionally brings about either p or not-p at t, she intentionally brings about p at t. This contention can be split up into two claims.

(1) If A at t has in her mind reasons the thrust of which makes true her claim that she ought to bring about p rather than not-p at t, then, if she at t forms a decisive desire to bring about either p or not-p at t, she forms a decisive desire to bring about p at t.

(2) If A at t forms a decisive desire to bring about p at t, then, if she at t intentionally brings about either p or not-p, she intentionally brings about p at t.

I have in Chapter 4 and in (1981) said what I have to say in favour of the conceptual connection between decisive desire and intentional action stated in (2); so the main topic of this discussion will be the formation of such a desire on the basis of reasons in one's possession, that is, claim (1).

(1) is backed up by the internalist construal of reasons and reasoning that I have offered. According to this account, A's at present having decisively stronger reasons for causing p than not-p is roughly tantamount to her beliefs representing p as definitely more conducive than not-p to realize what is the object of her currently strongest intrinsic desires. Under these conditions, if A on the basis of these beliefs decisively desires either to cause p or to cause not-p, she decisively desires to cause p.

However, if both (1) and (2) are necessarily true, it seems that weakness of will or *akrasia*, as acting against one's best reasons, is impossible. To be sure, this phenomenon is often differently formulated. It is said that *akratic* agents act contrary to what they think is best (for them) or to what they think they ought to do.[1] These formulations differ from the one here proposed in that they presuppose that akratic agents are self-conscious to the extent of being conscious of their current values or reasons *as* their values or reasons, and thereby their current desires.

For one cannot judge what is now of (greatest) value for one without being aware of one's present intrinsic desires, since, as I have explained, something's being of (intrinsic) value for one now consists in its fulfilling one's present (ultimately) intrinsic desires. Similarly, to think that one ought (in what I have called the rationally normative sense) to bring about p is to think that the reasons one has decisively support bringing about p. If so, it follows, owing to the desire-dependence of reasons, that a judgement about the thrust of one's present reasons for action presupposes an appraisal of one's current desires. This account of 'ought' in the practical sphere is confirmed by the fact that it could quite easily be generalized to cover occurrences of the word in the theoretical dimension. When we here say that p ought to be the case—for example that it ought to rain tomorrow—this is naturally construed as saying that there are best reasons to think that p is the case (or that it is probable that p).[2]

There are at least three reasons for preferring my formulation of the problem of *akrasia* to the latter two formulations which involve this self-consciousness of one's current desires. First, I believe it to be at least in principle possible that agents act out of weakness of will without being conscious of the desires they have at the time of action. One can clearly have in one's mind a reason for action without being conscious of having it, that is, one can think certain thoughts of a conditional form that have a causal impact on one's motivation without being aware (or thinking truly) that one is thinking these thoughts and that they have this motivational impact. If this is so, why would it not be weakness of will to act contrary to the best reasons that one *has* should this occur in the absence of the self-conscious reflection that one has them? I am prepared to concede that it might, for some reason, be the case that the *akrates* must have *the capacity* to monitor his current desires, but I fail to see why this capacity must be exercised at the moment of weakness.

Secondly, it seems to me clear that it is at least logically possible to judge (correctly) that it is best for one, or that one ought, to bring about p, and then on the basis of this judgement form a decisive desire *not* to bring it about. On the analysis of desire offered in Chapter 4, to have a desire to cause p is to be in a state that, in conjunction with a thought to the effect that one might be able to bring about p, tends to cause what one thinks is p. Now, it is in theory possible that one is in a desire-state that in conjunction with a thought that one might be able to act contrary to what one thinks is best for one, or what one thinks one ought to do, causes one to act in this contrary fashion. It is to be expected, though, that the world should contain few creatures who exhibit this defiant reaction to consciousness of the thrust of their own current reasons for action, because such creatures would be

---

[1] Sometimes it is assumed that these have to be moral judgements, but that is clearly a mistake.

[2] Cf. Edgley's contention (1969: ch. 4.10) that 'ought' expresses a pressure of reason consisting in there being good reasons for thinking or doing something.

singularly ill-suited to survival. If a species equipped with self-consciousness has been successful in the struggle for survival, it must be the rule that the response of its members to what self-consciousness informs them will most fully satisfy their current intrinsic desires will be a desire to pursue this course.

If we assume that a sentence of the form 'I shall cause p' is what I have called expressively normative and gives vent to a decision or the formation of a decisive desire (or intention) to cause p, then we should expect these imaginary self-destructive organisms to think things like 'I ought to bring about p, but I shall not bring it about'. On my descriptivist reading of (the rationally normative) 'ought', such a sentence is, logically speaking, perfectly coherent (as already remarked in Chapter 8). However, if one accepts R. M. Hare's prescriptivist interpretation of ought-judgements according to which they are not *statements* about what one has best reasons to desire, but *expressions* of decisive (universalizable) reason-based desires, this sentence will make doubtful sense. Since the sentence intuitively strikes me as meaningful, I see this as an argument in favour of my own descriptivist construal, as against Hare's prescriptivist one.[3]

But, as I have already indicated, I believe this cognitivist/non-cognitivist debate to be of marginal interest in the present context. There is clearly a need both for linguistic devices *describing* the order of strength among one's present practical reasons and for devices *expressing* (in a manner lacking truth-value) desires based on these reasons, that is, for what I have labelled rationally normative and expressively normative devices, respectively. It is of secondary importance which constructions are employed for which purposes, but it strikes me as most natural to stick to the terminology just proposed.

The fact that it is logically possible to respond to consciousness of what will maximize one's present fulfilment with a desire not to strive for this does not show, however, that weakness of will is possible. For all we know such a self-destructive desire to act contrary to what one takes to be one's own good or what one ought to do may be perfectly premeditated and cold-blooded and not at all a manifestation of weakness. So let us, in order to keep things as simple as possible, stay on the ground-level on which there is no consciousness of one's current desires.

The third reason for preferring to stay clear of talk of what is best for one or what one ought to do has to do with the fact that these judgements may be false: one could misjudge the thrust of one's desires or reasons. Of course, it is plain that if there is this discrepancy between judgement and reality, one can act contrary to one's judgement about what is best for one or about what one ought to do—by following the real thrust of one's motivation. This may seem to be a rather boring possibility, which has nothing to do with *akrasia*, but there is one variant of it that merits attention because it might create a false picture of the independence of evaluations of motivation. It is to the effect that,

---

[3] See Dunn (1987: chs. 2 and 3) for a discussion of Hare's prescriptive view of evaluative language from the perspective of *akrasia*. Dunn contends that the akratically relevant value-judgements neither entail imperatives nor are expressions of desires or intentions. He reads them as true-or-false statements about reasons for action, but appears to take an externalist view of reasons. Sometimes it is assumed that to be an internalist one must be a non-cognitivist, but this is because the necessary motivation is tied to the *holding* of a normative or evaluative judgement (rather than its truth): e.g. "if value judgements were capable of being true then they could have no logically necessary relevance to any choice of conduct" (Ibberson, 1986: 1).

owing to a hovering of 'reasons' between the apparent and the dispositional (or 'desires' between the occurrent and dispositional) reading, a judgement that was originally true in the 'apparent reason' sense may later, without one's noticing it, only hold true in the weaker, 'dispositional reason' sense.

Suppose that your judgement that you have best reasons to bring about *p*, read as a statement about apparent reasons, is originally in accord with the truth, but that, owing to, say, affective pressure, you lose sight of some of these reasons so that your strongest apparent reasons now support not-*p*, and you are consequently occurrently most motivated to bring about not-*p*. Then, since the original judgement may still be true, as a judgement about your dispositional reasons, someone who overlooks the ambiguity mentioned may erroneously conclude that the truth of the judgement at no time had anything to do with the state of your occurrent motivation. Thus, they may end up falsely believing that action at odds with the truth of the agent's judgement in its original sense is possible.

For these reasons, I avoid requiring that the *akrates* actually makes evaluative or normative judgements. Instead, he is taken just to have in his mind reasons that make these judgements true.

An Externalist Way Out

Of the two principles stated in the first section, (1) entails internalism, so one way to vindicate the possibility of *akrasia* is by espousing externalism. This is what Alfred Mele, for one, appears to do when he affirms that reasons for actions "have two importantly different dimensions: the agent's evaluation of them (when he does evaluate them) and their motivational force of valence" (1987: 95; cf. 37 ff.). Unless externalism is true, there could not be true evaluations of one's reasons that diverge from their motivational power. It is evident that a divergence of these dimensions provides room for weakness of will in the sense of agents' acting against their (true) judgement about what they have best reasons to do. For even though, given an ability and opportunity of acting, you must intentionally do what you are most motivated to do (1987: e.g. 13–14), the possibility of a misalignment between motivation and evaluation makes it conceivable that you act against your judgement about what you have best reasons to do. According to Mele, an intention to act (here and now) may be based on your evaluations (1987: 38–9, 103–7). But when your evaluations are not in harmony with your motivation such an intention may be defeated by a contrary intention arising from the motivational system.

By exercises of self-control this disharmony between the evaluative and the motivational system can be prevented, since self-control "is roughly the ability to master motivation that is contrary to one's better judgment" (1987: 54). Some techniques of self-control "involve the agent's altering his physical or social environment" (e.g. a smoker's destroying his cigarettes), while "[t]he operation of others is wholly internal to the agent" (1987: 54)—the latter including various strategies of directing one's attention to considerations that one otherwise risks overlooking in the heat of action. In my terminology, these attentive strategies have the function of ensuring that one's relevant dispositional reasons become apparent at the time of action, that is, that they manifest themselves in episodic thought and thus have a chance of affecting action. It will be seen that there is an important overlap between Mele's theory and the one I am about to develop because the gist of the latter is that akratic action is action against one's better dispositional reasons, but not against one's better apparent reasons at the time of action.

However, Mele embeds these insights in an externalist framework which I have dismissed in Chapter 8. I shall not reopen the externalism/internalism controversy. Let me just point out that a trouble with externalism in the context of *akrasia* is that it seems to make *too little* out of the problem: intuitively we feel there is something paradoxical about acting contrary to one's best reasons, but externalism makes this air of paradox vanish. According to this doctrine, acting against one's best reasons is not stranger than not doing what one recognizes to be, say, the conventional thing.

Loosening the Instrumental Relation

On my interpretation of the instrumental rule as constitutive of desiring, we *cannot* reject what we take to be means that are necessary and in the circumstances sufficient to our (dominant) ends. It lies close at hand to suggest that the solution to the problem of *akrasia* lies in diluting this impossibility into something looser or weaker. One form this dilution might take is externalist. It might be claimed that, though we have reason to adopt such means, we have to possesses *a desire to be rational* to actually adopt them. Thus, David Richards, who puts forth a set of normative principles of practical rationality that, among other things, commands one to choose the actions that most effectively attain one's ends (1971: 28), declares that "the agent may choose to act or not to act on rationality principles, as he wishes" (1971: 51), adding that "as a brute fact of human psychology, there is a widespread desire to be rational" (1971: 63).

This idea—that in order to derive a desire concordantly with the means–end relations that one has thought out, one stands in need of a second-order desire to derive desires according to this pattern—is exposed to the fatal objection that it erects an infinite hierarchy of desires. Suppose that, at t, you view p as an effective means to accomplish q which you desire. Then, *ex hypothesi*, to derive a desire for p you have to call on a higher-order desire to desire whatever is seen as an effective means to an end of yours. But you also need to recognize that the particular reasoning at hand is an instance of this general pattern, that p is an effective way of bringing about an end of yours. On the basis of this desire and recognition, you can at t derive a desire to form a desire for p. However if, on the theory under scrutiny, your derivation of a desire for p requires an appeal to a higher-order desire to execute this derivation, it would seem that the derivation of the desire to form a desire for p should do the same. Consequently, it would seem that this derivation demands a third-order desire to stand by the desire to desire effective means, and so on *ad infinitum*.

Hence, in loosening up the necessitation of instrumental reasoning, we must stop short of externalism. This is what Korsgaard attempts to do, for on the one hand she criticizes externalism—or "realism", in her terminology—along lines similar to mine (1997: 241).

On the other hand, she insists on the possibility of knowingly violating the rule of instrumental reasoning, as well as rules of theoretical reasoning like *modus ponens*. She claims that "it is perfectly possible for someone to fail to accept the logical implications of her own beliefs, even when those are pointed out to her" (1997: 222). Similarly, she holds that motivation will be channelled into what an agent takes to be necessary means only "*if nothing were interfering with her rationality*" (1986: 14 n.). It is, however, possible that "people's terror, idleness, shyness, or depression is making them irrational or weak-willed, and so that they are failing to do what is necessary to promote their own ends" (1997: 229).[4]

"How can there be an imperative which no one ever actually violates?", Korsgaard asks (1997: 228). Perhaps there could not, but it does not follow that there could not be *normative requirements* that no one could ever consciously violate. It must not be taken for granted that normative requirements must assume the expressive form of imperatives which allows for conscious violation, without having to be abandoned. This would beg the question against the view of theoretical and practical rationality advanced here. That view is that you are required to have, or not to have, certain beliefs and desires if you are to have beliefs and desires that have their proper direction of fit, that is, if you are to have any beliefs or desires at all. But if, for instance, you desire something while desiring to avoid what you take to be necessary means to it, your pair of desires cannot have their proper direction of fit if your belief has its fit to the facts, that is, they cannot mould the world to fit both of them. This notion of a requirement constitutive of desiring is not naturally rendered by anything like an imperative.

All the same, let us look closer at the case Korsgaard makes. She writes:

> If willing an end just amounted to actually attempting to realize the end, then there would be, so to speak, not enough distance between willing the end and willing the means for the one to *require* the other. (1997: 244)

So, she suggests, "willing an end just is *committing* yourself to realizing the end". This is "equivalent to committing yourself... to taking means to that end" (1997: 245). This "commitment to taking the means is what makes a difference between willing an end and merely wishing for it or wanting it" (1997: 252).

To begin with, I think that trying to understand willing an end as committing yourself to realizing it is to put the cart before the horse. To commit yourself is to perform an act that is necessarily intentional; thus, it presupposes the notion of intending or willing. Korsgaard also suggests that "to will an end *is a reason* for the end" (1997: 245). The phrase "is a reason for the end" is elliptical: it must mean 'is a reason for willing (pursuing etc.) the end'. However, we have seen that a reason for willing an end must be something which can *make* you will the end. But, obviously, your willing an end cannot *make* you will it. This also brings out that willing an end is ill-suited to give you a reason for it, since a reason can be demanded for willing it.

---

[4] In the same vein, Edgley maintains that "reason may fail to decide his conduct in this way . . . that he may not do y even though he intends to do x and thinks or knows that to do x he must do y" (1969: 144), and that this is the source of weakness of will (1969: 122, 144–5). But unlike Korsgaard and like me he holds that it is logically impossible to think that if p then q and p, but nevertheless not-q (1969: e.g. 121)

Moreover, even if these objections could be met, it seems Korsgaard's conception of willing would not help in explaining the possibility of *akrasia*. This is because willing an end seems to entail "attempting to realize the end" or being appropriately motivated to pursue it. (If it did not, we would be back with externalism.) Hence, to show that *akrasia* is possible, it must be shown that it is possible to attempt to realize an end while refraining from the use of what you take to be necessary means to it. Otherwise, there will not be that "distance" between the end and the means which a requirement that can be deliberately violated demands. However, construing willing as a commitment does nothing to establish this possibility.

If anything in Korsgaard's account achieves this, it is those factors that are said to "interfere with one's rationality", namely "terror, idleness, shyness, or depression". Obviously, all sorts of things can obstruct one's instrumental rationality, for example one could die or lose consciousness. The interesting question is, however, whether anything can make possible the formation of an instrumentally irrational desire, *without depriving one of one's access to one's reasons*. For weak-willed agents act contrary to reasons that in some sense they still possess. Loss of life or consciousness blocks access to reasons, but what about the factors Korsgaard cites? They certainly do not block the access to reasons anything as definitely.

Perhaps it is plausible to view them as doing their work by preventing one from fetching reasons that are in one's mind ready to be fetched. This is a suggestion I shall subsequently adopt. I shall propose that, owing to factors such as affective disturbances and weariness, we can fail to recall or episodically summon some of the reasons dispositionally stored in our minds, although they are highly relevant in the situation at hand. Since, as I contended in Chapter 4, it is in the considerations actually represented in episodic thought that occurrent desires and actions originate, this may issue in occurrent desires and actions contrary to the thrust of those of our dispositional reasons that are not apparent at the moment. But, again, this is a line of thought that is entirely independent of Korsgaard's construal of willing as a kind of commitment that supplies reasons.

It might be complained that the account I have just sketched does not show it to be possible to desire and act contrary to the thrust of reasons that are *in full view*. This is true whether or not the account is embedded in Korsgaard's theory. My proposal has been that, to the extent they can serve to make *akrasia* intelligible, the factors listed, such as depression, operate by obscuring or effacing the episodic representation of reasons that are dispositionally stored in one's mind, and in this sense still available to one. So we have not seen how it could be possible to form a desire for not-p, instead of deriving a desire for p, when one is episodically thinking that only if one brings about p then q and one occurrently desires q (and defeating circumstances concerning, for example other undesirable consequences are absent). To all appearances, viewing the instrumental rule as constitutive of desiring excludes this possibility. If both this view and internalism of reason and value are true, the ways of accounting for the possibility of *akrasia* are severely restricted. At least, it seems ruled out that *akrasia* could be action or desire contrary to the thrust of reasons in full view.

Davidson's Principle of Continence

There is, however, a type of theory—associated with the name of Donald Davidson[5]—that would accomplish precisely this. This theory tries to drive in a wedge between a desire which is the outcome of a reflection on all relevant reasons or considerations, a desire to bring about something *all things considered*, on the one hand; and on the other, an *unconditional* desire—or intention—to the same effect which is the immediate determinant of intentional action. Taking evaluative propositions to express the contents of desires and intentions,[6] Davidson distinguishes between judging one action better than another (or judging that one ought to do one action rather than another), *all things considered* or *on the basis of all available reasons* and judging this *unconditionally*. It is the latter, to repeat, that issues in intentional action. There is a "principle of continence", PC, that exhorts one to "perform the action judged best on the basis of all available relevant reasons" (1980: 41). The *akrates* violates PC: Davidson characterizes him as "holding that, all things considered, it would be better to do *b* than to do *a*, even though he does *a* rather than *b* and with a reason" (1980: 39).[7] Thus, according to Davidson, akratic action is possible in the sense of action against what one wants most, or judges most desirable all things considered, but not as action against what one unconditionally wants most, or unconditionally judges most desirable.

Nonetheless, it should not be thought that the *akrates* simply rejects PC. "Pure internal inconsistency enters", Davidson insists, "only if I also hold . . . that I ought to act on my own best judgment" (1982: 297). Should an agent who acts against his best judgement lack such a desire—of a dominant strength—then we could without any air of paradox explain his action by pointing out that this desire "was not as strong as his desire to do something else" (1982: 297).

However, this generates the following problem: how could it be that the weak-willed agent violates PC if he has a dominant desire to obey it? Davidson attempts to explain this with the help of this illustration: a man returns to a park to remove a branch that he has thrown into a hedge because he thinks it might project from the hedge in a dangerous fashion, although he regards the time and the trouble this costs him as a reason that outweighs the reason to eliminate the danger. The gist of Davidson's explanation is the

---

[5] See esp. 'How is Weakness of the Will Possible?' (Davidson, 1980: essay 2; and 1982).

[6] See Davidson (1980: essay 5, esp. p. 86) and Davidson (1985b). Thus, Davidson's evaluative judgements should not be construed as statements about one's desires, about what would satisfy them and the reasons to which they give rise. As indicated in Ch. 8, I regard Davidson's way of expressing himself as misleading, because it wrongly suggests that (*a*) to have a desire is like believing or having a thought that something is the case, in that it is an act of endorsing a proposition (or a proposition-like content), and that (*b*) practical reasoning, like theoretical, consists in a process of *inferring* propositions from other propositions endorsed. This would be to misunderstand the nature of desire, to overlook that it involves no element of endorsing a content over and above that which is of a straightforward theoretical kind and which ignites a behavioural tendency.

[7] Here, as in the formulation of PC, Davidson apparently assumes that the *akrates* performs another *action* than the one supported by his best reasons. However, as I shall explain in the next chapter, it is enough that the *akrates* forms a *decisive desire* (intention) that is contrary to his best reasons. Therefore, it would be better to say something like that PC enjoins one to form a decisive (unconditional) desire to act on the judgement about what is best (for one), given all available relevant reasons.

claim that the source of the irrationality lies in that "the desire to replace the branch has entered into the decision to do it twice over" (1982: 297)—first as a part of a reason competing with the superior reason not to return to the park and, secondly, when the agent has weighed up the reasons on this level, as a reason for ignoring PC and refusing to act on his best reasons. It is the second appearance which is responsible for the irrationality, for although this "motive for ignoring his principle was a reason for ignoring the principle, it was not a reason against the principle itself" (1982: 297). Obviously, this desire does not count against the validity of PC.

It seems clear to me, however, that this explanation fails to dispel the mystery. For if the desire to return to the park to remove the branch provides the agent with a reason or motive for disregarding PC, it would seem that his stronger desire to save time and trouble by not returning should supply him with an even stronger reason for heeding PC. Moreover, the latter reason is, *ex hypothesi*, backed up by an independent desire to respect PC. I do not see why the desire to return, when it makes its second appearance, does not come up against this combined opposition and, if it does, how it could conquer it. Thus, I believe that Davidson does not succeed in accounting for the possibility of weakness of will.

Mental Compartmentalization

A further type of theory suggests that the answer to the possibility of *akrasia* is found in an idea the origin of which can be traced back at least to Plato's *Republic*, to the idea put forward there that the soul has different parts or compartments. According to Terry Penner (1972) and Gary Watson (1977) the mind can be seen as being bifurcated into a part that is the seat of theoretical and practical reason or of the faculty of rational thinking or willing (desiring), on the one hand, and an appetitive section with its own capacity for desiring, on the other.[8] The former desires are necessarily in conformity with the weight of reasons, but the appetitive ones need not be so. Hence (1), of the two principles stated in the first section of this chapter, is not true, since one's strongest desire may be an appetitive one. A battle between rational and appetitive desires is thus conceivable. In the rational person the former are victorious, whereas in the *akrates* rebellious appetitive desires reign.[9]

At first blush this approach might seem appealing, but I think this impression evaporates when one tries to make the approach more precise. What are the defining characteristics of the rational and appetitive desires, respectively? Since Penner and Watson do not explicitly address this question, one will have to try to extract an answer from the

---

[8] Another writer who appeals to appetitive desires in this context is Davis (1986).

[9] One finds an echo of this dualistic view of the self in one of the interpretations that Hare puts on "backsliding", namely the one that comes to expression when he writes that the back-slider "is actually giving commands to himself, but unable to obey them because of a recalcitrant lower nature or 'flesh' "(1963: 81). Hare's other main strategy is, roughly, to doubt either the sincerity or the evaluative force of the judgement about what is best to do: the *akrates* "is, in his whole personality or real self, ceasing to prescribe to himself" (1963: 81).

exemplifications they provide. Penner lists as typical desires of the appetitive compartment sexual desire, the desires for food, drink, and warmth (1972: 109). To these Watson adds the aversion to pain and inclinations to excrete and sleep (1977: 323 n.). The desires so far listed may create the impression that what characterizes an appetitive desire is that it has its source in a bodily need. However, this cannot be right, for Watson is quite explicit in counting some desires that enter into emotional reactions as belonging to the appetitive section (1977: 320, 323). And contending that Plato did not take seriously the idea that emotions constitute an independent part of the soul, Penner apparently concludes that some emotions side with reason while others join forces with appetitive side (1972: 111–13). Indeed, it is reasonable to hold that one's being weak-willed can be put down to one's being in the grip of some emotion, for example fear.

This is, however, enough to wreck Watson's suggestion that the basis of the bisection "has rather to do with the *source* of the want", this source being *evaluations* in the case of rational desires (1975: 208). From the perspective of the subjective theory of value that I developed in Chapter 10, this proposal is objectionable in that it implies that values are independent of desires. But even if we waive this complaint and, for the sake of the argument, accept talk of values as sources of attitudes, there is another blow which awaits Watson, for then it becomes plausible to hold, as many indeed have done (see Chapter 5), that emotions, too, have their source in evaluations, for example that fear is induced by an evaluation of something as harmful or dangerous. So either values cannot be sources of any desires or they can be sources also of non-rational ones.

Against the background of the defeat of this proposal, the only way I can make precise sense of the distinction between rational and appetitive desires is to take it to boil down to the distinction that I have drawn between intelligent and non-intelligent desires. This interpretation implies that the *akrates* acts out of a non-intelligent desire and hence that the weak-willed action is not intentional. Now I am inclined to concede that some actions that can reasonably be characterized as resulting from weakness of will could be the upshots of non-intelligent desires. Suppose that someone expecting to be a victim of torture concludes that he has best reasons not to scream out during the imminent torture, but that he nevertheless fails to restrain his instinctive impulse to scream. Then (provided the impulse to yell out was not irresistible) it appears not unreasonable to describe the victim as being weak-willed, though his screaming was involuntary.

But we certainly do not want to say that every weak-willed act is the result of non-intelligent or instinctive desires: for instance, when somebody who thinks he has more important things to do nevertheless continues with a crossword puzzle, he may be described as being weak-willed, but of course his behaviour is not the outcome of a non-intelligent desire. So, in the idea under consideration we have at most a partial account of *akrasia*.

The notion of mental compartmentalization also figures in Davidson's writings, in particular (1982). Recall his example of the man returning to the park. Here the desire to remove the (possibly imaginary) danger created by the branch serves as a reason not only for removing the branch, but also for ignoring the principle of continence, PC, although it is not a reason to doubt the validity of that principle. This is, in Davidson's opinion, what makes it irrational to disregard the principle. A simpler example of wishful thinking, devised by Davidson (1982: 298), may make his point clearer. A young man believes that he has a well-turned calf because he wants to have one and wants this because it would give him pleasure. The desire causes the believing, but it is, of course, not a reason for thinking the content of the belief *true*—that is why the man's having this belief is irrational. (It is another matter that the desire—or rather the prospect of pleasure—is or could be an instrumental reason for, say, a prudentialist, to *have* this belief.)

Davidson is puzzled by this fact that one mental state can cause another without being a reason for endorsing its content; he believes reason-explanations to be "the only clear pattern of explanation that applies to the mental" (1982: 299). To find an intelligible model for how a mental event could cause another without being a reason for it, Davidson seems to think that he must turn to inter-personal cases in which my desire that you believe *p*—via intermediate physical events—causes you to believe *p*. Hence, Davidson concludes that in order to account for the causation involved in irrationality, "it seems we must assume that the mind can be partitioned into quasi-independent structures" (1982: 300).

This conclusion is curious, in view of the fact that Davidson himself points out that in "simple cases of association" "there is a mental cause of something for which it is not a reason" (1982: 305). Surely, this is also "a clear pattern of explanation that applies to the mental"—and, to all appearances, it applies within the confines of a *single* mind. That I have in the past seen *A* and *B* together and that I now see *A* would seem to make up a perfectly good causal explanation of why I now think of *B*, albeit thinking of *B* seems to be something for which one does not have a reason that makes it rational. So, to provide space for causal explanations that account for one mental state in terms of another, but which are not reason-explanations (of the sort that could make the *explanandum* rational), we should not resort to any partitioning of the mind (cf. Mele, 1987: 75–80).

Furthermore, it does not seem at all plausible to think that there is any mental division in cases of irrationality like the simple case of wishful thinking. Apparently, the irrationality is here dependent upon the desire and the belief being present in the very same mental entity—as Davidson himself stresses, there need be no irrationality when the desire is in one mind and the belief in another (1982: 300). I think one can explain wishful thinking without postulating boundaries dividing the mind, as follows. We have noted various ways in which a desire can affect the direction of one's episodic thinking. Among these ways, there is the one in which a wish that *p*—that is, a non-intelligent desire that *p* be the case though one is convinced that one can do nothing to bring it about—expresses itself in a tendency to direct one's attention away from the (compelling) evidence in favour of not-*p* and towards the weaker support for *p*. To the extent that such selective attention results, one may begin to think it true that *p* (cf. Mele, 1987: 125–6, for a more extensive list of techniques of deceiving oneself).

The Possibility of Simultaneously Having Contradictory Beliefs

So far there is nothing to suggest any mental compartmentalization, but it might be objected that I have left out an essential ingredient. It might be said that, if engaging in wishfully thinking p—or deceiving oneself into believing p—involves a desire to manipulate the relevant evidence at one's disposal so that it comes to support the truth of p, one must initially think or believe that this evidence does not really support this conclusion. However, if one ends up thinking that p is the case, it seems one must believe that the evidence at one's disposal indeed *is* sufficient for a belief p. Elsewhere Davidson explicitly maintains that it is this fact that people occasionally hold contradictory beliefs that necessitates divisions of the mind: "people can and do sometimes keep closely related but opposed beliefs apart. To this extent we must accept the idea that there can be boundaries between parts of the mind" (1985a: 147).

Mele's reply (1987: 129) to this claim is that the contradictory beliefs are not simultaneously held: the belief that the data are sufficient to make it highly probable that p *replaces* the belief that the data are not sufficient. Although Mele's reply may be right, I would like to argue that it is possible for one simultaneously to hold contradictory beliefs. I shall argue this in spite of earlier having claimed that it is impossible to believe an explicit contradiction, for example p and not-p. Hence, if I am to be consistent in allowing this possibility of someone simultaneously believing p and believing not-p, I must state conditions under which these beliefs do not coalesce into the conjunctive belief p and not-p. Furthermore, I shall have to show how one can 'keep them apart' without introducing any boundaries dividing the mind into compartments. For this divisive move has the drawback of making one wonder whether the irrationality is preserved, as there is nothing irrational about two persons simultaneously entertaining contradictory beliefs.

The clue to the solution lies in the fact that a belief p is a disposition to episodically think p, which need not be actualized even though a suitable occasion arises, for example even though one happens to be in a situation in which the truth-value of p is relevant. Consider the following illustration (and recall the case of buying parsley in Chapter 4). Suppose that I am used to hearing a certain bell strike at noon, but that some hours ago I was told that it will not strike today because it went out of order yesterday. So I know—and hence believe—that it will not strike today at noon. Nonetheless, I might still from habit slip into thinking or expecting that it will soon strike, and at least for the duration of this thought, I believe that the clock will strike at noon. But this does not mean that I cease to believe that it will not strike. When I catch myself and think 'Of course, it will not strike', I do not *acquire* a belief to this effect again; I have had it all along. Therefore, at the moment at which I am episodically thinking that the clock will strike, two contradictory beliefs can be ascribed to me. It is natural to suggest that this is possible, because at the time one belief does not manifest itself in episodic thought.

Nor can this failure of manifestation occur only when the truth of the belief is the object of merely marginal attention: it is not necessarily the case that, if its truth is at the centre of attention, a believer in p will episodically think that p and nothing explicitly incompatible with it. Our concept of belief allows us to say that we believe that p albeit at times we fail to think that p even when the question of its truth is of focal interest. For instance, suppose that I am misspelling 'supersede' as 'supercede' and that for a while it looks right to me; then for that moment I believe that this is the correct spelling of the word. But imagine that it soon dawns on me that the correct spelling is with an 's'; then it would be natural to say that all along—ever since I first learnt the spelling—I knew (and believed) this to be the correct spelling. So long as the failure to recall something is only temporary, we would not speak of a piece of knowledge being lost and then regained when one once again succeeds in recalling it. The situation is not one of forgetting and re-learning; the proposition is stored in my mind all the while. Our notion of having a proposition stored in one's mind, or possessing a belief or a piece of knowledge, is elastic enough for it to apply even in the face of temporary failures to retrieve the proposition. This provides room for the ascription of contradictory beliefs when episodic thoughts negating a not manifested belief momentarily occur.

These cases show that a disposition to believe or think p can fail to manifest itself in episodic thought even though one approaches the matter with an open mind, so to speak. In view of this, it should not be surprising that it could fail to manifest itself when, as in wishful thinking or self-deception, there is a desire that p not be true which influences the direction of one's thought. Yet, this is compatible with a belief p being ascribable to one even should one episodically think not-p. The explanation as to why the belief p and the belief not-p can coexist in the same subject without coalescing into a conjunctive belief that p and that not-p has already been indicated: they are not manifested in episodic thought at the very same time (or, strictly speaking, in immediate succession). They are kept apart in the sense of not being brought together in episodic thought and not in the sense of belonging to different compartments of the mind. Simultaneously having the belief p and the belief not-p entails having the conjunctive belief p and not-p only if both beliefs are manifested together in episodic thought.

Akrasia as Acting Against Dispositional Not Apparent Reasons

This account also provides the clue to an understanding of weakness of will, for, as for instance Davidson has stressed, there is a strong similarity between wishful thinking and self-deception, on the one hand, and *akrasia*, on the other: just as the victims of the former do not take into consideration all the relevant reasons for belief stored in their minds when making up their minds about what to think, so akratic agents have not in view all the relevant reasons for action stored in their minds when making up their minds about what to do. When one forms a decisive desire, that is, decides, one does so only on the basis of reasons that at the moment are represented in one's thought, that is, on the basis of what I have called apparent reasons; unrepresented propositions that one would succeed in calling to mind, given sufficient time and effort, are uninfluential in this respect.[10] So when only a sub-class of the relevant reasons stored in their minds is represented in the akratic agents' episodic thought, the decisive desires they form, and the intentional actions in which they issue, are not based on the best reasons they possess in a dispositional sense. We can then characterize akratic acts as not being determined by the agents'

---

[10] Contrast e.g. David Richards: "what acting for certain reasons implies is that these reasons are part of one's beliefs, not necessarily part of one's actual thoughts in conscious deliberation" (1971: 58).

best dispositional reasons, because their apparent reasons constitute only an inferior sub-class of these; some of the dispositional reasons remain dormant although they are of relevance.

So akratic acts spring from apparent reasons that, owing to causes which still remain unrevealed, do not adequately reflect the best relevant reasons that are dispositionally stored in the akratic agents' minds. They are thus not contrary to the preponderance of reasons that one faces in the fullest sense. I have rejected theories that try to accommodate such deviation by different measures: by the externalist separation of reasons from motivation, by allowing explicit violation of the instrumental rule of practical reasoning, by distinguishing reason-based desires from unconditional desires, or by distinguishing them from non-rational or appetitive ones. In contrast to these theories, I suggest that we keep apart reasons that one has in the narrower sense of them being the contents of one's episodic thoughts (apparent reasons) and ones that one has merely in a dispositional sense (dispositional reasons), and see one's decisive desires as being based on the former.

Like some of the other theories, my theory emphasizes the kinship between *akrasia* and phenomena like wishful thinking and self-deception. The possibility of the latter two phenomena also hinges on the fact that the relevant apparent reasons (in these cases reasons for belief) need not coincide with, but may be less comprehensive than, the dispositional reasons stacked up in one's mind. A desire based on a wishful thought will be irrational, though it need not exemplify *akrasia*. On the account here proposed, the practical irrationality of *akrasia*, and of the attitudes to be examined in later parts of the book, is an offshoot of the theoretical irrationality of biased representation.

The causal background of weakness of will must, however, be different from that of wishful thinking. I have tried to explain why certain propositions believed are not represented in thought, but remain dormant, by appealing to a desire to think true something that contradicts them. But it would seem inadmissible to account for the suppression of relevant reasons for action in cases of *akrasia* by a similar manoeuvre. For consider an akratic agent who omits to bring it about that *p*, though the course of bringing *p* about is supported by his best dispositional reasons. It would be fishy to explain why vital parts of the relevant dispositional reason-system of the *akrates* do not receive representation by referring to an occurrent desire of his to omit causing *p*. For why does the *akrates* have this desire rather than a (stronger) desire to bring about *p*? Surely, this must be due to a selective or partial representation of the reasons that are stored in his mind, for remember that the weight of these reasons favours the *akrates*' causing of *p*. And on pain of an infinite regress, this partial representation cannot be explicable by reference to a desire. In the next chapter, I shall attempt to show that such a bias of representation can be put down to other causes than the play of desires.

13

REPRESENTATIONAL
MECHANISMS

THE threatening regress mentioned at the end of the last chapter can be avoided, because what is episodically thought or mentally represented of the information dispositionally preserved in one's brain is not determined solely by one's desires. For instance, what one is thinking at a given moment is influenced also by what one *perceives* (or feels) at that moment, by what occurs in one's sensory fields at the time in question.[1] One cannot be thinking about, or attending to, everything that is simultaneously present in the field of a single sensory mode, for example the visual, let alone everything that is simultaneously present in all of one's sensory fields. Attention must be selective. In general, sudden changes in a sensory field more readily attract attention than what undergoes no change. An item noticed succeeds in lingering at the centre of one's attention by arousing a desire or interest: the pain caused by the sting of a wasp exercises a stronger hold on attention than the buzzing sound the wasp makes, an unfamiliar birdcall catches the interest of the birder, and so on.

It presents no difficulty to understand why the pain one is currently feeling should tend to capture one's attention. As was argued in Chapter 1, given the obvious fact that it is of survival value that sensations of pain have outward effects in the form of withdrawal behaviour, it is not hard to comprehend that the same must be true of their having an inner effect in the form of holding attention captured. For suppose that this was not the case, but that one could effortlessly think about other things. Since thoughts also have the power to affect outward behaviour, there would be a constant risk of the causal powers of painful sensations and of thoughts of other matters cancelling each other, thereby jeopardizing the evolutionary advantage of the arrangement of pains causing withdrawal behaviour. Furthermore, it is also clear that it would be advantageous if pains affected thinking not only by drawing one's attention to the sensations, but also by making one think about possible ways of eliminating or alleviating them.

---

[1] This presupposes a view for which I have argued elsewhere (1985a: ch. 3.1), that the sensory is distinct in kind from the conceptual, and so can be a causal factor determining it.

Akrasia and the Bias towards the Perceived

In the light of these considerations, let us look at a rather simple case of weakness of will which casts a sensation of physical pain in the role of the culprit. Suppose that I am suffering from some sort of neuritis which, as I am aware, will go away in a few weeks, leaving no bodily damage. A symptom of the disease is periodic bouts of excruciating pain. The only effective painkiller to which I have access is one that is very addictive, X. In a cool hour, before the pain sets in, I scrupulously envisage what feeling the pain will be like and carefully go through what I know about X-addiction. As a result of this, I form a decisive desire to abstain from resorting to X when the pain afflicts me. Nonetheless, shortly after the pain has started, I am seized with a stronger desire to get rid of the pain by injecting X, and act accordingly.

If it is not the case that this change in respect of desire can be put down to me having thought of some weighty new reason, how is it to be explained? The diagnosis I suggest is this. When the pain sets in, it more or less monopolizes my attention, so my mind is flooded by thoughts registering what the pain is like in detail and how it can be removed. Consequently, other topics—like that of the possibility and undesirability of X-addiction—receive scant attention. Since the strength of one's occurrent desires is determined by the propositions figuring in episodic thought, this leads to my desire to put an end to the pain increasing in intensity relative to my desire not to be addicted to X. Moreover, as the former desire is boosted and as the propositions about addiction dispositionally stored in my mind are jejunely represented, the risk of wishful thinking about addiction—to the effect, for example, that an addiction will develop less easily and is less harmful than I otherwise would think—increases. If wishful thinking of this sort should occur, the desire to be rid of the pain at the price of injecting the drug will gain further strength and possibly surpass the conflicting desire to endure it.

I shall summarize what has happened in this case by saying that I am subject to *the bias towards the perceived*, for short, the P-bias.[2] There are two ingredients in this bias. First, there is the fact that victims of it are episodically thinking more about some event—for example their feeling pain—when it is perceived than when it is not perceived (this process being set off by the fact that the perceived calls forth corresponding conceptual representations). Secondly, owing to this attention, there will be a stronger desire with respect to some event when it is perceived than when it is not perceived. This starts a process of spiral reinforcement in which this desire further amplifies the tendency to think more about the sensibly present, and what to do about it, producing thoughts which in their turn strengthen the desire connected with the event perceived, and so on. It is not difficult to understand how the upshot of this process can be a significant change in the relative intensity of some desires that were formed before one's perceptions became what they are at present.[3]

[2] Cf. Parfit's bias towards the present (1984: 145). However, at any moment, what is present to one's senses is only a tiny fraction of what is occurring at that moment, and what one is biased towards is strictly speaking only that tiny fraction (and not, e.g. what is occurring on the other side of the earth). So, rather than speaking of a bias towards the present (time), we should speak of a bias towards that of the present which one perceives.

[3] As we shall see in Part III, there is also a bias towards the near future, as opposed to the more distant future. It may be partly responsible for the effect in my example, since an addiction will take some time to develop.

It should perhaps be underlined that in order to put the P-bias into operation it is not necessary that one is feeling a hedonic sensation like that of pain or pleasure.[4] Sense-impressions from an ongoing activity in which one takes an interest will also do. Beforehand I have decided not to spend more than half an hour on some pastime, like a chess problem, before going back to work. But when I have begun engaging in it, I become engrossed in it and think little of work. So my occurrent desire to solve the chess problem becomes stronger than my desire to go back to work, and I carry on with the chess problem beyond the limit set. None of this is surprising in view of the fact that to be engaged in an activity in which one takes an interest is to be doing something that one wants to be doing for its own sake and that captures one's attention.

The phenomenon of weakness of will can be conveniently characterized in terms of the distinction between dispositional and apparent reasons. Briefly, a decisive desire that is initially based on a set of representations that seems to one to fully and fairly capture the reasons one thinks there are is *weak* when it is unstable or subject to fluctuation in strength as the result of these reasons subsequently being more fragmentarily represented in episodic thought, but one is still aware that these reasons are dispositionally stored in one's mind, and one would succeed in actualizing them were one to try hard enough. The cause of the inadequacy of the latter representations is in the example reviewed that one's perceptual environment favours the representation of some state of affairs at the expense of others. (I do not wish to claim, though, that at the root of weakness of will there is always the P-bias.) As the result of this representational slant, a desire (e.g. to inject the drug) is formed that is stronger than one's initial decisive desire. This new desire does not qualify as a decisive desire—or intention—since it is not formed by a decision that concludes a piece of deliberation.[5] There cannot be said to be any deliberation going on here, for there is no attempt to mobilize all the reasons one thinks one has. Quite the opposite, at the moment of action the *akrates* is, at least dimly, aware that some of his reasons remain partially dormant and, hence, to this degree causally impotent. This is also why he cannot properly be said to have *changed his mind*. Conversely, a decisive desire which is based on a full and undistorted representation of one's reasons is *strong* to the degree that it is constant, because one keeps in view all of one's reasons at every relevant moment, in spite of external pressures. So, there is no possibility of acting contrary to them.

This is a characterization of the type of weakness of will which culminates in intentional action, for the change in respect of apparent reasons results in a new intelligent desire being decisive. In the foregoing chapter, I mentioned the possibility of a weak-willed act being involuntary or the outcome of a non-intelligent desire. This type of akratic behaviour can now be seen to be closely related to the intentional variety. The non-intelligent desire, which is triggered off by a sensation of pain, for instance, can in

---

[4] Contrast Schiffer, who embraces the Aristotelian view that the pleasures of food, drink, and sex are the proper objects of *akrasia* on the ground that these give rise to reason-providing desires (r–p desires) and such desires fail to generate second-order desires for their own persistence (1976: 202). But by not classifying the desire to avoid pain as an r–p desire (1976: 198), Schiffer (counter-intuitively) implies that this sensation does not occasion *akrasia*.

[5] This is not noted by Holton (1999), who argues that weakness of will roughly consists in being over-ready to revise one's intentions.

two ways overpower an intelligent desire based on a certain episodic manifestation of dispositional reasons. It can do its work by 'infiltration', that is, by distorting the fashion in which these reasons are episodically represented. Or it can take the intelligent desire by direct assault, so to speak, by simply surpassing it in strength. In former case, the desire culminating in behaviour can be intelligent, and the consequent action intentional, whereas in the latter case the action will be non-intentional because the desire determining it is non-intelligent. It is, however, the former kind of *akrasia* that is of greatest theoretical interest, so the following comments will be made with it in view.

First, in order for one to exhibit weakness in causing *p* at *t*, one must at some time prior to *t* have deliberated and formed a decisive desire not to cause *p* at *t*. This distinguishes *akrasia* from recklessness in which one's decision at *t* is rash and ill-considered by being based on a careless assemblage of reasons. Weakness of will consists in a failure to *preserve* a decisive desire in the face of pressures like the bias towards the perceived.[6]

Secondly, from the characterization of weakness of will just adumbrated it should be evident that this phenomenon can occur in the absence of action (cf. Audi, 1979: 181–5). It is enough if a dominant desire, issuing from a distorted representation of one's dispositional reasons, replaces a decisive desire resting on a better representation of them. If in the example above I am paralysed just as I have formed a dominant desire to inject X, I have proved the weakness of my will. I need not inject X or even try to do so.

Thirdly, weakness of will is frequently taken to imply an action (or attitude) that is *contrary* to the one dictated by one's best reasons. But that does not seem to be necessary. To see this, add a new feature to the illustration of *akrasia* sketched above: imagine that I have a further reason for taking a shot of X—for instance, I am writing a dissertation on X as an analgesic and need some personal experience of the drug—and that this reason is weightier than the reasons against trying the drug. So on my best representation of my dispositional reasons, I form a decisive conditional desire to inject X when the pain sets in. However, when the pain afflicts me, the thought of this consideration in favour of taking the drug, as well as the reasons against this action, is swept from my mind, and I acquire a stronger desire merely on the basis of considerations having do with the awfulness of the pain. Then I am a victim of *akrasia* even though the desire on which I am acting is of the same orientation as the decisive desire shaped on the basis of the best representation of my reasons, for, no less than in the original example, this desire originates from an inferior representation of my reasons. The fact that there is this accidental coincidence may conceal the weakness exhibited by the subsequent desire, but it does not remove it, for it is still the case that it is based on a less comprehensive representation of the dispositional reasons.

Fourthly, in contrast to a person who acts out of a compulsory desire—for example a kleptomaniac—the *akrates* is responsible for his weakness. The *akrates* could have resisted

---

[6] Jackson (1984: 14–18) also stresses that weakness of will involves a change in respect of strength of desire which is *not* attributable to any change in probability resulting from the acquisition of new information. On this point, Jackson has been criticized by John Bigelow et al. (1990: 43) who argue that *akrasia* consists in acting on a desire that you do not want to act upon. But if, as these authors seem to hold (1990: 45), it is enough that this second-order desire be of some strength, and it is not required that it override conflicting ones, this account fails to state a sufficient condition, while if it is stipulated to be overriding, the mystery is unresolved. For another account of *akrasia* which relies on desires of different orders, see Schiffer (1976).

falling victim to the weakness, whereas the compulsive's desire is irresistible. The akratic desire is not so dominant that the subject would fail to represent episodically his full set of reasons were he to try.[7] That is why it is regarded as appropriate to blame and punish the *akrates*: it is reasonable to expect that this treatment will make him more inclined to make this attempt in the future and hence make him less likely to exhibit *akrasia*. On the other hand, the kleptomaniac and other compulsives will steal even though at the moment they are fully aware that there are stronger reasons for them to refrain. The compulsive ideas exercise such a powerful influence over the direction of their thinking that they cannot specify the stronger reasons and hold them before the mind sufficiently long for them to have proper impact on behaviour. Of course, it may in practice be impossible to draw a sharp line between compulsives and akratic agents, to settle in every case whether a desire was strictly irresistible or merely very hard to resist. There may be social norms roughly laying down what is a reasonable effort, and if such an effort is not enough to overcome a desire, it is deemed irresistible. (Compulsive desires will be further discussed in Chapter 33.)

Sensuous Representations

This analysis of *akrasia* puts us in a better position to gauge what rationalists are up against when they try to form para-cognitive attitudes that as far as possible are based on their view of the truth and nothing else. It is not enough that they try to acquire as extensive a system of relevant beliefs as they have reason to think they can acquire. They must also see to it that these beliefs are fairly represented in episodic consciousness when their attitudes are formed. For instance, rationalists must overcome the P-bias, and that is certainly no mean task. Thoughts registering the sensorily present can possess all the concrete specificity with which the perceived is endowed. It takes a great exertion of the powers of imagination to represent something not perceived with a vividness and richness of detail that parallel that with which the perceived is represented. If one has recently perceived something, it may not be that difficult to recall it in reasonable detail, but as time passes the vividness of memory-images usually fades, and this loss of content is accompanied by a loss in respect of motivational potency. Hume shows awareness of this fact when he writes:

> a drunkard, who has seen his companion die of a debauch, is struck with that instance for some time, and dreads a like accident for himself: But as the memory of it decays away by degrees, his former security returns. (1739–40/1978: 144)

Let me try to make more explicit what I take vivid representation to involve.

First, I assume that propositions can be mentally expressed not only in words, but also in images or representations that are so to speak isomorphic with the content of perception. Since the term 'images' suggests visual representations, and I do not want to exclude representations isomorphic to the contents of the other sense-modalities, I will in its stead speak of *sensuous representations* (cf. Persson, 1985a: ch. 3.2). To give a very

---

[7] Kennett (2001: ch. 6.2) claims that the *akrates* must have this power to actualize the better reasons, i.e. self-control.

simple example, the proposition that something perceived is a black cat can be expressed by this perceived thing calling forth a sensuous representation of a black cat. It is true that it is not altogether easy to understand how sensuous representations could capture the propositional feature of predication, for example the idea that blackness is predicated of a cat. The best I can do is the suggestion that the predicated property is expressed either by adding a sensuous representation of it to an already present representation of the subject or by focusing a hitherto diffuse aspect of the subject-representation, for example the blackness of the cat imagined.

Secondly, excepting abstract matters, sensuous representations offer a more economical or handier way of expressing information than do sentences. A content that it would take a large number of sentences to convey could be compressed into a single sensuous representation that could be present to the mind all at once. Thus, by putting matters in terms of sensuous representations one could survey a body of information that, if verbally expressed, would be too unwieldy to comprehend. (Indeed, as things stand, there are kinds of information that could only be sensuously represented—for example, our vocabulary of colours is scant compared to the millions of shades between which a normal percipient can discriminate. But I think that *in principle* everything that can be sensuously represented can be verbally formulated.)

Thirdly, the vividness of a sensuous representation consists in its conveying a great deal of information concerning matters of detail. Consequently, loss of vividness amounts to an impoverishment in respect of such information expressed, and it is thus comparable to words or sentences being deleted from a linguistic description. There is therefore nothing mysterious about a fading away of vividness bringing along a decrease of motivational power. The fact that a representation is sensuous rather than verbal neither adds nor detracts from its motivational potency; this potency is a function of nothing but the content represented.

It is possible to counteract this bleaching of sensuous representations by repeatedly calling them to mind. In general, this is what one must do to neutralize the P-bias: to try to impress on one's mind states of affairs perceptually absent by frequently dwelling on them in great detail.[8] I suppose one could also try to emphasize particularly important aspects of the sensuously represented states of affairs by codifying them in sentences. But the struggle to attain fair or unbiased representations of everything relevant dispositionally stored in the human mind seems to require superhuman efforts.

Some Principles of Association

We have seen how the skewed representation in which the bias towards the perceived consists can be responsible for weakness of will. Desire-relevant states of affairs that are perceptually experienced receive representation in episodic thought to a higher degree than do desire-relevant states of affairs that are believed, but not perceived, to obtain.

[8] Cf. Brandt's requirement that in undergoing "cognitive psychotherapy" information is to be "repeatedly represented" "in an ideally vivid way" (1979: 111).

But, as already indicated, it is not my belief that the P-bias is the only source of *akrasia*; so, let us look for other factors than perceptual experience that may single out some believed states of affairs for proportionally greater representation in episodic thought.

As may be gathered from Hume, there are some relations to what is perceptually experienced that may produce this effect. He first points to the fact that *resemblance* between something perceived—or merely episodically thought of—and something else may account for the mind's transition from the former to the latter (1739–40/1978: 11). Thus, the fact that I see, and attend to, a Rorschach blot may make me call to mind the image of a rhinoceros and certain facts about rhinoceros that are dispositionally stored in my mind, owing to the fact that there is a certain likeness between the outline of the blot and that of a rhinoceros.

As indicated by this example, a reference to likeness in some respect is, however, often not enough to explain why episodic thinking is given a certain direction by perceptual experience, for one thing is usually like countless others in one respect or other. Normally, one has to appeal to some other factor, like a desire of the subject. For instance, it may be the fact that I take an interest in rhinoceros that makes me 'see' the blot as such a crea-ture. In Chapter 4 I proposed that desires influence the direction of episodic thought by facilitating transitions from the subject matter of current thought to thoughts of the desired objective. The stronger the desire, the less of a resemblance between these is required for transition to take place. There is also a more indirect way in which the strength of a desire is relevant. The reappearance of thoughts of the desired objective is helped under way if it has been thought of rather recently and is comparatively fresh in memory. But the likelihood of this is greater if the desire is strong, since the objective of such a desire is more frequently thought of.

The second "uniting principle among ideas" (1739–40/1978: 10) that Hume mentions is that of *contiguity* (1739–40/1978: 11). Suppose that on some occasions you have per-ceived (with attention) two objects or events together (or have perceived two states of affairs to be the case), then, if you later perceive one of the objects or events, this tends to lead you to think of (something about) the other. Here the cause of the association lies not in likeness, but in the fact that in the past the things associated have occurred on the same occasion.

Two contiguous events may either be simultaneous or successive. Consider first a case in which they are simultaneous: the sight of a particular horse makes you call to mind the rider whom you have seen on the horse's back a number of times. Here calling to mind the rider will not take the form of thinking it true that he is sitting on the horse's back for that would blatantly contradict your visual experience. You will rather *imagine* him sitting there. When the contiguity is successive, there is of course not this obstacle to taking it for true that the consequent event will occur as long as only the antecedent one has occurred. We shall then take the representation as true, unless or until something makes us question it. It is not the case that it is first entertained before it is assented to. This is why we can so easily slip into thinking that something is the case against our better judgement.

According to Hume, it is only when contiguities are successive that we are led to assume causal connections between the relata (1739–40/1978: 75–6). He believes that, if in circumstances of kind C you have frequently perceived an event of type F (immediately) succeeding a contiguous event of type E, then, when you once again perceive an E-event in circumstances that you take to be C, you will automatically think of an F-type of event as occurring. The repeated experience of such "a regular order of contiguity and succession" or "constant conjunction" (1739–40/1978: 87) between two types of event creates the sense—which grows stronger with each instance experienced—that the later event follows *necessarily* on the prior and makes us regard the prior event as *the cause* of the later.

Leaving aside the question of how adequate it is as an analysis of causation, Hume's conception of the associative link arising out of the experience of constant conjunction seems to conflate some things that should be kept apart. First, he believes that "the habit" of thinking of the consequent event upon observing the antecedent "must acquire new force from each instance [of the conjunction] that falls under our observation" (1739–40/1978: 130). That is, the probability of our thinking of the succeeding event upon perceiving its predecessor increases with each observed pair. But, secondly, Hume also claims that every new observation of such a conjunction adds vividness to the representation of the later event which follows on the perception of the former; it is like "a new stroke of the pencil, which bestows additional vivacity on the colours" (1739–40/1978: 135) of the representation of the succeeding event. To say that the vividness of a representation increases is clearly different from saying that the tendency for it to occur is strengthened. It may be, though, that there is a causal relation between the two, that if a type of representation occurs more persistently, this makes (some instances of) it more vivid. Thirdly, Hume apparently confuses both of these things with the degree of *belief* in the truth of the representation, for he says that the habit of association grows in respect of force until "our judgment arrives at a full assurance" (1739–40/1978: 130); and, notoriously, he equates belief in an idea with its "force" or "vivacity" (1739–40/1978: bk. I, pt. III, § vii).

Now, it is plainly absurd to identify the vividness of a representation, at least as I conceive it, with the endorsement of it as true, though it must be admitted that we have an inclination to be taken in by vivid representations. It is also mistaken to identify the strength of the habit or tendency to, in some sense, think *of* an F-type of event upon perceiving an instance of an E-type of event with the degree to which, having observed the E-event, we are inclined to think (it true) *that* an F-event will follow. In the case of simultaneous contiguity considered above, seeing a horse may make you think of—that is, imagine—the usual rider as sitting on the horse's back, but you will of course not think (it true) that he is sitting there, since this flouts your sense-experience. Similarly, suppose (again) that for a long time I have been accustomed to hearing one clock strike just after another, but that I have just heard from a highly reliable person that the second one has recently broken down. Then upon hearing the first clock strike I can scarcely suppress the sensuous representation of the second clock striking or avoid hearing it strike 'in the head', but I will not think that it will soon strike.

It seems, however, that, if one has no independent reasons to think that an F-type of event will not occur, an experience of the occurrence of an E-type of event, with which the former has been experienced to stand in a relation of successive contiguity, will lead one to think that an F-type of event will occur and not merely to imagine it occurring. I call this phenomenon the *mechanism of spontaneous induction*, the MSI. In more primitive beings who possess no capacity to collect independent evidence in order to make reflect-ive inductive judgements—for example to the effect that the second clock will probably not strike—the MSI will win the day. We have, however, developed the ability to review critically the constant conjunctions we experience and investigate whether they are accidental or there is something, for example causal, connecting the events conjoined. If the verdict is that a certain conjunction is accidental, this weakens the propensity to give credence to the representation of the occurrence of the succeeding event which is called forth by the perception of its predecessor.

Notwithstanding this ability for reflection, the deliverances of the MSI may be power-ful, especially if we have frequently experienced a successive contiguity. It is likely that repetition always disposes us to overrate the probability of the consequent event's hap-pening in the face of contrary evidence. This is particularly so if the consequent event is the object of strong attitudes—for this is another factor determining how prone we are both to represent sensuously a consequent event as occurring and to take this representa-tion as true.

It may even seem that this attitudinal significance exercises a more powerful influence on the formation of tendencies of association than does repetition, for when they pull in opposite directions, the former often prevails. Imagine, for instance, that I have gone by air on a number of occasions and that everything has gone well, but that this time the aeroplane catches fire as it is about to take off. The fire is put out before anyone is injured, but nonetheless it manages to give me a serious fright. Under these conditions, it appears likely that the next time I enter a cabin, or even think of entering one, I shall in the first place represent to myself not what it has been like when all has gone well, but the scene when the plane caught fire. I shall also be inclined to overestimate the probability of this event happening. The explanation of this is presumably that, though I have experienced the former more frequently, the latter has aroused stronger para-cognitive attitudes in me.

Akrasia and the MSI

This illustration can be utilized to demonstrate how the MSI can be the cause of weakness of will and that therefore the P-bias may have an accomplice. Suppose that I am going to somewhere rather distant and that, after reflecting on different means of transportation, I have formed a decisive desire to fly. However, when I enter the plane or arrive at the air-port or even as the time of the departure draws closer, I find sensuous representations of the plane catching fire crowding my mind, at the expense of contrary evidence. As a con-sequence, I am seized by a fear of flying that is out of proportion to the actual dangers involved and by a tendency to go back akratically on my decision to take a flight to my des-tination. What happens here is that, since my mind is to such a large extent preoccupied with representations of a plane catching fire, I do not sufficiently attend to the evidence supporting the great improbability of such an event. As a result, it will now seem to me much more probable that an accident will happen than that it will in a cool hour. Hence, my unreasonable fear and my impulse to choose another means of transportation.

So like the P-bias, the MSI can be responsible for *akrasia*-generating distorted episodic representations of reasons dispositionally stacked up in one's mind. This account anticipates the account of temporal partiality that I shall develop in Part III. For it will be found that the MSI has a part to play in the form of weakness of will that takes the shape of preferring a lesser, temporally closer sensory pleasure to a greater, more distant one.[9]

So much for how weakness of will can be fitted into a theory which takes reasons for action and desire to have an internal relation to desire to the extent that compliance with apparent reasons is constitutive of desiring. I have spent some time on this phenomenon because it will serve as a model of the irrationality of attitudes that will be examined in subsequent parts. Some will probably object that the sense in which I have permitted *akrasia* is too weak, that this phenomenon can consist in acting against one's best current apparent reasons, that is, reasons that one faces in the strongest sense. Michael Stocker, for one, holds such a view, and he attempts to defend it by distinguishing between "a cognitive range of attention" and "an affective range of attention":

> The better act is still in the agent's cognitive range of attention and is still seen as better. But now the demandingness and the allure of the act . . . is either not felt at all or not felt with any considerable strength. Either it has entirely left the agent's affective range of attention; or if it is still there, it is there less vividly than the lesser act. (1989: 217)

However, I do not understand what could be meant by "an affective range of attention". In my view, attention is a cognitive or conceptual state, an act of thinking. Something affective or felt can only be an *effect* of attention (e.g. the more you attend to a pleasurable prospect, the more anticipatory joy you feel). Consequently, I do not think Stocker has succeeded in explaining how we could act contrary to the thrust of reasons that receive full (cognitive) representation at the time of acting.

Although most of the mechanisms that determine episodic thinking or representing—perceptual presence, logical entailment, common elements, experienced co-occurrence, and state of desire—do their work independently of the will, it should be kept in mind that representation can also be voluntarily controlled: there is such a thing as voluntarily thinking of something, imagining it, or visualizing it.[10] As we shall see, this is what makes possible the rationalist project of rectifying non-voluntary biases of representation. Prudentialists choose not to do this, but this would have been of no avail if dispositional belief in truth, independent of episodic expression, were the ground of para-cognitive attitudes.

---

[9] In his account of weakness of will which resembles mine in emphasizing the importance of selective attention or focus (1987: 87 ff.), Mele points to a factor that I shall discuss in Part III under the name of the bias towards the near, namely what he calls "the proximity of reward". This designates the fact that "a desire for a 'reward' of a prospective action, other things being equal, acquires greater motivational force as the time for the reward's achievement approaches" (1987: 85). Moreover, Mele—to my mind plausibly—suggests that the proximity of reward performs its function by affecting the direction of attention: "attention to the 'consummatory' or 'arousing' features of a desired item tends to increase as a function of the increasing proximity of the reward" (1987: 90). This is likely to bring along changes in the balance of motivational forces, since "increased motivation tends to be a partial function of this increased attention" (1987: 90).

[10] Note that the fact that episodic thinking is influenced by desire does not mean that it occurs voluntarily. That my possession of a certain desire was a causal condition of my blushing does not make the blushing voluntary.

PART III

Rationality and Temporal Neutrality

A man who sees too far, who is contemporary with the *whole* future, can no longer act or even move . . .

(E. M. Cioran)

14

INTRODUCTION: THE NOTION OF A TEMPORAL BIAS

THE stage is now set for an inquiry into what para-cognitive attitudes are rational in the light of philosophical reflection on certain general aspects of the world. I have tried to prepare the ground for this inquiry by examining the nature of attitudes in Part I and rationality with respect to them in Part II. In this part, I embark on the project of finding out whether it is cognitively rational to prefer (wish or hope for) one state of affairs rather than another merely because there is a difference in their temporal locations, for example that one is nearer in the future than the other. If it is, there are forms of *temporal partiality* that are cognitively rational, but if it is not, a *temporal neutrality* is a requirement of cognitive rationality.

If it is cognitively irrational to be temporally partial, as I shall contend, it follows, in the terminology explained in Chapter 11, that it would be relatively irrational for a rationalist not to be temporally neutral. But it is another thing whether it could be relatively rational for a prudentialist (fulfilment-maximizer) to exhibit this partiality. For the time being, I confine myself to the domain of prudence where acts and their consequences are considered only in so far as they affect oneself, that is, the fulfilment of one's own desires, since, as will transpire, it is in the case of one's own life that the temporal partialities are clearest. Prima facie, it might seem evident that to display at least some forms of temporal partiality—for example towards the near future—would be relatively irrational also given the prudentialist aim. For, surely, if one seeks to maximize the fulfilment of one's own life, it cannot matter when in one's life a quantity of fulfilment obtains: what is of sole importance is how great the fulfilment is. However, it might be generally true that, if one strives to purge one's attitudes of every trace of this form of temporal partiality and, once a state of neutrality is attained, endeavours to preserve it, one's life will contain less fulfilment than it would were one to leave one's natural temporal biases to some extent untrimmed. If this is the case—and in Chapter 17 I shall attempt to explain how it could be so—then it would be relatively irrational for prudentialists to try to attain and maintain a state of perfect temporal neutrality.

It might be wondered how I can censure such temporal biases as cognitively irrational when I have disowned the possibility of a critique of the irrationality of para-cognitive attitudes that extends beyond a critique of the irrationality of their cognitive bases. For there is in fact, and so it is not irrational to think that there is, *some* difference between two events which happen at numerically distinct times, and it is at least *conceivable* that for some subjects this difference suffices to make a difference in respect of their attitudes to the events. This must be conceded, but it could still be true that, given how *we* actually seem to be, it is *very improbable* that we would respond differently to purely temporal differences. The reason for this may well have to do with these differences being purely relational and not ones of 'quality'.

Although such recognitions of mere differences in timing by themselves conceivably *could* be the bases of temporal partiality, I shall maintain that this is in fact not so with respect to our partiality. If such differences in timing by themselves were the root of our temporal partiality, we should expect this partiality to rear its head not only when one considers one's own life, but to an equal extent when one considers the lives of others, for these are no less subject to time. But, as will transpire, this is not so. (Compare: in the foregoing chapter, we noted that the P-bias is a bias not towards the present, but towards what each of us perceives of it.) The ground for this partiality lies in a mechanism that is at work primarily when each of us views our own existence unravel through time. I hope to make it credible that this mechanism is inimical to rational deliberation. This is why I shall condemn our temporal biases as being cognitively irrational. It follows that if *we* are rationalists, we shall be rationally required to be temporally neutral, but that will not be so if we are prudentialists (or satisfactionalists of any other sort).

Two Temporal Biases

To be a bit more specific about our temporal partiality, there are two forms of it, or two temporal biases, the cognitive rationality of which I shall examine in particular. The first bias can be explained by the following example. Suppose that you face the option of having a smaller sensory pleasure in a minute or a somewhat greater one in an hour—for example of being served a smaller portion of ice-cream in a minute or a somewhat larger one in an hour (note that the option concerns experiences that you will have yourself). Suppose further that you have reason to believe neither that your desire for the pleasure will be stronger at one time than at the other nor that it is less probable that you will have the opportunity to enjoy the pleasure if you postpone it. In situations like this it often happens that subjects show a definite preference for having the smaller pleasure sooner. Apparently, they prefer to receive sooner something that will give them smaller pleasure than to receive later something that will give them a somewhat greater pleasure simply for the reason that they will enjoy the former *sooner*. Parfit calls such a preference *a bias towards the near (future)* (1984: 124). As a shorthand term, I shall use 'the N-bias'.

An objector might point out that in actual fact if one delays the enjoyment of the pleasure, it will normally be somewhat less probable that it will come to be: the risk that something will prevent the pleasure from materializing will be slightly greater. This is true, and it is admittedly very hard to devise a realistic example in which one can be quite sure that there is no distorting factor, such as a difference in probability. Nonetheless, it is implausible to put down the whole effect to the operation of such factors. The preference in favour of having one pleasure in a minute rather than another in an hour may be quite marked, while the risk that one will lose the pleasure by postponing it may be only marginally greater. Moreover, it has been found that if the source of the pleasure is actually perceived by the subject, the desire to have it sooner grows in strength,[1] though the (subjective) probability of its coming into the subject's possession could scarcely be held to be affected by this fact. I take it then to be clear that the preference to have a pleasure sooner cannot be fully accounted for in terms of some rational estimate of probability. At least partially, it is somehow occasioned by the mere thought of this pleasure occurring at a time that is closer to one's present. We do spontaneously exhibit a bias towards the near.

The question I intend to discuss in the next chapter is whether it is cognitively irrational to be subject to the N-bias. I shall contend that this bias indeed is irrational. My strategy will be to reach this conclusion by trying to construe the N-bias as the upshot of representional mechanisms of the sort studied in the context of weakness of will in Part II. In Chapter 16 I shall let another temporal bias, *the bias towards the future*, the F-bias—that is, our tendency to be more concerned about what happens in the future than in the past— undergo a similar treatment.

What the N-bias and F-bias have in common is that they are both tendencies to adopt different attitudes to things simply for the reason that they stand in different temporal relations to *one's present*. The N-bias and F-bias thereby represent forms of a temporal partiality that (though, as we shall soon see, somewhat misleadingly) could be called *perspectival* because they crucially depend on the subject's viewing things from a certain point in time, the present. In the case of the N-bias, one state of affairs is preferred to another because it will materialize at a time that is closer to one's present—a time indexically identified—than is the time at which another will be realized. And in the case of the F-bias, something affects one more because, in relation to one's present, it is in the future rather than in the past.

Some Strange Temporal Biases

It is possible to imagine a temporal partiality that is non-perspectival or *absolute*. Consider somebody who cares equally about all the parts of her life, with one exception: she is indifferent to what happens to her on Tuesdays. For instance, she would prefer having pain on a Tuesday to having pain on any other day, even though it would be much more severe if it were felt on a Tuesday. Such a preference is not perspectival, for the fact that certain days are Tuesdays does not depend on their having a particular relation to what is currently one's present.

---

[1] See e.g. the experiments reported by Brandt (1979: 62).

This is a modification of an example Parfit provides (1984: 123–4). He describes somebody who is indifferent to what happens to him on *future* Tuesdays. This man "cares equally about all the parts of his future", with one exception: "he never cares about possible pains and pleasures on a *future* Tuesday". "Throughout every Tuesday he cares in the normal way about what is happening to him." For this reason his attitude is not *purely* absolute. It has a perspectival element in that he cares about what happens to him on Tuesdays when they are *present*, but not when they are still future in relation to the present. Parfit presents this case to persuade us that an attitude can be *intrinsically* irrational, that is, can possess an irrationality which is not derivative from any irrationality in respect of the beliefs on which it rests. Thus, he assumes that his individual's attitude is not due to any false or superstitious beliefs about Tuesdays, or about anything else.

I think it is instructive to compare this "Future-Tuesday-Indifference" to a "Future-Tuesday-Incredulity". Consider someone who has normally inductive beliefs about what will happen to him in the future will be like, except when it happens on future Tuesdays. For instance, he believes that were he in the future to put his finger in a naked flame, he will feel intense pain, except if he were to do it on Tuesdays. He is not spontaneously inclined to believe anything about what he will feel on Tuesdays. So, he does not suspend his belief about what he will feel on future Tuesdays because he has any peculiar beliefs about the significance of a day being a Tuesday, or anything else.

Is this absence of belief irrational? Not if the mechanism of spontaneous induction is just a natural fact about us, and Humeans are right that we are not rationally justified in forming beliefs in accordance with it. If we do not have reason to form inductive beliefs that we shall feel pain if we put our finger in a naked flame on other days, we are not irrational if we fail to have this belief about future Tuesdays, even if we see no relevant difference between this day and other days. Similarly, I claim, if we have no reason to feel the spontaneous concern we normally feel for ourselves in the future (it would beg the question to assume that there is such a reason), but this is just a natural fact about us. We would then not be irrational, or defy reason, if we failed to exhibit this tendency as regards future Tuesdays, though we see no relevant difference between Tuesdays and other days.

Parfit himself points out that "there is a large class of desires which cannot be irrational", a class which includes, for instance, desires concerned with sensations that are pleasant or painful/unpleasant. As regards the "strong desire not to hear the sound of squeaking chalk" that many people have, he writes: "This desire is odd, since these people do not mind hearing other squeaks that are very similar in timbre and pitch. But this desire is not irrational" (1984: 123). It is not irrational, although there is nothing to justify our dislike of the sound of squeaking chalk, but not of similar sounds. It is just the way nature has designed us. It is in this class of attitudes that I would like to put the Future-Tuesday-Indifference: a very odd, but not irrational attitude. I do not see why this class could not in theory include attitudes whose objects are not felt sensations.

There is an indisputable difference in the content of one's thought when one thinks that one will experience a certain pain on a future Tuesday rather than on a present Tuesday or on any other future weekday. *Conceivably*, somebody could be so wired up by nature that this combination of the features of being in the future and being a Tuesday so to speak eclipses his concern about a pain he would otherwise be concerned about, though each feature on its own would not do so.

So described, the Future-Tuesday-Indifference would be, as Parfit puts it, "a bare fact" about its subject. In this respect, it seems just like the dislike of squeaking chalk, but not of similar squeaks, for this too seems a bare fact. There is nothing to justify either attitude. Just as we have no reason to dislike the squeaking of chalk when we do not dislike similar squeaks, the imagined man has no reason—not even a bad one—to be indifferent towards pains he will feel on future Tuesdays, for, *ex hypothesi*, he has no eccentric beliefs about the significance of a day being a future Tuesday. Both attitudes are just quirks of nature. But if there is this resemblance between them, and since Parfit agrees to exempt the dislike of squeaking chalk from the charge of being irrational, I do not see why we should not also exempt the Future-Tuesday-Indifference from this charge.

To be sure, if we were to come across an instance of this Future-Tuesday-Indifference, we would be strongly inclined to brand it as irrational. I think the reason for this is that we would be strongly inclined to surmise that it is not ultimately intrinsic, like the dislike of squeaking chalk, but based on some strange and irrational belief about future Tuesdays. For it is so unlike other ultimately intrinsic attitudes to which we are acquainted (these having simple objects like present sensations). But suppose we were to become convinced that no apparent reasons were in the offing; then I think we would be more inclined to regard his indifference as psychologically incomprehensible or unintelligible than as irrational. Although it seems incomprehensible that anyone should be indifferent to what happens to him on future Tuesdays when he is concerned about what happens to him on all days, even Tuesdays, when they are present and on all other weekdays when they are future, we would have to accept that nature has so designed this man that this peculiar combination of features turns off his concern. Hence, were this strange intrinsic indifference to occur, there seems as little reason to brand it as (intrinsically) irrational as there is in the case of the dislike of squeaking chalk.

Like the Future-Tuesday-Incredulity, the Future-Tuesday-Indifference is likely to be bad in general for the subject. These tendencies may lead subjects to prefer what is in fact greater pains on future Tuesdays to smaller pains on other days, and this is something that they will regret when it is Tuesday and the pains are felt. Thus, the subjects may have reasons to try to rid themselves of these tendencies, but this is not to say that they are tendencies to form attitudes that are *intrinsically* (cognitively) irrational. There may be special circumstances in which they are advantageous for the subjects. Suppose, for example, that the subject who is indifferent to pains on future Tuesdays faces the choice of undergoing a painful operation on a Tuesday rather than on some other day. Then the choice to be operated upon on a Tuesday will leave him in a trouble-free instead of an anxious mood until the day of the operation arrives, and so may be the better choice (even if the operation will be a bit more painful). The point is essentially the same as one that Parfit makes earlier on, namely that the existence of an ineradicable desire, even if it is not rational, may "indirectly" provide one with a reason for choice and action (1984: 120–1).

I think the Future-Tuesday-Indifference is properly classified as 'ineradicable'. For, as we have seen, this indifference cannot be based on any irrational beliefs, because its irrationality would then not be *intrinsic*, but would instead be derived from the irrationality of the beliefs. If it is not belief-based, however, one is as little able to rid oneself of this indifference by ridding oneself of any irrational beliefs, as one is able to rid oneself of the dislike of squeaking chalk by eliminating any beliefs. These attitudes seem equally 'ineradicable'.

In conclusion, we have found no attitude that is *intrinsically* irrational. If the Future-Tuesday-Indifference is conceived as ultimately intrinsic, it seems indistinguishable from attitudes which are admittedly not irrational, but rather psychologically odd. I see no need, then, to go back on my resolution to do without intrinsically irrational desires. Moreover, I shall leave aside temporal biases that are, partially or wholly, absolute, since it is unrealistic to think that anyone is the victim of anything like them. My concern here will be with purely perspectival temporal biases that undoubtedly occur. By being temporally neutral I mean, as already stated, being free of all sorts of temporal partiality.

Some writers, for example Parfit, have taken temporal neutrality to cover something wider than merely the absence of such biases. They have characterized subjects as having a temporally neutral attitude when they have the prudentialist goal of wanting to fulfil the desires of their entire lives in proportion to their strength and co-satisfiability, irrespective of whether they are past, present, or future. This goes beyond temporal neutrality as I conceive it, for it forbids something that temporal neutrality in my conception allows, namely that one gratifies a present desire rather than a stronger future one, because one judges *the orientation or content* of the latter to be base, depraved, etc.

The more far-reaching doctrine—that entails temporal neutrality, but is not entailed by it—is about *the inter-temporal maximization* of one's own fulfilment. It will be discussed in Part IV in connection with personal neutrality and the importance of a desire belonging to *oneself*. (I shall conclude that it is not rationally required.) The reason for this order of exposition is that, when one tries to vindicate the claim that it is (cognitively) irrational to refuse to fulfil one of one's stronger future desire because one now evaluates its content negatively, one may do this by arguing that it shares the most important property with one's present desires, to wit, the property of belonging to oneself.

Perspectival Biases and the Nature of Time

Turning now to the perspectival temporal biases, the N-bias and the F-bias, my claim that they are cognitively irrational will appeal to representational distortions caused by beliefs about the timing of events occurring to oneself. There is nothing irrational in these temporal beliefs themselves, I maintain, as they correspond to something in our temporal experience (to the effect, e.g. that one event is further in the future). It is not impossible that these temporal biases turn out to be irrational, though the beliefs underlying them make no irrational claims about time. For if these temporal claims were sufficient to explain the biases, it would be mysterious why the biases pop up only as regards events occurring *to oneself*, while the temporal claims could be made about events happening to anyone. There must then be something that explains why these biases crop up only as regards one's own life, and this could be wholly responsible for their irrationality.

When we perceive events, we perceive them as occurring, and when we perceive things, we perceive them as existing. Let us say, generally, that when we perceive something, we perceive it as *being present*. I claim that our temporal experience is essentially an experience of something *being present* and then *having been present* as something else *is being present*, and so on. This presupposes the notion of what *will be present* as the tense which that which is now being present had when that which now past was present. Being *present* is a primary notion which enters into the characterization of the past and the future: thus, the past is that which has been present, and the future that which will be present.[2]

In this sense, the temporal order we experience has a certain (irreversible) *direction* consisting in events and states successively becoming present. The succession of non-simultaneous events does not just consist in them being lined up 'next to' each other along an axis with dates, as it were. There is nothing that is present on such an axis, and consequently nothing that has just been present and nothing that will be present next.

What we experience we experience as being present and, so, as being simultaneous with our experiencing of it. But this does not imply that what we experience really is present, for the experience may be illusory rather than veridical. Consider seeing events far off in outer space through a telescope. About these events D. H. Mellor asserts:

> I observe the temporal order in which they occur: which is earlier, which is later. I do *not* observe their tense. What I see through the telescope does not tell me how long ago those events occurred. (1981: 26; cf. 1998: 16)

Certainly, what I see "does not tell me how long ago those events occurred". Therefore, I do not observe their tense in Mellor's sense, since by "tensed" sentences or statements he means "those that say, by verbal tense or otherwise, how near or far from the present, past or future, something is" (1981: 4). But to describe the temporal ordering I observe between events as "which is earlier, which is later" is to underdescribe it. For I observe one event, *e*, as *occurring*, and then another event, *f*, as *occurring*, that is, I observe one event after another as becoming *present* or as becoming such that *a verb in the present tense* applies to it. Granted, this entails observing *e* as being earlier than *f*, but it entails more, since the later statement will be true forever, but '*e* is occurring and then *f* is occurring' is false when both events are in the past. What is left out by the former is precisely what is expressed by the present tense.

---

[2] Cf. Spinoza's claim: "As long as a man is affected by the image of anything, he will contemplate the thing as present although it does not exist . . . nor does he imagine it as past or future unless in so far as its image is connected with that of past or future time" (1675/1949: III. xviii. demonstration). Spinoza's claim seems to imply that when we *imagine* something, we imagine it as being present. I think this is true as well. David Cockburn attacks this thesis of the priority of the present by arguing that what is present, if it is of any duration, however short, is divisible into a part which has been present and a part which will be present, until we reach something of no duration (1997: 174). But this is not true of the *experienced* (or specious) present which is at issue here: it is of *some*—indeterminate—duration. (Tye suggests that it is "at least 30 msecs long", 2003: 87.)

(I think it is arguable that a 'tenseless' understanding of relations like *being earlier than* presupposes an understanding of the direction of time or of experiences of particular events successively becoming present, that is, that one could not understand sentences like '*e* is earlier than *f*', unless one has already acquired an understanding of sentences like '*e* is occurring and then *f* is occurring'. The former seems to be a generalization or an abstraction from sentences of the latter sort which report particular experiences of temporal ordering. But if so, the relations to which tenseless theorists appeal involve the very feature they want to avoid: time's direction or the successiveness of becoming present.)

So, I claim that we observe events as (successively) occurring or becoming (or remaining) present, which is what we express by verbs in the present tense. Normally, we can rightly assume that when we perceive events as occurring, they are really occurring now, that is, at the time at which we are doing the perceiving. But Mellor's telescope example shows that sometimes this assumption is mistaken: sometimes when we (now) perceive events as occurring, they occurred thousands and thousands of years ago. We are then victims of a sort of perceptual illusion that may lead the untutored to false beliefs, to the effect, for example, that the stages of a process of a star they perceive as successively occurring now are really occurring now.

This temporal illusion is importantly disanalogous to the spatial illusion of something's looking to be closer than it is. Things generally look to be a certain distance from 'here', which is where the observer is. In some cases, the distance is so small that they may be said to look to be in the same place as the observer is. In contrast, things are never perceived as being located any temporal distance from the present, that is, as having occurred sometime in the past or as about to occur sometime in the future; they are always perceived as occurring in the present, that is, at the same time as the perceiving of them occurs. (This is one reason why it may be misleading to talk about a temporal 'perspective' from the present.) So Mellor is right that his example shows that we do not observe tense in his sense, where this entails observing "how near or far from the present . . . something is". But it does not follow from this that we do not observe tense in the ordinary grammatical sense in which it is something expressed by the tenses of verbs, for we do experience things as being present (now). My thesis is, then, that our temporal experience essentially involves experiencing events as successively being present. This is what I call the direction of (things in) time.

Parfit portrays (1984: 178) those who deny "time's passage" or "the objectivity of temporal becoming" as asserting that " 'here' and 'now' are strictly analogous" in the manner they refer to a place and a time, respectively: 'here' refers to the place at which this instance or token of 'here' is occurring, just as 'now' refers to the time at which this instance or token of 'now' is occurring. But there are here important disanalogies.

To begin with, 'here' refers to the particular place at which the producer of the token is situated. There are indefinitely many other places at which she could have been instead and at some of which other subjects are simultaneously situated. So, if we know only that a spatial world is experienced by some subjects in it, we cannot deduce what is 'here' for any of them. It would be absurd to argue that what is here in this spatial world is what is here for these subjects in it. For what is here for these subjects is not likely to be the same for all, as it is determined by their individual locations in space. Consequently, it is plausible to argue that, if there were no subjects in space, there would be no here in it (nor anything to the left or right, or near or distant, since these are relative to a here). In contrast, if we know that a temporal world is experienced by subjects in it, we can deduce what is now or present for these subjects. For in this case it is quite plausible to argue that what is now in this world is now for these subjects in it. No further information about their individual temporal location is needed for this inference. It follows that the argument that, if there were no subjects in time, there would be no now is correspondingly weakened. So, the assumption should be questioned that the parallel between the indexicals 'here' and 'now' shows that what is designated by the latter is subjective in the same way as what is designated by the former.[3]

Furthermore, even if 'now' could be replaced by 'the time at which this token of "now" is occurring', we have not got rid of the present tense. For this—the so-called token-reflexive—reference of a token to itself is possible only when the token *is now being produced*. In other words, 'this token of "now"' means 'this token of "now" *now being* produced', and this employs the present tense. Token-reflexive reference is only possible to a token one currently is in the process of producing.

Mellor has now given up this kind of account because it fails to cater for the truth of 'There are no tokens now' (1998: ch. 3.3). Instead he proposes that "what makes '*e* is present' true at any *t* is *e*'s being located at *t*" (1998: 2). Here '*e* is present' is meant to be the *proposition* that *e* is present, that is, a certain *type* of thought-content, of which individual beliefs, statements, etc. can be tokens. I have some misgivings, however, about saying that the proposition that *e* is present, as opposed to tokens of it occurring at *t*, is made true at *t* by *e*'s being located at *t*.

But my view of temporal experience gives me no reason to object to this way of stating the truth-conditions of tensed beliefs for, as Mellor concedes, it does not imply that they are "reducible to, or replaceable by" tenseless beliefs (1998: 58). As he points out (1998: 64), tensed beliefs are necessary for us to act intentionally. For example, my intention to start when the traffic light switches to green will only lead me to act if I acquire the belief that it is now switching to green. Suppose this belief is acquired on the basis of perceptual experience. On my view, the story might then be: I see the light switching to green and, having no reason to think otherwise, I take it for granted that what I now see as occurring is occurring simultaneously with my seeing, and form the belief that the light is now switching to green. If my assumption about the veridicality of my perceptual experience is correct, my belief is true.

Mellor would reject this explanation because he does not believe that the content of my temporal experience can be (present) tensed. To explain why our perceptual experience

---

[3] Equally questionable is the view that tensed statements are subjective in the sense of being perspectival and describing reality from a particular subject's point of view. Moreover, notice that this claim about the temporal categories of the present, past, and future being subjective is different from the Kantian sort of claim that time itself, even if tenselessly construed, is subjective, or mind-dependent, and is no feature of reality as it is in itself. The latter issue is irrelevant in the present context, for even if our temporal experience were mind-dependent that would not undercut the cognitive rationality of our temporal biases. Compare: it is not irrational to care about, e.g. pleasures and pains because they are mind-dependent; the aspect of them we care about—namely, how they feel—need not be mind-independent for us to care about it.

gives us now-beliefs he instead appeals to the survival-value of this mechanism: "It is only the habit of letting our eyes give us now-beliefs that lets us survive" (1998: 68). But this is not so: our survival chances would be as good if our experience instead had induced us to believe that what we perceive occurred a moment earlier than we perceive it (as is indeed the case). Mellor's explanation fails to account for why we acquire now-beliefs instead of such immediate past-beliefs. I can easily explain this, however: we acquire now-beliefs and not immediate past-beliefs because we perceive things as occurring, not as having occurred.

All the same, Mellor and I agree that now-beliefs—and other tensed beliefs—can be true and well-grounded, though we would spell this out in different ways. If so, then, to the extent these beliefs are responsible for our perspectival temporal biases,[4] these biases cannot be cognitively irrational. But the rationality of the underlying beliefs does not suffice to rescue the biases from the charge of being cognitively irrational. For, as already indicated, the basis of these biases involves more than tensed beliefs about temporal positions. If they had rested solely on such beliefs, the biases should be just as pronounced when we regard the lives of others as our own lives, for the lives of others are equally in time. But they are much more pronounced in our own case. So, something else is required to account for our biases, and this is a place where irrationality could creep in.

I shall argue that this 'something else' is representational distortions which are a feature of viewing one's own experiences spread out in the past, present, and future. One might say that the N-bias and the F-bias implicate the bias towards oneself, to be examined in Part IV. As these distortions are incompatible with the conditions of rational deliberation, these biases are indeed cognitively irrational. In the last chapter of this part, I shall go on to ask whether we should therefore attempt to rid ourselves of them. As will transpire, the answer will not be the same for rationalists and prudentialists. Thereby, we countenance a first dilemma over whether to keep a fundamental para-cognitive attitude, provided we are attracted to both rationalism and prudentialism.

For the time being, however, I only wish to question Parfit's assumption (1984: § 68) that the cognitive rationality of perspectival biases hinges on the metaphysics of time. It needs to be questioned, first, because tensed beliefs are indispensable, true, and well-grounded, irrespective of the outcome of the metaphysical debate about whether the tensed or the tenseless view of time is right. (On the other hand, if these beliefs were false and irrational had the tenseless view been correct, the rationality of the biases would depend upon the outcome not being that this view is correct.) Secondly, because the rationality of these tensed beliefs is not sufficient to ensure that these biases are not cognitively irrational, since something else is needed to account for them, and this extra element may inject irrationality into the biases.

---

[4] For want of a better term, I shall keep calling the N- and F-biases perspectival, though we have seen that it is misleading to talk as though things are experienced from the perspective of the present.

15

THE IRRATIONALITY OF THE BIAS TOWARDS THE NEAR

To find out whether the N-bias is cognitively rational, and so whether rationalists could allow themselves to be subject to it, let us compare three situations of choice. Suppose that (not irrationally) I strongly prefer strawberry to vanilla ice-cream, so that if I were facing the option of *at the same time* having either strawberry-flavoured or vanilla-flavoured ice-cream, I would without hesitation choose the former. (1) The choice I actually face is, however, between having vanilla ice-cream within a few minutes or having to wait another hour for the strawberry-flavoured delight. The slight discomfort caused by delaying the gratification of my desire for ice-cream is counter-balanced by the pleasure of anticipating the coming enjoyment of the strawberry ice-cream, for I have reasons to be as certain that I shall experience this enjoyment, if I choose it, as I have that I shall be served the vanilla ice-cream if that is what I prefer. Nevertheless, I now opt for the vanilla alternative. This pattern is (regrettably) familiar; it recurs often when we face analogous choices.

(2) Suppose instead that I do not face this choice now, but that I predict well in advance that I shall find myself in a situation of this kind. In order to form a well-grounded opinion about what I should choose when the situation arises, I try to imagine, as vividly as possible, myself being in this future situation and facing the choice. Given the way the situation of choice is described, I believe it highly likely that what I would *now* want with respect to this future situation is that I choose to be served, and am served, the strawberry ice-cream, for this is what would provide me with the greater pleasure. Note that I am here not trying to predict what I *would* want most *were* I in that future situation; I am trying to decide what I should *now* (decisively) desire that I do were I in it. I may well know, given what was said in connection with (1), that when I shall actually be in the situation I shall choose the vanilla ice-cream, and yet want now that I make the strawberry choice.

Could I regard both of these choices or preferences as cognitively rational? It may be held that I could if cognitive rationality is relativized to time: when I look at matters in advance, it is correct to judge that the strawberry choice is the rational one, whereas when the situation arrives, the right judgement is that the other choice is the rational one. However, if rationality is thus relativized, it would not be rational to make plans for future situations of the kind we have been discussing, for, inevitably, when they arrive, it will be rational to dissent from any rational plan formed in advance. But, although it is natural to think that such planning could be rational, it is not incontestable. So, this does not clinch the matter.

Let us therefore turn to another situation. (3) I here *imagine* facing the choice not at some future time, but *now* (I do not in fact face it). It seems to me clear that here, just as in (2), I would want that I choose the strawberry ice-cream—though, again, I may well know that were I *actually* in the situation I would plump for having vanilla ice-cream served within a few minutes. It is most unlikely that the fact that the situation is imagined to obtain now rather than in the future would make a relevant difference. Certainly, a difference as regards the temporal relation to the present moment *is* a difference, and it is not *logically* impossible that imaginative representations of things as being distinct merely with respect to such relations have different effects on our attitudes. Yet, given common-sense knowledge of what persons are actually like, it appears very improbable that anyone should think that this difference in timing by itself makes a difference.

But my judgement in (3), that it is irrational not to wait for the strawberry ice-cream cannot be reconciled with a judgement of mine in (1) that it is not irrational to choose to be served the vanilla ice-cream in a couple of minutes, by relativizing them to different times—the kind of reconciliation suggested above for the judgements in (1) and (2). For here the time is the same: the present. Nor could we claim that there is any relevant difference between the situation which is imagined in (3) and actual in (1), for *ex hypothesi* there is not: any relevant feature of the situation in (1) should—if possible—be incorporated into my imaginative representation in case (3). Therefore, one of my judgements must go by the board.

Which one should go? If we disown my judgement in (3), it would seem that we are committed to something like this: imaginative representations of an actual situation are necessarily inadequate; they miss something, which makes judgements based on them unreliable. This sceptical view seems hard to accept. Certainly, a situation imagined will be one imagined, and not (thereby) an actual one, but that is not a feature of the *content* of the imagination, rendering it unfit to match reality.

On the other hand, if we claim that the vanilla-choice I judge irrational in (3) *is* irrational, we must offer an explanation as to how *actually being* in the situation could entice one to make an irrational choice. I think this obligation can be discharged in the following way: actually being in a situation puts the P-bias, the bias towards the perceived, into operation, and this may distort one's representation of the situation in ways it will not be distorted when the situation is merely imagined. We have assumed that the discomfort or unpleasant tension of postponing the gratification of the desire for ice-cream is balanced by the pleasurable anticipation of the strawberry delight, but this requires that the prospect of this enjoyment is held in mind. But when the discomfort of having an unfulfilled desire is not merely *imagined*, but *actually felt* (as it will be provided the desire is sufficiently intense), the P-bias is brought into play, with the result that this discomfort comes to loom large in my mind, while representations of what it will be like to taste the strawberry ice-cream—how superior this taste is to that of the vanilla—will recede into the background. This will diminish the anticipatory pleasure of tasting the strawberry ice-cream and the preference to taste it. Consequently, I may form a dominant desire to have the vanilla ice-cream and thereby get rid of the unpleasant feeling of tension as soon as possible. In (3), where this discomfort is merely imagined, along with the taste-impressions, where the competitors both have the same status of imaginative representations, it is much easier to distribute attention fairly between them. Hence, at the root of the N-bias we discover the P-bias.[1]

In the light of this, it is intelligible why the N-bias is more pronounced when the lesser, closer pleasure itself, or a picture of it, is perceived. The P-bias then ensures that this source of pleasure is represented in great detail; consequently, the desire for the pleasure, and the feelings of frustration, will be strong. If a picture of the greater, distant pleasure is perceived along with a picture of the lesser one, it has been found that the capacity to resist the N-bias grows. The explanation of this phenomenon suggested by my account is that perceiving the picture of the greater pleasure helps one to maintain the expectation of it. However, it has also been found that if both sources of pleasure are perceived, the tendency to delay gratification again decreases. This may be due to the actual presence of the pleasures making the desire for pleasure grow to such a strength that delaying gratification becomes very hard (cf. Brandt, 1979: 62).

The Contribution of the MSI to the N-bias

I doubt, however, that this is a complete explanation of the N-bias. The MSI, the mechanism of spontaneous induction, is probably at work as well. Generally, it is the case that if one tries to predict what will happen in the further future, the events predicted will come out as less probable than if one tries to predict events in the nearer future. Thus, if one thinks of some event in the rather distant future, then, in accordance with the MSI, one will be spontaneously inclined to think that it is less probable than it would seem to one were it nearer in the future. By itself the MSI will not be able to overrule a reflective conviction to the effect that the more distant event is no less probable, but in a situation where one is under the pressure of feelings of an unfulfilled desire, it may facilitate one's wishfully thinking of the distant event as less probable, so that one is free to satisfy one's desire as soon as possible.

The contribution of the MSI becomes clearer in the negative case in which one prefers, for example, to undergo a greater pain in the more distant future to having a lesser pain in the near future. Clearly, if one prefers to postpone pain (at the price of making it worse),

---

[1] Cf. Shelly Kagan's suggestion (1989: 283–91) that it is the fact that one's beliefs about one's (more distant) future are 'pale' that makes one partial towards the near. By the way, it lies close at hand to hypothesize that also our bias to the *spatially* near—our tendency to favour beings in our neighbourhood to those in more distant places—rests, at least partially, on the P-bias, on the fact that the former are more regularly present before our senses. This mechanism will be further discussed in Part IV.

one does not fulfil the desire not to feel pain; so postponement does not bring along a bonus in the shape of ridding oneself of feelings of dissatisfaction and obtaining feelings of satisfaction in their stead. The explanation of the N-bias in the negative case cannot then appeal to the P-bias alone. I would insist, however, on the P-bias having a part to play here too, but it needs the assistance of the MSI. In the negative case, we are under the influence of sensations of a frustrated aversion towards pain (and possibly of sensations which are part of the felt somatic pattern of fear). The P-bias here consists in these feelings interfering with accurate representations of what the pains will be like, representations of differences in their intensity and the like. But it would be implausible to think that this by itself could mislead one to the extent of making one think that the more distant pain is no greater.

A more plausible conjecture is that the unfulfilled desire not to feel pain, and the unpleasant feelings to which it gives rise, with the assistance of the MSI, issue in one's wishfully thinking that by postponing the pain one increases the possibility of escaping it. Being in the grip of an unfulfilled desire not to feel pain, one looks around for ways of fulfilling it, and, given that one's power of reflection is hampered by sensations of frustration, the MSI manages to lead one to think that this might perhaps be achieved if one postpones the pain. Hence, at the basis of the N-bias we again we find the P-bias collaborating with the MSI.

But, as has been noticed by Parfit (1984: 160–1) among others, we also exhibit the opposite tendency: when we have become convinced that a certain pain is inescapable, we sometimes want to undergo it as soon as possible, in order to have it over and done with. How could this tendency exist side by side with the opposite effect of the N-bias? The explanation seems to be the following. When one's considered judgement that one cannot evade an imminent pain by pushing it further into the future is so firm that one cannot—with the help of the MSI—trick oneself into thinking that one might somehow get around it (when, for instance, one could only postpone it for a short period of time), one wants to undergo it as soon as possible. If one cannot reduce the intensity of the fear and of the feelings of the unfulfilled desire to avoid the pain, by making the pain appear less likely, one shifts tactic to wanting to reduce their duration. This tendency is thus complementary to the operation of the N-bias: when the N-bias cannot do its work because one's reflective judgement is incorruptible and withstands the pressure of the MSI, the tendency to get the unpleasant thing over and done with comes into operation.

Analogously, there is a propensity to postpone the enjoyment of a pleasure: when eating something delicious, one may be inclined to save the best bit to the last.[2] It is not hard to understand how this inclination can be reconciled with the operation of the N-bias. The anticipation of a future pleasure can generate two emotions: one can be glad or pleased that the future has this pleasure in store or, if a strong desire for the pleasure is aroused, one can long for the pleasure and feel the discomfort of unfulfilled desire. Suppose that the latter emotion is not felt—this may be so because one already is enjoying something pleasant (though perhaps of a smaller magnitude). Then it is natural to try to postpone the

---

[2] Cf. Slote's claim that "a good may itself be greater for coming late rather than early in life" (1983: 25). But Slote's examples involve complications arising from the fact that it is worse to be bereft of a good to which one has grown accustomed than to be without it when one has never enjoyed it (presumably because in the first case one is able to represent more vividly what being in possession of it is like).

pleasure anticipated, for in this way one prolongs the positive state of gladness or joy. (This, of course, presupposes that one is certain that one will not lose the pleasure by postponing it.) On the other hand, if one's predominant emotion is one of frustration (or of fear of losing the pleasure), one will naturally try to enjoy it as soon as possible—in other words, the N-bias comes into operation. It can now be seen why, when commencing the explication of the N-bias, I assumed that the desire for pleasure be so strong that frustration is felt. If this is not so, the inclination to postpone a (certain) pleasure prevails.

Against this background, there is nothing puzzling about the fact that sometimes when we fix the temporal order of a pleasure and a pain, we prefer to have the pain first. In this way, we reduce the duration of the feelings of the frustrated desire not to feel pain, or the fear of pain, and prolong the pleasurable anticipation of the pleasure.

Parfit argues that an account of the N-bias which, like mine, construes it as resulting from "some failure of representation, or some false belief" (1984: 161) does not succeed in explaining this bias, at least not completely. He rejects it as a full explanation on the strength of the following test case (1984: 161–2). A volunteer is to make up his mind whether to endure some pain for the sake of some pleasure. He knows that after making his decision he will be given a pill that causes him to forget his decision. (The purpose of this is to ensure that the tendency which opposes the N-bias will not come into play.) The volunteer is given a detailed description of what the pleasure and pain will be like, and he is asked to imagine as vividly as he can what it would be like to experience these hedonic sensations. He is, however, not informed about "the *timing* of this pain and this pleasure until just before he makes his decision" (1984: 161). Parfit imagines that the volunteer is first told that the pain will be immediate and the pleasure postponed for a year and that, in the light of this information, the subject mildly prefers to have neither. But then it is divulged that he has been misinformed: in point of fact, the timing is the reverse. Parfit thinks it likely that this will cause the volunteer's preference to change: he will now decide that it is worth enduring the pain for the sake of enjoying the pleasure. This reversal of preference cannot, Parfit claims, be the result of any changes in the vividness of the representations of the pleasure and the pain, since the subject had already imagined them as vividly as he could prior to being told about their timing.

I believe, however, that if the timing of the hedonic sensations is really disclosed *just* before the volunteer is to make his decisions, these taking place in rapid succession, then Parfit is wrong to think that there will be a change in his preferences. When the subject is asked to imagine vividly what the hedonic sensations will be like as a preparation to making up his mind whether the pleasure is worth the cost of the pain, he will probably—prior to knowing anything about their timing—make some preliminary decision simply on the basis of their respective intensity and duration. If he is required to make each of his two decisions *immediately* after being given each bit of information about the timing of the sensations, I am pretty sure that both decisions will coincide with the preliminary judgement. For the new information is allowed no time to work. So neither of the two conflicting pieces of information about the temporal positions of the hedonic sensations will cause any alteration in the subject's preferences (assuming, of course, that the postponement of one sensation for a year will not affect the subject's rational estimate of the probability of its occurrence).

Suppose instead that, in the case of each decision, some time is allowed to pass between the volunteer's being told about the timing and his having to make the decision; then the outcome Parfit envisages is not unlikely. But it could now be contended that this is due to the fact that the two pieces of information about the timing of the sensations have had time to influence the extent to which they are currently represented, so that, though they were first fairly represented, there is subsequently a distortion in favour of the closer sensation. Hence, I surmise that Parfit's example will seem to be a counter-instance to my explanation of the N-bias only if one conflates the two specifications of it that I have tried to separate.

On my explanation, awareness of something happening to one as being closer to the present does not directly cause a stronger desire. Rather, the desire evoked by this awareness is assisted by two intervening factors that distort representation, the P-bias, which pushes representations of what is not perceived in the background, and the MSI which lures one to see the more distant as less probable. On the strength of this explanation, the question at the outset of this chapter can be answered: the N-bias which governs my choice in case (1) is cognitively irrational. For it is irrational to give in to the P-bias which magnifies one's present frustration out of proportion and to the MSI which tempts one to go against one's reflective probability judgements. Since the P-bias can be experienced only in one's own case, this explains why the N-bias is much weaker, if not entirely absent, when one considers the future experiences of others, just as it is in the cases (2) and (3) described at the outset (because the P-bias exists only with respect to one's own *actual* present). That the N-bias shows up only in one's own case would be inexplicable if it were wholly due to the tense of some temporal belief.

Although it is of less consequence, it bears mention that we also exhibit a bias towards the near, as opposed to the more distant, *past*: we are more prone to think about, for instance, how we excelled, or disgraced ourselves, yesterday than last year. This is not due to the passage of time itself, but to the fact that it makes our memories fade and become less detailed, as already remarked in Chapter 13.[3] This in its turn decreases the power of our memories to call forth emotions and future recollections of the same event. Thus, the explanation of the bias towards the near past is similar to the explanation of the bias towards the near future in that it, too, appeals to the vividness of representation. The bias towards the near past may induce us to wish, irrationally, that we had refrained from a less disgraceful act in the immediate past rather than a more disgraceful act in the more distant past. But such wishes are of less consequence, since we know we can do nothing to affect the past.

---

[3] Cockburn objects that if we explain, e.g., the softening of grief, by the fading of memories, we are assuming that it "is not a completely appropriate development as a death recedes into the past" (1997: 31). But suppose that on the night after I have been informed of the death of a loved one, I fall into a coma and do not wake up until a year later. My memories are, however, as fresh as though the news were broken yesterday. Then, even if I am told that the event dates a year back, my grief will surely be as acute as if it had happened yesterday. Nor do I see any reason why my grief *should* be milder because the death is more distant in the past. This also applies to my reactions to events that do not personally affect me, for example my horror of genocides in the distant past: I cannot see why I should be less horrified simply because they are further back in history.

16

THE IRRATIONALITY OF THE BIAS TOWARDS THE FUTURE

PARFIT discusses another (perspectival) temporal bias that makes a stronger claim than the N-bias to be recognized as cognitively rational: *the bias towards the future*, the F-bias. We are the victims of the F-bias when the thought of, for example hedonic sensations "affects us more when they are in the future rather than the past" (1984: 160). In fact, we have already come across the workings of the F-bias when we noted the tendency to postpone pleasures and to get pains over and done with. If we prefer to have our pleasures ahead of us, and our pains in the past, it seems to be because the contents of our futures matter more to us than that of our pasts. So we want the better to be in the future and the worse in the past. Parfit provides a more striking illustration:

> I am in some hospital, to have some kind of surgery. This kind of surgery is completely safe, and always successful. Since I know this, I have no fears about the effects. The surgery may be brief, or it may instead take a long time. Because I have to co-operate with the surgeon, I cannot have anaesthetics. I have had this surgery once before, and I can remember how painful it is. Under a new policy, because the operation is so painful, patients are now afterwards made to forget it. Some drug removes their memories of the last few hours.
>
> I have just woken up. I cannot remember going to sleep. I ask my nurse if it has been decided when my operation is to be, and how long it must take. She says that she knows the facts about both me and another patient, but that she cannot remember which facts apply to whom. She can tell only that the following is true. I may be the patient who had his operation yesterday. In that case, my operation was the longest ever performed, lasting ten hours. I may instead be the patient who is to have a short operation later today. It is either true that I did suffer for ten hours, or that I shall suffer for one hour.
>
> I ask the nurse to find out which is true. While she is away, it is clear to me which I prefer to be true. If I learn that the first is true, I shall be greatly relieved. (1984: 165–6)

Generally, the F-bias is a propensity to prefer, hope, or wish that negative states of affairs, such as feeling pain, be in the past rather than in the future, while positive states of affairs, like feeling pleasure, be in the future rather than in the past (or a propensity to fear the reverse).

Parfit maintains that "most of us" would decline to regard this inclination as irrational (1984: 167).[1] At least, we are more likely to regard the F-bias as rational than the N-bias. For instance, Parfit's patient could very well adduce as *his reason* for preferring, hoping or wishing that he has had the longer operation that, since it is in the past, he does not have to go through it. That is, he may well present this as something justifying his preference. In contrast, when one succumbs to the N-bias and chooses the smaller, nearer pleasure, one would be loath to cite as *one's reason* for this choice the fact that the pleasure was nearer. For one would have grave doubts about the justifying force of this consideration. Certainly, the fact that the smaller pleasure was nearer was (roughly speaking) *the explanatory reason* why one chose it. But this explanation does not seem to explain by citing a reason that one views as justifying; it smacks more of an explanation of why one was weak and gave in to a temptation.

This debars me from using an argumentative strategy that I deployed in the preceding chapter. In analogy with the three situations depicted in the beginning of that chapter, consider the following two which are counterparts to (1) and (3): (1*) the hope, wish, or preference one would have were one actually in the patient's circumstances; and (3*) the hope, wish, or preference that one would now have as regards what be true of one if one imagined, counterfactually, that one now were in the patient's place. With respect to (3*) I find that I would now hope, wish or prefer it to be true that I be in for a one-hour operation later on the same day. Thus, for me there is a conflict corresponding to the one we discovered in Chapter 15. But I suspect that many would disagree and be inclined to view my judgement as being tainted by my commitment to a certain account of the F-bias.

To be sure, we could make the point that, if the F-bias is cognitively rational, this would pose a threat for the rationality of planning for the future. For surely, looking ahead to my treatment, it would be rational for me to hope, wish, or prefer that I will undergo a one-hour operation in the more distant future rather than a ten-hour operation one day earlier, because that would make my life better. But one would have to grant that, if the F-bias is rational, this ordering would contradict a rational preference that one will endorse when the ten-hour operation is in the past.[2] As pointed out in the foregoing chapter, however, this is by no means a decisive objection; it is possible to cheerfully accept this consequence for future planning.

To determine whether the F-bias is rational, one must provide an account of its nature. So if, on my conception of rationality, it is to be made out as a cognitively irrational aberration, it must be shown to have its origin in irrational cognitive or representational processes. I now turn to the task of sketching what these processes might be.

---

[1] Cf. Richard Kraut (1972) who argues that it is not irrational not to care about pains that one has had in the past.

[2] Note that the situation is quite different if the conflicting judgements of rationality would be due, not merely to the passage of time, but to changes in one's character. For the latter can be forestalled; one can strive to keep one's character constant. But conflicts that arise simply as the result of the flow of time cannot be avoided or mitigated.

An Asymmetry between Anticipation and Retrospection

First of all, we must remind ourselves of the account of temporal experience given in Chapter 14, namely, that it is an experience of events successively becoming present. This experience shapes our mental states in various ways. In detailing these, we must, however, take precautions to exclude the influence of an irrelevant factor: the direction of causation which leaves room for our present actions to affect the future, but not the past.

Consider *impatiently longing* for the occurrence of something, for example the holiday trip that one will go on some months in the future. Imagine this concerns nothing that one can affect: it is fixed when one will go on the trip. Accordingly, longing for something is to have a wish; more precisely, it is to have the wish that the successive becoming—that I have claimed to characterize our temporal experience—is 'speeded up', so that the event longed for happens sooner. Therefore, it makes no sense to long impatiently for something past (though one can impatiently long for knowledge about it). True, the nostalgic person is said to long for the good old days, but this is not the sort of longing that makes you impatient. It is just a wish to be back in the good old days, not a wish to speed up the passing of time so that they become present sooner. Thus impatient longing is an attitude that is, in Parfit's words, "essentially forward-looking in a way which cannot be explained by the direction of causation" (1984: 170).

For our present purposes, however, the most important effect of temporal experience on our attitudes takes a route via imagination. When we imagine a temporal sequence, we imagine it in an order from that which earlier became or becomes present to that which later became or becomes present (and, as we shall see, in the first instance, from the present to the future), that is, in the order we have experienced it or will or would experience it.[3] Thus, if I imagine hearing a tune I have heard, I imagine hearing the notes in the order I heard them.

Consequently, when, owing to the bias towards the perceived, I imagine events extending from the perceived present, I imagine them extending *into the future*. The MSI, the mechanism of spontaneous induction, exemplifies our tendency to imagine things rolling on from the present into the future in the kind of order we have experienced them, for it consists roughly in imagining that the future will be like that which, in the past, followed upon what was like what is now the perceived present. If in the past one has noticed that one sort of situation, S1 (hearing a certain bell), is immediately succeeded by another sort of situation, S2 (being served food), one anticipates that the perceived present will develop into one of the type S2 if one has observed it to be of the type S1. Hence, one projects into the immediate future an order of events of a kind that one has experienced in the past.

Even when we have not been struck by any important similarity between the present situation and some past situation, so that the MSI cannot supply us with any specific representation of what the future will be like, our habituation to the direction of time

---

[3] Cf. Hume's observation: "We always follow the succession of time in placing our ideas, and from the consideration of any object pass more easily to that, which follows immediately after it, than to that which went before it" (1739–40/1978: 430). Note that he makes this observation in the context of explaining a "phenomenon" which in effect is the F-bias.

throws us into speculations, daydreams, or reveries about what will develop out of the present situation.

No doubt, we have been equipped with the MSI and more generally this future-directedness of our imagination because it is of great survival value. For, as the direction of causality is from the earlier to the later, it is the content of the future that we can affect by our present actions, whereas we cannot in the present cause anything to have happened in the past. So, the future-orientation of our imagination is useful in that it increases our chances of acting in well-planned ways.

It follows from the above that what we call (imaginatively) looking backward to some (past) experience is not parallel to looking forward to one. Consider what it would be to look backward to something as we can look backward to something we have passed in space. Suppose I am moving towards a tunnel. When I look ahead to it, I see it from one direction to the other. Then I pass through it, and when I look back, I see it in the reverse direction. In contrast when I look backward to some past experience, I do not (spontaneously) imagine it in an order *reverse* to that in which I went through it, that is, from end to beginning. For I do not imagine the past *extending or stretching out* 'backwards' from the present as I am in the habit of imagining the future extending or stretching out from the present (and as I can imagine what I have passed in space stretching out behind me from my present point). For instance, when I look back on the experience of seeing a film I have just seen, I do not imagine the film from end to beginning, stretching out from the recent to the more distant past. Obviously, I imagine seeing it from beginning to end, just as I saw it. Temporally extended events have so to speak a fixed entrance and exit, through which we pass in and out of them and through which our imagination also enters into and exits from them.

But then '(imaginatively) looking backward' to an experience takes the form of imagining being *at some time(s) in the past* and looking *forward* to the experience, seeing it in a future which stretches out from that point. So we do not from the present point spontaneously look backward to experiences in the past, as we look forward to them from the present time—though, with great effort, we could accomplish a parallel instance of backward-looking in which events are experienced in a reverse order and as stretching out backward from the present. What we call looking backward to an experience is normally looking forward to it from a point in the past that we imaginatively take up.

Parfit asks whether there could be a "backward-looking counterpart" to anticipation (1984: 174). He does not give a definite answer to this question, but merely remarks that there could conceivably be "retrospection" of past pleasures and pains that is just as pleasant and distressing as anticipation of future pleasures and pains. I believe, however, that my analysis shows that, strictly speaking, there could *not* be a backward-looking counterpart to anticipation. Such a counterpart would have to have two features. (1) When we engage in it, we would imaginatively see the past as stretching out from the present (in an order reverse to that in which it has been experienced), just as in anticipation (of the imminent future) we see the future stretching out from the present. (2) Just as the pleasure or distress of anticipation is pleasure or distress at what will happen, the pleasure or distress of retrospection must be pleasure or distress at what has happened.

As regards (1), I have ventured the opinion that, though this is not how we spontaneously imagine things, we could with the greatest effort imagine them in this way, which would be the reverse of that in which we have experienced them. Of course, we would not spontaneously react to such reverse representations with pleasure or distress, but even if we suppose we did (which is logically possible, I take it), this would not be a reaction to *what has happened* (as, according to (2), it must be), for nothing has happened in that (reverse) order. Thus, at this point, if not earlier, the parallel between anticipation and retrospection breaks down, and it breaks down because of the direction of time.

To imagine what has happened in the past, I must then adopt the point of view of a time earlier than the present from which I can look forward to it happening. This yields an explanation of why, in feeling a pain, I am much more likely to desire to be rid of it, that is to desire that my future does not contain it, than to wish that I had not felt it for so long in the past.[4] For I spontaneously imagine or anticipate the pain extending from the present into imminent future, and this gives rise to a desire to prevent this from occurring. In contrast, I have to adopt another point of view than the present one, a point of view of the past, in order to look forward to moments of pain that are now in the past. But this point of view is usually *optional*; it does not force itself upon me like the present. This imaginary point of view and what follows subsequent to it are therefore less lively. Consequently, they do not arouse any strong para-cognitive attitudes. In the rare circumstances in which such a non-actual point of view forces itself upon one, as in the case of a traumatic experience, what follows upon it does indeed arouse strong reactions of fear, etc.

It is easily explicable in evolutionary terms why we normally do not automatically adopt a vicarious point in the past as the starting-point of imaginative representation, but rather proceed simply to imagine them from the perceived present as the point of origin. Again, it has to do with the fact that, while we are often able to influence what the future will be like, the past is fixed. There is a price to be paid for this imaginative anchorage in the present, though: when we become aware of a very bad future event as being unavoidable, we shall first feel great fear and a strong wish that it will not occur and then, when we have resigned ourselves to its unavoidability, a great sadness or despair.[5] These reactions would have been less violent had our attention been more evenly balanced between the past and the future and we could more easily adopt a past time as the starting point of imagination. I shall return to the question of whether this attitudinal slant towards the

---

[4] As can be gathered from what was said about wishes in Chs. 4 and 5, wishes with respect to the past can manifest themselves in suppressing knowledge of disagreeable events that have occurred and in daydreaming about agreeable events in their stead. As we have seen, even though we know something to be the case, it may temporarily fail to occur to us, and wishes can take advantage of these lapses to make it harder for consciousness about disagreeable events to recur.

[5] Usually, knowledge that one is powerless with respect to a future state has a harder time establishing itself than the corresponding knowledge about the past. Hence, fear of what one knows will happen to one is not easily replaced by (the resigned emotion of) sadness or despair that it will occur. This knowledge with respect to the future is more liable to be counteracted by wishful thinking. There is here the influence of the MSI to take into consideration: since one is so often capable of affecting the future, it lies close at hand to think, against one's better knowledge, that one *might* be so in the present case as well, especially if one very much wants this to be true. By undermining convictions of impotency, the MSI may even nourish (irrational) intelligent desires with respect to (what is in fact) unalterable aspects of the future, which it cannot do as regards the past. The upshot is that one is less inclined to be despondent and resigned as regards admittedly fixed features of the future than as regards the unalterable facts of the past.

future is an asset or drawback all things considered when I have examined its cognitive rationality.

The Cognitive Irrationality of the F-bias

The asymmetry between imaginatively looking forward and backward to events and the attendant greater concern about the future are in fact the F-bias that, in Parfit's words, consists in that events will "affect us more when they are in the future rather than the past" (1984: 160). We should expect that what one imagines will follow upon one's perceived present situation, in which one *actually* is, will be more vividly represented than what one imagines will follow upon a situation (e.g. in the past), that one has to *imagine* oneself being in. For the latter situation itself will be less vividly represented because it is not as steadily before the mind.[6] And, as has been repeatedly stressed in this book, the greater the vividness or detail of a representation, the greater its effect on our para-cognitive attitudes. So we have here the material of an explanation of our greater concern about the future.

Translated into the terms of Parfit's example, this means that the patient will quite vividly represent the one-hour operation that will happen later on the very same day, while the representation of the ten-hour operation which took place yesterday will be much fainter, since the act of imagining having to undergo it requires the adoption of an optional point of view in the past, located before the operation. Hence, no wonder that the possibility of having undergone this operation affects the patient less than the possibility of undergoing the shorter operation in the future, so that he wishes that the former possibility has been actualized.

Since a relative under-representation of the past (in comparison to the future) is the background of the F-bias, it is cognitively irrational. Note that this does not imply that the spontaneous future-directedness of our imagination is itself irrational. It means, however, that to form a rational judgement about matters it affects, one must take care to counteract it, by deliberately making the past vivid. For instance, to form a rational judgement about the relative desirability of the two operations, the patient must take care to imagine yesterday's operation from some past point of view—say, on the morning of that day—as vividly as he imagines today's operation from the present point of view. For being cognitively rational requires representing all relevant information equally vividly. If he does this, he will judge this operation worse and wish to have the shorter operation, for in the past he minded imminent pain just as much as he now does. Thus, were he to imagine the ten-hour operation with adequate vividness, he would fear it as much as if it were to occur later on today. So a rational person would not be F-biased and prefer, hope, or wish that a pain be in the past at the expense of being much longer.

---

[6] Contrast Hume, who argues that the less vivid representation of the past is due to our imagination here having to make the effort of reversing the temporal order (1739–40/1978: 431).

This reasoning can be applied to a more celebrated example on a grander scale. Following Epicurus, Lucretius in *De rerum natura* (book III, 972–7) points out that, although the fact that we shall die and our future lives are limited normally makes us depressed, we do not regret the parallel past fact that we were once born, that our past lives have limits, with the result that we have missed much in the past. If we are feeling a pleasure, we are more likely to want it to continue into the future than to wish that it had had a longer past duration, for the latter involves our imaginatively adopting the perspective of a past time from which we can imaginatively look ahead to a longer pleasure than we have in fact experienced. For analogous reasons, we are more inclined to desire the future continuation of our lives (and thus to regret death) than to wish their length backward to be greater. But here imaginatively to adopt a point of view from which we can imagine our past lives to have had a longer duration is an even greater feat, for such a point of view must lie before our birth, and the further something is removed from what is actually the case, the harder it is to imagine. Therefore, it is not surprising that we do not spontaneously regret the fact that our lives have not had a longer past duration or wish that this had been the case.

Suppose, however, that one were to imagine vividly and in detail how much richer one's life could have been if one had been born earlier—the interesting people this prolongation would have allowed one to meet, and so on—then I think one would find oneself wishing quite strongly that this had been the case. This is what we would do were we rationalists, and then we would lament the fact that we are mortal no more than the fact that we were once born, and it would be a matter of indifference to us whether we were at the beginning, in the middle, or at the end of our lives. In other words, Lucretius is right that it is not rational to bemoan more the fact that our lives have an end in the future than in the past.

On my construal, the F-bias is no less cognitively irrational than the N-bias. This may seem counter-intuitive for, as Parfit emphasizes, it is less plausible to maintain that the F-bias is irrational than that the N-bias is. The reason for this may be that in contrast to the latter, the F-bias cannot make us *act* in ways that are contrary to our own (long-term) good. In the patient's case, for instance, there is no possibility of putting the F-biased wish into effect, for there is nothing he can do so to arrange it that he had the ten hours of pain yesterday rather than that he will have the one hour of pain later today. The closest one can get to translating the F-bias into action is when *the recognition* that one will be under its spell in the future makes one prefer to have a certain pleasure after rather than before an unavoidable pain, so that one is able to enjoy the pleasure unperturbed by the pain at the time when the latter is in the past. This preference is, however, counteracted by the N-bias, and it will in any case not make one accept a much greater pain simply because it is earlier.

This fact, that the F-bias will not make us try to arrange things in ways that we will later regret, supplies one a reason for holding that it is not *bad* for us. But to condemn the F-bias as cognitively irrational does not imply that it would be better for us to be without it (this is rather true of what is relatively irrational for us). It has already been pointed out that, though the F-bias has a particularly obnoxious impact upon us when we are as impotent in regard to the future as in regard to the past, it has the beneficial effect of keeping us alert to the future when, as is usually the case, it is malleable in some respects. Thus it is not obvious that, on the whole, the F-bias is bad for us.

This is, however, Parfit's view (1984: § 67). As our lives pass, we have more and more to look backward to and less and less to look forward to. Given our F-bias, this will make us depressed, for it prevents us from fully enjoying our richer pasts, by riveting our attention to our shrinking futures. In contrast, if we had been equally concerned about the past and the future, we would better appreciate the swelling of our pasts and thus "greatly gain in our attitude to ageing and to death" (1984: 175). This is especially so since, in looking backward, "we could afford to be selective" and focus on what has been good. We need not be preoccupied with what is bad, as we must in the case of the future because we might here be able to do something to fend it off.

The main shortcoming of this argument is that it overlooks that, if we lacked the F-bias, we would probably be somewhat less keen to make the future as good for us as possible. The value of the future will appear less crucial as our capacity to extract happiness out of the past increases. For this reason our lives may go less well than they would were we F-biased. This makes me doubtful of Parfit's view that this bias is bad for us. His view would be more persuasive if the future were conceived as something that is largely impervious to our attempts to affect it.[7]

I do not have the ambition, however, to settle whether the F-bias is on the whole good or bad for us. Instead, I have tried to determine whether or not it is cognitively rational. Its goodness/badness is, however, relevant to a question I shall deal with in the next chapter, namely the question of whether we should attempt to rid ourselves of it. My claim will then be that it is relatively rational for prudentialists to keep it for it is so hard to eradicate that the loss of fulfilment will be greater than the gain. For rationalists it is, however, relatively rational to try to stub it out, despite the strain and effort this will cost.

On the account of the F-bias I have supplied, it is not the fact that we locate one of our painful or pleasant experiences in the past rather than in the future that *in itself* makes it affect us less. It is the circumstance that this leads to our being incapable of imagining it as vividly. Had we instead believed it to be in the future, especially the more imminent future, our imagination would quickly run ahead of time, making us vividly represent what it will be like to feel it. If we were not suffering from this time-directedness of the faculty of imagination, we would not exhibit the F-bias. That is the core of my case for the cognitive irrationality of this bias. It is not essential for my purposes that my diagnosis is the whole truth if any other factors causally responsible for the F-bias also are of a kind that would evaporate under the conditions of ideal representation.

In other words, my claim that the F-bias is cognitively irrational is not due to the consideration that a believed difference between having a past and a future location provides our reason for adopting this bias, and that a philosophical analysis of this difference undermines this reason. As we saw in Chapter 14, even on a tenseless view of time, such

---

[7] Parfit makes a concession in this direction when he restricts his view to "more passive types, who take life's pleasures as they come" (1984: 176), but this does not go far enough, for it does not deal with the risk that loss of the F-bias may have the bad effect of making passive types even more passive (with respect to the future).

as Mellor's, beliefs that employ the concepts of the past and future could be true and well-grounded (though I suggested that such a view is not true to our temporal experience). A further difficulty for this rival account of the irrationality of the F-bias is that, as we shall presently see, we exhibit it only when we look at our own life and not when we look at the lives of other subjects. This shows that no believed difference between a past and a future time could be the whole reason for our adoption of the F-bias, since any such temporal difference must exist also in the lives of others.

An Asymmetry between Oneself and Others

Parfit professes to detect an asymmetry between the case of oneself and that of others with respect to the past:

> I would not be distressed at all if I was reminded that I myself once had to endure several months of suffering. But I would be greatly distressed if I learnt that, before she died, my mother had to endure such an ordeal. (1984: 182)

He claims that he looks with *complete indifference* upon the pains that he himself has suffered in the past (1984: 173–4), while he is greatly distressed by the thought of the past pains of those he loves. If this reaction is universal, it means that, when we contemplate the lives of loved ones, the F-bias will not manifest itself at all, or at least much less forcefully. So, as Parfit remarks (1984: 183), if he were to learn that his mother's suffering had taken place in the past, and not was not to occur in the future as he earlier believed, he would not be much relieved. The fact that we might be a little relieved in such circumstances may be the result of the F-bias, so powerful in the case of our own life, affecting our attitudes to the lives of dear ones (1984: 183–4).

Parfit's reaction to the news about his mother fits nicely with my account of the F-bias, but badly with the hypothesis that the reason for it is a temporal belief, since this should make us expect that the bias was as strong in the case of others, when their experiences exhibit the same temporal relations. When you hear such news about a loved one, you imaginatively adopt some (indefinite) point of view of this person *during the suffering*, irrespective of whether it is that person's present point of view. In the circumstances Parfit describes, you cannot intentionally adopt the point of view that is this person's *present* one, since you do not know what her present circumstances are. So your concern will not take the form it does when you look forward from the perceived present, namely the form of a desire that the pain stop and does not continue into the future. Rather, it will take the form of a wish that the (entire) duration and intensity of the pain be less. Therefore it will not change much if you discover that the pain is now entirely in the past. If it makes a little difference, this may be due to the fact that there was earlier some taint of a forward-looking form of concern.

It would, however, be a mistake to think that we always feel this sort of concern about the pains of loved ones. Suppose that I were to see that my mother's facial expression is perfectly serene and untroubled as she describes her past sufferings (the explanation of her serenity being that she is subject to the F-bias).[8] Then it would surely be much more difficult for me to be distressed by her past suffering for I would be tempted to take up her present point of view and look ahead to her future.

Parfit claims it to be "hard to believe" that being distressed by the past pains of loved ones is irrational (1984: 185). But this claim would seem to sit ill with the view that the relative indifference in my last case is rational as well. Thus, it is a welcome corollary of the account put forward in this chapter that it construes this indifference as irrational, like indifference towards one's own past suffering.

This uniformity is welcome, too. For one should be ill at ease to maintain both that the complete indifference towards one's own past suffering is rational and that concern about the past suffering of others is rational if one wants to agree with the main contention of part III of Parfit's book (1984), namely the view that "personal identity is not what matters". Surely, this contention must rule out that rational beings take up one attitude to their own past sufferings, simply because they are *their own*, and another attitude to the past sufferings of other loved ones, simply because these sufferings are *not* theirs, but the sufferings of others. Since I shall in Part IV endorse this dictum, I am relieved to be able to deny the rationality of one of the sets of attitudes that make up Parfit's asymmetry. In rejecting the rationality of the F-bias, I have in effect rejected the rationality of being indifferent towards one's own past suffering.

Parfit's claim that we in fact view with *complete indifference* our past sufferings may seem surprising. For surely we can be distressed by some past pain that we remember having undergone, even if it occurred in the very distant past. According to an interview with the last survivor of the last Chinese Emperor's eunuchs, he was castrated without any anaesthetics by his peasant father. Although this was more than seventy years ago, the man confessed that he still shuddered when he recalled the excruciating pain. This man was certainly distressed by the memory of a pain he felt in the distant past.

It may be cases of this type that Parfit has in mind when he concedes that memories can be "painful" (1984: 172–4). The situations in connection with which he makes his claim about indifference are confined to ones in which we do not remember feeling the pain, but have to be reminded of it. It might be said that if we want a situation that is parallel to the ones we are in with respect to the past pains of others, we have to concentrate on ones in which we do not remember feeling our own pain, since we do not remember feeling the pains of others. But it is very doubtful whether this move sets up an adequate parallel, for when we do not remember feeling our own pain, but have to be reminded of it, we are aware of the situation as falling short of the normal one in which we do remember feeling our past experiences. This may make it seem unreal that we suffered the pain, and so be an obstacle to representing it vividly.

Thus, I think that if one wants to examine our attitudes to our past experiences (which is not exactly Parfit's objective in the paragraph from which I have quoted), one does best to consider, in the first instance, cases in which we do remember having them. Then the conclusion seems inevitable that we are *not* indifferent to them, especially not if they are

---

[8] Cf. the concession Parfit makes about a similar example (1984: 182).

in the fairly recent past. For when the events remembered are still recent, the memory of undergoing them is still comparatively vivid, whereas, as I argued in the last chapter, it fades in the course of time, making our reactions to it weaker.

The objection may be repeated that this procedure prevents a fair comparison to our attitudes to the past experiences of others which we do not remember having. Certainly, this procedure means that the case of one's own past experiences and that of the past experiences of others will not be on a par, but I am not convinced that this difference need mar the comparison. For I believe that what distinguishes remembering having an experience from imagining having it is mainly the existence of a special sort of causal connection (normally in the form of neural states) to a past experience. But as this connection is not part of what is represented when we are remembering, why should it influence our reactions? It may be objected that I have myself argued that the *absence* of this causal link may blunt our reaction. This is, however, a mistake: I have suggested that it is (an awareness of) the fact that a relation *falls short of what is standard* that makes a difference.

I conclude, then, that we are distressed by our own past pains when we recall having them and that if we are not distressed when reminded of past pains we have forgotten, this is the result of defective representation. It would be strange, I think, if people in their encounter with the past were totally indifferent towards the pains that they themselves then felt. For they usually strongly desire to escape whatever acute pains are avoidable, indeed they normally desire that they themselves escape pain more intensely than they desire that others do. But if one fails to accomplish that for which one has a strong desire, one will feel dissatisfaction, sadness, disappointment, and so on. So we should expect people viewing with these emotions pains that, in spite of their efforts to evade them, they have suffered in the past—at least as long as there is adequate representation, usually in the form of memories.

Is the distress here of the same strength as in the case of loved ones? The following variation of Parfit's patient example suggests a positive answer. Imagine that when I wake up I am told that either my very best friend in the room next door had the ten-hours operation and I the one-hour one, or it is the other way around. Then I would certainly not be concerned that I was the one who suffered the longer operation. Rather, I would not care much which was the case. In any case, as regards the past we do not find it difficult to achieve that neutrality between ourselves and others which is within the reach of so few of us when it comes to the future. This suggests that self-concern or the bias towards ourselves has to do with the fact that the present from which the spontaneous looking forward is conducted is perceived and vividly represented as it is in one's own case, that is, that it involves the P-bias. I shall return to this suggestion in the next part of this book.

17

THE DILEMMA AS REGARDS TEMPORAL NEUTRALITY

I HAVE contended that a temporal partiality consisting in the N-bias and the F-bias is cognitively irrational or, more precisely, that this is a set of attitudes that would not be sustained by an adequate representation of the facts. This entails that it is relatively irrational for *rationalists* not to try to overcome this form of partiality. The question then is whether the same is true of prudentialists. Pre-reflectively, prudentialists are *naïve* prudentialists whose aim to maximize the (experiential) fulfilment of their lives is subject to the two temporal biases described. Our present question concerns whether it is rational relative this aim of theirs to impose the rational constraints of temporal neutrality, that is, to be without the N-bias and the F-bias.

More specifically, there are two questions to be asked:

(1) Is the state of *lacking* these biases more conducive to maximizing the (experiential) fulfilment of one's life? In other words, would subjects lacking these biases be capable of leading more fulfilling lives than they would be were they in possession of them, *ceteris paribus*?

(2) Is it relatively rational for prudentialists to try to *get rid of* these biases, given the efforts and readjustments this would involve and the level of (experiential) fulfilment attainable when one is dispossessed of them (as stated in reply to the first question)?

My answer to both questions will be negative, though the answer to the first one is somewhat more tentative. Thus we here face the first dilemma between rationalism and satisfactionalism.

The Sense of Futility and Transience

Let me start by posing question (1) with respect to the N-bias. Doubtless, being free of this bias will have obvious advantages for prudentialists: it will mean that they are no longer tempted to fulfil weaker desires the fulfilment of which can be obtained sooner at the expense of leaving unfulfilled stronger desires the fulfilment of which lies further in the future. To this extent, being rid of the N-bias will promote the goal of maximizing the satisfaction of one's life.

However, to lack the N-bias means lacking the P-bias and the MSI; so, it must be examined whether the absence of these is also beneficial to the prudentialist pursuit. As concerns the P-bias, it is again evident that being free of it will to some extent be for the better, since, as I argued in Chapter 13, it plays a prominent part in the phenomenon of weakness of will. This advantage is so conspicuous that one may be led to wonder how it could be that well-adapted creatures display the P-bias in view of the fact that it is the origin of the detrimental effect of *akrasia*.

The material for answering this question has already been supplied. It is of survival value that thoughts directed at one's present hedonic sensations should motivate one and tend to monopolize one's attention, just as these sensations themselves do. Similarly, it is also of survival value that impressions of some activities in which one currently is engaged should attract one's attention; otherwise it would be much harder for immature individuals to expand their behavioural repertoire beyond instinctive patterns. However, it also enhances the prospect of survival if a power of mentally representing states of affairs beyond ones that are sensibly present—in particular possible future states—develops. But the more this power of envisaging possible futures is developed, the more of a drawback the P-bias will be, for it will prevent this representational power from having full impact on motivation. Thus, *akrasia* is the upshot of the conflict between two traits that each individually is of survival value. In better adjusted beings than actual human ones, the P-bias would be quite marked during the earlier stages of ontogenetic development, but would gradually loosen its grip as the capacity of mentally representing sensibly absent states of affairs expands and the power to estimate the probability of their materialization is refined.

The total absence of the P-bias will, however, have further effects. If one were rid of this bias, one would no longer be preoccupied with trying to prolong present pleasures and to abolish present pains. One would be able to look at the state of possessing desires for present experiences 'from a distance', that is, one would be able to represent vividly to oneself that these desires constitute only a small minority of countless similar desires that one has had or will have at other times in one's life. One would also be conscious that, once they are satisfied, one will think no more about them than one now thinks about similar desires gratified in the past, since they contribute little if anything to the fulfilment of later desires. Furthermore, one would be aware that, even if one succeeded in fulfilling all such 'local' desires in one's life, the fulfilment one's life would contain would still be negligible because the duration of one's life is vanishingly short compared to the time during which the whole universe will exist and oneself could in principle have existed and enjoyed fulfilment. Such a cosmic panorama, coupled with attachment to oneself, will engender occurrent desires or wishes to the effect that one enjoy pleasurable states of indefinite duration. Against the backdrop of such desires, the strength of one's desires *vis-à-vis* present hedonic sensations will dwindle, and the satisfaction experienced if they are gratified will correspondingly decrease. It will now stand in the shadow of the frustration caused by the unsatisfiable wide-ranging desires.

The situation will be parallel with respect to present desires to accomplish something that transcends the world of personal experience, for example to create some artistic or scientific work. As long as one is in the grip of the P-bias, one will not vividly represent to oneself how little accomplishing this work will contribute to the fulfilment of the many other strivings of one's life, that this work is only one among a countless number of similar works of other people, that sooner or later every trace of it, along with the traces of all other accomplishments of one's life and the lives of other humans, will be erased. Again, these reflections would no doubt, if vividly and steadily represented, weaken one's desire to bring about everyday changes in the external world, by giving birth to a stronger, occurrent desire to create something of more lasting—or even everlasting—duration and value. I shall term the weakening of occurrent desire that has its source in such reflections *the sense of futility and transience*, the SFT.

The sense in which the SFT reduces the strength of customary, more local desires should be made more precise. It is not that the intrinsic desires to obtain an ephemeral pleasure or to create a work occupying a humble position in space and time become weaker relative to the desire simply to forgo these things. No, these desires may retain their relative strength and, so, the states of affairs satisfying them their intrinsic value for the subject. But as a grander spatio-temporal vista is opened up by one's episodic thought ranging wider, they are coupled with a multitude of other states of affairs, giving rise to further occurrent desires. Some of these desires that appear on the arena are very powerful because they concern long-lasting goods. If these global, or even cosmic, desires cannot be fulfilled, the feelings of frustration stemming from this will swamp the feelings of satisfaction which come from the fulfilment of desires for the more local and ephemeral goods.

Compare: considered by itself, you may prefer making a smaller gain to not making it, and be glad if you make it. But suppose you couple these states of affairs with making a much greater loss; then though it would be rational to prefer the set containing the gain, the satisfaction you would get if this alternative materializes would be overshadowed by the sadness the great loss would occasion you. Similarly, the satisfaction you may get from winning small victories in life may be overshadowed by the sadness occasioned by the thought that soon all these victories will be forgotten and your life will not have culminated in anything of lasting value.

It is true that any sane person will realize that the desire to live an eternal life of high value cannot possibly be fulfilled, but this is compatible with the desire taking the shape of a wish. Certainly, if this insight fully permeates one, one will resign and not possess this desire even as a wish. But one could still feel sorrow and despair because this state of affairs is impossible, a sorrow and despair in which smaller pleasures and joys will drown. And even if these emotions eventually fade and are replaced by apathy and numbness, there is still a loss of felt satisfaction because local desires have been reduced in strength.

I surmise that what I have identified as the SFT is something that philosophers and literary writers have experienced when they have felt life to be meaningless. This can be illustrated by the manner in which this feeling of meaninglessness is expressed in Leo

Tolstoy's *A Confession*. Tolstoy writes: "Before occupying myself with my Samara estate, the education of my son, or the writing of a book, I had to know *why* I was doing it?" (1940: 16). Tolstoy confesses that he did not know why or for what he was doing these things. It seemed to him that all his pursuits would result in nothing, since eventually he would die and all his actions, whatever they were, would be forgotten. This insight "arrested" his life, brought it to a "standstill" (1940: 17).

In a comment on this reasoning, Anthony Flew remarks:

> to go on, as Tolstoi does, asking 'What for?' after you have already seen how your contemplated course of action is rooted in your fundamental sentiments and affections, might seem to be just silly, an indication of a failure to appreciate the scope and function of the question 'What for?' (1963: 111)

Flew's point is that the chain of one's reasons for doing some action cannot be endlessly long; something must be desired for its own sake. In stubbornly insisting on reasons for doing things that he presumably desires for their own sake, it might seem that Tolstoy betrays a failure to grasp this point.

It is certainly true that whenever one desires something, there must be something for which one has an intrinsic desire. But, as I pointed out in Chapter 8, it does not follow from this that, if one so far has desired p only for its own sake, it is a sign of confusion if one starts to ask for reasons for desiring p, since there might be *real* reasons either for or against desiring p. Admittedly, it would be a mistake were one to conclude, after finding that the reasons against are preponderant, that the thing formerly intrinsically desired was of *no* (intrinsic) value at all—the proper conclusion might instead be that it has an intrinsic value that is outweighed by its extrinsic disvalue. However, it is not clear to me that Tolstoy is guilty of this piece of erroneous reasoning. He might instead be taken aback by the fact that when the wider perspective raises the question of real reasons for his intrinsic desires, no good reasons can be found.

Flew appears to me to be on firmer ground when he maintains that for Tolstoy "all ordinary desires, affections, and satisfactions have lost their power and appeal" (1963: 111). But this is does not go far enough for we would like to know what the connection is between this frame of mind and the speculations about everything's ending in "real death—complete annihilation" (Tolstoy, 1940: 18). This is where the P-bias and the result of overcoming it, the SFT, enter the picture. The P-bias makes the regress of searching for reasons peter out and allows us to contemplate a sensibly present state of affairs in comparative isolation, without conjoining it with an indefinite number of other states of affairs. This isolation is necessary for desiring this state of affairs solely for its own sake and for this desire not to be swallowed up by other, stronger desires. If we resist this more or less exclusive concentration on some present (or imminent) sensation or activity and see the desire for it as a minute component of a life that is a minute component of the universe, this desire enters into competition with, and risks being overpowered by, other occurrent desires with more grandiose objects. That is what I have termed the SFT.

Flew correctly observes that Tolstoy is committed to the doctrine that "nothing can matter unless it goes on forever, or at any rate, eventually leads to something else which does" (1963: 113). He adds, however, that "there really is nothing at all ineluctable, or even especially profound, about this particular value commitment" (1963: 113). It is, of course, true that a state of affairs can be of intrinsic value, even though it is of limited duration. But the explanation of Tolstoy's state of mind that I have offered makes it comprehensible why a valuable state of affairs that is of infinite duration is of special significance: there is no wider temporal perspective from which it cannot be supported by any good reasons and from which it shrinks to next to nothing, by being coupled with more encompassing states of affairs. In fact, anything that is in any way limited could be placed in a wider context in which it becomes comparatively insignificant. Therefore, it is only if the life of each and every person makes a significant contribution to an all-encompassing state that the SFT could get no grip on them.[1]

As Thomas Nagel points out, the sense of the meaningless and futility of our lives often goes with a vision of us as "tiny specks in the infinite vastness of the universe".[2] But Nagel seems unable to explain the naturalness of this association: "Reflection on our minuteness and brevity appears to be intimately connected with the sense that life is meaningless, but it is not clear what the connection is" (1979: 12). I see it as a virtue of my account that it makes this connection intelligible. When one represents to oneself that the universe will continue to exist indefinitely after one's death, one's spontaneous self-concern will make one wish that one could go on enjoying life as long as the universe will exist, or at least produce something whose value will shine through eternity, and one will experience sorrow and frustration at the thought that this is impossible. Of course, none of this need rob one of desires that could be fulfilled within the span of one's life or of the joy consequent upon the realization of their fulfilment. In comparison to the unsatisfiable wishes, however, this amount of fulfilment is negligible: sorrow and frustration will by far surpass joy and satisfaction.

The mechanism is familiar from more mundane circumstances. You might be perfectly satisfied with your lot until it becomes vividly clear to you that other people thrive in much greater affluence. It is not that consciousness of these better-off people deprives your life of some or all of its value. What happens is that what you obtain is mentally put alongside all the affluence you miss. This awakens occurrent, unsatisfiable desires or wishes for more that are stronger than the satisfiable desires that have hitherto ruled. As a result, frustration and dissatisfaction gain the upper hand. Analogously, awareness of the cosmic perspective brings along the possibility of good things lasting indefinitely. The impossibility of achieving this is then coupled with the states satisfying more local desires. The result is that felt frustration arising from the unsatisfiable, cosmic desires or wishes supersedes the felt satisfaction arising from the more local, satisfiable desires.

It might be asked why we are not constantly aware of the cosmic perspective in this vivid fashion. The answer is, I think, that the facts constituting it are not present to the senses, and so do not receive the benefit of being supported by the P-bias. Moreover, our attention tends to focus on information newly discovered, and facts about our mortality and smallness in the universe do not have this status (though in the teenages, they strike us as relatively fresh, and consequently we feel more 'existential Angst' in this period). We are also prone to accept as part of an unalterable natural order conditions to which

---

[1] Cf. Nozick's speculations culminating in 'Ein Sof' (1981: ch. 6).
[2] 'The Absurd'; see the reprint in Nagel (1979: 11).

we have been accustomed all our lives; it takes a considerable effort to imagine such conditions to be otherwise. We can see this mechanism in operation in the impact comparisons of our lot to that of other human beings has. It is comparisons to more affluent neighbours and acquaintances rather than comparisons to even more fortunate people outside the range of personal acquaintances—oil tycoons, filmstars, etc.—that in the first instance make us dissatisfied and envious. This is presumably because it takes more of an effort to imagine vividly that we could have been in the place of the most advantaged. It takes even more of an imaginative talent—the talent of novelists and suchlike—to picture oneself enjoying a life of superhuman length and abundance.

As I have just indicated, being in the grip of the SFT does not amount to having the intensity of one's occurrent desires for more local goods reduced to nil, though it appears that this is sometimes assumed. If the intensity of one's desires is drastically reduced, one easily—out of despair—falls into the exaggeration of thinking that it has been reduced to zero. The fact that Tolstoy continues to live shows that he still has desires.[3] Here it might be objected that it is possible to live and (intentionally) act without having any desires. As remarked in Chapter 4, this is the view of Fleming. He is of the opinion that "we are acting intentionally if . . . we act because we know that we are performing that action" (1981: 218). Acting because of a piece of knowledge is not enough for the possession of a desire, since the latter also involves being affected or having feelings: "To have desire is to be affected in a way that tends to set in motion" (1981: 220). Acting without desire is not only possible but "the only pure case of acting" (1981: 220).

In Chapter 4 I argued that the point at which Fleming goes wrong is in believing that having a desire includes feeling or being disposed to feel something. It is possible to have a desire that is of such a low intensity that no frustration or tension is felt as long as it is believed not to be fulfilled and no satisfaction when it is believed to be fulfilled. This is no conceptual truth, but an empirical one resting on contingent facts about the working of our nervous systems, afferent and efferent pathways, and so on. Thus Fleming and I agree that intentional action without feeling is possible, but we differ in that Fleming—owing to his assumption that desiring includes feeling—describes this as acting without desire, while for me it is acting out of desire, but without feeling.

Nagel's diagnosis of the sense of absurdity or meaninglessness is, succinctly put, as follows:

> We cannot live human lives without energy and attention, nor without making choices which show that we take some things more seriously than others. Yet we have always available a point of view outside the particular forms of our lives, from which the seriousness appears gratuitous. These two inescapable view-points collide in us, and that is what makes life absurd. (1979: 14)

In other words, the sense of the absurdity of life is due to a clash between "the unavoidability of seriousness" and "the inescapability of doubt": on the one hand, we cannot

---

[3] There is also the mistake of thinking that, as the felt intensity of one's occurrent desires decreases, so does the value of the things they are for. Tolstoy's listlessness notwithstanding, his life surely contains many things of value for him, for example that his family is in good health, that his books are successes, and so on. His life would doubtless be worse had he been deprived of these things. But they become *comparatively* unimportant by being coupled with greater—unattainable—values.

help being wholeheartedly engaged in the down-to-earth matters of our lives, but on the other, in virtue of our power of reflection, we cannot escape occasionally adopting an external point of view that lets in doubt about this engagement.

It is not perspicuous to me what precise form this doubt allegedly takes. Like Flew, Nagel stresses that the fact that all chains of reasons must end somewhere, in something desired and valued for its own sake, does not supply any ground for doubting their justificatory power (1979: 12–13). (This is true but, as I have already remarked, if the wider perspective raises the question of real reasons for these desires, without supplying any, this may weaken their justificatory power.) The source of doubt that Nagel has in mind appears instead to be an idea examined in connection with Platts in Chapter 9, namely that if we imagine our desires and values to be entirely different, this threatens to make them lose their hold on us. For Nagel describes the external point of view as presenting us "as arbitrary, idiosyncratic, highly specific occupants of the world, one of countless possible forms of life" (1979: 21). But, as I made clear in the discussion of Platts, it is mysterious why reflection on the fact that there are possible worlds in which we or other beings have quite different desires and values should provide us with any reasons to give up our actual desires and values.

Nagel compares this doubt in the practical sphere with scepticism in epistemology (1979: 18–20). But it is precisely the aptness of this comparison that I would like to dispute, for while, if they are irrefutable, the sceptic possibilities—to the effect, for example that we might be deceived by an evil demon—would undermine the beliefs of common sense, it remains unclear how the feat of imagining ourselves to have other desires (and so values) could produce reasons for rejecting our actual desires, as they are not designed to fit the world. Therefore I believe that Nagel's diagnosis of the absurdity of life, though suggestive, fails in the end.

So much for the diagnosis of the feeling of the futility and meaninglessness of life. Supposing now that the removal of the P-bias leads to the SFT, would such a life contain more felt fulfilment than an otherwise similar life under the reign of this bias? In a life governed by the SFT, the satisfaction obtainable from local goods would be severely diminished. Hence, if these goods are largely attainable, the loss in respect of felt satisfaction would be corresponding, while if they are mostly unattainable, there will be a matching gain as regards diminished felt frustration. Since it is realistic to assume that for many prudentialists the former alternative will apply, it is immediately clear that a life under the reign of the SFT will be worse for them. Furthermore, it should be borne in mind that the SFT is allied with global or cosmic desires which, by the very nature of the 'human condition', must remain unfulfilled. Thus, it is doubtful whether the net balance of the change is positive even were the latter, pessimistic alternative to hold—and in any event, the resulting life would still contain a surplus of negative value and so be worse than non-existence. To conclude, the complete lifting of the P-bias apparently is not anything that would make life better for prudentialists—at least not if life beforehand is better than non-existence.[4]

---

[4] Michael Stocker argues that "psychic feelings are necessary . . . for a good life" that "(w)ithout them, one's life . . . is certain to be marred by such maladies of the spirit as meaninglessness, emptiness, dissociation, ennui, accidie, spiritual

The Sense of the Precariousness of Life

I shall now attempt to assess what it would be like to be without the MSI. Given that the world is subject to regularities, it would seem to enhance a subject's prospect of survival if it is equipped with the MSI rather than with no propensity to form ideas about what the future will be like. It should be expected that, when the states of affairs in question are also objects of desire, the MSI will gain additional impetus, since there is already a disposition to represent these states of affairs. On the whole, this would seem to be of survival value, although it is here more likely that anticipations will be erroneous than when they rest on repetition alone.

When a power of making more *reasoned* or *reflective* judgements of probability develops, however, it may appear that the MSI has outlived itself and lost its utility. As we have seen, it plays a role in weakness of will and it is responsible for the irrational phobias that rest on extrapolation from isolated instances (as in the example, discussed in Chapter 13, of the aeroplane catching fire). Thus, to this extent prudentialists—who are in possession of an ability to make more reflective judgements of probability—would be better off without the MSI. So far this parallels the findings about the P-bias.

But, again as in the case of the P-bias, liberation from the MSI will have more far-reaching consequences. One can never be absolutely certain what the future will be like in any contingent respect. At any moment serious misfortunes—like death and disabling diseases—might befall oneself or beings close to one. One is never in a position to predict with absolute certainty that such misfortunes will not happen within any substantial period of time. Yet, as long as one is in good health and in familiar circumstances, one will not represent to oneself the possibility of such mishaps, because the MSI will induce one to represent things as going well in the future as they have done in the past. For instance, when one takes one's bicycle to go to work, one will feel no fear or worry that one will be involved in some accident in the heavy traffic, though one knows that the risk of this is far from nil. In contrast, if one is unaccustomed to flying, one might feel fear as one is about to take a flight, even though one has no reflective doubt that the likelihood of an air accident is smaller. The reason is that the MSI is not at work here, leading one to represent vividly a future that is uniform with the past one has experienced.[5]

With the disappearance of the influence of the MSI, this sense of security felt in well-known surroundings will, however, vanish. Since reflectively one ought always to judge there to be some possibility of things going seriously wrong, one would never be without

---

weakness and tiredness" (1983: 6). Stocker's "psychic feelings" are "full-blooded", "feeling-laden" desires, desires that are felt as "pulls" (1983: 16), and the fulfilment of which is felt, too. My claim is that such feelings or desires are bound to disappear or grow weaker as the P-bias weakens its grip.

[5] Slote draws attention to the peculiar phenomenon that sometimes when we plan to go to an exotic place, we do not do it to *be* there, but rather to *have been* there; we wish the visit were already in the past. Slote wants to explain this by assuming that "some people unconsciously wish their whole lives over with" (1975: 23–4). I believe this assumption to be outlandish. It seems to me that the wish that the trip was already in the past is due—at least partly—to a fear of the unknown which results from the MSI not being in operation. (It is probably also due to various trivial inconveniences of travelling.) When we are in a position to look back on the visit, we are on the safe side. However, this fear is not so great that, overall, we do not want to go, for we believe the trip will enrich our lives (otherwise there would not be much to look back on).

some fear or anxiety that misfortunes would befall one. One would no longer rest secure in the conviction that things will go well as usual—that disasters will not suddenly happen to oneself—and one would be less confident that one will succeed in carrying out routine tasks.

How great should this fear or anxiety be? It may seem that it should be very slight, because, even though the misfortunes envisaged might be calamitous, they are most improbable. Our emotional life is, however, not so finely attuned that we are able to experience emotions that are perfectly proportioned to every degree of probability we are able to discriminate. The fear or worry that is likely to be occasioned by an elaborate representation of the possibility that one might die a painful death in the imminent future will presumably be out of proportion to the probability of the event, just as the hope of winning a large sum of money that an individual who buys a lottery ticket experiences is likely to be greater than his reflective estimate of the probability warrants. This fact about our emotional life should be kept in mind when the effects of not being subject to the MSI are assessed.

In any event, a blocking of the MSI brings along what one might call *the sense of the precariousness of life*, the SPL. The SPL should not be confused with the SFT, although they may both contribute to a feeling commonly described as one of the meaninglessness or absurdity of life. The former has rather to do with the uncertainty of attaining the goals that one sets oneself, whereas the latter concerns the insignificance of these goals in a cosmic setting. It seems to be the SPL that impressed those thinkers—for example the Stoics—who preached self-sufficiency and the independence of all the fortunes and misfortunes of the world as the ideal of the wise person.[6]

The SPL is based on certain presuppositions about the world. For instance, if one knew that the universe was ruled by an omnipotent being who was intent on seeing to it that everyone in it would achieve their aims, one would be relieved of the SPL. (The existence of such a being could also relieve one of the SFT if its concerns for one remained in force forever.) However, it would be no satisfactory antidote to the SPL if one's own knowledge and control of the world grew to the extent that one could predict not merely *that* one would attain a goal were one to set out for it, but also the details of *how* one would attain it. For we saw in Chapter 10 that the latter knowledge would inevitably undercut the curiosity the stilling of which provides a lot of the incentive for living. In the absence of the guarantee a benevolent, omnipotent being could deliver, it is, however, hard to see how we could gain the former assurance except at the cost of being burdened with undesirable excess knowledge.

Fear and worry accompany the SPL, but there are also things to be put on the credit side. We should not overlook something that Schopenhauer in particular never tires of emphasizing: the ever-present threat of boredom. The familiar easily becomes *too* familiar, with the result that the feeling of security is transformed into boredom, the state of having nothing to stimulate one's interest. If, freed of the MSI, one represents to oneself all sorts of unlikely things that may happen to one at any moment, everyday life will be

---

[6] In his discussion of a life under the reign of the Stoic virtue of *autarkeia* (1983: ch. 6), Slote suggests that "we should not want such an existence even if we were capable of having it" (1983: 137), because it would put out a lot of basic human strivings, bodily appetites, love, friendship, etc.

experienced as more of an adventure or gamble. The representation of the possibility that something other—be it positive or negative—than the usual thing might take place will stimulate one's interest, so that one becomes immune to boredom.

Will this positive effect of boredom evaporating offset the negative effect of fear increasing? Before we attempt to gauge this, there are some further considerations to be taken into account. It might be said that if one is also rid of the P-bias and, as a result, experiences the SFT, then one will be less concerned about one's own fate, since it will appear so trivial against the cosmic background. Consequently, one will not experience proper fear when envisaging possible misfortunes that may afflict one; one will instead be *thrilled*, that is, one will feel mere 'tickles' of fear that, because of their low intensity, are on the pleasant side. One would be in something like the position of somebody who watches a thriller and maintains a distance to what is happening to the people on the screen.

I am inclined to dispute the correctness of the claim that exposure to the SFT deflates one's interest in one's own fate. In my opinion, it is rather the kind of reflections on the nature of personal identity to be broached in Part IV that will take this effect. The natural reaction to SFT would instead seem to be—witness the case of Tolstoy and other writers plagued by existential torments—distress and despair due to the realization of one's cosmic smallness. It seems undeniable that this distress outweighs the greater resilience to boredom.

There are other positive effects of being without MSI, but it seems to me that they are counterbalanced by negative ones. For instance, it might be argued that if one consistently envisions unlikely mishaps then, though one will be more anxious, one will also be emotionally ready for them, so, if they in fact occur, they will be less of a blow. This is neutralized by the remark that, if one imagines unlikely fortunate turns then, though this may have the positive impact of making one more hopeful, one will also be less capable of enjoying them should they occur, for one will be acutely aware that at any moment one may be robbed of these benefits.

I do not think that this exhausts the considerations that could be put on either the credit or the debit side of the condition of lacking the MSI—in fact, this condition is so utterly different from any ordinary frame of mind that it is hard to envisage in detail what it would be like—but I can conceive of nothing that decisively outweighs what could be put on the other side. So I conclude, as I did with respect to the P-bias, that, in terms of the prudentialist goal, there is no reason to think the state of lacking the MSI better than our present state of being subject to it, but rather some reason to think that it will be tantamount to a deterioration. In other words, to maintain a state of being without the P-bias and the MSI—and, thus, the N-bias—is not rationally required relative to the goal of prudentialism.

Prudentialism and the F-bias

Let us next turn to whether being without the F-bias is more conducive to fulfilment than being ruled by it. As noted in the foregoing chapter, Parfit argues that we would be better off or happier if we lacked this bias (1984: 174–7). Because we cannot affect the past, "we could afford to be selective", Parfit observes (1984: 175) when looking backward; we could concentrate on rehearsing our memories of good things, and only remember bad events when this would enable us to avoid repeating bringing them about. But to a considerable extent we can shape the future by our actions; we can, for instance, prevent some bad things if, but only if, we pay attention to them. Had we allowed ourselves the luxury of selecting only the brighter aspects when looking forward, we would have lost this chance. Parfit concludes: "Since we ought not to be selective when looking forward, but could afford to be when looking backward, the latter would be, on the whole, more enjoyable" (1984: 175). And not being F-biased, we would be able to indulge more freely in the activity of looking backward.

In the last chapter I remarked that Parfit seems to fail to take due notice of the fact that, were we not enthralled by the F-bias, we would presumably be less keen to arrange the future to our advantage. Thus, without this bias our lives may be both shorter and less worthwhile. Furthermore, as construed in the foregoing chapter, the F-bias involves both the P-bias and the MSI: it is the spontaneous tendency to imagine things going on from the perceived present that makes us more concerned about this than what has happened in the past. Now, we have already concluded that loss of the P-bias is marred by the bad feature of leading to the SPL, and loss of the MSI by the bad feature of leading to the SFT. I think this clinches the matter, but some further speculations may be of interest.

I have hitherto assumed that a power of making reflective inductive inferences could fill the lacuna left by the MSI, but this may be an exaggeration. Perhaps the MSI can be profitably compared to short-term memory. To some extent, short-term memory is similar in kind to long-term memory: it is a capacity to recall something if the occasion arises. But at 'the end closest to the present' it may shade into something different: we know what happened in the most immediate past without having to recall it. This knowledge is a *sine qua non* of all coherent action, perhaps even of the act of recalling something past. If so, it cannot even in principle be replaced by the capacity of recalling in which long-term memory and more distant short-term memory consist. Similarly, it may seem that, although the MSI is continuous with the power of reflective induction, it shades into something which is not an inference from what is strictly present: our anticipation of the most immediate future, such as the anticipation that the floor will support one's next step or that a thing dropped will fall to the floor. Such anticipations, too, would appear to be a *sine qua non* of all coherent action, even the act of making inductive inferences. If so, there would be no adequate substitute for a *complete* loss of the MSI. Loss of it would be gravely incapacitating.

It is not obvious, however, that an obliteration of the F-bias requires a complete loss of the MSI, even if the P-bias is retained. It may require only that the grip of the MSI be less firm, for example that the MSI extends only to the most imminent future. So I shall put no weight on the considerations in the foregoing paragraph.

Summary

It is time to sum up the discussion and assess the fulfilment effect of the state of being without both the F-bias and the N-bias, that is, the state of having *no* temporal bias or of being temporally neutral. My conclusions about both the N-bias and the F-bias point in the same direction: the lifting of these biases is more likely to lower the level of felt fulfilment than that to raise it. The elimination of the P-bias (which is one of the props of the N- and the F-bias) would land one in the SFT, with felt frustration owing to unsatisfiable global or cosmic desires. In the absence of the MSI (which is the other prop of these biases), there would probably be an increase in anxiety owing to the SPL.

The case for holding that the removal of the F-bias is prudentially beneficial is the strongest, since it brings along the benefit of a greater capacity to derive pleasure from the past. But this is effectively counteracted by making us less disposed to see to it that the future turns out for the better. I need not argue, however, that being without the two temporal biases *diminishes* the amount of experiential fulfilment in life. It is enough for the rest of the argument if the answer to question (1) at the beginning of this chapter is that lack of the temporal biases does not amount to any *boost* of felt fulfilment.

For suppose that in being temporally neutral one would be on the same level of fulfilment as one was in the state of temporal partiality; then, even if prudentialists were in the position of just having to snap their fingers in order to get rid of their temporal biases, it would still not be relatively irrational for them to refrain from doing so. But we are obviously not in this position: the P-bias and the MSI are clearly features that are deeply ingrained in our psychological constitution, and they must be eliminated, or at least markedly reduced, if the N-bias and the F-bias are to disappear. To liberate oneself from these tendencies, one must consistently train oneself in the art of vividly representing states of affairs that are not perceived by one, of representing future states of affairs so that one's attitudes to them match one's reflective judgements of probability and past states of affairs so that they would evoke attitudes as powerful as the future-directed ones. To yield any results, this mental exercise must be engaged in constantly and consistently, as a way of life.

Perhaps even this will not be sufficient to counteract the tendencies mentioned; perhaps they are so well-entrenched that it is psychologically impossible for us to rid ourselves of them to the requisite extent. But it is at least clear that attaining this goal demands a stern, single-minded devotion that would mean that a lot of the subject's other desires would have to be left unfulfilled. In view of (a) this sacrifice of other avenues of fulfilment, (b) the great risk of succumbing in an unsuccessful attempt to attain the goal of temporal neutrality, and (c) the fact that, if this goal is attained, it is highly doubtful whether any compensating, fulfilment-enhancing factor comes into operation, it surely would not be relatively rational for prudentialists to endeavour to transform themselves into temporally neutral persons. Such is the answer to question (2) at the outset.

What prudentialists should do with respect to their temporal biases is rather to try to restrain their power somewhat. For, as we have seen, the N-bias frequently leads one to act contrary to the goal of inter-temporal maximization, for example by making one fall victim to *akrasia*, and the F-bias restricts the pleasure one could obtain from the past as well as making one excessively upset by inevitable aspects of the future. Prudentialists should endeavour to limit the influence of these temporal biases, and consequently their props, the P-bias and the MSI, to the extent that this serves the goal of making the felt fulfilment of their entire lives as great as possible. Unlike naïve prudentialists, rational prudentialists will take precautions to prevent themselves from giving in to the temptations of the near and from falling under the spell of irrational phobias. But rational prudentialists will not, for the reasons adduced above, try to *extinguish* the N-bias and F-bias.[7]

This is, however, the relatively rational course for rationalistists whose master-aim is to have attitudes that are cognitively rational in the sense of being formed in the light of rational thinking. Since these two biases are cognitively irrational, rationalists are required to try to overcome them, whatever the loss in respect of inter-temporal fulfilment. It follows that what is relatively rational for rationalists and for prudentialists will diverge. As it is reasonable to assume that most of us have both a deep-seated aim to form our attitudes in concord with truth and reason and a deep-seated aim to maximize the experiential fulfilment of our lives, this conclusion means that we are facing a disturbing conflict. The title of this book harbours an ambiguity that is designed to capture this dilemma. *Either* reason forces us to take refuge in something like the detachment of a retreat, by withdrawing from the temporal partiality of everyday life, and its attendant joys and sorrows, *or*, if we wish to preserve this involvement intact, reason is forced to retreat from the role of completely governing our lives. Whichever alternative is chosen, something precious to us—roughly speaking, truthfulness or happiness—is forsaken.

---

[7] Slote argues that common sense does not brand temporal biases as irrational, but views temporal neutrality as *more* rational or rationally *supererogatory* (1989: 124–30). I would be inclined to reinterpret this observation, if correct, as showing that common sense is not wedded to rationalism, but recognizes the rational legitimacy of prudentialism.

PART IV

Rationality and
Personal Neutrality

was this precious 'identity', to which he found himself so tenaciously clinging, of such supreme value after all

(Jocelyn Brooke)

18

INTRODUCTION: THE BIAS TOWARDS ONESELF

THE topic of this part is the cognitive rationality of another bias, *the bias towards oneself*, the O-bias. As a rule, if one knows that somebody will receive a benefit, one hopes, prefers, wishes, etc. that that being will be *oneself* rather than somebody else, however close the kinship or friendship with that being. Likewise, if someone will undergo some hardship, one usually hopes, prefers, etc. that this being will not be oneself, but rather some other being, however near and dear that being may be. This raises the question of whether the consideration that some being is (identical to) oneself provides one with a reason to be specially concerned about this being. This question is both about whether this consideration provides one with an apparent reason, actually motivating one's attitude, and about whether it provides one with a real reason, justifying it.

To be concerned about a being is to be concerned about how things go for this being; it is to want that things go well rather than badly for it.[1] So concern for a being implies that it is of a kind such that its existence or life can go well or badly for it; that is, it implies that it has consciousness. It does not imply, however, that life already goes well for it, that is, that it already has much, or any, of that which one is concerned, or wants, it to have. This can be put in Peter Unger's terminology (1990: 93–5) by saying that one can be concerned about, or matter to, oneself in the "prudential use", without one's life having much of what matters to one in the "desirability use" of what matters in survival.

This leads onto a distinction between being concerned about a being and *approving of* or *liking* it. Both entail having desires with respect to the being in response to a conception of it. But, as has already been indicated, to be concerned about a being involves conceiving of it as having consciousness, and being such that things can go well or badly

---

[1] Contrast Darwall's claim: "The object of care is the person *herself*, not some state or property involving her" (2002: 47). Darwall's argument that caring for another cannot be the same as to "desire intrinsically *that* another's good be realized" (2002: 2) can be met by requiring the intrinsic desire to be ultimately intrinsic. Also, in order to care for an individual, it is not sufficient to have an ultimately intrinsic desire that things go well for her on an isolated occasion (cf. Darwall, 2002: 69). Rather, care or concern for someone is a lasting disposition to have such desires (and related emotions of joy and sorrow when things go well or badly for this individual).

for it. In contrast, one can approve of or like something whilst conceiving it as an inanimate thing with, for example, appealing aesthetic properties. It is only required that one takes there to be something good (e.g. for oneself) *about* it; there need not be anything that can be good *for it*. Of course, this is reflected in the desires induced. Approval of or liking for a being implies desires to preserve what is good about it, but not desires that things go well for it. It may be what I will call *instrumental*.

It seems possible to be concerned about (how things go for) a being without approving of that being in any respect. If I see a stranger writhing in pain, I may be concerned that he be relieved of the pain without approving of him, though it may be that I would feel no concern were I to disapprove of him. In the case of oneself, however, concern and approval usually go together. One is not only especially concerned about oneself, but also especially approves of oneself. (The latter implies that one has something of what matters in the desirability sense, since things that are good about oneself, like the success one has had owing to one's intelligence and beauty, often make life better for one.) But, although self-approval and self-concern usually accompany each other, it follows from what has been said that self-approval may make one want to exist when self-concern does not, for example in a persistent vegetative state. Whether it may make one want to go on existing even when one's existence is intrinsically bad for one and self-concern impels one to commit suicide is another question.

Concern for one's future existence involves an *anticipation* of what one's future in some respects will be like for oneself 'from the inside', an anticipation of having some kind of experiences. This is because concern for a being, as opposed to approval of it, entails a conception of how things go for that being.

The central element of the O-bias, as I construe it, is self-concern, but I also take it to incorporate self-approval. The main question of Part IV is whether this bias is cognitively rational or whether it is based on irrational patterns of thought which will evaporate under conditions of cognitively and representationally ideal deliberation. Since the O-bias will be cognitively rational if our identity through time is such that it can justify this bias, an important part of this inquiry will be to analyse this identity.

It is of course (relatively) rational for rationalists to uphold the O-bias if and only if it is cognitively rational. Even if it is cognitively irrational, it is rational for prudentialists to uphold it. For prudentialists are archetypes who are governed by an aim constrained by the O-bias: their dominant aim is the inter-temporal maximization of experiential fulfilment, but, with greater or lesser emphasis, they give priority to the fulfilment of their own (intrinsic) desires because they are their own. The O-bias can be more or less pronounced, and to be a prudentialist it is not necessary to be biased to the degree that one maximizes the inter-temporal fulfilment of one's own desires at *whatever* cost to desire fulfilment overall. It is enough if one favours the fulfilment of one's own desires, because they are one's own, to the same or slightly bigger fulfilment of desires overall.

If the O-bias is cognitively irrational then, if satisfactionalists make their aim rational to the extent of disposing of this bias, they will be not only temporally neutral, like rational (as opposed to naïve) prudentialists, but also be *personally neutral* fulfilment-maximizers, like utilitarians. As we shall see, it is, however, not relatively rational even for these fulfilment-maximizers to try to completely rid themselves of their O-bias.

To repeat, to clarify whether the O-bias is cognitively rational, we need to explicate the concept of our identity through time: is the nature of this relation such that subjects who are perfectly clear about it will be more concerned about, and will like more, beings to whom they bear this relation than other beings to whom they do not bear it, however similar in other respects these other beings may be to the subjects? If so, an O-bias based on this relation will be cognitively rational. My point of departure, in Chapter 19, will be an account of the self or subject of experience which identifies it with our physical or material bodies. This view of our identity I call *naïve somatism*. I then turn to the most radical objection to this view: *immaterialism*, or the view that the conditions of our persistence consist in psychological relations which are entirely independent of the physical and have to do with, for example, the sameness of a mental substance.

After rejecting this challenge, I turn in Chapter 20 to theories which take the conditions of our persistence to consist in psychological relations with a material basis. They will be labelled *psychologist* theories. It will be found, among other things, that it is difficult to find any such psychological relation that is both in line with the intuition that we are things rather than processes and that is necessary for our persistence.[2] Further, the central psychological relation of memory presupposes an identity criterion which must be somatist. Thus, the somatist starting-point seems vindicated, and the question arises whether it can be satisfactorily articulated. Since our bodies are organisms belonging to the human species, this articulation must presumably take the form which has become known as *animalism* or *the biological view* of our identity. In Chapter 21, however, this view is found to involve two errors: it takes our human organisms to be the primary owners of our experiences, though these owners are in fact proper parts of them, and it implies that the essence of these organisms is such that they cannot cease to exist while our selves persist and perceive themselves.

The conclusion of this investigation is, then, that there are no coherent conditions of our persistence. In our commonsensical moments, we assume naïve somatism, but the animalist attempt to work out this view reveals that it involves two erroneous assumptions. Hence, we land in the view I will call *factual nihilism* about our identity, namely, that we are not identical to any one kind of thing. Of course, we all exist, so we are all identical to something: ourselves. There is a portion of matter that constitutes us, and it is essentially of some kind. The claim of factual nihilism is that neither this kind nor any other is essentially ours, that is, is such that if and only if something of this kind persists, then, necessarily, one of us persists. Certainly, since we every day make innumerable judgements of diachronic identity, we must have some notion of what it consists in. My conjecture is that this is given by naïve somatism which provides a criterion of our identity that works well enough in everyday life. Furthermore, we can refer to ourselves

---

[2] Cf. Thomas Reid: "I am not thought, I am not action, I am not feeling; I am something that thinks, acts and suffers" ('Of Memory', reprinted in J. Perry, 1975: 109).

by means of personal pronouns, but, as will transpire, this does not require that we know our essence and the precise conditions of our persistence.

On this nihilist approach to our identity, the claim that the O-bias is cognitively rational is indefensible, since our conception of our identity involves mistaken beliefs about our bodies. But I shall also examine whether its rationality could be vindicated were animalism or psychologism true. Clearly, the prospects for such a vindication seem brighter on psychologism than on animalism, since what we seem to value most in ourselves is our consciousnesses or minds. However, it will be found that psychologism, too, is incapable of propping up the cognitive rationality of the O-bias. Cases in the face of which it is difficult for it to defend this rationality include fission cases. 'Discontinuity' cases—in which there is dissolution into minute constituents quickly followed by the creation of a qualitatively identical individual from different constituents—present another obstacle. So, psychologism is virtually on all fours with somatism in failing to construe our identity as something that matters to us. All this is the business of Chapter 23.

On no theory of our identity, then, will it provide a rationale for the O-bias. This can be called *evaluative* nihilism about our identity. But not only is it the case that this favouritism towards ourselves comes out as cognitively irrational on all accounts of our identity, even immaterialism, we may wonder whether in everyday life we are so muddled-headed that identity-judgements—as understood by naïve somatism—in fact can be our (apparent) reason for being O-biased. From Chapter 23 onwards, I try to make credible the idea that these judgements are only the explanatory reason of why we are thus biased. They merely exercise a causal influence, consisting first and foremost in eliciting an anticipation of the having of experiences—that is, a spontaneous and vivid representation of them—but also by suggesting a resemblance in respect of features liked to oneself as one is at present. In Chapter 25 my objective is to explain also how this account is compatible with the amount of altruism that there actually is in the world.

The topic of Chapter 26 is to determine what, in the realm of prudence, are rational policies against the background supplied by the analysis of our diachronic identity. The main conclusion is that you are not rationally required to maximize your own experiential fulfilment inter-temporally, as prudentialism recommends, but may sacrifice it to pursue some *ideal* such as rationalism.

In Chapter 27, the possibility of idealism is carried over to the inter-personal case of *morality*, on strength of the rational insignificance of personal identity. If, in the intra-personal case of prudence, rationalists are at liberty to go against the goal of inter-temporal maximization of *their own* fulfilment, they must be equally free, in the inter-personal case of morality, to go against the goal of inter-temporally maximizing the fulfilment of *another*. To be sure, they have to pass a *rational requirement of universalizability* which implies rising above the O-bias, but by allowing idealism, this requirement does not constrain them to a personally neutral or utilitarian fulfilment maximization. It is only satisfactionalists who are led to this conclusion by the requirement. Although the requirement of universalization does not compel rationalists and satisfactionalists to endorse the same project, I suggest in Chapter 28 that the fact that agents are mutually dependent on each other for help in realizing their respective aims may make it relatively rational for them to co-operate.

Finally, in Chapter 29, I attempt to gauge whether it will be (relatively) rational for fully neutral satisfactionalists to shape their mental states in accordance with this requirement of universalization. The conclusion will be that, because the O-bias is so deep-rooted, it will be irrational for them to attempt to effect this remoulding, whereas of course rationalists are committed to it. Hence, in this sense, reason is required to retreat from the position of governing the attitudes of satisfactionalists, whereas it forces rationalists into a retreat in which they do less good to their fellow beings than they could have done had they not had the ideal of making their para-cognitive attitudes cognitively rational.

19

SELF AND BODY

WE are capable of referring to ourselves by means of tokens of the first-person pronoun, in the case of English, 'I'. Although it is not entirely uncontroversial (as we shall see), I shall take it that, if anything is one's self, it is the referent of these pronouns. There are at least two philosophical questions that can be asked about this self. First, when we employ 'I' to refer to ourselves, what are the properties of ourselves by means of which we attempt to pick ourselves out for purposes of reference? Secondly, what is the essence or identity of these putative selves of ours, that is , the entities we attempt to pick out? For this essence need not feature the properties which make it possible for us to be objects of first-person reference, since we can exist even when we are not the objects of such reference (for example in periods of unconsciousness).

In this chapter, I shall reply to the first question by suggesting that the properties by means of which we attempt to pick out ourselves when we use 'I' indicate that what we attempt to pick out are our material bodies. These bodies are obviously living organisms belonging to a certain biological species, *homo sapiens*. In Chapter 21 it will, however, be seen that the persistence conditions of these organisms are such that they may cease to exist, while the conditions for being a self allow that the same self persists, that is, the way in which these organisms are identified by first-person reference is inconsistent with their persistence conditions. It follows that we cannot be identical to these human organisms, that their and our conditions of persistence cannot be the same. For that of us which makes us selves surely cannot outlive that to which we are identical (even if, conversely, we can exist without being selves, that is, without being objects of self-reference by means of 'I'). But, as I also contend in this chapter and the next, there is no other kind of thing—for example no part of our organisms such as our brains—which matches the conditions of being a self. Hence, in Chapter 21 I draw the factually nihilist conclusion that there is no kind of thing to which we are identical, no philosophically defensible conditions of our persistence.

Conditions for Being a Subject of Experience and a Self

Whatever else is necessarily true of a self, it is surely a *subject of experience* in the sense that it is something to which experiential states (and normally dispositional mental states, like desires) are attributable. It is plausible to think that experiential states, like perceiving and thinking, must have a subject—something doing the perceiving and thinking—just as much as they need an object—something being perceived and thought. If anything is to be a self, it must be such a subject or, in other words, have consciousness. Something which does not have consciousness, like a rock or a rocket, cannot be, or have, a self. Let us call this *the owner aspect* of the notion of the self.

It is this aspect of the concept of the self that on a Humean 'bundle-theory' would have no persisting counterpart in reality (1739–40/1978: 252). A familiar difficulty besetting this theory is that if experiential states could not be attributed to any subjects, but were 'free-floating', how could we even in principle tell apart two simultaneously occurring qualitatively identical experiences that have the same objects? It would be of no avail were these experiences to interlock with other free-floating experiences to form 'bundles', for these bundles, too, could exist in duplicate. It would help, however, if experiences were not free-floating but ascribable to physical subjects that can be individuated by reference to their location in space (as well as in time),[1] and it will soon transpire how such subjects could emerge. Perhaps there is a way of construing a non-physical subject so that it could play this individuating role, but this is not something I would undertake to do.

A second aspect of selfhood or being a self is that the self must in some way *be aware of itself*. In a world like ours, there would scarcely be subjects having or owning experiences, unless being equipped with these features had had survival value. The fact that animals are capable of perceiving their environment, prey, and predators in the vicinity, increases their chances of survival. But it would not do so, unless they perceived *themselves*, that is, the subjects doing the relevant perceiving, in relation to surrounding objects. It would be of little use for the bird to perceive the stalking cat, unless it perceived the spatial relation in which the cat stands to *it itself*.

Let us call this aspect—that a self is necessarily capable of perceiving itself—*the phenomenal aspect* of the notion of the self. It concerns the self entering into the *content* of some of the states of (perceptual) experience that are attributable to it as their subject. It is this aspect Hume has in mind when he writes that there are philosophers "who imagine we are every moment intimately conscious of what we call our SELF" (1739–40/1978: 251). He repudiates this aspect, when he affirms that "there is no impression constant and invariable" (1739–40/1978: 251) as an impression of the self must be. But, to repeat, if we had not perceived ourselves in relation to an often hostile environment, we would in all probability not have lasted long.

It may be objected that, although this Darwin-inspired consideration shows that in *this* world conscious beings must have the capacity to perceive themselves, it does not show this to be a necessary truth, holding in every possible world. That is true, and I am willing to grant the possibility of 'self-blind' (or rather, as will be seen, 'self-numb') creatures. More specifically, I think there could conceivably be creatures who saw and heard things from mere 'points' which for them had no experiential content. Perhaps they could be said to be subjects of experience in virtue of conforming to the owner aspect. But they would not be subjects of experience in the full sense that is an amalgamation of the owner and phenomenal aspects, the sense in which the owner must be something

---

[1] A *locus classicus* for this line of thought is P. F. Strawson (1959: ch. 3).

phenomenally presented to itself. This is the more useful sense in our world which, as we have seen, will scarcely contain any 'pointillistic' subjects. To be a subject of, for example, perceptual experience, then, an individual must not only perceive, but must perceive things in relation to itself, as a perceptual object.

Being a subject of experience is, however, not sufficient for being a self. The reason why some subject, like the bird, is not a self is that, though it perceives itself, for example as standing in spatial relations to surrounding objects, like the cat, and, as this implies, perceives itself as having spatial properties, like shape and size, and related properties, like colour, the bird is not aware of itself *as an owner of experiences*. The bird does not attribute experiential states to itself: it does not think of itself as *seeing* the cat, as *thinking* that the cat is approaching, etc. I call this aspect—which in my usage drives a wedge between selves and subjects of experience—*the introspective aspect* of selves. Thus, a self must possess this third aspect, alongside the two aspects definitive of subjects of experience.

I conjecture that the introspective aspect presupposes the second, phenomenal aspect, that it is by (correctly) taking this phenomenal aspect as presenting a *physical* thing—in the sense of something capable of existing (also) unperceived—that one acquires the notion of a subject to which one can ascribe one's experiential states. This implies that the phenomenal aspect is a necessary condition for introspection of one's experiential states (so even if there were pointillistic subjects, they could never be selves). But it is not the case that this perception of oneself *is* introspection (the bird does not introspect). We should keep apart perceiving oneself as a spatial *object* among other spatial objects and being aware of oneself as a *subject* having experiential states, like perceiving oneself in relation to other spatial objects.[2] My hypothesis is that (correctly) taking the former self-perception, the phenomenal aspect, as veridical, as presenting a physical thing, is necessary for ascribing experiences to oneself, for being aware of oneself as a subject owning experiential states, that is, is necessary for introspective self-consciousness, as distinct from 'objective' self-consciousness.

Introspective self-consciousness is clearly a more sophisticated capacity than object self-consciousness, that is, self-consciousness to the extent of being aware that one possesses simple spatial and related secondary qualities. It is a more complex matter to conceptually register, for instance, *one's perceiving* a thing's standing in a certain spatial relation to oneself than this thing's standing in this relation (e.g. to think 'I see a cross in front of me' than to think 'There is a cross in front of me' on the basis of perception). For the content of the former act includes that of the latter plus the element italicized. I cannot here go into an analysis of perception (see instead Persson, 1985a), but will simply assert that possession of the concept of perceptual states presupposes possession of the concept of something physical serving as its subject. This hypothesis has the merit of explaining a fact we noted above: that mental states can be individuated only if they are attached to something physical, that there cannot be in this sense free-floating mental states.[3]

---

[2] In a way Michael Ayers does not seem to do when he speaks of the "physical or material self" as "the presented subject of experience and action" (1991: ii. 286). Cf. Cassam (1997: 51 ff.).

[3] As will transpire, the view that I have here tentatively advanced, that having the concept of an experiential state involves having the concept of a subject being in it, implies that Parfit is wrong when he claims: "because we are not

According to the proposal under consideration, this physical thing is obtained by regarding the phenomenal aspect of the body as presenting a physical body. If so, introspective self-consciousness presupposes objective self-consciousness. Contrary to this, Sydney Shoemaker maintains that introspective "self-awareness is not perceptual awareness, i.e., is not that sort of awareness in which objects are presented" (1984: 105). In his opinion, this self-awareness "is not mediated by anything analogous to a sense-impression [of ourselves]" (1984: 104). But those experiential states we are aware of ourselves as having in this self-awareness are attributed to *the very same entity*—namely ourselves—as those spatial attributes we perceive ourselves as having. While Shoemaker's view does not yield an explanation of why this should be so, mine has the merit of yielding a very simple explanation of this circumstance.

Also, my account provides a very simple picture of how the ascription of experiential states to oneself could get going. It is much harder to understand how this process could get started if these states are ascribed to something that is not physical or something physical that is not ordinarily perceived (e.g. the brain). Moreover, from the point of view of self-preservation or survival it would seem natural to suppose that our ability to differentiate ourselves from our environment is acquired rather early in our development, that it does not have to await the acquisition of the fairly advanced capacity of introspective self-consciousness.

The account proposed does not imply, however, that the concept of the physical is primary in relation to that of the mental. For we have also explained the notion of a physical object in terms of an existence independent of perception, that is, the concept of the physical involves the concept of something mental. So the notions of the mental and of the physical seem to come out as *inter-dependent* or *complementary*. A corollary of this inter-dependency is that there are concepts, for example of primary and secondary qualities, applicable to the content of perception that precede the distinction between the mental and the physical.[4]

As indicated above, the conceptual dependence of the mental on the physical is the reason why mental states cannot be free-floating. This may otherwise seem mysterious, unless one takes the physicalist or materialist position that mental predicates designate nothing but physical properties. If this reduction fails, it may be thought that experiences can have nothing but extrinsic and contingent relations to the physical.[5] The answer I have suggested is, however, that something can be described as mental only in contrast to something physical, to which it is attributed.

---

separately existing entities, we could fully describe . . . our experiences . . . without claiming that they are had by a subject of experiences. We could give what I call an *impersonal* description" (1984: 225). That is, that the truth of his reductionist view that we do not exist separately from our bodies and their mental states implies the possibility of an impersonal description of these mental states. This implication does not hold according to the view here proposed, for the subject which mental states require is the body, and nothing 'separate' from it.

[4] This is a matter I explore in (1985a) and (1999b).

[5] Cf. John Foster, who maintains that, *basically*, the subject of mental attributes could not also have corporeal ones (1991: 206–12). The inter-dependency between the mental and the physical indicated in the text is more fully spelt out in Persson (1985a: ch. 5.2).

To sum up, a self is something that (1) owns or has experiences (not to mention other mental states of a propositional and dispositional kind, like beliefs and desires), that (2) perceives itself, or enters into the content of some of its experiential states, and that (3) is aware of itself as something of which (1) is true. The introspective aspect, (3), involves taking the phenomenal aspect, (2), to be of something physical, in the sense of existing independently of perception. Thus, objective self-consciousness, (2), is a prerequisite for the introspective self-consciousness distinctive of selves, (3).

My starting-point was that, if the self is anything, it is that to which we refer by means of tokens of 'I'. Let us see how the account of the self given by (1)–(3) plugs into this starting-point. It is a commonplace that, just as, for example, the use of 'now' is governed by the rule that a token of it is to be used to refer to the time at which it is produced, so the use of 'I' is governed by the rule that a token of it is to be used to refer to the producer of it. This producer, as construed by (2), is a perceived spatial object, one's own body as perceived by oneself. Thus consciously to follow the rule is to use a token of 'I' to refer to the perceived body which is the subject or owner of the mental property of producing this token of 'I' in awareness of the rule.

According to this account, the self or the referent of 'I' is one's body, though it is identified by reference to psychological properties. If so, these psychological properties are not ones we *essentially* have, that is, we are not *essentially* selves in the sense that it is necessarily true that, were we to cease being selves, we would cease to exist.[6] So I can coherently assert 'I *shall* cease to be a self' or 'Once I *was* not a self'. But I contradict myself if I say 'I am not *now* a self', for my reference to myself by means of a token of 'I' implies that I am a self. Still, being selves is just a 'phase' we may pass through, like being adults. Nothing psychological is a necessary condition for our identity.

This corollary does not strike me as troublesome. We are quite ready to say things like 'If I were ever to sink into a persistent vegetative state, I want you to kill *me*', which presupposes that we could exist after having irrevocably lost all consciousness. Similarly, we are inclined to hold that we existed (prenatally) before acquiring consciousness. If you were to see a picture of the foetus in your mother's womb at the gestational period of, say, three months, when it has discernible human features, it is quite natural to exclaim: 'That's *me* in the womb. That's my left hand, etc.'

Proprioception and the Self

Let me now examine more closely how we perceive our own bodies. Michael Ayers maintains that we have "bodily sensations of ourselves as objects extended in space" (1991: ii. 285). The objects we tactually feel are also felt to be extended in (three-dimensional) space but, I submit, all of us perceive our own bodies, and only our own bodies, differently. Although what we tactually feel may present itself as three-dimensional

---

[6] Contrast, e.g., Robert Nozick's claim "that selves are essentially selves, that anything which is a self could not have existed yet been otherwise" (1981: 79).

when, for example we hold a ball in the palm of our hand, what we feel as three-dimensionally extended are two-dimensional surfaces: we do not feel the ball *filling* the space enclosed by its surface (though from its felt weight we might guess that it is not hollow). In contrast, we are proprioceptively aware of the *mass* of our own bodies as filling three-dimensional regions of space; we are aware of them as three-dimensional *solids*, of a rough human body-like shape.[7] This is the source of our notion of solidity and, thus, of a 3-D thing or body as something having this property.

Visual space is three-dimensional, too, but it is perceived as stretching out from a *single* point of view. In contrast, the felt three-dimensional solidity of our bodies is constituted by sensations from innumerable 'points of feeling' spread out in three-dimensional space, that is, from receptors distributed throughout the interior of our bodies. Neither vision nor tactile perception nor any other mode of perception of the external world can produce the unique impression of 3-D solidity or of filling through and through a 3-D region of space.

It is because one's proprioceptive or somatosensory awareness is an awareness not just of surfaces, but of this 3-D solidity, that one can feel bodily sensations—like pains and pangs of hunger—*inside* one's body, somewhere *in-between* where one feels, for example, a pressure on one's back and an itch around one's navel. A disturbance or damage occurring practically anywhere inside our bodies may cause us pain or some other sort of unpleasant bodily sensation in that region.

As this proprioceptive awareness includes kinaesthetic sensations, it is not surprisingly of crucial importance for our ability to execute intentional bodily actions. It supplies feedback information about the positions and movements of our limbs upon which we are dependent when we voluntarily carry out bodily acts. To lose it would be greatly incapacitating, though with practice other senses, especially sight, can partially fill the slack.[8]

Ayers further maintains that this proprioceptive awareness of our own body "essentially permeates our sensory experience of things in general" or is "integrated with the deliverances of each of the senses" (1991: ii. 285). Thus, one sees and hears things in relation to one's proprioceptive presentation of one's head, has tactile sensations on the surfaces of proprioceptive presentations of limbs in touch with objects, gustatory sensations in proprioceptive presentations of the mouth, and olfactory ones in the neighbourhood of proprioceptive presentations of the nostrils and palate.[9] This 'proprioceptive "body model" ', as Ayers terms it (1991: i. 187), is the common denominator of what we

---

[7] See Persson (1985a: ch. 4.5). For an elaborate analysis of bodily awareness, see Brian O'Shaughnessy (1980: i, chs. 6 and 7) and (1995). But, as opposed to me, O'Shaughnessy views bodily awareness as disanalogous to perception and as not presenting "an existent experienced entity" (1980: i. 230). In contrast J. L. Bermúdez argues that proprioception is perception of oneself (1998: ch. 6).

[8] This is dramatically illustrated by Oliver Sacks's account of "the disembodied lady" (1985: ch. 3).

[9] Contrast Evans's claim: "what we are aware of, when we know that we see a tree, is *nothing but a tree*" (1982: 231). In defending a similar thesis, Shoemaker contends that "we are so constituted that our being in certain states directly produces in us beliefs about ourselves to the effect that we are in those states" (1984: 104). But when we have a visual experience, we acquire not merely the belief that we see something, but that we see it *in some spatial relation to ourselves*, and how can such a belief be produced without perceptual awareness of ourselves?

perceive in all our sense-modalities: it is normally present whenever we perceive and are conscious of anything.[10] Therefore, it provides us with a centre around which we can spatially organize all our perceptual presentations of external objects, and on the surface of which or within which we can locate our bodily sensations. Moreover, its parts are involved in our kinesthetic sensations.

My claim is that this felt three-dimensional 'model' of our bodies, the centrepiece of our perceptual or phenomenal world, taken as presenting a real, physical thing, constitutes the subject to which we attribute our perceptual and other mental states. If correct, this account of the subject has the merit of undercutting scepticism about the physical world. As we have seen, the notion of an experiential state, for example the state of perceiving something, logically requires a subject. Now, if this subject can be obtained only by taking something in the perceptual content to be a physical thing, a general doubt about whether this content presents anything of physical reality would of course be ruled out. For asking whether a perceptual content presents something physical, that is, something that exists independently of it, requires a concept of the (perceptual) state of which it is the content, and this in turn requires a notion of a subject obtained by taking something in the content to be a physical thing. Therefore, a general scepticism about whether perceptual content presents physical reality would be undercut (though this is not a point I need for present purposes).

This would explain why we cannot doubt that the tokens of 'I' we produce with the intention to refer to ourselves succeed in so referring, though they refer to something physical. If (a) the producer of a (meaningful) instance of this token is perceived by me whenever one of these tokens is produced by me, as I have contended that my body is, and (b) I must take this perception to be of a physical thing to ascribe mental states to myself (as I must do to refer), I cannot doubt that my tokens of 'I' will successfully refer if they refer to my physical body.

Perhaps some would like to object to this identification of subject of experience and body that it is strange to say that our *bodies* perceive and think.[11] I believe this is like objecting 'It is not *men* but *policemen* who enforce the law'. The reason why it sounds odd to say that *bodies* perceive and think is, I conjecture, that if something is described as a 'body', it is 'conversationally implied' that it is a *mere* body, shorn of any mental capacities, just as if law-enforcers are described as 'men', it is implied that they are mere men, lacking the relevant authority. Moreover, note that it is not in the least awkward to say that *organisms* perceive and think but, surely, organisms *are* bodies (with a life-sustaining constitution, I shall contend in Chapter 21).

Nor can it be argued that since we say that subjects or selves *have* bodies, they cannot be identical to them. For we also say that our bodies have heads, trunks, and limbs, but evidently this does not rule out that they *are* a configuration of heads, trunks, and limbs. If we are that of our bodies which we perceive from the inside, these bodies *have* unperceived parts.

---

[10] There are aberrations; for an instance, consult again Sacks's account of "the disembodied lady" (1985: ch. 3). This unfortunate woman has a conception of herself, I maintain, only because she earlier perceived her body.

[11] See, e.g. E. J. Lowe (1996: 1).

Galen Strawson raises the different objection that one can

> well imagine a three-bodied creature that naturally experiences itself as three-bodied, and as receiving information (perhaps via different sense modalities) from all three bodies, while still having a strong sense of the single mental self, and thinking of itself as 'I'. (1997: 414)

So, although Strawson is prepared to concede that "ordinary human experience of oneself as a mentally single is deeply shaped by experience of having a single body", he denies that "any possible experience of oneself as a mentally single depends essentially on such experience".

I think the 'three-bodied' situation Strawson envisages must be further specified for it to become clear what, if any, challenge it presents to the view here proposed. Let me just say with respect to the proprioceptive awareness of our body as a 3-D solid, which according to my view constitutes the core of the phenomenal aspect of the self, that I cannot see how anyone could have such an awareness of three bodies that presents them *as separate*, that is, as separated by empty space. For this is an awareness of something (that offers felt resistance) *filling* a three-dimensional region. Such an awareness cannot represent the empty space between distinct bodies. So, if one had proprioceptive awareness of three distinct bodies, they would have to be experienced as adjoining each other and so forming a unity. One could, however, have proprioceptive awareness of one of the three bodies and awareness "via different sense modalities" of the two others, for example see things from the point of view of one of them and hear sounds surrounding the other. (If there was exteroception from more than one body, it might be difficult to put together the perceptual information to a coherent phenomenal space.) In these circumstances, my conjecture is that the proprioceptive awareness alone would provide the sense of the self as something single.

I would also like briefly to comment upon Strawson's remark that "ordinary human experience of oneself" is of "a mentally single". According to the owner aspect, the self is something mental in the sense that it has mental properties like perceiving and thinking. According to the phenomenal aspect, too, the self involves a reference to the mental, since it consists in one's body as given in proprioceptive awareness. However, none of this implies that the self is *essentially* mental, that its possession of some mental features are necessary and sufficient for the self's existence. But this conception seems to be what Strawson has in mind, for he asserts that the self exists "during any uninterrupted or hiatus-free period of consciousness. But . . . only for some short period of time" (1997: 425). So it seems to exist only so long as it is continuously experiencing or continuously experienced (or both). It is, however, unclear to me how such a self can be "deeply shaped by experience of having a single body".

As Strawson points out, however, this conception "offends against the everyday use of expressions like 'myself' to refer to enduring human beings" (1997: 21). Clearly, we take ourselves to be capable of persisting through periods of unconsciousness, for instance. I see this divergence from everyday use as a serious drawback because it is hard to find a less question-begging way of fixing what is the object of an investigation into 'the self' than by means of saying that it is the referent of tokens of the first-person pronouns.[12] Thus, in order to know what we are talking about, we should take the self to be that to which we refer by means of 'I', and this referent exists through periods of the blackest unconsciousness.

Immaterialist Theories of the Self

The position I shall call *immaterialism* denies that there are criteria for the persistence of us or our selves which refer to the identity of anything material (or physical, for present purposes it is not necessary to distinguish between these), that is, it denies the truth of what I shall term *matter-based* theories of our nature and identity. Immaterialists may positively affirm that these criteria are of something essentially mental, but, as we shall see, they may also hold that we are of a kind, distinct from anything material, of which it is improper or a category-mistake to ask for any criteria of persistence. Of whichever stripe, immaterialism is the topic of the present section.

Immaterialism is not simply the denial of materialism or physicalism of the mind, that is, the doctrine that mental predicates designate material or physical properties. It entails *property-dualism* in the sense of affirming that (some) mental predicates designate properties that are distinct from physical ones. But, whereas property-dualists can maintain that these mental properties belong to subjects that are essentially physical, immaterialists must reject this claim. Apart from this negative claim, they may hold that their subjects are essentially mental—this is *substance-dualism*—or that these property-exemplifications need not have any subjects—this is exemplified by the Humean 'bundle-theory'.

Now, to return to the problem of unconsciousness, can we really form a conception of anything essentially mental existing through such periods? There seems an acute risk that a self of this sort degenerates into something of which it is impossible to form any conception, like Kant's transcendental or noumenal self. It appears a mystery how we are able to attribute our experiences to such an elusive self.

Another approach to this problem, apparently favoured by the substance-dualist Descartes, is to suggest that 'thinking' goes on during periods of what we would ordinarily term 'unconsciousness', although this is thinking that we never remember.[13] This is, however, clearly an *ad hoc* move, designed only to save a cherished theory. It is not a move made because there is empirical evidence for there always being thinking which runs through periods of unconsciousness.

Richard Swinburne toys with the idea of denying the principle that "no substance can have two beginnings of existence" (Shoemaker and Swinburne, 1984: 33). This denial would permit us to hold that the person who wakes up from unconsciousness is the same mental substance as someone who was earlier knocked unconscious. But if numerically the same substance can have two beginnings, what difference is there between this and

---

[12] The importance of making clear what the topic is when 'the self' is discussed is made clear by Olson (1999).

[13] For references to relevant passages of Descartes and criticisms of his view, see Unger (1990: 15–16, 45–7) and G. Strawson (1994: 125–7).

the state of affairs consisting in one substance ceasing to exist and being replaced by a distinct (but qualitatively similar) one? Swinburne's proposal threatens to eradicate this difference.[14]

John Foster launches a proposal that might appear to dispense with the idea of a mental substance persisting through a span of unconsciousness. He suggests that when a lacuna of unconsciousness separates a stream of consciousness, ending at an earlier time, from one commencing at a later time, they belong to the same subject if and only if they have "the potential for being phases of a single stream" (1979: 179; cf. 1991: 251–2), that is, if and only if they would have formed a continuous stream if the earlier stream had gone on until the later one started. Strictly speaking, however, what has the potential of fusing these two streams is not the streams themselves, but something else that actually made them separate and instead could have made them continuous. If this is proposed to be a mental thing or substance, we are still stuck with the problem how it should be conceived. If, more realistically, it is taken to be something physical, presumably, something in the brain—a hypothesis to which Foster seems to help himself (1979: 180)—the immaterialist position is surrendered. Our identity has then been made parasitic on the identity of some physical entity.

A more radical non-substantialist way of trying to deal with the problem of how to understand a mental owner of experiences is advocated by Geoffrey Madell. He is of the opinion that personal identity can only be understood from a subjective or indexical point of view, and he castigates substantialist immaterialism (along with matter-based views, of course) as manifestations of an unsound "tendency to treat persons as just another sort of object"(1981: 134).[15] He distinguishes between the first-person (or subjective) perspective and the third-person (or objective) perspective. As I interpret him, the first-person stance is adopted when one identifies things indexically as 'mine' and 'yours' or persons as 'me' and 'you', whereas no indexicals can figure in descriptions from the third-person view. He claims then that "the nature of the identity of a person over time is not to be spelled out in terms of what the third-person eye can perceive" (1981: 139), that is, I presume, in terms of what is formulable in an indexical-free way.

Speaking of a break in consciousness, he asserts: "Quite simply, we have the same self before and after the break, if the experiences both before and after the break are mine" (1981: 137).[16] The postulation of a "continuing ego", or of something material, to fill the slack is condemned as examples of an unsound "objectivisation" of persons. Gaps of unconsciousness would be in need of filling only if minds were located in objective time.

This is a startling view, but there is a grain of truth in it. For, as we shall see, we can refer to ourselves by means of 'I' even if we are not essentially of any kind and there is no criterion of our persistence. But this means only that we can single out ourselves *in the*

---

[14] H. D. Lewis likewise has no qualms about supposing that "in the event of strictly dreamless sleep we cease to be" (1982: 89), only to find ourselves to be the very same persons when consciousness is regained. But how do we know that those waking up are not merely the same *sorts* of persons?

[15] Cf. Unger's discussion of the "subjective view" he finds in the philosophizing of common sense (1986).

[16] Cf. the implications Lynne Rudder Baker draws from her "Constitution View" (2000: 132–8).

present without these means; it does not imply that we can make past- or future-tense judgements about ourselves without applying some criterion of our transtemporal identity. I believe this criterion to be a somatic or bodily criterion which, on closer inspection, turns out to be untenable. But I cannot see how one could possibly make a past- or future-tense judgement about oneself—a judgement implying that someone existing in the past or future is identical to the current thinker—without appealing to some criterion of transtemporal identity, without tracing the continuity of some kind of entity through space and time. That is, however, what Madell seems to affirm.

In one passage (1981: 137–8), he suggests an analogy between 'the *property* of being mine' and the property of being red. Given the aptness of this analogy, I should be able to identify a subject directly, that is, without the application of any criterion of identity, in the past or future as me and its experiences as mine. But the analogy is certainly suspect: 'being me' and 'being mine' do not express anything *universal* as 'being red' does. If there was not this contrast between indexicals and universal predicates, it would follow, for instance, that the distinction between the first-person and the third-person point of view, on which Madell places such a weight, would collapse.

Since these immaterialist attempts to get along without the notion of mental thing or substance persisting through periods of unconsciousness are unsuccessful, let us return to the problems of this notion. These can be made more specific than the accusation that the notion is obscure. If this thing or substance is supposed to exist not only when perceived, but also unperceived, it seems to be a physical rather than a mental thing or substance. For we have seen that it is plausible to define a physical object as an object that exists not only when perceived—as does a mental object like an after-image or ache—but is also capable of existing unperceived. We have construed the perceptual world as spatially arranged; so, if the self is perceived, it would seem to have to have spatial features and be located either within the limits of the body-model or outside them. If such a perceived object exists also unperceived, it is hard to see how it can fail to qualify as physical.

Our conception of the mental seems to be either of certain states—of perceiving, thinking, etc.—or of entities that exist only so long as they are the objects of such states—like after-images. The mental thing or substance is neither. It is not just an object of experience, since it can allegedly exist when not experienced, through spells of unconsciousness. Although it is a subject or owner of states of experience, it is not essentially in such states, precisely because it can persist during unconsciousness.

Against this background, it is not surprising that those who take the mental self to be introspectively revealed have nothing illuminating to say about its nature. For instance, after declaring that in introspection he is immediately aware of "being a certain kind of thing—a sort which characterizes me independently of my mental condition", Foster adds that the content of this awareness of one's self cannot be verbalized, except in words that are "ostensively" interpreted (1991: 234).[17]

---

[17] In a similar vein, H. D. Lewis writes that "there is nothing I can say about myself beyond the affirmation that I am the person I find myself to be" (1982: 57).

Continuity of Consciousness and Identity of Subject

Vinit Haksar, for one, has claimed that a "permanent self" "provides unity to our experience both at a time (synchronic unity) and over time (diachronic unity)" (1991: 37). We have seen that there are two levels at which our experience could be united: the ownership level, at which states of experience are united into different consciousnesses by being owned by the same subject, and the phenomenal level, at which their objects are united into coherent phenomenal worlds. So far, we have focused on synchronic or momentary unity. The main claim has been that the objects perceived at one moment are spatially organized around the subject's body perceived from the inside, as a 3-D solid. To provide unity or structure at this phenomenal level, there seems no need for the subject to present itself experientially in any other way than as a (spatial) body. Hitherto, we have proceeded on the assumption that it is this body, taken as physical, which strings together (simultaneous) states of experience, with objects spatially organized in the way indicated, into separate consciousnesses; thus the phenomenal and the owner aspects are tied together. (In the next chapter, we shall see that the assumption of the body as the owner is problematic, but these problems do not support the idea that the owner of experiential states is mental.)

But perhaps reasons to revise this picture emerge if we turn to experiences which are temporally extended and to the *diachronic* or *transtemporal* unity or continuity of the subject or self. Here, too, we must be alert to the distinction between the ownership level, where a relation between experiential states are at issue, namely the relation of being owned by something, and the phenomenal level, which concerns their objects or content. As regards the first level, there is a *continuity of consciousness*, CCS, consisting in a stretch of consciousness, or series of conscious states, which is not interrupted by any moment of unconsciousness. This continuity may stretch over a whole day. It should be distinguished from a *continuity of content*, CCT. There is this continuity if, for instance, one perceives a change, for example the flight of a bird across the sky, as smooth and continuous, and as not containing any sudden 'jumps' of the bird from one spot to another. In some respects, this continuity often lasts a day, too: there is normally a large amount of continuity in the perceptual content, though one's thoughts may shift from one theme to another.

Now, Foster maintains that the "double overlap" of what is in effect CCT and CCS

> provides the sensible continuity of sense experience and unifies presentations into a stream of awareness. And it is in the unity of a stream that we primarily discern the identity of a subject.[18]

The subject is construed by him in the "Cartesian" fashion "as a simple and genuine mental continuant" (1979: 174; 1991: 233–4).[19]

But, although I agree that "the sensible continuity of sense experience" is *normally* provided by the joint forces of CCT and CCS, I want to stress their separateness. In

---

[18] (1979: 176). More recently, Foster has restated what I take to be the same account (1991: 240–61).

[19] Similarly, Swinburne claims that "my experience of continuing change is the experience that my experiences of certain small changes are experienced in succession by a common subject" (Shoemaker and Swinburne, 1984: 44). Cf. also Campbell (1957: 76–7).

particular, I would like to insist that, however comprehensive its content may be, one could not tell from CCT whether or not it composes CCS, that is, whether it forms an unbroken stretch of consciousness (let alone that the subject is the same which, as we shall see, does not follow from CCS).

It is as a rule reliable to infer CCS from CCT (and we have to resort to *inferring* our own CCS, since, of course, it does not show up introspectively). This may lead us to overlook the difference between the two, or think that CCT ensures CCS, but that would be a mistake. Suppose that my perception of, say, a moving vehicle was interrupted by a period of unconsciousness lasting a few seconds, but that the vehicle's motion also came to a halt for the same period. Then my perception might exhibit CCT—the vehicle's motion may still be perceived by me as continuous—though I do not exemplify CCS.

The following admittedly fantastic case demonstrates the divide between CCT, on the one hand, and CCS and identity of subject, on the other. It is conceivable that the microparticles composing the body of a person A are suddenly scattered, but that some other particles almost at once come together to constitute the body of a person B who (at least in macroscopic aspects) is qualitatively indistinguishable from A. Imagine that this whole sequence of events occurs so rapidly that human senses cannot detect that for a fraction of a second there was no body of a person in the relevant spatial region. In reality, however, there has been a brief period in which no macroscopic body existed, and for that reason the bodies of A and B are not numerically the same body (as I hope to make clearer in Chapter 22). Although there is CCT between the states of these persons, to the same extent that there would be if there had been no physical discontinuity, they are surely distinct subjects and there is no CCS between them.[20]

There is indeed CCT between the conscious states of these persons. If B is not informed about the behaviour of the elementary particles, she would think that what A experienced the moment before was experienced by herself. If A perceived a continuous movement, the phase of that movement that B perceives will fit in as nicely as it would have done had the bodies of A and B been identical and there had been CCS, for, *ex hypothesi*, the discontinuity is too brief to be registered by human sense-organs. Notwithstanding this, we would be inclined to say that the consciousnesses of A and B are distinct as well as that A and B are distinct subjects, because of the bodily discontinuity separating the underpinning of consciousness.

It may be claimed that, although there is a discontinuity in physical existence, the same mental substance continues to exist right across this gap. This would allow A and B to be the same subject. But here one would like to know how one can tell that the same mental substance continues to exist rather than that one such substance is annihilated and another one created. The reply that the extreme briefness of the physical discontinuity makes it unreasonable to assume the latter is obviously unsatisfactory: why should only longer physical breaks put an end to the sameness of mental substances? Nor will it do to retort that there is a single mental substance when and only when the successor is a perfect replica of its predecessor, for then there is again a tendency to slur over the difference

---

[20] Cf. a similar argument directed against Chisholm in Wachsberg (1983: 36).

between there being a single substance and there being distinct, successive instantiations of its type. In Chapter 22, we shall see that continuity at some level is necessary for the numerical identity of physical things, and there is no reason to think that the situation could be different for mental things.

Consequently, I see no way of denying the claim that, in the case envisaged, there is not CCS and subject identity. Once CCT and CCS are distinguished, it is obvious that the appeal to phenomenology, to which the appeal to the former is tantamount, cannot establish CCS or identity of subject. Furthermore, even when there is the "double overlap" that CCT and CCS together supply, this seems not to ensure identity of subject, *pace* Foster. The logical possibility of a consciousness dividing into two 'branches', each occupying a body of its own, demonstrates this. Suppose that each hemisphere was a double of the other so that a state in each was sufficient for every conscious episode. If there were this sort of overdetermination then, if the two hemispheres were separated, a consciousness could be divided into two without any discontinuity in content resulting. At least if each hemisphere was located in a body of its own, the outcome would be two distinct subjects of experience, but it seems quite natural to say that they are linked by CCS to a common source.[21]

When discussing fission cases (1991: 258–61), Foster plumps for the heroic course of claiming that the two consciousnesses have the same subject, are consubjective, and hence belong to the same person. (He also denies that fusion creates a single subject.)[22] But surely, if "it is in the unity of a stream [of consciousness] that we primarily discern the identity of a subject", Foster should discern two subjects in two streams. It is true of a mental subject, as he writes, that "we lose our grip on what it is ... unless we think of it as having, at any time, an integrated mind, whose contents are accessible to a single centre of introspective awareness" (1991: 257).

These considerations show that an experience of change does not necessarily involve experience of the persistence of the same mental subject, for it is compatible with there not being identity of subject. Moreover, whether or not there is identity of subject has turned out to depend upon the identity of physical things. I have earlier in this chapter suggested that it is a matter of the identity of the whole body rather than of the identity of parts of it, such as its brain, but in the next chapter this assumption will be queried. For the time being, the conclusion is just that immaterialism is false and that the truth lies with matter-based theories of our identity.

Reductionism and Non-reductionism

In arguing against immaterialism, I have argued against some views that Parfit classifies as *non-reductionist*. However, immaterialism in my vocabulary is not co-extensive with

---

[21] See Unger (1990: 51–4) for a variant of this example and another that supports the same conclusion.

[22] Other immaterialists or non-reductionists, e.g. Haksar, take the track of contending that a splitting of *consciousness* is not a "physical" or "technical" possibility (1991: 148–9) and so has not *actually* been produced, e.g. in commissurotomy cases (1991: 107 ff.). As will transpire in the next chapter, I believe this to be a mistake.

non-reductionism in his. On the one hand, immaterialism does not imply non-reductionism: for instance, the Humean bundle-theory may be a form of immaterialism, but it would presumably not qualify as non-reductionism in Parfit's terminology.[23] On the other hand, non-reductionism may not imply immaterialism: E. J. Lowe's view that persons comprise "a basic sort, for which no adequate criterion of identity can be formulated" (1989: 135) qualifies as non-reductionism, but it may seem not to be immaterialist, since persons are said to "have bodily characteristics, in a strict and literal sense" (1989: 112; 1996: chs. 1 and 2).[24]

A basic claim of reductionism, as conceived by Parfit, is something like:

(R) Our existence and persistence just consist in the existence and continuity of certain physical/organic bodies and/or the inter-relations among their various psychological events.[25]

Reductionists, in the sense of adherents of this constitutive claim, can however go beyond it by putting forward the following identificatory claim:

(M) We are identical to our bodies, that is, this is that to which personal pronouns, as used by us, refer.[26]

This *identificatory* reductionism can also take the form of what we have called matter-based psychologism:

(P) We are identical to that which is the minimal owner of our minds which must be something material.

But Parfit's reductionism is distinct from both (M) and (P); it is an *eliminative* reductionism which, to begin with, declares

(S) We are *distinct* from our bodies and the psychological events which compose our minds, that is, personal pronouns as used by us do not refer to that in which (R) says we consists.

Now, (S) may seem to threaten (R): the fact that personal pronouns cannot be construed as referring to those psycho-physical entities to which (R) alludes lets in the non-reductionist

---

[23] Haksar takes the difference between reductionism and the bundle-theory to be "merely verbal" (1991: 1). Probably, this is because he tends to concentrate on pure psychological versions of reductionism: cf. his repeated use of the analogy that on reductionism "a person is really like a group" (1991: p. xiv). Clearly, this analogy becomes less natural if one regards us as *bodies*. (Thus it may be that Haksar, too, associates reductionism with the rejection of substantialism: see n. 26.)

[24] I suspect, though, that Lowe's position should really be classified as immaterialism, since he concedes (personal communication) that persons have bodily characteristics only *derivatively*, by being embodied (the possibility that they might be disembodied is not excluded). Lowe then seems to face the same difficulties that I have argued that (other) immaterialists face, regarding the possibility of conceiving of the identity of persons independently of everything physical.

[25] This formulation is gleaned from (1984: 210–11), with some innocuous additions.

[26] *Pace* Cassam who suggests that what is definitive of reductionism is instead that it takes our identity to consist in continuities that "are not *constitutive* of the persistence of a person *qua* substantial being", that its core is the "rejection of substantialism" (1993: 25). Cf. also his later claim: "For Reductionism, the ontological status of persons is akin to the ontological status of nations, and nations are not substances" (1997: 172–3). This leads, as Cassam realizes, to some views which Parfit would like to classify as reductionist becoming non-reductionist, namely, some forms of what I have called identificatory reductionism. It also has the opposite effect of making some views Parfit classifies as non-reductionist, reductionist, for instance Madell's view (1981).

possibility that they refer to some *"separately existing entities"* (Parfit, 1984: 210), perhaps mental substances. Hence, Parfit is led to a further claim (which is what justifies the adjective 'eliminative'):

(I)   The psycho-physical entities mentioned in (R) "can be described in an *impersonal* way" (1984: 210), that is, without a referential use of personal pronouns, in particular 'I'.

Thus, (I), which has generated a lot of controversy, is not an essential component of reductionism—not of identificatory reductionism. My own nihilistic position is of this brand; it comes closest to (M). But I add the qualification that the reference of our personal pronouns to our bodies is based on some assumptions about them that are in fact false. This may explain the attraction of (S), I think.

Parfit concedes that, "if the Non-Reductionist View was true", I would have "a reason to be specially concerned about my future" (1984: 310). Suppose that, notwithstanding the above objections, there are mental substances and that our identity consists in the persistence of such substances. Then it seems to me that it could still be asked whether we would have a real reason to be O-biased, to favour particular persons simply because they are ourselves. Readers of Locke (1689/1975: II. xxvii. 14) should not be surprised by the suggestion that the identity of mental substances may be just as rationally unimportant as the identity of material substances (to anticipate the upshot of the Chapter 23). It certainly needs to be shown that it is more reasonable to be favourably disposed towards a future person who is numerically the same mental substance as the subject of my present experiences than towards a perfect replica who is a distinct mental substance (of the same type). But this question could be pursued only if, contrary to fact, we had possessed a coherent notion of a mental substance.

20

PSYCHOLOGICAL THEORIES
OF OUR IDENTITY

A POSSIBLE response to the foregoing chapter is to agree that immaterialism is false and that some matter-based theory of our nature and identity is correct. But, it might be said, for us to persist, no more of our bodies need persist than that which is *minimally sufficient* to sustain (some subset of) the mental capacities composing our minds. This view—*psychologism*—gives short shrift to the phenomenal aspect of the subject and construes this notion purely in terms of (causal) ownership: the subject is not the phenomenally presented body, but only that in the body which is minimally sufficient for there to be a capacity for having experiences. If it assumes the identificatory instead of the eliminative form (see the end of the last chapter), it takes the referent of a token of 'I' to be only that in the body which is minimally sufficient for this capacity.

Psychologism and the Owner of Experiences

That this minimally sufficient ground is far less than our whole bodies is indicated by the much-discussed thought-experiment of a 'brain-transplant':

> Case I. A perfect replica of my body—apart from the fact that it has no brain—is made. Since several vital organs of my body, though not my brain, are about to collapse, my anaesthetized brain is removed from my body, placed in the skull of the replica and properly connected to this body, so that a human being (seemingly) having all my mental dispositions results (e.g. he seems to remember as much of what I have experienced and learnt as I would have done had I survived in the normal fashion, and he has my traits of character).

Here it is hard to resist the view that I am the post-operative person. If so, we would have to reject the somatic view that sameness of body is necessary for our identity.

This identity judgement implies that, strictly speaking, case I is not an instance of a *brain*-transplant, but rather of a *body*-transplant. If a new heart is transplanted to my body, I am the one who receives the heart. Similarly if lungs, kidneys, etc. are added to the heart. According to the identity intuition, case I is an extreme instance of this spectrum, an instance in which I at one go receive a whole new body apart from a brain.

We should, however, not let these considerations lead us to a 'cerebralist' view that takes us to be identical to *things* like brain(-part)s.[1] For, strictly speaking, what is minimally sufficient for the persistence of one's mind is not any part of the brain, but certain *states* or *processes* taking place in them. Imagine that my brain is so gravely damaged that my capacity for consciousness is irrevocably lost; then, according to psychologist theories, I have ceased to exist. Consequently, I cannot be identical to anything neural—such as my brain or of its parts—that persists under these conditions. Instead I must be identical to certain states or processes which were found in these things as long as my capacity for having consciousness was present, but which are no longer found in them now that this capacity is lost.

The following thought-experiment brings home the same point. Suppose that each hemisphere of the brain is sufficient to house the processes sustaining every psychological capacity or disposition of a person. They are, however, not at work simultaneously, but in shifts: one hemisphere does duty one day, but during sleep it goes blank, and the other, identical hemisphere is activated in its stead. That is, the neural processes sustaining one's mental powers drift from one hemisphere of the brain to another. The fact that on one day one hemisphere is the seat of the mind and on the next another hemisphere is compatible with identity of mind, since the underlying neural states or processes are identical, having merely moved from one hemisphere to another. (Such movements clearly do not disrupt identity of a process: for instance, a wave can move from one portion of water to another.)

Imagine now that today my inactive hemisphere is replaced by a duplicate of it. Tomorrow, when this duplicate has taken over the responsibility for my mental functions, the other hemisphere is removed, and another blank one implanted in its stead. I think it must be granted by psychologists of our identity that these transplants will not have disrupted the identity of my mind, though the cerebrum which now harbours my mind is entirely new. For the underlying neural states or processes have retained their identity, though the transplants have made them 'migrate' from one cerebrum to another, by means of their wandering between hemispheres. Thus psychologists must reject the identity of any material thing, such as any part of a brain, as necessary for our identity in favour of the view that what is necessary are certain neural states or processes. These are what is really minimally sufficient for our minds.

However, there is something counter-intuitive about this conclusion. For, as already Thomas Reid pointed out (see the quotation in Chapter 18), we are surely things or substances which undergo states and processes and which have capacities. We are neither the states or processes that some thing, for example our organisms, undergo, nor any capacities they have. Yet, on identificatory psychologism, this is what we would have to be identical to. In contrast, insisting on the phenomenal aspect of the notion of a subject

---

[1] Forms of cerebralism are advocated by J. L. Mackie (1976: ch. 6), Thomas Nagel (1986: 37 ff.), Mark Johnston (1987), Michael Lockwood (1985), Michael Tye (2003: ch. 6), and in most detail by Jeff McMahan (2002: ch. 1).

captures the Reidian intuition, for if that which owns our mental states is something perceived, our body or organism is the most likely candidate.

Some writers who embrace the biological or animalist view that we are identical to our organisms—Carter (1989), Snowdon (1990: 91 ff.), Ayers (1991: ii. 283–4), and Olson (1997: 106–9)—have protested that psychologism is committed to an objectionable doubling of the subjects of experience. For, surely, human organisms or animals can also be said to think and have experiences. Therefore, if the minimal owner of the mind does so too, it follows that when I think and have experiences, there are *two* distinct entities doing so, a certain human animal and the minimal owner.

As I have argued at length elsewhere (1999a; cf. McMahan, 2002: 92), this is not really absurd. For, although these subjects of thought and experience are distinct, they are not *independent* of each other, according to the views under consideration: on the contrary, one—the animal—thinks and has experiences *in virtue of* the fact that the other—the minimal owner—does so. These are not independent owners of mental states because one of them—the animal—cannot be in any such states unless the other one is. Rather, its being in such states is simply a logical consequence of the minimal owner of the mind being in them. In other words, mental predicates are *derivatively* applicable to the whole animal because within it there is something to which they are *primarily* applicable, in the sense that it is minimally sufficient for their application. Therefore, no absurdity, such as each subject having its own stream of thoughts and experiences, is implied.[2]

So construed, the practice of attributing psychological properties to animals is of a piece with an exceedingly common pattern. We observe that something exercises some power, for example that a liquid or a gas poisons or intoxicates us. Only much later do we discover that it does so in virtue of containing a certain chemical, that is, that the applicability of these predicates to it are to be construed as derivative from the applicability of them to the chemical. Similarly, we observe that animals think and have experiences (or, if you prefer, that they behave in ways that make this hypothesis credible). It is only later that science establishes that they do so in virtue of having certain parts or organs, that is, that the applicability of these predicates to them should be understood as derivative from the applicability of them to these parts which strictly speaking do the thinking and experiencing.

I think, then, that the 'double subject' objection does not show that psychologists cannot with impunity separate minimal owners of minds from their organisms. That such a separation is possible is brought out by brain-transplant cases. Moreover, as we shall see in the next chapter, there are further cases in which it is hard to refuse to distinguish that to which thoughts and experiences are strictly speaking attributable from the whole organism. These are cases in which one organism seems to have two minds or

---

[2] Lynne Baker so defines the distinction between derivative and non-derivative attribution that only persons have person-making properties non-derivatively, whereas their organisms and their parts have them only derivatively (2000: e.g. 97–8). However, Baker's view has a counter-intuitive implication, noted by her (2000: 101–5): since their organisms will non-derivatively have simpler mental properties, like feeling physical pain, these will non-derivatively belong to another subject than the person-making properties. Consequently, when I am introspectively aware of a pain I am feeling, I am aware of a pain that is really felt by a subject distinct from me who performs the introspecting.

consciousnesses. Yet an awkward bulge crops up when psychologists identify us with these minimal owners, for they turn out to be of the wrong category: they are not things or continuants, as we intuitively take ourselves to be, but rather states, processes, or capacities. This is no problem for somatism and immaterialism in the form that identifies us with mental substances.

What Psychological Relations are Necessary for Identity?

Psychologism is, however, freight with graver problems, and some of these surface when we consider the question of the nature of the minds or consciousnesses minimally supported, and the associated question of how minds or consciousnesses that exist at different times must be related to each other to share the same subject. On one version of psychologism—*personalism*—these minds must exhibit *personhood* or be *personal* minds. This is the thesis that we are identical to *persons*. To be a person, one must be *self-conscious* in the sense characterized in the last chapter, that is, one must not only perceive and think, but be conscious of oneself as perceiving and thinking. Furthermore, one must also conceive of oneself as existing as a self-conscious being at *other times than the present*, and be able to appraise the *rationality* of one's propositional attitudes. This virtually coincides with Locke's well-known description of a person as "a thinking intelligent being that has reason and reflection and can consider itself as itself, the same thinking thing in different times and places" (1689/1975: II. xxvii. 9).

The term 'person' is, however, ambiguous. In another sense, it applies to the referent of 'personal' pronouns, like 'I', whatever its nature. We may safely take it that this referent must be a person in the Lockean sense at least to the extent of being self-conscious *at the time* at which it refers to itself by means of 'I'. But it is an open question, the answer to which we shall now try to determine, whether it has to be a Lockean person to this extent at *every* time of its existence, that is, whether it is *essentially* a Lockean person at least to this extent. (To anticipate, the answer will be negative.)

What sort of (psychological) relations must hold between Lockean persons, existing at different times, for them to be numerically the same person? Locke himself appealed to memory: one person must remember things about the other. It is helpful to make a rough distinction between two kinds of memory, *experiential* memory and *factual* memory. Two speakers of English share a welter of (true) beliefs about the conventions of English, and in all probability they have also in common innumerable beliefs about various other general aspects of the world. These beliefs are held, not because they are supported by what is perceived at present, but because there is memory of things learnt in the past. Generally, the contents of these beliefs—which take a propositional form— do not concern what things are like from a certain subject's point of view; they do not represent what a subject has perceived or thought *from that subject's perspective*.

In contrast, the content of experiential memory represents what experiencing something was like from a particular subject's point of view. I have such a memory when I remember what it was like to feel that awful headache a week ago, to step on a snail, etc.

As a matter of fact (though, as we shall shortly see, things could have been otherwise), no other subject has experiential memories of my past. No other subject remembers how a pain felt like to me or what my stepping on the snail was like to me at the time; experientially, other subjects only remember such things as how I looked to them when I felt the pain or how my verbal report of it sounded to them, that is, experiences that they themselves had. This is because my sense-impressions cause me to have (lasting) dispositions to represent how they presented things.

Owing to this fact, experiential memory has been thought of as something that could constitute our identity. It is obvious, however, that it would be far too strong to demand that I, who am existing now, can only be identical to someone existing at an earlier time if I remember something that happened to the latter. For instance, I am certainly identical to some toddler, though I may have no experiential memories of his situation. To remedy this defect, Parfit introduces the notion of *psychological continuity* defined as "the holding of overlapping chains of *strong* connectedness" (1984: 206). There is strong (psychological) connectedness "if the number of connections, over any day, is *at least half* the number of direct connections that hold, over every day, in the lives of nearly every actual person" (1984: 206). Psychological connections consist in psychological dispositions, like being able to remember the experiences of someone.

This move saves the idea that experiential memory can enter into the conditions that make it true that I am identical to a certain toddler, since I have a lot of memories of the experiences I had yesterday, and yesterday I remembered a lot of the experiences I had the day before, and so on all the way back to the toddler. But there are other counter-examples. Consider so-called fugues, cases of amnesia in which it appears that all experiential memories are suddenly extinguished, and persons, entirely oblivious to their pasts, set out for new lives. Surely we would not say that a person who suffers this loss of memory that blots out all experiential memories ceases to exist (cf. Brennan, 1988: ch. 9 and Wilkes, 1988: 104–5). Perhaps in some cases of amnesia the patients regain their lost memories, and then the connection to the past could be said to be provided by the recovered person who remembers both the phase of amnesia and the past beyond it. We need not wait for this recovery to occur, however, to affirm identity.

The case of temporary amnesia brings to light a complication that should be mentioned at least in passing. Victims of this condition seem unable to remember certain experiences in the sense that they will not succeed in calling them to mind even if they try as hard as they can. Yet these amnesiacs are not in the state of having lost memories irreparably and having to re-learn; they are in a state in between these, a state of being capable of regaining some of their experiential memories. We might ask whether this state rather than the actual possession of memories is necessary for our identity.

Such a broadening would not, however, make other psychological connections redundant since, to repeat, in instances of fugues we do not have to wait for the return of memories to declare identity. So it may be proposed that psychological connections having to do with factual memory and likeness in respect of traits of character can step in and fill the slack left by experiential memory.

Unfortunately, not even a disjunction of the psychological connections mentioned seems to be a necessary condition for our identity. A return to the psychological continuities, CCS and CCT, mentioned in the last chapter, could bring out this point. Short-time experiential memory is involved in these continuities, since in them memory of what one was conscious of moments immediately before meshes with what one is currently conscious of. It is plausible to think that, on psychologism, CCS and CCT must be sufficient for our identity (provided that there is no branching of consciousness). Yet if this is so, not only Parfit's strong notion of psychological continuity (which is not presented by him as a necessary condition), but also much weaker notions, fail to be necessary for our identity.

An adaptation of a case described by Parfit himself (1984: 229) serves well to show why. I am in the hands of a sadistic neurosurgeon. He causes me excruciating pain. While the pain is going on, he removes my experiential and factual memories, my interests and traits of character, by tampering with my brain. (It is unlikely that a subject suffering acute pain will notice this loss by vainly trying to actualize memory dispositions.) The psychological connections and/or continuity between the subject before and after this tampering will be very weak: the connections may boil down to one, the continuous awareness of the pain. Yet this will surely not lead me to believe that the subject experiencing the pain after the tampering will not be me. Surely, I cannot go out of existence in the midst of consciousness of a continuous pain inflicted on my body (there is not even any rough answer to the question *when* I would go out of existence that is plausible).

This sort of example undermines also a proposal like Peter Unger's. Unger distinguishes the psychology "distinctive" of the person from a "core psychology", that is, those psychological dispositions that are common to *all* normal human beings and a lot of subnormal ones (1990: e.g. ch. 4). He thinks that it is only a sufficiently continuous physical realization of a core psychology that is necessary for our identity. Albeit not confidently, he holds that *being a person*, in something like the Lockean sense outlined above, is an essential property of us to the extent that, once we have acquired it, we cannot lose it without going out of existence (1990: 196, 249). But surely, even if the neurosurgeon removed also those dispositions constitutive of my personhood, during the duration of the pain, it would still be me who is feeling all this pain. If I have been a non-person once, why can I not be one again? In this case I am certainly to be pitied both for having to suffer all this pain and for having most of my (distinctive and core) psychology wiped out.

Having gone this far, it seems that we can take a further step. Imagine that the neurosurgeon puts me to sleep after torturing me for a day. He intends to see to it that tomorrow the same organism will be conscious again and subject to the pain stimulus. Will this subject be me only if there is some psychological connection between him and me suffering today, for example only if he will remember today's agony? No, for it seems natural to think that, if he fails to remember, what he then fails to remember is that *he* felt pain yesterday.

Against the background of this example, it seems a psychological criterion would do best to hold that we can exist as long as there is *any* consciousness at all, even the most rudimentary consciousness restricted to the present. More precisely, such a criterion would lay down that a necessary condition for me to survive in the future is that in the future there be someone whose capacity for consciousness is underpinned by numerically the same neural processes that underpin (some of) my current mental capacities. That is, although the (neural) link to the past must sustain mental capacities, it need not sustain any such capacities that connect one to the past, as does memory in allowing one now to remember what happened in the past. As pointed out by McMahan (2002: e.g. 47), this criterion has the advantage of letting us survive severe neural degeneration, as in the final stages of Alzheimer's disease. Let us term this view (which is a rival to personalism) *broad* psychologism.

It may, however, be doubted whether even broad psychologism goes far enough. Suppose that, having tortured me enough, the neurosurgeon gives me anaesthetics. Then he removes the last psychological dispositions from my brain. Now, just as it seems natural to say, at the outset, that he is starting to deprive *me* of my psychological dispositions, it seems natural to say that, at the end of the series of operations, he has deprived *me* of all of my psychological dispositions. Looking ahead to a persistent vegetative state, we find it quite natural to express requests like: 'If I were to sink into such a state, I want to be killed'. But this presupposes that we can exist without having any capacity for consciousness whatever. If so, even broad psychologism is false.

Generally, it seems strange that we can unnoticeably—both to ourselves and to others—slip out of existence when what is most palpable about us, our bodies or organisms, persist virtually intact. This intuition causes as much trouble for broad psychologism as for narrower views that insist upon the necessity of some psychological connections to other times.

We must not lose sight of the fact that in everyday life we routinely make judgements about our diachronic identity. This fact makes it likely that we should take our identity to consist in something that is ascertainable in everyday circumstances. Whether there are any psychological connections or even any capacity for consciousness is, however, a much more elusive matter than whether one and the same human body or organism persists.[3] Our knowledge of the brain is not extensive enough to exclude all situations in which even neurological expertise is unable to tell whether someone's state of unconsciousness is permanent. This uncertainty may linger for decades. Then, on broad psychologism, it will be unsettled for decades whether some of us are still around, despite the indubitable presence of their living bodies. Clearly, this is a startling consequence which jars with what we would ordinarily say. We would definitely be inclined to say that they are still around, though it is unclear whether they have been robbed of all their psychological faculties.

Concordant with this is the observation, made in the foregoing chapter, that we also seem inclined to hold that our existence antedates our acquisition of any capacity for consciousness. It is likely that our nervous system does not develop to the point where it is able

---

[3] Cf. Johnston's claim that "considerable implausibility attaches to any theory that cannot reconstruct as wholly justified the easy and uncomplicated ways in which we reidentify people on the basis of their physical appearance and manner" (1987: 63). In my opinion, however, this implausibility ironically attaches to Johnston's own view: "The kind *human being* is such" that "the tracing of the life of a human being gives primary importance to mental functioning" (1987: 79).

to sustain any capacity for consciousness until half-way through pregnancy, but, though it is debatable exactly when we begin to exist,[4] surely we exist earlier than that. Consider, for instance, a 12-week-old foetus with a discernible human shape, with a head, limbs, etc. The most reasonable thing to say is that it is you or me, that its head, limbs, etc. are yours or mine. It is odd to think that somebody else had these body parts before we acquired them.

Problems about Fission Cases

So far I have explored the reasons for doubting the *necessity* of even the most tenuous psychological conditions for our identity. Let us now turn to a thought-experiment that poses problems for the *sufficiency* of even the most extensive of psychological connections, like Parfit's strong connectedness:

> Case II. Suppose that each hemisphere of the brain is capable of sustaining normal day-to-day psychological connectedness. Suppose also that the hemispheres could be severed from each other, by cutting the *corpus callosum*, without destroying their capacity to sustain this connectedness.[5] Now *two* brainless replicas of my body have been created. My anaesthetized brain is taken out of the cranial cavity, is split into two, and each half is successfully transplanted to one replica. As a result, two persons, A and B, emerge from the transplants.

Because the psychologically connectedness is as strong as in case I, there is reason on psychologism to judge that here, too, I am identical to A and B. However, this identification will have one of the following strongly counter-intuitive consequences: either identity is not both symmetric and transitive or A and B are identical, or there were two entities of my sort sharing my mental states and body even before the division.

Some personalists have chosen the last alternative. They accept something that has been called *multiple occupancy thesis*, to the effect that at least two distinct entities of the very same kind can occupy the very same space at a time—in the present case, that before the fission of my brain there were (at least) two persons or mental entities of my kind at the time sharing a single body and stream of consciousness. This is because on this view persons are *four-dimensional entities* which alongside their spatial dimensions have temporal extension.[6]

---

[4] Cf. Olson (1997: ch. 4) and Persson (2003a). A popular answer is that we begin to exist at conception, but what if monozygotic twinning later occurs? So a better answer might be: some 14 days or so after conception when the so-called primitive streak forms in the place of the spine and monozygotic twinning is ruled out. True, at this point conjoined twins can still result. This shows that we cannot be certain whether one or more human beings exist at this stage. But this uncertainty cannot be a reason for denying that a human being exists, since even when they are fully grown, it may be uncertain whether a pair of conjoined twins constitutes one or two human beings (as we shall see in the next chapter). However this may be, I think it is very plausible to hold that a human being has begun to exist at least at the point I consider in my example (12 weeks).

[5] Some writers, e.g. Robinson (1988), insist that lower parts of the brain, such as the brainstem, are essential to consciousness and that they cannot be divided without losing this function. Although this may in fact be true, it is still *logically* possible that the brain be such that a suitable bisection of it would result in two halves each of which is sufficient to sustain all ordinary psychological relations. This logical possibility is all that is needed for the thought-experiment, though I shall not argue for this claim, since the possibility of dividing consciousness is not crucial for my central purposes.

[6] A view of this sort has been advanced by John Perry (1972), David Lewis (1976) and Harold Noonan (1989: chs. 7, 9, 11).

An overall assessment of the four-dimensional framework would take us too far afield. But as even some of its adherents—like Noonan (1989: 168)—confess, the multiple occupancy thesis has counter-intuitive implications. It fits badly with what we ordinarily take ourselves to know about ourselves. I take myself to know that there is now only one entity of the sort I am where my body now is, regardless of what happens later on. For we assume that a subsequent fission, were it to occur, would produce a duality (of minds and their minimal subjects) *at the time it occurs*; it does not make it true that there was a duality even before it occurred. But on four-dimensionalism, a future fission means that there are already two entities of my kind and, so, that I could be fundamentally deluded about myself.

Furthermore, suppose that I could predict that I will undergo fission in the future. Then, looking ahead, I cannot report in the first person singular what will happen to the fission-products, A and B, after the fission—if what is true of one is false of the other—but I know that, looking back, both of them could use 'I' to refer to me! For instance, suppose that A starts smoking, but that B never does. If I predict this before the fission, I cannot announce 'I shall start smoking', but I know that A, looking back at my prediction, could report '*I* predicted that *I* would start smoking'.

I believe, therefore, that psychologism would be an awkward position if this were the best version of it. A credible psychologism cannot identify me with both A and B. Since it appears gratuitous to identify me with one of the two fission-products, the best course is to identify me with neither. I no longer exist, but have split into A and B who now exist in my place. It then follows that something alongside psychological connectedness/continuity is required for our identity, since both of the fission-products are thus related to me. According to many psychologists—for example Parfit (1984: 216, 262) and Shoemaker (Shoemaker and Swinburne, 1984: 90)[7]—what is needed is what might be called a *non-branching constraint* to the effect that the psychological connectedness/continuity constituting personal identity must take a *one–one* or *non-branching* form: if I am psychologically continuous with a person existing at *t*, I am identical to him only if there is *nobody else* at *t* with whom I am psychologically continuous.

There is a difficulty here which may in the end prove to be merely technical. Parfit writes that it "does not follow, and is in fact false" that A and B "are psychologically continuous with each other" (1984: 302). The reason he supplies is that although "psychological continuity is a transitive relation, in either direction in time", it "is not a transitive relation, if we allow it to take both directions in a single argument" (1984: 302). This is puzzling for it implies both that psychological continuity is a temporally directed relation—like that of remembering—and that it can run both from the earlier time to the later one and vice versa—unlike that of remembering.

If the post-operative person A later *remembers* having some of my present experiences, there is *another* relation holding in the reverse direction, namely that some of my experiences *are remembered* by A. Neither of these relations can run in both directions. Of course, we can stipulate that there is psychological connectedness (and so continuity) if (and only if) *either* of these relations obtains between two persons existing at different

---

[7] A structurally similar theory is Nozick's "closest continuer" theory (1981: ch. 1).

times. We then have a relation of connectedness which can be said to run in both directions. Furthermore, this relation will be *symmetric*—which seems necessary if, like Parfit, one takes it to be what identity consists in (identity, of course, being a symmetric relation). But how can one then disallow that it run in "both directions in a single argument"? It must do so if there is to be symmetry. Therefore I cannot see how Parfit can avoid the conclusion that, in case II, A and B are psychologically continuous.

The unwanted conclusion that A and B are the same person then follows, unless the non-branching constraint excludes this. Now, we can easily set up matters so that in its present formulation it does not exclude this. Just imagine that A and B do not exist simultaneously. Suppose, for instance, that A is short-lived and only exists for a day or two and that the brain-half that goes to constitute B needs a few days of repairing before it is capable of sustaining a mind. Then, as formulated above, the non-branching constraint does not rule out that I am identical to both of them and that A and B are identical to each other, for there is no single time, t, at which both A and B exist. Certainly, the constraint may be amended so that this consequence is blocked, but it is not immediately apparent how this should be done.

Another corollary of the non-branching constraint is that *the thesis of the intrinsicality of identity* must be rejected as false. Here is Nozick's formulation of this thesis:

> If x at time t_1 is the same individual as y at later time t_2, that can depend only upon facts about x, y, and the relationships between them. No fact about any other existing thing is relevant to (deciding) whether x at t_1 is (part of the same continuing individual as) y at t_2. (1981: 31)

To bring out the intuitive force of this thesis, imagine that in case II it is clear that one transplant will succeed, but that it remains uncertain for a while whether the other transplant will issue in the existence of a conscious being. Then, during this period of uncertainty, the identity of the first person will be unsettled: he will be identical to me if the other transplantation fails, but not if a person emerges here as well. This unclarity seems counter-intuitive: surely the identity of the first patient cannot hinge on the fate of the other. Suppose both operations succeed; then one could say to either of the resulting persons: 'Count yourself lucky: if the other person had not existed, you would not have existed either!' For if only one transplant had been a success that person would have been me and so would not be the one he now is (cf. Noonan, 1989: 159–60). That seems queer.

This does not amount to a knock-down argument against theories that operate with something to the effect of a non-branching constraint, but it brings out some of the intuitive strength of the intrinsicality of identity. It would definitely be desirable to be able to define our identity in terms of a sort of continuity which *must* assume a one–one form. Instead of fastening on a form of continuity that could split into branches each being fit for identity had it been the only one, and thereby necessitating the stipulation that there is identity only when such a branching in fact does not occur, one would do better to opt for a continuity which, if it holds between two relata, guarantees their identity, regardless of their relations to other things existing simultaneously.

At the root of the problem of branching lies, I believe, the mistake of taking our persistence conditions to be those of a process, like our minds flowing on or our mental activities continuing. A process, like a stream, can divide, without creating any identity problems. If a stream divides at t, there is no question of the two processes starting at t being identical to the original stream. They are simply two distinct processes that continue a process which began before t, just as a single stream after t would do if there had been no division. The same holds for the 'stream' of mind or consciousness. But the same answer will not do for the likes of us, since we are not processes, but things undergoing processes. We cannot say that both branches, though not identical to us, are continuations, or temporal parts, of us, just as each of them would be if it had been single. For being things, we do not have temporal parts, according to the everyday three-dimensional scheme. Moreover, if there had been just a single branch, there would be identity. So we are faced with the anomaly that it is the mere existence of a second branch that rules out identity, and thereby with the denial of the intrinsicality of identity.

Despite suspicions to the contrary (e.g. Noonan, 1989: 18–19, 150), we should not be forced to this denial if we took our identity to be that of some physical things, like our bodies. For even though a body can be divided, the results of the division are strictly (spatial) *parts* of the body. (This is no less true if the division is the eventual outcome of a growth in two directions: the two offspring are each identical to one part of the ancestor just prior to its division.) And it is necessary that the stronger the claims of one branch to identity, the weaker the claims of the other. If a body is divided into a minor part, for example an arm or a heart, and the rest of the body, the latter makes a very strong claim to be identified with the body, but the claim of the arm or heart is proportionately weaker. Therefore, we cannot have the problematic situation of two offshoots each raising as strong a claim for identification as if there had been no division.[8]

Of course there is no sharp cut-off point at which a progressively amputated human body can no longer be counted as a human body and as identical to the body that existed before the amputations. But this is to say that the identity of a body is *indeterminate*, not that it is not intrinsic. Our uncertainty as to the identity of the entity from which parts are progressively subtracted is not due to any ignorance as to whether they are assembled elsewhere (in the event of which there may be a rival for identity). It is due to the fact that, although less than the persistence of the whole body is necessary for its identity, it is indeterminate how much is necessary. But we do know, at least, that if a body is to be said to persist even though what is strictly speaking only a proper part of it persists, that part must constitute more than half of it, and this is enough to ensure that we shall never face a situation in which a body is divided in such a fashion that *both* of the resulting items could count as identical to it.

Notwithstanding these scruples, suppose we agree to add a non-branching clause to the psychological conditions. Then we face another problem, namely that the branching of our minds or consciousness does not seem sufficient to destroy our identity. Consider:

> Case III. In respect of assumptions about the capacity of the brain, this case is similar to case II. The difference is that, after the bisection, the brain halves are put back into my body—which we now imagine to be healthy—and reconnected to it (though not to each other).

---

[8] I will say a bit more to support the intrinsicality of identity as regards material things in Ch. 22.

Here it seems that one could hold that my *mind or consciousness* has divided into two, without being committed to the view that *I* have divided. Compare the case of actual split-brain patients who have undergone commissurotomy—that is, have had the bridge between their hemispheres cut—in order to relieve severe disorders like epilepsy. Again, there is reason to hold that the number of minds or consciousnesses has doubled,[9] but, as I think descriptions of such cases evidence, we tend to recoil from speaking of the number of *patients* being doubled. If this is so, however, it seems that *we* would not have divided, since we are potentially patients of this surgery. Analogously, I would not have divided in case III, only my mind would have.[10] But, unless qualified, psychologism would imply that we cease to exist by division in such cases, since the non-branching constraint is infringed. (In the next chapter, we will see that this possibility of two minds in a single organism creates problems for animalism, too.)

A further case similarly suggests the pertinence of bodily requirements:

Case IV. This is like case III. The difference is that after the bisection only one of my brain halves is reconnected to my body, the other is transplanted into a replica of it.

It is hardly satisfactory to maintain that I do not survive here because the non-branching clause is not met. A more plausible view is, as Nozick suggests, though with some hesitancy (1981: 40), that I am the individual with my old body and half of my brain. Nozick writes that on his

closest continuer view, a property may be a factor in identity without being a necessary condition for it. If persons conceivably can transfer from one body to another, still, bodily continuity can be an important component of identity, even (in some cases) its sole determinator. (1981: 35)

The idea might be that it is primarily psychological continuity that determines which continuer is the closest one, but that bodily continuity enters secondarily, to cut ties in

---

[9] That there is a division of minds or consciousnesses here is accepted by most. One dissident is van Inwagen, who denies that there are two consciousnesses for the reason that there is only a single organism (1990: 188 ff.). This depends upon van Inwagen's view that composition requires life which I criticize in my review of his book (1993). For another dissident, see Wilkes (1988: ch. 5). She appears to agree that commissurotomy causes disunity of consciousness, but holds the to my mind (consciousness?) implausible view that it is indicative of a "disastrous over-emphasis on *conscious* mental processes" (1988: 165) to take this disunity as sufficient for a duality of *mind*. A sounder ground for denying that there are two minds here would seem to go *via* the denial that there are two separate consciousnesses because the brain stem is still intact; see Robinson (1988). But this is not conclusive because, although the brainstem may be *necessary* for consciousness, higher parts of the brain, too, have a role to play. If so, division in the latter region may still be enough for division of consciousness. I think this interpretation of commissurotomy cases is the most plausible, but this cannot be argued here.

[10] This coincides with Parfit's view about a similar example (1984: § 87). In supporting this view, he states that "there was only one body" (1984: 256), although it is unclear why this should be a reason for there being only one person on his psychologist view. Another reason for holding that there is only a single person is given by Tye, who writes that the consciousness of a split-brain subject "is unified except in certain very special experimental situations" (2003: 128). But, first, it seems much more plausible to say that the experimental conditions *reveal* a split that is already there (produced by the commissurotomy) than that they *produce* it. Secondly, since there are two consciousnesses, even if only briefly, there must be two subjects of consciousness where there was only one before which, on psychologism, is identical to one of us. As in other cases of fission, it seems reasonable to hold that, since the old subject cannot be identical to both of the new ones, and it would be arbitrary to identify it with one of them, it—and one of us—has ceased to exist.

respect of psychological continuity or even—as the last bit of the quotation suggests—to determine identity in its absence. This would explain not only why we incline towards identity in case IV, but also why we incline towards it in cases of permanent unconsciousness (as we have seen above).

The problem with this proposal is that it makes it mysterious what *kind* of thing we can be identical to. If we are the kind of thing that can go with our brains in brain-transplant cases, how can bodily continuity in other respects be an "important component" of our identity, and perhaps even a sufficient condition for it? Nozick deliberately leaves "the measure of closeness" undecided. He thinks that there is no measure valid for all, but that each person may fix it "in accordance with how much he cares" (1981: 69; 105–10),[11] but, as we shall see in Chapter 23 and onwards, what determines the closeness of continuity is quite different from what determines care.

The Circularity Objection

Although we have seen that, when put under pressure, psychologists can hardly retain the view that experiential memory is indispensable for our identity, psychological criteria surely owe a lot of their intuitive appeal to it. This is enough to motivate a review of a famous objection to regarding it as a necessary ingredient of our diachronic identity. But this review will issue in further support for a somatist view. The objection can be traced back to Bishop Butler.[12] It has been articulated by contemporary philosophers like A. J. Ayer (1956: 196) and Bernard Williams;[13] more recently, Marya Schechtman (1990) has developed a version of it, Noonan (1989: ch. 8) has provided some support for it, and Gareth Evans (1982: ch. 7.5) has argued for its pivotal contention. It has been called *the circularity objection*, since it is to the effect that it is viciously circular to appeal to experiential memory in explicating our identity through time, because experiential memory presupposes identity between the subject having the memory and the subject who had the experience being remembered.

After examining a reply given to this objection, I shall conclude that the objection can indeed be met. But I shall then go on to argue that there is a weaker version of the circularity objection—to be called the *ad hominem* version—in which it holds good.[14] This version does not show that, on pain of a circularity, the notion of experiential memory cannot function as the criterion for the persistence of *any* beings who are like us in having experiential memories. It only establishes the weaker conclusion that it cannot in fact be

---

[11] According to the theory Nozick tentatively defends, "there is no preexisting I; rather the I is delineated, is synthetized around that act of reflexive self-referring" (1981: 87). This theory is supposed to explain that "it is part of the essence of selves that they are selves or have the capacity to be selves, to reflexively self-refer, though this capacity may have been blocked temporarily or not yet have been developed" (1981: 78). But how can a self have this (as yet) unexercised capacity of reflexive self-reference if it is not "preexisting", i.e. existing prior to and independently of such acts of self-reference? On the other hand, if *actual* acts self-reference are required for there to be a self, it seems it will not last through, e.g. a period of dreamless sleep. So, we should take the self to be "preexisting" and the question arises what kind of entity it is.

[12] See 'Of Personal Identity' from Butler's *The Analogy of Religion*, e.g. in J. Perry (1975).

[13] 'Personal Identity and Individuation', see the reprint in Williams (1973: 4).

[14] This reproduces an argument I give in (1997*b*).

our criterion of our persistence because we make identity-judgements in which we apply this criterion before we acquire the notion of experiential memory. We make these judgements on the basis of *what* we experientially remember—this explains our feeling that there is an intimate relation between experiential memory and our identity—before we acquire the capacity to make judgements to the effect that we engage in the activity of remembering. Consequently, the criterion we apply in making identity-judgements on the basis of the content of our experiential memory cannot involve our making judgements to the effect that we engage in the act of having such memories. As we shall see, this criterion must rather be a somatic criterion of some sort.

The circularity objection may be formulated as follows. Remembering having an experience E at some time, t, in the past is remembering *oneself* having E at t. A reference to oneself, now remembering, enters into *the content* of the memory-experience. If this is so, then, since it is possible to remember only what has in fact occurred, I can remember (myself) having E at t only if I in fact had E at t. Suppose I have an experience which to me is like remembering having E at t—it will here be called a memory-like experience or an apparent memory—but that I did not in fact have E at t or any other time. Then I do not really remember having E; it merely *seems* to me that I do. Thus, in order to establish that I really remember having E at t, one must consult a criterion of personal identity, which yields the verdict that I had E at t. A vicious circularity would obviously result if, to apply this criterion, one would have to establish that I remember having some experience. Therefore, the applicability of this criterion of identity cannot entail that experiential memories obtain.

Of course, that I have an experience which is like remembering having E at t and that I in fact had E at t are not sufficient for me to remember having E at t. It is commonly, but not universally, agreed that the latter fact must *cause* the former. As is well known, however, any causal relation will not do, but it is quite tricky to specify the requisite one.[15] Let us call this specific causal relation which must obtain between these facts for there to be memory 'the M-link'.[16] Alongside the other two conditions (that a memory-like experience occurs and that it corresponds to an actual past experience), then, the presence of the M-link (between them) seems to give rise to a sufficient condition for remembering having some experience.

Now causal theories of reference may suggest the idea that, if remembering having E is necessarily remembering *oneself* having E, this is because the M-link cannot hold in the absence of identity, that this necessary reference to oneself in the content of what is remembered is due to the memory-experience *perforce* being M-linked to an experience oneself had. For suppose it could logically be M-linked to an experience that somebody else had: suppose that I have a memory-like experience of having E at t, the content of which in every respect corresponds to somebody else's, A's, having E at t, and that the M-link obtains between my present memory-like experience and A's having E at t. Then it seems that there is no reason to deny that I *remember A's having E at t*, for my relation to his having E at t is just the same as it would be to my having E at t were I to remember having this experience.

[15] For a classic attempt to do so, see Martin and Deutscher (1966).
[16] Cf. Sydney Shoemaker's "M-type causal chain" in (1970: 278).

Certainly, in the former case the subject who had the experience in question is not me, but that seems no reason to deny that my relation to the experience is one of memory. Rather, it seems a reason for saying that *the object* of the relation of memory is not myself, but another, that it is 'other-memory' instead of 'self-memory' (just as the fact that the object of my emotion is myself does not rule that it is of the species contempt or pity, but rather implies that it is of the sub-species *self*-contempt or *self*-pity if it is of this species).

It may be objected that our everyday notion of experiential memory could still be that of 'self-memory', that it could entail, as a constraint independent of that of the M-link, that the experience being remembered must have been had by the subject doing the remembering. But if so, that would be a trivial restriction. We can then construct a notion—called 'q(uasi)-memory' (Shoemaker, 1970: 271; Parfit, 1984: sec. 80)—which is like that of the everyday notion save that it does not involve the identity-constraint mentioned. Since this constraint is logically independent, lifting it cannot result in an incoherent notion.

Against the background of what has been said it is, however, also comprehensible how it could *seem* to be a necessary truth (even if it is not) that remembering having an experience is remembering oneself having it. This could be because, as a matter of fact, whenever we remember having an experience, the memory-experience always corresponds to and is M-linked to an experience that we ourselves had. It is easy to confuse such an exceptionless empirical uniformity with a conceptual necessity. This is enough to justify a certain reluctance to using the term 'memory' without qualification about the retrieval of the experiences of others, for it would carry the conversational implication that the experience retrieved was had by oneself. But this is an implication that can be cancelled, by coining a term of art, 'q-memory', and expound our criterion in terms of it.

There are, then, two aspects of the claim that experiential memory presupposes an identity of subject and, furthermore, these aspects are connected. There is (1) the claim that remembering having E is necessarily remembering *oneself* having E. This is a claim about *the content* of experiential memory, to the effect that a reference to oneself necessarily enters into it. But there is also (2) the claim that the requisite M-link presupposes an identity between the subject remembering an experience and the subject who had the experience remembered. This is a claim about *the relation* between *the having* of the memory-experience and *the having* of the experience being remembered. My hypothesis has been that if (2) is false, if the M-link is not identity-constrained, the content claim (1) cannot be sustained, either. With this in mind, it is natural to begin by trying to determine whether or not the M-link entails the identity-constraint in question.

In the literature, there are two sorts of case lending credence to the view that the M-link does not presuppose identity between the subject who had the memory-experience and the subject who had the experience being remembered. Shoemaker (1970: 280 ff.) appeals to the cases of fission we have just discussed. As we have seen, on most plausible accounts of our persistence, these fission-products will not be identical to me. Yet it seems most natural to say that they remember having experiences that I had. It is natural to hold this because the causal mechanism underlying their apparent experiential memory can be the same as the one that underlies my experiential memory. Suppose that the bisection of my brain never took place because just before it I had an accident that destroyed one of my hemispheres. This does not rule out that, when I regain consciousness, I remember having experiences I had before the accident in virtue of still possessing the one intact hemisphere. But if it is granted that there is experiential memory here, and so that the M-link holds, it cannot be denied that it holds in the case of (at least one of) the fission-products (though we may prefer the idiom of 'q-memories' to avoid misleading implications).

Another kind of case which supports the same point is Parfit's "Venetian Memories" (1984: 220).[17] The fission case assumes that the seat of experiential memory is in some states of the two hemispheres. It does not assume that individual memories can be mapped onto specific parts or processes of these hemispheres. Suppose this is the case; then it should be possible in theory to remove these parts or processes from one brain and transplant them to another. This is what happens in my adaptation of Parfit's case. Some of the 'memory-traces' of Jane's brain are removed and instead she receives some from Paul's brain.[18] After regaining consciousness, she apparently remembers having some experiences that Paul had during one of his visits to Venice. Again, it seems plausible to maintain that the M-link is present here, for Jane has her apparent memories in virtue of having the same neural structures in virtue of which Paul would remember his experiences (though on no theory is she identical to Paul). Thus, if we deny that Jane remembers having some of Paul's experiences, it seems we are guilty of the trivializing move of adding an independent identity-constraint.

It may be objected that the kind of transplant here envisaged is not merely technically impossible, but nomologically impossible because individual memories cannot be mapped onto specific neural traces in the way we have imagined. Every memory involves larger neural tracts that overlap with tracts other memories involve (see Wilkes, 1988: ch. 1, esp. p. 39). This may be so, but could it reasonably be claimed that such an assumption is enshrined in our concept of experiential memory? If future neuroscience were to discover that the mapping was after all feasible, would that necessitate a revision of our concept of memory? It is surely more likely that this concept possesses a 'neural neutrality' which permits us to vary these underlying factors without upsetting it.[19]

In view of cases of these two sorts, it seems very plausible to conclude that (2) above is false, that the presence of the M-link does not ensure identity between the subject having the memory-experience and the subject who had the experience being remembered. Consequently, if my conjecture above about the relation between the claims (1) and (2) is

[17] Note that Schechtman's argument falls short of establishing the general claim that experiential memory presupposes identity by her bracketing simple visual memories of the kind exemplified in this case (1990: 81). Strangely, she also fails to discuss the serious threat that fission cases pose to her position.

[18] It is an adaptation because Parfit speaks of a "copying" of the memory traces.

[19] I cannot see that Wilkes has presented any reasons for claiming that this supposition brings us to a world so utterly different from ours that "it does not allow for philosophical conclusions to be drawn" (1988: 46). The alterations imagined here are located below the surface of the everyday experience which largely determines the content of commonsensical concepts. It is true that these concepts may embody causal assumptions about what occurs below this surface, but these are scarcely specific enough to rule out, e.g. the mapping envisaged. (For an explication of the M-link that fits these specifications, see. n. 23) Therefore, I fail to see how this thought-experiment could disrupt the use of these concepts to the extent that no reliable conclusions about them can be established.

correct, it follows that it is only trivially true, if true at all, that if I remember having an experience E, I necessarily remember *myself* having E. We can clearly conceive of a phenomenon at most marginally different from memory—quasi-memory—for which it is not true.

We should not, however, leave the matter at that, for there is a further problem. Remembering having E is remembering this experience *from the inside*, it is remembering *what it was like* to have E,[20] and it is arguable that remembering E from the inside is remembering E *from the point of view of a subject* or that remembering what it was like to have E is to remember what it was like *for a subject* to have E. Now, it is far from transparent how this subject should be construed, and what its relation to the subject currently having the memory-experience is.

At this juncture, we should recollect the account given in the foregoing chapter of the notions of a subject of experience and self. If whenever we perceive something, we perceive it in relation to our bodies, perceived as three-dimensional objects in which our bodily and kinaesthetic sensations are located—we should expect that when we remember one of our perceptual experiences, we remember it in relation to our bodies, as experienced from our bodies, thus perceived. For it would be extraordinary if we could entirely forget this ever-present ingredient, though, of course, we do not in detail remember what it was like on individual occasions. Thus my suggestion is that, when we remember having an experience, we remember what it was like having this experience from the point of view of a proprioceptive body model.

Normally, this model will, of course, be a model of one's own physical body, as it was on some past occasion. In the case of Jane's "Venetian Memories" it is instead a model of *Paul's* body, since it was he who had the experience being remembered. In other words, the identity of the subject(-body) of the content of a memory(-like) experience is determined by who (if anyone) was the subject of the past experience, to which it is M-linked, that is, by whose body, perceived from the inside, it was around which the content of the past experience was organized. If the subject as represented by the memory(-like) experience also matches the subject who had the past experience, then this subject is the one to which the content refers.

If this is correct, the identity of the subject of a memory(-like) experience is determined in the same fashion as the identity of any 'object' of such an experience. Who is the passenger I remember sitting next to me (or my body perceived from within) on the train earlier on today? If she is identical to any real human being, she is clearly identical to the one who was actually sitting next to me when I had the visual experience I now remember, that is, the human being who played a prominent part in the causing of my original experience and, thereby, in the causing of my memory experience. (Just as the identity of the train I remember sitting on is determined by what actual train caused other ingredients of these experiences.) But in order for this human being to be the one remembered, the representation, as far as it goes, must also at least roughly match her.

---

[20] Thus, remembering having E should not be confused with a piece of factual memory, remembering that E occurred, which does not entail that E is remembered 'from the inside'.

Consequently, I suggest that whose, if anyone's, experience one remembers having is determined in the same way as other aspects of what, if anything, one remembers.

Let me sum up. I have made the point that there is a great credibility in the view that a—memory—experience of what something is like from the inside must be an experience of what it is like from the point of view of a subject. Although remembering having E may not be remembering oneself having E, it is remembering *somebody* having E. An account of this subject has now been offered: it is a proprioceptive body model from the perspective of which the external world is perceived and in which bodily and kinaesthetic sensations are located. Furthermore, an account of the identity of this subject(-body) has been provided according to which it is fixed by causal considerations and the fit of its properties (as represented) to an actual body. In other words, we have found corroboration for the conjecture advanced above, that only if the M-link is identity-confined can there be an essential reference to the subject having the memory(-like) experience in the content of this experience.

Since we have concluded that the M-link is not thus confined, we can conclude that it is not deeply true that when one remembers having E, one remembers oneself having it. One remembers this experience from the point of view of a proprioceptive body model, which in the actual world is always a model of one's own body, but which may conceivably be of somebody else's body (as it is in the cases of fission and Parfit's Venetian memories). So, though one necessarily remembers somebody having E when one remembers having E, this subject need not be oneself. Therefore, the circularity objection is invalid: the concept of experiential memory does not presuppose identity between the subject having the memory and the subject who had the experience being remembered.

A New Version of the Circularity Objection

Although the circularity objection can thus be laid to rest, it would be premature for the memory theorist of our identity to rejoice. For, as I shall now argue, there is another circularity objection which I shall call, a bit frivolously, the *ad hominem* (circularity) objection.[21] It establishes a weaker conclusion than the traditional objection: not that, on pain of a circularity, the identity criterion of *any* beings could not appeal to their experiential memory, but that the criterion *we in fact have* of our own persistence could not do so because of the way we acquire the notion of this memory. It will transpire that, in accordance with the above account of the subject of the experience remembered, our criterion of our persistence is instead a *somatic* or *bodily* one.

We can reliably make (and know to be true) judgements to the effect that our pasts were thus and so only because we in fact *remember* our pasts being thus and so. Call these *memory-based claims*. For instance, I can reliably make the judgement that I sat down in this chair an hour ago only because I remember sitting down in this chair an hour ago.

---

[21] I formulate this objection somewhat differently in (1997b).

Now, it seems that one's ability to *describe* oneself as remembering, to make *memory-claims* to the effect that one *remembers* this or that happening to oneself, presupposes one's ability to make memory-based claims to the effect that this or that happened to oneself. This is because a memory-claim makes a causal claim to the effect that one's present capacity to imagine or mentally represent oneself V-ing (where 'V' represents some verb construction like 'sitting down in a chair') is caused—in the constrained way that we have designated as 'the M-link'—by one's V-ing in the past. That is, one's V-ing in the past not only caused one to have a capacity to be aware of it while it was occurring, but also a lasting capacity to represent it afterwards.[22] Obviously, this is a judgement one could not make unless one had the ability to judge that one V-ed in the past.

Notice, then, the compatibility between saying that (*a*) one's ability to make memory-based claims presupposes that one *in fact* has memories and that (*b*) one's ability to *describe* oneself as having memories presupposes one's ability to make memory-based claims. Similarly, one's ability to make perception-based judgements about one's environment to the effect, for example, that there is something white and rectangular in front of one presupposes that one *in fact* perceives those things. Yet one's ability to *describe* oneself as perceiving such things presupposes one's ability to make the corresponding perception-based judgements. For instance, judging that one *sees* something white and rectangular in front of one obviously presupposes that one can judge that there is something white and rectangular in front of one, since the content of the former judgement includes that of the latter and more.

When one makes memory-based claims to the effect that something happened to one in the past, for example that one sat down in a chair, one assumes oneself, who now produces the relevant token of 'I', to be *identical* to someone existing in the past and undergoing the event remembered, for example sitting down. What (constitutive) criterion of one's identity does one apply when one makes such identity-claims, that is, what is the content of these assertions? On pain of a circularity, it cannot involve that there is a chain of memories linking oneself in the present to someone in the past. For, as (*b*) states, one's ability to describe oneself as remembering presupposes one's ability to make the memory-based claims that entail the identity-judgements in question.

One's criterion must, however, be such that its satisfaction guarantees the truth of the causal claim that memory-claims embody, that is, the holding of the M-link, for it is surely the fact that one is able to make memory-based identifications that enables one to acquire the concept of memory and thus to ascribe memories to oneself. The suggestion that my discussion is leading up to is that this criterion is a *bodily* one, to the effect that the body now proprioceptively given is identical to one figuring in the content of the

---

[22] Thus I think that the gist of our concept of the M-link is of a single, intrinsically unspecified, state that both (1) enables us to have memory-experiences (which, I think, intrinsically are like imaginings), and (2) is (directly) caused by some subject having a corresponding experience (typically, but not necessarily, the subject who had this experience and the one who has the memory-experience are identical; hence, the possibility of quasi-memory). So the M-link involves identity of an underlying state, but not identity of subject. (Neuroscience is now beginning to spell out what this state is intrinsically like.) To remember an experience is to imagine having the experience as an actualization of a state with this origin; it does not involve the (memory-)judgement that one's imagining has this source.

memory, as the centrepiece of the scene remembered. Clearly, if there is bodily identity, the M-link will normally hold, that is, there is normally identity of those brain structures underlying memory.

But equally clearly, the M-link could logically obtain in the absence of our identity—say, because of a transplant of tissue from one brain to another. Thus, it is in principle possible to establish that one remembers someone's undergoing something in the past prior to, and independently of, establishing whether this subject is identical to oneself. This is why the traditional circularity objection fails.

In fact, however, this is not the way we proceed. It is only now, when neurophysiology is beginning to close in on what the M-link is, that we can *directly* ascertain that it obtains. Earlier we relied on *inferring* its presence from the fact that one is identical to someone existing in the past who underwent some event one now remembers. This procedure implies that our criterion of our identity is such that (*a*) it can be applied independently of our being able to make memory-claims and that (*b*) the presence of the M-link is inferrable from its applicability. Both conditions are satisfied by a bodily criterion, but obviously a memory-criterion violates (*a*).

So it is not the case that our identity cannot be defined in terms of memory-links because these links necessarily involve our identity. In principle, it would have been possible for us to acquire the concept of experiential memories prior to, and independently of, acquiring the concept of our identity. But in fact our procedure has been the other way around: we make memory-based claims about our own pasts prior to, and independently of, making memory-claims about ourselves. If so, the identity-criterion applied in our memory-based identifications of ourselves cannot be a memory-criterion. This is the *ad hominem* version of the circularity objection.

On this proposal, these identity judgements about the subject of memory would be of a piece with countless memory-based identity judgements we make about material things. I am strongly disposed to think that the chair I am now sitting in is numerically identical to the one I remember sitting in a few moments ago because of a continuity and resemblance in respect of perceived features. Similarly, I suggest that I am inclined to think that I am identical to the being whom I remember sitting in a chair a few moments ago because of a continuity and resemblance in perceptual and proprioceptive respects.[23]

In all probability, such transtemporal identity-judgements made by us are manifestations of an innate disposition that is actualized at a very early age, for they are of utmost survival value. A creature that was not capable of knowing that *it* a few moments ago was threatened by *that* now distant animal may again draw closer to it, with a fatal result. Consequently, we should expect that our basic conception of ourselves is such that, when one of us is able to discriminate the body she perceives from within from objects

---

[23] Contrast Johnston, who characterizes experiential memory as "something whose internal phenomenology makes it seem like a faculty suited to picking up only mental connections between earlier and later mental states" (1987: 77). I do not understand what he means by "picking up" here. In remembering (myself) having E at t, I normally do not *remember* any mental connections between my having E at t and my present experience, though my having this memory guarantees that there *is* such a connection. Learning to make memory-claims is learning to "pick up" or ascertain the presence of such connections.

surrounding it, and is able to identify that body with one presented as perceived from within by her short-term experiential memories, she is also able to discriminate and re-identify herself. Hence, as the formation of reliable beliefs about what has happened to ourselves in the past is of such a great survival value, we should expect the capacity to form them to be in our possession before we acquire the rather sophisticated ability to ascribe psychological states, like memories, to ourselves. In view of its importance, it is more plausible to hypothesize that it is part and parcel of the comparatively rudimentary capability to identify and re-identify our bodies among the bodies of our current perceptual experience.

This argument also effectively disposes of the idea that the identity criterion involved in our memory reports appeals to other psychological properties than experiential memory, such as a continuous realization of traits of character, of Unger's "core psychology" or of any mental disposition or capacity. For, obviously, judgements about such mental faculties and the continuity of their (neural) realization are far too advanced to enter the picture at this rather elementary stage: a child certainly acquires the capacity to make memory-based claims involving its own identity before acquiring such notions.

It might be objected to this that it is wrong-headed to construe memory-based claims about one's own past as involving a (separable) identification of oneself now judging with someone in the past undergoing the event remembered. The memory-based claim that I was F cannot be divided into the two claims that such-and-such an individual was F and that I am this individual (see G. Evans, 1982: 237 ff.).[24] If this division was possible, the first claim could be correct, while the second is mistaken. But, according to the objection, memory-claims are immune to such errors of misidentification.

If this objection were correct, it would be logically impossible to remember the pasts of other subjects (contrary to my argument in the foregoing section). This would resurrect the original circularity objection, and a memory-criterion would be untenable for that reason. On the other hand, if there is a separable element of identification, the criterion used in it cannot be a memory one, for the reasons I have argued. So, whichever is the case, a memory-criterion cannot be correct.

I do not think Evans's denial of the separability of identification is tenable, however. His argument in favour of it is as follows (1982: 244–5). Suppose that 'memory-traces' could be transplanted from one brain to another. I wake up after such a transplant, not knowing what has happened, and making what I take to be the memory-based judgements that I was F, etc. Then I discover that I was in fact not F, etc. Suppose I then retreat to the general judgement 'Someone (such-and-such) was F, etc.' Then, according to Evans: "*These judgements could not possibly constitute knowledge*" (1982: 244); they would be mere hypotheses which could be falsified.

But, even if this is correct, it seems to me that it could still be true that I *remember* that someone (such-and-such) was F, etc. Evans speaks of memory as involving "a non-conceptual informational state, whose content corresponds in a certain respect with that

---

[24] Similarly, Shoemaker denies that such identifications are made "on the basis of bodily criteria" (Shoemaker and Swinburne, 1984: 103).

of some earlier informational state of the subject (a perceptual state)" (1982: 239). It might, however, be said that a perceptual or sensory state is not tantamount to knowledge, but is rather normally a *basis* for knowledge—though it may lead us to error, as hallucinations show. Similarly, it might be said that a memory provides merely a generally reliable *basis* for knowledge about one's past—though, in some cases, such as the transplantation case, just described, it leads one to error. It then leads one to error because we all have a strong tendency—which is massively confirmed by experience—to believe that the subject of the experience remembered is ourselves now remembering.

Evans himself grants that "it is possible for memory to *serve as the basis* for . . . knowledge about the past" (1982: 245). For instance, if I am informed that I have received 'memory-traces' from A, this information, alongside my "apparent memories", provides me with *inferential* knowledge that A was F. But, Evans insists, this is different from the 'direct' knowledge of ordinary memory-based claims about one's own past. Certainly, but what is at stake is not whether these situations are different, but whether they are different in that one involves a separable element of identification and the other does not, or in that, while both involve identification, it is inferential in one situation and direct in the other. I have argued that the difference is of the latter kind.

According to my view, memory involves a non-conceptual informational state of imagining someone being in a situation, along with a spontaneous tendency, "underwritten by evolution", as Evans puts it (1982: 245), to identify the subject of that situation with oneself. This tendency is not put out of operation if one is told that the non-conceptual state in this particular case is the result of one's having received 'memory-traces', since the enormous support it has received throughout one's life has made it too well-entrenched. But there will nevertheless be a countervailing reflective judgement that this subject is the one from which the 'memory-traces' have been received. I do not see how Evans can resist the description of the normal case as involving an ingredient of identification once he has conceded that both normal and abnormal cases share a non-conceptual state—he talks of "apparent memories" in the latter case—and that there is room for identification in the latter case. It may be that we are *psychologically* incapable of inhibiting the (tendency to the) belief that it is we who are the subjects of the events remembered, but this belief is nevertheless *logically* separable from what constitutes our experiential memory. It is a belief *about* the content of what we remember rather than an ingredient of it.

An Explanation of the Appeal of Psychologism

Let me summarize this exploration of psychologism. (1) It turns out that matter-based psychologism views us as processes rather than as things, as we intuitively take ourselves to be, for it is neural processes that are the minimal ground of our psychological capacities. (2) It was then seen that it is difficult to maintain that the persistence of any such capacities is necessary for our persistence, since we can apparently persist without any of them, for example in persistent vegetative states. (3) To handle the problem that what constitutes our identity can branch, psychologism is forced to introduce a non-branching clause that violates the intuition that identity is intrinsic. This difficulty was traced to the fact psychologism takes the conditions of our persistence to be that of (psychological) processes rather than of a thing. Furthermore, it is considerably less clear that the branching of our minds or consciousnesses means our division when it occurs in circumstances of bodily identity. (4) The fact that our ability to make memory-based claims about our own past is primary in relation to our ability to make memory-claims implies that the identity-judgements entailed by the former claims cannot apply psychological criteria appealing to memory. Instead, it seems likely that they apply a somatist criterion. This is also a conclusion which fits in with the other considerations.

But if our criterion of identity is a somatist one, whence the adamant intuition that, in cases like I, in which our brains are transplanted to new bodies, *we* receive these new bodies? We have noted our deeply ingrained tendency to assume that the subject who underwent the event remembered is identical to the subject now having the memory representation. Powerful as this tendency is, we have seen that it could scarcely be taken as invariably reliable: most of us would agree that it would deceive us in fission cases, for instance. I suggest that it is deceptive also in brain-transplant cases like I, for there is no identity of the subject in the phenomenal aspect: the body proprioceptively given after the transplant is not identical to the body thus given before the transplant.

In contrast to what is true in fission cases, in the latter cases there is, however, identity of the primary owner of the mind, the owner shorn of its phenomenal shell and whittled down to what is minimally sufficient for the sustenance of consciousness or mind. But this can explain why we are strongly tempted to think that we go with our brains only on the assumption that we are strongly tempted to identify ourselves with this owner; and why is that? One reason for this is, as I shall argue in the next chapter, that underlying our everyday identification of ourselves with our bodies is the erroneous assumption that our bodies are the primary owners of our experiences. When this is seen not to be the case, for example by thought-experiments about brain-transplants, we may stick to identifying ourselves with that which is the primary owner, in disregard of the fact that this owner does not live up to the phenomenal aspect (which the body does). This move may be facilitated by the fact that when we refer to ourselves by means of a token of 'I', we refer to ourselves as the producer of this token. It is easy to slip into thinking that we refer to ourselves *only as that, whatever it is*, that produces this token, whereas, I have contended, we refer to ourselves as a phenomenally apparent body producing this token.

This reduction may also be helped under way by a liability to equate our *value* with the value of our minds or what is minimally sufficient for the production of our thoughts and experiences. This manifests itself, for instance, in that I would be as strongly biased towards the post-operative person in case I as I would be towards myself had I survived in the usual fashion (at least if the post-operative body is in macroscopic respects indistinguishable from my own). It seems that I would not find it worse that the post-operative individual comes into being and receives a benefit than that I would enjoy ordinary survival and receive it. Undergoing a brain transplant therefore seems as good as ordinary survival.

This adds further impetus to the temptation to think that *we* go with our transplanted brains. For there is a tendency, when a proper part of a complex is the source of more or less the whole value one attaches to the complex, to express this evaluation by saying that the part *is* the complex, though such an identification is literally absurd. (This inclination may be made easier by there being, as we have noted, a looseness in our mereological talk which allows us to identify a sufficiently big part with the whole.) For instance, somebody who more or less equates the value of Swedish cinema to that of the films of Ingmar Bergman may well say that Swedish cinema *is* (the films of) Ingmar Bergman. Analogously, we tend to identify ourselves with the parts of ourselves that we see as the source of most of our value, namely our minds. Of course, the emotional or evalutative identification of Swedish cinema with Ingmar Bergman would fool nobody, but in the case of more complex and perplexing entities like ourselves, such an emotionally exaggerated identification could easily be literally interpreted.

Not infrequently, this tendency to shrink ourselves to that in ourselves which we find particularly precious is carried to such extremes that it loses all pretension to be taken literally. For instance, we sometimes speak as though we would cease to exist, 'would no longer be ourselves', were we to lose our most passionate interests or leading ideals, such as our religious faith or political convictions.[25] I suggest that, partially, the psychologist project of 'whittling down' the bodily component of our identity is evaluatively fuelled just as these declarations are.[26]

My suggestion is, then, that the identity intuition in brain-transplant case like I is an illusion generated by these mechanisms. In this case, I do not go on existing, only something in me—*my mind* (and its primary owner)—does, but this is what I regard as most valuable about me.

Although, on psychologism, our identity and what matters in it would not part ways in these brain-transplant cases, it should be stressed that, in the end, this view fails to align identity and what matters. Parfit has argued (1984: § 90)—to my mind persuasively—that if one considers the matter carefully, one would care roughly as much about both of the branches A and B in the fission case II as about the single product in case I. For, in important respects, each branch is as intimately connected to oneself as a single product would be, and this connection is enough for the concern for the post-operative individuals to be as strong as for oneself.

But, unfortunately, there are accidental features that may distort one's judgement about what matters in fission cases. First, as is often pointed out, a person's life normally contains values that cannot be shared with anyone else (e.g. being exclusively favoured by a particular individual such as one's spouse). We must then take care not to imagine branches whose lives are made worse than the ancestral one because of values for which no compensation can be made.

---

[25] Cf. Parfit (1984: 304–6) on "successive selves", though he has in mind a loss of psychological connectedness *simpliciter* rather than a loss of it in respect of just traits valued.

[26] It is in this light, I think, that we should look upon the ambiguity of 'human being' or 'human' often remarked upon in ethical contexts. For instance, Peter Singer (1993: 85–7) has claimed that these predicates can designate either a member of the species *homo sapiens* or a person. The former use is the basic or original one, I hypothesize, and the latter one is an evaluative shrinkage of it which restricts the term to the most valuable traits of members of the human species. This shrinkage can go even further, as it does when we say of somebody 'She is a real human being', meaning that she exhibits valuable intellectual, emotional, or moral qualities to an *exceptional* degree.

Second, the duality may bring about a loss in respect of what Unger calls "the focus of one's life" (1990: 268 ff.). Again, this loss is not necessarily related to the loss of identity, as is shown by the fact that it can be reduced more or less to zero without identity being restored. Suppose that one branch dies a couple of seconds after having awakened. We may reasonably regard this as a misfortune, but surely not for the reason that our concern for the remaining branch could not now be as great as it would be if the other transplant had been a total failure! It is a misfortune simply to the extent that one life that might have been worthwhile is lost.

Due to these complications, and to the fact that Parfit has already forcefully deployed the fission case (cf. also R. Martin, 1998: ch. 3), I shall in Chapter 23 rely on another type of case which, in addition, has the merit of implying a break of identity even for advocates of the multiple occupancy thesis.[27] But before going into the question of what evaluatively matters in our identity, I should complete my analysis of it in the next chapter.

---

[27] Note that, contrary to what is sometimes suggested, it is not clear that multiple occupancy theorists can lay claim to the merit of reconciling the fact we care as much about both branches as about ourselves with the view that identity is the relation that matters. For concern is normally forward-looking and, as already noted, we cannot before the fission identify both of the branches with ourselves, i.e. refer to both of them by means of 'I'.

21

SOMATIST THEORIES
OF OUR IDENTITY

In Chapter 19 I advanced what I take to be a commonsensical account of our selves according to which they are identical to our bodies. Then I tried to meet the most radical challenge to it, namely that of immaterialism. In Chapter 20, I progressed to scrutinizing the less radical, but still lethal, threat of psychologist theories that specify the conditions of our persistence in terms of matter-based psychological relations. The conclusion of this investigation was that the somatist starting-point emerged fortified.

A somatist view offers the comfort of simplicity in that it regards our identity as a species of a genus of identity we must countenance in any case, namely that of material things without minds. It does not propose a set of criteria which is especially designed for beings with minds, as do its main contenders, immaterialism and psychologism. This is not to say that the persistence conditions of material bodies are a simple matter. As Chapter 22 shows, they are not.

The question is, however, whether a somatist view can be defensibly worked out. Pre-reflectively, we identify ourselves with our physical bodies. More precisely, we identify ourselves with our bodies as the owners of our minds and as they are presented by proprioception, and other modes of perception. This is a presentation of them as bodies pure and simple, that is, as three-dimensional entities having mass and a certain tangible shape. Furthermore, if we are to ascribe mental states to ourselves, this proprioceptive and perceptual awareness must be taken as veridical, that is, as being of something physical in the sense of something existing independently of our awareness.

Our bodies are, however, not merely material, but also *organic*. In other words, they are organisms or, more specifically, animals. These animals belong to a certain biological species, *homo sapiens*. So, if the commonsensical identification of us with our bodies is to be sustained, the conditions of our persistence must be those of human animals. That is, the position known as *animalism* or the *biological view* of our nature and identity must be correct.[1]

---

[1] The term 'animalism' was coined by Paul Snowdon (1991: 109). Other important animalist contributions are Snowdon (1990), Ayers (1991: ii. ch. 25), Wiggins (1980: ch. 6) and Eric Olson (1997). The human animal or organism of animalism must of course not be confused with a human being in Mark Johnston's sense, i.e. "an unspecified kind of locus of (perhaps reflective) mental life" (1987: 71).

It should not be taken for granted that the somatism that, I have argued, common sense embraces coincides with animalism. Nor, if it does not, that there is a defensible form of somatism distinct from animalism. For the commonsensical view may be in a pejorative sense a *naïve* somatism which identifies us with our bodies on the basis of untenable assumptions. This possibility is not to be excluded, since, as will be seen, we can pick out something by means of an indexical like 'I' without knowing the kind of thing it essentially is. It may be that science has to explicate our nature. There is no guarantee that this explication will reveal something of a kind that necessarily persists as long as do our selves, that is, the entities picked out by 'I'.

The upshot of this chapter is that the commonsensical identification of ourselves with our bodies is indeed naïve in that it rests on two erroneous assumptions. First, that these bodies are the primary owners of our minds or consciousnesses, so that identity of mind entails bodily identity. Secondly, that identity as regards the phenomenal aspect also entails bodily identity. So, all in all, naïve somatism assumes that our selves are our bodies, and that the identity of the owner and the phenomenal aspects of the notion of a self each implies bodily identity (though, of course, bodily identity does not imply identity in either of these aspects, since the body can exist without mind). Now, if it turns out that we cannot be identical to bodies of the kind we pick out by means of 'I', because of the falsity of these assumptions, we are not identical to things of any kind, and there are no coherent conditions of our diachronic identity or persistence. That is, we land in the view I call (factual) *nihilism* as regards our nature and identity.

Animalism and the Concepts of an Organism and Species Membership

Before we draw this radical conclusion, we must examine animalism or the biological view, according to which we are essentially *organisms* or *animals of the human species*. This necessitates a clarification of the notions of being (1) an *organism*—or a member of *some* biological species—and (2) a member of a *certain* biological species, like *homo sapiens*.

With respect to (1), there is obviously some connection between the concept of an organism and that of biological life (i.e. life in a sense in which it could be attributed to plants, too). But we should not assume that it is as straightforward as that an organism is perforce alive at every moment of its existence. For that would be refuted by cases of 'suspended animation'. It is a routine in laboratories to freeze micro-organisms so deeply that their life processes come to a halt. When there is need for it, the organisms can be warmed up to the point at which their life processes start again. During the deep freeze, they are not alive (though it does not follow that they are dead), but they are still organisms (of the same species).[2]

---

[2] Note that, although these organisms are not alive, they are still *living things*: in one sense, 'living thing' seems to mean organism rather than thing that is alive (now).

At the present state of the art, it is not possible to freeze and thaw out complex organisms like human beings. But this impossibility seems merely technical, and we can imagine humans undergoing the same treatment. This would cause them to cease to be members of the human species who are alive, but it would surely not cause them to cease to be human animals. (So, fortunately for animalists, they are not compelled to say that the freeze would cause us to cease to exist.)

In the frozen state, the organisms are still *capable of* coming to life, and it may be suggested that it is this capacity for life (whether or not exercised) which is essential for being a member of a biological species. To say that something has a capacity for life is not to say that it is—empirically or naturally—possible that it will live. For suppose the equipment or chemicals needed to thaw out the frozen organisms were lost; then they would not thereby have lost their capacity for life (to regain it if the chemicals were retrieved). Their capacity rather consists in their *internal* state or constitution being such that, if certain (possible) external conditions were to obtain at a suitable time and place, the organisms would come to life.

The proposal that an organism or member of some species essentially has a capacity for life seems, however, to face a devastating objection. For as, for example Fred Feldman has contended, there is "no reason to suppose that biological organisms lose their species membership merely by dying" (1992: 104). A human corpse still belongs to the human species, just as a dead dog or dolphin is a dog or dolphin. (So, on animalism, we would often exist after our deaths.) In other words, they are still organisms (of the same species) as before they died. As Feldman remarks (1992: 94–5), we can point to such a dead body and truly say, 'This was formerly alive'. That is, the thing which is now dead is the very same thing as one that was earlier alive. But it was, presumably, an organism which was alive; thus this organism still exists (though as we shall shortly see, this is not undisputed). It seems, however, patently false to hold that the dead organism has a capacity for life.

A weaker proposal would be that a dead organism is an organism so long as it retains *most* of the internal constitution in virtue of which it was capable of life (cf. D. Mackie, 1999: 236–8). This constitution can persist to a large extent even though the capacity for life is lost: materially small changes can be functionally decisive, making it impossible to pair the internal state with any external circumstances that would result in the revival of the individual. If so, it can be maintained that an organism is a material thing with (most of) an internal constitution that enables *or enabled* it to be alive.

Of course, there is no sharp cut-off point at which this constitution has been destroyed, say, by decomposition, to the degree that the organism no longer exists: is it on animalism correct to say, as we sometimes do, for example, '*Lenin* should be moved from Red Square'? But I do not regard this vagueness as a good objection to animalism since, as will appear, on any credible theory of our identity, it is in some circumstances indeterminate whether or not we persist.

Another approach suggests that a dead organism is an organism so long as it retains (most of) a bodily constitution which *it has acquired by having been alive*. Ayers writes: "Life is essential to a thing in so far as it is inconceivable that it (*this* thing) should have come into existence as a non-living thing" (1991: ii. 224). It is a central theme of his book that, as our sense-experience presents matters, "there are naturally discrete and unitary objects waiting to be picked out by us as the primitive subjects of predication" (1991: ii. 4), some of these being organic. In the case of these objects, their discreteness and unity are not *constituted* by their being alive (for then they would dissolve at the moment of death), but, according to Ayers, they are *caused* by their having been alive, and this is a non-contingent matter.

A stronger and a weaker claim should be distinguished here. According to the stronger claim a living thing or organism must be alive when it comes into existence.[3] According to the weaker one, an organism need not be alive at this stage, but it is inconceivable that an organism, which in fact was alive when it came into existence, would not be alive when it started to exist. The stronger claim is more relevant in the present context, but Ayers may endorse only the weaker one. I am, however, inclined to think that both claims are false. Hark back to the micro-organisms in the state of suspended animation: surely some scientist could in theory put together an animal out of such micro-organisms and then make it alive by reviving them.[4] This animal would exist before becoming alive. As regards the weaker claim, it seems to me plausible to hold that an animal we have before our eyes is the same one, regardless of whether 'its' existence began in the way just sketched or in the normal way.

Despite the fact that it is hard to spell out the link between the concept of an organism and that of biological life, it nonetheless seems clear that there must be some such link. This raises the question of the purport of the concept of life here invoked. Although this issue is notoriously controversial, a reasonable proposal is that to be alive consists in something like acquiring materials from the environment—by eating, drinking, and breathing—and making them part of one's own body.[5] As a counter-instance to such a proposal, Feldman adduces the case of a moth which neither eats nor drinks (though, presumably, it breathes). But it is still absorbing material from a "reserve of stored energy" (1992: 30) which, at an earlier stage, it has extracted from its environment. Thus, the possibility is left open to define being alive in terms of this absorption or assimilation of alien material which is or has been acquired from the environment. It is this absorption that underlies the growth and development characteristic of living organisms.

According to this explication, life-processes—and, hence, organic status—would not be open to everyday observation. For although we observe that we breathe, eat, drink, and excrete some products, we do not observe that our bodies absorb material from what we take in. As far as everyday observation goes, what we consume might just have supplied us with the energy needed to keep our mental and bodily activities going. In other words, as far as this observation goes we could have been inorganic, cleverly constructed robots with consciousnesses. For present purposes, this, and not any more

---

    [3] By a "non-living thing" in the quotation above, Ayers presumably means a thing that is not alive rather than something inorganic (to appeal to the distinction just drawn).

    [4] I shall not attempt to explain the distinction between an organism and an animal, though I take it that an animal is a complex organism which perhaps must be capable of locomotion.

    [5] Cf. Olson, who equates the life of an organism with "the sum of the metabolic activities the organism's parts are caught up in" (1997: 136).

specific details about its analysis, is the important point about the concept of life, and it appears very credible.

Let us now move on to question (2), about what it is to belong to a specific biological species. It is common to distinguish between *morphological* and *genetic* criteria of species membership. It seems safe to say that the former criterion, which discriminates between species on characteristics observable in everyday circumstances, is not sufficient for the job: for instance, if we happened to look exactly like creatures found in a very distant region (e.g. another planet), though the genetic dissimilarity was great enough to rule out interfertility, we would hardly view them as conspecific with us. Appeal to genetic relations appears inescapable in a definition of species membership, though morphological characteristics probably also have a part to play (e.g. as fixing the reference to the underlying genetic ones).

A third criterion appeals, in Ayers's words, to "all that is involved in the members of one species forming a historically related, unitary group" which is a matter "of the interbreeding and common origin of members of the group" (1991: ii. 85). Consequently, he claims that "however accurately the morphology and genetic structure of *Tyrannosaurus rex* were reproduced, the result would still not be a member of that species, or of any species" (1991: ii. 85), if it were synthesized by us, for it would not have the right origin. I shall later suggest that this third criterion merely gives a factor that as a matter of fact explains common genetic structure.

After this attempt to clarify the purport of the terms central to animalism, I shall now begin to probe its tenability.

The Human Organism Not the Primary Owner of Consciousness

In connection with the 'double subject' objection, which, as we saw in the last chapter, animalists launch against psychologists, we noted that animalists take the subjects of our experiences to be our animal organisms. It is not hard to understand why they insist on this point, for if these subjects were distinct from our organisms, there would be a good case for saying that we are distinct from these organisms, since we are surely identical to the subjects of our experiences. I suggested, however, that psychologists can plausibly argue that our organisms are only derivatively the *owners* of our experiences, that these experiences belong to these bodies only in virtue of there being something in them—for example (processes in) their brains—to which they non-derivatively belong. They belong non-derivatively to these entities in the sense that they are minimally sufficient for them.

To be sure, this is not enough for these entities instead of our whole organisms to be the *subjects* of our experiences, for they do not face up to the phenomenal aspect: they do not crop up in the content of experience. A subject of experiences must weld the owner and phenomenal aspects. It is not an owner of experiences in a purely causal sense, but something that takes on the phenomenal aspect so that self-ascription of experiences is possible. It is, however, rather the whole body that matches this aspect.

Here it might be objected that the whole body must then be the primary owner of our experiences, must be that to which we in the first instance ascribe our experiences. Yes, but only in an *epistemic* sense; in an *ontic* sense, it is merely derivatively the owner. To satisfy the owner aspect, something must, however, be the non-derivative owner of experiences in an ontic sense. This is a demand which our bodies fail to live up to, and a reason why animalism is untenable (which is not to say that the rival psychologist conception is correct).

Since some are sceptical of science fictional thought-experiments, like brain-transplants, it bears mention that nature produces counter-examples to this animalist claim, in the form of human organisms with two minds or consciousnesses. Consider cases of conjoined or Siamese twins. They form a continuum as regards common bodily parts. At the one end there are instances in which the overlap is only a patch of skin: every bodily member exists in duplicate, from two heads, each with a functioning brain, down to two sets of legs. Clearly, here are two human animals which could easily be surgically separated. Hence, animalists will readily agree that there can here be two subjects of experience, one thinking p and the other not thinking p (but perhaps not-p), one suffering from a headache and the other being pain-free, and so on.

But consider cases near the opposite end of the spectrum, in which the twins share most bodily organs, though each has its own head filled with a functioning brain. These brains may receive sensations from, and exercise control over, one half of the body each (this body may have two arms and legs as a normal body). Obviously, the fact that these twins have most bodily parts in common, limbs, intestines, etc., provides a reason for saying that there is only one human organism here. Since there is a single set of vital organs, like heart, lungs, digestive tract, there is no possibility of a division into two organic entities each viable on its own. And the requirement of independent viability seems a plausible way of distinguishing an organism from other biological entities like (a collection of) organs.

A failure to meet this requirement, however, provides *no* reason for maintaining that there now has to be only one mind or consciousness instead of two. The facts that earlier made us both apply and withhold the predicates 'thinking p', 'suffering from a headache', etc. to a pair of twins—that is, the fact that there are two functioning brains, each control-ling a mouth which utters psychological sentences that contradict those of the other mouth—still obtain. So, to all appearances, there are still two minds or consciousnesses.

As opposed to what is true as regards the organisms, these consciousnesses are physically separable. Imagine that one twin's head is chopped off and successfully grafted onto a human organism whose brain-dead head has been detached. Animalists will admit that there are now two minds or consciousnesses around. But surely this duality was not *created* by the transplant; it was present before, when the heads were still sitting on the same torso. If, however, there are two minds or consciousnesses, there must be two physical owners of them, since they cannot be 'free-floating'. As there is only a single human organism, these minds or consciousnesses cannot belong (except derivatively) to it, but must rather belong to two distinct parts of it.[6]

---

[6]   This argument is elaborated in Persson (1999a).

Consequently, I take it that nature in the shape of such conjoined twins supplies cases that decisively show that the conditions for the individuation of minds and their organisms are such there can be more than one mind and, thus, mind-owner in a single (human) organism. If so, we cannot in man-made cases, like the commissurotomy cases considered in the foregoing chapter, reject the view that there are here two minds or consciousnesses simply on the ground that there is only a single organism. We must rather approach them with an unprejudiced mind. Perhaps cutting the bridge between the two hemispheres is sufficient to give rise to two consciousness. It may be hard to tell because there is not one mouth through which each can express itself. In any case, it seems indisputable that the existence of two normal brains is sufficient for two consciousnesses, though it is not sufficient for there being two organisms.

I conclude, then, that animalists cannot avoid conceding the possibility of there being a single (human) organism with two minds or consciousnesses. Therefore they must admit the distinctness of non-derivative mind-owners and their organisms, if they admit, as I claimed in Chapter 19, that minds cannot be free-floating, but must be owned by something (physical). The distinction between derivative and non-derivative ownership is disguised by the fact that normally there is at most a single mind per organism.

We must, however, be careful not to overstate this conclusion. It has *not* been contended that, in the case of these conjoined twins, there are two *subjects* or *selves*, for, to repeat, these notions also comprise a phenomenal aspect. On the other hand, the number of human organisms does not necessarily settle the number of phenomenal objects. It may be arguable that, even in some cases of conjoined twins with so extensive a bodily overlap that they form a single human organism, they still compose two distinct, but partially overlapping, phenomenal objects. For these distinct phenomenal objects may consist not just of parts that are duplicated, like heads and necks, but also of different parts of a shared body, if they are connected to different brains. This may supply enough of phenomenal distinctness for there to be two selves or subjects, that is, two referents of the tokens of 'I' which come out of the two mouths of the twins.

It does not follow that there are two subjects also in the cases in which a brain has been divided and put back in the original body, as in case II in the foregoing chapter, even on the proviso that the two hemispheres are connected to different parts of the body. The fact that there is here no abnormal bodily duplication—of heads or whatever—may make us settle for the view that there are not two *subjects* of *selves* here, although there are two mind-*owners*, in the causal sense. This is something I shall not try to settle, since I believe it may be indeterminate how many selves there are, just as it may be indeterminate how many human organisms there are. The point I am out to make is a negative one about mind-ownership, namely, that animalists are wrong in claiming that the whole human organism is the non-derivative mind-owner (in the ontic sense). This undermines their claim—which they share with naïve somatists—that the subject or self is identical to this organism.

As regards the owner aspect, psychologism is closer than animalism to the truth, but psychologism suffers from the shortcoming of neglecting the phenomenal aspect. It asserts not merely that brains, or brain-parts, are mind-owners, but in effect that they are subjects or selves, since it concludes, for example, that we go with our brains in brain-transplant situations. But the power of the phenomenal aspect can be felt if one imagines, as in Daniel Dennett's well-known thought-experiment,[7] that my brain is taken out of my body and kept alive in a vat distant from my brainless body. By radio transmission my brain receives impulses from this body, so there is still proprioception of it and exteroception by means of its sense-organs. Here we are torn between saying that I am where my brain is and that I am where my body is. This conundrum is due, I hypothesize, to the fact that what carries the owner aspect is rather the brain, while the rest of my body aspires to fill the phenomenal aspect. The source of the conundrum is not simply that my body is 'scattered', by one part of it being distant from the rest (*pace* Garrett, 1998: 47). For there would be no conundrum if, say, it was instead my bowels that had the location of the brain; the isolated part has to be the owner of my mind. Nor would there be a conundrum if there were not also a tendency to identify oneself with the phenomenal aspect.

Given the latter tendency, whence the common conviction that in brain-transplant cases we go with our brains or with that piece of matter which is minimally sufficient for our minds? It is presumably due in part to the rough coincidence in space between the owner and phenomenal aspects causing a failure to separate them and to realize that identity in each respect is necessary for our identity. This effaces the significance of the fact that there is not identity in the phenomenal aspect because after the operation a numerically distinct body is playing the phenomenal role. (Further explanatory considerations were offered at the end of the preceding chapter.)

If the conviction that we go with our brains in transplant cases were right, we would need an explanation of why we do not unequivocally hold that in the foregoing case our location is that of the brain in the vat. Moreover, what would explain the fact, noted earlier, that we are inclined to hold that we can persist in a state of being permanently unconscious? This may be the state of the donor body after the removal of its higher cerebral parts, which are the mind-owner, and we cannot identify ourselves both with the transplanted brain-parts and with the body left behind.

To conclude, we have discussed cases which necessitate a distinction between our bodies or organisms and the primary owners of our minds. Although these cases imply that our selves cannot be identical to our bodies, they do not show, as is often thought, that our selves can outlive our bodies (which entails that there can be identity in both the owner and the phenomenal aspects without bodily identity). I now turn to a second argument against animalism that attempts to show precisely this.

How our Selves Might Outlive our Organisms

If animalism holds good, the self, that is, that which we pick out by means of 'I', must be identical to a human organism and the criterion of our persistence must be that of such an organism. This would mean that we could not conceivably cease to be either human

---

[7] See 'Where Am I?' in Dennett (1978).

or organisms without ceasing to exist. I shall first examine whether we could cease to be organisms.

The thought-experiment to which I shall appeal presupposes that it is not a necessary truth that a self or subject of experience is an organism. Snowdon mentions a "psychological animalism" to the effect that "any psychologically endowed thing must be an animal" (1990: 83). If this doctrine were true, it would indeed be necessary that the subject of experience is an animal or organism: its being conscious and perceiving itself would vouchsafe its being organic. But as he confesses, the defence of psychological animalism would be "an enormous task" (1990: 104). And the onus of proof is surely on psychological animalists for, prima facie, it appears to be no more than a contingent truth—if it is a truth at all—that all psychologically endowed things are animals. (It is not true if those who claim that computers literally have minds are correct.)

Thus, the most reasonable conclusion seems to be that, though the physical bodies, which are selves or subjects, are in fact organisms, this is not deeply necessary: in other possible worlds at least some of them would be inorganic. Now, could the organisms we in fact are be replaced by such inorganic things in such a way that it would not be true that we go out of existence? If the answer is affirmative, the criterion of our identity cannot be organic, since we can linger in existence without being organic.

Let us take a look at what such a replacement—or transformation, if we do not take this term to presuppose the identity of the bodies involved—might be like. As there is no reason to believe psychological animalism to be true, we can imagine there to be some inorganic material that has the power to sustain minds and behaviour like ours and that is supplied with energy by the substances we consume. If the organic material of our bodies bit by bit were transformed into this material, the resulting bodies would be subjects whose experiences could be 'seamlessly' continuous with our experiences, that is, there would be both CCS and CCT.[8]

Moreover, this change from organic to inorganic might go unobserved by our proprioceptive and exteroceptive systems. We have seen that the concepts of an organism and that of (biological) life are—albeit tenuously—linked, and that life roughly consists in taking up material from the environment and integrating it into the organism. This integration, we noted, takes place deep inside the body and is therefore not open to the view of everyday proprioception and perception. Although we perceive that we eat, for example, we do not perceive that some material consumed is transformed into bodily matter rather than used up as energy for our activities. On the basis of everyday observation, we are consequently unable to tell whether we are living organisms or life-like robots with consciousness. Since we are unable to monitor life processes inside our bodies, and externally, our bodies would look and behave in the same manner, the metamorphosis could occur unobserved. Thus, the veridicality of our everyday observations of our bodies guarantees only that they are three-dimensional things occupying certain spatial zones, not that they are organic.

---

[8] Recently, Garrett (1998: 49–50) and Baker (2000: e.g. 11, 106) have called attention to the possibility of such a transformation.

Suppose that one were informed of these changes going on below the observable surface; then one would hardly exclaim 'Help, I'm in fact about to disappear!' For, introspectively, it appears to one that one goes on existing, and, as we have seen, the first-person pronoun refers to the perceptually (mainly proprioceptively) given aspects of the physical body that is producing the current token of it. There is identity in these aspects if certain regions of physical space are continuously filled. This can be the case, though an organism is about to vanish and be replaced by an inorganic thing which maintains its consciousness. So our organisms do not really match up to the phenomenal aspect. To do that, it is not enough that they are perceived; rather, they must be 'fully' perceived in a sense in which something is fully perceived only if all essential parts of it are perceived, so that it cannot pass out of existence without perceiving that it does. (This is analogous to the claim that for our organisms to match up to the owner aspect, our experiences must be *non-derivatively* ascribable to them.)

It might be useful to compare this thought-experiment to brain-transplants that are often thought to show that our identity is not that of an organism. As regards brain-transplants, I have argued that they do not really preserve numerically the same subject of experience or self because there is no identity in the phenomenal aspect. This objection is not valid against organic–inorganic transition. There is here identity in the phenomenal aspect because the perception we have of our bodies—as something, with morphological human features, filling three-dimensional regions of space—is veridical: there really is something with these human features continuously occupying the relevant regions of physical space, whatever goes on in the unobservable depth of this occupant. (Analogously, a 'view' of, e.g. landscape picks out certain visible aspects, so that there is numerically the same view, as long as these aspects persist, whatever happens to other parts of the material things which have them.)

It may instead be complained that in the organic–inorganic metamorphosis, identity of the owner aspect is not really preserved. For although, as we have seen, the phenomenal aspect of our bodies is that to which, in an epistemic sense, we first ascribe our experiential states, the ontically non-derivative owner is something lying beneath this phenomenal aspect, namely (something in) the brain. Since the brain goes out of existence with the organism, to be replaced by some inorganic surrogate, it may be doubted whether there is really CCS or identity of mind in this case, as opposed to what may be true in the brain-transplant case.

I do not think this objection can be sustained, however. For, as I remarked in the foregoing chapter, identity of brain(-parts) is not necessary for CCS or psychological continuity, since the neural processes supporting mental states can move from one brain to another. Now, if such states can be supported by inorganic material, it seems they can move from a brain to some inorganic entity. There could then be CCS and identity as regards the primary owner of mental states in the organic–inorganic transition, provided the transition is gradual and slow enough.

A more radical objection to the possibility of the metamorphosis (and a support for psychological animalism) can be gathered from van Inwagen, who claims that (*a*) there is something that simples compose if and only if their activity constitutes a *life* (1990: § 9) and that (*b*) if there is thinking and feeling "there must be a thing, one thing, that is doing the thinking and feeling" (1990: 12; cf. also § 12). It follows that non-living collections of simples cannot think or feel. But van Inwagen cannot plausibly mean that, when an organism dies, it loses its unity in the sense that, to our sense experience, it no longer presents itself as a unitary thing, for evidently a dead organism may to our senses be indistinguishable from a living one. Ayers is surely right that the unity of the "objects waiting to be picked by us as the primitive subjects of predication" is not constituted by their being alive. Thus (*a*) is false: the phenomenal unity that is the subject can persist, though the life-processes that pumped it up peter out.[9]

Therefore I conclude that the metamorphosis envisaged may preserve identity both in respect of the phenomenal aspect and the owner aspect of the self. Hence it may preserve the identity of our selves. It follows that it may preserve our identity, since that which makes us selves surely cannot outlive us (albeit we can cease to be selves). But since it does not preserve the identity of our organisms, we cannot be identical to these organisms.

Underlying this argument is the assumption that we can perceptually pick out ourselves by means of 'I' without knowing what kind to which the thing intended to be picked out essentially belongs. In this respect, first-person reference is similar to demonstrative reference: in both cases, it is enough that one is able perceptually to single out the thing intended from its environment (cf. Cassam, 1997: 136 ff.). For instance, to demonstratively refer to 'that worm-like thing' I perceive, I certainly do not need to know its kind and the conditions of persistence, for example whether they allow its transforming into a butterfly. This is something that science may establish much later. It suffices that I am able perceptually to tell it apart from its environment. The same is true of the producer of a current token of 'I' which stands out from the environment by being the only object proprioceptively given as a thing filling a 3-D region.

But there is a crucial difference between these cases. Suppose that I am informed that, underneath the qualitative continuity I perceive, the 'worm-like thing' undergoes a radical change from an organic to an inorganic state; then I shall have to retract the identity-judgement that I am spontaneously inclined to make, to the effect that I perceive one and the same thing. For I cannot specify any sort of thing such that the thing is the same thing of that sort. In contrast, I have argued that we need not retract our judgements that we, or our selves, persist in the same circumstances. We need not retract these judgements as long as there is identity in the phenomenal and ownership aspects entailed by the concept of the self. These aspects makes the self, as Roderick Chisholm has put it, "transparent".[10] This transparency obstructs the identification of the self with anything

---

[9] A complication is, however, that van Inwagen might be prepared to count something as a living thing, although it is not made out of organic material (1990: 137–8). For further criticism of him, see Persson (1993).

[10] He continues: "to know that I perceive the cat to be standing, I must know that I perceive a proper part of the cat . . . but to know that I perceive myself to be thinking I need *not* know that I perceive a proper part of myself" (1994: 100). That is, I need not know that my body has other, possibly essential, parts. This is why it is the case that to know whether I perceive the same cat, I must know what happens to parts of the cat that are not currently visible to me, but to know whether I go on existing, I need not know anything about unperceived parts of my body: it is enough if the perceived parts and the consciousness attributed to them go on existing.

of a natural kind whose essence is hidden from the consciousness that the self necessarily possesses.

The independence the self has of hidden essences seems to spill over to the artefacts we create: the essential properties of these artefacts appear to have to do rather with the function and shape they are made and perceived to have than with the material out of which they are constituted. Consider, for instance, a statue made of some sort of metal. Suppose it is scooped out, leaving only a thin 'shell' instantiating its form. Later the cavity inside it is filled with a new quantity of some sort of metal, the same or different. It is plausible to say that the same *statue* or *work of art* survives this procedure. But in the end we certainly do not have the same *lump of metal* as we had in the beginning (if the 'shell' is composed of only a tiny portion of the metal). The conflict is due to the fact that the identity conditions of things of artefactual kinds have to do with their observable features, like their form, which is suited to the function for which they are designed, whereas these conditions of things of natural kinds rather have to do with their composition.

Now, we have of course not created ourselves by our conscious efforts, and there is no (created) 'form' or 'function' that need be retained for our identity to be preserved. But in a less forcible way our consciousnesses nevertheless 'impose' themselves on our organisms, by selecting those aspects of them given especially in proprioception, roughly their being 3-D solids. If there is constant surveillance from the inside of a physical continuity in these respects, we persist, irrespective of the changes in other perceptual respects or in the unobservable depth of our bodies.

Why We Are Not Essentially Human

We have seen that species membership is not decided on the basis of morphological criteria solely—in our case the criterion of having a characteristic human 'shape'—but that appeal must be made also to facts unobservable in ordinary circumstances, namely genetic ones. Therefore we could run an analogous argument in favour of the conclusion that, putting aside whether we are essentially organisms, our species membership is not essential. If deep inside our organisms genetic changes took place which led to them no longer being classifiable as human, it would surely be as counter-intuitive to infer that occurrences of 'I' in the relevant continuous streams of consciousness will change their reference, as it was in the case of the organic–inorganic transition.

Ayers agrees with the claim: "To identify the species of a living thing is to go beyond its sensible appearance" (1991: i. 190), but, as remarked, he accords a prominent place to the historic criterion of belonging to a certain interbreeding group. Let us see what effect this criterion would have on inter-specific transitions as the one envisioned. To discuss this, we need not confine ourselves to human cases, because the animalist claim that we are essentially human is an instance of the more general claim that every organism essentially belongs to its species or, as Ayers puts it, that "biological individuals do not change kinds" (1991: ii. 87). As a possible counter-instance to this principle he speculates about a horse that has "its DNA so altered by some experiment in genetic engineering or by radiation (or whatever) that it grows in all respects to be like a deer" (1991: ii. 86). His conclusion is that "the resultant creature does not have the right origins to *be* a deer . . . It is a horse which has suffered deformity, not a deer which has replaced a horse" (1991: ii. 86).

Suppose that (*a*) it is the same individual animal that undergoes this metamorphosis. Then, if we assert that (*b*) species membership is essential, we are obliged to conclude with Ayers that (*c*) the resultant creature is a horse. But (*c*) requires that the criteria for species membership are not just morphological and/or genetic; what is called for is rather that (*d*) they are primarily historic as he makes them out to be, so that a deer must spring from parents which are deer. For morphologically and genetically the resultant animal is doubtless a deer rather than a horse.

I find it hard to believe in (*c*), however. Imagine that the resultant creature reproduces with deer; it seems to me wildly implausible to classify the offspring as a crossbreed between a deer and a horse. Surely, they are deer. So, either both parents are deer or a deer can spring from parents at least one of which is not a deer. In either case, doubts are thrown on (*d*). The most natural conclusion seems to be that the criteria of species membership are just genetic and morphological and that common proximate ancestors are only something that generally explains genetic similarity. (The more distant the common ancestors are, the greater the genetic dissimilarity could be; otherwise, species could not evolve out of each other.) But if so, we must reject either (*a*) or (*b*). I think we can reject (*a*): we want to say that the horse becomes, or is transformed into, a deer, but this does not entail (*a*). It only entails that the matter composing a horse is so transformed that it comes to compose a deer. Compare the way a statue of a horse can become a statue of a deer when a lump of clay is remodelled. The lump survives this transformation, but not the statue of the horse.

This identity of constituting matter is enough to allow for the possibility of it being one and the same consciousness that first is the consciousness of a horse and then of a (numerically distinct) deer. That is all I need for my thought-experiment. Of course, the inclination to speak of the same consciousness is strengthened if there is introspective self-consciousness, as in the case of humans. So, I claim that we can conceivably cease being human and become members of another species, though no biological organism could undergo such a metamorphosis. Hence, we are not essentially such organisms.

Conclusion: Factual Nihilism

The conclusion we have arrived at is, then, that we are of necessity neither human nor animal, that 'human animal' describes a 'phase' that we could logically leave behind. In this argument, my point of departure (in Chapter 19) has been similar to that of Ayers, but I have turned it against his animalism. For I believe there to be a tension between his starting-point of taking our experience of ourselves "as being a material object among others" as a guide and the animalism of his conclusion. One source of this tension is that we do not experience our own bodies as human organisms, but rather as material things or bodies with superficial, morphological human features. This means that our bodies do not face up to the phenomenal aspect of being fully perceived.

Qua being physical or material things of a certain shape our bodies do face up to this aspect, but this does not specify a kind of thing with distinctive conditions of identity. Our shape must be allowed to be changeable, gradually, out of recognition. And, as been pointed out, for example by Wiggins (1980: 63–4), the (dummy) 'sortal' *physical (material) thing* is so general and unspecific that it is pointless to trace the identity of anything under it: through suitably gradual changes (e.g. a series of deletions of tiny parts until only a small portion of the original thing remains and then a series of additions of other tiny parts), it allows a physical thing to be identical to a physical thing from which it is intuitively distinct. So this view would permit us to persist indefinitely. Moreover, what meets the owner aspect is something different that may not even be a thing (or 'continuant'), but may rather be some (brain-)processes. These two 'satisfiers' are lumped together only because of their relation to something external, the mental features constitutive of selves, not because they together form a material kind.

The proper conclusion to draw is that the somatism of common sense is a naïve one that overlooks two distinctions: that to be our selves it is enough neither that (*a*) our bodies are that to which we (epistemically) first ascribe our experiences; they must be the (ontically) *non-derivative* owners of them, nor that (*b*) our bodies are perceived; their essence must be perceived, so that they cannot go out of existence without this showing up. The first oversight rarely makes itself felt in everyday life—only in some cases of conjoined twins and, possibly, of split-brain patients—while the second never does, since our bodies never cease to be human organisms. Thus, when we routinely re-identify ourselves, we can safely employ the criterion of the identity of our human bodies, for the situations in which this criterion lets us down practically never occur. Therefore, it takes philosophical imagination to reveal its shortcomings.

John Locke, who more than anyone else could claim to have initiated the discussion of our identity, famously distinguished the man, or human animal, from the person (1689/1975: II. xxvii). We have now rejected both sorts of account of our identity, animalism and psychologism, which can be traced back to this distinction, along with the immaterialism, spurned by Locke. The fact that we have self-conscious minds does not supply us with an identity-criterion on its own, but it does have the effect of ruling out any tenable somatist criterion, since that in the physical world which satisfies the constraints it imposes does not form any kind of thing.

Although my account of the notions of a subject of experience and a self is incompatible with both animalism and psychologism, it explains the attractions of both. The body which appears to satisfy the phenomenal aspect is in fact a human organism. This body also promises to satisfy the owner aspect, though scientific discoveries have disclosed that it does so only derivatively, in virtue of something it contains. Scientific discoveries have also revealed the gulf between the identity conditions of such organisms and what is phenomenally apparent, and, thus, made us alert to the possibility of such thought-experiments as the organic–inorganic transition. These facts apart, it seems quite plausible to put trust in a somatist criterion, as we do in everyday life. Hence the attractions of animalism.

But once it has been made clear that our organisms own our consciousness only in virtue of having certain parts, the pull of psychologism is felt. This is the result if one takes one's lead from the owner aspect and neglect or misinterpret the phenomenal one. An inventory of the penalties for this is found in Chapter 20; it includes such things as violating the intuition, supplied by the phenomenal aspect, that we are things rather than processes, the intrinsicality of identity, and overlooking that judgements of our identity are prior to claims of having experiential memory.

This conclusion may seem absurd for, if we are not identical to things of any kind, it seems we do not exist. But even though tokens of 'I' do not correctly identify the material things they are supposed to identify, our human organisms, there is something about these organisms of which the identification is true. Therefore these tokens do have reference, and we exist, after all! But what is identified does not belong to any kind with its own conditions of identity. Thus, we exist, but are not identical to things that form any kind. This is what I call the *nihilistic* view of our diachronic identity or persistence.

The nihilism I have described is a *factual* or *descriptive* one as opposed to an *evaluative* nihilism, according to which we are not any sort of thing whose identity *matters* or is of *value* to us. Factual nihilism prepares the ground for the evaluative nihilism for which I shall argue in Chapter 23: since we are not identical to things of any kind, we cannot be identical to things of a kind that is valuable to us, that is, it cannot be cognitively rational to be O-biased.

My brand of factual nihilism should also be distinguished from some other, related claims. One such is that we *are* things of a certain kind, though this kind is such—fuzzy or open-textured—that in some circumstances it is indeterminate whether or not something is of this kind or whether or not it is *the same* individual of this kind. I think this claim is true, too, but mine is more radical.

Another is that "any item we single out may be said to fall under several distinct sortals, and it therefore has different identity conditions as a specimen of (i.e. relative to) each of those sortals" (Zemach, 1987: 223). That is, many different ways of carving out any item of reality are conceivable. It seems to me to be a *non sequitur* to conclude from this that "there is no one thing which 'I' denotes . . . hence, in a very real sense, I do not exist" (Zemach, 1987: 226). For even if many sortal-classifications of us are *conceivable*, there may be one which is most *natural* to us, given our perceptual apparatus and other cognitive assets, and this would be enough for there to be things of one sort that 'I', as used by us, *does* denote (even if other denotata are *possible*). But this is what I deny.

22

THE IDENTITY OF
MATERIAL BODIES

ON our pre-reflective conception, naive somatism, we take ourselves to be identical to our bodies because we assume that they satisfy both the ownership and the phenomenal conditions for being the subjects of our experiences. But in fact neither our bodies nor physical things (it has to be physical things) of any other kind play this double role. So naïve somatism cannot be articulated into a philosophically defensible criterion of our persistence. Still, it supplies a rough-and-ready criterion serviceable in everyday circumstances. According to it, our persistence consists in the persistence of a material body. I shall now look into the notion of the persistence of such a body. Although I think that it will emerge that this notion is probably basic and indefinable, this investigation will throw up some findings that makes it a useful prelude to a discussion of the importance of our identity.

A Sufficient Condition of Material Identity

I have here and there in earlier chapters assumed that the diachronic identity of a material thing entails some sort of spatio-temporal continuity. Now, it is a commonplace that for every material thing, m, there has to be some kind or sort, K, to which m essentially belongs, that is, which is such that m must be a K at every time at which it exists. Is it also the case that, if m begins to exist at a time t_1 in a region r_1 and ends its existence at t_n in r_n, it will have to exist, as a K, at every time between t_1 and t_n in some series of regions linking r_1 and r_n in space? Presently, we will find that this is not so: the requisite spatio-temporal continuity is less stringent.

In the foregoing, I have employed the commonsensical framework of enduring things that successively exist (in their 'entirety') at different times until they cease to exist. Such a framework is presupposed when we speak of a thing (identified as) existing at one time being identical to a thing (identified as) existing at another. This identity is thought to be consistent with the thing undergoing a lot of changes in the course of time. Some changes, however, rule out diachronic identity. To ask for the necessary and sufficient conditions for m_1 at t_1 being identical to m_n at t_n is to ask: what changes between t_1 and t_n are such that if and only if they occur, m_1 will not be identical to m_n? For instance, are these changes precisely the ones that are incompatible with there being, at all times between t_1 and t_n, something of the kind to which m_1 and m_n essentially belong?

The three-dimensional commonsensical framework has a rival, four-dimensional conception that in place of the notion of a thing operates with the notion of the whole of its existence or 'career'. Accordingly, any shorter time during this period will be only a 'stage' or 'slice' of the thing. The thing has 'temporal parts', or other stages, making up its existence at other times. In contrast to spatial parts, these temporal parts or stages seem to be instantiations of the same kind as the thing of which they are stages, for example, a stage of a ship or sheep is apparently itself a ship or sheep. If the duration of a ship or sheep had been shortened from twenty years to twenty minutes, the result would still be a ship or sheep. In this four-dimensional framework, the problem of diachronic identity will take this form: what conditions are necessary and sufficient for different stages being stages of the existence of one and the same more lasting thing?

The four-dimensional framework could in this fashion be used to rephrase the issue. But it should be borne in mind that the existence of a thing is not the same as the thing itself. For instance, a (material) thing is composed of matter, but its existence is not; its existence has duration, but the thing itself does not. And a thing cannot be identified with the whole of its actual existence, since the thing could have existed for a shorter, or longer, period and still be the same thing. It follows that we need to make up our minds whether a 'stage' of a thing is a shorter bit of its existence or the thing considered as existing only at this time. If, however, we are not guilty of these confusions, there may be no harm in employing the four-dimensional framework in discussing diachronic identity.[1]

It may seem that we must take the relata of the relation of diachronic identity to be *momentary*, that is, the times at which things are identified to be moments, times having no duration or extension. For if they have extension, one can distinguish an earlier and a later part of the things existing during them which are related precisely in the manner to be analysed. Within each of these parts, one can in turn separate an earlier and a later part, and so on. It is only if we at last arrive at something momentary, and the analysis is applicable to it, that we have succeeded in giving a general, non-circular analysis of what makes a thing persist or retain its identity through time.

Unhappily, there seem to be serious problems besetting such attempts to understand transtemporal identity or persistence in terms of relations between momentary things.[2] But even if, in response to these difficulties, we scrap the notion of a momentary thing and grant that, however far the regress is pursued, the relata will be of some, albeit very short duration, it does not follow that the explication, though non-reductive, will be vacuous. It can be informative to be told that two things existing at different times are

---

[1] But see David Oderberg who argues that "it is precisely the conflation of a persistent *with* its life-history which permits the stage-theorist to give the appearance of revealing the existence of a novel ontology" (1993: 127–8).

[2] See Saul Kripke's unpublished, but widely known, lectures on identity over time.

identical if and only if they stand in a certain relation R to each other, although these relata are persisting things that in turn are divisible into things that stand in R to each other, and so on *ad infinitum*. (Compare: it can be informative to be told that someone is a human being if and only if both of his/her parents are human beings.)

At most, what we can aspire to do may well be, then, to spell out such a relation R that makes identical two things which themselves persist for some period. As already indicated, it is often suggested that the persistence of a material thing, m, consists in the spatio-temporally continuous existence of something of the kind of which m essentially is, that is, that this relation is R. Granted, since the notion under analysis is very pervasive, it is hard to get rid of suspicions that it crops up in various places in the *analysans*, reducing it to circularity. For instance, it has been argued both that the requisite place-identifications presuppose the identity of persisting objects and that the notion of an essential kind does.[3] But, in line with the concession in the foregoing paragraph, let us waive such worries and merely ask whether a continuity analysis along these lines could give a condition that, albeit non-reductive, is both necessary and sufficient for two persisting material things being the same K.

An obvious, and serious, difficulty with this analysis as a necessary condition—a difficulty to which I shall return later in this chapter—is that a thing may fall to pieces without the thing's identity being definitely obliterated. If so, then for m_1, existing in r_1 at t_1, to be the same K as m_n, existing in r_n at t_n, there need not be a K at every time between t_1 and t_n in some series of regions connecting r_1 and r_n.

Another difficulty for such a necessary condition concerns the matter of precisely specifying the relevant spatial path. This is due to the fact that, from one moment to another, a thing may lose or acquire large parts while retaining its identity: for instance, a big branch could be chopped off a tree without its ceasing to be the same tree. This would, of course, make it occupy a different region, even if it is immobile.[4] Clearly, it is indeterminate how much of a thing could be lost without it ceasing to exist. This would be true even if the issue was a purely quantitative one of the size or mass of the parts at stake, but it is further complicated by the fact that parts are often more or less central to a thing (e.g. the trunk is more central to a tree than the branches).

Some have thought it paradoxical to identify, for example, a tree, T, with the tree that exists after a branch has been chopped off it. Suppose that the branch is cut off T at t. Then, it might be urged, the tree existing after t, T^*, must be identical to an undetached part of the tree existing before t, namely, this tree minus the branch, $T - B$. For all their parts are identical. But this undetached part, $T - B$, is not identical to T existing before t which possesses the additional branch, B.

I reply by denying that T^* is identical to $T - B$ rather than to T. T and T^* are things of the same kind, trees, so they can be the same thing of this kind, the same tree. In contrast, $T - B$ is not a tree, but a proper part of one, which T^* is not. What about the claim that T^* must be identical to $T - B$ rather than to T, since T^* and $T - B$ share all proper parts

---

[3]   See, for example Oderberg (1993: 6–10 and 50–2 respectively).

[4]   For further discussion of this difficulty, see Hirsch (1982: ch. 1).

(while T and T^* do not)? As shown by other cases, like that of the ship of Theseus discussed below, the fact that the parts of x at one time and of y at another are identical does not entail that x and y are identical, even if they are of the same kind, as they are not in the present case. If T^* were identical to $T - B$, it could not survive the loss of a further branch which it clearly can. Instead, $T - B$ wholly *composes* T^*, whereas it partly composed T.

More fundamental is, however, the problem that a condition to the effect that there be something of a certain material kind without any spatio-temporal interruption seems not sufficient for the transtemporal persistence of a single material thing or body of this kind. Sydney Shoemaker has devised a thought-experiment to this effect:[5] he imagines there to be both machines that instantaneously destroy tables and machines that instantaneously create them. Suppose that a 'table destroyer' annihilates a given table (along with its constituents) at t, but that a 'table producer' creates a qualitatively indistinguishable table on the same spot, r, the very next moment. Then there will continuously be a table in r, but, as Shoemaker—to my mind correctly—maintains, it will not be one and the same table. So, a spatio-temporal continuous existence of something of table-kind does not suffice for diachronic identity of something of this kind.

He goes on to argue that an analysis in terms of continuity "has to be replaced or supplemented by an account in terms of causality" (1984: 241). The gist is that what is missing in the situation envisaged is that the fact that there is a table in r just after t is due, not to there being a table in r at t, but to the operation of an external cause, the table-producing machine. If the table existing just after t had been the same table as the one existing at t, one would be able to say truly that there was a table just after t *because* there was one at t, and not because of any external cause. Following W. E. Johnson, Shoemaker thinks that what is at work here is a special form of causality, "immanent causality", distinct from ordinary, "transeunt" causality which relates events (1984: 254).

Now, it seems to me to go against the grain to say, for example, that there being a certain sort of table somewhere was *caused* by there being a similar table in the same place just before. It seems strange to me to hold that such a static state as there being a table in r at t, could be a cause of anything, let alone the state of there being a table in the same place just after t. Instead, I think the full causal explanation of there being a table in r just after t is that at (or before) t a table was placed or created in r, and just after t no cause has as yet removed or destroyed the table in r. There is an external cause of why there begins to be a table in r at a certain time and of why this state ends at a later time. But there is no positive cause of there being a table in r at any intermediate time. The only causal explanation of this seems to be, negatively, that *no* external cause has as yet removed or destroyed the table. That is, the only possible causes of there being a table in r are *external* ones. A thing's persistence cannot, then, be defined in terms of any "immanent" causation internal to it.

These observations, however, suggest another way of making the continuity condition sufficient: the table existing in r at t is identical to the table existing in r just after t if there is a table in r just after t because no external causes have removed or destroyed the

---

[5] See 'Identity, Properties, and Causality', repr. in Shoemaker (1984).

table existing in r at t (and created or placed a table in r just after t). That is, the continued presence of a table does not require any external cause to sustain it, but only the absence of causes that would prevent it. I think this may capture the notion of persistence exemplified in our sense-experience, in particular, in proprioception or the perception of our own bodies from the inside. For instance, the experience I have of the persistence of my body, while sitting and writing this, is of there being a body in a certain chair from one moment to another, without this state being sustained by any external cause.

It may be objected that it is conceivable that tables causelessly cease to exist and pop into existence. That is true, but this possibility requires that there be some discontinuity, I think. It seems no coherent possibility that, without any cause, a table has ceased to exist and another table has popped into existence at the very same time in the very same place.

A graver difficulty is, however, that there are two crucially different ways of 'destroying' tables: one that is compatible with their retaining diachronic identity and one that is not. As already indicated, and as we shall soon see in greater detail, an artefact can be dismantled in such a way that it can be 'resurrected' if the parts are properly put together again. This means that were we to turn our sufficient condition into one that is necessary as well, we would have to rule out this type of destruction. We would have to specify that the relevant destruction and creation mean that a *numerically distinct* thing of the same kind would exist instead. But, of course, that would be blatantly circular.

Still, despite its shortcomings the analysis proposed provides some insight. For it brings out a difference between the continuity of a physical *thing* or *body*—that is, an entity that possesses mass, has a tangible shape, and fills a three-dimensional region of space—which is not causally sustained by anything external, and the continuity of other physical entities or phenomena, like purely visual entities, for example, shadows, and auditory ones, which is causally sustained by something external, namely proper things. In the case of the latter, too, spatio-temporal continuity fails to make up a sufficient condition, but here the extra element can probably be understood in terms of the continuity being causally sustained by one and the same external thing. So, as in Chapter 20 I suggested about the identity of the mind, I now suggest that the identity of these phenomena is parasitic upon the identity of proper things which may be basic and indefinable.

To simplify matters, we might as well formulate the sufficient continuity condition at which we have arrived in the following openly circular fashion:

(C) m_1 existing at t_1 in r_1 is identical to m_n existing at t_n in r_n if, at every time between t_1 and t_n and in some series of regions joining r_1 and r_n, there is something of the same kind as m_1 and m_n to which they are both identical.

The Pragmatic Dimension of Material Identity

But, as already indicated, we face the problem that (C) fails as a necessary condition. Imagine that a ship that exists at t_1 is dismantled at t_2 and that the planks and so on are stacked away. Some time later, at t_3, a perfectly similar ship is built out of these. It would be quite natural to assert that the original ship which existed at t_1 has been rebuilt, that the ship existing at t_3 is numerically the same ship as the one that existed at t_1. But this shows that (C) is not necessary, since the *ship* is identical to no ship at t_2.

It will not do to retort that the ship is identical to something at t_2, namely a heap of planks and so on: that this is a ship, though a ship in pieces. For suppose that a ship had never again been constructed out of these. Then we would not say that the ship which existed at t_1 exists as long as the heap does; clearly, we would hold that it went out of existence at t_2 when it was dismantled. So we should admit that this example demonstrates that (C) will not do as a necessary condition.

It might be suggested that a simple revision of (C) will take care of the difficulty: suppose we add to it the disjunct (D) 'or a greater number of the parts constituting m_1 exist at every time between t_1 and t_n in regions linking r_1 and r_n, and no later than t_n they have been joined to constitute m_n that is of the same kind as m_1'. I do not think, however, that this revision will meet all difficulties, for we do not believe that a thing retains its identity whenever its constituents, after being separated, later come together to compose something similar in kind.

Suppose, for instance, that the elementary particles composing the ship were dispersed, but that some time later they resume their original positions and constitute a similar ship. This sequence is, we further imagine, irregular: sometimes something of the same kind as the decomposed thing is created, but quite often this does not happen. When it happens, it happens long after the dispersal. Under these circumstances, I think we would be hesitant to identify any ship later created with the one which earlier disintegrated. We would be uncertain whether the original ship has reappeared or whether it been replaced by a new ship resembling it.[6]

Why this uncertainty? I do not believe that the reason for it is that the disintegration is more radical here, that the constituents into which the ship is decomposed are smaller here. Nor do I think that the length of the interval between annihilation and creation is the decisive factor. Instead I think the reason for hesitancy is that the radical disintegration is a process that we do not control and we cannot predict its outcome (whereas removing planks from a ship and putting them back is of course a process under our control). Imagine that the outcome of the radical disintegration was regular and predictable, that the particles dispersed *always* rejoin to compose a qualitatively identical thing, or that our knowledge of micro-cosmos grew to the extent that we learnt a method of steering the paths of particles so that we could at will cause macroscopic objects to come into and to go out of existence. Then I think we would be willing to proclaim the thing that later appears identical to the one earlier decomposed, even if it takes a long time to appear. This is, I think, the explanation of the readiness of some SF-writers and philosophers to speak of things being 'tele-transported'—a description that presupposes identity—when they are dissolved into their micro-constituents and these are sent in a stream to another place where they are reassembled into their original structure (see e.g. Tye, 2003: 147).

---

[6] So, we have no unwavering faith in Hirsch's "compositional criterion" (1982: 64–71).

If this speculation is correct, it suggests that there is a *pragmatic dimension* to identity across time. It is not the nature of a particular sort of disintegration itself which determines whether it is destructive of identity; it is our knowledge and control of it. When we learn to control a process of decomposition so that we can recombine the parts it separates from each other, or at least reliably predict that such recombination will occur, we are prepared to speak of the original thing as coming back into existence, in spite of our earlier being inclined to see this sort of decomposition as destroying the original thing. This consideration is noteworthy because it supports a main contention of mine—to which I shall come in Chapter 23—namely that diachronic identity is not a deep relation that carries any greater importance.

There is another consideration showing the disjunct (D) to be inadequate. Imagine that, before building a ship at t_3, we had used its components to build a shed; then I think we would be inclined to take this intermission as ruling out identity between the original ship and the new one. But (D) does not harmonize with this verdict, for the parts of a ship continue to exist even if they make up a shed.

The hitch seems to be that a shed is a structure which rivals that of ship: nothing can be both a ship and a shed. In contrast, something may be both a collection of planks and a ship because the planks constitute the ship. Furthermore, in some conditions there is a tendency to identify the planks as 'parts of a ship' even when they do not constitute a ship—but not any longer when they have been used to build a shed. Then the possibility of numerically the same ship reappearing is also ruled out. If we did not take the interference of rival structures to block identity, we might, for instance, hold ourselves to be reappearing if, after millions of years during which the elementary particles composing us have helped to constitute other organisms and inanimate objects, they predictably come together to make up organisms indistinguishable from our organisms as they were at the time at which they were disintegrated. But this is surely absurd.

A necessary and sufficient condition that captures these complications would run along the following lines:

(C⋆) m_1 existing at t_1 in r_1 is the same K as m_n existing at t_n in r_n if and only if:

(1) m_1 and m_n are identical to something K existing at every time between t_1 and t_n in regions connecting r_1 and r_n *or*, if (1) does not hold:

(2) most of some set of parts constituting m_1 exist at every time between t_1 and t_n in regions linking r_1 and r_n, and are parts which (*a*) predictably and no later than t_n are united to constitute m_n that is a K just as m_1 is, and which (*b*) have not between t_1 and t_n constituted anything of a kind incompatible with K.

In (C⋆), (2) is intended to be a subordinate condition which comes into operation only if (1) is not satisfied. For this reason the ship of Theseus poses no difficulty for (C⋆). According to the story, the planks and other components of this ship, s_1, existing at t_1, are gradually replaced by new ones, so that the ship s_2 existing at t_n has none of the original parts. These original parts have, however, been hoarded and a ship similar to the original one, s_3, is built out of them at t_n. Now which of s_2 and s_3 is identical to s_1? According to (C⋆),

s_2 is. The fact that if s_2 had not existed, we would have identified s_3 with s_1 is accounted for by the conditions (a) and (b) of (2) which come into play when (1) is not met.

This does not violate the intrinsicality of identity (mentioned in Chapter 20), for whether s_1 is identical to s_3 does not depend on s_1's relations to anything existing *simultaneously* with s_3, at t_n, but on what happens *in between* t_1 and t_n. This is shown by the fact that, if just before t_n s_2 had been destroyed, s_3 would still not be identical to s_1, despite the fact that it has no contemporary competitor for identity. Therefore, psychologists of identity cannot defend their rejection of the intrinsicality thesis by appealing to its breakdown in cases like that of the ship of Theseus.

I do not want to insist on the details of (C*), since I believe identity across time to be a fluid concept which cannot be captured by any precise necessary condition. But I do want to emphasize that the diachronic identity of a material thing consists in the spatio-temporally continuous existence of material things of *some* kind. In the first instance, this condition takes the form described in (1): an earlier thing is identical to a later thing if it is identical to something of the same kind existing at every time in between. Whether or not this condition is fulfilled is sometimes indeterminate, since, as we have seen, it is not clear how much of a thing can be lost without it going out of existence.

If this condition is not satisfied, we can fall back on a second form of continuity: continuity as regards the existence of components. Were we to give up this constraint, it seems that the notion of diachronic identity has been loosened to the point of dissolution.[7] When this continuity is responsible for the identity of the whole, identity becomes even less determinate since, apart from the indeterminacy as regards the requisite extent of the persisting parts, there may be uncertainty as to whether a disintegration–reconstitution sequence is of the right sort. This fuzziness of the distinction between the identity and distinctness of material things is worth underlining because it supports a main claim of this part of the book, to wit, that our identity in itself is nothing of importance. (It will support this claim even if we accept a psychological account of our identity, since, as I contended in Chapter 19, psychological accounts must assume a matter-based form.)

Of relevance for my argument for this claim in Chapter 23 is also the leading idea behind (C*), that continuous existence of things of some kind is a *sine qua non* for diachronic identity. Every macroscopic thing is constantly involved in a process of having its microscopic constituents successively replaced. Generally, as the size or number of the parts replaced at one go increases, persistence becomes more and more dubious. There is no definite point at which a replacement is sufficiently extensive to bring the whole thing out of existence. (Nor is there a definite answer as to how short the time-interval between each permissible replacement in a series may be without destroying identity.) But if *all* of a thing's constituents are replaced at one shot, it certainly goes out of existence. Any macroscopically indistinguishable thing that succeeds it will then be numerically distinct from it. To repeat, if it is affirmed that numerically the same thing

---

[7] Thus I am unmoved by Hirsch's speculation (1982: 216 ff.) that numerically the same macroscopic object can go on existing even if there is a simultaneous replacement of all or most constituents on the micro-level.

can make a comeback after everything of it going out of existence, it is hard to see what distinction there can be between such a comeback and it going out of existence to be replaced by a numerically distinct, qualitatively identical thing.

Since this is of some importance for what follows, let us take a somewhat closer look at someone who adopts a contrary position. Andrew Brennan imagines scientific investigations showing that in what is apparently a hill enjoying continuous existence, there occur brief intervals of non-existence (1988: 92 ff.). Still, this gappiness would, Brennan claims, prevent us neither from saying, in his favoured terminology, that the hill survives nor from holding the different hill appearances to be causally connected.

But Brennan's view leaves it unclear how he can uphold the distinction between one and the same thing continuing in existence and its ceasing to exist and to be replaced by another, similar one. I cannot discern a more plausible basis for this distinction than one that makes it turn on the presence or absence of the spatio-temporal continuous existence, if not of the thing itself, then of components of it. It seems reliance on causality will not do the trick, for one also wonders how the hills on opposite sides of the discontinuity are supposed to be causally linked. It does not seem intelligible to suppose that the former hill causes the latter to exist before it goes out of existence, a while before the latter begins to exist.

Secondly, Brennan's view forces one to surrender the intuition that diachronic identity is an intrinsic relation between the relata. For suppose that a hill disappears at t_1, but that a similar hill appears in the same place a fraction of a second later, at t_2. Brennan claims that such a discontinuity does not necessarily rule out identity between the hill existing at t_1 and the one being present at t_2. But it is conceivable that another, perfectly similar hill appears elsewhere at t_2. The hill existing at t_1 can scarcely be identical to both of these hills; so, if one cannot come up with a reason for identifying it with one rather than the other, identity is excluded in this case of duplication. But then, contrary to the intrinsicality thesis, the identity of the hill at t_1 and the one appearing in the same place at t_2 depends on the relation of the first to what happens in other places at t_2, on hills not suddenly coming into existence in them at that time.

Brennan can hardly escape this conclusion by contending that the fact that one hill appears in the same spot as the one that disappears presents a conclusive reason for picking out that hill for identification. For he allows that a thing may 'hop' not merely in time but in space as well, and it would indeed seem arbitrary to permit jumps in one of these dimensions, but not in the other.

For such reasons, I insist that the diachronic identity of a thing involves spatio-temporal continuous existence at least in respect of components composing it.

23

THE RATIONAL INSIGNIFICANCE
OF IDENTITY AND CONTINUITY

WE have concluded that there is no kind of thing to which we are identical, no defensible conditions of our persistence. In everyday life, we take ourselves to be identical to our bodies because we believe them to be such that neither the phenomenal aspect nor the owner aspect of the notion of the self can outlast them, that is, we believe them to be the subjects of our consciousness once we acquire this notion. This is what I have called naïve somatism. But both aspects can outlast our bodies, and there is no other kind of thing that matches both of these aspects of the notion of being the subject of our consciousness.

This enables us to answer quickly the question of whether the O-bias is cognitively rational, that is, of whether it is cognitively rational to be biased towards an individual for the reason that it is identical to oneself. Plainly, this cannot be rational. Once it is established that there are no coherent conditions of our persistence, para-cognitive attitudes, whose cognitive rationality hinges on it being rational to believe that these conditions are satisfied by our relations to somebody, cannot be cognitively rational. Factual nihilism, as regards the truth-conditions of our identity, leads onto evaluative nihilism, a denial that our identity can justify the O-bias.

This may, however, be thought to put too much trust in the correctness of the nihilist account of our identity given here. What if it is wrong? There are conflicting animalist and psychologist strands or ingredients of naive somatism. The animalist strand is that we identify ourselves with our bodies. We may imagine that, contrary to what I have contended, this identification stands up to a closer scrutiny. Would the O-bias then be cognitively rational? We may also imagine that that psychologist strand of identifying us with the primary owners of our minds, though they fall short of the phenomenal aspect, can be vindicated. Would this make the O-bias cognitively rational?

These are the questions I shall now attempt to answer, in turn. Because we are F-biased, it is our attitudes to individuals in the *future* that are particularly revealing. As we saw in Part III, with respect to individuals in the past, we find it easier to be neutral between ourselves and others.

The Irrationality of the O-bias on Animalism

Reconsider case I of Chapter 20 in which my whole brain is transplanted into a new, indistinguishable body (those who believe it makes a difference to organic identity may assume that only the higher brain underlying consciousness is transplanted, not the brainstem and suchlike). As has already been indicated, it is plausible to think that if I were cognitively rational, I would be as favourably disposed and biased towards the person resulting from the transplant as towards my future self had I lived on in the ordinary style. I would be as concerned about the fate of the brain recipient for in him my consciousness flows on, and there is no reason to like him less when, alongside his being as tightly psychologically connected to myself at present as I would be in normal survival, his observable physical characteristics are exactly similar to mine. Yet, this would not be rational if it were the fact that somebody is identical to oneself—as this is interpreted by animalists—that rationally justifies the O-bias, since the post-transplant human organism is distinct from mine.

In fact, the animalist construal of the justification of the O-bias is committed to an even more implausible corollary than that it would not be rational to be as biased towards the post-transplant individual as towards oneself. Animalists are committed to the view that, if a new and different brain is transplanted into my body, it would be irrational not to be biased towards the resulting individual as I would be towards myself in ordinary circumstances, since that individual is myself. This is because, on the animalist view, organic identity is not only necessary, but also sufficient for our identity. But this corollary is very difficult to buy.

Even if the extreme claim that organic identity with an individual is sufficient for the rationality of being O-biased towards it is rejected, there might be a lingering reluctance to give up the claim that it is necessary. It might be suspected that, while this view might be true of someone like me—a philosopher whose interests are predominantly cerebral—it is not true of, for example, body-builders, who take a keen interest in their bodies or organisms. These individuals might approve of and value their bodies not only on account of their appearance—that they look powerful and beautiful—but also because this appearance is the result of their own efforts: these bodies are so to speak a monument of their owners' determination and perseverance. But if the body-builders' bodies are replaced by replicas, as happens in case I, it will no longer be true that the bodily vehicles of their minds are the outcome of their earlier efforts. So, it might be concluded, body-builders would reasonably not be biased towards the brain recipients as they are towards themselves.

I want to reply to this argument by disputing the claim that the new bodies or organisms are not the result of the body-builders' efforts. In a more indirect way they are such a result: if it is part of the transplantation policy to give the patients bodies that are replicas of the bodies they originally possessed, then the body-builders' prior efforts determine what sort of bodies they will receive, by determining the kind of bodies the body-builders had at the time of the operation. Admittedly, this dependence is less direct than when organic identity is preserved, but why should this greater degree of mediation matter even to a body-builder?

To be sure, collectors are notoriously more interested in originals than in replicas. But in the actual world replicas are not perfectly similar in respect of intrinsic properties to their originals—if they were, experts would not be able to tell them apart. Consequently, if one wants to be certain that one does not miss any valuable or interesting feature of the original, it is rational to go for nothing less than it (if one can afford it).

This sort of example actualizes a distinction. Often, we are interested in the numerical identity of originals not simply for its own sake, but because these originals are equipped with certain relational properties that 'fakes' usually lack: for instance, a painting was made by a certain artist, a rock-star played a particular guitar, etc. However like fakes may be originals in respect of intrinsic features, they will lack these relational properties. We may draw the same distinction as regards our own bodies, between interest in their numerical identity, or the continuity of their path through space and time, for its own sake and for the sake of something else to which it links us. We may then propose not the extreme view that the identity of our bodies matters simply for its own sake, but also because it makes our current bodies identical to the ones we had when certain important events in our biography occurred, for example, when we met the love of our lives or finished our *magnum opus*. Even on this less extreme view, it would be rational not to have the same bias towards the post-transplant individual as towards ourselves.

It must be admitted that, intuitively, we are strongly inclined to assign this derivative importance to identity, as regards both our own bodies and other material things. I think, however, that this is due to the fact that, intuitively, we are strongly inclined to imagine that material identity involves an immutability 'all the way down', an identity of all of constituents. If we were permeated by vivid realization of what is actually the case, that there is a constant exchange of constituents, so that after a period of time all constituents have been substituted as surely as if there had been replication, it seems to me most likely that it would no longer matter to us whether there is identity or replication. (This is especially so on the hypothesis explored in the Appendix, to the effect that it is only the most basic constituents that exist in reality, that is, independently of perception.)

It should be stressed, however, that this is just an empirical conjecture: it is conceivable, though I believe very unlikely, that some of us who clear-headedly envisage the incessant change that underlies the apparent unchangeability of macroscopic things, continue to regard their numerical identity as important. If so, then, on the account of cognitive rationality I offered in Chapter 11, their attitude cannot be condemned as irrational.[1]

The Irrationality of the O-bias on Psychologism

I now turn to the question of whether the cognitive irrationality of the O-bias would also hold good were some form of psychologism correct and our identity consisted in the identity of the primary owners of our minds. One relevant line of counter-argument has already been canvassed in Chapter 20. We saw that, in the face of fission cases, the best

---

[1] Cf. the similar view taken by Martin (1998: 15 ff.).

option for psychological theorists is to introduce a non-branching constraint: if the identity of our minds were constituted by psychological continuity, it would have to be added that the continuity take a non-branching or one–one form. As noted, Parfit contends (1984: sec. 90) that it does not rationally matter whether or not the non-branching constraint is met, provided that the lives of the two brain-recipients are each as good as the life of the single brain-recipient. So he concludes that, in virtue of the fact that our identity involves the requirement that psychological continuity must assume a non-branching form, identity is not what matters.

Instead he believes that it is psychological connectedness and continuity that matters in ordinary survival, but although Parfit thinks that both of these psychological relations are of importance, he argues only for the view that psychological connectedness is important, that continuity alone is not enough (1984: 301–2).[2] His argument does not rule out, however, that what matters is not psychological connectedness in itself but merely psychological *resemblance*. For instance, he claims that if I strongly want to achieve certain aims, "I would regret losing these desires, and acquiring new ones" (1984: 301). This may be true if I lose my desires and acquire new ones of a *different kind or content*, desires which I value less, but suppose that I lose a desire and acquire a numerically distinct desire of the same kind or content. In earlier chapters I have contended that psychological states, including psychological dispositions, must have physical bases (in the brain) and that their numerical identity depends on continuity in respect of these bases. What we are now imagining is that there is no such continuity, but that one such basis after a brief gap is replaced by a numerically distinct one that sustains, qualitatively, the same psychological disposition. It is a natural extension of what I have just said about the rational insignificance of bodily identity to propose that it would be a matter of rational indifference whether numerically the same desire continued to exist, owing to a certain physical continuity, or was swiftly replaced by a qualitatively identical desire. In other words, whether there is connectedness or just resemblance in respect of psychological dispositions should not rationally matter for our attitude to the resulting being.

Since Parfit agrees that a loss of psychological connectedness might be welcome, namely if it consists in one's losing some unwanted desires (1984: 299), he would agree that the value lost in a loss of connectedness can be outweighed if the improvement in quality is sufficiently great.[3] He would then presumably agree that the change for the better can be so great that one would like more the person emerging than one would like oneself had one continued to exist unaltered. This greater liking may nurture greater concern.[4] But he does not go into how great this improvement must be to counterbalance the loss of connectedness; hence, it remains unclear how much importance he assigns to connectedness. Nonetheless, Parfit implicitly rejects the view I favour, namely that it is rational to hold it to be *no better* to retain numerically the same disposition than

---

[2] Presumably, this is partly due to the fact that this view is essential for a later argument of his (1984: sec. 103).

[3] Martin (1998: chap. 4) certainly agrees.

[4] Thus, it should not be thought that we are here engaged only with Unger's desirability use of what matters. We should not rule out that prudential concern is at least partly underpinned by one's possession of desirable features.

to acquire a qualitatively (and numerically) distinct one to which one attaches *the same* value when he declares:

> The value to me of my relation to a resulting person depends both (1) on my degree of connectedness to this person, and (2) on the value, in my view, of this person's physical and psychological features. (1984: 299)

According to this passage, connectedness adds an independent value; so, in my example, one should prefer to retain numerically the same disposition. But Parfit offers no argument for this claim.[5] He just assumes the falsity of the view I defend, namely that it is not irrational to like as much and be as concerned about an unconnected replica as about a connected continuer or, in other words, that psychological connectedness rationally matters only to the extent it can be relied on to ensure qualitative psychological similarities between oneself in the present and in the future.[6] (Note that from this it follows that psychological continuity does not matter, either.)

I would like to support this view by the following thought-experiment:[7] imagine the world to be such that, occasionally and at random, the elementary particles composing the body of a person are suddenly dispersed, but a fraction of a second later *altogether different* particles join to constitute a body that in (macroscopic) physical and psychological respects is indistinguishable from the prior one. The replacement takes place so rapidly that it is undetectable to (unamplified) human senses. Nonetheless this brief discontinuity, during which there exists no human being and person at the relevant place, is enough to prevent those existing at each side of it from being identical. This denial of identity does not rest on how our identity is construed: on whether it is construed as organic or as psychological or on how loose the physical mechanism underlying the identity-constituting psychological relation is permitted to be (as long as it exhibits some sort of continuity).[8]

I have stressed that the particles composing my 'successor' be altogether different from the ones composing me the moment before because in Chapter 22 I allowed that if they are (largely) the same, identity may not be broken. I suggested the possibility that there may be a pragmatic dimension of identity to the effect that if we had grown accustomed to, and learnt to control, the processes of radical disintegration and reconstitution, we could speak of the very thing which disintegrates as reappearing after a period of non-existence.

But could not the pragmatic dimension of identity make us extend the notion of numerical identity to cover even the case in which there is no sameness of constituents,

---

[5] In private communication Parfit has admitted that, at the time, the view here advanced had not occurred to him.

[6] If one abandons the view that connectedness has any value over and above the value of the properties it preserves, one sidesteps some of the criticisms Susan Wolf (1986) offers of Parfit. There is no need to abstain from projects that diminish connectedness if, in terms of one's own values, one turns into a person as good as, or better than, the one one used to be.   [7] For an earlier version of this argument, see Persson (1985b).

[8] Parfit is inclined to think that psychological connectedness/continuity can have *any* cause (1984: 208). (Accordingly, he assumes that there is psychological connectedness/continuity in, say, cases of tele-transportation.) Apparently, he infers this from his belief that, from an evaluative point of view, it does not matter what the cause is. But this inference is invalid, for our conceptual scheme may comprise distinctions that are evaluatively insignificant. (Cf. an objection by Noonan, 1989: 203 ff.).

assuming we had gained control over the processes involved? I do not think it could or should because this would seem to erase the distinction between numerically the same thing persisting and it going out of existence, quickly to be replaced by a qualitatively identical one. Also, it would mean surrendering the intrinsicality of identity, for in order to ascertain identity we would then have to trace the paths of the original constituents to ensure that they do not come together to form a duplicate elsewhere. Thus in the situation I described one does not persist, but is succeeded by a replica.

Would it rationally matter to us whether we underwent this replacement or survived in the normal way? One irrelevant factor must be put out of play. Owing to the MSI, we have a spontaneous fear of dissolution, since in our experience dissolutions of humans are never followed by their reappearance. To block the influence of this factor, we must assume that we are as certain about having a successor as about normal survival. It may be objected that, if the replacement is random, we cannot in advance have a rational assurance that it will occur after the disintegration. Perhaps it is correct that, under these circumstances, we cannot have a *rational* certainty of this, but that it is not necessary for my thought-experiment. It is enough if we can be—perhaps irrationally—certain or confident that replacement will follow upon dissolution, and this we can be.

Suppose that there are on record countless cases of instantaneous disintegration and that in all of them there have been replication; then, through the MSI, one may well feel certain that this will also happen in the next case facing one—whether or not this certainty is rational or justified in the absence of a theory of a mechanism that explains the replication. I do not need rational certainty that replacement succeeds disintegration for I am asking whether it is rational to bother about whether there is normal survival or radical disintegration provided one is confident that the latter is followed by replication. If one feels confident, whether rationally or not, that there will be replication in the latter case, there will be no anxiety to distort the picture.

In support of an answer that this would be as good as ordinary survival, one could argue as follows. In nature, the difference between cases in which there is identity and ones in which there is not is merely one *of degree*. So the all-or-nothing distinction between identity and non-identity is *conventional*, or something that belongs to the conceptual or linguistic level. When the distinction is applied, there is a range of conceivable cases in which it is either left indeterminate whether or not there is identity or, if a sharp dividing line is drawn, the application will be arbitrary.[9]

For instance, in my example, all one's constituents are replaced at one go, but there is only a gradual difference between this situation and what happens in the ordinary run of things where one's body is caught up in an incessant process of successive replacements of cells and other micro-particles. The difference between these situations is just the number of constituents replaced 'at one shot'. It is easy to construct a case in which it is indeterminate whether or not one survives—say, if 40 per cent of one's particles (including those composing each of one's psychological dispositions) are simultaneously replaced. Of course, we could put an end to this indeterminacy by adopting a fairly

---

[9] Parfit argues at length that our identity is indeterminate (1984: secs. 83–6).

precise convention to the effect that, for example, at most 30 per cent of the constituting particles can be replaced at one go if our identity is to be preserved. But that would be arbitrary: why not 25 or 35 per cent?

In the light of these facts, it seems reasonable to say that it does not matter whether the particles instantly replaced are, say, 80 or 40 or 20 per cent. What is of sole importance is what the outcome will qualitatively be like and the certainty of it occurring; so one should like as much and be as concerned about the individual emerging whatever the percentage of the replacement. But suppose someone insists instead that when 80 per cent is replaced there is definitely not identity, so that here it would be improper to be O-biased towards the outcome, whereas when 20 per cent is replaced there definitely is, so that here it would be proper to be O-biased. In cases in between, one's attitude should perhaps be hesitant and vacillating. We should not expect that, on my conception of rationality, such a position could be conclusively refuted, but it appears artificial.

This becomes clearer if we make it clear that there are two dimensions of indeterminacy of relevance to psychologism. My remarks so far bear rather on (*a*) the indeterminacy concerning the persistence of a mental disposition owing to replacements in its physical basis. But in Chapter 20 I mentioned (*b*) the indeterminacy regarding the number of mental dispositions required for one's persistence on the psychological view. (I have also in Chapter 19 touched upon (*c*) indeterminacy as to what counts as a mental disposition of a certain kind, for example the disposition of being able to remember something, but this may be left aside for the sake of simplicity.) Imagine that, according to the conventions adopted, a mental disposition definitely survives if at most 40 per cent of the constituents of its basis are exchanged at one shot and that if there is to be identity each link of the chain of connectedness must consist in a retainment of at least 60 per cent of the mental dispositions. Suppose further that this is barely true of the relation between myself at present and some possible future being, *A*, and that the other 40 per cent of *A*'s dispositions have bases that are not at all continuous with the bases of my dispositions. There is, however, an alternative future for me: I could instead be succeeded by another possible future being, *B*, who will inherit slightly less of my dispositions, 55 per cent (according the above convention), but the underlying physical continuity will here be stronger, for example, less than 1 per cent of the constituents are replaced at one go. As regards the remaining 45 per cent of *B*'s dispositions, they barely fail to be identical to mine because, say, 45 per cent of the constituents of their bases are simultaneously replaced.

Now somebody who espouses the view that it is rational to be biased towards someone who has the same mind as (and therefore, on psychologism, is identical to) oneself will have to say that, given the choice, I should prefer to be succeeded by *A* rather than *B*. But to this it could be retorted that there is (mental) identity here only given our present conventions, and that there are alternative conventions that are equally defensible. We could instead adopt a convention which tolerates a 45 per cent instant replacement of constituents, but which requires that the number of dispositions shared must be greater than 60 per cent. According to this alternative convention, I would instead be identical to *B* and should prefer to be succeeded by him rather than by *A*. As this convention is no less defensible, this attitude is no less defensible.[10]

No doubt, there are other conventions no less defensible, but none is rationally required, it would seem. The rational course certainly appears to be to disregard whether a process possesses the continuity that, on some form of psychologism, turns resemblance into identity, and bother only about how reliable it is and the quality of its outcome.

The Anticipation of the Having of Experiences

In arguing that only qualitative relationships, and no continuity of process, between oneself now and someone in the future, rationally matters, one is likely to come up against the objection that a sort of normal *anticipation* will be missing here.[11] It may be protested that, in the case of radical disintegration, one could not or at least normally would not anticipate *having* the experiences of one's successor as one would anticipate having the experiences one predicts that oneself will have in the future if one survives in the everyday fashion. Hence, it may be concluded, one could not or would not be biased towards a discontinuous successor as one normally is biased towards oneself. Now, if one *could* not be biased towards such successor, it seems that one cannot be rationally required to be so (for 'ought' implies 'can').

It must be admitted that anticipation of the having of experiences—experiential anticipation—may not readily occur in situations like that of radical disintegration. But what relations to future individuals are necessary and sufficient for one's being ready or able to anticipate the having of their experiences? Is it identity, on your preferred criterion, or what would be identity were there no branching? The argument would then be that (*a*) only identity (or identity-constituting continuity) elicits experiential anticipation and that, as (*b*) the O-bias encompasses this anticipation, (*c*) the O-bias is restricted to cases of identity. It follows that one could not be rationally obliged to adopt the same sort of attitude to individuals to whom one is not identical. I shall now argue that, contrary to (*a*), experiential anticipation is not so intimately linked to identity that we cannot be rationally obliged to extend it to others and, consequently, to broaden our O-bias to them.

More precisely, I shall argue for the following three claims. (1) It is possible to construct cases which show that you can anticipate having experiences that, as you correctly believe, only somebody else will have; so this sort of anticipation does not presuppose identity. (2) These cases suggest that anticipating having an experience is an instance of *vividly imagining (from the inside) what having the experience will be like*, an instance which is *non-voluntary* or *involuntary* (plus a belief to the effect that the experience will in fact be had by someone in the future). (3) This analysis of experiential anticipation makes it understandable not only why, in the normal course of events, we anticipate having only

[10] This argument occurs in my review (1992*b*) of Unger (1990) who vigorously puts forward the view here criticized.
[11] This is something emphasized by Martin (1998).

our own experiences and not those of others, but also why this anticipation may not easily occur in certain scenarios distant from those of real life, like the disintegration case. It leaves open, however, the possibility of a *voluntary* counterpart to anticipation—that is, a voluntary act of imagination—which rationally should be directed to others than oneself.

(1) Suppose that, for a long time, I have been hooked up to A's afferent pathways in such a way that all impulses that have to do with his bodily sensations in his left foot are transmitted to my brain, too. (The foot is still his, since it is attached to his body. We may also assume that there are no efferent links from my brain to A's body.) Thus, when he feels a pain in his foot, I shall also feel a pain in his foot. If, under these circumstances, I come to believe that A will soon feel an intense pain in his foot, I shall surely (fearfully) anticipate having the pain in his foot as firmly as I would (fearfully) anticipate having a pain in my own body, for I expect to feel a pain in A's foot no less than a pain in my own body.

Now imagine that, having been hooked up to A's nervous system for many years, ever since I was a child in fact, I am suddenly disconnected, so that I shall no longer feel pains in his foot. Immediately afterwards I notice some oddities of A's behaviour that during the period of being hooked up were an infallible sign that he was about to have a bout of excruciating pain in his foot. Although I know that I shall no longer share these pains, it is surely reasonable to think that, habitually, I shall (fearfully) anticipate having the pain in his foot, just as I was doing before the disconnection. If so, it follows that I can anticipate having a pain that I (correctly) believe that *I* shall not feel on any reasonable criterion of my identity.

It may be objected that this is not so if I *know* that I have been disconnected from A and *know* that I shall no longer feel pains in his foot. This objection, however, is not well taken, as an ordinary case of Pavlovian conditioning demonstrates. Suppose that in the past I have regularly experienced a severe pain after hearing the sound of a bell. I am then told by the experimenter, whom I trust, that in the future the sound of the bell will no longer be succeeded by a sensation of pain. Even if this convinces me that I shall not have any pain, it is a plain matter of psychological fact that the next time I hear the bell, I shall have an experience which, save the absence of the belief that pain will be felt, is like (fearfully) anticipating having the pain. It will take several negative instances to extinguish the tendency to have this experience; merely acquiring the belief or conviction that the pain will not occur is not enough. If it were, irrational fears (like the one about the plane catching fire discussed in Chapter 13) would be much more uncommon, or even non-existent. For the same reason, I shall for a while after the disconnection continue to have this experience which is like (fearfully) anticipating having pains in A's foot when I perceive the oddities in his behaviour, even though I no longer believe that I shall feel the pains.

It is immaterial whether the absence of this belief makes it improper to speak of anticipating having the pain, because anticipating having an experience is anticipating *oneself* having an experience. Suppose that this is so because anticipating having an experience incorporates a belief that one will oneself have the experience. Then we could simply introduce the term 'quasi-anticipation' to designate the phenomenon which occurs in my thought-experiment above and which is like anticipation save that it does not include any belief that oneself will have the experience in question (a move which is parallel to the proposal to introduce 'quasi-memory' considered in Chapter 20). It will not do to retort that, because of this missing element, quasi-anticipation, unlike anticipation, will not sustain the attitudes that compose the O-bias. For in fission cases whether you anticipate having the experiences of the post-transplant persons hardly turns on whether there is identity here, on your preferred criterion. This being so, I shall ignore the distinction between anticipation and quasi-anticipation.

(2) It is, then, not identity that provides experiential anticipation with its distinctive character—which distinguishes it from, say, mere imagining from the inside of the having of an experience—since it is possible to anticipate having experiences that one knows that only someone else will have. It must instead be some factor that is present in the case in which I anticipate having the pain of my former 'affective associate', A. Here I do imagine from the inside what the pain in A's body will be like, but this imagining is not *voluntarily* produced as it normally would be in a case in which I imagine what the pain of another would be like. For, normally, I would have to make a considerable voluntary effort to imagine vividly the experiences of another. But in the connection example, as in cases of Pavlovian conditioning, vivid sensuous representations of what having the experiences will be like crop up *non-voluntarily* and perhaps even *involuntarily*: I may not succeed in suppressing them even if I should make an attempt to do so.

Instead of being produced by an act of will, the sensuous representations are here automatically produced by experiences I have had in the past. If on each of the frequent occasions in the past when a stimulus S (the behavioural oddities of A, the bell sounding, etc.) has obtained, I have experienced E, then, when I now perceive that S obtains again, or otherwise believe that it obtains or will obtain, vivid sensuous representations of what it is like to experience E will crop up in my mind—as the result of the mechanism of spontaneous induction, the MSI. Hence, if we add that the vivid imagining of what having E will be like from the inside must occur non-voluntarily or automatically, then, I claim, we have caught the quintessence of anticipating having E (leaving aside the belief that E will be had by somebody in the future).[12]

(3) On this analysis, it is not mysterious why, in the ordinary course of events, we anticipate having only experiences that we are aware that we will have ourselves. For it is only in this case that the awareness is followed by actually having the experience, and it is this

---

[12] Martin objects both to this analysis of experiential anticipation and to the example with which I have supported it. He thinks there is something he calls "appropriation" of an experience which involves in some sense thinking of it as one's own (1998: e.g. 67). In one passage (1998: 111), he suggests that in my example in the text I do think of A's pain as my own in this sense, though in a more straightforward sense I do not. If this response is not tenable, my example refutes the claim that experiential anticipation involves appropriation. He also points out that the kind of imagining I characterize does not ensure sympathy (1998: 103). I agree, but I do not see this as an objection to taking experiential anticipation to consist in this sort of imagining, since I take sympathy to be *based on* anticipation rather than included in it.

Although David Velleman's view on anticipation is altogether different from mine, I derive partial support from the following claim of his: "Surely, a position from which I must deliberately project myself into a life is not a position on the inside of that life" (1996a: 76). I maintain that it is the fact that the imagining is non-voluntary which gives it the urgent 'feel' of being concerned with oneself.

that makes automatic the imagining making up experiential anticipation. One's imagination so to speak leaps ahead to the experience one believes one will have. Since cases of being hooked up such as the one I have imagined do not actually occur, the experiences we have are exclusively our own. For instance, as I have never in fact experienced pain in your body when you are subjected to a painful stimulus S, my thought that you will be exposed to S will never act as a cue which non-voluntarily evokes in me vivid sensuous representations of what the pain in your body will be like. The peculiar feature of the example of being hooked up is that in it I *have* had experiences of pains in some else's body, so my thought about his present situation *can* (without the assistance of my will) elicit forceful sensuous representations of what the pains he will have are like.

Moreover, the exercise of our intellectual capacity which allows us to predict that we will have a certain experience is by itself enough to call forth anticipation. For instance, the thought 'I shall feel pain' will cause me to call to mind sensuous representations of what feeling pain is like, since I have been in many situations in which the pain was first in the future and then experienced. But my thought that you will feel pain will not automatically make me imagine what your pain will be like for when pains in your body have been in the future, it is not the case that I have experienced them later, since I have not been hooked up to you. Of course, I can voluntarily call up vivid sensuous representations of what your pain will be like, but the fact that these representations are voluntarily produced robs them of that distinctive, instinctive character which provides the 'feel' of experiential anticipation.

Against the background of this account of experiential anticipation, it is perfectly intelligible why it does not occur in certain 'fantastic' cases like that of disintegration followed by replication. In ordinary cases, the automatic imagining of what it will be like to have E, which constitutes the core of anticipating having E, is derived from repeatedly experiencing S, and then living on in the normal fashion—which involves bodily and psychological continuity—to experience E. It is an imaginative projection into the future elicited by one's registering yet another instance of S. Naturally, this projection is disturbed by the information that one will not live on in the normal manner until E arrives. The greater the deviation from normal survival, the greater the obstacle to this automatic projection.

Thus, there is some resistance to anticipating having the experiences of the post-operative person in a case in which one's brain has been transplanted, for there is not the usual bodily continuity. Still, there is psychological continuity and some measure of bodily continuity to cling to. These rails are also present in the fission cases in which one's brain is divided and transplanted to two new bodies, but here there is the complication of duality: one cannot simultaneously anticipate having the experiences of both fission products, at least not if they are qualitatively different.[13] In the example of decomposition and replication there is, however, a gap that cannot be imaginatively filled with any of the material composing everyday survival, for there is a period in which neither one's body nor any similar body exists in the relevant place. This gap prevents the imagination

---

[13] This is in my view the explanation of Unger's "loss of focus" (1990: 268 ff.).

from running smoothly from the observation of S on one side of the gap to the experience of E on the other. It does not help much to postulate that it is the same constituent particles that participate in the reconstitution. There is nonetheless a chasm of non-existence on the everyday macroscopic level that separates oneself from the being reconstituted, a chasm that imagination does not spontaneously bridge.

Suppose that we come to the conclusion that our identity is preserved in the latter sort of cases.[14] Then I think we have a case in which it is harder to anticipate having the experiences of ourselves than of successors to whom we are not identical, for anticipation seems to occur less easily here than in the fission case. (On my view, there is not identity in the single track brain-transplant case, either; so this comparison could also serve to illustrate the point.)

As regards experiential anticipation, the case of disintegration and reconstitution is roughly on a par with cases of tele-transportation in which my organism is destroyed after a scanner has recorded the states of all of its cells and transmitted the information to a replicator that creates a replica of me as I was at the time of the scanning. For there is here equally little of continuity in respects to which we are accustomed. Experiential anticipation is harder in Parfit's *branch-line* variant of it in which the scanner does not annihilate one's body after recording its condition (1984: sec. 97). Here the replica will exist alongside oneself in the future (I assume that we shall not hesitate about whom we are identical to in this situation). As one will live on in the normal fashion, one will anticipate having the experiences that one will oneself have rather than the ones the replica will have. Thus one will fear one's own death in a way one will not fear the death of the replica. Even more problematic is the case in which the replication is now in the past. One cannot then *from one's present point of view* anticipate the experiences of the replica, but must imaginatively return to the moment of branching. This is like anticipating having another subject's experiences in ordinary situations in that it involves imaginatively adopting another point of view than that one currently occupies.

Whereas imagining what it will be like from the inside to have certain experiences occurs non-voluntarily in anticipation, it takes a voluntary effort in these cases. For instance, in the case of radical decomposition and replication, one can make a voluntary effort to imagine vividly what it would be like for one's successor to have the experiences he will have. In fact, one is rationally required to make this effort, for, as I have argued earlier in this chapter, the fact that this being is not identical to oneself is without rational importance, and his experiences are just as real as one's own would be. If one fails voluntarily to represent the experiences of this successor as vividly as one would non-voluntarily represent the experiences of one's future self, and as a result is less concerned about the successor, this difference in concern is cognitively irrational. The rational thing to do would be to try to overcome the exclusiveness of instinctive anticipation by voluntarily imagining as vividly what it would be like for the successor to have his experiences, and, as a consequence, care as much about him as one would about one's future self.

---

[14] I do not insist on any particular view here, provided it is also taken to apply to mindless material things. I do find curious the position of Unger (1990: 23–7, 131–4), who argues that, though our identity is disrupted in these cases of reconstitution with sameness of constituents, that of mindless things is not.

The selectivity of normal experiential anticipation and, consequently, of the O-bias is a product of evolution: it is just what one would expect to find in a world in which beings are programmed to propagate their genes. There is nothing to make cognitively rational the selection of particular individuals, be they ourselves or, as Parfit argues, those to whom we are psychologically connected/continuous. As opposed to what Martin believes, there is no "cut between those who are appropriate beneficiaries of narrowly self-interested choices and those who are not" (1998: 123), to be explained.

This is not to say, however, that were one to imagine what it would be like to have the experiences of *any* other subjects than oneself as vividly as one anticipates having one's own, one would necessarily be as concerned about them as about oneself. For, in contrast to the successor we have envisaged, these subjects may be qualitatively very different from oneself, and nothing so far adduced excludes that this can provide one with a legitimate reason to favour oneself at their expense.

As I have indicated, there are two elements of the O-bias, self-concern and self-approval, alongside experiential anticipation. In my explication of the latter, I have assumed that it generates concern. This link is one thing I shall try to explain further in the next chapter. My other aim in that chapter is to try to elucidate the second component of the O-bias, self-approval; that is, I shall try to explain why people tend to approve specially of or to like their own present features, such as their appearance and their desires and associated abilities, as well as their future ones, without relying on the fact that these features are *their own*. As will appear, this will yield a basis for rationally favouring oneself, not because of one's identity, but because of certain contingent properties, for example certain interests and abilities, that one attributes to oneself. By implication, it will reveal features that could block concern.[15]

My objective in the present chapter has been to contend that the O-bias is not cognitively rational, that is, that it is not cognitively rational to have a special concern and liking for a subject simply for the reason that it is identical to oneself. I have argued that this is so not only on the nihilistic view that the notion of our diachronic identity encapsulates false assumptions, but that the same conclusion would hold if animalism or some form of psychologism were true. Thus the O-bias, conceived as being based on considerations about our identity, cannot be cognitively rational.

I have also explained why in the actual world we anticipate having only our own future experiences and, as a result, are specially concerned about ourselves. Some have thought that in order to understand this, we have to have recourse to some immaterialist belief, for example, a belief that we are mental substances or pure egos. I argued in Chapter 19,

---

[15] Jennifer Whiting suggests that "the psychological continuity theorist might take friendship as a model for how psychological continuity can justify concern" (1986: 557). She spells out the analogy: "The idea here is that our prospective friends and future selves may have characters we admire or projects and desires of which we approve—that is, characters, projects and desires which we regard as making them worthy of our concern" (1986: 572). But then it is after all not psychological continuity that justifies self-concern, but rather the qualitative considerations of the sort I have indicated. Given the parallel with friendship, this is not surprising, for although there are causal relations between the psychological states of friends, there is not the psychological continuity that goes into personal identity. In ch. 26 I shall scrutinize Whiting's further claim that "a concern for our future selves is a *component* of psychological continuity and so . . . of personal identity" (1986: 552; my italics).

however, that these notions, which have absolutely no foothold in experience, are so radically unclear and confused that attributing to us belief in them can have no explanatory value. On my account, anticipating having an experience chiefly consists in non-voluntarily imagining vividly what it would be like to have it. It is true that this piece of imagination is facilitated by the belief that one will in the normal way be the subject who has this experience. But it is in principle possible voluntarily to imagine with the same vividness the experiences of others to whom one does not (believe oneself to) have this link. Moreover, one is rationally required to do this, since their experiences are just as real, and our identity is unimportant.

24

SELF-CONCERN AND SELF-APPROVAL

THE preceding argument points to the conclusion that the consideration that a future individual will be identical to oneself is not merely no real reason that justifies one's special concern for this individual, but also that it does not supply one's apparent reason for displaying this concern. It is rather the explanatory reason why there is that experiential anticipation which in turn activates concern. We have also seen that the core of this anticipation is a non-voluntary act of imagining having an experience, and that this is an act which, in principle, can be directed at the future of others. I shall now try to explain how this anticipation gives rise to concern.

Self-concern

As I remarked in Chapter 1, it is to be expected that, if a subject who is instinctively averse to the sensations of pain it is currently feeling develops the ability to think that it will in the future have such sensations, to which it will then be averse, it will respond with a second-order concern that this aversion be relieved by the elimination of the painful sensations. This is not logically necessary. It is even logically possible that a subject respond to awareness that it is currently feeling sensations of pain, to which it is averse, by indifference or even a desire that this aversion be frustrated, for a desire is only contingently—causally—attached to such awareness. But such a response would be disastrous from the point of view of survival: a creature having it would be paralysed or stymied by constant conflicts between its first- and second-order desires. Thus a well-adapted individual will be so wired up that the thought that it will in the future have a painful sensation to which it will then be averse will induce in it a second-order desire—a *sympathetic concern*—that this aversion be relieved.

Now, will any desire that one foresees having elicit this sympathetic concern that it be satisfied? Not necessarily, for it may be a desire one thinks one should not have, or has most reason not to have. If reasons are desire-dependent, as I have construed them to be, it is, however, not possible to hold rightly that one ought not have those desires that are *currently* the strongest ones that one has. It does not follow, though, that one must be sympathetically concerned that the strongest desires, one is *conscious* of currently having, be fulfilled, for these need not *in fact* be the strongest. But cognitive mistakes aside, the order of strength among one's current lower-order desires will be reflected in a simultaneous concern about their fulfilment in self-conscious being like us.

The same is not true of desires one correctly represents oneself as having *at other times*, actual or hypothetical. For, of course, the desires that one has at present, and the relations of strength between them, may differ from the desires that one accurately portrays oneself as having at another time. Suppose that I predict that at some future time t my decisive desire will no longer be for p (e.g. that the rest of my life be dedicated to some cause, like doing philosophy), but for (something entailing) not-p, and that my desire at t for not-p will be stronger than my present desire for p at t. Then my present desire for p supplies a reason that may block my sympathetic concern that my desire for not-p fulfilled be at t. Owing to my present desire for p, I may now regard desiring not-p as so low or base that I now prefer p's being the case at t, even though I know that I shall then be conscious of this fact and shall as a result feel frustration.

Of course, this is not what always happens when there is a clash between my current desires and the ones I take myself to have at another time. For I may see this change not as a degeneration, but as the result of an improvement, of my becoming wiser by discovering reasons of which I am now oblivious. Then I shall be concerned that those desires be satisfied, though I am not yet ready to share them.

Furthermore, having strong, unfulfilled desires engenders sensations of tension and frustration, whereas the satisfaction of them, if conscious, produces sensations of pleasure. If one foresees having strong desires that one cannot prevent oneself from having, these sensations provide reason for being concerned about the fulfilment of the desires, though they may be desires one does not want to have. These sensations provide reasons if—or, rather, because—one currently dislikes having sensations of tension and frustration and likes having sensations of pleasure. For prudentialists (and satisfactionalists generally), these reasons will win the day if the frustration of contravening one's current desires is not greater. So far we have, however, seen no reason to bow to the prudentialist claim, that one's dominant aim should rationally be to inter-temporally maximize one's own satisfaction. But the discussion will continue in Chapter 26.

Then we shall also continue the discussion of whether it is rationally required that sympathetic concern be self-regarding, that is, whether it should be activated only by thoughts to the effect that it is oneself who is the subject of the desire, or whether it may be other-regarding, directed at others than oneself. In the foregoing chapter, it was implied that it *can* be other-regarding since, as I argued, experiential anticipation can be directed to other subjects than oneself, for this anticipation is what evokes the benevolent second-order desire of sympathetic concern. I believe this possibility of other-regarding concern to be borne out by familiar phenomena about which I shall say a bit more in the next chapter.

If I now desire that p be the case at t, though I realize that I will not then desire it, this desire of mine cannot be, to use a label introduced in Chapter 10, implicitly conditional upon its own persistence. It must be a desire that I not only desire to be fulfilled as long as I have it, but which I want to retain or like myself to keep—for its own sake and as a means to experiential fulfilment—if I believe this matter to be within my control to some extent. It need not, however, be that, if one wants to fulfil a desire one has, one wants to retain this desire. As long as I have the desire to wear my hair long, I may be concerned to fulfil it, even though I have no desire to see to it that I preserve this desire to wear long hair. But sympathetic concern is counteracted when the desire is one I do not want to have.

Desires that are not conditional upon their own persistence are then desires that one normally desires to have or keep or that one likes oneself to possess. (Consequently, they are also desires that one likes, though I imagine that one can like a desire without liking *oneself* to have it: one may like only someone else to have it.) For if one now has such a desire that p be the case at a future time t, one will regard the fact that p as being of value at t independently of the desire-fulfilment that it could then supply one with. So, by keeping the desire for p until t, one will be able to contribute to a state of affairs that one sees as valuable. In addition, the materialization of this state of affairs will make one satisfied rather than frustrated.

Our most serious interests and causes—including the rationalist desire—provide illustrations of desires that are not conditional upon their own persistence. I refer to them as 'ideals'. Desires that are instead conditional upon their own persistence are often also conditional on their yielding experiential fulfilment (to call upon another category introduced in Chapter 10): that is, we want their objects to obtain at future times only if we believe not just that we shall still desire them then, but also that we shall then be conscious of the factual fulfilment of our desires and feel consequent pleasure. In the case of such desires, if we want to retain them, we do so not for their own sakes, but because we see them as avenues of experiential fulfilment. We are sympathetically concerned that they be satisfied only if their satisfaction can be experienced, whereas we are concerned about the fulfilment of ideals even if their fulfilment is purely factual.

So, we do not mind losing experiential fulfilment-based desires if they can be replaced by other desires that promise at least as much experiential fulfilment. We may want to preserve the desire for sex for this reason, that we imagine that the loss of it cannot be compensated for by the acquisition of another desire which would yield as much felt satisfaction. (But we may also want to retain it because we view life without the intimacy of sexual relationships as jejune.)

This is, then, one ground for self-approval or self-liking: that one is conscious of oneself as possessing desires that one approves of, likes or intrinsically wants oneself to keep. That one likes oneself to keep a desire is, however, not a necessary condition for a sympathetic concern that it be fulfilled. This concern also envelops, for example, desires conditional upon their yielding experiential fulfilment. But in both cases this concern can be blocked or stifled by the fact that one also carries around conflicting desires that make one dislike, and want to change, the state of one's having these desires.

Self-approval

Let us hunt for further properties which could serve as grounds for self-approval. There is a class of features associated with ideals that adds to this ground, namely talent or ability as regards pursuit of these ideals. It should not be hard to understand why one could like oneself because of prowess in the pursuit of some currently held ideal: the greater one's ability, the more efficient an instrument one is in furthering the ideal. Moreover, the greater one's ability, the more stimulated and stronger one's endorsement of the ideal is likely to be, and hence, the greater the potential for fulfilment. I shall not dwell on these matters, however, but rather turn to another set of properties whose service as grounds for self-approval must be accounted for in a different way.

Consider observable physical properties that one has, in particular one's looks. I suggest that these features constitute another important class of features that one tends to like and because of which one tends to like oneself as one is at present. To like such a characteristic is to want to experience or to go on experiencing it, and therefore to want that they continue to be exemplified. Consequently, approval of one's conspicuous physical features will provide one with reasons for fulfilling those basic needs whose fulfilment is necessary for survival. Similarly, since dislike or disapproval of one's prominent physical characteristics will mean that one does not want to continue to experience them, this attitude may supply reasons for doing things that are contrary to survival (if plastic surgery to remove the characteristics is not available!). In view of this, we should expect well-adapted creatures to like rather than dislike their prominent physical features. I believe that experience bears out that we like features of our looks more than we would had they belonged to others.

What is the mechanism behind this? I propose that human beings along with higher animals have a general tendency to like that to which they have been accustomed since the start of their life and, as a result, to dislike anything markedly different from this. Of course, I am not suggesting that habituation is the only factor that determines what perceptible properties one comes to like. One will like perceptible features that strike one as beautiful, and what one finds beautiful is conditioned by other factors than habituation, probably some having to do with what are conducive to the survival of the species and that are thus common to all normal members of it. It is therefore quite possible to find ugly and repulsive a lot of that to which one is accustomed. The point is just that habituation is *one* condition that influences such approval. This is enough to explain why beings in general like their external appearance more than they would if it had been possessed by some other beings, for one has as a rule been more frequently exposed to one's own appearance than that of most others. (Granted, it is possible that one's appearance has recently undergone a radical change, so that one is not at all used to it. But that is the exception rather than the rule: usually the appearance of sentient beings changes only slowly and gradually, so that the effect of habituation is not disturbed.)

Here it is essential to be on one's guard against a misleading formulation. The idea just laid out may be summed up by saying that one is inclined to like one's own appearance because it is one's own appearance. This might, however, entice one to believe that there is an experience of oneself as distinct from one's appearance, as a bare or featureless subject, and that one likes one's appearance because one associates it with this bare subject. Such an account would imply that liking for this subject—one's pure ego or self—was a source of liking for oneself, that is, precisely the doctrine that I am out to combat. The argument could run: if certain qualities matter to me because they belong to me now, my synchronic identity matters; and if my synchronic identity matters, my diachronic identity should also matter, since it, too, is my identity.[1]

But I want to suggest that one should read the plausible claim that one tends to like one's own present gestalt because it is one's own as an oblique way of stating that one likes it because one has frequently been exposed to it and has grown used to it, as the result of it belonging to oneself. In this there is no appeal to identity or a pure ego as the basis of self-approval. Consequently, one can—without incurring any circularity—go on to assert that one likes oneself partly because of one's present gestalt. (Certainly, as I will soon claim, one will also like the appearance of one's future self in so far as it resembles one's present appearance.)

By way of summary, I have tried to lay bare two main grounds for our approval of ourselves as we are at present: (1) the desires we may have that are not conditional upon their persistence, and talents associated with them, and (2) conspicuous features of our appearance to which we have grown accustomed. I need not claim that this inventory of the grounds of self-approval is exhaustive. To make it credible that it is possible to account for our special liking for ourselves without postulating any experience of a pure self as a source of this liking, it is enough to present an account that captures a significant portion of these grounds.

It should also be emphasized that these grounds are designed to explain why we *in general* like ourselves as we are at present. They do not rule out the possibility of some thoroughly disliking the present state of themselves. For it is possible (though highly unlikely), first, that one's self-consciousness is selective in such an infelicitous manner that one is not aware of one's dominant present desires, but only desires of a lower intensity. Then one could dislike *all* of one's current desires of which one is conscious. (Given that there are grounds for liking oneself, like those suggested above, it is more likely that attention is focused on features of oneself that one likes—thereby boosting one's self-approval beyond what is justifiable.) Secondly, it is also possible that one's appearance recently has been radically disfigured by an accident, so that one finds one's present appearance both unfamiliar and ugly. Thus, it is conceivable that one dislikes oneself at present both because of one's desires and because of one's appearance. But although this is conceivable, it is the exception rather than the rule.

---

[1] Cf. Stone (1988: 527). The dilemma that Stone tries to force upon us—namely, that "either we must embrace an extremely dubious ontology [that of non-reductionism in Parfit's sense], or we must face the fact that we don't exist" (1988: 520)—rests upon two assumptions that I reject: first and foremost, that we are essentially persons, but also that the term 'person' is inextricably tied up with attitudes which are groundless if non-reductionism is false. But these disagreements should not obscure the similarities between Stone's view and mine.

The O-bias Explained

We are now equipped to explain the O-bias, our special concern and liking for ourselves in the future, without assuming that in itself our belief in identity is our reason for it. As we concluded in the foregoing chapter, this belief is the reason why anticipation of the having of experiences is triggered off. For instance, as regards an experience one expects to have later on today, one effortlessly imagines one's consciousness running on (as short-term memory informs us that it has been running on until the latest moments) until it connects with the future experiences. We should expect such representations of imminent experiences to evoke a sympathetic concern that is almost as strong as that evoked by representations of one's current experiences. If the experience expected is some day distant, the explication of the bias towards the near in Chapter 15, implies that anticipation and, hence, concern will be somewhat fainter. Thus, the present account of self-concern ties in neatly with the account of temporal biases, for the MSI underlies both.

Furthermore, identity normally guarantees that the future person will greatly resemble oneself as one is at present. Accordingly, this individual is likely to have a physical appearance with which one is familiar and which one likes.[2] For the same reason, it is unlikely to have a greater number of desires that one dislikes (one cannot dislike most of one's current desires, since this dislike must stem from desires that one currently has.) Thus, when there is identity to somebody existing in the foreseeable future, there will in general be little to obstruct the sympathetic concern called forth by experiential anticipation. In virtue of this link to resemblance, belief in identity, though not in itself a reason for approving of a future person, will imply the presence of such reasons. So, it is confirmed that in itself the belief that one is identical to some future individual is not one's reason for being O-biased towards it. It is at most an explanatory reason, a factor that figures in the explanation of the O-bias, on the strength of what it brings in its wake, namely, experiential anticipation and qualitative resemblance.

The relative constancy or unchangeability in respect of features observable in everyday circumstances with which identity usually coexists may, however, make identity appear more portentous than it really is. This may give rise to the impression that the difference between identity and, for instance, decomposition-and-replication is bigger than it really is. For, as remarked in Chapter 23, we tend to unreflectively assume that identity goes 'all the way down', that there is identity in respect of all constituents, too. Thus, our diachronic identity may acquire the appearance of involving a deep immutability. But this immutability is an illusion. On imperceptible micro-levels we are constantly involved in processes of successive replacements. (Perhaps the truth is that, as entities existing

---

[2] Note that what I am saying is that it is important that there be similarity in respects *valued* to future stages, not that similarity itself is of importance, so that the more of it the better. The latter view is absurd, as Ernest Sosa points out: "If one's life has contained intense suffering and little else, one will want rather difference than similarity for future stages. What one wants for such future stages relative to one's present stages would seem to be primarily high quality of life" (1990: 313). As should be clear, my view, with its provision for concern, is concordant with Sosa's claim that we want a high quality of life for future stages, though, as we will see in Ch. 26, not necessarily maximal fulfilment.

independently of perception, we are only what we are on some such level—a topic I shall take up briefly in the Appendix.) Hence, there is in fact only a difference of degree between the most pedestrian case of diachronic identity and decomposition accompanied by replication, consisting in that elementary particles are successively replaced in the former case, but at one go in the latter. If this is realized, and the appearance of deep immutability is dispelled, it may be easier to rid oneself of the feeling that identity *has* to have rational importance, *must* be a reason for being O-biased.

Some writers who are committed to the importance of identity believe that a theory like mine cannot deliver a proper construal of the concern that one will not feel pain in the future. Since the aversion to pain is normally not a desire that one likes, and because of which one likes oneself, they may think that my type of view would have to hypothesize that one is concerned to comply with this aversion only because one would otherwise be less capable of satisfying desires that underpin one's self-approval. Such an instrumental construal of the concern that one not feel physical pain certainly has an implausible ring.[3]

In view of the above distinction between concern that a desire be satisfied and approval of it, it should be evident that this criticism is misguided. It seems to embody the mistaken assumption that one can be concerned that a desire be fulfilled only if one approves of it and sees it as a reason for approving of oneself, but this is, as we have seen, erroneous. The approval of a desire ensures that there is nothing hindering the concern that it be fulfilled; but it is not indispensable for the existence of the concern. For concern to be evoked, it is, other things being equal, enough if one anticipates having a desire that one does not want to be rid of.

It should be stressed that the account here given does not imply that we would be as concerned about ourselves in the future as about ourselves in the present were there a perfect similarity in respect of mental and physical features valued. We must not forget that we are subject to the P-bias, the bias towards the perceived. The P-bias consists in a proclivity to represent the perceived present more vividly than what is not perceived. It will result in one's present sensations being more vividly represented than the sensations that one expects to have in the future, even when it is imminent. As an upshot of the P-bias, one will have a stronger concern for oneself at present than for oneself in the future, simply for the reason that one's present situation is more vividly represented than the one which is merely anticipated.

This appeal to the P-bias suffices to explain not only why one would be more concerned about oneself at present than in the future, but also why one spontaneously would be more concerned about oneself than about a perfect replica existing alongside oneself in the present, for of course its pains and so forth are not perceived by oneself. This parallels the fact, noted in the foregoing chapter, that one would be more concerned about oneself in the future than about a co-temporal perfect duplicate, which is

---

[3] See Madell (1981: 110–15). Madell directs this objection at the doctrine about what matters in identity that John Perry (1976) advocates (more recently, Perry has been criticized in a similar way by Martin, 1998: 36–9). My view is so similar to Perry's that perhaps it can be read as an expansion of it. If so, I think that the most significant addition is the account of experiential anticipation and the sympathetic concern based upon it.

separated from oneself at present by an identity-disrupting discontinuity, because nature has wired up us in such a way that we readily anticipate having the experiences of the former.

In both cases of replication, there is an obstacle in the form of a non-voluntary tendency of our imagination that we can in principle surmount, by voluntarily imagining from the inside what the experiences of the replica will be like. Needless to say, this voluntary act of imagination will not have the same 'feel' as that of experiential anticipation—let alone the power of the P-bias—but this distinctiveness of experiential anticipation is nothing that gives it a privileged status from the point of view of rationality. Quite the contrary, it is a representational distortion which is foisted upon us by evolution and which we must strive to overcome if we want our attitudes to be cognitively rational (as do rationalists). If we succeed in this, we shall care no more about ourselves in the future than about co-temporal qualitatively indistinguishable beings. Similarly, we shall not care more about ourselves in the present than about these future individuals, since this partiality is due to our slavery to the P-bias. For if we want our para-cognitive attitudes to be cognitively rational, we must counteract the P-bias by representing to ourselves what it would be like to be those future persons as vividly as we represent our present conditions (as future circumstances are more vividly represented, perceived ones will be less vividly represented, since there is a limit to what we can vividly represent). As a result, we shall be under the spell of the O-bias with respect neither to the present nor to the future.

Nothing so far adduced implies, however, that were our attitudes to become cognitively rational, we would stop favouring ourselves at the cost of others, *as they actually are*. For nothing so far adduced excludes that preferential treatment of ourselves can rationally be based on *qualitative* differences in psychological and physical respects between ourselves and others. This is a matter to which I revert in Chapter 27. Analogously, nothing rules out the rationality of treating one's present self better than one's future self on such grounds. I turn to this topic in Chapter 26, after a brief excursion on other-directed concern and liking in the next chapter.

25

CONCERN FOR AND
APPROVAL OF OTHERS

I HAVE argued that the O-bias—to the effect that oneself rather than others be benefited—is neither justified by the real reason that the individual benefited is identical to oneself nor explained by one's having an apparent reason with this content. In conformity with this conclusion, I shall now argue that the bias-constituting attitudes of concern and liking for *others* never rest on reasons that have to do with the numerical identity of these individuals. This would have made these attitudes non-transferable to any other particulars, however similar.

Loving Another Individual

My view is contrary to how some have conceived of love of others. Robert Kraut defines love directed at a particular in terms of its being non-transferable to any other being with any set of features in common with the first: "love is directed toward a particular person *iff* it is directed toward that person non-transferably" (1983: 51).[1] Suppose that a man is transported to a twin-earth on which a perfect replica of his wife lives; if he then transfers his love from his wife to the new woman, that shows, on Kraut's view, that he really loves *none* of the women, but rather a set of characteristics that they have in common (1983: 49–50). This kind of opposition is clearly analogous to the one I earlier faced when I argued against the view that self-directed attitudes are supported by the recognition that the being favoured is oneself. Both contestants affirm the irreplaceability and uniqueness of the object.

In a vein similar to Kraut, Robert Brown insists on "the difference between loving a person and loving that person's manifestation of certain qualities or properties" (1987: 45). According to Brown, the former is not even "reducible to an unrepeatable instantiated

[1] Cf. also Unger's claim that he would not want his wife to be replaced by a perfect replica even if he were to earn a hundred million dollars in the process (1990: 276).

complex of qualities" (1987: 106)—although such reducibility would not introduce replaceability. What allegedly blocks this reduction is the fact that love is an "open-ended relationship": in loving someone you are "prepared to love the person in the future despite—or because of—the many changes that may take place in the character and circumstances of the beloved" (1987: 107). But this claim seems entirely beside the point: that you are prepared to love a being in the future, although it will undergo changes, need amount to no more that your future love will be based on different properties of the object, and this is fully compatible with it *now* being based on a definite set of features.

This does not amount to a denial of the distinction upon which Brown insists, namely, that there is a difference between loving a person and loving some aspects of that person. It is, of course, true that there is a distinction to be upheld between loving certain aspects of a person—loving her voice, wit, loving to travel or to talk philosophy with her, etc.— and loving the person. But I hold that this is a difference of degree, that if you love enough of the aspects of a person, love of them so to speak suffuses the whole person, so that one can properly be spoken of as loving the person. For if love is to be love of a particular person, it must be caused by (awareness of) that person. There must be something that attaches the love to this person rather than anyone else, and it is hard to see what could provide this attachment if it is not causality. But when a thing causes something, it is always in virtue of having certain features. Hence, when you love somebody, you love her in virtue of her having certain features. In other words, it is the instantiation of those features you love.

Even if love of a particular is reducible to love of some properties it exemplifies, it may be suggested that love of a particular is non-transferable to any other particular, simply due to the fact that the features on which it rests are unique and non-shareable. Now Brown is of the opinion that in so far as love of a particular is property-based, its basis includes such properties:

> when the agent loves another person . . . the agent is cherishing, in part, a particular complex of instantiated qualities. It is a complex, however, that is made unique for the agent and the partner by occurring at certain times and places, and by thus having an unrepeatable career or history. (1987: 106)

This seems to imply that love of a person can be non-transferable in virtue of the fact that its basis encompasses such relational features as that the beloved has a shared history with the lover or has stood in certain relations to the lover in the past. For instance, the fact that I am in love with a particular woman may be causally dependent on my having spent some time with her at a particular beautiful place, having done some historically or biographically important work with her, etc.

These relational properties are such that if they belong to A, they cannot later belong to B. Nonetheless, they are not essential to A: they could instead have belonged to B to begin with. I could instead have spent the same time at the same place with another woman that (in intrinsic respects) could have been a replica of the woman I in fact spent this time with. If so, I would surely have loved the replica instead. Once this is realized, however, it seems irrational not to transfer or extend my love to the replica.

Kraut also grants that love of a particular is "in part a function" (1983: 53) of the properties that the particular possesses, and he spells out this dependence in causal terms, but a peculiar feature of his account of the genesis of love is that he appears to believe love to originate in the characteristics that the beloved *in fact* has rather than in ones that the lover *thinks* that she has. He suggests that "the intentionality of emotion is to be understood on the model of the intentionality of perception" (1983: 43), and what makes an act of perceiving the perceiving of a particular physical object could plausibly be held to be its involving a state caused by some actual features of that object. Rather than love being based on beliefs about the beloved object, it is, Kraut proposes (1983: 45, 55) the other way around: the emotions guide one's beliefs about the object.

This view strikes me as so implausible that I hesitate to offer it as an interpretation of Kraut:[2] surely, it is a patent fact that love is conditioned by how one sees its object and not directly by how it in fact is; for instance, if I am attracted to a woman by her beauty, I must have perceived it (and noticed what I perceived). It is true, as Kraut observes, that one's love may induce one to ascribe flattering attributes to the beloved, but this tells against rather than for Kraut's account, since surely these ascriptions will enhance one's love. Contrary to what both he and Brown (1987: 45, 103) seem to believe, it does not tell against the thesis that love is propositionally grounded, since love can be aroused by fairly accessible features (e.g. physical ones) and influence one wishfully to ascribe less accessible ones (e.g. long-term traits of character).

I conclude, then, that love of an individual is based on (real or apparent) reasons that ascribe properties to this individual. These properties are not such that nobody else could conceivably have them, though it could be that once they belong to somebody, nobody else could later have them. So, love on this basis could have been directed towards other individuals, and once this is realized, it will be transferable to other individuals who do not possess these features, but who are similar in other relevant aspects.

I must dispose of a misunderstanding of this thesis. In connection with Gabriele Taylor's advocacy of the thesis here subscribed to, Brown objects that a lover often cannot say why he or she loves a particular object and that when he or she claims to be able to do this, there "is no reason why we must accept the agent's account of why he or she loves someone" (1987: 45). This is true, but irrelevant: it is one thing to say that we have reasons for our para-cognitive attitudes and quite another to say that we know what these reasons are. The second claim in no way follows from the first one, for our thoughts or beliefs can evidently exercise influence on us without our being conscious of this.

The view here advocated may seem emotionally disturbing in that it makes the beloved object replaceable by another one similar in respect of relevant properties. Does this not turn love into something more superficial? I think the depth of love has to do with the width and richness of the array of properties attributed to the object in the propositions that constitute the reasons for the love, as well as with how important those

---

[2] In a later paper of his, there is a remark that is at odds with this interpretation: "Emotions tend to be caused by beliefs, judgments, and evaluations in a way that perceptions are not" (1986: 419). I cannot but think that Kraut is inconsistent here. In a postscript to this paper, Kraut also expresses doubt as to whether he has not gone too far in trying to exorcize cognitivism with respect to emotions.

features are judged to be by the object and others. If this array is reasonably wide and rich, the love is deep and there is no replaceability in practice (not even in the case of identical twins). It should be emphasized, though, that the fact that replaceability is not possible does not guarantee that love is deep. Love is not deep when the irreplaceability is due to a shared history, but it is the case that anyone who was like the beloved in rather trivial respects would have been as much loved now had she happened to be at the right place at the right time to share this history. This love has a shallow basis in a restricted set of intrinsic features of the beloved, and the fact that she is now irreplaceable should not flatter her. It only goes to show that it matters to her lover that someone has had certain relations to *him*; thus, this love is at bottom egocentric.

Grounds for Having Concern and Liking for Others

If other-oriented love—and liking—are based not on considerations of identity, but on features that conceivably could have belonged to other particulars than they in fact do, what are these features? Of course, these features are so multifarious that it will be possible only to skim the surface. I will focus on those that parallel ones we discussed in the foregoing chapter.

Consider first liking because of look or appearance. To begin with, it is obvious that other beings can share such features that one has grown to like by constantly experiencing one's own exemplification of them. But the mechanism of habituation can certainly also be set in motion by the repeated experience of the appearances of other beings, especially if it occurs in emotional situations. It seems clear that such encounters play a part in the genesis of the liking that members of the same family often exhibit for each other. But we should keep in mind the point earlier made, namely that the liking for perceptible properties is not determined solely by habituation. We like perceptible properties that we find beautiful, but other factors than habituation condition what we experience as beautiful. Some experimental findings even indicate that there are something like universal standards of human beauty.

Intriguingly related to the liking that is aesthetically based, there is sexual liking, liking somebody because he or she makes one sexually aroused. Sexual liking is different from the other forms of liking something for the sake of its appearance. Liking in the latter case means wanting to perceive or experience the appearance, but sexual liking also involves a desire to engage in sexual activity with the object. But let us here concentrate on what is the common core of liking based on appearance, to wit, the desire to (continue to) experience or be in the presence of the appearance.

This is a desire to seek out things that are equipped with the appearance in question, but—if such things threaten to lose this appearance—it is also a desire to take measures that are calculated to prevent this. Thus, from this desire there will flow derivative desires to fulfil those desires the fulfilment of which is essential for survival of the beings shrouded in the appearances liked, that is, a form of derivative concern. This concern should, however, not be confused with genuine altruistic concern, concern that the desires of others be satisfied *for their own sake*. Instead it constitutes an *instrumental* concern that builds on considerations of what the consequences of the satisfaction for oneself will be.

A similar story could be told about liking and concern for others because of shared interests. A special case of this is when others show an inclination to do good to oneself. Naturally, this will result in a liking for these do-gooders and a concern that their desires be fulfilled in return (this is what is called gratitude).

Analogously, it is easy to comprehend that if one likes oneself partly because of one's interests in the arts, sciences, sports, etc.—which includes wanting oneself to retain these interests—one will like and seek the company of people who share these interests. For the company of such people tends to promote and stimulate one's own interest. But the aid of these people is likely to be most effective if one is oneself willing and capable of giving them something in return. So it lies in one's own interest to fulfil some of their desires, for example, those desires whose fulfilment is necessary for the pursuit of the interests. We see here in outline a mechanism of reciprocal reinforcement that could create quite strong unions between people.

The desires for others so far studied are instrumental: desires to fulfil the desires of others because of the benefits that will accrue, or has accrued, to oneself. But there is also genuine altruistic concern—desires to satisfy the desires of another as an end in itself—to take into account. Take the simple case of concern for another who is suffering from physical pain. As both everyday experience and psychological experiments bear out,[3] it is especially hard to be indifferent to the suffering of another when one perceives that being. The explanation of this seems to be that one is induced to imagine vividly from the inside the experience of having a frustrated desire to get rid of a pain upon observing the behavioural signs of the having of this experience (just as one is induced to mimic facial expressions, etc.). Thus, if one perceives another writhing in pain, one tends to automatically imagine the other's feeling pain and being averse to it more vividly than one would do if one merely heard it verbally reported that this being is suffering pain (though perhaps not as vividly as when one anticipates one's own pain). This vivid representation then gives rise to a proportionally stronger wish or desire to alleviate the pain of the other for its own sake (cf. Darwall, 2002: 66–8).

I do not put forward this illustration to suggest that only awareness of ubiquitous desires, like the desire to avoid pain, could elicit sympathetic concern. Any desire of another that one is disposed to share, or can envisage what it would be like for oneself to be in the grip of, could serve this function. If one has experienced a desire to complete a bigger work and has been frustrated by how slowly it goes, or a desire to recover from a long-lasting illness, one readily feels altruistic concern that such desires of others be satisfied when one witnesses their efforts to satisfy them.

This enforces the argument of the foregoing chapters, to the effect that one is not sympathetically concerned that one's own current desires be fulfilled because they are

---

[3] I here have in mind, e.g., Stanley Milgram's famous experiments (1974). Darwall refers to some other experiments relevant to empathy and sympathy (2002: ch. 3).

one's own. If sympathetic concern is also occasioned by consciousness of the desires of others, this lends support to the view that it is not crucial whether a desire is ascribed to oneself or another. Sympathetic concern arises upon a vivid awareness of a desire, be it a desire of oneself or another.[4] That such concern is more common with regard to oneself—especially oneself at the present time—is due to the fact that a vivid representation of one's own desires is easier to come by—indeed, it commonly forcibly imposes itself upon one.

There are, however, also other factors that explain why sympathetic concern is more pronounced in one's own case: there is less to block or counteract the operation of this concern with respect to oneself, since one generally likes oneself more than others. Thus, in the case of others, there is a greater probability of disapproval of personality or gestalt counteracting sympathetic concern. Disapproving of beings because of their characteristics is wanting to rid oneself of their presence. In the case of others, this desire naturally generates desires not to fulfil their desires to have the most elementary comforts of life. So one's sympathetic concern that they not suffer from pain, hunger, thirst, cold, etc. is obstructed.

The outcome of this is of course that as a rule there is a greater sympathetic concern for others of which one approves than for others of which one disapproves for the reason that concern flows freely in the former case. Approval or disapproval of the features of others could, however, affect sympathetic concern for them in a more indirect and devious fashion than by supplying reasons that let through or counteract the concern. I have pointed out that, if one approves of others—irrespective of whether this is because of their appearance or interests—one tends to seek their company, while if one disapproves of them, one tends to avoid them. As a consequence, it is likely that other individuals approved of will be in the presence of one's senses more often than individuals disapproved of, and it was noted above that the perceptible presence of others encourages one to imagine vividly their experiences, with the result that a stronger concern is aroused in one.

Needless to say, this disparity in respect of vividness and detail of the representations of mental states of beings liked and disliked is unacceptable from the perspective of cognitive rationality. From this perspective, a mental state must be represented with the same degree of vividness regardless of whether it belongs to the present or some other time, to oneself or another, or to a being liked or disliked. In the following chapters I shall, however, argue that, if one represents the attitudes of a being disliked—whether this be another being or oneself at another time than the present—as vividly as one represents one's own present attitudes, then, if sympathetic concern is not strong enough to overpower the reasons in its way, supplied by properties disliked, it is not cognitively irrational to let this resistance have its way.

Although an account of the basis of concern and approval should explain the apparent fact that these attitudes are occasionally felt as strongly towards others as oneself, such an

---

[4] Cf. Nagel's idea that a person's awareness of how bad a pain is "does not essentially involve the thought of it as his. The desire to be rid of pain has only the pain as its object" (1986: 161).

account must also make intelligible the prevalence of the O-bias in the actual world (in which others are qualitatively different from oneself). Let me summarize what I have offered on this score. First, there is the fact that one's own mental states are more vividly represented by one. In the case of oneself at present, this is the work of the P-bias, whereas in the case of oneself in the future, this is to be put down to the fact that a belief in identity (at least on the naive somatist account of it) readily triggers off the imaginative devices of experiential anticipation.[5] Secondly, there are facts that make one more inclined to approve of one's own (present) appearances and attitudes than those of others. There is the mechanism of habituation and the fact that one is more likely to approve of attitudes that are possessed by oneself and so are constitutive of one's (current) values. Many of these properties are ones that one will have in the future as well. Hence, it is more probable that there will be something to block the sympathetic concern to fulfil desires had by others than desires had by oneself at any time. Some other individuals, however, share many of the features of which one approves in oneself (they may also possess other properties that one values), and this supports empathy directly as well as indirectly, by making one seek the company of them. This ensures a free flow of a sympathetic concern oriented towards them. Hence the strong altruism we sometimes observe.

The condition that has to do with the inadequacy of representation by itself indicates that the tendency to favour oneself may be—and presumably normally is—bound up with cognitive patterns that are irrational. In the next two chapters, I turn to the conditions under which it is cognitively rational to favour oneself at present both over oneself in the future and over others, in the present as well as in future. As will transpire, it would be rash to assume that we are rationally required to care for ourselves in the future and for others to the extent commanded by the demands of inter-temporal and inter-personal maximization, respectively. We must keep apart a temporal and personal *neutrality* from an inter-temporal and inter-personal *fulfilment-maximization* and not assume that if the former pair is rationally required, so is the latter.

---

[5] Cf. Kagan's claim that "it does not seem implausible to suggest that an agent's bias in favor of his own interests may simply be a function of the fact that his interests are more vividly represented than are the interests of others"; so were the interests of others as vividly represented, one "would tend to act in accordance with the objective standpoint" (1989: 292). But, as will become clear in the following chapters, I take exception to the suggestion that "the objective standpoint" requires inter-temporal and inter-personal maximization.

26

PRUDENCE: MAXIMIZATION OR IDEALISM?

I HAVE discussed two different kinds of 'pro-attitude' towards oneself: (1) sympathetic concern for oneself, that is, intrinsically wanting things to go well for oneself in response to an imaginative representation of what things are like for oneself; and (2) approval of oneself because of some features that one exemplifies, that is, intrinsically wanting to preserve oneself in response to a belief that one exemplifies those features. Concern for oneself at a time may be aroused by one's vividly representing desires that one possesses at that time. In the case of oneself at present, this is the work of the P-bias, whereas in the case of oneself at a future time it assumes the shape of anticipating having experiences that one thinks one will have at that time. This anticipation is non-voluntarily imagining what having these experiences will be like (from the inside). It is usually triggered by the belief that one will survive in the normal, naïve somatist fashion up to the relevant time, though survival of the primary mind-owner, that is, certain brain-parts, may fill the same function. This belief makes one vividly imagine having the future experiences one will have, since one is accustomed to future experiences becoming present. Due to the fact that we are under the spell of the P-bias and represent the future less vividly than the present (and generally less vividly the more distant it is), the concern one will have for oneself in the future will be weaker than the concern for oneself in the present (and weaker the more distant the future is).

As regards approval of oneself, the properties that constitute its ground include both observable physical ones, such as one's appearance, and psychological and psycho-physical ones, such as one's being equipped with certain desires, and abilities correlated with them. With respect to the former, I have argued that habituation is an important, though not the only, causal factor. With respect to the latter, my argument has been that awareness of a desire one currently has does not invariably give rise to approval of one's having it as it gives rise to concern that it be fulfilled. Nonetheless, one cannot overall disapprove of one's own current desires—as one can of the desires of others—since this second-order attitude must be grounded in first-order desires that one currently has.

Identity normally brings along an extensive similarity in respect of both physical and psychological properties. Therefore, the fact that a future subject is identical to oneself makes it less likely that one will find something to dislike about it than if it had not been identical to oneself. Since it is dislike that blocks concern, there is less to block one's concern for oneself not only in the present, but also in the future, than there is in the case of others. Add to this that, in the latter case, the concern evoked will be weaker to start with, because representation from the inside will be less vivid, and I claim that we have an adequate explanation of the O-bias, as we in fact find it in ourselves (though not a rational justification for it).

According to this account, the recognition that some future or present subject is *oneself* is not in itself one's reason for being O-biased. This recognition operates, first, by non-voluntarily triggering an act of vivid imaginative representation from the inside that in principle can be voluntarily directed to others. Secondly, it operates with the assistance of certain features that *contingently* and often not even uniquely belong to one—features that, conceivably, one could be deprived of and that other beings than oneself could possess and, if they admit of degrees, could possess to a greater extent than does oneself. In contrast, the property of being (identical to) oneself is a property that *essentially and uniquely* belongs to oneself, that is, it is a property that one cannot be without,[1] and that others cannot share.

Self-oriented Attitudes Grounded in Contingent and Universal Features

In the case of some properties, it is controversial whether they are essential to their bearer. To fix the reference of a term, we need a definite description that singles out its referent. It might be contended that the properties mentioned in some such description that identifies a subject must be essential properties of that subject. For if the subject in question lacked these properties, no reference to it appears possible, and this seems tantamount to saying that it does not exist.

This inference to the existence of essential properties may, however, well be premature. The fact is that there are several alternative descriptions by means of which the reference to a subject can be fixed. For instance, the (rigid) reference of a proper name to a human subject can be fixed with the help of either a description that specifies the time and place of her birth or a description that picks her out as the human being *now* being at a certain place and doing certain things. If the former is assumed to fix the reference of 'Womanina' to her, Womanina's life after birth could consistently be imagined to have taken an altogether different course from the one that it actually has followed; while if the latter description is chosen to fix the reference of the name, the circumstances of her birth and subsequent life up to the present could conceivably have been quite different

---

[1] Note that this is a stronger sense of an essential property than the one employed in ch. 19.

from what they in fact have been. Consequently, neither the property of being born at a certain time in a certain place nor the property of being now at a certain place and engaged in certain activities may be an essential property of Womanina. I believe, though I need not argue for it, that the fact that there are alternative descriptions by means of which an individual could be identified undermines the idea that there are essential properties of it sufficient to single it out.

Even if some of these reference-fixing properties were to be essential characteristics of the referents, it would not follow that I am wrong in claiming that self-directed attitudes rest on features that are contingently possessed. For a reference-fixing description succeeds in selecting one only by citing some of one's spatio-temporal positions, and it would clearly be eccentric to have a particular concern or liking for oneself because of some such positions. Also, those of one's intrinsic features that these descriptions mention need only be highly general ones, such as that one is conscious or human, and of course such properties cannot make up the reason why one likes or is concerned about oneself *in particular*. Thus we can rest assured that, on my construal, self-directed attitudes have a contingent basis.

I believe it to be legitimate to take a further step and maintain that the properties on which self-oriented attitudes are founded are not merely contingent, but *universal*. A universal property is a property that involves no relation to anything particular. The point can be put linguistically. Let us roughly distinguish terms that *express* or *rigidly designate* properties from ones that *refer to* or *non-rigidly designate* them. The term 'greenness' expresses the property of greenness, while the description 'the colour of chlorophyll' or 'the national colour of Ireland' refers to it. In terms of this distinction, we can say that a universal property is one that can be expressed without reference to anything particular or individual.

Of course, a property can contingently belong to one without being a universal property: the property of desiring to imitate the ways of that great man Manek or of being the brother of him are contingent, non-universal features. Suppose that one approves of oneself because of these properties. If I have been right about the insignificance of identity and of spatio-temporal specifications, then, in so far as these characteristics serve as the bases of self-approval, they must be replaceable by universal ones, for example, the properties of desiring to imitate the ways of a man that is excellent in certain ways.

On the strength of such considerations, I believe we could assume that the basis of self-directed attitudes is constituted by features that not only contingently belong to oneself, but which are also universal. But it is not of crucial importance that the latter claim be conceded. What is vital for what follows is that these foundational features be ones that one could conceivably lack and that some other beings could conceivably possess (to a higher degree). This is ensured by the contingency of ownership alone. In this chapter I shall contemplate the possibility of oneself deteriorating in value in one's own eyes, by losing some features liked at present, while the possibility of others possessing or acquiring disliked characteristics will be dealt with in the next chapter.

The Possibility of Idealism

Suppose that one of the main reasons why Philo approves of himself is that he has a desire that philosophical progress be made and that, to whatever extent this is possible, he makes a contribution to this end. Philo predicts that, at some future time t, he will no longer have this desire; in fact, he foresees that he will then be averse to the idea of philosophical activity. Nonetheless, he *now* desires that philosophical progress be made at t and that he then does whatever he can to contribute to it (and perhaps is punished if he does not). We have seen in Chapter 10 that there are such desires that are not implicitly conditional on their own persistence. Let us make the further assumption that the matter is considered only to the extent that it falls within the domain of prudence, that is, that only the consequences for the agent's own good or desires are taken into account.

Now, suppose that, in the light of representations that are as vivid as one could wish, Philo goes on desiring that philosophical progress be made at t and that he be instrumental to it, even were he to believe that at t he would be averse to this end and that the frustration occasioned by the promotion of it then would be incompatible with the inter-temporal maximization of his (experiential) fulfilment. Then I shall say (as foreshadowed in Chapter 24) that this desire constitutes an *ideal* that Philo now has in the domain of prudence and that Philo to this extent is an *idealist*. To uphold an ideal in this domain, one must desire something more than one desires to attain the prudentialist goal of inter-temporal maximization of one's own fulfilment, that is, more than one desires to lead a life containing as much (experiential) fulfilment as possible. But note that the pursuit of an ideal could *in fact* turn out to be compatible with the inter-temporal maximization of one's fulfilment, since, definitionally, an ideal is something that *would be* pursued even *were it believed* to go against maximization.

Ideals can be as various as interests are, but a possible ideal of particular importance in a philosophical context is the *rationalist* ideal. It is, however, of importance in the present context also because rational constraints can be imposed upon the satisfactionalist goal. Other possible ideals are the aims to create a great work of art and to be among the best athletes in the world. Note, however, that, on my definition of an ideal, the goal of inter-temporally maximizing one's own fulfilment cannot make up an ideal in the realm of prudence, for obviously this goal cannot be pursued though it is seen to be contrary to the inter-temporal maximization of one's own fulfilment.

It is not uncommon to take it for granted that, in this realm, the supremely rational course is to aim at this prudential goal. On a conative theory of motivation, one necessarily acts on one's strongest current desires. This *explanatory* claim may be confused with the *teleological* claim that one necessarily acts with *the goal or aim* of fulfilling one's strongest current desires. If one then makes the mistake of overlooking the existence of desires that are not conditional upon their own persistence, one may conclude that whenever one wants something to happen at a time, one does so because one thinks it will then satisfy a desire one has at the time. Laying down a rational constraint of temporal neutrality may then yield the result that the rational course is that of inter-temporal maximization of one's own fulfilment.

But the conative theory of motivation imposes only a *formal* constraint on theories of practical rationality, namely, that they must be "present-aim" theories, in Parfit's terminology (1984: secs 34–5). It is only confusions, such as the ones mentioned in the foregoing paragraph, that can make this theory seem to entail the *substantial* claim that our present aims must concern the fulfilment of our own desires. So it cannot be that in conjunction with a requirement of temporal neutrality the conative theory prescribes the prudentialist aim.

Such a conclusion would be tantamount to denying the rationality of ideals in the sphere of prudence. In opposition to such view, I shall in the present chapter contend that having ideals in this sphere is not in any sense irrational. For instance, it is not irrational to have the rationalist aim of wanting to live in the light of truth even though this will make one's life unhappier than it could otherwise be. I shall not argue that one is rationally *required* to have any ideals, since I believe it to be a rationally *permissible* stance in the realm of prudence to aim at the prudentialist goal of inter-temporally maximizing one's own fulfilment. Since, as we saw in Part II, ultimately intrinsic desires cannot, as such, be irrational, it cannot be irrational to have such a desire for (felt) satisfaction that is stronger than one's ultimately intrinsic desire to be cognitively rational.

True, I have earlier in this part concluded that the O-bias is cognitively irrational. So it would seem to follow that the prudentialist aim, which is a temporally neutral satisfactionalism restricted by the O-bias, must be a partly irrational aim. But in Chapter 11 we saw that, although an attitude is cognitively irrational, it need not be relatively irrational for everyone to have it. To be a prudentialist will be relatively irrational only if one's rationalist desire is stronger than one's satisfactionalist desire. Suppose that, spontaneously, the latter desire takes the prudentialist form that I am particularly concerned that my own present and future desires be fulfilled, for these are the desires that my P-bias and my habit of experiential anticipation represent to me. Imagine that I am then brought to realize that the exclusiveness of these modes of representation cannot be rationally justified, but that I should represent the mental states of others as vividly. Then, relatively to my prudentialist desire, it may still be irrational to attempt to break this exclusiveness, that is, to abandon the O-bias—for it may bring me less fulfilment—and this desire may be stronger than my rationalist desire relative to which this move is rational.

Moreover, it should be kept in mind that in this chapter we confine ourselves to prudence, where, definitionally, the beings who count are reduced to oneself. Thereby, the restriction of the O-bias is vacuous. Things will stand differently when, in the next chapter, we move onto the intersubjective domain of morality in which the effects of one's actions on other beings than oneself count.

It should be apparent from this that one's ideals possess a certain independence of one's desires or preferences: Philo's philosophical ideal is independent of the desires that he foresees that he will have at t, though he can uphold this ideal at present only if he at present possesses desires that correspond to the ideal.[2] Ideal-constituting desires stand in contrast to desires that are conditional upon their own persistence (as we saw in Chapter 10,

---

[2] Cf. what Gordon (1986: 112–13) calls transcendent values.

a desire for p is of this kind if and only if one desires that p obtain only at times at which one envisages that one will still have a desire for p). Therefore, they also stand in contrast to desires that are conditional upon their yielding experiential fulfilment. Such desires are mere means to experiential fulfilment: one wants to have them because of this fulfilment and would be prepared to exchange them for equally satisfiable ones. In contrast, if Philo is prepared to desire that philosophy be pursued at t, although he realizes that he will then be adversely affected by its pursuit, he will naturally wish that he could have preserved his interest in philosophy.

Ideals in my sense do not presuppose any objectivist account of value; the subjectivist strategy of defining what is of value in terms of what one (ultimately) intrinsically desires or would desire does not impose on one the rejection of idealism. All subjectivism constrains Philo to do is to concede that at t, when he no longer desires philosophy, it will be of no value for him (in the broad subjectivist sense). But Philo's concession that at t philosophy will be of no value could not force him to surrender his *present* desire that philosophy be pursued at t or his *present* assessment of philosophy as valuable. This desire or assessment is the result of his now preferring the growth of philosophy to his maximizing his own fulfilment, and subjectivism does nothing to show that this preference order is misguided.

As I indicated in Chapter 3, if, in its claim about homogeneity in respect of the objects of ultimately intrinsic desires, hedonism had been correct, idealism would be undercut. For the object of my present desire to promote philosophy would then ultimately have to be pleasure or satisfaction, that is, my desire for philosophy would not be ultimately intrinsic, but would have to be derivative from something like a desire for pleasure or satisfaction. If that had been the case, it would be relatively irrational for me to desire to do philosophy when this would bring me less satisfaction. And if it were irrational relatively to the prudentialist policy, it would be irrational relative to the only possible ultimate goal in the realm of prudence.

Further, we have in Part III established the cognitive rationality of temporal neutrality but, I claim, this falls short of implying that, in the realm of prudence, prudentialism is the only rational policy. Nor can an appeal to the importance of one's identity do the job, for there is no such importance.

Nagel and the Timelessness of Reasons

Let us review some arguments that could be cast as supporting the view that, in the sphere of prudence it is irrational to reject the prudentialist, inter-temporal maximizing policy. There is an argument that can be construed as being to the effect that it is irrational to have ideals, since that would involve a violation of some sort of temporal neutrality. Thomas Nagel espouses the view that "the influence of reasons is transmitted over time" (1970: 46); in particular he claims that

> there is a reason to do not only what will promote that for which there is presently a reason, but also what will promote something future for which it is expected that there *will* be a reason. (1970: 36)

To the extent that I have understood Nagel's argument in support of this thesis, it is unten-able.[3] Moreover, it is questionable whether he consistently sticks to an interpretation of the timelessness of reasons that is incompatible with it being rational to have ideals. For instance, in discussing a man who foresees that he will change from valuing sex, spontane-ity, frequent risks, etc. to valuing security, status, wealth, etc., Nagel writes that this man

> may be strongly enough convinced of the worthlessness of his inevitable future values simply to refuse them any claim on his present concern. He would then regard his present values as valid for the future also, and no prudential reasons would derive from his expected future views. (1970: 74 n.)

If, as Nagel says, this man's position "would be formulable in terms of timeless reasons" (1970: 74 n.), the timelessness of reasons will not exclude the having of ideals. For this man seemingly treats his present values as ideals in my sense.

The man in the example will now have reasons to do things that he knows he will later have reasons to try to undo. Nagel maintains that a system of practical rationality that allows such consequences

> not only fails to require the most elementary consistency in conduct over time, but in fact sharpens the possibility of conflict by grounding an individual's plottings against his future self in the apparatus of rationality. (1970: 40)

In a similar spirit, John Rawls maintains:

> the claims of the self at different times must be so adjusted that the self at each time can affirm the plan that has been and is being followed. The person at one time, so to speak, must not be able to complain about the actions of the person at another time. (1971: 423)

As remarked, if Philo's desire—that philosophical progress be made and that, to the best of his ability, he be instrumental in promoting it—is an ideal of his, he will naturally want that he keep this desire, and do what he can to accomplish this, for by retaining this desire he will more effectively contribute to philosophical progress and avoid frustration. So, if he later abandons this ideal, it is because his future character is not entirely under his control. It is plausible to think that if a theory of practical rationality exhorts one to *create* for its own sake situations in which one at the present time has reasons to do what one knows that one will later have reasons to undo, that theory is defective. But what is here in question is a claim which covers situations in which such a conflict arises because some things are beyond one's control. I do not see why it must be irrational in such situ-ations to prefer that philosophical progress be made to that one's future desires be (max-imally) fulfilled. To hold this to be irrational would seem to be like saying that when the enemy is so superior that it cannot be defeated, the only rational course is to collaborate with it—to which a reasonable reply is: not if what it stands for is sufficiently bad. Certainly, it is unsatisfactory that in the future one will have desires that cannot be fulfilled, but in terms of Philo's present desire it will be even more unsatisfactory if philosophical progress is hampered.

***

[3] For this argument, see Persson (1988*b*).

It should be noted that Nagel concentrates on *future* reasons and their power to generate present reasons. But if "the influence of reasons is transmitted over time", the fact that one once *had* certain reasons should also provide one with present reasons.[4] To take an example of Parfit's (1984: 152): imagine that for fifty years one of my leading ideals has been that Venice be saved and that I be one of its saviours, but that I have now lost this ideal. If the force of reasons really extends over time, it would seem that I still have a powerful reason to try to save the city, though I am now indifferent—or perhaps even averse—to the survival of the city. Given the duration and the strength of my desire to save Venice, the reason it generates may be stronger than other present reasons of mine. As Parfit remarks (1984: 152–3, 157), most of us would, however, find it hard to believe that we could in this way be rationally committed to act in accord with our past desires. This view is tantamount to holding that changing one's mind is always pointless, since it cannot have point to change one's mind if one afterwards must heed the desires one had to the same extent as before the change. So it does not appear to be a general truth that "the influence of reasons is transmitted over time".

Parfit's example, however, presents no difficulty for the prudentialist aim construed as that of inter-temporally maximizing *experiential* fulfilment,[5] since the fulfilling of a past desire cannot produce any feelings of fulfilment. For this reason, prudentialists may entertain mostly desires that are conditional upon their yielding experiential fulfilment. They may entertain unconditional desires only when this is consistent with the inter-temporal maximization of their experiential fulfilment (e.g. desires that concern the time after their death.)

But I believe that Parfit's example may not constitute an insurmountable obstacle even for those who advocate the broader view that factual fulfilment should be maximized. This is because I have suggested that experiential fulfilment counts for more even for these theorists, as it involves in addition (at least) the factual fulfilment of the hedonist desire to experience fulfilment. If this hedonist desire is strong enough, it will generally be rational to fulfil one's current desires instead of past ones.

Is Idealism Temporally Partial?

Rejecting Nagel's claim about the transmission of the influence of reasons over time and endorsing some ideal may, however, seem to involve a questionable temporal partiality. This charge can be elaborated as follows.[6] To elevate some of one's present desires to the status of an ideal is to assign a greater weight in one's present deliberation to them than to future (or past) desires, even though the latter may be of greater intensity. For one acts concordantly with the ideal rather than with them. If any of these other desires had

---

[4] Harrison (1981–2: 53 ff.) defends the thesis that if one desires that something obtains at a time at which one realizes one will no longer desire it, then one has just as strong a reason to satisfy this desire even when it is past. It does not matter to him whether the desire disappears because of the death of the subject or a change of mind.

[5] Hare's introduction of a "requirement of prudence" is a move to a similar effect (1981: 105).

[6] The following argument repeats some points made in Persson (1990).

instead been held at the present, it might have constituted one's present ideal. Thus, a desire is elevated to a present ideal at least partly because it *is possessed at the present time*. In other words, when a desire is embraced as an ideal, it is given priority in virtue of its temporal position. So, to uphold an ideal is to violate a rational requirement of temporal neutrality.

This argument trades on an ambiguity in the claim that a certain desire is given priority 'because it is possessed by one at present', an ambiguity noted above between an explanatory and a teleological sense. Imagine that one were to make up one's mind about what to do in the following fashion. As far as possible, one tries to represent to oneself the desires that one will have in different temporal parts of one's life: that is, one strives to predict what desires one will have in the future, to introspect present ones and to remember past ones. Then one decides to fulfil one's strongest present desires rather than the perhaps stronger past or future ones simply for the reason that, *as the desires have been represented by one*, they are the strongest desires that one *now* has. This gives the teleological sense: one has a *goal* which is biased towards the present time. It amounts to an irrational breach of temporal neutrality if the reasoning in Part III is correct.

But this is not the way in which idealists would proceed. What Philo has in mind as his goal or objective when he pursues his ideal to promote philosophical progress is, obviously, to promote this progress. He need not be conscious of the fact that at present he has a desire to this effect, and hence, he need not be aware of the fact that by acting as he does he fulfils a present desire of his. Often, though, an idealist will be conscious of these facts. All the same, if the desire acted on is an ideal of the agent's, it cannot be that these deliverances of self-consciousness adds crucially to his motivation—that without them the ideal-constituting desire would not animate him. For, definitionally, ideals are pursued independently of any thought of the fulfilment their pursuit would bring: they are not conditional upon their own persistence and fulfilment.

This unravels another sense in which one could be said to act on a desire 'because it is possessed by one at present', namely the causal or explanatory one. A desire that one has at present can constitute an explanatory factor of one's present action simply in virtue of the fact that one *possesses* it at the present time. It is not dependent on being *represented* in one's self-consciousness as being possessed by one—being in the foreground of deliberation, as Pettit and Smith (1990) put it—in order to have this power. Contrast a desire that one will have in the future: it can affect how one acts at present only by being currently represented by one. The mere fact that one will *have* some desire in the future cannot causally influence one's present behaviour unless one is aware of this fact.

However, this leads to another construal of the charge that idealism involves temporal partiality. Idealists are temporally biased, it may be urged, in that they let their behaviour be determined by certain desires simply in virtue of currently *having* them. When idealists act on some present desire of theirs rather than on a perhaps stronger future one that they predict they will come to have, this is because the former is a desire that they *in fact have*. Idealists may try to justify their decisions by claiming that the future desire is base, ignoble, etc., but these evaluations only reflect the desires that they *at present possess*.

By permitting themselves to be affected by present desires through an avenue that is closed to desires of other parts of their lives, idealists are guilty of a temporal partiality.

So, to be temporally neutral in the sense now recommended, one must ensure that one's present desires influence one only in a manner in which desires of other temporal stretches of one's life can also influence one, namely, via being represented by one at the present time. Rational deliberation in the prudential sphere, the objection goes on, consists in representing to oneself as exhaustively as possible the desires that one will have in different parts of one's life and then deciding to fulfil those desires the fulfilment of which will make one's entire life contain as much fulfilment as possible. The temporal location of the desires should not enter into the grounds of the deliberation. Evaluation of the desires as better or worse, or higher or lower, should be avoided, since it will inescapably reflect the state of one's present desires. The only relevant ground is what contribution the satisfaction of a desire will make to the total satisfaction of one's entire life.

This yields the idea of a temporally neutral or inter-temporal *maximization* of fulfilment which is the prudentialist goal if fulfilment is specified as experiential fulfilment.[7] It should be sharply distinguished from the notion of temporal neutrality in Part III. Inter-temporal maximization evidently includes temporal neutrality, but goes beyond it: it entails temporal neutrality in its demand that rational deliberators should ignore the temporal location of the desires represented, but it transcends temporal neutrality in its constraint that deliberators should be affected by their desires only to the extent that they are represented and not at all by the fact that they actually possess some of them. Hence, one can consistently deny that rationality demands inter-temporal maximization, and so prudentialism, even if one holds that it demands temporal neutrality.

One thing about this way of arriving at inter-temporal maximization should be emphasized straightaway. It is strictly *impossible* to be affected by one's present desires only via the avenue of representation. If one follows the decision-procedure just sketched, then one does so because one *has* a dominant desire to maximize one's inter-temporal fulfilment. This desire determines one's behaviour, although it is not mentally represented by one. Hence, inter-temporal maximizers cannot demand that one be influenced by one's present desires only to the extent that this impact is transmitted via one's consciousness of them. Their requirement must rather be that, in the sphere of prudence, one be directly affected by no other present desire than the one to the effect that one's fulfilment be inter-temporally maximized.

But this concession provokes a question: what is it that makes it rational to be directly influenced by the inter-temporally maximalist desire, but not, for example, by the desire that philosophical progress be made, as our idealist is? To this question the following reply may be suggested. If I fulfil my present desires (ideals) at the cost of frustrating my

---

[7] In the literature—see Sen (1979: 470)—there is also a temporal *egalitarianism* which insists that value or fulfilment should be equally distributed over the periods of a life even if this clashes with maximizing the quantity of value or fulfilment of the entire life. Might there then in the realm of prudence be a conflict between maximization and justice / equality as there is in the inter-personal case of morality? I do not think so because, throughout one's life, one's concern for one's whole life is so powerful that one would at no time object to having less if this were in the name of overall maximization (cf. ch. 37). For this reason, Rawls's demand that selves located at different times have to be able to affirm a life-plan leads to inter-temporal maximization.

stronger future ones, I treat myself, as I am at present, *better* than myself as I will be in the future. This preferential treatment can be justified only if the present 'slice' or 'stage' of myself is better, or more worthy of having its desires gratified. But this cannot be the case, for—at least to myself—by far the most valuable property of me is that I am (identical to) myself, that I have the feature of being me. When I desire to fulfil my own desires, I do so precisely because I recognize these desires as *mine*. But desires that I have in other temporal stretches of my life than the present one are to an equal degree equipped with this spellbinding property of being mine, of belonging to stages that are stages of me. Therefore there can be no justification for me to prioritize my weaker desires of one period over my stronger desires of another unless, as is unlikely, this promotes an increase in quantity of fulfilment of my whole life.

This argument was, however, undermined in Chapter 23. It was there contended that the fact that something belongs to oneself is, by itself, a matter of rational indifference. I have argued that cognitively rational persons—and, indeed, even actual persons—are concerned about and like themselves not because they recognize themselves to have the feature of being themselves, but because of certain mental and physical attributes that they see themselves as contingently possessing. Consequently, we are not rationally required to treat every temporal slice of ourselves as of equal significance simply for the reason that they are all slices of ourselves. Depending on the contingent features of these slices, it could be rational to place higher or lower value on past or future slices than on the present slice of oneself.

Therefore, it is not irrational to have ideals. When Philo promotes philosophical progress in spite of the fact that he realizes that it is at odds with the inter-temporal maximization of his fulfilment, he implicitly treats his desire for philosophical progress as more worthy of being satisfied than some of his stronger desires held at other times. This presupposes that desires do not become equally worthy of being fulfilled by him in virtue of belonging to him, that the fact that an individual is him does not present a (superior) value to him that is independent of his contingent properties, such as his desires and appearance. Of course, the fact that he will cause himself frustration in the future will arouse his sympathetic concern to mitigate this frustration, but this concern will be offset by the fact that this frustration is occasioned by desires that are in conflict with his present ideals, and so are disapproved of by him at present.

Hare and 'Self-endorsement'

There is a further line of thought that could support prudential inter-temporal maximization. With respect to the following two statements:

(1) I now prefer with strength S that if I were in that situation x should happen rather than not, and

(2) If I were in that situation, I would prefer with strength S that x should happen rather than not.

Hare claims that one "cannot know that (2), and what that would be like, without (1) being true, and that this is a conceptual truth".[8] I shall refer to this claim as *the principle of hypothetical self-endorsement*, the PHS. It would have the effect of ruling out idealism. For it means that when Philo represents to himself that at the future time *t* he will have desires that conflict with his present desire that philosophical progress be made, he will form present desires—of the same strength—that these desires be satisfied. So if the future desires are stronger than his present putatively ideal-constituting desire—as they must be if this is to be a case of idealism manifesting itself—then also the generated present desires to the effect that the represented ones be fulfilled must be superior in respect of strength. Consequently, Philo will act on them and be a prudentialist inter-temporal maximizer instead of an idealist.

Let us examine what could be adduced in favour of the PHS. It seems altogether incomprehensible that my taking up of a cognitive attitude now could *logically* or *conceptually* constrain me to form a certain preference. (Of course, if I *realize* that I currently have a certain preference, it will follow that I *have* the preference, but that is not because my taking up of a certain cognitive attitude entails that I have some preference. It is because this cognitive attitude cannot be described as an act of *realization* unless its content is *true*.) It is, however, reasonable to read Hare as denying that (2) is purely descriptive and, consequently, that 'knowledge' of it is an entirely cognitive affair. He suggests that " 'I' is not a wholly descriptive word but in part prescriptive" (1981: 96). This suggestion is expanded as follows:

> In general, when I say that somebody who would be in a certain situation would be *myself*, in so saying I express a concern for that person in that hypothetical situation which is normally greater than I feel for *other people* in the same situation. To recognize that that person would be myself is already to be prescribing that, other things being equal, the preferences and prescriptions of that person should be satisfied. (1981: 221)

Apparently, the idea is that when I take some person, who exists in some hypothetical situation, to be the same person as myself, I do not merely make a certain factual claim—to the effect that certain factual criteria of personal identity, such as "bodily continuity, continuity of personal characteristics, and linked memories" (1981: 96) are satisfied—I also adopt a certain attitude of sympathetic concern: I desire that the desires of this person be fulfilled in proportion to their intensity.[9]

If this is so, what could my reasons be for adopting this concern for myself? Since the concern I feel for myself "is normally greater than [the one] I feel for *other people* in the

---

[8] (1981: 96). The following discussion of Hare's argument draws on the one in Persson (1988b).

[9] Compare Whiting's idea that since we take "concern for our friends as a component of the friendship relation", her analogy between self-concern and friendship bids us to hold that "concern for our future selves is a component of psychological continuity" (1986: 560–1). But the problem is that the latter concern seems to presuppose that which it is supposed to constitute, for it presupposes that a future being has been identified as (being psychologically continuous with) oneself. (In contrast, concern for a friend does not presuppose that one identifies the friend as 'a friend'.) David Brink, who champions a similar idea (1997: 103–4), suggests the remedy that the concern constitutive of identity be thought of as 'quasi-self-concern' on the model of quasi-memory (n. 13). But then the upshot seems to be that identity will be broader than it is ordinarily conceived to be and will hold, e.g. in fission cases.

same situation", it is presumably (at least partially) based on such reasons as 'this person is psycho-physically continuous with me' (supposing this continuity to constitute the factual element of our identity). The reason cannot be to the effect that the person *is identical to* me, for, given that Hare is right about personal identity, this entails that I have already adopted the attitude in question. In contrast, it would be a *synthetic* truth, if it is a truth at all, that if I take somebody to be psycho-physically continuous with me, I would as a consequence adopt the attitude that his desires be fulfilled in proportion to their strength.[10] Thus, we arrive at the conclusion that, at the bottom of Hare's claim about (1) and (2), there lies the assumption criticized in Chapter 23, namely, the assumption that the consideration that some subject is linked to oneself at present by identity-constituting continuities provides one with the best of reasons for being concerned about the satisfaction of the desires of this subject.[11]

What could have led Hare to endorse this assumption that we found so unconvincing? Well, Hare starts by considering one's attitudes to one's *current* states of mind. In this connection he declares the following to be "a conceptual truth": "If I am suffering, I have a motive for ending the suffering" (1981: 93). It is indeed conceptually true that, if I am suffering because (I am aware) *p* is the case, I have a desire that *p* cease to be the case. Hence it follows that, in virtue of the "stage" of the person doing the representing being the very same stage as the stage represented, the former has a desire for not-*p*. This case is then significantly different from the one in which I represent myself as suffering at *another* time than the present because of *p*, for in that case there might be a discrepancy between the desires of the representing subject and those of the represented one. It is therefore hazardous to extrapolate from the case of monitoring one's present states of mind.

For instance, if I am aware of myself suffering at present because *p*, I form a *second-order* desire that my desire for not-*p* be fulfilled and, so, that the negative affective state of suffering be brought to an end. I have argued that this is a contingent truth. It is *conceivable* that there be creatures so ill-adjusted that they lack the disposition to form such second-order desires. But actual human persons are not like that. When I register the fact that I am suffering, my sympathetic concern will be elicited. Moreover, since the representing subject here will share the represented being's desire for not-*p*, there will be no disagreement in respect of desires to block the sympathetic concern. But the case in which I

---

[10] This argument is tantamount to employing against Hare himself a tactic that he has frequently used against descriptivism about the meaning of moral words: insisting that if the meaning of a word comprises both descriptive and evaluative components, these components must be separable in principle.

[11] In one place (1988: 216), Hare appeals to another type of consideration in support of PHS, namely, that a representation of a desire cannot be perfect unless it *is* a desire. This contention seems different, since it does not turn on my identifying the subject of the desire represented as *myself*. Timothy Sprigge, however, explicitly links representing an experience perfectly with representing it as one's own: "it is built into the very nature of our separate individualities that, in thinking of an experience as someone else's rather than mine, I think of it as not having quite the same intense reality as it would if it were mine" (1988: 180). He adds that "representations of an experience can never be completely adequate, since if they became perfect icons they would simply be those experiences" (1988: 203). I have already adduced all of the arguments I possess against the first claim. As against the second one, I shall only point out that it seems to rests upon a Humean division of experiences into impressions and ideas according to which the difference is only a matter of intensity.

represent myself suffering at another time than the actual present one does not necessarily include this feature: here it is indeed possible that I now strongly detest that state of affairs which I desire at the time represented and the absence of which then induces me to suffer. And this current dislike might (legitimately) counteract my sympathetic concern.

There are then crucial disanalogies between the case of being conscious of one's present attitudes (towards one's experiences) and representing or imagining the attitudes one would have (towards one's experiences) at times that are not now actual. If one overlooks these disanalogies and assumes that what is true in the former case is true in the latter case as well, it might well seem to one, I surmise, that the explanation of this fact is something like the PHS.

Prudentialism and Higher and Lower Qualities of Fulfilment

My argument has only been to the effect that the maximalist or prudentialist reaction prescribed by Hare's PHS is not rationally *required* in the realm of prudence, not that it is in any sense irrational or rationally impermissible.[12] The idealist option of wanting something more than the inter-temporal maximization of one's own fulfilment is also rationally permissible. To assess properly the denial of a requirement to accept prudentialism, it should be remembered that the prudentialist aim of inter-temporally maximizing one's own experiential fulfilment need not be understood in a purely quantitative fashion, as it often has been, but could allow for a differentiation between higher and lower fulfilment, as remarked in Chapter 10. This follows from the rejection of the arguments in favour of prudentialism given in the foregoing sections.

Imagine that we discover a drug which slows down our life-processes and which, thereby, enables us to live lives more than ten times as long as our present lives. The drug, however, has the side-effect of making our mental faculties duller; they are reduced to the level of, say, pigs (as we have seen, such a transformation would not destroy our identity). But, in our present advanced state of technology, we also have the power to arrange the environment so that, were we to turn into pig-minded beings, we could live satisfied throughout our long pig-lives. No doubt, under these conditions the average life of a pig would contain quantitatively much more fulfilment than an average human life in an affluent country now does.[13]

Nevertheless, prudentialists need not advise us to take the drug. For, even if they vividly imagine how overwhelmingly pleasant, quantitatively speaking, a pig-life would be, it is possible for prudentialists to prefer a life in which they could fulfil some of the more sophisticated desires they currently possess, but would lose were they to turn

---

[12] Hare's earlier position (1963: 121) seems closer to mine, for here he claims that it would be a mistake "to try to incorporate ideals into a utilitarian theory". This is exactly what my argument will result in, when in the next chapter, it is extended into the inter-personal domain of morality.　　　　[13] Cf. Parfit's "Drab Eternity" (1986: 160).

pig-like. This is possible because, even though a desire is conditional upon its yielding experiential fulfilment, not only the intensity and the duration of the fulfilment, but also its quality, that is, its object, may be a reason for preferring its satisfaction—even at the cost of the satisfaction being shorter or less intense. Thus, the goal of fulfilment-maximization could be interpreted in a (to my mind, at least) more plausible way than it sometimes is. Idealism, therefore, has a worthy opponent.

27

THE REQUIREMENT OF PERSONAL NEUTRALITY

THE subject-matter of prudence is the consequences of one's actions in so far as they affect only one's own (ultimately) intrinsic desires. The question of how to live here takes the limited form: 'In the light of philosophical truth, what life have I most reason to lead, taking into account only my own intrinsic desires?' A traditional reply is an inter-temporally maximizing one: I should lead the life that contains the maximal felt fulfilment of such desires over time. This is prudentialism which features a requirement of cognitive rationality that demands temporal neutrality—a requirement defended in Part III. In the last chapter, I pointed out, however, that this temporal neutrality (which prohibits preferring one thing to another simply because of its temporal position) does not rule out (prudential) *idealism*. Nor is there any other consideration—as, for example, the truth of hedonism or the importance of one's own identity—that shows this idealism to be cognitively irrational. Hence, rationality does not force upon you the aim of inter-temporal maximization of experiential fulfilment in the domain of prudence. You could rationally adopt some ideal, like rationalism, which conflicts with prudentialism.

The subjectivism or desire-relativism of value espoused in Part II allows that it is best for you now that p is true at a future time, t, although it is the case that, because of changes in your desires, it will at t be best for you that not-p is true then. This raises the question of whether you rationally should bring it about that p or that not-p at t. If inter-temporal maximization were a rational requirement, there would be no doubt about the answer: you should rationally do that which maximizes the desire-fulfilment of your whole existence. But, if the argument of the preceding chapter is right, and rationality does not rule out idealism in the realm of prudence, this sort of fulfilment-maximization is not required.

Extending Idealism into the Inter-personal Realm

In this chapter I lift the artificial restriction to prudence and introduce the complementary dimension which spans the consequences of your actions in so far as they affect the fulfilment of the intrinsic desires of all *other* beings than yourself. It is apposite to do so, since the foregoing discussion of personal identity shows that there is a rational requirement of *personal* neutrality which demands neutrality between different persons or conscious subjects, like the requirement of temporal neutrality demands neutrality between different times. Thus, in the inter-personal or intersubjective domain of morality, there operates a requirement of personal neutrality which extends the requirement of temporal neutrality, in force in the intra-personal domain of prudence, across the lives of different individuals.

If they want their aim to be cognitively rational, this new requirement will force satisfactionalists to abandon prudentialism in favour of a fulfilment-maximization that is personally neutral as well as temporally neutral—a *utilitarian* fulfilment-maximization. Will it also force rationalists to surrender, in the inter-personal realm, their idealism? No, it bans personal partialities like the O-bias; so, if one is to be cognitively rational, one cannot favour the fulfilment of the desires of somebody at the expense of the fulfilment of those of another simply because the first individual is oneself. This parallels the fact that one cannot rationally prefer the fulfilment of one desire to another simply because it is in the nearer future. But just as giving up temporal biases does not make it cognitively irrational to be an idealist in the prudential case, giving up the O-bias does not make it irrational to be an idealist in the moral case. Ideals upheld in the intra-personal domain of prudence can be rationally transferred to the inter-personal domain of morality.

My argument for this transference is not hard to extract. I have urged that, in the name of an ideal, it is rationally permissible to go against the fulfilment of desires that oneself will have in the future, and thus against the goal of the inter-temporal maximization of one's own fulfilment (a goal which one may embrace in the future). In Chapter 23 I contended that the relation of our diachronic identity, and the material and matter-based psychological continuities that allegedly compose it, are in themselves rationally trivial. It follows that what one may rationally do to somebody to whom one bears these relations one may do to another, otherwise similar being, to whom one does not bear these relations. Therefore, it is rationally permissible to go against the prudentialist goal of another, similar individual, and thus against the goal of utilitarian maximization, just as it is permissible to reject the goal of inter-temporal maximization of one's own fulfilment. But we must also take care to separate this idealism from a discreditable egoism which is under the sway of the O-bias,[1] as in the domain of prudence we must keep apart idealism from a violation of the constraint of temporal neutrality that expresses itself, for example in the bias towards the near.

The position in which my argument in this chapter issues is what I shall call a *moral individualism*, to be distinguished from the *prudential* individualism which was the upshot of the preceding chapter. If rationality had demanded inter-personal and inter-temporal fulfilment-maximization, rationality would have been able to restrict the theoretical

---

[1] When Susan Wolf argues that, from the "point of view of individual perfection" (1982: 437), it would not be "particularly rational or good or desirable for a human being to strive" to be a moral saint (1982: 419), I think she does not do enough to distinguish what has the sanction of this point of view from what we find (un)attractive merely as a result of the "egoistic, hedonistic side of our natures" (1982: 496).

possibility that value-subjectivism leaves open of the same persons at different times, and different persons at the same or different times, making conflicting true claims, relative to their different sets of intrinsic desires, about what is best to do. It would have been possible to reach a consensus about what real reasons exhort one to do. But we saw in the previous chapter that, in the domain of prudence, rationality leaves open the choice between idealism and inter-temporal fulfilment-maximization. We shall now see that this individualist choice extends into morality owing to the rational insignificance of identity.

Some will think that such a moral individualism is absurdly weak. For they hold there to be demands of rationality strong enough to establish a consensus about what should be done in the moral realm. It is, however, hard to see how this could be feasible even if there were objective values. I believe that it should even then be agreed that both living in the light of truth and living a fulfilling life are on the list of objectively valuable aims. But then, if these aims diverge, it can hardly be denied that there is room for individualism in the sphere of prudence at least to the extent that one may rationally prefer one of these aims to the other. However, given the rational insignificance of identity, this individualism must extend into the moral sphere in which others are affected.

In any case, according to moral individualism rationality does not settle the choice between idealism and fulfilment-maximization. Cognitive rationality does not do it, and there is no other form of rationality that could do it. Moral individualism allows the different personalities or individualities of people to articulate themselves morally, in the shape of some form of idealism, like rationalism, or in a satisfactionalist rejection of all ideals. As I shall attempt to bring out in the next chapter, there is something attractive about this idealism, but it has the drawback of making pressing the question of how to cope with disagreements about what is morally right or wrong. So, in the next chapter, I shall also point to some contingent facts about us that may help us to deal pragmatically with these disagreements.

My characterization of morality as an inter-subjective sphere, as opposed to the intra-subjective sphere of prudence, needs to be further clarified in some respects. Although this conception of morality implies that one cannot act morally rightly or wrongly so long as only one's own desires are affected, it does not imply that the attitude of others to one's behaviour towards oneself is beyond the pale of moral judgement. Suppose that, in the name of some ideal, I am (rationally) about to make my life short and poor in respect of fulfilment. Then a utilitarian may correctly regard it as *morally* right for her to intervene because, to her, I am another and my behaviour is at odds with a requirement of fulfilment-maximization that she applies to all. It would be morally wrong of her to let me go ahead, but it does not follow that I am acting morally wrongly towards myself.

Michael Slote claims that "ordinary moral thinking seems to involve an asymmetry regarding what an agent is permitted to do to himself and what he is permitted to do to others" (1984: 181). For instance, according to common-sense morality, it is, he writes, "quite permissible to sacrifice one's own greater benefit to the lesser benefit of another" (1984: 180), but not another's greater benefit to save one's own smaller benefit. If an agent were to treat another better, his action could be described, in Slote's words, as "irrational", "stupid", and "gratuitous" (1984: 180). But, according to common sense, it would not be *morally* wrong, for he has done nothing wrong to *others*.

I agree that this behaviour would be irrational if the agent's reason is simply that the other is distinct from himself, but on the idealism I will espouse it would not be irrational if his reason consists in some qualitative difference that could constitute an ideal of his. On this idealism it could also be rationally permissible to favour one's own smaller benefit at the expense of a greater benefit of another. So, to be in line with what is rationally permissible, common-sense morality must allow some exceptions in one's own favour, as many think it does (cf. Samuel Scheffler's "agent-centred prerogatives", 1982: 5). In contrast, it never seems to count favouring others at one's own expense as morally wrong, though it may be irrational. Hence, what is morally wrong is at odds with what is irrational when oneself is disadvantaged.

Even if moral wrongness requires that another being than oneself is wronged, there need, contrary to Slote's feeling (1984: 185), be no tension between, on the one hand, the idea that one cannot act morally wrongly by sacrificing one's own greater good and, on the other hand, the idea that one has stronger moral obligations to people closer to one— kin, colleagues, etc.—than to strangers. For however closely related other people may be to one, they are still numerically distinct, and this fact may (allegedly) provide a foothold for moral obligations one cannot have to oneself. But if violations of a requirement of rationality, of personal neutrality, cannot be described as morally wrong if the agents themselves are disadvantaged, the word 'moral' is used to signal a distinction between oneself and others which we have found to be rationally unimportant. This is likely to make the word unsatisfactory for some systematic purposes, but it does not matter in the present context. For here we shall be exclusively concerned with the permissibility of actions that negatively affect others and, so, are indisputably qualified for moral appraisal.

A Requirement of Universalizability

Let me now state the rational requirement of impartiality or personal neutrality to which I have alluded. Suppose that *A* is biased towards herself rather than towards some other being *B* because, according to *A*'s view, she herself has the universal, or at least contingent, properties $P_1, \ldots, P_n$ that *B* lacks. This particular bias could manifest itself as follows: when *A* eliminates her own present pain rather than the more intense pain of *B*, she claims to do so because, in contrast to *B*, she is equipped with $P_1, \ldots, P_n$. Now, this bias satisfies the requirement of personal neutrality only if it is *universalizable* or can be extended to all others who possess the properties mentioned. So, in terms of such a bias, this requirement generates a (rational) *requirement of universalizability* that can be expressed as follows:

(RU)   *A*'s being biased towards herself rather than towards *B* because she, *A*, has $P_1, \ldots, P_n$
        which *B* lacks is cognitively rational only if: for every *X* not identical to *A*, if *A* were
        to contemplate a situation in which *X* is endowed with the properties $P_1, \ldots, P_n$, and

A lacks them, then, with respect to that situation, A would be as much more strongly biased towards X than towards herself as A now is more biased towards herself than towards B.

Thus, A's preference that her own milder pain be put to an end rather than the more intense pain of B, who lacks $P_1, \ldots, P_n$, is sanctioned by RU only if she would prefer that the milder pain of B rather than her own stronger one be relieved, if B had possessed $P_1, \ldots, P_n$, and A herself had been without them.

Against ideas similar in spirit to RU advanced by Hare, it has been objected—for example by Dancy (1981: 375–80)—that it is never possible to formulate sufficient reasons for a person's particular concern or liking for an object. For however fully one specifies the reasons, it is always possible to point to some further feature such that were it possessed by the object, it would undermine the attitude towards it, that is, such that its absence should be cited in the sufficient reason for the attitude.

In response to this objection, it should be noted, first, that, given a causal analysis of attitudes, this can be a problem only if there is in general a problem about specifying sufficient causal conditions. It would appear that, in practice, formulations of sufficient causal conditions must always encapsulate an 'other things being equal' clause, but it is not clear that the inclusion of such a clause would make them so indeterminate that one cannot as a rule settle what they are meant to exclude. Secondly, it should also be noticed that there is an alternative way of stating RU that sidesteps the need to spell out the grounds of A's attitude. As suggested by Hare, we could speak of 'every X which is similar to A in every respect save those that are essential to A's numerical identity'.[2] That many of the properties here alluded to would be irrelevant to A's attitude does not matter.

In whichever of these ways RU is formulated, it presupposes that one's bias towards oneself is not based on some property that in principle can belong only to oneself, such as the property of being (identical to) oneself. For if the bias were based on such a property, RU would bid one to contemplate a self-contradictory scenario—hence the indispensability of my argument to the effect that self-concern and self-approval are based on universal features of oneself, or at least on features that contingently belong to oneself. These are properties that one could conceivably lack and that some other beings could possess.

Against the background of this thesis about the motivational impotency of considerations of numerical identity, it may seem mysterious how RU could be a substantial constraint on para-cognitive attitudes, how it could rule out any attitudes, for its efficiency as a test appears to imply that a mere shift in respect of numerical identity could affect attitudes. When A imagines being in B's position of lacking $P_1, \ldots, P_n$, the only change that need occur would seem to be the shift in the numerical identity of the individual being without these properties. Thus, if this feat of imagination alters A's attitude towards the individual without $P_1, \ldots, P_n$, it seems the alteration must be occasioned by the change in respect of numerical identity. But this collides head-on with my thesis about the basis of attitudes.

---

[2] To be precise, Hare talks about exact similarity in respect of universal properties; see e.g. (1981: 63).

The effectiveness of RU cannot, however, depend on anything like A's imagining there to be identity-constituting continuities between herself at present and the being imagined to lack $P_1, \ldots, P_n$. For there would in fact be such continuities of which one must be conscious were one to consider how to act against oneself in the future, and yet, as I have indicated, one can be accused of failing to put oneself into the place of this future individual. The charge here would, however, not be to the effect that one has failed to imagine what it would be like if *oneself* were to suffer as the being at the receiving end will suffer, but rather that one has ignored imagining what it would be like if oneself were *now* to suffer like the patient.[3]

This charge gives the clue as to how RU could be an effective check on attitudes. It performs this task by demanding that one rectify the selectivity of representation involved in the P-bias and experiential anticipation, by *voluntarily* executing an act of imagination: by imagining having the universal features of another being as vividly as one represents one's present circumstances. This is not imagining that the *particular* subject of experience that is oneself has those features—that could easily be self-contradictory. But one is also *a* subject of experiences. When one imagines what it would be like to be in the place of another subject (or oneself in the future) and have the experiences that they have, one views oneself just in this respect, as *a* subject of experience which one imaginatively equips with whatever experiences and other features that the other subject is believed to possess. Thus what one imagines is a subject of experience having the experiences that another subject than oneself in fact has and perhaps being embodied the way it is. If one does not confuse imagining a subject having certain experiences with imagining *perceiving or experiencing* an (embodied) subject having these experiences, one realizes that the first is imagining what it is like 'from the inside' to have those experiences.

Pace Hare's conception of this procedure (a conception that was scrutinized in the foregoing chapter and to which I shall soon revert), I do not see it as essential that the subject doing the imagining keeps any properties which enable it to retain its numerical identity. Therefore, it is possible without any trace of incoherence for it to imagine being an individual who has a life-history that is entirely different from its own.

This is the test that RU demands that one's attitude to every affected being should be capable of passing. Briefly put, RU requires one to overcome the P-bias that makes one under-represent one's own future and the exclusiveness of experiential anticipation that makes one under-represent the future experiences of subjects to whom one is not related by ordinary survival. As the motivational impact of a representation is proportionate to its vividness or richness of detail, it is plain that to rectify the slant or selectivity of representation which defines the P-bias and experiential anticipation, by voluntarily imagining in vivid detail being in the positions of other affected parties, as RU demands, could alter one's attitudes towards these parties. In particular, it could augment one's concern for them.

---

[3] Schopenhauer maintains that when I am seized by compassion I feel the suffering of another "*as my own*, and yet not *within me*, but *in another person*" (1841 / 1995: 165). What if one pities oneself because of the suffering one will feel in the future: is this pain felt as mine, though not in me-now, but in me-in-the-future? No. The suffering which arouses compassion is not felt, but imagined, and it is imagined not as mine, but as the suffering of another. So there is no need to postulate that the numerical distinctness between us is ultimately unreal, as does Schopenhauer.

To exemplify, the fact that B lacks the valued properties $P_1, \ldots, P_n$ may have hindered A from vividly representing how intense the pain of B will be; perhaps A has just had the *verbal* thought that B will suffer a pain more acute than her own. If A now represents B's pain in all its concreteness, her sympathetic concern for the relief of this pain will be boosted. The result may be that it becomes so strong relative to A's concern to relieve her own present pain that the concern to relieve the pain of B is victorious. If this is the case, then, if A actually prefers to mitigate her own lesser pain, through a failure to subject herself to RU, she is governed by the cognitively irrational O-bias.

It should, however, be stressed that it is possible for A to stick to the preference to relieve her own lesser pain, although she has undergone the test laid down by RU. This is what happens when the having of $P_1, \ldots, P_n$ constitutes an ideal of A's. Suppose that the experience of pain interferes with the continued exemplification of these properties (suppose, for example, that one property is that of successfully pursuing philosophy). Then A's preference for relieving her own lesser pain for the reason that she is equipped with $P_1, \ldots, P_n$ will be defensible from the perspective of cognitive rationality if it can be sustained in the light of a vivid representation of the inside of B.

This situation, when the pain *interferes* with the esteemed activity of doing philosophy should be distinguished from that in which an eminent philosopher is feeling pain, but it does not interfere with her philosophizing. The ideal that the cause of philosophy be furthered only legitimizes that a smaller pain be relieved in the first situation. In the second situation, one could try to argue that such an eminent person *deserves* better than to suffer pain, but in Chapter 34 I shall contend that the concept of desert lacks application. I see no way of justifying the judgement that somebody pursuing an ideal be better off when this does not further the ideal pursued.

This is also my reply to Frances Kamm's claim that "those who resist the effect of vividness may do so because believe they have a *right* not to sacrifice themselves" (1996: 232; my italics). I shall try to undermine the applicability of the concept of a (natural) right in Chapter 34. But I would now like to stress that, even if we had rights to various things, RU would be in operation. For even if I had a right to something, X, it is reasonable to think that it would not be morally permissible for me to keep it to myself if somebody else needed it sufficiently much more than I do. And I think RU should be used to determine whether another's need for X is sufficiently stronger.

To sum up: in the foregoing chapter it was argued that it is not irrational to be an idealist in the domain of prudence. This rationally permits one, at the price of a greater pain that would be felt by one in the future, to favour the elimination of one's own present, lesser pain, if this better promotes one's ideals. As I have already argued, this is consistent with holding that temporal neutrality is rationally required, for this requirement must not be conflated with the prudentialist goal of a temporally neutral or inter-temporal maximization of one's own fulfilment. Now, I have also contended that a personal neutrality is rationally required in the sense that mere differences in respect of numerical identity of individuals are rationally insignificant. But again, it does not follow that in the domain of morality A could not relieve her own milder pain at the expense of B's more intense pain without violating personal neutrality by being O-biased. For A may not favour the mitigation of her own pain for the reason that the pain is *her own*, but for the reason that it is the pain of a person of a certain *universal type*, a person who has $P_1, \ldots, P_n$. If so, she is neutral as regards *particular* subjects or *personally neutral* or, in other words, she has risen above personally biased representation. *A* then exhibits the personal neutrality of RU, but, like what holds, *mutatis mutandis*, for temporal neutrality, personal neutrality does not commit one to a personally neutral maximization of fulfilment.

Peter Singer quotes J. L. Mackie's claim that, even if a person rejects objectivism and admits that things are of value only in so far as they are (or would be) desired, he "has no need to degrade an ideal which he endorses to the level of a mere preference, saying 'This matters only because I care for it' " (1988: 151). In opposition to this claim, Singer argues that subjectivism with respect to values undermines ideals:

> as long as we reject that there can be objectively true moral ideals, universalizability does require that we put ourselves in the place of others and that this must then involve giving weight to their ideals in proportion to the strength with which they hold them. (1988: 152)

It is precisely this inference that I have contested. In the context of a subjectivism of value, RU does *not* force the aim of a personally neutral maximization upon everyone. This aim only follows if one postulates a satisfactionalist aim that one accepts to subjugate to this requirement (as well as the requirement of temporal neutrality).

A Remark on Hare's Approach

My explanation of the procedure of imaginatively putting oneself into the place of another is profitably contrasted with Hare's account of the principle of hypothetical self-endorsement, PHS, outlined in the preceding chapter. Although he also insists on the importance of the vividness of representations (1981: 92), Hare assumes that the act of imagining oneself being in the circumstances of another has special effects which are due to the fact that the person in the imaginary situation is *oneself*. This assumption comes to light in his speculation about the prescriptivity of 'I'. It also surfaces in his explicit denial that the PHS involves the claim that the concern is directed onto the person actually in these circumstances (1981: 99).

In the foregoing chapter I argued that Hare's construct of the PHS is defective precisely because it encapsulates this assumption to the effect that self-directed attitudes are based on the representation of some being as *oneself*. I shall now supplement this with an argument to the effect that *if* Hare's explication had been correct, this would bring along certain consequences that are disadvantageous for him, consequences that will be absent if I am right about how imaginative identification works. These awkward consequences have to do with the fact that the PHS-generated sympathy exclusively concerns oneself in a hypothetical situation and is not transferable to the individual who *actually* is in this situation.

Some passages of Hare's efface the problem. Consider this succinct formulation of a central argument in (1981) which turns on the PHS and RU:

> To become moral is, first of all, to contemplate the hypothetical situation in which what are actually going to be the states of another person would be states of oneself, and thus to acquire a hypothetical concern for the satisfaction of oneself in that hypothetical situation, and then, because of universalizability to find oneself constrained... to turn this merely hypothetical concern into an actual concern for the satisfaction of the preferences of the actual other person. (1981: 223)

Clearly, a requirement of universalizability cannot constrain one to turn one's PHS-generated concern for oneself in a hypothetical situation into a concern for the actual person in whose situation one imagines being. This is impossible because the PHS-generated concern is supposed to be rooted in one's identification of the hypothetical individual as *oneself*, and the property of being oneself is not one that another individual can possess. As we have seen, RU can get a grip on an attitude only if it rests on the attribution of universal or at least contingent features. A PHS-generated attitude cannot be universalizable, since one cannot even imagine another individual with the property on which such an attitude is grounded, namely the property of being identical to oneself. (So if, as Hare claims, universalizability is a necessary condition for an attitude being moral, the proper conclusion to draw is that the PHS-generated sympathy is not a moral attitude.) In contrast, on my construal of the attitudes aroused by imaginative impersonation or identification, they will be based exclusively on universal properties of the actual individual whom one imagines being. Consequently the attitudes elicited will concern this actual individual.

The fact that there is no possibility of transmitting the PHS-produced concern to the actual beings impersonated has significant repercussions on Hare's project of going from universal prescriptivism to a version of utilitarianism by means of steps "all based on the logic of the concepts involved" (1981: 176; cf. 4, 111). For utilitarianism to result, it is plainly crucial that one be required to add up the strengths of preferences that have to do with different persons. Justifying this requirement poses no difficulty in the case of sympathetic preferences concerning actual beings, but, as I have argued elsewhere (1989), it does when they are directed to hypothetical beings who exist in different possible worlds.

Further Remarks on RU

I see, then, as little reason to hold that one is rationally required to maximize fulfilment and to abstain from ideals in the inter-personal sphere of morality as in the intra-personal one of prudence. So far as I can find, even if there is adequate vividness of representation, there is nothing to make irrational favouring the fulfilment of one's own present desires over the stronger desires that oneself will have in the future or that another has or will have, provided there is some qualitative difference that could constitute a reason for the preference. Just as the fact that temporal neutrality is required by cognitive rationality must not be taken to imply that a temporally neutral *maximization* is required, so the fact that a personal neutrality, as codified by RU, is required by cognitive rationality must not be confused with a personally neutral *maximization* being required. As we have seen, this would have been required if hedonism had been true and pleasure or satisfaction the only object of ultimately intrinsic desire.

Although prudence and morality are parallel to this extent, the latter brings along complications. One of them has to do with the way in which most of us thinks that *the number* of the patients involved affects the outcome of deliberation. Suppose that Sophie has the ideal that philosophy be furthered and that, without infringing rationality, she can prefer that she herself, who is a competent philosopher, escape having a milder pain when she is philosophizing at the price of one other individual who is not a philosopher, undergoing a somewhat intenser pain. Even so, there is, realistically (though not necessarily), some finite number of patients n such that Sophie cannot, without being irrational, prefer that she herself avoid the milder pain at the cost of each member of an n-membered group of non-philosophical patients suffering a somewhat intenser pain. This is so because, by subjecting herself to the procedure of imaginative identification, Sophie will form, for each other affected party, a desire that it not suffer pain, and so the opposition to her ideal will grow in strength with each party.[4]

Bringing in multilateral cases in which there are at least two (other) patients adds impetus to an objection that may have occurred to some readers. To carry out the activity of imaginative impersonation is surely a taxing task. Ideally, one should represent to oneself the experiences—of pain, etc.—of another as vividly as that individual itself represents them, for otherwise this experience has no chance of affecting one's own attitudes to the same degree as the attitudes of the other. But, it might be protested, we are incapable of performing such feats of imagination, and, as a result, our other-regarding desires will be weaker than they should in fairness be. Moreover, this defect is magnified if there are several patients to take into consideration. Besides, is there not something absurd about the idea of moral deliberation including a huge number of acts of imaginatively putting oneself into the position of another?

There is indeed, but a moral deliberator could get by, albeit not infallibly, without having to go through the procedure of sympathetic identification, except occasionally; it may function merely as an expedient to help one get hold of data from which one can extrapolate. Suppose that one knows, in an abstract way, how many the affected parties will be and the extent to which they will be affected; then, if in a single instance one has acquired something like a full sense of the innards of another, and knows what impact this has had on one's desires, one is equipped to calculate what impact a full sense of the reactions of all affected would have on one. (If the number of affected parties is n and their desires are equally strong, one knows, without having to go through n sympathetic acts, that the opposing desires will be n times as strong as would have been the case were

---

[4] This is so because, in contrast to the PHS-generated desires, these other-regarding desires can be added together since they are co-satisfiable; see Persson (1989).

there just one other party.) Given an intention to act on a deliberation that fairly takes everyone involved into account, this guess is sufficient to enable one to act roughly as one would act were one to act on the basis of such a deliberation (cf. Kagan, 1989: 288–91, 297–300). Of course, one is more than likely self-deceptively to underestimate the feelings and responses of others, but this is a shortcoming of ours that any moral method comes up against. The point here is just that the trick of imaginative identification is not useless by having an all-or-nothing character; it can be employed sparingly, in single instances, to quicken one's concern for others and thereby supply one with a ground for extrapolations that cater for more complex scenarios.

It should be noted, however, that talk of imaginative identification or impersonation is misleading because, when one imagines being in the place of another, one typically brings to bear a cognitive perspective wider than that of the target. For instance, if I put myself into the place of someone who is slandered behind his back, I have a piece of information that he necessarily lacks, namely, that he is slandered behind his back. (Indeed, such extra information is required to deal with the situations of several patients who might be unaware of each other.) Thanks to this extra bit, those desires that are capable only of factual fulfilment can be brought within the ambit of this method. This is as it should be since, as I contended in Chapter 10, such fulfilment is of value to the subject.

So, if we want to confine ourselves to the consideration of experiential fulfilment, this must be for other reasons. Hare wishes to do so when he "provisionally" excludes what he terms "external" preferences from the utilitarian calculus (1981: 104). But this exclusion is not necessitated by his construal of imaginative impersonation, the PHS, for if the basis of concern is that, in some hypothetical situation, one recognizes a desire to be *one's own*, external desires ascribed to oneself must also elicit concern, since they are as much one's own.

The method of moral deliberation that I have outlined presupposes that it is possible to gain knowledge of the strength of the desires of others in relation to the strength of one's own desires. Even if we suppose that it is possible to have knowledge of the minds of others to the extent that it can be ascertained that they possess certain desires and of how, intra-personally, they are ordered in respect of intensity, the inter-personal comparison is still troublesome. I shall not attempt to resolve any of these difficulties. Let me just point out that the method here sketched shares these difficulties with utilitarianism and with other plausible theories of morality, for surely they all have to weigh up the preferences of different subjects. We have to acknowledge that the subject matter of ethics is such that it would be illusory to hope for a decision-procedure that could be mechanically applied.

In conjunction with our tendency to be O-biased, the absence of any clear-cut way to make inter-personal comparisons of the strengths of desires is likely to make us overestimate the intensity of our own desires relative to the intensity of the desires of others. On the other hand, it should be borne in mind that we are here dealing with subjects who are willing to place themselves under a demand of personal (and temporal) neutrality. We do not need a foolproof method that even those who are O-biased to the point of not wishing to subject themselves to cognitive rationality in the inter-personal domain would have no chance of applying in a self-deceptive manner. Such a method would be of little use, since it is anyway relatively rational for O-biased persons to refrain from acquiring cognitively rational attitudes in this domain. It is therefore enough if we have a procedure that anyone who is honestly prepared to try to be personally neutral can reliably employ. I think that the method here espoused could satisfy this desideratum.

If I am right in that ideals are rationally permissible in the intersubjective or moral realm, and so that a personally neutral or utilitarian maximization does not follow, unless one has a satisfactionalist aim that one is willing to constrain rationally, what I have termed moral individualism results. Ideals are expressions of one's personality or individuality. They can be as multifarious as interests. They include not only the familiar, noble aims such as that human knowledge of the universe grow and that beautiful objects be created, but anything—such as diverse forms of athletics and craftmanship—in which we can take an interest intense enough to make us sacrifice fulfilment. Of course, anyone of us can have several ideals—or none, and so have the satisfactionalist master-aim of maximizing fulfilment. Thus, if ideals are legitimate in the moral sphere, the personality of each and every one of us can receive rational expression in this sphere. The result may seem likely to be a wide-ranging disagreement. To many this will look like a grave disadvantage of moral individualism, and indeed it is, though it may still be true that there is nothing stronger to put in its place. In the next chapter, I shall turn to the question of whether there are any factors that could mitigate the moral disagreement individualism makes possible and what I think is a compensating virtue of individualism, namely, the room it leaves for autonomy.

28

MORAL INDIVIDUALISM: AUTONOMY AND AGREEMENT

MANY believe in, or hope for, a *moral monism* to the effect that, if we were rational and fully informed, we would necessarily reach a consensus about what general principles of action (like the principle of utility) to apply in the intersubjective sphere and so, given that we also agree on factual matters, about what it is morally right to do in every situation. The theory towards which I have worked my way, however, contradicts such a monism. Instead it amounts to what I have called a moral individualism to the effect that no matter how rational and well-informed we are, we may disagree about what the correct principles are, and so about what it is right to do in concrete situations. Analogously, my theory of prudence allows that what one at one time correctly judges to be the best way one's life could go may conflict with what one at another time correctly judges as regards this matter. In this chapter, I shall suggest first that it is a merit that morality is under the reign of individualism, and secondly that the conflicts individualism allows may not be much of a problem in practice, since the aims of idealism and fulfilment maximization converge to a great extent.

Consider the following two claims that I have put forward:

(1) A (value-theoretical) *subjectivism* according to which what is of (non-derivative) intrinsic value is always of intrinsic value *for* some subject in the sense that it consists in the satisfaction of some (ultimately) intrinsic desire of a subject (remember, though, that this relativity leaves room for a distinction between personal and impersonal values).

(2) The possibility of *idealism*: although cognitive rationality requires that we be temporally and personally neutral in our moral or inter-personal concern about desire fulfilment (just as, with respect to prudence, it requires that we be temporally neutral as regards the fulfilment of our own desires), this does not rule out

idealism and constrain us to inter-temporally and inter-personally maximize fulfilment.[1]

As we have seen, some who accept subjectivism (or reject objectivism) believe this stance to leave no room for ideals (in the last chapter I quoted Peter Singer to this effect). Consequently, they have been led to endorse moral monism in the shape of utilitarianism (and in the prudential sphere in the shape of inter-temporal maximization). This is mistaken, but it is true that the value-theoretical relativity of subjectivism does not exclude monism, for it can be consistently coupled with the hedonist assumption that there is a homogeneity in respect of what are the objectives of ultimately intrinsic desires to the effect that pleasure and the avoidance of pain (etc.) are the only such objectives. If so, idealism would be ruled out, and, according to the argument so far (which leaves out considerations of justice to be introduced in Part V), rational people would land with the utilitarian aim. On the other hand, the value-theoretical absolutism or non-relativity of objectivism can scarcely entail monism and exclude individualism. For objectivists should surely acknowledge both the aims of rationalism and satisfactionalism, and it is unlikely that there would be an objectively valid ranking of these aims, so that all rational subjects (as conceived by objectivists) would necessarily resolve conflicts between them in the same way. Thus idealism stands in the way of monism, and it does not presuppose subjectivism. I have proceeded on the basis of subjectivism because I have no hold on objective values or reasons.

On my view, then, there is no guarantee that there be any unanimity among rational beings on what is morally (or prudentially) right. It could still be claimed that, although the aims of rationalism and satisfactionalism cannot rationally be ranked, only one of them—say, satisfactionalism—could properly be called 'moral' when it is constrained by temporal and personal neutrality. But this would merely be a linguistic circumstance of a rather shallow sort that would not change the fact that there is a disagreement which rationality cannot resolve. More important is the possibility that such a unanimity between rational persons about what is right in the intersubjective sphere of morality may still *in fact happen* to result. This is not excluded by moral individualism, for the purport of the claim that a theory is of this form is just that this unanimity is not ensured by what the theory entails. One chief claim of this chapter is that the inter-personal conflicts which individualism lets in, by providing room for ideals, can be resolved in favour of a policy which (setting aside considerations of justice) approximates to what utilitarianism recommends.

An Appeal to Autonomy

Before arguing for this claim, I would like to stress what I believe to be a merit of moral individualism. According to this doctrine, to make up one's mind rationally about what is morally right in an inter-personal situation is never just a matter of ascertaining the facts,

[1] As will appear in Part V, I believe that there is a dimension of morality to which there is no parallel in prudence, namely, justice. It is my view that cognitively rational satisfactionalists should accept, alongside a universal maximization principle, a principle of justice requiring equality. This is consistent with the present point which is that the requirements of neutrality are not sufficient to yield universal maximization.

for example, about what course of action will procure maximal fulfilment of all desires affected. It crucially involves one's own conative response to these facts. It is, to employ a Kantian turn of phrase, a matter of one issuing, upon the basis of one's desires, universal laws in the light of these facts. Autonomy in this sense enables moral individualism to sidestep an objection to which utilitarianism is exposed.

Consider, for instance, Bernard Williams's plea for the importance of "ground projects"—a person's ground projects being projects "which are closely related to his existence and which to a significant degree give a meaning to his life" (1981: 12). Williams criticizes the "impartial" moral theories of utilitarianism and Kantianism for their requiring, in the event of a clash between a ground project and a moral demand, the agent to give up the former. According to Williams,

> it is quite unreasonable for a man to give up, in the name of the impartial good ordering of the world of moral agents, something which is a condition of his having any interest in being around in that world at all. (1981: 14)[2]

If we assume that ground projects are universalizable, then, on moral individualism, they can be rationally accepted by individuals as guidelines in inter-personal or moral affairs. Hence, moral individualism provides room for something which is analogous to that feature of common-sense morality which Samuel Scheffler has called "agent-centred prerogatives" (1982: 5) in that it allows you to give greater weight to some of your aims than the goal of a wholly neutral maximization would. By means of its requirement of universalizability, RU, moral individualism supplies a means of distinguishing such favouring of oneself from immoral egoism or selfishness.

But moral individualism is not only capable of providing room for a sort of favouring of oneself, it also caters for the moral permissibility of the opposite trait we mentioned in the foregoing chapter: sacrificing a greater benefit to oneself to secure a smaller benefit to another. Again, this permission is given on the assumption that the reason for the sacrifice is that the other possesses some feature that passes RU, so that one would sacrifice the greater benefit of another to secure a lesser benefit to oneself were one instead to be equipped with this feature. Altruism, too, can be excessive, though this is of course much rarer than the excessiveness of egoism.

I am not claiming that common-sense morality and moral individualism provide space for autonomy in the shape of permissibility of both self-favouring and self-sacrifice for the same reason. As I noted already in the last chapter, common-sense morality seems to accomplish this by investing the distinction between self and others with moral significance. Moral individualism rejects this distinction as rationally unimportant, and by this means offers to set limit to what is acceptable self-favouring and self-sacrifice. In contrast, it is not clear how common-sense morality sets these limits. But the main point in this connection is that, according to moral individualism, the idea of autonomous choice gets more elbow room in morality than some monistic moral theories, like utilitarianism, allow for.

---

[2] Cf. Susan Wolf's objection to the goal of becoming a moral saint, i.e. a person who is "dominated by a commitment to improving the welfare of others or of society as a whole" (1982: 420) to the extent that one denies oneself as "an identifiable, personal self" (1982: 424).

The Possibility of Agreement

This allowance of autonomy is compatible with there *in practice* being an extensive convergence between idealism and fulfilment-maximization in the inter-personal domain. The main reasons for this convergence are the obvious facts that people are reciprocally dependent upon each other to achieve their aims and that they can influence the extent to which they will obtain the aid of other persons by giving aid in their turn. In other words, they can profit by entering into *reciprocal agreements* with each other to the effect that if one helps others in the pursuit of their aims, one will be helped by them in return. None of them is powerful enough to *coerce* all others to a subordination which is as effective in promoting one's own goals.

Let us consider a simple illustration of how this can work out: a conflict between an idealist whose position is that rationalism should be furthered as far as possible and a utilitarian. Imagine that both are in possession of unpleasant truths about the other, that is, truths that, if divulged to the other, would prevent the inter-temporal maximization of that individual's fulfilment, and thereby, we may assume, fulfilment overall. Then compliance with RU could sanction both the rationalist's telling the truth to the utilitarian and the utilitarian's withholding the truth from the rationalist. If both the rationalist and the utilitarian in this way, without infringing requirements of rationality, hinder the other's pursuit of her master-aim, they both lose out.

This is, however, a loss they need not incur. If both parties are sufficiently intelligent, they will adjust their treatment of the other to how they have been treated or to what they expect will induce the treatment they want to receive from the other. They will have an incentive to co-operate with each other, to enter into reciprocal agreements to the effect that one party should aid the other party in the pursuit of its aim, provided that the service be returned. For this will enable them to fulfil their respective master-aims to a greater extent than would be possible in the original situation of conflict. The rationalist may get the utilitarian to tell the truth about her if she suppresses the truth about the utilitarian.

So, as soon as some contingent facts—namely, the inter-dependence of rational agents and the possibility of a mutually advantageous co-operation—are put in place, an escape from the predicament sketched opens up. These facts make it relatively rational to enter into an agreement that resolves the conflict. Of course, it is not guaranteed that there be this happy resolution of all conflicts. But perhaps there is a conjecture which bolsters optimism: the variations in personalities and interests which give rise to these conflicts have been allowed to evolve, by and large, to the great extent we actually find among human beings only because they have a capacity to co-operate which enables them to profit collectively from this variation.

It should be noticed that the above agreement does not yield what is best from a utilitarian perspective: it will maximize the fulfilment of the rationalist's *present* desires, but that is not to say it will *inter-temporally* maximize her fulfilment which may necessitate abandonment of the ideal of rationalism. This agreement rather maximizes the success individuals have in leading the lives they at present autonomously choose. But since what people choose is often not wildly out of line with what will make their lives contain as much fulfilment as possible, and since violating people's autonomy is something of great personal disvalue, there may not be much difference in practice between these maximizing aims. Thus, in fact, the upshot of a theory that allows individualism in the moral or inter-personal realm may be pretty similar to that of a moral monism which prescribes utilitarianism.

This brings out one respect in which the parallel between prudence and morality breaks down (another is the respect of justice, to be broached in Part V): since the flow of causality is from the past to the future, there is an asymmetry in prudence which is lacking in morality. Later stages of oneself are in one's present hands to a greater extent than other people normally are, and one cannot properly collaborate with these stages of oneself. Hence, morality differs from prudence in that—apart from the requirement of imaginative identification with affected parties—it also includes taking into account how one's treatment of them will influence their future behaviour towards oneself and how one can meet these repercussions. Hence, the question arises how, taking these facts into account, it is relatively rational for one to act, given one's intrinsic aims, and it may be that how it is relatively rational for different parties to act tend to coincide.

The pragmatic way out of disagreements here outlined must not be confused with another sort of proposal. Many philosophers have appealed to our mutual dependency and ability to co-operate in attempting to lay *the foundation* of morality. This is a *constructivist* (or contractualist) approach to morality one of whose main historical proponents is Thomas Hobbes. As the name indicates, this position sees morality as analogous to law, as a device *constructed* or *invented* to solve inter-personal conflicts. It is an arrangement that it is relatively rational for us to adopt to achieve a reconciliation that suits our ends. The approach outlined here, however, is congruent with there being a morality consisting in inter-personal requirements and relations that hold independently of any such agreements.

There are two differences between constructivism and the agreements to which I have here appealed. Traditionally, constructivists regard the disagreements to be overcome as issuing from the unregimented desires of largely self-regarding or selfish persons. On the present proposal, since the relevant conventions do not create morality, the conflicts they may be a means of resolving may already be classifiable as moral, by virtue of being between desires that conform to certain inter-personal requirements. Secondly, I have been talking about *actual* agreements, but if constructivism is to avoid the well-known trap of failing to offer adequate moral protection for those who have weak negotiating positions, they have to talk about agreements under some suitable *hypothetical* circumstances. This move seems unable to deal with the even harder problem of protecting sentient beings incapable of entering into agreements. But I will not attempt to explore the prospects of constructivism.

I believe that there is a common-sense morality which comprises the following elements. First, there are, fairly weak, moral reasons of *benevolence* and, perhaps somewhat stronger, reasons of *compassion*, that exhort us to aid others and, in particular, relieve their suffering. Secondly, common-sense morality provides space for *autonomy*, not only in respect of one's own life, but also in respect of treatment of others, as we have just seen. Thirdly, this morality has *deontological features*, expressible in terms of the act-omission doctrine and the doctrine of the double effect, which imply that we are more responsible for what we actively cause, especially if it is intended. Fourthly, it endows us with *rights* and corresponding *duties* or *obligations*, generally of a negative kind. Fifthly, common-sense morality takes us to be more or less *deserving*. The last two elements are subsumable under the category of *justice*.

In my view, it is the task of moral philosophy first to articulate these elements and then to explore how they fare in the light of requirements of reason, like RU. How they fare in the light of these requirements is a matter of fact that has nothing to do with any agreements. In this part of the book, I have to some extent tested the rationality of the second idea of autonomy, and in the next part, I shall to some extent do so with respect to the last three features, especially the notion of desert. But, as I made clear already in the Introduction, no fuller picture of morality is attempted.

Nor do I here wish to argue about what the meaning of the term 'moral' is. I have used the word to designate the domain in which sentient beings other than oneself are affected. I am also inclined to think that if others are treated worse than one treats oneself owing to some form of cognitive irrationality, this treatment is morally wrong. So far as I can see, such a use would not prejudge any questions of substance. For instance, in claiming that O-biased maximization in the intersubjective sphere, which is cognitively irrational, is morally wrong, one would not be insinuating that this position is inferior in any way that must matter to adherents of it. All that matters to them is to be relatively rational in implementing their O-biased ends, not whether these ends are cognitively rational. I would concede that it may be rational for prudentialists in the only sense of rationality that need impress them—that is, the relative sense—not to comply with morality.

True, it is conceivable—as will be indicated in the next chapter—that prudentialists be placed in such circumstances that it will be relatively rational for them to be more personally neutral. But it is not the topic of this book to explore these circumstances, just as it is not its topic to fully explore the circumstances, outlined above, under which relative rationality can overcome the disagreements made possible by moral individualism. The topic of this book is to explore what the application of requirements of cognitive rationality—in this part, the requirement of personal neutrality or impartiality, RU— entails for rationalists and satisfactionalists, respectively. The conclusion is that it does not drive rationalists, as it does satisfactionalists, in the direction of a fully neutral maximization because for the former idealism is possible in the inter-personal sphere of morality, no less than in the private sphere of prudence. The next question to be raised is the central one of whether the aim of a fully neutral maximization rationally requires as strict an observance of personal neutrality as does rationalist idealism.

29

THE DILEMMA AS REGARDS
PERSONAL NEUTRALITY

SINCE the notion of our identity involves false assumptions about our bodies, to the effect that they are identical to the subjects of our experiences, the O-bias, which is a bias towards an individual simply because that individual is oneself, cannot be cognitively rational. Moreover, this bias would not be rational even if animalism, some form of (matter-based) psychologism, or immaterialism were correct accounts of our identity. But a belief in identity is not in itself our reason for being O-biased. We exhibit this bias because the P-bias and the selectivity of our capacity for experiential anticipation make us represent what things are like for other affected beings less vividly. This causes us to violate RU.

It might be that if we were to conform to RU, we would still be in a position to favour the fulfilment of our own desires. But this favouritism would then no longer rest on a selective representation triggered by the belief that the being favoured is oneself, but on certain universal features which we believe ourselves to possess. This would no longer be the O-bias as I understand it, but would be a personally neutral attitude in concord with cognitive rationality.

Now, we cannot here raise a question with respect to RU which is parallel to a question that in Part III was asked about the rational requirement of temporal neutrality. There it was asked whether it would be relatively rational for prudentialists, who have subjected their goal to this requirement, to rid themselves completely of all temporal biases that naive or untutored prudentialists display, for example, when they succumb to weakness of will in the shape of choosing a smaller, closer good. It was concluded that, though it would be relatively rational for these prudentialists to try to become more cognitively rational by restraining their natural temporal partiality towards the present and near, it would not be relatively rational for them to try to live up more fully to the requirement of temporal neutrality, by ridding themselves completely of all temporal biases, for the gains, if any, in respect of fulfilment when this goal of temporal neutrality is attained could not possibly outweigh the sacrifices incurred on the way to this goal. Thus, relatively to prudentialism, it will be rational only to try to check inborn temporal biases to *some* degree, to internalize or instil some rules demanding a limited temporal neutrality. Consequently, prudentialists will part ways with rationalists who of course are rationally required to strive to be fully cognitively rational, whatever the cost in respect of their inter-temporal fulfilment.

We cannot here raise a parallel question as regards the rational requirement of personal neutrality. For, unlike the requirement of temporal neutrality, this requirement dissolves the prudential goal with its personal bias. If this requirement of personal neutrality is imposed, this goal will transform into the goal of inter-personal maximization. So we should not be asking to what extent it could be relatively rational for prudentialists to try to comply with the requirement of personal neutrality. In some unusual circumstances, it may be rational for them to achieve some compliance in this respect. This might be so if they were placed in a society of altruists to whom their motives were transparent and who possessed effective means to retaliate on anyone cheating.

The question we should be posing is instead whether it is rational for inter-personal fulfilment-maximizers, who have imposed the requirement of personal neutrality, RU, along with that of temporal neutrality, on their satisfactionalist aim to try to rub out their O-biases completely. We shall arrive at a conclusion analogous to the one drawn in Part III with respect to prudentialism and temporal biases: relative to this aim, it is rational to restrain these biases, but not to make the great effort of totally obliterating them.[1]

Rationalists will not ultimately strive to make *themselves*, their own attitudes, as cognitively rational as possible, but to make it the case that there is as much rationality in the world as possible. Thus they may fulfil the rationalist aims of others no less than their own. Suppose, however, as I think may well be true, that they can promote the rationality of the world most efficiently by improving in the first instance on the rationality of their own para-cognitive attitudes. Then it will be relatively rational for them to seek a perfect attitudinal compliance with the requirement of personal neutrality.

It would not be rational for inter-personal fulfilment-maximizers to seek this. Granted, if these maximizers could instantaneously purge themselves of the O-bias (and of temporal biases), it might be relatively rational for them to do so, because they would thereby transform themselves into more efficient instruments to the cause of inter-personal maximization. But, of course, such instantaneous changes are not actually possible. Quite the contrary, it is obvious that we are so thoroughly infected with personal and temporal biases that to disinfect ourselves we must spend a great part of our lives single-mindedly or fanatically pursuing a rigorous programme of self-training. It does not seem unreasonable to conjecture that during this period one's contribution to satisfaction overall will be so far below one's maximum that it will not be compensated for by one's later possible prowess as a do-gooder. Add to this that, since the state of neutrality is so hard to attain, one must reckon on a sizeable risk of failing miserably and causing oneself to suffer some sort of mental breakdown or disorganization. It will then be realized that,

---

[1] Cf. Parfit on how theories like the self-interest theory and consequentialism may be "indirectly self-defeating" (1984: ch. 1).

with the possible exception of some extraordinary specimens who can be confident of their exceptional moral fibre, it will be relatively rational for aspiring inter-personal maximizers to set their aim lower than that of having para-cognitive attitudes that are perfectly personally neutral.

Like prudentialists who strive to combat temporal biases only to the extent that they manifest themselves in harmful instances of *akrasia*, the would-be personally neutral maximizers should try to internalize rules that prevent merely the grossest forms of neglect of the fulfilment of others. These agents should not attempt to be motivated only by reasons that pass such requirements as RU. In order for it to be relatively rational for one to attempt to abolish the O-bias completely, it is necessary for one to endorse rationalism as an ideal. It is not rational relatively to the master-aim of fully neutral fulfilment-maximizing, that is, satisfactionalism bridled by the rational constraints of temporal and personal neutrality.

At this juncture, it might be interjected that not even the most devoted rationalists could rationally strive to conform to RU because it imposes obviously excessive demands on the powers of imagination: we cannot ever completely neutralize the P-bias and represent the phenomenal world of *one* other being as vividly as our own, but nonetheless RU requires that we put ourselves into the places of hordes of other individuals! As already remarked in Chapter 27, however, RU requires nothing as grossly impossible as our simultaneously having big clusters of phenomenal worlds before our minds. In order to find out whether my initial preference to favour myself at the expense of several other (not relevantly dissimilar) beings passes the test of RU, I could proceed as follows. I first imagine what, subjectively, the favoured course of action would be like to one individual in this collective. I then compare the strength of this subject's aversion to the treatment proposed with that of my original preference for it. Suppose that the latter comes out slightly ahead. It is then most unlikely that it will come out ahead if the number of other parties is more than one. So, in all likelihood, my initial preference will prove not to be a rational one.

It may be true that we cannot entirely counteract the P-bias, by representing the inner worlds of others as vividly as our own present one, and that this fact is likely to make us prey to a selfish partiality that will distort our generalizations and consequent moral judgements. Still the hardest part is, I think, to stick to these impartial judgements in action and not give in to the P-bias. Imagine that one reaches the conclusion that, rather than relieving one's own excruciating pain, one should relieve the equally acute pains of several others (this is not a conclusion that is difficult to arrive at). When the pain is at its worst, it requires an almost superhuman effort not to backslide and relieve one's own pain. It is this task, of making personal neutrality motivationally dominant by keeping the relevant judgement steadily before the mind, that will present the greatest obstacle to prospective rationalists.

It might be helpful to end with a review of possible stances as regards personal and temporal neutrality. By nature, we are naïve prudentialists who are in the grip of cognitively irrational personal and temporal biases. From this point of departure, there are the following stages of ascending rationality:

(1) prudentialists who are cognitively rational to the extent of imposing the requirement of temporal neutrality on their satisfactionalist aim and who restrain their temporal biases to the extent that is rational relative to this aim;

(2) inter-personal maximizers who are cognitively rational to the greater extent of imposing also the requirement of personal neutrality on their satisfactionalist aim and who put a restraint on their temporal and personal biases to the extent that is rational relative to this rationally purified fulfilment aim;

(3) rationalists who uphold rationalism as an ideal and who suppress their temporal and personal biases to the extent this aim makes relatively rational, for example, even when this conflicts with the satisfactionalist aim stated in (2).

In this fourth part I have claimed, first, that there is a requirement of cognitive rationality demanding personal neutrality. Secondly, that this requirement will not lead to an acceptance of inter-personal fulfilment-maximization unless we are satisfactionalists. Thirdly, that it is rationally permissible to endorse rationalism as an ideal that contravenes the satisfactionalist aim. Fourthly, that whereas this ideal makes it relatively irrational not to try to overcome the O-bias completely, this is not so given the satisfactionalist goal of inter-personal maximization. On the rationalist alternative, reason forces us into a retreat far from everyday life and feeling; on the satisfactionalist alternative, reason itself is forced to retreat from the claim to shape our para-cognitive attitudes fully.

In the next part it will emerge that there are further deep-seated attitudes, that have to do with desert and responsibility, which reason in the form of cognitive rationality demands that we sacrifice. The outcome of this fifth part will be that the goal of inter-personal (and inter-temporal) maximization is rationally defective in leaving out of consideration justice in the form of equality.

PART V

Rationality and Responsibility

the pursuit of ideal justice seems to conduct us to such a precipice of paradox
that Common Sense is likely to abandon it

(Henry Sidgwick, 1907/1981: 284)

30

INTRODUCTION

Iᴛ has been thought that a non-reductionist or immaterialist view of us is necessary for us to be free in the sense required by the ascription of full responsibility, that is, responsibility which entails desert and makes proper certain attitudes like resentment, gratitude, indignation, etc. For instance, Galen Strawson writes:

> There must be a 'mental someone' if there is to be a free agent, because it is the mental someone that is the true subject and object of our attitudes, ascriptions, and practices of approval and disapproval, responsibility and desert, and praise and blame—the true subject, most generally, of our interest, in so far as we are interested in what we take to be a truly responsible agent.[1]

A "mental someone" is "a thing which has some sort of singleness considered purely in its mental aspect—even if it also has, and believes itself to have, singleness considered in its physical or overall psycho-physical aspect" (1986: 155). It is in fact a mental substance in my sense of something mental that transcends and exists independently of its particular mental states (cf. Strawson, 1986: 324–6). Strawson does not deny that, if there is a "mere bundle of beliefs, desires, attitudes, and so on, tied to a single body" (1986: 162), this is sufficient to constitute a "single agent", but without a mental substance there cannot be free agency (in the above sense).

This non-reductionist view of personal agents enters into the free-will controversy because it may seem indispensable for a defence of a sort of *ultimate self-determination* without which there cannot be responsibility in the full desert-entailing sense. Suppose that determinism is true, that is, that given the total state of the world at any past time and its laws, it is (causally) determined what the future of the world will be like. Then, if you are responsible for having a certain property *F* (e.g. for having performed a certain action), this will be determined by the exemplification of certain responsibility-giving properties. You may be responsible for the exemplification of these properties, too, but since you have not existed forever as a responsible agent, this regress of responsibility cannot be infinite: there have to be some properties, the exemplification of which determines your being responsible for having *F*, though you are not responsible for their being

---

[1] (1986: 163). Strawson here intends to depict the view of common sense and not to express his own view.

exemplified. In other words, *ultimately* you are not responsible; you do not have that ultimate self-determination, which will be seen to be required for desert-entailing responsibility.[2]

Nor will ultimate responsibility be salvaged if gaps of indeterminism are merely inserted into this story, e.g., if responsibility-giving properties, for which you may not be (fully) responsible, are thought not to determine fully the outcome that you have F.[3] For it is not clear how you can be responsible for having F because this is partly a matter of chance. We need something—the mental substance that is you—to step into the gap of indeterminism and see to it that you will have this property. If this entity's interference is not caused by any events, your responsibility for having F will to some extent be ultimate. In view of its ontological status, this (mental) substance rises above the fateful dichotomy of the determined and the merely random if it makes no sense to ask whether its operation is caused (by events).

This line of thought is central to this part of the book and it will be more carefully scrutinized in Chapter 34, a chapter devoted to showing that we are not in fact equipped with that sort of ultimate responsibility and self-determination to which our ascriptions of desert commit us. It might be asked why we employ notions, like that of desert, which presuppose such extraordinary conditions as that of ultimate responsibility to be applicable. In Chapter 36, I use the conclusions of Chapter 6 to argue that the cognitions of agent-oriented emotions encapsulate a less fanciful notion of *epistemically* ultimate self-determination. The causes of some of our properties are so evasive that, pre-reflectively, we abstain from inquiring into them. When, at a more reflective stage, we do inquire into these causes, this epistemic notion of ultimacy is of course left behind, but, as the argument indicated above shows, there is no applicable notion of *ontically* ultimate self-determination to replace it.

The outcome of this rejection of ultimate responsibility and self-determination is that we deserve nothing, no praise and blame, no reward and punishment, and that emotions like anger and gratitude, pride and shame, admiration and contempt cannot rationally be felt towards us. In Chapter 37 I explore the possibility and rationality of revising our reactions in accordance with these findings. It is not hard to see that we have here entered into yet another area in which there is a clash between rationalism and satisfactionalism: rationalism makes life hard for us by requiring us to uproot cognitively irrational ways of thinking and feeling that are quite central to our human nature. Daniel Dennett, for one, is then wrong in believing, in the context of the free-will issue, that "the common wisdom about our place in the universe is roughly right" (1984: 19). The concepts of ultimate responsibility and self-determination and desert, embraced by "the common wisdom", must be discarded, and for rationalists this makes imperative a disturbing

---

[2] However, the logical possibility of agents with an infinite past for which they have been responsible makes it arguable that the notion of ultimate responsibility or self-determination—contrary to Strawson (1986: 29)—is not *logically* absurd.

[3] G. E. M. Anscombe (1981) and van Inwagen (1983: 138–41) have argued that 'causes' does not imply '(causally) determines (or necessitates)', but this view seems to leave it unexplained why 'causes' is a success-verb, which entails the occurrence of that which is said to be caused. Therefore I shall take indeterminism to mean that the exemplification of nothing causes your having F, though something may cause this to be possible and probable.

attitudinal adjustment. A more reflective and scientific outlook therefore poses a genuine threat to the common-sense world-view.

None of this is, however, meant to establish that the *whole* of concept of responsibility is rendered inapplicable; in fact, the argument against ultimate responsibility presupposes the applicability of a concept of responsibility, 'direct' responsibility. In Chapters 32 and 33 I shall start to unravel the concept of responsibility from an angle which is clearly compatible with the world being deterministic. If I say that you are responsible for the occurrence of some event, I make a normative claim to the effect that you are related to this occurrence in such a way as to make it *right* or *justifiable* to let you respond, or answer, to criticism for it having occurred. Like the word 'criticism', I think there is a negative slant to 'responsibility'; it is more at home when the event is of a kind that makes blame or punishment proper. But for systematic purposes it is convenient to talk of responsibility also in cases in which it is proper to give positive criticism, that is, to praise and reward the agent. I shall henceforth refer to this practice of applying positive or negative sanctions as 'the R(eward)–P(unishment) practice'. Negative sanctions may then be felt to be more closely associated with the notion of responsibility;[4] the reason for this could be that they are apt when some requirement is contravened, whereas the fact that there is compliance with a requirement may not be sufficient to make praise or reward in order. This may take something 'beyond' what is required, something supererogatory.

How do you have to be related to an occurrence to be responsible for it, that is, for it to be right or justifiable to let you respond to (positive or negative) criticism for it? First, you must in some way have causally contributed to it or, in other words, be causally responsible for it. Secondly, you must be capable of understanding why your being causally responsible for this occurrence is thought to justify this criticism of you. Thirdly, the state in virtue of which you are causally responsible for this event must be modifiable in the light of an understanding of this criticism, so that you may act differently in the future, for example a reward will encourage you to engage in similar types of conduct, while punishment will discourage you.

Applications of the R–P practice may be justifiable by reference to such behavioural consequences, if they are beneficial overall. This sort of *forward-looking* justification is obviously compatible with determinism, and Chapters 32 and 33 will be dedicated to the spelling out of such compatibilist conditions that are sufficient—indeed more than sufficient—for the applicability of the R–P practice from the forward-looking perspective. One objection to this analysis is answered in Chapter 35, namely, that it needs to be modified to account for the deontological intuition according to which we are more responsible for what we do or actively cause than passively let happen and for what we do with intention than with foresight.

For present purposes, a more serious objection to the justification of the R–P practice from a forward-looking perspective is that it is not enough for the attribution of responsibility. It is also necessary, some will hold, that we *deserve* to be rewarded or punished or that it is *just* so to treat us. In other words, a justification from the point of view of justice is requisite, too. As we shall see, this form of justification is typically *backward-looking*: it demands that there be something in the past in relation to which applications of the

---

[4] This fact is also noted by Wallace (1994: 61).

R–P practice are justly proportionate. This justification requires more than that one be responsible in virtue of a state that is modifiable in the light of criticism, that is, direct responsibility; it requires that one be responsible in virtue of such a state and for this state not to be caused by any states of one which are not in this way modifiable, that is, ultimate responsibility. Otherwise, applications of the R–P practice cannot be just.

It would not be just, for instance, to reward those babies who cause their mothers little pain when born and punish those who cause much pain, for this is due to circumstances for which the babies cannot be responsible. But if determinism is true, then everything about us adults is in the end due to such causes for which we are as little responsible as neonates, since these causes must be present before we even begin to exist. That is to say, we cannot exhibit that ultimate responsibility and self-determination which the backward-looking justification of applications of the R–P practice (as deserved and just) demands.

There are, then, two parts of the determinist challenge to responsibility, a prospective part and a retrospective part. Looking ahead and deliberating about what to do, we must believe that more than one alternative is open to us. Determinism might seem to undercut this belief. As will transpire in Chapters 31, 32, and 33, it does not. Despite determinism, deliberation can occur and exercise an influence on action. The forward-looking justification of responsibility is on safe ground. But since this vindication is compatibilist, and does not establish that it is causally possible for us to act otherwise, it implies that there may be causes of the conditions of this direct responsibility which we can trace backwards until we reach causes beyond our responsibility. So we may have to conclude that we are not ultimately responsible if determinism is true. This would undercut the backward-looking justification of responsibility. Hence, the compatibilist rebuttal of the prospective challenge leaves the door open for the triumph of the retrospective challenge.

It might be interjected that modern physics gives us little reason to believe that determinism is true. For this reason, I shall in my argument against ultimate responsibility only assume that determinism is true to the extent that our practice of holding people responsible and the applicability of causal notions of our practical vocabulary (such as the notions of para-cognitive attitudes and intentional action) are not threatened. Some—for example Hobart (1934)—have thought that responsibility requires the truth of determinism, but others have convincingly argued that the control presupposed by responsibility can be reconciled with indeterminism in some respects. For instance, I think that the "modest libertarianism" put forward by Alfred Mele (1995: ch. 12), according to which there is a doxastic indeterminism consisting in it being undetermined which beliefs become occurrent in deliberation, does not upset direct responsibility. But indeterminism to this extent cannot rescue ultimate responsibility.

When in everyday contexts there is talk of responsibility, or it being justifiable to apply the R–P practice, both the forward-looking and the backward-looking justifications are called into play. This means that if it is revealed that one type of justification is impossible, we may feel—as incompatibilists apparently do—that there is no responsibility, that the R–P practice cannot be justified. But this is not the whole truth, for the forward-looking justification is possible, and so in an attenuated sense we are responsible. We are, as I shall put it, directly, but not ultimately, responsible.

31

PREDICTABILITY AND THE EXPERIENCE OF FREEDOM

It might be thought that if the sphere of mind and action is under the dominion of determinism, the activity of deliberation is threatened. If determinism reigns to this extent, it is not both causally possible that you perform a certain action and causally possible that you refrain from it. But it may seem that you can deliberate about whether to perform an action or to refrain from it only if you believe that you can perform it and believe that you can refrain from it. If it is settled what you will do, what is the point of deliberating?

The reply might be that the 'can' presupposed by deliberation does not express a causal possibility. Instead it may express an *epistemic* possibility, that something is a possibility relative to your beliefs. Even if it is only causally possible that you act in one way, it might be both epistemically possible (relative to your beliefs) that you act in this way and epistemically possible that you refrain from this act, if you are ignorant of the causes that determine the outcome.

Nonetheless, this defence is brittle if there is no principled ground for why you must be ignorant of these causes. For then the possibility of deliberation hinges on the contingency of your ignorance. If you had been omniscient, like God, deliberation would have been ruled out.

Events that are Unpredictable in Principle

I shall now argue that there is such a principled ground for ignorance. More precisely, I shall defend the following claim about unpredictability in principle:

(P) At every time at which there exist predictors, there is some mental event the occurrence of which is not in principle predictable for them *at that time*, namely, what they themselves will think the very next moment.

This is so, I shall contend, because at every time the full proximate causes of what these predictors will think in the most immediate future are in principle outside the reach of their knowledge at that time.

The fact that these causes cannot be known in principle at every time clearly does not imply that they are not there to be known, however. If nothing could be a fact unless, at every time, it were in principle possible to know it to be a fact, it could not be a fact that there are no conscious beings in the universe at some time, for it is in principle impossible that this be known to be a fact at that time. But that this is in principle knowable at other times suffices to show that it can be a fact. Likewise, if, as I think is the case, some mental event has sufficient causes that are in principle unknowable at one time, but are in principle within the ambit of knowledge at some other times (earlier or later ones), these causes are there to be known. Therefore (P) does not tell against the truth of determinism.

The train of thought lying behind (P) runs along the following lines.[1] Whatever the content of the thought p, in thinking p one logically cannot think that one is currently thinking p. It follows that, for at least some of one's current thoughts, one cannot think of or be conscious of having them. For suppose that the content of all my present thoughts is p; then, if I think that the content of all my present thoughts is p, it will no longer be just p, but p *plus* the proposition that the content of all my present thoughts is p.

Moreover, if there is some present thought of one's such that it is necessarily true that one cannot at present think that one is having it, one cannot think that the effects of one's having it may be this or that. Consequently, if I were to ransack the contents of my mind and were to base on the upshot of this inventory (among other things) a forecast of my future conscious life and its behavioural embodiments, there would be things that I would necessarily have to leave out: the making of this inventory, the prediction based on the content of the inventory, and the possible effects of these mental operations. Now, since I know that some of my thoughts have effects on my future thoughts and behaviour, I cannot a priori exclude the possibility that my making the inventory and the prediction has such an impact. Therefore, it would be irrational of me fully to trust the accuracy of my prediction: a prediction cannot be regarded as completely reliable if it leaves out of consideration some factor that may be of relevance to the event predicted. The conclusion of the present argument is, then, that one is logically barred from reliably predicting one's own future to the extent that it could be influenced by one's present thoughts. (Of course, the argument does not show that it is in principle impossible to predict aspects of one's own future that are independent of one's thoughts or will, for example one's swallowing involuntarily or perspiring.)

In reply to this it has been contended that, although *I* cannot reliably forecast thought-sensitive aspects of my future, *other* persons could logically do so. To be sure, these persons could not reliably forecast thought-sensitive aspects of their own futures, but it would seem possible for them to take precautions that will rule out that their futures mingle with mine. Therefore, the considerations adduced do not suffice to show that

[1] The ultimate inspiration for these reflections is the remarks on "the systematic elusiveness of 'I'" in Ryle (1949: 195–8). For a recent exposition of this argument, see Bok (1998: 79 ff.).

thought-sensitive aspects of my future are in principle unpredictable; they only demonstrate that they are in principle unpredictable *by me*.

This reply does not go to the heart of the matter, however. For it grants that, for every predictor, there is something that is in theory unpredictable, namely, the predictor's own thought-sensitive future. Now, we can form the conception of an event or state of affairs that will encapsulate the thought-sensitive futures of *all* predictors. This event or state of affairs cannot be reliably predicted by *anyone* (on the proviso that the argument presented is sound). It is in principle beyond the reach of reliable prediction.

Since this reply does not remove the obstacle to predictability, but merely so to speak blows it up on a larger scale, let us return to the simpler personal case of people who predict their own futures. Another objection to the argument against predictability in this case is this. As John Thorp (1980: 79) points out, instead of trying to base my prediction on what is true of me (and my mind) *at present*, I could erect it on what was true of me at some time *in the past*, say, a minute ago. If determinism is true, there will be at this past time, no less than at the present time, a sufficient cause of what will happen to me from now onwards. But there is no bar in principle to my having exhaustive information about the content of my mind at some time in the past, for here the mental act of reviewing is not part of that which is to be reviewed.

This objection is sound, but it can be circumvented. It might be retorted that in order reliably to predict my thought-sensitive future right back to the moment *immediately succeeding the present one*, I need information about what my mind is like at present, for what is present to my mind now will also be present—in short-term memory—to my mind the very next moment. The continuity of conscious content, CCT, consists in something more intimate than one mental episode immediately succeeding another; in the succeeding state, there is also short-term memory of its immediate predecessor. But we have seen that I cannot possibly be exhaustively informed about the present content of my mind. Hence I cannot reliably predict my thought-sensitive future up to the present moment, because I cannot have full knowledge of its proximate cause, and this cause is reflected in the event to be predicted. That is, (P) is true.

I believe this reasoning to be irrefutable. In conjunction with the argument three paragraphs back, it entails that there is at least one state of affairs that, at present, cannot be reliably predicted *by anyone*, to wit, how the thought-sensitive futures of *all* predictors will be the very next moment—and the following moments so long as the inaccessible elements are mentally reflected.

For deliberation, it is, however, the principled unpredictability of one's own immediate, thought-sensitive future that is crucial. It ensures that it *must* be for one both epistemically possible that one (intentionally) performs a certain act the next moment and epistemically possible that one abstains from this. Thereby, it guarantees the possibility of deliberation.

I surmise that this impossibility of predicting one's own thought-sensitive future back to the present moment, of devising a prediction in accordance with which one's immediate future will unswervingly unfold is to a great degree responsible for the impression we have of our immediate thought-sensitive future as being free in a contra-causal sense, of ourselves as a kind of entity

> which is in some way essentially over and above all its particular motives, and which is therefore capable of making decisions independently of, and in the light of, those motives. (G. Strawson, 1986: 61–2; cf. Searle, 2001: ch. 3)

We could perhaps imagine ourselves to have a sort of split consciousness that allowed us to monitor our own current deliberations and their behavioural effects. But if so, this monitoring must be thought to be insulated from having any effects on our future thoughts and (intentional) behaviour. Then, in theory, if determinism is true, predicting one's future thoughts and intentional behaviour could be on a par with predicting that one will soon break into sweat when one has been locked up in a sauna or that one will soon blink when a dazzling light is about to be flashed into one's eyes (though in practice the former predictions will turn out to be a much more complicated matter). Under these circumstances, I think we would not feel much freer or self-determined in respect of our future intentional actions than we now do *vis-à-vis* our breaking into sweat in the sauna or blinking when we are subjected to a dazzling light. We would not feel our future intentional actions to be self-determined, because we would see our future intentions and the consequent acts as flowing from external events like the sweating and blinking.

In fact, our introspective awareness is itself causally potent. So we must react to this awareness in one way or another (even if it will be by indifference), and our reaction will not be a reaction determined simply by the thoughts of which we are aware. Thus we cannot see our thoughts and intentional actions as flowing inevitably from these thoughts of which we are aware, along the channels we may have predicted. At least partially, I think this accounts for the feeling of freedom with respect to them. But of course the fact that it is beyond our capacity to see our future thoughts and intentional actions as a causal outflow does not prove that it is false that they *are* such an outflow. Our intuitive feeling of being free or undetermined should not be taken as a proof that we *are* free and undetermined, since on the explanation I have offered we would have this feeling even if determinism were true.

It should be noted, though, that there is a way of making predictions of thought-dependent aspects of one's future that is immune to the difficulty discussed above: rendering them conditional. Suppose that I have made an inventory of the current content of my mind and other factors that may be relevant to the question of whether I shall perform a certain intentional action. Suppose further that I cast my prediction in a hypothetical form: *if* I and my environment are as described in the inventory, I shall perform the action. Such a prediction cannot be rendered unreliable or false by the possibility of my making this prediction altering the outcome; it can only prevent me and the circumstances from meeting the specifications of the antecedent.

The fact that we are in a position to make hypothetical predictions of different sorts is important. If we had not been able to predict, in some detail and with some degree of probability, what would happen if we were to perform a certain action, we would have been in possession of no reasons for or against performing it; rational deliberation about whether or not to execute it would be impossible.

Mental Events not Experienced as Causally Related

There are, however, other circumstances that probably contribute to our sense of freedom as regards the thought-dependent aspects of our future. I believe that the common-sense concept of a cause, or causal necessitation, derives from the proprioceptive awareness of our own bodies interacting with external physical reality. I have in mind such experiences as of a heavy weight forcing your arm downwards or of your body pushing another body aside or being warmed up by the presence of a source of heat. There is here a tight spatio-temporal contiguity consisting in one quality—motion, heat, etc.—spreading from one object to another, which is lacking in the case of visual and auditory impressions (that, as we saw in Chapter 1, do not involve bodily feeling).

It is also lacking in cases in which a mental episode like the having of a perception or a thought is an effect or cause.[2] When the having of a sense-impression, for example of an after-image, is caused by something in the physical environment, or when a thought is caused by a perception or another thought, we have no sense of a spatio-temporal contiguity propagating any quality. We could not in going from the thinking of one thought to the thinking of another be aware of the first thought causing the second for a very simple reason: thinking a thought is not being aware of the fact that one is thinking it, and it is the fact that one is thinking something, rather than the thing thought, that causes it to be a fact that one thinks something else. Certainly, we can retrospectively be aware of having had certain thoughts, but if we were not at the time of having them aware of them as causing, or causally necessitating, each other, we cannot insert this relation retrospectively. Instead we simply experience a thought temporally succeeding another thought when its content is related to the content of the former in one of the ways I tried to describe in Chapter 13. Likewise, we experience having thoughts whose content is related to the content of our perceptions. The experienced connection in these cases is 'contentual' rather than causal. It is only because thoughts have neural correlates, which are nodes in a causal network, that thoughts can be described as causes and effects. Therefore, we do not feel freer when we have thoughts that pop up without having any relation to the contents of earlier thoughts. These thoughts do not appear to us to be causally undetermined to any greater extent.

It follows that we cannot, either, observe how our thoughts cause our bodies to move when we move our bodies as the result of our thoughts. Here, too, the connection observed

---

[2] I partly, but not wholly, agree with Sprigge's suggestion that the Humean dogma about the unobservability of causal connections is due to a concentration on visual perception at the expense of "bodily and emotional feeling" (1988: 141). Proprioception supplies impressions of causal influence in a way that visual impressions cannot do. Consider the difference between *feeling* an alien object pressing against one's own body and forcing it to move and *seeing* the same thing happening to another body than one's own. It seems a palpable fact that the latter impressions leave it open that the body just *happens* to move when the moving object touches it. (It should be stressed, however, that the fact that we have this impression of causal influence does not ensure that there really is this causal influence in the world, for the impression we receive might be due to some defect or lack of acuity in our senses which debars us from detecting microscopic discontinuities.) But, in opposition to Sprigge, I deny that we experience the having of sensations of pleasure or pain, and thoughts of them, as exercising a causal influence on our actions. In my view, it is only in the *objects* of bodily feelings that we experience causality, not in the connection between *states* of feeling.

runs via content, as was implied in Chapter 4: we experience the thought that it is possible for us to bring about *p* being succeeded by us bringing about what we think is *p*. The thought is not observed to necessitate the behaviour causally as the action of another body may be observed to do. In this connection, it should also be kept in mind that thoughts are not by themselves causally sufficient to spark off bodily behaviour, but do so only with the assistance of desires, and desires are not mental episodes, but non-introspectible, neural states. Thus our inner experience of the domain of mind and action is non-causal.

We can imagine that we could retrospectively plumb the depths of our brains and monitor the electric impulses that are correlated with the having of one thought that gives rise to the having of another thought. Perhaps this would provide us with consciousness of causality. But we could not conceivably execute this scanning of neural correlates while engaging in the thinking of a thought, for at that moment we could not even be aware of the thinking itself (in contrast to the content of the thought).

I hypothesize that this non-causal character of the content of our (introspective) self-consciousness joins with the principled impossibility of prediction, expressed by (P), to give us a powerful impression of being free or causally undetermined in the domain of thought and action, even if determinism is true. Both these features have a common denominator in the fact that, in thinking a thought, one cannot simultaneously be thinking that one is thinking it.

To summarize the discussion of this chapter, I hold it to be possible to give an account of the possibility of deliberation and of our experience of freedom that is compatible with determinism in the realm of mind and action. But I want to stress that, in contrast to, for example, Honderich (1988), I am not assuming the truth of such a determinism. As remarked in the foregoing chapter, I am willing to grant that there may be loopholes in the causal network to an extent which does not jeopardize responsibility, for example those loopholes which Mele's modest libertarianism posits (1995: ch. 12). But I would be loath to admit an indeterminism to the extent that, for example, it would be a mere coincidence that we succeed in executing our intentions when we have the ability to do so (cf. Mele, 1995: chap. 11). This would render the formation of intentions pointless.

Also, I am granting the applicability of the concepts of desire, emotion, and intentional action though, as I argued in Chapters 4 and 5, they are imbued with causal assumptions. The concept of desire may be especially useful in illustrating the strength of the commonsensical urge to think in causal terms, for here an unobserved factor is *postulated* for the purposes of causal explanation. But I do not think that common sense assumes that all mental states or episodes are caused. Quite the contrary, both this chapter and the account given of emotions in Part I imply that there are mental phenomena into whose causes we do not, and even cannot on pain of a regress, delve. As will transpire, such a lacuna in respect of causal awareness is what enables us to employ the concept of desert-entailing responsibility and to have associated emotions, though it does not rationally justify this. Before we come to that, however, we shall in the next two chapters see how the fact that it is both epistemically possible that one executes an action and epistemically possible that one refrains from this enters into a compatibilist or forward-looking notion of (direct) responsibility.

32

COMPATIBILIST FREEDOM
OF ACTION

To salvage the possibility of deliberation is not to salvage the possibility of responsibility. Arguably, responsibility requires a sturdier sense of being able to act in alternative ways than an epistemic one, perhaps a sense implying that this is causally possible. But I shall in this and the next chapter engage in the familiar—compatibilist—undertaking of showing that there is a sense in which agents can be held (directly) responsible for their actions that is compatible with the truth of determinism.

I claimed in the foregoing chapter that to say that one is responsible is to say, roughly, that one is in a state such that the R–P practice can justifiably be applied to one—the R–P practice being the practice of rewarding and punishing, praising and blaming. Now, since justifications of the forward-looking type—that is, theories that try to justify the R–P practice by its beneficial consequences with respect to the agents themselves and/or other subjects, the encouragement rewards give and the discouragement punishments give—enjoy a widespread reputation for being suitable for compatibilist purposes, it is natural to look in their direction. To be sure, there is the problem with such justifications that they may appear too weak, and justify an R–P practice that functions as a mere conditioning device (like rewards and punishments applied to animals to teach them tricks). This is a trap I shall be wary to avoid.

Schematically, there are three transitional stages at which there could occur interferences that would rob us even of the forward-looking type of responsibility:

(A) The cognitive stage. If the R–P practice is to serve the function of inciting agents to perform some actions and deterring them from performing other actions, these agents must obviously have a capacity to form reliable beliefs to the effect that they are rewarded and punished for these actions. When there are promises of rewards and threats of punishments, they must be able to tell to what actions these promises and threats are attached. Likewise, when they are actually rewarded or punished, they must be able to ascertain for what. This is required also when the R–P practice functions as an instrument of mere conditioning, but when the practice is bound up with ascriptions of responsibility, something stronger is, as will transpire, necessary, namely, that agents conceive of their actions as being good and bad for others, and interpret the rewards and punishments as befalling them because of this goodness and badness, respectively. Furthermore, agents must not only be equipped with this capacity of belief-formation, they must also be capable of episodically representing the contents of these beliefs with a degree of vividness sufficient for them to take motivational effect.

(B) The stage of desire-formation on the basis of reasons. The R–P practice is designed to provide agents with reasons for acting. For agents who possess the cognitive capacities demanded in (A), applications of the practice will present not only real reasons, but will be *their*—dispositional and apparent—reasons. But this is of little avail if the strength of these agents' (intelligent) desires cannot reflect the breadth of their reasons, for it is their desires that are manifested in their intentional behaviour. Hence, the R–P practice will not be an effective means of shaping the intentional behaviour of agents whose (intelligent) desires cannot mirror the full array of their (apparent) reasons. In other words, for the R–P practice to be effective, it is essential that the strength of (intelligent) desires can be a function of the force of episodically represented reasons.

(C) The stage of intelligent desires manifesting themselves in (intentional) action. Suppose that intelligent desires did not issue in (overt) behaviour, except perhaps accidentally, that how agents behaved in every situation was fully determined by conditions that had nothing to do with whether or not they formed any intelligent desires, it being just a matter of coincidence were they to behave in a manner that accorded with their decisive desires. Then the R–P practice could not be justified on the ground that it increased the likelihood of beneficial forms of behaviour and decreased the likelihood of harmful ones, for it would have no power to change the behaviour of agents; it would only affect impotent desires. (It might reasonably be argued that beings who knew they were inhabiting such a world would form no desires and intentions; I ignore this possibility in order not to make my exposition unnecessarily complicated.) Thus, if the R–P practice is to be justifiable on forward-looking grounds, intelligent desires, and intentions, must regularly manifest themselves in (overt) behaviour.

Compatibilist Conditions of Responsible Action

I shall examine what must obtain more specifically when things run smoothly at these three stages. It will be expedient to reverse their order and begin by considering the transition from intelligent desire to intentional action. Not least in the light of what has just been said, it lies close at hand to hypothesize that a sufficient condition for A's being responsible for it being the case that p must include that this results from an intelligent desire in a way that makes p being the case intentional:

(1) A intentionally causes that p (or lets it be the case).

To be sure, (1) is not minimally sufficient. In Chapter 8 it was remarked that it is possible to desire p, realize that if p then q, and not desire q. Suppose that A causes p and q under these conditions. Then, it may be said, she causes that p intentionally, but she does not cause q intentionally, for this is nothing desired—nor, consequently, intended—by her. She causes q *knowingly* or *wittingly*, but not intentionally. Nevertheless, she would appear to be as responsible for q as if she had caused it intentionally.[1] Hence, if (1) is to stand any chance of being necessary for responsibility, it may be that it should rather require that A knowingly or consciously causes p. But even if this objection is sound, I shall not revise (1). For my objective is not to state a necessary condition for responsibility, and (1) in its present form is more convenient for expository purposes.

In any event, even if revised, (1) would not be necessary in all cases of responsible action, for one can be held responsible for actions that are not knowingly performed. For instance, a doctor can apparently be held responsible for the death of a patient, even though she performed the fatal operation firmly believing that it would restore the health of the patient, provided that, being a doctor, she *should* have realized how hazardous the operation would be. When one accepts the social role of being, say, a doctor, one puts oneself under certain obligations that go with it. The fact that one is not competent to carry out those obligations is nothing that relieves one of the responsibility for failing to do so. Incompetence in carrying out the obligations of some social part should prevent one from shouldering this role but, once it has been accepted, incompetence does not relieve one of being responsible for failures to fulfil the associated obligations.[2]

It should be clear from this, however, that responsibility in such situations depends on other acts being responsible in a sense that presupposes the truth of (the revised) (1): in the present example, the doctor would not be responsible for the faulty surgical proced-ure unless she had intentionally (or knowingly) placed herself under the obligations of surgeons. But since I am not interested in necessary conditions for responsible action, I need not bother about such cases of derivative responsibility.

Something that is of concern to me is that (1) is compatible with A's being subject to causes outside herself and her control. The causal analysis of the concept of intentional action hinted at in Chapter 4, provides no reason to believe that such a condition of control must be met. Since it portrays the intentional behaviour as being caused by certain thoughts and desires, it is inconsistent with a radical indeterminism that takes such behaviour to be uncaused. But because it leaves open the causal origin of these

---

[1] This is denied by deontologists who endorse the doctrine of the double effect. Similarly, deontologists who endorse the act-omission doctrine deny that we are equally responsible for what we let be the case. The discussion of these doctrines can be postponed to ch. 35, since it is not crucial for the task of finding conditions that are sufficient for us to be responsible for something.

[2] The distinction here drawn is sometimes presented as being between prospective and retrospective responsibility; see e.g. Zimmerman (1988: 1–2).

causes, it is compatible with them ultimately being the effects of causes outside the control of the subject in question.

We must push further, however, since (1) is not by itself sufficient for responsibility. Many have held *avoidability* to be a *sine qua non* of responsibility; more precisely, that *A* could be responsible for causing *p* only if:

(2) *A* could have avoided causing *p*.

If this is correct, it seems plain that (1) cannot be sufficient for responsibility because it does not entail (2). An illustration might bring out this. Suppose that *A* forms a decisive desire or intention to pull the trigger of the gun in her hand and that, as a direct result of this, she pulls the trigger. If the causal route between the desire and the action is in no way deviant, this is sufficient for her to have *intentionally* pulled the trigger. This is, however, perfectly consistent with its also being the case that had *A*'s desire not issued in this result, a twitch would instead have caused her finger involuntarily to pull the trigger at the same time. Perhaps if the outcome of her deliberation had been an intention not to pull the trigger, her cramped finger would have twitched with dire consequences when she was about to loosen its pressure on the trigger. Thus, even in the absence of an intention to pull the trigger, *A* would have pulled it (involuntarily). In other words, she could not have refrained from pulling it, despite the fact that she pulled it intentionally. Therefore (1) does not entail (2).

Yet, it seems reasonable to contend that *A* is all the same responsible for having pulled the trigger, provided the act is intentionally executed. So, it appears that the fact that she could not have avoided pulling the trigger at the time does not absolve her of the responsibility of (intentionally) having pulled the trigger. Surely, the question of whether *A* is responsible for her act is answered by attending to what actually lies behind her act. What would lie behind the act in a certain hypothetical situation seems relevant only to whether she would be responsible for her act in this hypothetical situation. So, (2) is not necessary for responsibility.

This is roughly the conclusion Harry Frankfurt reaches in his celebrated paper 'Alternate Possibilities and Moral Responsibility' (reprinted in Frankfurt, 1988). Of course, Frankfurt's contention has not gone unchallenged—see for example van Inwagen (1983: 162–82)—but as I think that Frankfurt has defended himself ably,[3] and it is not crucial to my concerns that he is right, I shall not dwell upon the matter.

Frankfurt suggests that the claim that (2) is necessary for responsibility strikes us as plausible because we tacitly assume that, when an agent cannot but perform an act, this fact enters into the explanation of the act, in which case it will not be responsible (1988: 9). This leads up to the proposal that a necessary condition for responsibility is that *A* does not cause *p* *because* she could not avoid causing *p*. But Frankfurt does not believe that this revision yields a tenable condition (1988: 10), and an elaboration of my example supports his view. Imagine that the desire and the twitch work simultaneously to

---

[3] See 'What We Are Morally Responsible For' in Frankfurt (1988). For other defences of Frankfurt, see Klein (1990: ch. 2) and Fischer (1994: ch. 7).

produce the pulling of the trigger, both being in conjunction with the prevailing circumstances, but independently of each other, sufficient for this effect—that is, the pulling of the trigger is overdetermined. So far as I can see, this overdetermination rules out neither that A acted intentionally, nor that she acted responsibly. Surely, the fact that A happens to be afflicted by a twitch at the crucial moment cannot be allowed to let her off the hook of responsibility when her state of desire was such that she would have pulled the trigger even in the absence of the twitch.

The view Frankfurt favours is instead that an agent is responsible only if she does not perform her action *only* because she could not have done otherwise and not at all because she wanted to do so (1988: 10). In the elaboration of my example, it is still true that the agent pulled the trigger partly because she (decisively) wanted to; so this requirement would not exclude responsibility here. But we have now a condition that adds nothing to (1): that a responsible act must be done at least partly because the agent (decisively) wants to perform it is entailed by the demand that it must be executed intentionally.

In my opinion, there is, however, more to be said about responsibility and avoidability, and this surfaces if one does not concentrate on what has to be true on each and every occasion of responsibility, but ask instead what must *generally* be true with respect to avoidability for there to be responsibility. I have asserted that to say that an agent is responsible is to say that she fulfils conditions that make it justifiable or appropriate to apply to her the R–P practice (conditions which I am in the process of unravelling). We have this practice at least partly for, as we believe, the beneficial effects it promotes, in the form of reinforcing some patterns of behaviour and counteracting others. But it has already been implied that the R–P practice could effectively fulfil this function only if the outward behaviour of agents often is what it is only because their intelligent desires are what they are. Imagine that how A would behave throughout her life was fixed by sufficient conditions that had nothing to do with the state of her intelligent desires; then there would be precious little point in subjecting her to the R–P practice. So a presupposition of our adhering to the R–P practice is that we believe that it is frequently the case that we will cause something if, but only if, we form a decisive desire to do so.

Moreover, it seems evident that we would not bother to form decisive desires to act in different situations unless we believed that, for those actions in those situations, it is true that we will then perform these actions if we desire to and will refrain from them if we so desire, that is, that our performance of those actions in those situations is conditional on what we (intelligently) desire. Since what will happen must be causally possible, we can also say that, conditional on what we desire, we can perform actions and can also abstain from them: we can perform them if we want to, and can abstain should we so desire. As already remarked, it is pointless to deliberate about whether to form a decisive desire to cause p, or not to cause it, at a certain time t, if it is held to be certain that whether or not one will cause p at t is fixed by factors independent of one's desires.

Now this belief in our conditional capacity could be false for some actions in some situations. Occasionally, nervous twitches or other factors may operate alongside a decisive desire or may intercept it, as in the examples above. But it is, I submit, extremely improbable that this belief is false in all cases or even in a majority of cases. By far the most credible explanation of why we have this belief is that it is generally true. I grant that it is *conceivable* that a philosophical sceptic would be right in claiming that we are always deluded in this respect, but I would insist that we have *no reason* to believe that this is so. So I would claim that the fact that in many situations we form intelligent desires to act makes it very likely that, in a great majority of those situations, we actually have a conditional capacity to perform and to forbear, that is, that it is the case that what decisive desire we form makes a crucial difference to our conduct.

Plainly, this reasoning does not salvage (2). It does not support the contention that responsibility can only justifiably be attributed when *A* could have acted differently on the very occasion in question. Even if a decisive desire is rendered superfluous or intercepted by another factor which is sufficient in the circumstances of the action, the fact that the desire was formed is enough to make it meaningful to encourage or discourage its formation, provided that on a great number of other occasions such a desire would be a non-redundant ingredient of a sufficient condition for a certain type of action.

If I were out to specify the necessary conditions of responsibility, I would have to formulate a condition that catered for all these complexities. But since I am interested in only a sufficient condition, I shall propose a condition that is merely an explication of (2):

(2*)   *A* could have avoided causing *p* if she had had an intention, that is, decisive desire, to avoid causing *p* (instead of an intention to cause it to materialize).

In other words, the conjunction of (1) and (2*) lays down that, if *A* causes *p* because she intends this, but would have avoided causing *p* had she intended to, then she is responsible for having caused *p*. Without this intention, she would not have caused *p*, non-intentionally.

By explicating (2) as (2*), I have expressed my view that the avoidability germane to responsibility is *implicitly conditional*. But the claim that 'could have avoided' can be *expanded* into something of the form 'could have avoided if . . .' should not be confused with the claim that it is to be *analysed* as something like 'would have avoided if . . .'. I think that 'could have' expresses a causal possibility, but then 'could have avoided if . . .' cannot *mean* the same as or be *logically* equivalent to 'would have avoided if . . .'.[4] True, in a deterministic world, these constructions are *materially* equivalent, for here whatever is causally possible—and only this—will happen. This may have misled some to conflate the expansion and the analysis theses.

J. L. Austin once argued against the conditional analysis by invoking the case of a golfer who misses "a very short putt", but nonetheless remains convinced that he "could have holed it" (1970: 218 n.). His suggestion was that "a modern belief in science, in there being an explanation of everything . . . is not in line with the traditional beliefs enshrined in the word *can*" (1970: 218 n.). I do not think Austin's example proves this suggestion to be true, but I do not want to exclude its truth. This is achieved by favouring a conditional expansion instead of a conditional analysis. That it was causally possible that the golfer

---

[4] This accounts for the fact, which Laura Waddell Ekstrom (2000: 61) adduces as an objection against analysing 'could have' in terms of 'would have if', that one could reply to the question of why one failed to do what one intended by saying that one could not do it.

would hole the putt were he to try is perfectly compatible with his trying and failing (causelessly). It is only on the assumption that the world is deterministic that the fact that he could hole it, were he to try, implies that he would.

On the other hand, the conditionalization of the capacity to act otherwise, or of the causal possibility to act otherwise, makes the latter compatible with the truth of determinism. Evidently, it is consistent with determinism that it is causally possible that A causes p if certain conditions C—including A's having an intention to this effect—obtain and that it is causally possible that she omits causing p given the obtaining of certain other conditions C^*—including the absence of such an intention. For this does not imply that either her causing p or her not causing it will be without a sufficient cause that determines it. What is inconsistent with determinism is, of course, that, at a time, it be *unconditionally* causally possible that A causes p and causally possible that she not causes p. Hence, the addition of (2^*) constitutes no transgression of the bounds of compatibilism.

An Argument Against Compatibilism

The availability of the concept of a conditional capacity of acting otherwise rebuts a *prima facie* compelling argument to the effect that, in a deterministic world, one cannot act differently than what one in fact does.[5] Let 'p' represent the proposition that A performs some act, say, moves a finger. If p is true in a deterministic world, there will be some description, q, true of the world prior to the existence of A such that q, in conjunction with some laws of this world, r, entails p. That is, letting 'N' express 'it is necessarily true that' we obtain:

(A) N (if q & r then p).

Consider now this proposition:

(B) If N (if q & r then p), then A can make it false that p only if she can make it false that q & r.

To appreciate the force of (B), imagine that A makes it false that p—that is, imagine that she omits moving the finger at t. In this possible world, it must be false that q & r, for otherwise this world would contain a contradictory state of affairs. So, it would seem that A can see to it that p is false only if she can see to it that q & r is false. Obviously, from (A) and (B) it can be inferred that:

(C) A can make it false that p only if she can make it false that q & r.

Now it appears plain that it is in A's power neither to alter the state of the world before she began to exist—that is, to make it false that q—nor to break the natural laws of the world, that is, to render it false that r. Thus, we apparently get:

(D) A cannot make it false that q & r.

---

[5] For elegant formulations of the argument, see van Inwagen (1983: ch. 3). This type of argument is thoroughly discussed by Fischer (1994: chs. 1–5).

From (C) and (D) we can deduce:

(E) *A* cannot make it false that *p*,

in other words, that she cannot abstain from moving the finger.

The crucial premise in this argument is (D), that *A* cannot make it false that *q* & *r*. It can be interpreted in a stronger and a weaker way.[6] The positive version of the strong reading is roughly this:

(S) *A* can make it false that *q* & *r* = *A* can *cause* it to be false that *q* & *r*.

According to this interpretation, (D) is certainly true. The weaker interpretation is this:

(W) *A* can make it false that *q* & *r* = *A* can perform some act such that if she performs it, it is false that *q* & *r*.

Can she perform such an act? *If* she can avoid moving the finger in the conditional sense, she *can* execute such an act. For contemplate the world in which this forbearance can take place: as already remarked, this must be a world in which it is, *by hypothesis*, false that *q* & *r*. Note that the conjunction *q* & *r* is here not *made* or *caused* to be false by *A*'s making it false that *p*—as is required by (S)—but that its falsity is *assumed* in order to make room for it to be the case that she can make it false that *p*.

Consequently, for us to have a reason to endorse (D), it must be read in accord with (S). But, then, if the argument is not to trade on an equivocation, the same sentence in (C) must have the same meaning. The trouble is now that, whereas (C) had been uncontroversial if this sentence had been read along the lines of (W), it is questionable on the (S)-interpretation. It is false if '*A* can make it false that *p*' is read as implicitly conditional on some states of affairs, such as her desiring to abstain from moving the finger. For *A*'s power of making it false that *p* is then *conditional on* its being false that *q* & *r* (since this conjunction entails that she intentionally moves the finger, it must entail that she forms a desire to this effect). Hence, in order to be able to make it false that *p*, *A* does not have to be able to *make* this conjunction false in or by making it false that *p*. Thus, if (C) is to be endorsed as true, on the (S)-reading, the sentence '*A* can make it false that *p*' must be understood as expressing an *unconditional* (causal) possibility (or at least a possibility that is not conditional on anything which contradicts *q* & *r*).

Given this, the argument goes through, and we reach the conclusion that *A* cannot make it false that *p*, that is, that it is not unconditionally possible for her to render it false that *p*. This is not an unexpected conclusion: surely, it is obvious that in a deterministic universe it is not unconditionally (causally) possible that agents act differently from how they in fact act. But, as I, along with many others, have tried to show, the argument will convince only those who are already convinced,[7] for it assumes without argument that the power of acting otherwise is not conditional. If this power is (implicitly) conditional on, for example certain motivational states of the agent, (D) is undercut.

---

[6] Cf. David Lewis (1981), who distinguishes between a stronger and a weaker sense of being able to break a law.

[7] Cf. the "dialectical stalemates" Fischer lands in (1994: ch. 4), though he thinks there is a "basic version" of this type of argument which escapes these stalements (ch. 5). Thus, he concludes that we do not have the "regulative control" which implies that we can do otherwise. Cf. also the view of Kane (1996: 44–52). These books also contain a lot of references.

33

COMPATIBILIST FREEDOM
OF WILL

IT has been contended that a conditional analysis or expansion of 'could have acted otherwise' merely gives us freedom to *act* in accordance with our will, not freedom of will. In other words, it merely pushes back the problem one step, from whether we could have done otherwise to whether we could have (decisively) desired otherwise. More precisely, it might be said that if

(a) A could have avoided causing p

is to be viewed as an ellipsis for

(b) A could have avoided causing p if she had intended, that is, decisively desired, to avoid causing p

then (b) must be taken as presupposing

(c) A could have intended to avoid causing p.

This is so, since (b) is compatible with

(d) A could have avoided causing p *only if* she had intended to avoid causing p.

The circumstances could be such that the only condition that would make it causally possible for A to avoid causing p would be an intention to avoid this. (It changes nothing in principle if this avoidance is conditional upon several distinct sufficient conditions, for then the disjunction of these is necessary.) Now, if (b) does not presuppose (c), it is compatible with its negation, namely,

(e) A could not have intended to avoid causing p.

But (d) and (e) apparently entail the negation of (a), namely that A could not have avoided causing p.[1] So, if (a) is to be elliptical for (b), (b) must be incompatible with the conjunction of (d) and (e), and this will be the case if (b) is taken to presuppose (c).

---

[1] This is an adaptation of a classical objection, expressed, e.g., by Chisholm (1966).

I believe this objection to be sound. Surely, if it is maintained that the possibility of acting otherwise is implicitly conditional, that it obtains if, and only if, certain conditions are fulfilled, then these conditions must be such that it is possible in some suitable sense that they be satisfied. Otherwise it would be highly misleading to state the power to act differently elliptically as in (*a*). So I propose to regard (*a*) as an ellipsis for (*b*) and (*c*); in other words, to let (*c*) be added to the set of conditions sufficient for *A*'s being responsible for causing *p*. The following set is then obtained:

(1) *A* intentionally causes *p*,

(2) *A* could have avoided causing *p* if she had intended to avoid causing *p*, and

(3) *A* could have intended to avoid causing *p*.

In view of the fact that we are thus forced to introduce a new seemingly unconditional 'could'-statement, are we caught up in a regress, the regress of having to expand '*A* could have intended to avoid causing *p*' into '*A* could have intended to avoid causing *p* if she had intended to intend to avoid causing *p*' and so on? It would be premature to conclude that we are caught up in this regress. The action of causing *p* is intentional, that is, it necessarily results from an intention to this effect. This involvement of an intention in the genesis of intentional action is the basis of the claim that a capacity to execute such an action is conditional upon the presence of an appropriate intention. The state of intending (or desiring) something is, however, not an (intentional) action. Therefore there is not the same reason to think that a power to have an intention is conditional upon the presence of a second-order intention, an intention to intend.[2]

An intention (or desire) cannot reasonably be construed as an action, but Thomas Pink has argued that a decision is a "second-order action", that is, a (deliberate or intentional) "action which generates action by way of constituting the formation of an intervening action explanatory psychological state" (1996: 3; cf. Mele, 2003: chap. 9). What makes a decision an action is, according to him, that it "is governed by reason in this distinctively practical way" (1996: 8; cf. 48) which "comes to *means–end justifiability*" (1996: 8; cf. 50–2).

But deciding is not anything one *does in order to* achieve something. To decide is to succeed in deliberating (thus, only beings who can deliberate can decide). Deliberating or trying to make up one's mind about what to do is indeed an action or activity, something you can do in order to achieve something (a state of intending). Your decision is your succeeding in this undertaking, and succeeding in something is not an action. Nor does it make sense to say that you succeed in order to achieve something. When you try and succeed, you do not do two things: a trying and a succeeding. So deciding to do something is not an action (nor is choosing, since it is deciding to go for one alternative rather than another). Similarly, deciding what to *think true* is the successful culmination of trying to find out what to think true. It would be strange to hold that such theoretical deciding is doing something in order to achieve something (presumably a state of believing).

It is another matter that an intention (or desire) could be intentionally *caused*, and the claim that *A* could have refrained from *causing* the intention mentioned should be

---

[2] The difficulty one encounters by taking this line is fully discussed by Shatz (1986).

understood as implying a condition concerning second-order intentions such as 'if she had intended to refrain from causing herself to have the intention'. But we must not conflate 'A could have had another intention' and 'A could have *caused* herself to have another intention'. It does not follow from the fact that the latter is conditional upon second-order intentions that the former, too, is.

How shall we then understand (3)? We can conclude from Chapter 31 that if A's intention to cause p was an outcome of deliberation, then it must have been the case that, relative to her information, it was epistemically possible that she would avoid causing p— more precisely, that this avoidance would be a possible *outcome of her deliberation*. But then it must have been epistemically possible that she would form an intention to this effect. This is, I suggest, the sense in which A could have intended to avoid causing that p. In other words, 'could have' in (3) expresses an *epistemic* possibility: given the information available to A at the time of deliberation, it was possible that she would end up intending p and possible that she would end up intending not-p. Both of these possibilities were open to her because of the impossibility in principle of predicting one's immediate thought-sensitive future. For this reason, in asserting a claim like (3), we can endorse as justified the deliberative uncertainty the agent experienced.[3]

In general, then, when we assert that people can do something in the 'all-in' sense of having both the ability and the opportunity, we mean that they can do it—that is, that this is causally possible—if they intend (decide) to do it and that their intending to do it is epistemically possible.

Irresistible and Merely Strong Desires

This brings us to an important topic, that of *irresistible* or *compulsive* desires (as will appear, I do not regard these terms as perfectly synonymous, but take the latter as entailing the former). The main point of tacking a constraint like (3) onto (1) and (2) is surely to preclude that A's decisive desire to cause p is irresistible. If A's desire to cause p were irresistible, she could not have decisively desired to avoid causing p and could not for that reason have avoided causing p. For instance, if A is a kleptomaniac and possesses an irresistible desire to steal, then, owing to this desire, she cannot form a decisive desire not to steal. It is presumably true that *if, per impossibile*, she had formed such a desire, she could—and would—have abstained from stealing. So when we assert that A could not have refrained from stealing, we do so because we take the view that a constraint to the effect of (3) is not fulfilled.

Does the account here given imply that someone with an irresistible desire like the kleptomaniac's could not have decisively desired otherwise, and for that reason should be let off the hook of responsibility? I think so, for in this case it is not in principle

---

[3] Cf. Persson (1981: 4.2.2). Essentially the same account is found in Bok (1998: 107 ff.). But, at bottom, I see her further attempt to establish that "from a practical point of view" our decisions *are* genuinely up to us because in deliberation we are constrained to *regard* them as such as unconvincing as concluding that "from a practical point of view" we *are* immortal because we will never be in a position correctly to *regard* ourselves as dead.

impossible for the agent to predict what she will end up decisively desiring: this will inevitably be what she irresistibly desires. If a desire really is irresistible, the outcome of no prediction can possibly overthrow it. Hence, acknowledgement of an irresistible desire precludes genuine deliberation.

It might be objected that the same is true of cases in which people act out of over-whelmingly strong desires, but are nonetheless rightly held responsible. It might seem that when Martin Luther declared that he could not act otherwise in Worms, he was acting on a desire so powerful that no considerations, or predictions, could sway him to form a contrary decisive desire. Yet, this fact surely does not absolve him of responsibility for his behaviour in Worms. It would be preposterous if people who act on their leading passions or ideals were held not to be responsible for their actions!

There is, however, a significant difference between a desire such as Luther's and the kleptomaniac's desire to steal, though they have in common the feature of being of over-powering strength. This is that the former, but not the latter, is held only because it reflects the strength of (the most extensive set of) the agent's relevant reasons.[4] Even if Luther knew it was risky for him to behave as he did in Worms, he would still take himself to have best reasons to do so. It may be that these reasons are so strong that it would be unrealistic to imagine him finding stronger reasons on the other side. But this is still logically possible, and *if* he were to hit upon such reasons, he would form a decisive desire to behave otherwise. In contrast, the kleptomaniac's desire to steal, if really irresistible, is independent of the thrust of what she sees as her reasons: she would still have an over-powering desire to steal even if she were to believe that she has best reasons to refrain from stealing. It is pointless for Luther to go on deliberating, for the reason that it is very unlikely that he will strike upon weightier reasons on the other side, but it is pointless for the kleptomaniac to deliberate for another reason, namely, that whatever conclusion she reaches, it will be ineffective. Moreover, deliberation is *impossible* for someone who *knows* she has an irresistible desire in the sense of an overpowering desire that is sealed off from the thrust of her reasons. This is like deliberating about whether to blink or swallow when one knows that one will do so involuntarily.

It follows from this that, from a forward-looking perspective, it would be unjustifiable to subject people like the kleptomaniac to the R–P practice, since it cannot have any effect on the desire upon which they act. It would be useless, by meting out punishment, to try to make vivid the reasons for not stealing, for the overruling desire to steal is insulated from reasons. The problem with these people is that there is a malfunctioning at the second stage of the three that were distinguished at the outset of the foregoing chapter— that of desire-formation. Perhaps, if the punishment imposed on kleptomaniacs were severe enough to cause traumas—say, if it consisting in burning or chopping off their

---

[4] In the process of expounding her "Reason View", Susan Wolf puts forward an "Asymmetry Thesis" to the effect that, whereas responsibility for a bad act requires that it could be avoided, responsibility for a good act does not (1990: ch. 4). This thesis gains credence by a failure to compare like with like, e.g. a reason-based desire such as Luther's with a reason-independent desire like the kleptomaniac's. In the sense I am specifying, it is only the latter subject who cannot act otherwise. For further discussion of Wolf's thesis, see Mele (1995: 162–4) and Fischer and Ravizza (1998: 55–61).

hands—it might deter them from committing this offence. But such severe punishments are not conducive to promoting the most beneficial consequences overall.

As opposed to this, it makes sense to apply moderate doses of punishment to people like Luther in an attempt to amplify their reasons for acting, because the intensities of their desires is a function of the thrust of their reasons. Certainly, the reasons these measures supply may in fact be insufficient to overturn their leading desires, but, since their desires are reason-sensitive, it still has a point to ensure that they make clear to themselves what relevant reasons there are.

I propose to employ the term 'irresistible desire' so that it does not cover overruling desires like Luther's. To be irresistible, it is not sufficient that a desire possesses overpowering intensity; this intensity must also not stem from the thrust of the agent's reasons (if it does, there will be unpredictability in principle). That is to say, I suggest a definition like this:

(IR) A desire D of A is irresistible if and only if: D is stronger than any (set of) competing desires of A's, and it is so independently of whether it is supported by what she conceives to be her best reasons.

Notice that, according to (IR), an irresistible desire might by coincidence accord with what A's best reasons recommend. The superior strength of a desire could be overdetermined: it could be the strongest desire both because it is supported by A's best reasons and because of a sufficient condition independent of this. For instance, a heroin user's craving for the drug could be due both to the fact that he is addicted and to the fact that he sees addiction as the most attractive way of life.

There is a clear parallel between actions resulting from such an addict's craving and (a case considered in the foregoing chapter) the action of pulling the trigger when it is overdetermined by having one sufficient condition comprising an intelligent desire and another comprising a nervous tension. In both cases, I am inclined to view the agents as responsible for their behaviour, though they could not have refrained from their behaviour.[5] Thus, acting out of an irresistible desire—and being incapable of acting otherwise for that reason—is not sufficient to relieve one of responsibility. Being a presupposition of (2)—about the possibility of acting otherwise—(3)—about the possibility of desiring otherwise—is as little necessary for responsibility as is (2).

But, as I have emphasized, we are interested in building a sufficient condition the components of which need not be necessary. The interpretation of (3) that my reasoning has led up to is this:

(3*) At the time of her deliberation, it was epistemically possible that A would decisively desire (intend) to avoid causing p, for her desires in this matter are determined solely by her reasons and so are in principle unpredictable for her.

It seems conceivable that A might mistakenly take her desires to be solely determined by her reasons, and thus engage in deliberation, when her strongest desire to cause p is not

[5] Cf. Frankfurt's conclusion concerning the "willing" addict in 'Three Concepts of Free Action' in Frankfurt (1988: 51–2). Contrast the view of Don Locke (1975), to which Frankfurt's paper was originally a response. Recently, Haji (1998: 71) has adopted Locke's view.

so determined. Then we cannot endorse as justified the deliberative uncertainty or openness she experiences, that is, she cannot really have a contrary decisive desire, though she thinks so. But even so, she may be responsible in a forward-looking sense.

If an agent's desire is based on the reasons she in fact has, there are *normally* contrary reasons that would make her respond by forming decisive desires based on them. But this response is not strictly necessary. First, because there might be the overdetermination we have already noted. Secondly, there might be something about an agent which makes her impervious to other reasons than her actual ones. For instance, it seems that the fact that someone is so tender that she would respond to nothing as a sufficient reason to hurt anyone would not disqualify her from being responsible for her intentionally refraining to hurt someone. Therefore, I think Fischer and Ravizza (1998: chs. 2 and 3) are mistaken in relying, in their explication of the reasons-responsiveness involved in responsibility, on the construct of agents' acting otherwise in some alternative scenario in which their reasons are different.[6]

The 'Externality' of Compulsive Desires

In contrast to what is true of irresistible desires, I shall make it necessary for responsibility that agents do not act out of a *compulsive* desire. For a compulsive desire, as I conceive it, is an irresistible desire that is unsupported by *and* goes contrary to what one realizes is dictated by the thrust of one's reasons. Thus, if one is in the grip of a compulsive desire, one is the victim of a conflict of desires in which the desire for which, as one is aware, one has best reasons is opposed by a stronger desire which is independent of these reasons. Since it is scarcely possible, except perhaps in theory, to be the victim of such a conflict without being conscious of it, and without being conscious of the irresistible desire forcing itself upon one, I shall include this when speaking of a person as having a compulsive desire.

A compulsive desire is, then, necessarily at war with a desire viewed as being reason-grounded. The latter desire will naturally generate a second-order desire not to act on the compulsive desire. Of course, this second-order desire is doomed to frustration. For Frankfurt this is a situation in which one lacks freedom of will. He claims that it "is in securing the conformity of his will [that is, his effective desires] to his second-order volitions [desires concerning his will] . . . that a person exercises freedom of will".[7]

According to this conception, the willing addict is not equipped with freedom of will, since if he wanted his will to be different, he would not succeed. Nevertheless, Frankfurt characterizes him as acting of his own free will. He thinks it is a mistake to believe that a person "acts of his own free will only if his will is free" (1988: 24). This strikes me as a counter-intuitive way of speaking. Apparently, Frankfurt describes the willing addict as acting freely or of his own free will because he likes to think of freedom as a *sine qua non* of responsibility. But for reasons that will surface later, I reject the latter assumption.

---

[6] For a similar account, see Haji (1998: ch. 4).
[7] See 'Freedom of the Will and the Concept of a Person', repr. in Frankfurt (1988: 20).

The experience of a compulsive desire is, it feels natural to say, an experience of something 'external' to one's self that imposes itself on one and drives one in a direction that one regards as undesirable. In my opinion, the root of the compulsive desire's 'externality' is its dominance independently of what one takes to be one's best reasons. Contrary to what Bernard Berofsky seems inclined to hold (1987: 40), a resistible desire cannot be experienced as an external force impelling one in an undesirable direction, for a resistible desire is either not dominant or would no longer be dominant were one to reflect on one's reasons. But if a desire, whose dominance would persist independently of what one takes one's reasons to be, accidentally happens to have the support of those reasons, its externality remains latent or dormant. It breaks out into the open only if these reasons come to generate a desire of a conflicting orientation.

A different view of the externality of desires is, however, tentatively offered by Frankfurt. His suggestion is roughly that a desire is rendered external by one's taking up of a second-order stance towards it, to the effect that it not be acted upon, that is, that it not be one's will. In 'Identification and Externality' Frankfurt recognizes a point that critics of his earlier papers have urged,[8] namely that construing the internality/externality of a desire in terms of a higher-order attitude of acceptance or rejection threatens to start an infinite regress, for the same question 'internal or external?' seems to arise for the second-order attitude. The fact that a desire is accepted in a second-order attitude as one's will can guarantee its internality only if the second-order attitude is itself internal, and if this is to be determined by its acceptance in a third-order attitude, we seem caught in a regress.

Frankfurt tries to sidestep this objection by conceiving the second-order stances as *decisions* that certain first-order desires (not) be effective: "It may be that a decision of this kind ... lies behind every instance of the establishment of the internality or externality of passions" (1988: 68). This is alleged to be possible for the following reason: "Decisions, unlike desires or attitudes, do not seem to be susceptible both to internality and to externality" (1988: 68 n.). Decisions are necessarily internal. (I think the content of the decisions must be to *try* to put certain desires into effect, because if one is up against a desire that one has reason to believe to be irresistible, one cannot decide to resist it—this presupposes a degree of confidence in success that one does not here possess.)

It seems to me that there is something correct in Frankfurt's feeling that decisions cannot be external, but this feature of decisions is in need of clarification. My conjecture is that it is due to decisions being necessarily linked to deliberations or considerations of reasons (cf. Klein, 1990: 111–12). Thus I believe that if A is capable of deciding to (try to) implement her desire to cause p, it is because she has best apparent reasons to implement this desire, that is, best reasons to (want to) cause p. But if the distinction between the internality and externality of desires at bottom has to do with whether they are reason-dependent or reason-independent, it becomes unimportant to insist that the second-order stance be a decision rather than a mere desire. Indeed, there is a basis for classifying a desire in respect of internality/externality irrespective of whether any

---

[8] See Frankfurt (1988: 65–6). Many critics have followed in the wake of Watson (1975: 217–19) and (1987: 148–51).

higher-order stance is actually adopted towards it. There is a case for saying that the adoption of such a stance of accepting or rejecting a desire as effective is a form in which a latent internality or externality manifests itself.

The account here proposed of compulsive desires is in some respects like that of Gary Watson's, which views such desires as being "more or less radically independent of the evaluational systems of these agents" (1975: 220). But while I (roughly) regard what is best as (implicitly) relative to some set of intrinsic desires, as that which fulfils them, Watson may well take an objectivist view of values. He sees evaluations as a *source* of desires (1975: 211), as something from which desires spring or arise (1975: 208). They are, however, not the only source of desires, on his view. As was noted in Chapter 12, Watson presents a dualistic picture of the self, according to which reason—within the province of which the making of evaluative judgements lies—constitutes one source of desire and appetite the other. One problem with this dualism is to explain why desires springing from reason should be authoritative relative to desires having their origin in the appetitive part of the self: why should one try to overcome the latter desires (cf. Piper, 1985: 178–81)?

But supposing that we construe what is at present of value for A as what would fulfil her present, intrinsic desires, how can we then explain the occurrence of compulsive desires, that is, overruling desires that are contrary to what she sees as best? We have already accounted for a similar discrepancy in cases of weakness of will by maintaining that one can temporarily overlook some of one's dispositional reasons that are relevant enough to be episodically represented. This will, however, not do when it comes to compulsive desires, for here one is fully conscious that the compulsive desire runs counter to one's best reasons: as has been remarked, this desire is experienced as an external force dragging one in an undesirable direction. None of this is true of the *akrates* who is momentarily oblivious of the fact of acting contrary to his best dispositional reasons. If it had occurred to him at the crucial moment that he was about to act against his best reasons, he would have resisted this, because he would then episodically represent these reasons. The compulsive subject cannot do this, I suggest, because the compulsive desire is so strong that its objective monopolizes attention. He is currently aware that he *has* better reasons that point in the opposite direction, but, owing to the strength of his compulsive desire, he fails to *spell out* or fully and vividly represent to himself what the contents of these reasons are. Therefore, they are prevented from taking their proper effect.

It is true of the weak-willed agent that he possesses dispositional reasons such that, if prior to the situation in which the weakness took place, he had vividly represented these reasons to himself, he would have been able to recall them at the crucial moment, and if he had done so, he would have refrained from falling victim to *akrasia*. In this sense, the *akrates* could have avoided being weak. Punishing or blaming the *akrates* could have the effect of strengthening his motivation to take such precautions in the future. Therefore, there is a forward-looking justification for holding the *akrates* responsible. In contrast, the agent who is in the grip of a compulsive desire could *not* have resisted this desire: however vividly he represented his reasons before the onset of the compulsive desire, he would fail to retrieve them after its onslaught. In view of the strength of the desire, the content of the compulsive desire exercises such a hold on attention that thoughts of nothing else can gain a foothold. Hence, it would be useless, from a forward-looking point of view, to punish or blame this agent.

An illustration might be of assistance. Hark back to an example of *akrasia* given in Chapter 13: *A* takes a painkiller when a severe pain sets in, although, as she realized beforehand, she has better reasons not to. Here it was assumed that if *A* had prepared herself for the possibility of backsliding by trying to impress on her mind that she must not later fail to think of certain salient reasons, she would not have succumbed to the temptation to inject the painkiller. This is the import of the claim that *A* could have abstained from this act. Suppose, however, that the pain had been excruciating, so intense that however great an effort *A* would have made to think of something else, she would have failed. Then it would not help; whatever precautions she had taken to facilitate the future representation of her best reasons, she would still have failed to represent them with sufficient vividness for them to take proper effect. That is, *A*'s desire to get rid of the pain is irresistible, and she cannot avoid acting on it.

To sum up: in order for *A*'s causing *p* to be a responsible act it is necessary that it not be done out of a compulsive desire to cause *p*. It is, strictly speaking, not necessary that the desire that *A* acts out of on this particular occasion be resistible (not irresistible), but it is necessary that, *as a rule*, the desire out of which responsible agents act be resistible or sensitive to the agents' reasons. Otherwise there could not be a forward-looking justification of the R–P practice. The argument here is analogous to the one presented in the last chapter as regards condition (2) of responsibility. But let us for the time being eschew these complications and concentrate on the conditions at a particular time of action. Since we are concerned only with a sufficient condition of responsibility, we can rest content with (3*) given above.

Coercion and Acting of One's Free Will

There are further considerations bearing on ascriptions of responsibility. I have in mind considerations to the effect that the agent was *forced* or *coerced* to act or acted *under duress*. Coercion can be 'physical'. Suppose that a stronger man pushes me off the pavement, with the result that I knock over a bicyclist. Then I am certainly not responsible for having knocked over the bicyclist (at least not if I have done nothing to provoke the man to force me off the pavement). It is not hard to understand why this is so. For even if I can be said to have acted in some sense when I knock over the bicyclist, I obviously do not act intentionally or knowingly. In other words, condition (1) suffices to explain why there is no responsibility here. So we need not waste any time on physical coercion.

We should rather focus on cases in which the agent's *will* is subjected to coercion. A case in point would be the one discussed in Chapter 4, where a cashier hands over money to a robber, because he is convinced that the robber will otherwise carry out his threat and kill him. It seems incontestable that there is a sense of 'acting of one's own free will' in which it is not applicable to the cashier in this situation. It is not applicable to him because he acts under duress or is forced or coerced to act as he does by the robber's threat. Moreover, it seems plain that the cashier's behaviour can be described in this fashion even if he does not act out of a desire that is compulsive or irresistible, but it is true of him that he complies with the robber's threat simply because he judges that course of action to be best for him under the circumstances.

In 'Coercion and Moral Responsibility', Frankfurt grants that such an agent could properly be described as acting "under duress" (1988: 37). In this sense, one is forced to do something if that is the only *reasonable* thing to do, if other alternatives would be, as one realizes, far worse at least for oneself. Under these conditions, however, one *could* strictly speaking have willed and performed an alternative action: the effective desire was not irresistible. Had one's view of one's reasons or good been different, one would have acted accordingly. Now Frankfurt prefers to employ the term 'coercion' so narrowly that an agent is coerced only if his effective desire is irresistible and, more precisely, compulsive. He stipulates that "coercion, as here understood, may be said to deprive its victim of free will" (1988: 42 n.)—where "free will" carries the meaning expounded above, namely, a will that is controlled by one's second-order volitions. Frankfurt's reason for understanding 'coercion' so narrowly is that this understanding is indispensable if coercion is to annul responsibility (1988: e.g. 39).

This is true: if 'coercion' is so liberally used that the cashier can be described as being coerced when he submits to the robber's threat, not because he is seized with an irresistible or compulsive desire to save his life, but because he sees this course as the one he has best reasons to choose, then a plea of coercion does not exempt him from responsibility. However, even if the threat here does not relieve the cashier of responsibility, it qualifies, as we shall soon see, *what* he could justifiably be held responsible for. Thus, the wider sense of coercion has some bearing on responsibility, and this justifies my taking a closer look at what lies behind this talk of coercion. Furthermore, since I have already investigated irresistible and compulsive desire, I can now concentrate on cases of coercion that fall outside the scope of Frankfurt's narrow notion.

One difference between a compulsive desire, like the kleptomaniac's, and the desire that the cashier is forced or coerced to have is that the cashier is forced to have this desire only given some *other desire* that he possesses. The cashier is forced to want to hand over the money only because he has a desire to hang on to life and, as he is aware, the latter desire can be fulfilled only if the former state of affairs obtains. So far as the case has been described, the clerk is, however, not forced to desire to go on living, for this desire is not presented as being derived from some other desire of his. Hence, if one describes the cashier as doing what in the present situation will keep him alive, one attributes to him an action that he executes of his own free will. There is no other threat—for example, to the effect that the clerk's children will be tortured to death if he does not submit to the first threat—which forces him to do what in the present situation will keep him alive. Nevertheless, he is forced to hand over the money to the robber; this is not anything he does of his own free will, although it *is* that which in the present situation will keep him alive.

Against this background, it should be readily comprehensible that coercion does not *remove* responsibility, but merely qualifies that for which one is held responsible. The action for which the clerk is held responsible should not be described as simply 'handing over the money to the robber', but as doing this in circumstances in which this action was necessary to save his life or, in other words, as 'saving his life at the expense of giving away the bank's money'. For it is only in the special circumstances in which giving money to the robber is a means of staying alive that the clerk wants to do this action. Of course, blame and punishment might be withheld from the clerk, because it is agreed that his appraisal of the situation was reasonable, that his life is indeed of greater weight than the money. But this does not alter the fact that he has performed an action for which he can intelligibly be held responsible: somebody who dissents from this appraisal could intelligibly urge that the cashier be blamed and punished.

So freedom of will in a sense that excludes coercion or duress is not necessary for responsibility.[9] Thus no clause requiring this freedom of will need be added to the three conditions for responsibility so far established. A requirement to this effect can, however, easily be built into the conditions. Acting intentionally is acting at will or voluntarily, in one sense. Clearly, acting of one's own *free* will or acting voluntarily, in another sense, entails acting at will. Hence we can incorporate the requirement mentioned by replacing (1) by

(1*) *A* voluntarily causes *p*,

where 'voluntarily' carries the second, stronger sense. This substitution ensures that *A*'s responsibility for causing *p* does not rest on any special circumstances obtaining at the time of action.

One further matter should be cleared up. I have claimed that the statement that the clerk is forced or coerced to—want to—hand over the money to the robber presupposes his having some other desire from which this desire is derived. But obviously, not every derived desire is one that one is forced or coerced to have, so it must be asked: what distinguishes derived desires that one is coerced or forced to have? If we let the term 'the will' designate the capacity to form desires, including derivative ones, the problem can be formulated as follows: when is the will coerced?

The answer was sketched in Chapter 4. Prior to the issuing of the threat, the bank clerk has both a firm desire not to give the bank's money to anyone who is not entitled to it and a firm desire to stay alive. This is possible because until he was threatened these desires were co-satisfiable. The threat obstructs this co-satisfiability and brings them into conflict. Since the desire to go on living is the strongest, the cashier forms a derivative desire to give away the bank's money in this situation. Because of his aversion to this conduct, in view of what it normally brings along, he reluctantly forms this derivative desire. That is why he is described as being coerced or forced to—want to—hand over the money. As we saw, offers can be coercive just like threats. If I am strongly averse to eating worms, but do

<hr>

[9] This is argued, e.g. by Don Locke (1975) and Slote (1980: 147–9).

so to earn a million dollars, I can be described as being forced to—want to—do this action in order to earn the million dollars.

In contrast to what is the case as regards the cashier, however, it goes against the grain to deny that I eat the worm freely or of my own free will. The question why that is so was earlier left unanswered. I think that the reply is that, whereas a threat makes the alternatives of action facing the agent *worse*, an offer *improves* them. Therefore, all things considered, the agent *welcomes* the offer: I welcome the offer to make a million dollars, because—in spite of the unpleasantness of having to eat the worm—it opens up new possibilities of living a more fulfilling life. In contrast, a threat *restricts* these possibilities. Prior to the introduction of the threat, the cashier could fulfil both his desire to stay alive and his desire to guard the bank's money; after its introduction, he can fulfil at most one of these desires. Hence the cashier *regrets* the fact that the threat has been issued. My conjecture is, then, that one is said to be deprived of freedom of will when one is forced to form a desire as the result of circumstances (beyond one's control) that one regrets obtaining. Being subject to a compulsive desire and being coerced or forced to have a desire in a sense that entails the negation of freedom of will are then similar in that in both cases there is in the offing a wish or desire that one be without these desires.

As Slote points out (1980: 143–7), it follows from this account that it is a relative matter, depending on the variable psychological make-up of subjects, whether or not some external circumstance eliminates freedom of will. For instance, suppose that, by repeatedly dwelling on the causal necessity ruling all events in the world, the cashier has developed an attitude of calm acceptance of everything that happens. As a consequence, when he is threatened, he does not regret the fact that he is put in a situation where he must (want to) hand over the bank's money to a robber; it does not appear to him that his alternatives of action have been substantially restricted. Then he cannot be said to have been divested of his freedom of will. It should be noted, though, that this avenue to freedom opens up only to those willing to pay the price of being attached to few things.

Forward-looking Justification and Mere Conditioning

It is sometimes suggested that a forward-looking justification of the R–P practice reduces it to a mere conditioning device that has nothing to do with responsibility. For instance, Susan Wolf argues that to justify rewarding and punishing in this way

> is to justify these practices in the same way that we justify the praise and blame of lower animals—in the same way, that is, that we justify the reward and punishment of pets, of pigeons in the laboratory, of monkeys in the circus. It is to justify these practices only as a means of manipulation and training. (1981: 389)

In expounding condition (3) as (3*), I have already gone some distance towards meeting this objection, for this move reveals this condition to entail that A has to have conceptual resources to deliberate and form reason-based desires, and this is a power that some of Wolf's "lower animals" certainly lack. It is possible, however, to be equipped with these resources without being able to ascribe desires to other beings than oneself—or, for that matter, to oneself at other times than the present—and hence without being able to form a conception of the weal and woe of these beings. But I believe having a conception of the weal and woe of a being to be necessary for being responsible for what one does to it.[10] Remember that in Chapter 30, when I expressed the view that one's being responsible for something, for example a deed, was tantamount to it being right or justifiable to let one respond or answer to criticism for this deed, I claimed that this presupposes one's understanding of assessments of the deed for which one is criticized. In other words, responsible subjects must have a general understanding of why praise and blame, rewards and punishments are distributed; they must understand judgements such as 'You are blamed (punished) because you have acted wrongly to somebody'. Thus we should add a constraint like the following:

(4) *A* is conceptually equipped to view the R–P practice as being applied to herself because she has caused something good or bad for some being (usually other than herself).[11]

This is not a requirement for *every* application of the R–P practice being justifiable from a forward-looking perspective. It can be justifiably applied to conscious beings that lack the capacity of attributing desires to other creatures, and that, as a consequence, have no conception of what is good or bad for these beings. But for *responsibility* to be attributable we should demand that the R–P practice perform its useful service *in a certain way*: through the subjects' understanding that the sanctions befall them for the reason that they have brought about something good or bad for somebody. Doubtless, the R–P practice can effectively be used on beings that lack this understanding, to reinforce certain forms of behaviour and to counteract others. For this use, it is only necessary that the being to whom it is applied experiences the sanctions as pleasant or painful and that it correctly links them to actions performed by it. I claim, however, that under these conditions—that is, if (4) is not satisfied—the justifiability of the R–P practice is not sufficient for responsibility. It is then just a method for manipulating the behaviour of non-responsible agents.

It may be asked whether we should not strengthen (4) to require that *A* is conceptually equipped to view the R–P practice as being *justifiably* applied to herself. This is in effect to require that to be responsible one must oneself have the concept of responsibility.[12] But this requirement threatens to make the account circular by assuming that an understanding necessary to *make* applications of the R–P practice justifiable have to be to the effect that they are justifiable.

Putting together the four conditions, we obtain the following conception of responsibility. (4) demands that the responsible agent *A* is endowed with cognitive and conceptual powers

[10] There is no need for punishment if one causes harm to oneself *now*, for then the effect itself fulfils the function of punishment.

[11] For similar ideas, see Stern (1974). Wolf's book on the subject (1990) makes it clear that she favours a clause requiring *knowledge* of moral goodness. Her "Reason View" maintains that "part of freedom and responsibility lies in the agent's ability to form or revise her deepest values in light of the truth" (1990: 140–1). But it seems to me that responsibility requires no more than (true or false) *beliefs* about what is good and bad.

[12] Cf. Galen Strawson (1986) and Fischer and Ravizza (1998: 220–3).

that allow her to register certain facts of the world, namely, how her actions affect the good and bad of other creatures, and that the R–P practice is applied to her owing to these facts. Obviously, if A cannot associate the application of this practice with some of her behaviour, the R–P practice cannot supply her with reasons for action. (3*) ensures that the strength of A's reasons is mirrored by her intelligent desires. If this were not the case, providing her with reasons by bringing the R–P practice to bear on her would not be a reliable way of influencing her intelligent desires. (1) states that A's intelligent desires are manifested in action, and (2) that if she instead had desired to avoid the action, this would have been possible. If intelligent desires were not as a rule non-redundant components of sufficient conditions for action, the R–P practice could not efficiently serve the purpose of reinforcing and counteracting forms of behaviour. In sum, there must be malfunctioning at none of the stages (A)–(C) distinguished at the beginning of Chapter 32.

Direct and Ultimate Responsibility

It may be objected that the conditions (1)–(4) cannot be sufficient for responsibility because it is possible that A has been made to satisfy them by the manipulations of another agent. Suppose that, initially, A was not at all inclined to intentionally cause p, but by manipulating her brain the neurosurgeon B has transformed her into such a person that when she deliberates about whether or not to cause p, she forms an intention to cause p which she also implements in action. (Note that this is not a case of implanting into A's brain a compulsive intention or desire, whose strength is independent of her reasons. This would not satisfy the conditions (1)–(4).) It may seem that if the causal background of A's satisfying the conditions (1)–(4) is of this kind, she is not responsible for causing p (e.g. something very harmful).

On the basis of such considerations, some writers—for example Mele (1995: ch. 9) and Fischer and Ravizza (1998: 194–201)—have argued that responsibility is a "historical" notion: only if the history behind the fulfilment of conditions like (1)–(4) is of a certain kind, do we have responsibility. The libertarian Robert Kane has concluded that the manipulation I have sketched rules out an *ultimate* responsibility which involves "the power to be the ultimate *source* or *origin* of one's ends or purposes rather than have that source be in something other than you" (1996: 70; cf. Pereboom, 2001: 110 ff.).

We shall turn to the notion of ultimate responsibility, and the attendant backward-looking perspective, in the next chapter, but for the time being my point is that the motivational manipulation in question does not undercut justification of the R–P practice from the forward-looking perspective. From this perspective, it is perfectly possible to hold B responsible for causing A *responsibly* to cause p. This may be put by saying that, alongside the notion of ultimate responsibility, the forward-looking perspective provides space for a notion of *direct* responsibility, for which (1)–(4) are sufficient.

True, if B's manipulations of A's motivational states are very frequent, for example daily, it would be pointless to subject A to the R–P practice. (Under these circumstances, we should concentrate on applications of this practice to B.) But then it is the *frequency* of the manipulations that has this consequence, not the mere fact that A's mind has been manipulated by someone else. If A is left alone after an instance of manipulation, it makes perfect sense to apply the R–P practice to her to consolidate or improve her ways. This brings out that the R–P practice is designed to be applicable to people who exhibit something like the psychological stability we encounter in the actual world. (It follows that to make our set of conditions strictly sufficient, we need to add some such 'stability' condition. But I refrain from explicitly doing so because it is obvious that it can be done consistently with determinism. Similarly, I have not tried to state the other conditions, (1)–(4), as carefully as possible, but only precisely enough to make it plain that they are compatible with determinism.[13])

If this is correct, direct responsibility is not a historical notion. But hitherto I have confined myself to justification of responsibility from the forward-looking perspective. I have deferred the question of justification from the backward-looking perspective which needs to be addressed to make applications of the R–P practice deserved and just. As will transpire in the next chapter, the notion of ultimate responsibility with which this perspective operates *is* a historical notion. Now, that A is ultimately responsible is indeed excluded by the manipulation we have considered.

In fact, the mere truth of determinism suffices to exclude it. For, as Kane remarks, irrespective of "whether the sources of your ends or purposes lie in nature or in other agents, *they do not lie in you*" (1996: 71). It would be hard to insist on a wedge here, for it does not appear crucial that the manipulation is executed by an agent acting intentionally. Surely, A would not be more (than directly) responsible if the cause of her mental transformation were some natural force, like radiation (as conceded by Mele, 1995: 168–9). Nor would A be more responsible if B had *created* her with her present attitudes instead of letting her undergo a mental transformation (cf. Mele, 1995: 168). But, if neither of these aspects is essential for manipulation to rob us of responsibility, what could plausibly be held to make manipulation but not determinism responsibility-robbing? The next chapter implies that this challenge cannot be met, for there I shall give a general argument to the effect that determinism is incompatible with our being ultimately responsible. Moreover, in opposition to Kane, I shall try to show that ultimate responsibility is undermined by indeterminism, too. Neither determinism nor indeterminism can give us this deeper responsibility which, alongside direct responsibility, is a part of the commonsensical concept of responsibility.

Thus, the exploration of responsibility is forced backwards yet another step. I started by examining the sense in which responsibility has been held to require that one can *act* otherwise. I found that this presupposes a sense in which our deliberation can issue in another *decisive desire or intention* than the actual one. According to my explication, the latter notion is epistemic, boiling down to that the upshot is in principle unpredictable, owing to the fact that it is based on our reasons which, necessarily, are partly outside our

---

[13] Double puts it well: "Although the task of arriving at the *best* compatibilist account may be indefinitely perplexing, the compatibilist's strategy promises to ever more closely approximate the best account" (1991: 61). I think, though, that Double's "autonomy variable account" (ch. 2) demands too much in respect of mental powers such as rationality and self-knowledge. It seems to me to state necessary conditions for being free to a high degree rather than being responsible.

purview. It will be seen in Chapter 36 that this explication is of importance for my interpretation of responsibility in the desert-entailing sense. For the time being, however, I want only to emphasize that this explication does not force us to postulate any degree of indeterminism (though it does not exclude it). Consequently, we arrive at a sense of responsibility—direct responsibility—that is compatible with determinism. But it has emerged that there is a stronger sense of responsibility—ultimate responsibility—which forces us to move further backwards and plumb the causal background of the conditions of direct responsibility. Since these conditions are compatibilist, there must be such a background to plumb.

34

RESPONSIBILITY AND DESERT

I HOPE now to have outlined a plausible forward-looking justification for ascriptions of responsibility that is compatible with the possibility that determinism rules in the sphere of mind and action. That there should be such a justification appears likely in view of the fact that so many thinkers have embraced compatibilism, that is, the thesis that determinism is compatible with *full* responsibility, for it seems unlikely that all of them have gone completely wrong. By analogy of reasoning, however, the fact that libertarianism and incompatibilism have also found a great number of adherents indicates the existence of an alternative way of justifying the R–P practice that transcends the bounds of determinism. If this conjecture is correct, neither compatibilism nor incompatibilism represents the whole truth about the relationship between responsibility and determinism. Both of them rather reflect complementary aspects of this relationship, although both err in denying aspects discerned by their opponents.[1]

In Chapter 30 I characterized the backward-looking justification of the R–P practice now to be considered by saying that, according to it, applications of the practice are *deserved* and, thereby, *just*. What I shall now attempt is to make good the claim that this kind of justification can be reconciled neither with determinism nor with indeterminism. To accomplish this, the concept of desert must be analysed in some detail.

The Structure of the Concept of Desert

In a ground-breaking study of desert, Joel Feinberg remarks: "If a person is deserving of some treatment, he must, necessarily, be so *in virtue of* some possessed characteristic or prior activity".[2] That in virtue of which someone deserves something—*the basis* of desert—"must be facts about that subject" (Feinberg, 1970: 59). A plausible candidate for being the basis of *A*'s deserts are actions of his that are responsible in something like the

---

[1] This sort of 'compromise' has been defended in different forms by Honderich (1988: chap. 8), Double (1991: ch. 6), and Smilansky (2000: ch. 6). [2] (1970: 58). See also Kleinig (1971: 73).

meaning explicated in Chapters 32 and 33, that is, roughly, actions that are voluntary and that result from non-compulsive desires of an agent who has a conception of what is good and bad for other beings than himself at present.[3]

Secondly, when one is deserving, there is *something* that one deserves—it might be termed a *return* (deserved). Feinberg maintains that returns

> have at least one thing in common: they are generally 'affective' in character, that is, favored or disfavored, pursued or avoided, pleasant or unpleasant.[4]

It seems to me closer to the truth to say that a return must be something that is (regarded as being) of positive or negative (personal) *value for the subject*. For suppose that A deserves a reward; then it would scarcely be felt to be apposite to give him something that he desires (favours, pursues) only because he holds some erroneous belief.

We have, then, reached this position: when A is a subject of desert, there is something deserved, a return, that is of positive or negative value for him, and there is some feature F of him—say, a responsible action—in virtue of which basis he is deserving of the return. We have also noted that *desert* is a consideration of justice, that is, that it is just that A receives the return he deserves in virtue of the basis.

What must the basis of desert, for example a responsible action, be like if such a claim is to make sense? In a typical case, we think that A can deserve a positive or negative return on the basis of an action that affects for better or worse *another* individual than himself, and the personal value of the action's result for A is discordant with its personal value for others. For instance, imagine that A is a criminal who profits by actions that bring pain and misery to others or a do-gooder who undergoes hardships in order for others to flourish. Here the claim of desert seems to amount to something like that A receive returns the personal value of which to him *equals* the personal value of the desert-basis for others: when the basis is an action that has culpably made the life of some other being worse and A's better, the claim is that this advantage be removed and he be made to suffer like his victim, whereas if the basis is an action that has improved the condition of some other, the claim is that A be compensated for any personal loss incurred and be made as much better off as the beneficient has been.

This idea is rough and in need of refinement (which is not surprising given the attitudinal embedding of desert that I shall sketch in Chapter 36). Suppose, for instance, that the basis of A's desert is of different value to different other subjects—should the return deserved then equal the higher or the lower value or perhaps some mean? I shall not grapple with such refinements, since it is not essential for my purposes that the common-sense concept of desert can be spelt out with tolerable precision.[5] My objective is to marshal a certain argument against the applicability of the concept of desert and for that

---

[3] But if we go by everyday discourse, it is too restrictive to claim, as does J. R. Lucas: "Deserving is tied to doing" (1993: 125). For people are said to deserve to win beauty contests in virtue of their beauty and to deserve privileges in virtue of their noble ancestry. I am also inclined to hold, against Lucas, that the distinction between 'desert' and 'merit' is philosophically insignificant.

[4] (1970: 61); cf. also Kleinig (1971: 73). As Kleinig points out, it follows from this that inanimate things cannot literally deserve anything.   [5] Even champions of desert, like Cupit (1996: 55–7), concede its indeterminacy.

I only need to delineate the contours of the concept. It is, of course, entirely consistent with this project that the concept be embroiled in other difficulties.

However, the basis of desert is not perforce anything that makes a contribution to what is of value for others. Imagine that a farmer makes great efforts to get a good crop, but does not get it, owing to hailstorms; then he might deserve a good crop.[6] For he seems to deserve a return whose value for him equals the value his efforts were designed to produce, although the latter value is relative to him rather than to others. But if the farmer is to deserve a positive return, his endeavour must at least not be harmful or morally unjustifiable. If his aim had been harmful to others, say, if he had planned to waste land, we would not regard him as deserving success if he had failed; rather he deserves the frustration he gets (and probably more).

This example introduces the complication of actions that fail to achieve their purpose. It reveals that we can be persuaded to assign desert, not in proportion to the result an action actually brings about, but rather to what it is designed or intended to bring about. Consequently, if A performs an action designed to improve the lot of others, but it fails to do this, through no fault of his, we seem inclined to hold that he deserves a return the value of which for him is equal to the value of what the action was designed to bring about rather than what it in fact brought about.

At this point, it becomes necessary to draw a distinction between *motivational* desert—which includes *moral* desert—and what (thinking of the etymology of the term) one may call *technical desert*.[7] The basis of motivational desert is meant to be purely motivational; it seems to be, in Kantian terms, the good will that is all-important, one's skill in putting it into effect being irrelevant. Surely, one does not deserve *moral* censure if one causes bad effects by failing to implement one's good intentions because, through no fault of one's own, one is handicapped or incompetent. In contrast, technical desert brings in skill or ability as well: a scientist cannot become deserving of the Nobel prize merely by being strongly motivated to make a ground-breaking discovery, nor can an athlete deserve to win an Olympic gold medal merely on the basis of a firm will to win. On the other hand, scientific or athletic skill or ability is not sufficient by itself; it is necessary that it be put to use. Normally, the use of the ability must issue in success (e.g. a scientific award is given to somebody who has actually made some great discovery), but success seems not strictly necessary: a runner in a clear lead who trips just before the finishing line allegedly deserves the victory, despite the fact that she does not win. Perhaps the fact that

---

[6] Here one should be alert to the distinction—noted by Feinberg (1970: 56–8, 64–5, 85–7) and Kleinig (1971: 74–5)—between what one deserves and that to which one has *a right* or is *entitled*, though it is not clear-cut. I do not think it correct to say that the farmer has a right or is entitled to the crop he does not get owing to some misfortune, though he may deserve it. For no one owes it, or is under an obligation to give it, to him. On the other hand, if he were exceptionally lucky, and got a very rich crop, he has a right to it or is entitled to it, but he may not deserve it. Thus, I believe Gaus (1990: 411–13) goes wrong in asserting, generally, that one *deserves* "the fruits of one's labour". If the farmer works single-handedly on his own land, then (assuming the applicability of the concepts) he has a right to whatever crop he gets—even if it is bigger than the one he deserves. Others are under an obligation not to lay their hands on it. I shall return to this distinction later in this chapter.

[7] The varieties of desert are extensively discussed in Sher (1987). In contrast to the view here expressed, Sher believes that desert-claims can be justified.

success often appears to be the basis of technical desert is owing to its being good *evidence* of an underlying condition that is the real basis.

The term 'technical desert' is somewhat misleading for I want it to cover also cases in which the basis of desert has nothing to do with the exercise of any capacity, but concerns rather some property like being beautiful (cf. n. 3).

The Argument from Ultimate Responsibility against Desert

Although this survey brings out that the concept of desert is both complex and nebulous, I nevertheless think it allows us to extract the following entailment from it:

(D) If A deserves a return R in virtue of having F, then, as the result of his having F, it is just that he receive R because his receiving R will make things as valuable for him as his having F makes things for others or is designed to make things for others or for himself.

Now what conditions must A's having F satisfy if, for example, this equivalence between the value of it and the value of R for him is to make it just that he receive R? A plausible proposal is, as already indicated, that this must be something for which he is *responsible* (in something like the sense characterized in Chapters 32 and 33). Suppose that A's having F consists in his doing some action for the beneficial result of which he is not responsible; luckily, some circumstances he did not foresee effected this result. Then it surely cannot be just to reward him in proportion to the value of this result. Imagine that B acted with the same intention as A did, but that no unforeseen factors collaborated to make the result of her action as beneficial; then it cannot be just to give A a bigger return in virtue of his having F. Analogously, if A and B are not at all responsible for their behaviour. For instance, if they are two new-born babies, it cannot be just to reward A for having caused his mother little pain while he was being born and to punish B for having caused her mother a lot of pain, for this difference is due to genetic and environmental factors for which they have no responsibility. In fact, it is hard to think of any property of neonates—or non-human animals—that could make it just to treat some better than others and, thus, which makes some more deserving than others. The most likely explanation of this fact seems to be that there is nothing for which they are responsible. Thus,

(R) It can be just (because deserved) to reward or punish A on the basis of his having some feature, F, only if he is responsible for having F.

When you are responsible for having F, however, you are necessarily so in virtue of having certain properties—call them 'responsibility-giving features'. These features need not comprise every feature that is causally necessary for your being responsible for having F; they need not comprise those that are necessary for your very existence, for example such general conditions as the occurrence of the Big Bang or the presence of oxygen. Rather, they may consist only in features that, given your existence in the world, are causally necessary for the properties you possess to include the particular property of being responsible for having F rather than an alternative one. Since at this point I am assuming determinism, I also imagine these properties to be sufficient to determine whether this property is included.

As we have seen in foregoing chapters, if you are responsible for having F, this may be something that you have intentionally brought about. But intentionally to bring about that you have F, you must have a character which, in the circumstances, inclines you to intend to bring about this, abilities that allow you to execute this intention and information that you now have an opportunity to exploit these abilities, and so on. Granted, it is possible that you are also responsible for your having these particular responsibility-giving features, G. But if so, this must be in virtue of having certain other responsibility-giving features, H, which make you responsible for your having G. Evidently, this regress of responsibility cannot be infinite in the case of temporally finite beings like us. Instead,

(−U) The responsibility-giving properties in virtue of which individuals are responsible are ultimately ones for which they are not responsible.

In other words, even if A is responsible for having F, he is not *ultimately* responsible for it, that is, he is not responsible for the exemplification of *every* responsibility-given feature of his having F, however distant in time (for a similar conception of ultimate responsibility, see Kane, 1996: 35). This is compatible with his being, as we have put it, *directly* responsible for having F (in the sense roughly explicated in foregoing chapters). Now, it follows from (R) and (−U) that

(−JU) It cannot be just to reward or punish A on the basis of his having the ultimate responsibility-giving properties.

Surely, this can be just as little as it can be just to punish and reward us in accordance with whether we cause our mothers much or little pain while being born. In both cases, the explanations of the alleged bases of just distribution refer to genetic and environmental forces beyond the subjects' responsibility. However,

(−J) If it cannot be just to reward or punish A on the basis of these ultimate responsibility-giving properties, it cannot be just to reward or punish A on the basis of something for which he is responsible in virtue of them, such as his having F.

For this is indirectly to reward or punish him on the basis of the ultimate responsibility-giving properties on the basis of which it is agreed that it cannot be just to reward and punish him. It cannot be just to reward or punish him, and thereby make him better or worse off than others, on the basis of properties he is guaranteed to have by properties he is not responsible for exemplifying and others are prevented from exemplifying by lacking these properties beyond their responsibility.

Now, (−J) and (−JU) entail that

(−JR) It cannot be just to reward or punish A on the basis of something for which he is responsible, such as his having F.

Finally, (R) and (−JR) entail the conclusion

(C) It cannot be just (because deserved) to reward A on the basis of any feature he has.

That is, all prima facie bases of desert are undermined. So, the responsibility condition on the desert-basis is really stronger than (R) which requires only direct responsibility:

(UR) If A's receiving a return in virtue of having F is to be deserved and, thus, just, he must be *ultimately* responsible for having F.[8]

This is, however, a condition which cannot be satisfied by any temporally finite being like us. The rationale for (UR) is that if A is to deserve a return R in virtue of having F, this must be just because the value for him of R is equivalent to the value of his having F. But the justice of this equivalence presupposes that A's having F is *entirely* due to what he is responsible for, so that its value flows from nothing external to his responsibility. This is after all why responsibility for the desert-basis was required to start with. But if A is not ultimately responsible for having F, his having this feature must have an external source in the end. Since no temporally finite being like us can satisfy this condition, (UR), it follows that the concept of desert is not applicable to us.

As I have argued in preceding chapters, direct responsibility is sufficient for a forward-looking justification of the R–P practice, in terms of the beneficial consequences of this practice for A and other beings. But to say that applications of the R–P practice are deserved and just is to say that they can be given a backward-looking justification which requires ultimate responsibility because of the implied justice of a value-equivalence between a return and some fact about the recipient.[9]

Geoffrey Cupit denies (R), that desert in general presupposes responsibility and suggests the following explanation of why this may seem so:

> Desert can easily seem to presuppose responsibility for it is easy to make the mistake of transferring to the notion of desert what is properly associated only with some of those modes of treatment which can be deserved. The modes of treatment which do presuppose responsibility—in particular, punishing and rewarding—are, after all, a very significant subset of the forms of treatment which are said to be deserved. (1996: 171–2)

---

[8] Predecessors of this argument against desert have been advanced by Sidgwick (1907/1981: 283–4), Nagel 'Moral Luck', reprinted in Nagel (1979), and by Galen Strawson (1986: 28–30 and 1999). Strawson does not seem to emphasize specifically what it is about desert—namely, that it involves justice—that generates the regress of responsibility. This enables Mele to respond that responsibility may be conceived as an "emergent" property rather than one which is "transmitted" from underlying states that are also responsible (1995: 224–5). But I have to confess that it is beyond my abilities to flesh out any plausible way in which justice could 'emerge' along the track. Of course, there is direct responsibility, but it is not sufficient to make applications of the R–P practice just.

[9] Feldman (1999: 144–5) may be right that desert-bases need not be located in the past. The essential point may instead be, I think, that they have to be *fixed*. The deserved return may be something designed to fit something fixed. This 'direction of fit' distinguishes considerations of justice from those of utility. The latter are designed to fix or determine something which, because of the direction of causality, will have to be future in relation to them. In contrast, what we know to be fixed is normally in the past. The rationale for the label 'backward-looking justification' need, however, not be that desert bases must be in the past, but could be that it encompasses ultimate responsibility which involves tracing responsibility backwards.

We do, however, speak of rewarding and punishing non-responsible beings, like small children and pets. Surely, we do so because it is the same "modes of treatment"—doing something that is good or bad for the subjects—applied for a similar reason—their behaviour being good and bad, respectively—as when we speak of rewarding and punishing in the case of responsible agents. But, then, the relevant "modes of treatment" presuppose only sentience or consciousness, not responsibility. It is not these modes themselves, but their being *deserved* which requires responsibility—indeed, as we have seen, even ultimate responsibility.

It has also been argued, for example by Fred Feldman (1999: 141–2) and Owen McLeod (1999: 63), that when we become worse off without being responsible for it, by being mugged or contracting some disease, we deserve compensation or aid. But this seems to me to be so only if we do not deserve to become worse off because there is nothing for which we are responsible in virtue of which we deserve to become worse off.

A Closer Look at Some Responsibility-Giving Features

Let us now look in more detail at the paradigm desert basis, a responsible action, to ascertain that its conditions—the responsibility-giving features—are such that the agent cannot be ultimately responsible for the basis. These conditions can be divided into three groups: (1) the agent's intention (or whatever one sees as the proximate motivational antecedent of action) that is implemented in the action, (2) the agent's ability to perform the action, and (3) the agent's awareness of an opportunity to act. An 'opportunity' designates circumstances external to the agent which allow him to exercise the ability: for instance, the presence of a legible text which allows one to exercise the ability to read. Awareness of these circumstances makes the agent actualize dormant dispositions.

To begin from behind, sometimes the opportunities we have are the result of our responsibly having placed ourselves in certain situations. But these responsible actions are in their turn determined by action opportunities we had earlier on. These opportunities may also be the outcome of responsible actions on our part, but eventually we reach opportunities for which we cannot have any responsibility, for example opportunities we happen to have because we were born in a certain place at a certain time.

The same clearly applies to the ability which is the second condition for the successful implementation of an intention. It may be responsibly acquired as the product of training, but the training activity obviously presupposes other abilities, and so on until we reach some potential 'given' to us by our genes and early environmental influence. Hence, to unearth something we can be ultimately responsible for, we must bracket both ability and opportunity and concentrate on (1), the intention implemented.

To do this is to focus on moral desert—or, more broadly, motivational desert—as opposed to technical desert. The bases of technical desert include abilities or skills: what the artist or athlete deserves certainly depend upon their artistic or athletic abilities. So they are eroded by the above argument. But if we assume that the basis of motivational desert is purely motivational and that it is immaterial for this assessment whether the motivation materializes in action, perhaps a proper basis for such desert can be isolated. (On the other hand, if the basis of motivational desert is eroded, so are the bases of technical desert, since we would hardly consider anyone deserving because of some capacity which others have induced, say, by drugs.)

A moment's reflection reveals, however, that the actual formation of an intention is also dependent on opportunity. The characters of two people, A and B, may be equally courageous, but only A is in fact placed in a situation in which, say, he will have the occasion to form an intention to save lives at the risk of his own. But the character of B is such that, if he had been in A's situation, he *would* have formed the same intention. If so, it seems clear that he is as deserving of praise as is A, that it cannot be just to treat A better than him.

True, given a policy of rewarding only people who actually save lives, A alone may be *entitled to* (or have *a right to*) a reward. But, and this is a point to which I shall come back, 'is entitled to' does not mean the same as 'deserves'. We should also notice that one may be entitled to something, *given a policy*, without being *morally* entitled to it, for the latter presupposes the moral propriety of the policy.[10]

The upshot of the discussion so far is this: when matters beyond our responsibility are peeled off, the true basis of our motivational desert can include at most our *traits of character*, conceived as standing dispositions to have various intentions and desires in suitable circumstances. The basis cannot be the actual formation of these intentions and desires, since this is prey to accidental and fortuitous circumstances. This conclusion seems, however, to break violently with the everyday practice according to which claims of desert are apparently based on what is intentionally and responsibly accomplished. For instance, in a court of law, the grounds for conviction are responsible actions and not traits of character. Does this prove that we have removed ourselves from the common-sensical notion of moral desert?

No, because epistemological considerations may account for the discrepancy. If moral desert bases in their purest form are the characters of persons, it will be very hard to ascertain their moral deserts, since their characters are hidden from view. The best guides to or indications of the characters of persons are their responsible actions which express their intentions: we can scarcely know that somebody is bad enough to murder unless he actually murders. Consequently, even if our moral deserts are *in fact* fixed by our traits of character, it is normally possible to make *an epistemically justified claim* as to what they are only on the ground of our responsible actions. Since it is especially imperative that judgements of desert be well founded in courts, it is not surprising that nothing less than responsible action will do as a ground for conviction. To sum up, the discrepancy between the view that character is the proper basis of moral desert and everyday practice may vanish if we keep in mind the distinction between desert-claims that are true and ones we are in a position to know or justifiably believe to be true.[11]

---

[10] For this reason, I am not convinced when Cupit argues that desert does not presuppose responsibility by claiming that competitors can deserve to win without being "responsible for possessing those attributes which enable them to win" (1996: 161). I think they can only be entitled to the winner's prize, given the rules.

[11] For further elaboration of this point, see Norvin Richards (1986). Richards draws this distinction in order to defend the view that "when we are concerned with what a person deserves, we are interested in his behaviour *as a display of character*" (1986: 200). It seems to me, however, that Richards errs in not gauging the full implications of his concession that character could be a basis of desert only if it is "one's own artefact" (1986: 202) and in construing desert as a forward-looking notion.

Of course, this practice leaves much to be desired because it leaves open the possibility that our actual opinions of people's moral desert might be grossly erroneous and unfair: owing to good or bad luck, they might never have strayed into 'opportunities' that reveal the depravity or excellency of their characters. But let us concentrate on the question of how well character stands up as a desert-basis, given that we know it. Imagine we know the characters of A and B to be equally bad; both are equally prone to commit acts of malevolence and cruelty. But, while A has up to the present point lived in a social milieu that is more advantageous than the average, B was born into a violent environment in which he has been constantly maltreated by parents and peers. Here it is tempting to judge that B deserves less in the way of punishment than does A, because of his earlier maltreatment. Then it would follow that their *present* characters cannot be the bases of their respective moral deserts, since these characters are alike.

However, this conclusion would be too rash. I think that the truth is rather that B deserves less *further* punishment, for he has so to speak been punished in advance by his miserable upbringing.[12] If we discount in rough proportion to the suffering in his upbringing that has helped to produce his character, it is evident that less future punishment is needed to make B's life as much worse as his character would make the lives of others (given suitable circumstances) than is requisite to establish the same equilibrium in A's case. So the badness or misfortunes of one's past life are relevant to one's present moral deserts if there is a causal connection between them.

All the same, this case has the virtue of directing one's attention to the fact that one's present character may be moulded by environmental factors that are beyond one's responsibility. To the extent that it is, it cannot be a proper basis of moral desert. To the extent that it is responsibly shaped by one's earlier doings, the same question arises about the character behind these doings, and so on until we reach a character, or a proto-character, close to our origin. But it is certainly fixed by one's genes and early environmental influences beyond the range of one's responsibility.

This concludes our attempt to extract something for which we are ultimately responsible out of the three kinds of determinant of our responsible actions: motivation, ability, and opportunity. In every case we find that when we have filtered out what is not ultimately our responsibility, nothing is left. In other words, $(-U)$ is established. By means of (UR), it follows that there is no proper basis of desert, nothing that can make it deserved, and just, that someone is treated better than another.

It should be noticed that this determinist argument against responsibility does not employ what Jay Wallace has called the "generalization strategy" (1994: 16–17). It does not do its work by showing that the 'compulsory' kind of obstacle to responsibility that, say, an irresistible desire constitutes, is *always* present when we act intentionally. This would undermine even a forward-looking justification of (direct) responsibility. The generalization strategy attempts to eliminate the importance compatibilists attach to the distinction between being caused and being compelled to act intentionally to the effect that the latter but not the former undercuts responsibility. In contrast, the present argument grants the importance of this distinction and that we are directly responsible, but

---

[12] Cf. what Klein calls "the payment-in-advance-condition" (1990: 84).

contends that we do not have the ultimate responsibility required by backward-looking justification.

It is also wrong to suggest, as does Fischer (1994: 149), that determinism threatens responsibility only by implying that we cannot act otherwise. For determinism to threaten the responsibility which it does threaten—ultimate in contrast to direct responsibility—it is not sufficient to show that we cannot act otherwise in the determinist sense, that is, that it is not causally possible for us to act otherwise. If beings with an infinite past as responsible agents populate a determinist world, it is causally impossible for them to act otherwise, but this does not establish that they are not ultimately responsible. Nor, as we shall soon see, is showing that it is not causally possible for us to act otherwise necessary for the conclusion that we are not ultimately responsible: indeterminists, too, fail to rescue our ultimate responsibility.

Three Objections to the Argument against Desert

An Appeal to Rights

My argument against desert does not invoke the assumption that bases of desert must themselves be *deserved* (like the argument attributed to Rawls, for example by Sher, 1987: ch. 2). Against this sort of argument, Nozick protests:

> It is not true, for example, that a person earns Y . . . only if he's earned (or otherwise *deserves*) whatever he used (including natural assets) in the process of earning Y. Some of the things he uses he may just *have*, not illegitimately. It needn't be that the foundations underlying desert are themselves deserved, *all the way down*. (1974: 225)

But my argument does not rely on the assumption that "the foundations underlying desert are themselves deserved". The nub of it is that subjects must be ultimately *responsible* for their desert bases, not that they must ultimately deserve them.

When Nozick speaks of things that we "may just *have*, not illegitimately", he means things we have acquired without violating anyone else's (natural) rights or entitlements, and so things to which we ourselves have a right or are entitled.[13] Now, if one has a right, or is entitled, to X, it is just that one have it and it would be unjust to deprive one of X and to transfer it to someone else (unless one consents to this). This is so even if others deserve to have X (which goes to show that rights trump desert as considerations of justice). Hence, like desert, rights invoke justice. (Nozick's entitlement theory is presented as a theory of *justice* (1974: 150–82).)

Nozick's theory is a descendant of the Lockean theory of natural rights. Locke famously writes:

> every man has a property in his own 'person'. This nobody has any right to but himself. The labour of his body and the work of his hands, we may say, are properly his.

---

[13] Nozick explicitly states (1974: 153) that it is not among his aims to supply a ground for his rights or entitlements. By 'natural' rights I mean moral rights that are grounded in some natural fact as opposed to conferred by some conventions.

Whatsoever, then, he removes out of the state that Nature hath provided and left it in, he has mixed his labour with it, and joined to it something that is his own, and thereby makes it his property (1690/1990: II. v. 27).

Locke seems to make two principal claims here. *(a) the self-ownership claim*: we own, or have property-rights to, our own bodies, and their psychological capacities (some of which make these bodies embody persons). Locke here apparently ignores his famous distinction between the person and the body (1689/1975: II. xxvii), in so far as he effortlessly moves from speaking about having property in one's *person* to the labour of one's *body* being one's own. There might seem to be something paradoxical about the notion of having a right to oneself, since it might seem that right-holders would have to be distinct from that to which they have a right. But let us grant that each of us may be said to become the owner of a certain body by being "the first occupant" of it (cf. Kamm, 1992: 101), in the sense of being the first (and normally the only) one to exercise voluntarily control over it and to receive proprioceptive sensations from it.

This brings us to the second claim, *(b) the property-acquisition claim*: in virtue of the fact that we have a right to our bodies, we come to own virgin natural resources by being the first ones to 'mix' our labour—that is, something to which we have a right—with them. (Properly speaking, the labour seems to be the mixing rather than that which is mixed, as Jeremy Waldron points out (1988: 185–6), but never mind.)

There are many difficulties in this theory, some of which I have earlier tried to bring out (1994, though I am no longer altogether happy about the details of this presentation). First, the ultimate responsibility argument that above was mobilized against desert applies to rights as well. As remarked, that individuals have rights to something entails that it is just or fair that they have it. But in order for it to be just that individuals have that to which they have rights, the basis of rights—which we have construed as first occupancy or appropriation—must consist in something for which right-holders are ultimately responsible. Individuals cannot, however, be ultimately responsible for whether the bodies of which they are the first occupants are richly or poorly endowed and, hence, for what they are able to accomplish by the use of them on unowned natural resources that happen to come in their way.

A possible objection is that individuals may be said justly to get the bodies they are born with because, prior to existence, everyone has *equal chances* of receiving richly and poorly endowed bodies. This reply will not do, however, since assigning equal chances to non-existent individuals requires that they can be identified independently of their bodies, and this is not so on the view of our nature developed in Part IV. Furthermore, from the point of view of justice, assigning equal chances to benefits and burdens is acceptable only when the benefits and burdens themselves cannot be equally distributed. But in the case of initial bodily equipment, it is hard to see why it could not have been more equally distributed.

In order to present the second argument against rights, we have to examine some of the differences between rights and desert. These differences are indicated, for instance, by the fact that while it is perfectly natural to think that we have rights to our bodies and the psycho-physical resources materialized in them, it would be peculiar to hold that we *deserve* these things. So Nozick has a point (though, *pace* him, it is hardly natural to say that we are *entitled* to our bodies and their assets; 'entitlement' seems a narrower notion, suggesting perhaps the presence of conventions).

There can be nothing in virtue of which we deserve our bodies and their assets. If you deserve a return R in virtue of a basis B, R and B are distinct in the sense that you may possess B without possessing R. Your possession of B is rather designed to make it just that you possess something of value for you that you may not already possess. Hence, if you were to deserve possession of B, it would have to be because of your being in possession of something distinct, B^*. There is clearly nothing that could play this role in the case of your deserving your body and its resources. In contrast, the basis of a right to B—the first occupancy of B—is not something distinct from B that you could possess (as a property) without possessing B. The basis of a right to B is something that puts you in a position to enjoy or make use of B. This sort of basis therefore does not exclude that you have a right to your body, as the basis of desert excludes that you could deserve your body.

This is also, I think, the explanation of why rights—that is, 'claim' rights which are not mere liberties or permissions—are correlated with *obligations or duties*. Rights are had against others (who are capable of recognizing them). It is reasonable to think that general rights, which are held against everyone,[14] like your rights to yourself and your property, are *negative*. They are, then, rights against others that they do *not* harmfully interfere with your use of your bodily-based assets and property. The corresponding duty of others is consequently the negative duty not to make this interference. But you can deserve something without anyone being under a duty to let you have or use it, for example the farmer may deserve a good crop, though no one has duty to let him have it (cf. Sher, 1987: 195; Zimmerman, 1988: 162). For nobody may be capable of giving him this crop (and 'ought implies can'). The crop he has a right to is however the crop he in fact gets if he single-handedly cultivates his own land (cf. n. 6 above). The fact that he has already acquired it sits well with that the grounded right, and the correlated duty, have the negative content of avoidance of harmful interference. If you have acquired something, you do not need positive help to be put in possession of it.

Also connected with this grounding of rights is the fact that rights can be *waived*, that is, you can give up your possession of something you have acquired and release others from their duty of non-interference if you wish. But what you deserve need not be similarly optional—as the deserved punishment of criminals illustrates.

The second argument against rights—it may be called 'the constitution argument'— focuses on the fact that the basis of a right is supposed to put you in possession of the thing to which you are said to have a right. The pivotal premise of this argument is:

(P) One has a right to X only in so far as one a right to all of its parts.

If X has proper parts, y, z . . . to which one does not have any rights, then, strictly speaking, one has a right to X minus y, z . . . If X can be divided into proper parts to none of which

---

[14] As opposed to special rights which are had against certain individuals who have done certain things to the right-bearers, like having made promises to them or having brought them into existence. This distinction was introduced by Hart (1955).

one has a right, one cannot have any right to X. It would be vacuous to claim a right to X under these circumstances, for one part after another could be removed from X without one's right being infringed, until there was nothing left of X.

Now, it seems that one's body can be divided into parts to none of which one has a right, for example the elementary particles of physics. For one is not the first to occupy or appropriate them (if indeed one can be said to have occupied or appropriated them at all), since they constituted other things before they came to constitute one's body. Nor is it the case that earlier occupants and alleged right-holders voluntarily transferred them. Hence it transpires that one does not have any right to these constituents of one's body. In conjunction with (P), this entails that one does not have a right to one's body. Furthermore, as we have remarked, this claim, the self-ownership claim, is presupposed by the property-acquisition claim; so it follows that one cannot have a right to anything.

While the constitution argument highlights the self-ownership claim, a third argument— 'the generation argument'—highlights the property-acquisition claim. To repeat, the property-acquisition claim presupposes the self-ownership claim. The generation argument asserts that, in conjunction with an evident fact, the former claim also implies the falsity of the latter claim. This evident fact is

(G) Parents produce their children out of material that belongs to them.

In conjunction with the property-acquisition claim, (G) entails that parents own their children—at least until they voluntary transfer their ownership to their children. By the same argument, the parents would be owned by *their* parents, since they are themselves children of other parents. A fatal regress that would undercut everyone's ownership of themselves thus threatens. It is true that the regress could be avoided by parents always voluntarily transferring the property rights to their children, say, when they attain majority or before the children produce their own offspring. But suppose that they do not do so (perhaps because they do not realize that they have these property rights).

Hillel Steiner tries to solve this paradox by maintaining that parents do not fully own their offspring because their "production required them to mix their labour with natural resources in the form of germ-line genetic information transmitted from ... grandparents" (1994: 248), that is, the production involves material that does not fully belong to the parents. As a result, their ownership of their children is not full, and this means, according to Steiner, that it is temporary and liable to expire when the children attain majority (1994: 248, 275). At that time, the children allegedly become self-owners. But this does not explain why children—that is, anyone of us—become self-owners instead of being something owned by nobody. For they are constructed in accordance with genetic information which, *ex hypothesi*, is not theirs, nor anyone's. Further, the 'construction material' used in the building process in accordance with the genetic blueprint cannot be theirs because they are not fit to own anything—or anyone's, since we have all been in the position of children. So, how is it that anyone owns anything?

On the strength of these arguments I claim that it will not do to appeal to (natural) rights in support of the notion of desert. Rights should be rejected alongside desert, for partly the same reasons.

An Appeal to Indeterminism

In my ultimate responsibility argument against desert I presupposed the truth of determinism, but in fact my conclusions hold good irrespective of whether determinism or indeterminism is true. On reflection, it seems rather obvious that, if determinism holds true in the sphere of responsible action, it is impossible to insulate anything for which we are ultimately responsible, since, ultimately, every condition of our actions is the product of causes that exist prior to us. But it is in fact not much less obvious that desert cannot gain any foothold on the indeterminist assumption that its basis is partly due to chance. For to the degree that something is ascribable to chance, it is as little within the range of our responsibility as if it had been caused by factors prior to our existence. Hence, it cannot be just to let us prosper or suffer in proportion to its value.

To illustrate this in somewhat greater detail, consider the indeterminist or libertarian theory of free will recently presented by Robert Kane (1996).[15] The central notion of Kane's theory is that of "self-forming willings", or acts of will (1996: 124–5). We may here content ourselves with looking at self-forming willings in the shape of decisions or choices occurring in situations of moral or prudential conflict. Moral or prudential reasons are here pitted against reasons favouring the immoral or imprudent course, the comparative strength of these sets being such that neither is "decisive" (1996: 127). As a result of these sets of reasons, there occurs an "effort of the will" to resist the temptation to act immorally or imprudently. *That* such an effort occurs is determined by there being reasons for and against, but the effort is in other respects *indeterminate* (1996: 128). Since the effort is indeterminate, it is both causally possible that it terminates in a choice or decision to act morally or prudentially and causally possible that it terminates in a contrary choice or decision to act immorally or imprudently. Thus, the choice or decision which actually occurs is *undetermined*.

To explain how this indeterminacy of efforts may be possible, Kane draws on quantum indeterminacy and chaos theory. He imagines that "the neural processes occurring when the efforts are being made are chaotic processes . . . In chaotic systems, very minute changes in initial conditions grow exponentially into large differences in final outcome" (1996: 129). If this "chaotic amplification" works on quantum indeterminacies in the brain, it may issue in indeterminacies in respect of macro-neural processes that, experientially, are efforts of will. For moral and prudential conflicts "stir up chaos in the brain" (1996: 130).

All this is empirical speculation that may eventually be falsified. The question I want to ask is, however: supposing it is true, will it provide us with desert-entailing responsibility? It seems not, for surely I cannot reasonably be held responsible in this sense for whether or not my effort to resist the temptation to act immorally or imprudently is successful. I cannot reasonably be held to deserve praise if it succeeds and blame if it fails, as it is a

[15] This theory is a development of theories earlier put forward by Kane, e.g. in (1985, 1989). For references to criticisms of these theories, see Kane (1996: esp. ch. 10). Kane makes further additions to his theory in (1999), but I ignore these since they are irrelevant to my objections. Other libertarians, like Ekstrom (2000: ch. 4), have put forward theories that appear to be exposed to the same sort of objections.

matter of chance whether it succeeds or fails. It seems that my responsibility can extend no further than to having assembled reasons and, as a result of that, having made an effort. In one causally possible development from then on, my effort is successful; in another it is a failure. Which development actualizes, however, is not up to me, but a matter of chance, or (good or bad) luck. Surely, it cannot be just to let my future lot depend on such a random outcome.[16]

Compare this with another example of Kane's in which chance interferes after a decision to act has been made (1996: 55): a nuclear facility employee plants some radioactive material in a drawer of an executive's desk with the intention that she be exposed to harmful dose of radioactivity. It is, however, a matter of chance how much radioactivity the executive will be exposed to when she is at her desk. But if the executive happens to be exposed to more rather than less radioactivity, the employee cannot deserve harsher punishment than he would deserve if the material had happened to emit less radioactivity. This harsher punishment could not be just, since it is genuinely a matter of chance how much radioactivity the material will expose the executive to. (Harsher punishment would also seem difficult to defend from a forward-looking perspective.) To be sure, what the employee is described as being responsible for depends on the actual outcome; so, if the degree of radiation is high, he is responsible for a greater threat to the health of the executive. But it does not follow that he is more blameworthy, since he is not responsible for whether this degree is high or low, as this is the result of an undetermined process.

This responsibility requires something that Kane himself admits but that indeterminism rules out, namely "Antecedent Determining Control": "the ability to be in, or bring about, conditions such that one can guarantee or determine which of a set of outcomes is going to occur before it occurs" (1996: 144). He insists, however, that "this limitation [of control] is a requirement of free will" (1996: 144) and, hence, responsibility. But, as we have just seen, this limitation of control over the outcome is instead something that restricts our responsibility.[17]

There is one further complication that should be mentioned. Kane argues that we must not assume that it is always as probable that agents will succeed in overcoming temptations as that they will fail to do so (1996: 177). They can increase the probability of success by making "character-building" choices, that is, choices to resist temptation that succeed (1996: 180). If, as the result of such character-building, it is more likely that some agents succeed than others, he considers them more deserving.

But there is a problem with this idea: to begin with, before any character-building could occur, was it equally probable that all agents would succeed in their efforts? If it was not, it seems that those for whom success is more probable, owing to no efforts of their own, cannot be more deserving. Consequently, if, as the result of this head start,

---

[16] Kane replies to the similar objection that his theory implies, absurdly, that when one of two agents, who have exactly the same life-history and who have made exactly the same effort, succeeds and the other fails, the former is more deserving than the latter (1996: 171–2). His reply is that 'exactly the same' has no sense for worlds in which there are the indeterminacies he is hypothesizing. But it is not essential to this type of argument that the phrase carries the qualitative sense. It could have the numerical sense, i.e. we could consider two possible futures of a single individual, as I have done.

[17] O'Connor (1993) criticizes earlier theories of Kane's and two other incompatibilist theories on the similar ground that they cannot provide for an adequate notion of agent-control.

they have succeeded, by making character-forming choices, in raising even further the probability of their efforts being successful, their level of desert cannot correspond to the high probability of their now being successful. Suppose, instead, that originally it was equally probable that the efforts of all would succeed. If the probability of success later varies between agents, this is the outcome of their past efforts being successful. But whether these efforts are successful is a matter of chance and so, according to the argument above, nothing which can make our responsibility greater or less. Hence, whatever the origin of the possible variations in respect of the probability of making successful efforts, they cannot be the basis of responsibility in a desert-entailing sense.

It might be objected that the situation in which all have equal chances of succeeding in their efforts is like that of participants in a lottery in which everyone has equal chances to win, and there is no objection from the point of view of justice to such a lottery. I would concede that, if a benefit cannot be equally divided, it is fairest to give everyone an equal chance of winning it. But in many cases benefits can be equally divided. Moreover, it is not just to let the fact that someone has won once increase that individual's chance of winning the next time, as one would have to hold to maintain that someone's character-building choices can boost desert.

The introduction of indeterminism, then, does nothing to render the concept of desert-entailing responsibility applicable. Certainly, it endows agents with a contra-causal power to act otherwise and thereby effectively undercuts the possibility of predicting and manipulating their behaviour. This is important for Kane, who thinks that the possibility of "nonconstraining control" removes a kind of freedom (1996: 64 ff.).[18] My present argument has been to the effect that the kind of freedom which is removed by determinism and the possibility of this control, but invited by indeterminism, is not of the kind that underlies desert-entailing (or any morally relevant sense of) responsibility.

An Appeal to Agent-Causation

In Chapter 30 I remarked that I am not certain that it is *logically* impossible that there be agents who exhibit ultimately responsible self-determination. This is because I take it to be logically possible that there be responsible agents who have existed forever. Suppose that such eternal agents inhabit a deterministic world. Their present responsible actions can be determined by present responsibility-giving features which in their turn can be determined by earlier responsible actions of the agents which are determined by other responsibility-giving features of these agents, and so on *ad infinitum*. If so, there would be responsibility-giving properties of these agents for the exemplification of which they would be ultimately responsible in the sense that however deeply one probes their genesis, one does not move outside the range of their responsibilities. Such agents may be proper subjects of desert.[19]

---

[18] But he also thinks that libertarian freedom is a precondition for many other things we value, including the reactive attitudes I shall discuss in ch. 37. I shall there argue that, along with desert, these attitudes will be banned by rationalism, regardless of whether determinism or indeterminism is true.

[19] I think these speculations reveal that Klein is right in her claims (1990: 56 ff.) that ultimate responsibility (what she terms "the U-condition" (1990: 51)) is separable from a condition demanding a contra-causal power to act otherwise. For it

But let us leave these fanciful speculations aside and turn to an idea which could make *us* subjects of desert, although we have evidently not existed forever as responsible agents. So far I have assumed that causal relata are events or facts, so if an event or fact does not have a sufficient cause in other events or facts, it is in part causally undetermined. To be sure, in ordinary discourse, we often appoint a thing or continuant the cause of something, for example, the rock is said to have caused the window pane to break. But it is arguable that these statements can be rephrased as statements that cast events or facts in the role of causes, for example the fact that the rock was hard and moved at such and such a speed when it hit the pane caused the latter to break. Following Roderick Chisholm (1966) and Richard Taylor (1966: chs. 8 and 9),[20] a number of modern philosophers have, however, rejected such translatability for cases in which we act intentionally or responsibly. They maintain that alongside causation by events or facts (so-called transeunt causation), there is another form of causation, *agent-causation* (or immanent causation) in which we then engage. We then make causal contributions that are not reducible to what is caused by events or facts with us as subjects. It is, strictly speaking, *we ourselves* who cause something here.

Most of these writers—Thorp (1980: ch. 6), Foster (1991: 273–80), Clarke (1995), and O'Connor (1995b, 2000)—have endorsed Chisholm's view that agent-causation is necessary to save our responsibility in the full sense, though Bishop (1983) takes the different line of Taylor's that this construct is requisite to uphold our status as intentional agents.[21] These argumentative strategies are importantly different. If the postulation of agent-causation were necessary to account for the intentionality of our actions, that would provide a stronger reason for its postulation than if it were necessary for our being fully responsible. For it is a matter of controversy whether we are responsible to this extent, but it cannot sensibly be doubted that we act intentionally. Unfortunately, as will be seen, it is harder to understand how agent-causation could perform the service of making intentional action comprehensible. But let us start by examining the more popular strategy.

If the notion of agent-causation is to supply the sought-for ultimate self-determination demanded by desert-entailing responsibility, there cannot be sufficient event-causes for exercises of agent-causation, or for the events that are agent-caused. Nor can it be that these exercises merely *happen* to lack such a cause, for then they run the risk of being out of control like other undetermined events. The operation of an agent-cause must rather be an event that could not *intelligibly* be caused by any other events. This is why it holds

---

would not be causally possible for the agents with infinite pasts whom we are now considering to act otherwise. Pereboom (2001: ch. 1) argues that the condition that a responsible act "is not produced by a deterministic process that traces back to causal factors beyond the agent's control" (p. 3) does not imply an ability to act otherwise. But, contrary to my view, his argument is to the effect that "moral responsibility requires that the action's actual causal history have certain indeterministic features" (p. 37), and that this implies the former condition but not ability to act otherwise.

[20]   Both have since given up this approach, see Chisholm (1982) and Taylor (1982).

[21]   In his more recent book (1989), Bishop has abandoned the agent-causalist doctrine in favour of an event-causalist analysis of intentional action. In fact, Bishop's "sustaining cause" version of this analysis is akin to the one espoused by me (1981: ch. 6).

out the promise of being a way out of the fatal dilemma: either accidentally undetermined or ultimately determined by something external to the agent's responsibility.

In conformity with this, we find John Foster claiming that

> for a subject to be the agent of a certain mental event is for him to be involved in it in whatever way it is which makes events of that type intrinsically autonomous. (1991: 277–8)

An event (e.g. a decision) is of a type which is intrinsically autonomous if and only if it is of a type such that "its intrinsic nature excludes the possibility that either it or any of its components is causally determined by prior conditions" (1991: 277).[22] Of course, as Foster himself concedes (1991: 279), the notion of there being a type of event whose intrinsic nature makes it logically impossible that it be caused by other events is highly peculiar. But this is not all, I want to argue, for it leads onto further peculiarities, namely, the doctrine that the agents exercising this sort of causation must be mental (or immaterial) substances.

It is believed that (a) agent-causation is the prerogative of material things with a mind that is involved in the production of their acts; inanimate things, or even simple conscious beings, are not agent-causes. But if it is also believed that (b) a thing's having a mind consists in nothing but a set of mental events that have this body, and no mental substance, as their subject, one wonders why (a) should be true, why the introduction of mental *events* as causes, should give rise to *agent*-causation (which is irreducible to event-causation).

In response to this puzzlement, O'Connor suggests that the property of being an agent-cause could be an *emergent* property of ours in the sense of

> a macroproperty that is generated by the properties of an object's microstructure, but whose role in the causal processes involving that object are not reducible to those of the microproperties (1995b: 179).

This emergentist view is particularly problematic if one also, like O'Connor, believes in the above-mentioned doctrine that "no answer *could* be given to the question of what was the cause of a given agent-causal event" (1995b: 186; cf. 2000: ch. 3) because the cause here is no event but "an enduring agent". Even if an exercise of agent-causality is not reducible or identical to the microstructure that constitutes or realizes it, it is hard to see how it could make perfect sense to ask for the (event)-causes of this microstructure, whereas the same question as regards the constituted or emergent macroevent is "ill framed" (O'Connor, 2000: 58).

In fact, O'Connor's suggestion that it is incoherent to think of an exercise of agent-causality as either caused or uncaused tempts one to think that it is incoherent to assume that there could be such an event. Surely, if one hears that something can neither be caused to happen nor be said to happen uncaused, the most reasonable thing to think is that it cannot happen at all. At the very least, if agent-causalists cling to the belief that an

---

[22] Cf. also Thorp, who claims that when a decision is agent-caused, it is neither the case that it has a sufficient cause in mental events—albeit it may be more or less influenced by reasons (1980: 131–7)—nor that it is correlated with a neurophysiological event that has a sufficient neurophysiological cause.

exercise of agent-causality is essentially beyond the reach of event-causality—which they must do if it is to yield that ultimate self-determination which is required by desert-entailing responsibility—they cannot see it as an emergent property. They must rather see it as a property of another substance than the material one. Hence, *pace* O'Connor, Taylor (1966: 134–8) and Thorp (1980: 119–22), I think that agent-causation must go with a belief in mental substances that play the role of agent-causes.

If the conception of free agents as agent-causes presupposes that they are mental substances, this conception is of course heir to all the difficulties raised against the latter notion in Chapter 19. To these should be added difficulties special to the agent-causalist hypothesis, for example why should the causal operations of these substances be in line with physical laws? (The special difficulties of aligning agent-causality with the event-causality we know from experience merit a fuller discussion than they can receive here; see for example Kane, 1996: 120–2, 187 ff., and Pereboom, 2001: ch. 3.) It is hard to swallow that the intuition that we have desert-entailing responsibility could be strong enough to justify all these extravagancies.

When critics object to the unclarity of the notion of agent-causation, some advocates of it reply that it is no worse than event-causation. "The nature of transeunt causation is no more clear than is that of immanent causation", Chisholm writes (1966: 22). Similarly, Thorp holds that "the event causality with which we seem so comfortable is itself unfathomly mysterious", so the agent-causalist "is not introducing mystery alongside clarity, but mystery alongside mystery" (1980: 106). This appears to me exaggerated, but it is true that the controversy which surrounds event-causation makes it trickier to establish that agent-causation is incoherent. Since any more substantial claim about event-causation—for example that it involves constant conjunction or counterfactual dependence—is bound to be contestable, we cannot successfully argue that agent-causation is incoherent because the same claim about it makes no sense. But if we cannot argue that the concept of agent-causation is a contradiction in terms, we can at least argue that it is vacuous or empty of content.

Admitting that they have no definition or verbal characterization of the concept at hand, agent-causalists sometimes appeal to experience. For instance, Foster writes that the concept is one "which we can only grasp introspectively" (1991: 278; cf. Thorp, 1980: 106–10). That is, it is a primitive and indefinable concept which, like, for example, the concept of a colour, is derived from experience—in this case the experience from the inside that one has of oneself acting intentionally. Now I am willing to grant that one has an experience from the inside of what it is like to execute an intentional action (about which I have tried to say something in Chapter 4). So, *if* it had been proved that in acting intentionally we engage in agent-causation, I would concede that we do have an experience of ourselves as agent-causes, an experience from which our concept of an agent-cause could stem. This has not been proved, however. Hence this appeal to ostensive definition can be successful only if it can be shown that the introduction of agent-causation is necessary to account for intentional action. If so, Chisholm (1966: 22) would be right that, given that our concept of causality derives from our experience of our own acting, the concept of agent-causation is primary in relation to that of event-causation.

Agent-causalists like Taylor (1966) and Bishop (1983) have contended that what makes the doctrine of agent-causation worthy of consideration is that event-causalists have failed to state necessary and sufficient conditions for the occurrence of intentional acts, the conditions put forward being insufficient to exclude, for example, wayward causal chains that are incompatible with intentionality. Here I can do no more to rebut this charge than to express my view that it seems to me that the concept of intentional action can be elucidated along the (event-causalist) lines sketched in Chapter 4.

What should be emphasized, however, is that even if this account is found insufficient, agent-causation cannot supply what is missing. As C. D. Broad pointed out long ago (1952: 215), a reference to an enduring agent as a cause cannot explain why that agent acted at a particular time of its existence rather than at any other. Nor, as Carl Ginet adds (1990: 14), can it explain why the agent at that time performed one action rather than an alternative one. O'Connor replies that an agent-cause does not act on its own, but that "a full explanation of why an agent-caused event occurred will include, among other things, an account of the reasons upon which the agent acted" (1995: 184; cf. 2000: ch. 5). The agent-cause provides a "mechanism of control that 'hooks up', so to speak, the agent's reasons and consequent decision (and action)" (1995: 195; cf. 191).

But this amendment does not leave agent-causes with any genuine explanatory function. For the construct of the agent itself as a cause cannot explain why some of the reasons rather than other ones that the agent had led to action, nor why they led to action at any particular time rather than another one at which the agent existed. Whatever the agent's reasons upon which he acted and whatever the time of his action during his existence, agent-causalists can declare *post factum* that agent-causation stepped in and did its 'hooking up'. So, the notion of agent-causation does not, and cannot, constitute any genuine addition to an (indeterminist) action-explanation in terms of the agent's reasons. It is a vacuous or empty notion.

This is conceded by some agent-causalists, for example Randolph Clarke, who writes that "affirming agent causation would not improve our ability to predict and explain human behaviour" (1995: 210).[23] Clarke instead rests the case of agent-causation on its being a *sine qua non* for moral responsibility (1995: 210–11). We have seen that this tactic cannot succeed, since it can reasonably be doubted whether we really are responsible in the full, desert-entailing sense required. It might, however, be pointed out that we indubitably *possess the concept* of such responsibility. How have we acquired this concept if we are not ultimately responsible by being agent-causes? Later on in this part, I shall try to show how our possession of the concept of desert can be explained without relying on any assumptions to the effect that we have ultimate responsibility or are agent-causes.

---

[23]   Clarke adds that "there is no observational evidence that could tell us whether our world is an indeterministic world with agent causation or an indeterminstic world without it." But Pereboom argues persuasively that available evidence rather supports the latter hypothesis (2001: 79–86).

Conclusion

The attempt to introduce a form of causation special to intentional or responsible action, therefore, ends in failure. Let me pull together the threads of the reasoning in this chapter. (1) Alongside the forward-looking interpretation of responsibility expounded in Chapters 32 and 33, there is the idea that applications of the R–P practice can be justified in the sense of being deserved and so just. (2) As stated by (UR), one can deserve a return only if there is something for which one is ultimately responsible, that is, something which is due to no responsibility-giving condition for which one is not responsible, in the forward-looking sense. (3) Excepting responsible agents having infinite pasts, agents cannot be ultimately responsible for anything if they are subject to event-causation, irrespective of whether it is fully deterministic or partially indeterministic. (4) It has been suggested that they could be ultimately responsible if there is such a thing as (irreducible) agent-causation which they exercise. A precondition for their exercising agent-causation is, however, that they are conceived as mental substances. This conception of responsible agents is therefore heir to all the difficulties of immaterialism with respect to persons; but, apart from that, the notion of a substance, which makes a causal contribution over and above what is attributable to events or facts, that have it as a subject, is vacuous. (My conjecture is that the notion of agent-causation reflects a misunderstanding of the experience of freedom and action described in Chapter 31.) From this we may infer that the application of the R–P practice to temporally finite agents cannot be deserved and just.

So we arrive at this conclusion about responsibility. To say that agents are responsible is to say that the R–P practice can be justifiably applied to them. Of the two points of view from which applications of this practice has been thought to be justified, the forward-looking one and the desert-entailing backward-looking one (the latter being backward-looking in view of its reliance on something for which the agent is ultimately responsible), only the former remains. If an assignment of responsibility is to be defensible, it cannot mean more than that an application of the R–P practice can be justified from a forward-looking perspective.

However, the common-sense conception of responsibility apparently welds the two accounts of why the R–P practice is justifiable. Once one of them is discovered to be untenable, we shall experience a certain conflict in ascribing responsibility: we shall feel such ascriptions to be unjust because undeserved. (In Chapter 37, I shall suggest that, when desert is rejected, justice will consist in equality, and applications of the R–P practice will come out as unjust by counteracting equality.) It does not follow, however, that such ascriptions cannot be *morally justified*, for the 'yes' of forward-looking justification may outweigh the 'no' of backward-looking justification: the consequences of holding someone responsible may be good enough to offset morally the injustice of the procedure. This is a matter I cannot pursue any further. Let me just stress that the fact that applications of the R–P practice can never be deserved, and for that reason declared just, makes us unable to attribute responsibility as whole-heartedly as we did when we were philosophically innocent.

35

THE DEONTOLOGICAL ELEMENT
OF RESPONSIBILITY

THERE is a further aspect of our commonsensical notion of responsibility which, as we shall presently see, is linked to the notions of desert and of rights. When delineating a compatibilist conception of responsibility in Chapters 32 and 33, I did not raise the question of whether we can be as responsible for what we passively let happen as for what we actively do or bring about and as responsible for what we do with foresight as with intention. This was harmless, since the purpose was to set forth conditions sufficient for our being responsible for something. But it is contrary to two familiar deontological doctrines: *the act-omission doctrine*, AOD, and *the doctrine of the double effect*, DDE.

One could easily make the mistake of assuming that, if it is shown that a backward-looking justification of responsibility must give way to a forward-looking—also termed 'consequentialist'—justification, it follows that what we are responsible for must be understood in a consequentialist or non-deontological way. But these are separate issues: the first is about the sense in which we are justifiably subject to the R–P practice when we are responsible, while the second is about what we are responsible for. Claiming that the sense of justification cannot be the backward-looking one because of its reliance upon ultimate responsibility is one thing, and claiming that the two deontological doctrines are wrong about what we are responsible for is another. So we should not without discussion exclude the possibility of a forward-looking justification of responsibility for something that is deontologically construed.

For my own part, I believe, however, that the deontological doctrines mentioned are false, and I shall briefly indicate why.[1] My discussion will be brief because in the present context it is of less importance whether deontology is true. The reason is that our primary interest lies in the psychological cost of attaining rational compliance with the truth as regards responsibility. Since we have concluded that this compliance requires the disposal of what is part and parcel of backward-looking, desert-entailing responsibility, it

---

[1] For a penetrating criticism of these deontological doctrines, see Kagan (1989: chs. 3 and 4).

does not matter at what this responsibility is directed. It would have mattered if this form of responsibility could have been salvaged, for then the question would arise at what it is rational to direct it. True, this question also arises with respect to the responsibility which is given a forward-looking justification: should it attend as much to what we merely let happen and foresee as to what we actively cause and intend? But this sort of responsibility comprises no spontaneous reactions which it would be psychologically costly to redirect from a deontological to a non-deontological target.

All the same, the range of forward-looking responsibility needs to be determined. It is also pertinent to insert a short discussion of deontology for the reason that, as I shall try to bring out, deontological thinking is allied with the thinking that underlies desert and rights. Let me start with AOD, which takes the performing of certain actions, for example killings, to be morally worse, or harder to justify morally, than letting them occur, so that there are circumstances in which it is wrong to kill, but permissible to let die or be killed the same kind of individuals. As I shall now argue, AOD is an integral part of the theory that our general rights to ourselves and our property are negative.[2]

The Act-Omission Doctrine and Rights

We saw in the last chapter that these rights are rights against other people (i.e. beings capable of recognizing rights) that these people do *not* harmfully interfere with how right-holders make use of their psycho-physical assets and property. Being claim-rights, these rights are correlated with duties on the part of the others that they do not interfere in this way. The fact that these rights (and, hence, the correlated duties) are negative and include no positive rights to be helped to make use of one's life, limb, or property is congruent with the fact that the ground for these rights lies in right-holders' acts of occupancy or appropriation which are designed to enable them to control, in the natural course of events, the things to which they have rights. This entails that there are no positive duties to help right-holders to make use of themselves or their property in the natural course of events.

But there could still be positive duties to prevent other people from *violating rights* by depriving right-holders of life, limb, and property. The idea of negative rights could consistently be so construed that it yielded such duties of protecting people against the right-violations of people other than oneself (and oneself at other times than the present). One would then have a duty to violate a right to life by killing one person if one could thereby prevent two or more violations of this right. This would amount to what Nozick calls a "utilitarianism of rights" (1974: 28). The fact that the theory of negative rights is not construed in this "utilitarian"—or, rather, consequentialist—fashion is, I think, due to AOD. Thus, I am inclined to think that AOD adds something to our theory of negative rights that this theory need not entail, namely, that it is morally worse now to violate a right than to let it be violated.

---

[2] This is discussed further in (Persson, 2005*b*).

My hypothesis is that AOD can make this addition because it involves the intuition that you are morally responsible for what you actively cause in a way or to a degree to which you are not responsible for what you passively let happen (cf. McMahan, 2002: 461). I will call this intuition AGR (short for 'activity generates responsibility'). As it is reasonable to think that our duties are restricted to that for which we are more responsible, AGR will not let them include the prevention of killing as well as killing.

AOD, however, consists in more than AGR. For the fact that we actively cause something does not always have the same moral repercussions. If it did, it would follow that, in Jeff McMahan's words,

> the significance of the distinction between doing and allowing should be reversed in cases in which the outcome is good rather than bad. If doing harm is worse than allowing harm to occur, actively benefiting someone should, in general, be better than merely allowing someone to be benefited. (2002: 461)

But if the greater responsibility for the good that we can actively cause made us shoulder an obligation to cause it, just as a harm that we can actively cause places us under an obligation to refrain from causing it, we would after all not be permitted to refrain from doing good, as AOD lays down. We would have a duty to kill one in order to save two, since this would be an instance of actively benefiting the two. Hence, if AOD is to be sustained, there must be something to it, over and above AGR, that explains why there is no duty actively to do good, why actively doing good does not have the same moral bearing as (actively) harming.

This is where the theory of negative rights not to deprive beings of things in their possession such as life, limb, and property, fits in. For, according to this theory, there are duties not to harm by deprivation of these things, but no duties positively to ensure the possession of these things. (In addition, the appeal to this theory of rights explains why the causing of certain harms, e.g. by getting a promotion or victory that somebody else would otherwise have got, is not wrong: there are no claim-rights to these things.) Hence, there is an intricate interplay between AOD and the theory of negative rights.

It follows from this that if, as I argued in Chapter 34, this theory of rights should be rejected, AOD must also go by the board. But there are also arguments against the AGR-component of AOD that I have developed elsewhere (2004a), arguments to the effect that AOD is involved in a paradox springing from the fact that the killing which you may now be permitted to let occur may be a killing by yourself. I shall here just summarize a part of my argument. Imagine that you foresee that if you let a spasm run its course, it will cause your finger to contract around the trigger of a gun, with the result that you will shoot and kill Vic. Imagine further that you are in a situation in which you are permitted to let Vic be killed, but you would not be permitted to kill him. (AOD must imply that there are such situations—for example when you have to let Vic be killed in order to have time to save two people—because it takes killing to be worse than letting die.) Then, if it so happens that Vic will be killed by you, you are permitted to let Vic be killed by yourself, that is, you are permitted to let yourself kill Vic. On the other hand, it would seem that, if it would be wrong of you to kill Vic now, you cannot be permitted to let yourself kill Vic now. If this is so—I support this premise in (2004a)—AOD is entangled in the paradox that you are both permitted and forbidden to let Vic be killed in certain circumstances.

The most promising way out of this paradox might seem to be to restrict AOD so that it does not apply to killings performed by yourself now. It might be said that to let yourself kill now is not permitted like letting other agents kill, but is instead as wrong as killing now. Let us call this move *the self-exception claim*. The first thing to notice about the self-exception claim is that it is tantamount to abandoning AOD, by giving up its AGR-component. For this claim implies that the morally significant distinction can no longer be that between killing and letting die or be killed, since one instance of the latter (namely, letting be killed by yourself now) is on a par with killing.

Secondly, the self-exception claim is also incompatible with the deontological bedfellow of AOD, DDE. Suppose you could quell the spasm that will cause you to shoot Vic only by intentionally squeezing the trigger and thus kill him intentionally. Then this claim implies that whatever you do is wrong. According to DDE, however, you should rather let the spasm run its course, foreseeing that it will lead to Vic's death, than intentionally kill Vic.

Defects of the Doctrine of the Double Effect

While AOD is based upon the AGR-intuition that there is a responsibility for harms you actively cause or do which is lacking as regards harms you let occur, DDE is based upon the intuition that with respect to harm you actively cause, you have a responsibility for that harm which is intended, as a means or as an end, which is missing as regards that harm which is merely foreseen. So, it may be permissible to bring about a greater good and a lesser harm if and only if this action is such that the greater good could be the (intended) end of it without the lesser harm being an (intended) means to the good, but the harm is instead merely foreseen as a side-effect of a neutral means or of the good. There is an affinity between AOD and DDE in that what you intend in doing something gives the descriptions that motivate you or move you to act (derivatively in the case of means), whereas what is merely foreseen is motivationally inert.

DDE is, then, naturally construed as a qualification of AOD, a qualification which has the effect of permitting some causings of lesser harm in the pursuit of a greater good, namely, lesser harm which could be merely foreseen as opposed to lesser harm which must be intended (as means or end). If DDE were to be accepted without AOD, the result would be a morality which would be more or less as demanding as consequentialism is commonly chided by deontologists for being. For we would then be allowed to let harm happen only when pursuing an end which is a greater good—a permission the better-off could rarely benefit from in a world with so much suffering as the present one.

On the other hand, DDE is needed to qualify AOD. One reason for this is that the latter may place us in situations in which the performance of some forbidden action is unavoidable: either I drive on straight ahead and kill five people or I steer to the side and kill a single one. Here DDE permits me to steer to the side, with the end of saving the five and merely foreseeing that I will kill the one. (As remarked, it is more problematic to use DDE to qualify AOD if the latter is restricted by the self-exception claim.)

Since DDE is most plausibly construed as operating upon AOD, it is less urgent to assess it critically so long as AOD is not in place. But a quick assessment is still in order.[3] The main problem with DDE is that while it is clear that intending harm as an end when one acts is worse than merely foreseeing that it will result, it is not at all clear why intending harm as a means is worse. For harming somebody as a means is quite compatible with a concern about the welfare of that person—it only implies that one's concern for the good end is even greater—whereas harming somebody as an end is not (cf. Kagan, 1989: 167–9). It is true that when we harm as an (intended) means, we are, derivatively, activated by the thought of harm, but it is not clear why being derivatively activated by the thought of harm is wrong. When we intend harm as a means to a greater good, we may in a perfectly good sense *put up* with having to do harm just as we do when we bring it about with foresight.

Furthermore, there are cases that show that the fact that harm is done as a means is neither necessary nor sufficient to make an act worse than an act with the same good end would be were the harm merely foreseen. As in illustration of the former difficulty, consider a case—call it *Blow up*—provided by Kamm (1996: 151): it appears to be wrong, according to our deontological intuitions, to blow up a runaway trolley which will otherwise kill five people if, as a (foreseen) side-effect, an innocent bystander is also blown up. It appears to be more or less as wrong to blow up the bystander here as it would be were it a means to saving the five (e.g. were he to block the entrance to a hole in which the five are dying).

Note that in *Blow up* not even *the bystander himself* (as opposed to the harm to him) is used as a means. In this respect, *Blow up* differs from some other cases in which the smaller harm is mistakenly thought to be intended as a means. Thus, consider *Push* in which you accomplish the end of stopping the trolley from ploughing through the five by pushing Vic in front of it. Although it is commonly believed that DDE declares pushing Vic to be wrong here, the harm to him need not be intended. If, miraculously, the trolley bounced off Vic without hurting him, you could have achieved everything you intended, since this suffices to save the five.

Friends of DDE might try to make the doctrine condemn the pushing by claiming that, although harm is not a means here, there is still a use of *the person Vic* as a means in a way that is harmful to him. Such a revision would, however, not suffice to bring DDE in harmony with our intuition in *Blow up*. Nor will it do to reject this intuition because the bystander is not involved as a means. For suppose he were thus involved: suppose that when throwing the explosives, you have to aim for the bystander's steel helmet from which they will bounce to the trolley and explode, again with the side-effect that the bystander is blown up, too. Your action here would hardly be worse than it is in *Blow up*, though the bystander now is harmfully used as a means.

---

[3] DDE is more fully discussed in (Persson, 2005a).

A further objection to DDE is provided by cases which demonstrate that using as a means Vic in a lethally harmful manner—or, for that matter, doing harm as a means—to save the five is not *sufficient* for wrongness when producing this harm as a foreseen effect would be permissible. One such case is when the harm would have resulted whatever is done; another is when the harm is an effect of a first saving of somebody, but a means to a second saving of them without which the first saving would be pointless. To illustrate, suppose the five are placed in front of Vic on the track along which the runaway trolley hurtles. The five can only be saved from death by being lifted off the track with the help of a crane which will unavoidably drop them further along the track behind Vic. So, the five will only be saved because Vic's body functions as an effective buffer. In *Double saving I*, all six will be killed if you do not operate the crane because then the trolley will crash right through the five and kill Vic as well. (Perhaps the crane is so connected to the track and the trolley that operating it will slow down the trolley.) If so, it seems clearly permissible, *pace* DDE, to save the five by lifting them off the track, though this involves harming Vic as a means, for he will be as much harmed whatever is done.

In *Double saving II*, we suppose, more realistically, that the trolley will not plough through the five and kill Vic, too, if the five are not lifted off the track. If used to save the five, the crane will, however, still unavoidably dump them behind Vic, so that the five will be saved from being hit by the trolley at a slightly later time only because his body stops it. Hence, when you lift the five with the intention of saving them, you must intend this use of Vic as a means. Therefore, DDE declares this action wrong. But again, this seems mistaken, for Vic would have been as much harmed if his death had been only a foreseen effect of saving the five—that is, if the crane had dumped the five on the track at a time *after* which Vic has been hit and the trolley would have passed the place of the drop if it had not been stopped. Under these circumstances, DDE would allow the saving, but surely it cannot make any moral difference at what time the five are dumped, since the harm that befalls Vic is the same.

Hence, DDE must be rejected. Deontologists may nourish the hope of discovering a sound replacement for it. In search for a replacement, Kamm maintains that, in cases like the following one that might be referred to as *Delayed death*, killing the bystander by blowing up the trolley to save the five is permitted (1996: 202 n.). Here the explosion, which does away with the trolley, instead kills the bystander by releasing some chemical that slowly and unnoticeably undermines the bystander's health so that he dies a week later. Since *Delayed death* appears to differ from *Blow up* only in respect of how directly the bystander's death is brought about, any possible moral difference between these cases must have to do with this fact. This is also essentially the line Kamm takes when she puts forward for consideration a principle that "permits lesser harm to come from greater good, but only permits lesser harm to be an indirect effect of a means that directly produces a greater good" (1996: 202 n.). But, apart from the fact that one wonders how it could make any moral difference how directly harm is caused (if this does not affect the certainty of it which is a factor that determines responsibility), this principle is in conflict with our intuitions in cases like *Double saving*.

So, not only must DDE be rejected, the chance of finding a tenable replacement for it seems very slim. I suggest that DDE may be supported by two related mistakes about intention. First, that some events which are really immediate side-effects of the means are intended as means (as illustrated by *Push*). Secondly, that it is wrong to intend harm as a means because it is wrong to intend it as an end (probably because the thought of harm is assumed to activate us in both cases).

A Purely Causal Sense of Responsibility

Let us return to the self-exception claim which was introduced as the most appealing way out of a paradox that AOD faces. The fact that this claim is the most appealing way out indicates that what, according to AGR, we feel specially responsible for is not just our intentional actions, but what we do in a broader sense which includes what we do non-voluntarily, on reflex, etc.—that is, doings that are not intentional under any description. For the self-exception claim makes it wrong to let oneself do certain things in this broad sense, for example pull a trigger as the result of a twitch. The opposite of acting in this sense is not what we *let* happen, which is intended or at least foreseen. It is rather the wider category of what we do not do, but could (broadly) do. This is the reason why we can let ourselves act in the broad sense, which in turn is the source of my paradox.

The concept of responsibility at work when we take ourselves to be responsible for our actions in the broad sense is a purely causal one. It is symptomatic of a tendency to overlook the contribution of negative causal conditions. Pre-reflectively, we think of causes as *changes* (genuine changes, not so-called Cambridge changes) that produce other changes. I have suggested that this concept of a cause is derived from our proprioceptive experience of ourselves acting upon—and being acted upon by—the environment. It is in particular that which, against the background of the perceptual field, stands out as marked changes that are candidates for being causes (and effects). As opposed to this immediate awareness of causation, it takes counterfactual reflection to realize that the fact that we do *not* act to stop some ongoing process, when we could have done so, is also a causal condition of a negative sort: the process continues because certain changes do not occur.

To illustrate that, intuitively, we feel a special responsibility for things we do which are not done intentionally or knowingly under any description, consider a case of a so-called innocent threat who is in no way morally responsible for the damage she is about to cause. Imagine that she is being hurled at a victim and can be directed away from him only at some cost to herself, such as a broken leg. About such a case, Kamm writes: "the innocent threat has a greater responsibility to bear this cost, because she is headed to where she should not be, on the victim, who has a right not to be occupied" (1992: 47). So, even if the damage the human threat would cause the victim was somewhat smaller, it would still be right to deflect the threat at the cost of her breaking her leg.

I agree that this is how the situation might intuitively strike us: at first blush, we are indeed inclined to view the active cause as more responsible, though its activity is beyond intentional control. But, I contend, on reflection this intuition should dissolve. For if the threat is not, in something like the sense outlined in Chapters 32 and 33, responsible for being a threat, she is no more responsible for the damage caused by the collision than is the victim. It is no more true that "she is headed to where she should not be, on the victim" than that the victim is where he should not be, in a place where he blocks the threat's trajectory. Suppose that, by accident, our two vehicles collide and that, owing to forces beyond our control, either you or I will be hurled out and hit the other, with the result that the target's leg is broken. Suppose further that you are hurled out and could be deflected away from me only at the cost of somewhat greater injury than I would suffer by being hit. Clearly, it cannot be just and right to let you bear this cost, for your being the one who was hurled out was just an accident.

The feeling of responsibility for what we actively cause even if it is unintentional and could not reasonably have been foreseen is also at work in the emotion which Bernard Williams has called "agent-regret".[4] This emotion may be strongly felt by, for example, a lorry driver who unintentionally runs down a child he could not reasonably expect would dart out in front of his vehicle. Nothing similar would be felt by anyone who unwittingly failed to prevent the accident by not delaying the child before it reached the site of the accident.

This has been disputed. Judith Thomson argues that there is an emotion analogous to agent-regret with respect to things one is not aware of being able to prevent and, therefore, does not prevent. Her example is that, unbeknownst to her, a mother leaves her baby on Thomson's doorstep on a cold night (1990: 241). When Thomson discovers the baby on the following morning, it is dead. Her regret and sorrow will naturally be much more intense than it would be were she to read about such an incident in a newspaper. She will think, 'If only I had known it was there. I could easily have saved it.' Yet she cannot reasonably be blamed for not saving the baby, since she had no way of knowing that it was on her doorstep.

I think, however, that this regret is different from Williams's agent-regret in that there is no element of responsibility and guilt in it.[5] Suppose that there had been ten people in Thomson's house each of whom could have saved the baby just as well as Thomson. I conjecture that this would not have made Thomson less upset, though it would decrease a feeling of responsibility and guilt. Contrast the situation in which you along with ten other people unintentionally cause someone's death (e.g. unaware of each other, each of the ten pours a painkiller in someone's cup and together these contributions make up a sum which is minimally sufficient to kill the victim). Here one would

---

[4] See 'Moral Luck', reprinted in Williams (1981: 27 ff). Cf. also Williams (1993: 69–70 and 93). In the latter book, Williams writes that agent-regret "can be psychologically and structurally a manifestation of guilt" (p. 93). He also maintains that it is a mistake to condemn this guilt feeling as irrational for the reason that it is guilt for something for which one is not responsible, because one has not intentionally or knowingly brought it about. However, regret—which, as we saw in ch. 6, is a wish that something be the case which is caused by the conviction that it is not the case—is not the same as feeling guilt. To the extent that the lorry driver is feeling guilt along with regret—and this combination does not appear uncommon—it is irrational. For, as remarked in ch. 6, to feel guilt is something like to feel that one *deserves* to be blamed or punished, and this presupposes a wrong for which one is responsible.

[5] As I argued in the foregoing note, this is a reason for thinking that Williams's term 'agent-*regret*' is infelicitous.

feel less 'agent-regret' than if one had single-handedly killed the victim by mistake. Nothing corresponding seems true in Thomson's case. In my opinion, this case just illustrates the fact that we are much more upset when something tragic happens close to us than when it happens far away. It makes evolutionary good sense that we should be equipped with a mental set that inclines us to care more about what happens around us, since we can more often effectively influence this.

The Williams example may lead us to think that at least the driving which causes the accident must be intentional, for you would not feel agent-regret if, for example, by being forcibly shoved off the pavement, you involuntarily knock over a bicyclist, causing her a cranial fracture. This is so, though the origin of the concept of cause in bodily experience, as proposed in Chapter 31, suggests that you would indeed see yourself as a cause of the cyclist's fall. But in this case of involuntary movement, you do not view yourself as an epistemically ultimate cause, because you immediately trace the causes of your movement to something external to yourself. Since you are aware of your own movement, but not of the push you are given, as being causally necessitated, you are more bent on taking the latter as a causal starting-point and hypothesize that, if the push had not occurred, the cyclist would not have been injured than that this would not have happened if you had resisted the push. Thus, you here see yourself as a means to rather than as an ultimate cause of the accident.

In some cases of involuntary action, however, you may well feel causally responsible. Imagine that an irresistible twitch suddenly causes you to pull the trigger of the gun in your hand, with the result that you shoot and kill somebody. Here you will probably feel agent-regret. The reason is, I surmise, that in this case the causes of the twitch may be sufficiently unobtrusive for it to be possible for you to spontaneously view yourself as an epistemically ultimate cause. But when an intention starts the action, the impression of ultimacy is even deeper, making the agent most inclined to hypothesize that if the action had not occurred then . . . (e.g. the lorry driver inclined to hypothesize that if only he had driven a tiny bit more slowly then . . .).

We have here an explanation of why we do not see ourselves, for example, as having killed or violated a right to life if we cause somebody else to kill *responsibly*, but why we may well do so if we cause them to kill involuntarily by giving them a push. In the former case, an epistemically ultimate cause—in the shape of the affected agent's deliberations— enters and breaks the causal chain, which has its ultimate source in us, and this new cause initiates its own chain of events.

To sum up this discussion of the responsibility of which AGR and, by implication, AOD and DDE speak, it is a responsibility for changes that we see ourselves—that is, something about us—as the epistemically ultimate causes of. At the most basic level, it is a responsibility for what we actively cause. When self-consciousness emerges, it becomes in particular responsibility for effects that are intended, since intentions activate us, as opposed to what is merely foreseen. Since this is responsibility for something of which we are epistemically ultimate causes, it is naturally responsibility in the desert-entailing sense. I have suggested that this view on responsibility is wrong both in taking us to be responsible for events for which we are not responsible—events we unwittingly cause—and in relieving us of responsibility for events for which we are reasonably responsible, namely, what we let happen and the merely foreseen consequences of what we actively cause. The 'active' form of responsibility deontology rests upon should be replaced by the notion of responsibility sketched in Chapters 32 and 33.

As already indicated, however, it is of less interest in the present context to critically scrutinize the scope of this active, backward-looking responsibility, since it has already been concluded that it must be rejected because of its appeal to ultimate responsibility and self-determination. If it turns out, as I argue, that the concepts of natural rights and of desert as well as the attitudes of anger, gratitude, pride, shame, etc. will have to go by the board if there is to be rationalist compliance—because they are underpinned by a notion of (epistemically understood) ultimate self-determination—we need not ask whether their orientation is misguided, to compute the cost of achieving rational compliance. They would have to go by the board even if their orientation had been impeccable. So this inquiry into orientation would be most pressing if the states in question were well founded. Certainly, the proper range of forward-looking responsibility should be determined, but this is an issue of minor interest for the present purpose of estimating the psychological cost of rationalist compliance.

It is still of interest to see a bit more precisely how deontology, as codified by AOD and DDE, fits into the notions of desert and natural rights. From the picture here painted, it emerges that it is not just a historical accident that the rejection of these notions has tended to go with the rejection of deontology, as they have done in utilitarianism. (Utilitarianism also rejects personal and temporal biases, as I, too, have done but, unlike me, justice as well.)

36

THE EMOTIVE GENESIS
OF DESERT

THE agent-oriented emotions of *anger* and *gratitude* are expressions of the 'tit for tat' strategy which has been found to be conducive to survival in populations in which it is reasonably spread.[1] Roughly, when harm is done, for example pain is inflicted, anger, which includes a desire to inflict pain in return, is induced. On the other hand, when a favour is done, for example pleasure is caused, this may occasion gratitude, which encompasses an inclination to do good in return. Other emotional expressions of this strategy are *feelings of guilt*, for example if one fails to repay somebody who has done one a favour; *shame*, for example if one fails to retaliate against harm done; *pride* if one succeeds well in this; *admiration* of others who succeed well in the same enterprise; and *contempt* for those who fail; *forgiveness* if somebody shows *remorse* for having done wrong. *Benevolence* (sympathy) or *compassion* (pity) may also play a role in starting the exchange of favours, by sparking off an initial beneficial act. But let us here focus on the pair anger and gratitude and, especially, on the negative emotion of anger.

The hypothesis I would like to put forward is that we ascribe desert to each other (and to ourselves) because we exhibit the agent-oriented emotions of, in particular, anger and gratitude.[2] A sentence like 'I'll give him what he deserves' expresses what we feel like doing when we are in the grip of anger. The equivalence between the value of desert-bases and of returns based on them, which desert-claims demand, is a refined conceptualization of the cognitive-behavioural tendencies that are involved in these emotions.

As we saw in Chapter 6, anger comprises a tendency or (primarily non-intelligent) desire to engage in behaviour designed to cause something of negative value, primarily pain, to someone who (one thinks) has in some way made things worse for (first and foremost) oneself. (If one is less personally involved, indignation may replace anger.)

---

[1] For a brief review and some references, see e.g. Wright (1994: ch. 9).

[2] To my knowledge, this hypothesis was first put forward by Adam Smith in *The Theory of Moral Sentiments* (1759); see, e.g. the excerpt in Pojman and McLeod (1999).

Presumably, we have a disposition to exhibit this emotion because it is of survival value, by discouraging future aggressors. Analogously, gratitude promotes survival by encouraging future benefactors, by demonstrating to them that it pays to do good. These reactions pay back 'in the same coin' in the sense that they return bad by bad, and good by good. But it is also important to see that they pay back in the same coin in another sense, that *the amount* of the bad or good returned roughly equals that of the bad or good initially caused.

The response of anger is more serviceable if the initial aggressor, the responding agent, and possible bystanders are all prone to react to the same degree of harm inflicted by paying back with roughly the same amount of harm, if there is a common perception of what degree of retaliation is proper to what degree of aggression. For suppose that a substantive number of (potential) aggressors would view many acts of retaliation as involving too little harm caused to them; then they would not be deterred from future acts of aggression. On the other hand, if they take the offended to cause too much harm, there is a greater risk of escalation of aggression, by them or bystanders siding with them. Hence, the survival value of the propensity to pay back or retaliate will be optimal if there is more or less a uniformity in reaction. Now, the simplest way to establish this balance between action and reaction would seem to be if everyone responded to harm caused by inflicting what they agree would be a roughly *equal* amount of harm on the initial agent ('an eye for an eye, etc.').

Consider now beings endowed with this response-propensity who acquire the capacity to ascribe mental states—including desires and emotions—not only to themselves at present, but to others as well. (As was indicated in Chapter 6, one can experience anger without having this conceptual capacity.) They would then be capable of seeing not only the harm caused to themselves by aggressors as harmful to them, that is, as something that is of personal disvalue for them, but also of seeing the harm they cause or tend to cause others in their acts of vengeance as harmful to the others. They would thereby be able to articulate conceptually the value equivalence between the harmful action which elicits their reaction and their vindictive reaction itself. These judgements constitute judgements of desert of the most primitive kind. (We shall soon see that more sophisticated judgements have a more refined conception of the desert-basis than what is involved in anger.) As there is a rough uniformity with respect to assessments of vengeful responses, these desert judgements of different subjects will roughly agree with each other.

This explains not only why we are *capable* of making desert claims, that is, claims to the effect that the value of a return matches that of an initial action, but also why we *want* individuals to get what they deserve, why we regard, for example, the fact that somebody has injured another as a reason to pay back with an equal quantity of harm. For having the propensity to experience agent-oriented emotions is to be so wired up that one non-intelligently or instinctively *desires* to return equal for equal (and, I argued in Part II, desires generate reasons). Letting a wrongdoer have what he deserves therefore satisfies common desires of ours—desires that Honderich names our *grievance-desires* (1988: 571).

Honderich's view is that, in so far as claims about punishment being deserved provide reasons for punishing, they are tantamount to the fact that the distress this punishment involves "satisfies a desire to which the offender has given rise by his offence" (1988: 571). I agree that a claim about what punishment wrongdoers deserve would not supply any reason for distributing the punishment to them (and that we would not employ the concept of desert) were we not prone to feel grievance-desires. But, as Honderich may well admit (1988: 574–5), a claim about the satisfaction of grievance-desires is scarcely part of what we *mean* when we assert that somebody deserves punishment—if it were, the meaning of 'desert' would not be the same when a reward is deserved. In my opinion (with which Honderich may not agree), the connection to grievance-desires is consistent with the traditional view that the content of a claim such as that A deserves a return R in virtue of possessing F has to do with an equivalence between the value for him of R and the value (normally for others) of his having F. Given the attitudinal background of desert-claims here sketched, establishing this evaluative equivalence will gratify grievance-desires (and their positive counterparts).

This account of desert as rooted in agent-oriented emotions can be expanded to explain why we tend to restrict the ascription of desert to agents who are responsible in the deontological sense laid out in the foregoing chapter, once we have acquired the capacity to ascribe mental states like intentions. Suppose that A unintentionally inflicts pain on me by hitting me with a stick: he had no way of knowing that I would turn up within the ambit of the stick's movement, at a time when he could still stop the movement. At first blush, when I have registered only observable causes, I shall be angry with A and want to deal him a blow which is as painful as the one I have received. The concept of responsibility I then apply is the causal one encoded in AOD. But, since I am endowing A with a mind, I shall also think that he deserves the painful payback.

Imagine, however, that it is then brought to my attention that he had no way of knowing that the swinging stick would hit me; then I shall be inclined to retract my judgement of desert, and my anger with him will subside. This is, I surmise, because I no longer see him as the cause of my pain when I realize that he was not actively seeking to inflict pain on me. To intend or desire is, as we have seen in Chapter 4, an active state, a state of being disposed to bring something about. When I understand that A did not intend to hit me (and was not even aware of the fact that he would do so), I shall rather attribute the pain to unlucky circumstances. So, once we have acquired a more refined understanding of the mental causes of behaviour, we shall tend to censure as cognitively irrational our outbursts of anger, unless they are directed at agents who are responsible in the full deontological sense, which includes DDE. And we shall consider it proper to allocate desert only to agents who are responsible in this sense.

This attitudinal embedding of desert gives a clue to the genesis of the idea that the basis of desert must be something in respect of which one is *ultimately* responsible— an idea that was spelt out and disputed in Chapter 34. In Chapter 6, I argued that the object or target of agent-oriented emotions is a cause whose operation is conceived as causally *blank*, that is, neither as caused nor as uncaused, because it is situated at a point at which causal inquiry ends. I contended that, from an evolutionary point of view, this arrangement was more advantageous than that of agent-oriented emotions which are geared to a conception of the target as being endowed with a consciousness in which the causal chain starts. This arrangement brings along a propensity to view any agents, the cause of whose activity is sufficiently obscure, as ultimately responsible in a certain sense, and as deserving once they are endowed with minds.

Now, as long as a responsibility-giving state of an agent is assumed to be causally blank in the sense indicated, the fateful dilemma between it being outside the agent's ultimate responsibility either by being determined by causes that extend beyond the agent's responsibility or by being (partially) undetermined does not arise for it. For the relevant assumption of blankness does not consist in a *positive* belief that in respect of any of his states the agent is ultimately responsible in the sense of being responsible for all of its responsibility-giving conditions, however distant in the past they are. Instead the assumption consists merely in *the absence* of beliefs about the causal origin of responsibility-giving states, in the fact that the question of their causal genesis never occurs. This is the sense in which it is 'blank'.

An agent who is the subject of this assumption of blankness is ultimately responsible only in an *epistemic* sense, in contrast to the *ontic* sense of ultimate responsibility just outlined (at best, only agents whose responsibility has had infinite duration can have ontically ultimate responsibility). The epistemic ultimacy of a cause within an agent is, however, volatile: as soon as there is reflection upon what might have caused its activity, it will evaporate. Its activity will then be seen either as ultimately deriving from causes external to the agent or as partly uncaused.

In replying to an argument to the effect that "determinism undermines the concept of desert" (1999: 135), David Miller claims that, in ascribing desert and having attitudes like admiration and gratitude, which, like me, he sees as closely related to desert, "we look no further than the present qualities of the individuals concerned. We do not inquire into their past histories" (1999: 136). This is precisely what I mean to express by saying that we see the exemplification of these qualities as causally blank; hence Miller's claim falls short of meeting my construal of the threat of determinism. For it may be that desert and these para-cognitive attitudes depend upon this absence of causal speculation, so that the acquisition of any belief about the causal genesis of this property-exemplification undermines them. That is, the incompatibilist claim to be met need not, and in my opinion does not, take the form that desert and desert-entailing attitudes depend upon some positive anti-deterministic belief.

The Causal Elusiveness of Mental States

An instinctive, pre-cultural belief is hard to rid oneself of. So, even after reflection on the causal antecedents of responsibility-giving states, we may find that we can hardly refrain from believing that there are desert-bases for which we are ultimately responsible. This reluctance may be misinterpreted as evidence that we are ultimately responsible in an ontic sense, and this may in its turn lead onto extravagant ideas such as agent-causation (or doctrines, like that of *karma*, which take the beginning of our existence as responsible agents to extend beyond our present existence). I have here attempted to demonstrate that to understand our commonsensical attitude to desert, we need not have recourse to such fanciful measures—just as, in Part IV, I set out to give a genetic account of the bias towards ourselves which does without appeal to any beliefs in selves or minds that are not based in matter.

But my account of the network of desert will work only if the responsibility-giving mental states can possess epistemic ultimacy, for desert can only be attributed to agents with minds (since the return must have value for the recipient). So we must check whether, in particular, the causes of the mental antecedents of responsible actions are sufficiently unobtrusive to be beyond knowledge, though a concept of responsible action which refers to these antecedents has been acquired.

As was pointed out in Chapter 31, we do not experience our episodic thoughts as being causally determined or necessitated to occur or as causally determining our behaviour. At most, they are experienced as temporally succeeding other thoughts or perceptions to which their contents are related in ways I tried to describe in Chapter 13. (They may, however, also pop up without any such contentual connections to predecessors.) Similarly, as we saw in Chapter 4, when we act on the basis of an intelligent desire, the connection between thought and behaviour has to do with content rather than with causal mechanism: our being such that the thought that it is possible for us to bring about *p* leads to our bringing about what we think is *p*. These mental events can be fitted into a causal network only because they have neural correlates.

In this respect, there is a contrast with how we experience our bodies acting upon, and being acted upon by, external objects: we feel our bodies pressing against these foreign bodies, moving or being moved by them, being heated or chilled by them, and so on. Since we do not experience the causal influence we exercise by our abstentions from acting, we spontaneously see ourselves as causally responsible only for that which is actively caused.

If our thoughts are to be introspectively traced to a source external to us, it has to be via their content, as when a thought registers something perceived in the external world. When such thoughts lead directly to action—as in acting on reflex—we do not feel free and responsible. For instance, we do not feel free and responsible when we reflexively withdraw from a source of pain, in spite of the fact that we do not even in these cases experience our behaviour as being causally necessitated by our thoughts. But our more abstract thoughts cannot in any obvious way be linked up with what is external to us (except perhaps when we have them as the result of reading), and they lead to behaviour only via deliberation. The unpredictability of such thoughts also discourages us to seek their causes. It is not until scientific advances make credible the idea of correlating all thoughts with brain processes that there arises the idea of fitting all thoughts into a causal network that transgresses our boundaries. This picture also makes us look around for external causes of our states of desire. We cannot look for such causes until science has led us to identify with certain neural structures that about us which makes us respond with appropriate behaviour to thoughts about what we can do.

If this is on the right track, it is comprehensible that there is a stage of conceptual or cognitive development at which we can sustain a notion of our being epistemically ultimately responsible as regards motivational states such as thoughts on the basis of which we act. It is such a stage for which we are looking: a stage at which we can restrict responsibility to actions that are intentionally or wittingly performed, but at which there is no opinion on the causal ancestry of these responsibility-giving motivational states that rules out the epistemic ultimacy that desert demands. To repeat, my hypothesis is that it is an absence of causal theorizing rather than any positive belief in some sort of ontically ultimate responsibility that, pre-philosophically, nourishes our belief that ultimate responsibility can be desert-entailing.

The concept of desert cannot be applied as long as there is no capacity to ascribe mental states to other beings, and agent-oriented emotions are directed indiscriminately at animate and inanimate things which are seen as causally responsible for various pleasant and unpleasant effects upon us. This concept requires a stage at which this capacity of mental attribution has developed, at which agent-oriented emotions towards beings without a conception of the welfare of others will be regarded as unreasonable (though they will persist), and sub-types of these emotions, like resentment and indignation—whose propositional underpinning involves the attribution of mental states to others, for example, their targets—have emerged. This is the stage at which common-sense thinking is located.

At a future, higher level of cognitive development, the scientific picture of mental episodes as being nomologically correlated with neural events and thereby connected to the vast network of physical causality could pervade the inquiring mind. The formerly blank mental causes would then be thought of as flowing from an origin external to our responsibility. Epistemic ultimacy would be abandoned, but there is no ontic ultimacy in which desert-entailing responsibility, and associated emotions, can be rooted; so their irrationality must be countenanced. Thus, the level at which desert-entailing responsibility and the more sophisticated agent-oriented emotions flourish occupies an intermediate position between the 'scientific' level and a level at which only the simplest forms of anger and gratitude are felt because there is no conception of their targets being in any mental states.

Along such lines, I think we can make it comprehensible why common sense employs the concept of desert without invoking any obscure postulates of mental substances that possess ontically ultimate responsibility, just as in Part IV we explained the O-bias without appealing to any beliefs in such substances. Indeed, in these accounts there is no appeal to any positive beliefs about our natures. Instead of positive beliefs, these explanations draw upon *gaps* that spontaneous representation leaves. In the case of the O-basis, the gap is between the much fuller representation of our own present situation compared to that of others (the P-bias), and its extension into the future by means of the MSI. Now they rather concern the way our present situation shades into the past.

Of course, the latter explanation purports to *justify* the employment of the concept of desert, as little as the former purports to justify the O-bias. Instead it disqualifies the backward-looking justification of desert and leaves the whole ground for the forward-looking justification of the R–P practice with which it has so far coexisted. But this coexistence is one more thing to account for: given that common sense employs a concept of desert to justify applications of the R–P practice, could this justification fuse with the one built around forward-looking considerations? Are these two justifications not so dissimilar that there is a conspicuous tension between them?

No, for let me repeat a fact already noted: nature has endowed us with the agent-oriented emotions—that is, the emotions which nurture the concept of desert—because they have beneficial consequences in terms of encouraging and discouraging certain patterns of future behaviour. We should therefore expect a considerable degree of harmony between the verdicts of backward- and forward-looking justification. In light of this, we can see forward-looking justification as a symptom of the fact that our reason has developed to a point at which we can take in our own hands something that nature has hitherto done for us, namely, to design our responses towards conscious agents in ways that are useful to us. We engage in this enterprise by specifying the beings to which the R–P practice is applicable along the lines suggested in Chapters 32 and 33.

The circumstances in which the forward-looking approach issues in judgements of responsibility—roughly, the circumstances in which one's motivation and behaviour are such that they can be influenced by reasons that stem from applications of the R–P practice—in general coincide with the circumstances in which the backward-looking justification allegedly delivers such judgements, the latter circumstances being those in which the external influence on one's mind is elusive enough to leave room for epistemic ultimacy. When the external influence is most apparent and direct—for example a terrifying situation causes someone to act in panic—the mental states induced tend to be inflexible and insensitive to the operation of the R–P practice. Conversely, when one's motivation is flexible and sensitive to reasons flowing from this practice, it is normally the case that it is the result of deliberation upon which the external pressures have been comparatively unnoticeable. Hence, when we are directly responsible and the R–P practice is justifiable from the forward-looking standpoint, it also seems justifiable from the backward-looking standpoint since, epistemically, we are ultimately responsible. The two justifications, then, are harmonious enough to pass together in the common-sense conception of responsibility.

An Extension to Rights

A story similar to the desert story could be told for natural rights which, as we found in Chapter 34, are involved in the bases of desert. Rights are not purely a cultural product. Like the concept of desert, I believe the concept of a right to be a primitive notion which is the expression of behavioural reactions that we have in common with higher animals, reactions such as the animals' defending with a special fierceness their turf or the prey they have hunted down. It is not difficult to see how such patterns of behaviour could have survival value, nor how they could be fitted into the type of account supplied for desert. The (e.g. genetic) causes of the psycho-physical capacities with which we find ourselves are sufficiently elusive for it to be possible to view the fact that we have these capacities as ultimate and thus to view them as originally belonging to us. Therefore, it may appear unjust to deprive us of them and transfer them to someone else, without our consent. When, by virtue of these capacities, we lay our hands upon other things, not already belonging to subjects who enjoy their value, these things, too, are seen as becoming attached to us, so that it becomes unjust to prevent us from making use of them.

The concept of a right, however, occupies a smaller place in this book than the concept of desert. This is because it is not involved in our emotions to the same extent. The explanation of this fact may be found, I surmise, in an observation made in Chapter 34 when the concepts of a right and of desert were compared and contrasted: that to which you have a right is normally in your possession, while there is often a discrepancy between what you deserve and what you have. Therefore, there is in general more reason to be moved to action by the thought of what someone deserves than by the thought of what someone has a right to.

The pre-cultural concept of a natural right may have been consolidated by the fact that it happened to fit in with some influential cultural products, like the Judaeo-Christian world-view. According to this picture, a morally perfect, omnipotent being is responsible for the natural order and supervises the distribution of assets and defects to every creature. If so, there is reason to believe it to be just and right that we have the assets and defects with which we in fact find ourselves. The concept of a natural right is, however, rendered inapplicable by the modern scientific outlook which traces our possession of these capacities to external causes that has nothing to do with justice.

This does not mean that we must give up speaking of rights altogether. Owing to the fact that the concept is so well-entrenched in our ways of thinking, to discard it will cause a lot of frustration and confusion. Because the effects of abolishing the concept would be devastating, it can contended that we should implement rules laying down that we have conventional rights roughly corresponding to the natural rights we spontaneously think we have. Since our belief in natural rights is instinctive and so deeply ingrained in us (and since we have other mental limitations), it will in general have better consequences if we act not in the light of the truth about the groundlessness of rights, but on the basis of rules roughly copying our natural rights. Therefore, it might be that we should have a rule-system that confers upon us conventional rights that in their core correspond to the natural rights in which we intuitively believe.[3] In this way we could keep rights, just as we could hang onto desert ascriptions if we reinterpret them in a forward-looking way. But this is a topic for the next chapter.

---

[3] For a consequentialist justification of rights, see L. W. Sumner (1987: ch. 6).

37

THE DILEMMA AS REGARDS RESPONSIBILITY

IF we are cognitively rational, we will not entertain the epistemic conception of ultimate responsibility which sustains ascriptions of desert and the possession of agent-oriented emotions like anger, indignation, resentment, and gratitude. We shall believe either that determinism is true to the extent that directly responsible actions are fully determined by events outside our responsibility or that these actions are partially undetermined, and to this extent beyond our responsibility. In either case, it is cognitively irrational to think of individuals in terms of desert and as fit for agent-oriented emotions. Consequently, to the degree that we are rationalists, we are constrained to rid ourselves of this way of thinking and of these emotions.

The idea that the acceptance of determinism will have a profound effect on our attitudes has a long history. For instance, Spinoza believed that the endorsement of this doctrine would affect the attitudes which he designates as "love" and "hatred", but which he construes rather as I have construed gratitude and anger. His view (1675/1949: pt. III, props. 48 and 49) is, however, that the determinist creed has the effect of dispersing "love" and "hatred" over several objects rather than of extinguishing them by removing their propositional foundation. He argues that the "love" and "hatred" felt, for example, toward Peter, on account of the joy and sorrow he is seen as having caused, "are respectively diminished as we imagine that Peter has not been their sole cause", while the "love" and "hatred" toward him would have been at its greatest if he had been seen as free—that is, uncaused—in causing the joy and sorrow, for then they would focus on him alone.

Spinoza's view is plausible for simultaneous causes that jointly produce an effect, for example a gang which kills somebody by each member inflicting on the victim a non-lethal stab. Here one is likely to be less angry at each member than if he had been the sole killer. But for sequential causes this view has the counter-intuitive corollary that, if a man beats me with his fists, I should be more angry at him than were he to hit me with a stick, for in the latter case part of my anger should be directed at the stick, too, since it is also a cause of my pain. Obviously, this is not so: in both situations my whole anger is typically focused on the man.

Generally, if one conceives of something as causing one pain by the use of some instrument, one's anger is not divided between the two causes, as Spinoza's views seemingly imply, but concentrated on the (epistemically) ultimate one. This is true also if the 'instrument' is a human being: if a neurosurgeon implants in somebody a compulsive desire to hurt, and I am hurt as planned, my anger will be directed solely at the neurosurgeon. In Chapter 6, I supplied an evolutionary explanation of why this is so. The arrangement of agent-oriented emotions that is directed at ultimate causes has greater survival value than alternative ones, like their being directed at mental causes. For although the aim of the emotions will be somewhat less accurate, their distribution will be so much wider. Now, given that ultimacy in the ontic sense is too fanciful, it has to be epistemic, to the effect that *no* view about the causal background of the target's activity be entertained, that it be seen neither as caused nor as uncaused, but be regarded as a blank cause that is, say, hurtful.

Rationalists will also try to quash remorse and feelings of guilt occasioned by the thought that they themselves have done something wrong, since these emotions are also cognitively irrational. Like the intuitive impression of freedom, these emotions are nurtured by the unpredictability described in Chapter 31 and the fact that mental episodes present themselves to introspection as contentually and temporally linked rather than as being related by causal necessity. This appearance is, however, compatible with there being an underlying, neural causal necessity. But even if there be gaps of indeterminacy, there will not be the ultimate responsibility these emotions presuppose.

Furthermore, rationalists will have to undertake to stub out the comparative emotions of pride, shame, admiration, contempt, embarrassment, and envy, for, according to a claim of Chapter 6, they are cognitively irrational in that they rest on thinking that one's exemplification of some feature is causally blank. For instance, the possibility of being proud of oneself because of one's beauty or intelligence hinges on seeing one's possession of these attributes as ultimately self-determined because it involves taking oneself to be praiseworthy in virtue of them. The moment one vividly represents to oneself that one's being equipped with these qualities is due to genetic and environmental factors that are outside the range of one's responsibility and a matter of luck, pride evaporates and is replaced by humility (which of course is not the same as shame).

The link between comparative emotions and the concept of desert seems to me to be indisputable. For if one is proud of oneself because of some feature, one will think that, in view of that feature, one is more deserving or worthy of being favoured, rewarded, etc. than members of some reference-class. Similarly, if one feels contempt for somebody for some reason, one will think that, for that reason, that person is deserving of worse treatment than others. Moreover, there seems also to be a link between these emotions and the concept of a natural right: if one is proud of one's assets, it seems one must think one has a right to them, whereas if one is ashamed of them, it seems one must think one has a right to them but nothing better.

Thus, when rationalists take to heart facts about the causal ways of the world, the emotional adjustment required would change them almost out of recognition. They would, however, not be forced to give up the assignment of responsibility to agents, for, as I contended in Chapters 32 and 33, there is a viable conception of responsibility, direct responsibility, that is compatible with determinism. The practices of rewarding/praising and punishing/blaming can be retained, but they will now have to be squarely put on a forward-looking foundation, that is, they will have to be justified solely by reference to their future effects (and they will cover omissions no less than actions). As remarked, this is not tantamount to reducing them to the status of mere conditioning devices.

Justice as Equality

It is, however, important to emphasize that rationalists would not be constrained to surrender the notion of justice along with that of desert and natural rights, as utilitarians apparently tend to assume. For we may reasonably take there to be a formal principle of justice to the effect that a state is just with respect to what is good and bad for them if and only if all individuals have equally much of what is good and bad for them, unless there are grounds that make it just that some are better off than others—such grounds precisely being deserts and rights. If these grounds are then undermined, justice remains in the form of the *egalitarian* demand that all individuals have equally much of what is good and bad for them, for the formal principle of justice still stands. Thus rationality does not require us to dispose of our well-entrenched notion of justice along with the companion notions of desert and rights which are designed to make just divergences from equality.[1]

This means that in the inter-personal domain the rational satisfactionalist aim is not the utilitarian one of a personally and temporally neutral maximization of fulfilment. Since there is no reason to evict justice as equality, this satisfactionalist aim includes seeing to it that the distribution of fulfilment is equal. So the aim is to the effect of seeing to it that everyone is as equally well off as possible on as high level of well-being as possible (this is subject to a qualification added below).

Notice that if justice consists in equality rather than in getting what you deserve, the friction between justice and fulfilment-maximization, for example as regards justifying applications of the R–P practice, is likely to increase. For in view of the fact that what people are responsible for differs widely—some being responsible for beneficial deeds to their fellow beings, while others are responsible for heinous crimes—forward-looking applications of the R–P practice are likely to create or amplify inequalities and, thereby, injustice. There would not be this tension if, contrary to fact, justice instead could have consisted in receiving the reward and punishment you deserve in virtue of your (ultimately) responsible actions.

It may be asked why considerations of justice enter into the inter-personal domain of morality, but are absent as long as we confine ourselves to prudence. I think this is because justice presupposes the competing claims of distinct individuals who do not

---

[1] I discuss this matter at greater length in my paper 'A Defence of Extreme Egalitarianism' (2004c). I discuss other aspects of egalitarian justice in (2001) and (2003b).

identify with each other and do not regard benefits to others as adequate compensation for their own losses, but demand to receive something themselves in return for favours rendered to others. This is confirmed by the observation that a pre-reflective expression of justice is the 'tit for tat' strategy. It is also confirmed by the existence of groups of individuals who care as much about each other as about themselves, so that benefits are voluntarily transferred to the group members who are worst off. Since there are no competing claims within this group, it can for the purposes of just distribution be treated as single unit, like single individuals whose distribution of benefits over their own lives is regarded as being outside the sphere of justice.

This point may be clearer if we turn from bilateral to unilateral voluntary transfers of benefits. Suppose, for instance, that in a situation in which, justly, all are equally well off, one voluntarily transfers a benefit to another, thereby making her better off. Then the resulting inequality is not unjust.[2] We should here remind ourselves of a remark made in Chapter 27: it is not morally wrong to make oneself worse off than others (provided dependants are not affected). Since creating an unjust inequality would be morally wrong, other things being equal, this inequality is not unjust. But neither is this inequality just; merely voluntarily choosing to benefit somebody cannot make this just. A voluntary transfer of a benefit is, then, in itself neither just nor unjust. That is to say, a distribution can be beyond the pale of justice; so we must not infer from the fact that it is, say, not just that it is unjust.

In respect of being beyond the pale of justice, this distribution is like distributions over one's own life. As noted in Chapter 27, intra-personal distributions are in themselves neither morally right nor wrong; they are rather simply rational or irrational (or, more colloquially, wise or stupid). They can be irrational because, as we have seen, self-concern spontaneously diminishes with temporal distance and dissimilarity. But, as we have also seen, the fact that such a distribution is not in itself morally wrong does not imply that other people cannot be morally right to interfere. For if these distributions are grossly irrational, or have very bad effects on dependants, interference would be morally justified. Analogously, others may be morally justified in interfering with voluntary transfers of benefits to others which create inequality, though these transfers cannot be classified as unjust. They may be justified in so doing if the transfers give rise to reasonable envy or have other bad consequences.

Thus there are voluntary transfers of benefits between people which are beyond the pale of justice. An example of such a transfer would be if parents make their children better off than themselves (I am assuming that, in accordance with justice, the families in question are on average equally well off). These transfers are analogous to intra-personal distributions in which people postpone the enjoyment of benefits until later in life. In neither case is the concept of justice applicable to the outcome because the givers distribute benefits they justly possess without harming others. The upshot of this reasoning is that a qualification needs to be inserted in maximalist egalitarian demand

---

[2] Compare with the judicial practice of some countries which gives victims, or their relatives, the power to pardon criminals from the punishment to which they have been sentenced, though this punishment is presumably thought to be deserved and just.

sketched above: everyone should be as equally well off on as high a level as possible, unless they autonomously choose to be worse off.

Now, the principal question here is whether it is rational relatively to this rationally constrained satisfactionalist aim, the maximalist egalitarian one, to purge ourselves of desert-thinking and of agent-oriented and comparative emotions, alongside personal and temporal partialities, as it is rational to do relative to the rationalist striving. It seems clear that it is not, that these attitudes are so firmly implanted in our natures that to uproot them would require a single-minded devotion and rigorous regimentation that would shut us off from others. This is bound to be detrimental to the pursuit of the satisfactionalist aim.[3] So it is rational relative to this aim to go on thinking and feeling in terms of desert and rights, possibly to a reduced extent, though this frame of mind is cognitively irrational. Thus it is not only the case that it can be morally justifiable to punish some and reward others, albeit this has a tendency to increase inequality, because it is conducive to utilitarian maximization. Satisfactionalists can also interpret this practice in terms of the residual desert attitudes that it is rational for them to keep.

We have, then, encountered yet another dilemma between rationalism and a rationalized satisfactionalist aim (I think the latter can lay claim to be *fully* rationalized, though this is not something I can prove). To repeat, both of these aims are rationally permissible. Thus, we can distinguish two models of being relatively rational in the inter-personal realm: philosophical idealists, who renounce the world to make their own characters conform to the requirements of cognitive rationality, and philanthropists or do-gooders who are intent upon perfecting themselves as means to a rationalized satisfactionalism.

Honderich and the Possibility of Reform

It is instructive to compare the stance here adopted with respect to the attitudinal consequences of determinism with that of Honderich (1988: pt. 3). Honderich and I share the view that commonsensical thinking about responsible agency is to a significant extent consistent with the truth of determinism, but that in no less vital parts it transgresses the bounds of this doctrine. In Honderich's terminology, common-sense thought about responsible agency encompasses both *voluntariness* and *origination* (1988: 390). If one fastens exclusively on the first notion, one will respond to the challenge of determinism with the attitude Honderich calls *intransigence*: the truth of determinism affects very little, if at all, the attitudes that matter to us (1988: 399). On the other hand, if one emphasizes the importance of the idea of origination to our attitudes as regards responsible agency, the reaction will be one of *dismay*: in the face of determinism, more or less no attitude of significance can be sustained (1988: 391). But, according to Honderich, there is a third response that supersedes both intransigence and dismay, namely, the response of

---

[3] The beneficial effects of sustaining illusion about desert-entailing responsibility are elaborated by Smilansky, who even contends that it may be hard to go with compatibilism as far as it goes without this illusion (2000: 190).

affirmation (1988: 493–4, 516–17). In contrast to intransigence, the purport of affirmation is that, if we are to come to terms with determinism, some attitudes of value for us will have to go by the board, for they rest in part on the idea of origination; but, as opposed to dismay, it insists that enough is left for our lives to be satisfactory.

One difference of consequence between Honderich and myself lies in how we interpret the commonsensical idea of origination. Honderich regards the notion of there being in each of us "an ongoing entity or attribute which originates decisions, and hence actions" (1988: 208) as not being *entirely* without content. In other words, he thinks that (*a*) there is "hardly any positive content" in the non-reductionist or immaterialist view of persons, but that there is still "a thin idea of a unity of a wholly unspecified ontological kind" (1988: 198); and that (*b*) the idea of the activity of such a unity "is thin *nearly* to the point of non-existence" (1988: 207; my italics). Whatever thin content Honderich finds in this notion he stuffs into the commonsensical idea of origination. For my own part, I am unable to detect *any* coherent content in this notion; hence, I am disinclined to charge common sense with it. Instead I take the commonsensical 'idea' of origination (or ultimate responsibility) on which desert-claims and desert-entailing emotions rest to consist merely in an epistemic lacuna, an *absence* of causal hypotheses and assumptions. I have distinguished two stages here: a more primitive stage when there need be no capacity to ascribe mental states to the subjects in question, and a more sophisticated one when these states are ascribed, and there is a more or less articulate notion of responsibility, but these states baffle and confound the pre-scientific mind to the degree that there is no causal speculation about their antecedents. The latter is the stage at which the concept of desert is applied.

This difference has repercussions on the question of the feasibility of the response of affirmation, that is, for the assessment of the difficulties involved in stamping out the para-cognitive attitudes based on the everyday idea of origination/ultimate responsibility. Honderich can plausibly hold that the concept of "an ongoing entity or attribute which originates decisions" is a cultural product on a level with pantheistic or animistic beliefs (1988: 534). The road is, then, paved for the contention that there is "a practical possibility of our making the response of affirmation, and living in accordance with it" (1988: 534). The picture alters if one instead takes the commonsensical 'idea' of origination, in so far as it underlies agent-oriented emotions, as consisting in an instinctive pattern of thinking that we share with non-human animals also capable of experiencing these emotions. This interpretation of the 'idea' of origination (as epistemically ultimate responsibility) seems inevitable if we are to conceive of the 'idea' as underlying emotional responses that we have in common with many non-human animals. But then, what we are up against in making the response of affirmation is eradicating something that is much more deeply rooted in our natures than a certain culturally conditioned idea and its effects; it is certain *instinctive* patterns of thought and feeling. *Pace* Honderich, adopting the response of affirmation is of the same order as altering "the fact that we are desiring creatures" (1988: 534).

I am not asserting that such a change is practically impossible. As Galen Strawson observes, to cleanse themselves not merely of emotions like anger, but of all desires is a goal set up by Buddhists, and we should not reject out of hand their claim that some of their saints have attained this goal (1986: ch. 6.6).[4] But the difficulty of this undertaking can scarcely be underestimated: it requires a lifelong dedication to reach fruition. Since this is likely to be at odds with the satisfactionalist aim of maximizing the fulfilment, whether it be of just one's own life or of the lives others as well, it follows that we have hit upon another area of conflict between the aims of rationalism and satisfactionalism.

Strawson and Bennett on "Reactive Attitudes"

It is also worth comparing these conclusions to those of a celebrated approach to the topic of the impact of determinism on our attitudes to responsibility, namely, the one initiated by P. F. Strawson in his classic paper 'Freedom and Resentment' (reprinted in Strawson, 1974), and subsequently elaborated by Jonathan Bennett (1980; 1984, esp. §§ 78–9). According to this account, what Strawson terms *reactive* attitudes have a central role to play. These attitudes are described as "essentially natural human reactions to the good or ill will or indifference of others towards us, as displayed in *their* attitudes and actions" (1974: 10; cf. 6). Such attitudes are exhibited when one feels "resentment, gratitude, forgiveness, anger or the sort of love which two adults can sometimes be said to feel, reciprocally, for each other" (1974: 9). The class of reactive attitudes is subsequently broadened to include "self-reactive" attitudes like shame and "moral" ones that we vicariously feel on behalf of others because of attitudes adopted towards *them* (1974: 13–16).

Strawson believes that only by taking reactive attitudes into consideration can we bring out "*all* we mean, when speaking the language of morals, we speak of desert, responsibility, guilt, condemnation, and justice" (1974: 23). According to him, reference to these attitudes is absent from the forward-looking justification of the R–P practice in terms of its effectiveness as an instrument of behaviour control. By leaving out the element of reactivity, the forward-looking view lands in an attitude that Strawson sees as profoundly opposed to reactive attitudes, namely, the objective one. This stance is characterized as one of seeing "the agent as one posing problems simply of intellectual understanding, management, treatment, and control" (1974: 17), of "understanding 'how he works', with a view to determining our policy accordingly" (1974: 12).

Having presented the two opposing stances around which Strawson's—and Bennett's—account revolves, I now take a closer look at some salient points.

(1) In contrast to the view here expressed, a central tenet of Strawson's is that the truth of determinism is not something that undercuts the propositional basis of reactive

---

[4] I believe, however, that Strawson exaggerates the consequences of this change when he suggests that it means losing one's sense of self. The reason why Strawson makes this suggestion is that he supposes that, at least for "any recognizable human sense of self" (1986: 99–100), conceiving oneself as ultimately self-determined, as an originator, constitutes "an *essential* aspect of what one is mentally considered" (1986: 96). But it seems to me undeniable that there is a conception of oneself as something *passive* which is at work when one is aware of oneself as perceiving or as having thoughts simply occurring to one. This is not a conception of oneself as causing anything—*a fortiori*, it is not a conception of oneself as *originally* causing anything—but it is oneself "mentally considered" in that the attribution of mental properties is involved.

attitudes, and thereby lets in objectivity (1974: 12–13, 18–19). This negative claim is supplemented by a positive thesis: it is the applicability of various 'pleas' or 'excuses' that paves the way for objectivity by preventing us from adopting reactive attitudes, pleas to the effect that the agent is acting under post-hypnotic suggestion, that he is beside himself or mentally deranged or under age (1974: 7–13, 16–19). There are objections to both the positive and the negative claim.

As regards the positive thesis, we should remind ourselves that we do feel reactive attitudes—like anger, gratitude, and love—towards beings who fall under Strawson's pleas, for example the mentally deranged, children, and non-human animals. Strawson's reply might be that in these cases some component is lacking which is present when these types of emotion are felt towards responsible beings (cf. 1974: 9). But to specify this component might well turn out to be exceedingly hard. Alternatively, it could be retorted that "civilized people" would adopt reactive attitudes "only towards things they regarded as not merely sentient but personal" (Bennett, 1984: 341). But although, say, anger directed at an inanimate thing can be censured as 'uncivilized'—because it is patently ineffective—there is not the same reason for calling anger with a child uncivilized (if it does not go out of control), for it can be effective in changing the child's future behaviour. In short, I find it very difficult to defend the claim that there is a species of, for example, anger that is appropriately felt only towards responsible beings.

In maintaining that the applicability of the pleas mentioned makes it suitable to take up the objective attitude, Strawson tends to slur over a distinction highlighted in Chapter 33, namely, the distinction between an employment of the R–P practice to influence behaviour by means of a mechanism that involves one's interpreting it as something that is inflicted on one because one's actions have been beneficial or harmful to others and an employment of the practice that bypasses such interpreting. The former employment is excluded by the applicability of excuses to the effect that one is mentally deranged or under age. So, if Strawson takes it for granted that it is with these excuses that the objective standpoint comes into operation, he must tacitly assume that the R–P practice as put to work by the objectivist is a mere conditioning technique. In other words, he would without argument rule out the richer meaning that a forward-looking justification of the R–P practice can carry, thereby of course making it seem more or less incontrovertible that there can be no responsibility within the confines of objectivity, that responsibility essentially comprises a reference to reactivity.

Of greater importance for present purposes is the falsity of the negative claim. Strawson's supports this contention by arguing that in everyday circumstances we do not cite the truth of determinism as a reason for withholding reactive attitudes. This is true, but the explanation might simply be that, being an abstract doctrine, determinism is precisely the sort of doctrine that is not likely to come up for review in everyday life. It is significant that when, in our philosophical moments, we *do* reflect on determinism, we do feel a tension between it, on the one hand, and responsibility and at least some of our reactive attitudes, on the other. Why is that if determinism does not contradict the propositional underpinning of these attitudes?

Strawson's suggestion is that this tension has to do with the opposition between the objective attitude and reactive ones. This suggestion is elaborated by Bennett, who praises as the "single greatest achievement" of Strawson's paper that it construes the question whether we should cleave to reactive attitudes as having no "strict dependence upon a perpetually troublesome theoretical question" (1980: 30), to wit, the question of whether determinism reigns in the sphere of human actions and reactions. In Bennett's opinion, the conflicts commonly felt between seeing a person's conduct as externally caused and taking up a reactive stance toward it "are not logical conflicts between propositions, but an incompatibility between two frames of mind" (1984: 340), namely, the objective and reactive frames of mind. For Bennett it is a *practical* question whether we should retain reactive attitudes (1984: 341), a question to be settled by calculating the gains and losses of this retention to human life rather than by asking whether these attitudes are in accord with the facts of the world.

The hypothesis that the felt clash between determinism and responsibility/reactivity is in reality an opposition between the objective and the reactive frame of mind needs, however, to be fleshed out. First, how is this opposition to be understood more precisely? Bennett is forced to confess that he cannot explain this (1980: 28–30; 1984: 340). Secondly, even if it is granted that reactivity is opposed to objectivity, it still needs to be explained why it is felt to be opposed to *determinism* if the truth of this doctrine does not undercut the propositional foundation of reactivity. On this point, too, Bennett acknowledges defeat. In view of this, I think it is fair to conclude that the Strawson-Bennett view fails to explicate why determinism should be felt as a threat to reactive attitudes (or rather some reactive attitudes, namely agent-oriented and comparative ones).

One reason Bennett adduces for rejecting accounts which construe determinism as contradicting the propositional ground of reactive attitudes is that they would be hard put to explain why "the impulse to blame someone for an action tends to fade out . . . also in the face of a cool, careful thought of it as not determined" (1984: 340). I hope it is clear that the view I have delineated escapes this objection. It is, however, not unlikely that Bennett's resistance to the kind of account here set out derives from his inclination to believe that the conflict which is the leitmotif of this inquiry—the conflict between having cognitively rational attitudes, conforming to truth and reason, and having ones that are rational relative to a satisfactionalist aim—cannot arise:

> We cannot be obliged to give up something whose loss would gravely worsen the human condition, and so reactive feelings cannot be made impermissible by any facts. (1980: 29)

I take it that Bennett here assumes that we are all under the rationalist obligation to surrender any *belief* that is shown to be untenable, that, in his words, falsity is a "price nobody will pay" (1984: 342). But then it strikes me as a piece of wishful thinking to assume that the world must be so arranged that the attitudes most deeply entrenched in us cannot rest upon what we have to surrender as falsehoods. So far as I can see, Nietzsche could be right that "it could pertain to the fundamental nature of existence that a complete knowledge of it would destroy one" (1886/1973: § 39).

(2) The Strawsonian class of reactive attitudes is heterogeneous in the crucial respect of its relationship to determinism. It comprises agent-oriented emotions—for example anger, gratitude, resentment, feelings of guilt and remorse—and comparative emotions, such as pride, shame, admiration, etc. These are emotions the propositional underpinning of which is undercut by determinism. However, the class also encompasses love—"the sort of love which two adults can sometimes be said to feel reciprocally, for each other" as Strawson puts it—and presumably its opposite, hate. These attitudes, I shall now contend, are not threatened by determinism.[5]

As stated in Chapter 6, to love some individual consists in having, as a result of perceptions and thoughts about that individual, a complex set of desires directed onto it. In this set, two main kinds of desire were distinguished, namely, instrumental desires to engage in various rewarding relations with that individual and a concern for the well-being of it for its own sake. In so far as the love of an individual has a physical basis, the former include desires to look at it, to caress it, to have sex with it, etc. It is patently absurd to think that such desires could be undercut by the conviction that the being's physical assets, its beauty, sex appeal, etc. have causes external to its responsibility.

If this variety of love is affected by the truth of any philosophical doctrine, it would presumably be the doctrine that naive realism is false, that in reality material things are not as they appear to our senses. I am inclined to think that it would affect one's physical love of a being if one came to be convinced that what one finds beautiful and sexually appealing is not really (the surface of) that being, but sense-impressions *caused* by that entity. One could still be said to like or love that being, but there is a difference between liking or loving something for what it is in itself and liking or loving it because of its effects. After the conversion from realism, one would like the being more as one likes an apparatus which produces enjoyable experiences by electrically stimulating one's brain. I will take up this topic in the Appendix. What is at issue now is the effect of determinism on physical enchantment, and this effect cannot but be non-existent, since this attitude surely does not rest on any assumption to the effect that the features attributed to the object as it is in reality are ones for which it is ultimately responsible.

Consider next love to the extent that it is based on less observable traits like mental qualities such as being generous, witty, forgiving, etc., and abilities, for example to draw, sing, philosophize, or play chess well. Love will here encapsulate wanting to seek the company of the object because one wants to benefit from the manifestations of these traits. Clearly, the realization that the object of the emotion is not ultimately responsible for its possession of these traits should not drain one of such desires; for this fact makes the object no less generous, witty, etc.

Finally, there are intrinsic desires for the well-being and fulfilment of the being loved and, consequently, pity or compassion when this being suffers, and joy when it is happy. As, Bennett for instance, brings out (1984: 341), pity is unaffected by determinism. Spinoza thinks otherwise, arguing that "sorrow for the loss of anything good is diminished

---

[5] Cf. Wallace who narrows down reactive attitudes to the "central cases" of "resentment, indignation and guilt" (1994: 30). Pereboom takes a similar line (2001: 199 ff.)

if the person who has lost it considers that it could not by any possibility have been preserved" (1949: pt. V, prop. 6; cf. Ben-Ze'ev, 2000: 198–9). So, he continues, we do not pity humans because they have to spend several years in infancy, since this is necessary for all of them. But we *could* pity them for this reason, just as we can have pity for humans because they have to die. It is just that in the first instance we reserve pity and compassion for those who are *especially* unlucky, for example those who die prematurely. It is a bad thing that a being suffers, or a good thing that it enjoys itself, irrespective of the causes of these states.

Hence, I conclude that love—and by implication, hate—is not undermined by the truth of determinism. Certainly, love can mingle with emotions that are opposed to determinism, for example admiration, and hate can be blended with contempt. If so, the resulting attitude will, of course, not be immune to a conversion to determinism. But to concede that some ingredients of certain instances of love and hate are under a determinist ban is clearly not to imply that the residue would not qualify as love and hate.[6]

In view of this heterogeneity one may wonder why Strawson and Bennett circumscribe the class of reactive attitudes in the way they do. This is not easy to understand, especially as they fail to define reactivity, as Bennett admits (1980: 38–9; 1984: 340). Bennett supplies three clues to reactivity, however. Two of them have already been criticized; they concern that reactive attitudes are directed at *persons* and that they are opposed to objectivity and causal thinking. The third is that they are "responses to actions or attitudes or active dispositions" (1984: 341). This is plainly not true of every instance of the attitudes listed: it is, for instance, not true of pride of one's own beauty or noble ancestry. It would be too weak to be of any service to demand that it must be possible for a reactive attitude to be a response to an active disposition, for that is equally true of many attitudes that are not counted as reactive, for example fear (one can fear another being because of its intention to cause one harm).

---

[6] The position arrived at here has a certain affinity with Honderich's when he argues that, although "there is a kind of personal feelings to be given up" in the face of determinism, it is also true that "we can persist in personal feelings of another kind" (1988: 521). But it seems to me that Honderich's view is only that there are *certain instances* of reactive or personal feelings that are discredited by determinism. In contrast I assert that there are certain *types* of emotions—agent-oriented and comparative ones—such that *every* instance of them is impugned by determinism.

In this connection, it is also worth mentioning Jonathan Glover's view that determinism cannot undermine "the aesthetic-cum-sexual responses we have to people's appearance, or to their style and charm" or "aesthetic responses of another kind to people's intellectual qualities: to their being imaginative, independent, or quick on the uptake" (1988: 191). For these responses are not desert-based. In my opinion, Glover fails to gauge fully the difference in respect of propositional underpinning between responses of attraction/repulsion and desert-entailing ones. He points out that "[t]here can also be aesthetic responses to people's motives and character" and that one can judge actions performed by oneself or others "aesthetically as admirable or appalling" (1988: 191–2). But then he takes himself to have established that "[a]esthetic responses parallel to the old desert-based ones could grow up" and that, on closer inspection, faithfulness to determinism "incorporates responses which look less and less different from the desert-based attitudes it repudiates" (1988: 192).

The mistake here seems to be in an assumption to the effect that if two kinds of attitudes are both oriented towards characters, motives, and actions, there can be no significant difference in respect of their propositional content. But in Chapter 6 I argued that there *is* such an important difference between the contents of attraction/repulsion (liking/dislike) and desert-entailing reactions in that the latter involves the notion of a blank cause, and I also tried to explain why we should expect there to be this difference. This difference remains, however intimately intertwined these two sets of responses may be in practice.

All the same, talk of the opposition between reactivity and objectivity carries considerable intuitive appeal, and an attempt should be made to clarify why that is so. As in the case of emotions generally, the behavioural responses included in reactive attitudes are, in Bennett's words, of the "impulsive uncalculated" (1984: 341) variety, that is, they are responses designed by nature, responses dispositions to which are encoded in our genes. In contrast, the objective stance could be conceived as one where we exhibit only behaviour designed *by ourselves* to have the best consequences. Obviously, objectivity as here conceived would go with the making of causal inquiries, since it puts into effect the knowledge obtained in such inquiries. So understood, the opposition between the reactive and the objective would be a species of a more general tension between engaging in behaviour that is instinctive or designed by nature and behaviour that is calculated or designed by ourselves. (The latter may eventually become habitual and so superficially come to resemble instinctive behaviour.)

From this objective or teleological point of view, instinctive behavioural reactions can be appraised with respect to how well suited they are to the ends for which they have been designed and to other ends that we endorse. We have seen that we are probably equipped with, for example, the disposition to react with anger because this reaction increases our chances of survival by deterring future acts of aggression. Now, in view of our reflective or scientific understanding of human nature, we may find that we are able to correct our reactions so that they would be even better suited to this end. The objectivist recommendation would then be to suppress the response of anger and not to hit anyone out of anger, except when, according to our own calculations, this treatment will have the best effect on the recipient's future behaviour. Similarly, there could be recommendations to help anyone out of compassion only when such aid would comply with justifiable principles of, say, maximizing fulfilment and distributing it fairly, not to love anyone except in proportion to how well they perform as judged by acceptable standards. The rationale behind such projects of attitudinal modification—which would transform us into more 'objective' and less spontaneous beings—would be that the new calculated patterns of behaviour which replace the old instinctively triggered ones would be better adapted to aims we cherish.

However, these considerations do not settle the matter for, as Strawson and Bennett would not be slow to emphasize, we must also take into account—on the debit side—the frustration and strain it would cost us to try to quell our instinctive reactions (at least as long as we are not in command of the art of genetic engineering to the extent that we are capable of creating future generations that lack the undesirable propensities). It is certainly true that, in Bennett's words, "reactive feelings can have a considerable place in our lives only at the risk of our sometimes not acting in the most fortunate manner" (1980: 22). But it might be that this risk is offset by the likelihood of the disruption and confusion that any large-scale attitudinal re-shaping certainly involves, and by the probability of a mental breakdown following in the wake of undertaking this project.

No doubt, it would not be an easy matter to determine on which side the scales tip here. But this need not detain us, for our objective is to investigate the effects of disposing only of attitudes that are made cognitively irrational by the fact that their propositional ground is in conflict with determinism (and indeterminism). We are not examining whether we should strip ourselves of attitudes like love, hate, pity, and fear because it is relatively irrational to exhibit them giving certain aims.

This should be borne in mind in assessing Strawson's claim that it is "practically inconceivable" (1974: 11) for us to get rid of our reactive attitudes, that this is something that "it is not in our nature to (be able to) do" (1974: 17). I think this claim is highly dubious; it seems to me that we know far too little about human nature to set any definite limits to what can be achieved through lifelong efforts. But, in any event, the attitudinal modification required of rationalists when determinism is taken to heart is not as far-reaching as discarding all the attitudes classed as reactive. What is at stake is extinguishing only those attitudes that are rendered cognitively irrational by this backdrop, for example agent-oriented emotions like anger and comparative ones like pride. Now, this is precisely what many saints and ascetics have described themselves as having achieved, and there seems no stronger evidence to pit against their testimony. On the other hand, it should be stressed that attitudinal compliance with determinism is harder to attain than Honderich imagines, since it involves a reshaping of our pre-cultural nature.

(3) Strawson also contends that

> if we could imagine what we cannot have, viz. a choice in this matter [of whether or not to retain reactive attitudes], then we could choose rationally only in the light of an assessment of the gains and losses to human life, its enrichment or impoverishment ... and the truth or falsity of a general thesis of determinism would not bear on the rationality of *this* choice. (1974: 13)

In opposition to this claim, I want to insist that the truth-value of determinism *does* bear on whether it is (relatively) rational to retain reactive attitudes—because their cognitive rationality turns on this truth-value—though it does not *settle* this question. Suppose that determinism is true and that agents are in the grip of causes external to their responsibility; then many reactive attitudes would be cognitively irrational. This would force a loss upon those of us who want both to have cognitively rational attitudes and to avoid the strain of eradicating their inborn reactive attitudes.[7] Suppose on the other hand that determinism were false and that, *per impossibile*, personal agents were ultimately responsible. Then this dilemma would disappear.

This does not settle the question of whether it is relatively rational to keep up these reactive attitudes. It will, of course, be irrational given the rationalist enterprise of achieving attitudinal conformity with determinism, but, as we have seen, not given satisfactionalist aims even if they be fully rationally constrained. The more deeply ingrained these reactive attitudes are, the more likely it is that it will be relatively rational for satisfactionalists to retain them. They might well stick to thinking in terms of desert and rights and continue to be carried away by agent-oriented and comparative emotions. To exterminate these tendencies will be relatively rational only for rationalists whose

---

[7] Galen Strawson seems to take a similar view (1986: 90–2). The line of thought here developed also resembles A. J. Ayer's view (1980: 12–13).

supreme aim it is to be pervaded by truth, however deeply ingrained in our being the resistance to this may be.[8]

Susan Wolf, however, appears to deny that there could be any reason to try to let reactive attitudes vanish and to withhold the concept of desert, even if they are contradicted by the acknowledged fact of determinism:

> even if determinism is true, and even if this implies that as a matter of metaphysical fact we are not free and responsible beings, this gives us *no reason at all* to regard ourselves as unfree, unresponsible beings. That is, we have no reason at all to abandon our reactive attitudes and to adopt the objective attitude in their place. (1981: 393–4)

She supports this remarkable claim by the assertion that

> it is only rational to take some particular attitude toward ourselves in the context of the belief that we are, at least in our capacity as attitude-takers, free and responsible beings. (1981: 403)

This is true no less of the attitude that we are *not* free and responsible beings. Hence it would be irrational and self-contradictory were we to adopt this attitude, for in so doing "we would be asserting ourselves *as* free and responsible beings" (1981: 399). Let me refer to this presupposition as *the presupposition of responsibility*, PR.

In response to this argument, I would like to yet again remind the reader of my distinction between the forward- and the backward-looking justification of responsibility. Now, Wolf introduces PR with the help of a case of a "willing addict" who can legitimately be held responsible, because he declares himself to be free and responsible by endorsing his irresistible craving for a drug by a higher-order attitude (1981: 394–5). But since it was concluded in Chapters 32 and 33 that the forward-looking conception could cater for responsibility in such cases, Wolf's argument could at most show that PR holds if 'free and responsible' is accorded this sense. (Wolf appears blind to this possibility, probably because of her view, expressed in a quotation in Chapter 33, that there is nothing left of responsibility if desert and the emotions in which desert is embedded are subtracted.) If so, it is not self-contradictory to take up the reflexive attitude that one is not free and responsible in the desert-entailing way.[9]

This conclusion is important also because it suggests that it is unfounded to fear that, if determinism is true, it follows that we cannot distinguish between what we ought to

---

[8] It should be noticed that P. F. Strawson does not, and could not consistently, express this line of thought when, in an adjunct footnote, he writes that even if "we should be nearer to being purely rational creatures in proportion as our relation to others was in fact dominated by the objective attitude", "it would not necessarily be rational to choose to be more purely rational than we are" (1974: 13). By a "more purely rational" being he cannot mean a being that has rid itself of certain attitudes made cognitively irrational by the conversion to determinism, since he denies that reactive attitudes embody beliefs contradicted by determinism. Rather, he means—see Strawson (1980: 261)—something like a being whose power of ratiocination is less impeded by affects than ours.

[9] Wolf also holds the curious view that were we to stop thinking of ourselves in terms of responsibility, we would also have to give up thinking in terms "that would allow the possibility that some lives and projects are better than others" (1981: 400). But it is surely sensible to hold that the lives of human infants and non-human animals can be better or worse for them, although they lack the mental powers requisite for responsibility.

do and what we ought not do. For it is reasonable to think that, just as the distinction between what we have reasons for and against believing presupposes only direct responsibility, so does the distinction between what we have reasons for and against doing.

I conclude, then, that to the extent that we are rationalists, we have decisive reasons to withhold claims of desert and of natural rights. Consequently, we must also to try to rise above the emotions in which such claims are nested and to put the R–P practice on a purely forward-looking basis. But to the extent that ours is a satisfactionalist aim, even if it be one that is fully cognitively rational, we have better reasons to retain thinking in terms of desert and rights and to sustain the emotions mentioned, though they are cognitively irrational, for they are deeply rooted in our natures and to pull them up would cost a lot of effort and strain. These attitudes will probably have to be corrected in some ways to better suit our purposes, for example by becoming less deontologically oriented. But, when we punish somebody, say, we would do so out of a vindictive anger that we regard as cognitively irrational, though we would do so on an occasion and to an extent in which it is rational, given our satisfactionalist aim, to give vent to this emotion. Rationalists would, however, have none of this cognitive irrationality in their behaviour. Accordingly, there again arises a dilemma between rationalism and satisfactionalism of a sort to which we are by now accustomed.[10]

---

[10] I first presented this dilemma in (1991).

Conclusion

THE CONFLICT BETWEEN RATIONALISM AND SATISFACTIONALISM

> Between the extremities
> Man runs his course
>
> (W. B. Yeats)

WE have an ultimately intrinsic desire that pleasure and satisfaction be felt. Thus, vividly represented pleasures and experiential desire-fulfilment evoke our desires. As it is normally our own present or future desires that we vividly represent, satisfactionalism takes a prudentialist shape. From an evolutionary point of view, this certainly makes sense.

We also have an ultimately intrinsic desire to be rational, to gain knowledge about the world, and to have this knowledge shape our para-cognitive attitudes. This is clearly of survival value, too, for it increases the probability of our desires being coherent and realistic. So, up to a point, the prudentialist desire to maximize our own fulfilment and the rationalist desire to live in the light of truth should be co-satisfiable.

As we saw in the Introduction, at least some ancient philosophers took the view that letting one's attitudes be informed by philosophical truth would improve the prospects of leading a fulfilling life. The leitmotif of this essay has, however, been that rationality in this sense goes against, rather than with, not merely the pursuit of prudentialism, but even the pursuit of a rationally regimented form of the satisfactionalist aim. This is because making our para-cognitive attitudes cognitively rational in the sense of being formed in the light of philosophical truth would amount to such a huge remodelling of ourselves that it might well mentally wreck us. It is not surprising that there should be this chasm between our everyday attitudes and those that are cognitively rational, for the patterns of thought which permeate our everyday lives, and in which our ordinary para-cognitive attitudes nest, are likely to be discordant with our reflective, science-based picture of the world. If so, to reform our attitudes to cognitive rationality might effect such an upheaval of our settled ways of reacting that our efficiency to promote satisfactionalist goals would drastically drop.

We display the P-bias, the tendency to conceptually represent what is at present perceived in much greater detail than anything absent to our senses. As the result of this bias, we may fall victim to the cognitive irrationality of preferring a lesser, perceived pleasure to a greater, unperceived one. We are also subject to the MSI, the mechanism of spontaneous induction, that unreflectively causes us to imagine that our future will be like the experienced past. The MSI is responsible for many irrational phobias. Consequently, prudentialism would be served were we freed of the distorted representations for which the P-bias and the MSI are responsible. To this extent, the projects of prudentialism and rationalism are in harmony.

When the matter is further pursued, it will, however, be seen that this harmony breaks down. If the P-bias is lifted, we are exposed to the SFT, the sense of futility and transience. This sense consists in being unable to focus on the fulfilment of more local desires when other desires, to the effect that we achieve more lasting objectives that do not dwindle into insignificance *sub specie aeternitatis*, crowd in on us. The pleasure formerly felt when local desires were gratified is flooded by the frustration, despair, and, eventually, resignation induced by the unsatisfiability of these grandiose desires. Moreover, were we to put the MSI out of operation, we would run the risk of being constantly exposed to the sense of the precariousness of life, the SPL, that is, of being afflicted by anxiety and insecurity, since there is an ever-present possibility of disasters. However, even if these admittedly tentative speculations about a frame of mind very different from ordinary ones exaggerate the negative aspects, it seems indisputable that this frame of mind cannot be so much more conducive to our fulfilment that it can compensate for the losses incurred in the long combat to divest oneself of the P-bias and the MSI. This suffices to establish the conclusion that the aims of rationalism and prudentialism conflict as regards the P-bias and the MSI.

Now the P-bias and the MSI nurture two temporal biases: the N-bias, the bias towards the near (future); and the F-bias, the bias towards the future. Since they have their source in such representational distortions, it follows that these temporal biases are cognitively irrational. (Thus they are not irrational because they are based on an untenable conception of time. For then we would exhibit these biases not only when we consider our own lives, but also the lives of other individuals, which are equally in time, and we do not.) Therefore it is rational relative to the aim of rationalism to dispose of these temporal biases. But, although it may seem to be rational relative to prudentialism to rid oneself of at least the N-bias, this is not so. For this would involve ridding oneself of the P-bias and the MSI and, according to the reasoning of the preceding paragraph, it is not rational for prudentialists to try to annihilate these tendencies. Thus, rationalists and prudentialists are bound to disagree about the relative rationality of having the N- and F-biases.

Another irrational bias is the O-bias, the tendency to prefer that oneself be fulfilled rather than somebody else, however this other individual may be related to oneself. An analysis of our transtemporal identity demonstrates that the commonsensical identification of us with our bodies presupposes two false assumptions about these bodies that are necessary to make them identical to our selves or the subjects of our experiences. These assumptions are to the effect that our bodies satisfy the owner and the phenomenal aspects of the notion of a subject. Since the notion of our diachronic identity is philosophically indefensible, it follows that it cannot be cognitively rational to be biased towards somebody in the future for the reason that this being is identical to oneself. Nor, as we have seen, would it be rational if the notion of our identity had consisted in the identity of our organisms or in some psychological continuity.

Furthermore, a belief in identity is in fact not even our (apparent) reason for being O-biased. We are biased towards future stages of ourselves because the mechanism of experiential anticipation—a form of the MSI—makes us vividly imagine what our future experiences will be like from the inside. Also, there are generally strong similarities in respect of psychological and physical characteristics between ourselves at present and ourselves in the future; so the approval or liking we have of the former, on grounds partially explored in Part IV, is transferred to the latter. Our identity, then, is not in itself our reason for being O-biased. It merely puts this bias into operation by triggering experiential anticipation and by guaranteeing similarities.

To form a cognitively rational attitude towards oneself in the place of the O-bias, one must counteract the tendency to imaginatively overrepresent one's own present and future situation, by a voluntary effort to imagine the situations of others as vividly as one's own. Although such an elimination of the O-bias may bring along some prudential advantages, it is plain that it cannot overall be an improvement from the prudentialist viewpoint, since this bias is the very axis around which this viewpoint revolves. But this elimination might still be thought to promote a kind of satisfactionalist aim: the one which results if prudentialism is abandoned by the imposition of a requirement of personal neutrality or universalizability, RU (alongside a requirement of temporal neutrality). This would be tantamount to the utilitarian maximization of the fulfilment of all alike. But, as in the case of prudentialism, we find that rationalism advocates a cleansing of irrational para-cognitive attitudes beyond what is rational relative to this rationally rectified satisfactionalist aim.

This does not mean that this rationalist pursuit is irrational. For, first, it is not irrational to pursue something as an *ideal* in the sense of pursuing it although it is contrary to the prudentialist goal of inter-temporal maximization of one's own fulfilment. Had the hedonist claim to the effect that only pleasure is intrinsically desirable been true, this would have been irrational. Secondly, owing to the rational insignificance of personal identity, this idealism can rationally be extended from the domain of prudence to the inter-personal domain of morality. The fact that there is room for these two idealist moves is what I have called prudential and moral individualism, respectively.

I have argued that individualism is not dependent on the subjectivism or desire-relativism of value here adopted. Even on objectivism it would be hard to defend either the view that not both rationality and satisfaction are valuable aims or that one is superior to the other. For not being called for by the direction of fit of desires, objective values can scarcely be claimed to have the evident authority needed to settle conflicts between such widespread aims. But, although individualism is inescapable, it is checked in the inter-personal sphere by the usefulness to everyone of co-operation.

A third area of conflict concerns a set of emotions the propositional contents of which encompass an idea of 'blank' causation or epistemically ultimate self-determination—an idea which can be preserved in the face of belief neither in determinism nor in indeterminism. This set comprises the agent-oriented emotions of anger, gratitude, remorse, and feelings of guilt and the comparative emotions of pride, shame, admiration, and contempt. Since this epistemic notion of self-determination cannot be entertained in a rational frame of mind, these emotions are cognitively irrational. Hence, rationalists must be shorn of them, but it is another matter whether the same is (relatively) rational for satisfactionalists whose aim is correspondingly rationally constrained.

As the concept of desert also involves the notion of epistemically ultimate self-determination, this aim cannot comprise justice conceived in the traditional terms of getting what one deserves. But, contrary to utilitarian assumptions, justice conceived as equality can remain in place if desert—along with natural rights, the other ground designed to make inequality just—is discarded. The fully rational satisfactionalist aim would, then, be a combination of maximizing the fulfilment of all and distributing it equally. But, since temporal and personal biases, desert-thinking, and related emotions are such fundamental elements in our psychological make-up, to divest ourselves of them is likely to cost so much in the way of time and energy that we would less proficiently serve the rationalized satisfactionalist aim than we otherwise could have. As rationalism demands this elimination, there is a collision with this satisfactionalist aim, too.

In the three areas examined, the source of the cognitive irrationality of our attitudes lies in the dominance which the perceived exercises over thought-processes. This is obviously so in the case of the P-bias. The MSI is a tendency to imagine that the future will be like what it has been perceived to be in the past. Agent-oriented and comparative emotions are due to a tendency not to reflect on causes that are not perceived. The act-omission doctrine, AOD, springs from the perception of causal connections. (In the Appendix we shall come across our disposition to take the perceived as real rather than to construe it as something caused by an underlying reality.) The cognitive irrationality of the para-cognitive attitudes we have investigated is not to be attributed, then, to any more abstract beliefs that we irrationally endorse.

In all cases an abstract belief that would stand any chance of justifying the attitudes would, at best, teeter on the brink of unintelligbility. As regards temporal biases, it seems downright impossible to produce any conception of time that would justify the N-and F-bias—in particular as they manifest themselves to a much stronger degree, if not exclusively, with respect to one's own life. We have also found that no conception of our identity, not even the immaterialist one, could vindicate the O-bias. Finally, an ontically ultimate self-determination which might render comprehensible agent-oriented and comparative emotions is incoherent (at least for agents with finite pasts). These attitudes are, then, caused by the influence perception exercises over thought rather than by abstract, perception-transgressing thought.

To sum up, the list of these attitudes that are cognitively irrational and that rationalists must do without includes a considerable portion of the attitudes that characterize normal human beings. It includes agent-oriented or comparative emotions, the N-, F-, O- and P-biases and, therefore, all those fluctuations in respect of plain emotions—such as hope, gladness, fear, sadness, etc.—that are characteristic of beings in the grip of these biases. (As we shall see in the Appendix, it may also include desires for physical contact.) Rationalists will dwell in a retreat of reason in which few of the attitudes we know from everyday life will remain.

The rationalist aim has been pitted against a series of satisfactionalist aims, increasingly rationally constrained: prudentialism that (unlike naive prudentialism) is temporally neutral, inter-personal or utilitarian maximization which (unlike prudentialism) is personally neutral as well, and egalitarian maximization which (unlike utilitarian maximization) encompasses the justice of equality, resulting from the removal of the incoherent notion of desert. In all cases we have found that it would not be rational for satisfactionalists, of any stripe, to go as far as rationalists to extirpate the relevant attitudes, though it may be rational for them to restrain them. There is a limit to their engagement in mental exercises of imaginative representation aimed at breaking the dominance of the perceived and making the truth impregnate their affective-conative nature. Relative to their satisfactionalist aims, it would instead be rational for them to let reason retreat from the role of forming their attitudes to completely suit the mould of cognitive rationality.

The Possibility of a Retreat of Reason

It might be thought that this latter retreat or withdrawal of reason is impossible, that if one realizes that an attitude is cognitively irrational, one cannot maintain it. But it is one thing (a) to gain an insight and another (b) to dwell on adequate representations of it to a degree necessary to shape one's attitudes. It seems that it is a blurring of this distinction which at one point leads Hume to reject a prudentialist approach to philosophy. He points to a

> singular and seemingly trivial property of the fancy, by which we enter with difficulty into remote views of things, and are not able to accompany them with so sensible an impression, as we do those, which are more easy and natural. (1739–40/1978: 268)

As a result, "[v]ery refin'd reflections have little or no influence on us". He then asks whether this is as it should be, whether we should "establish it for a rule, that they ought not have any influence" (1739–40/1978: 268). He provides two reasons for thinking that it is not. It would mean that

> you cut off entirely all science and philosophy . . . And you expresly contradict yourself; since this maxim must be built on the preceding reasoning, which will be allow'd to be sufficiently refin'd and metaphysical. (1739–40/1978: 268)

Hence it appears that we should be (more?) influenced by "refin'd reflections". But this leads Hume into an impasse, for he also argues that

> the understanding, when it acts alone, and according to its most general principles, entirely subverts itself, and leaves not the lowest degree of evidence in any proposition. (1739–40/1978: 267)

That is, there are no reliable "refin'd reflections" to guide you.

If, however, the distinction between (a) and (b) is observed, the two reasons quoted are displayed as irrelevant, and the first horn of the dilemma dissolves. You can still engage in science and philosophy to gain insights, even if you resolve not to make any endeavour—by systematically contemplating the insights in vivid detail—to have them affect your para-cognitive attitudes and actions. Secondly, there is no inconsistency in affirming, on the basis of a "refin'd" piece of reasoning, either that such reasonings should not *forthwith* be pursued or that, if they are not discontinued, no attempts should be made to put their results into practice by "cognitive psychotherapy" (to borrow Brandt's term).

So prudentialism can be combined with continued scientific and philosophical undertakings, as is only too obvious from everyday experience. In fact, it appears to be the course that Hume himself adopts in the end. As he describes it, "nature herself" comes to his rescue and cures him of "this philosophical melancholy and delirium" (1739–40/1978: 269). He dines, plays backgammon with friends, in short enjoys himself and does not return to philosophical speculation until he feels "naturally *inclin'd*" to do so, until he can truly say to himself that "by attaching myself to any other business or diversion, I *feel* I shou'd be a loser in point of pleasure; and this is the origin of my philosophy" (1739–40/1978: 271). Thus could prudentialists speak; and, given a scepticism such as Hume's, rationalism—even of the negative or destructive kind I have practised—would scarcely be a viable alternative: it would hardly be rational to try to attain attitudinal compliance with some inconvenient deliverances of philosophy if they are no more likely to be sound than those of common sense.

It takes a somewhat greater confidence in the philosophical enterprise to create the conflict or dilemma in the philosophy of life that has been the centrepiece of this study. Philosophical truth—for example about the persistence of the self and its capacity to determine itself—must be seen as something which is in some measure accessible to us. Then the dilemma between satisfactionalism, on the one hand, and rationalism, on the other, that I have tried to expound can make itself felt. People can have other interests than the rationalist one that can compose ideals of theirs; for instance, they may have artistic or athletic ambitions of this kind. But, as remarked in the Introduction, the rationalist ideal of letting one's attitudes be shaped by philosophical truth is especially pertinent in an investigation into philosophical truth. Moreover, these truths have the power to modify the satisfactionalist aim though, as is now clear, these modifications will not effect a desirable harmony between rationalism and satisfactionalism.

As I also noted in the Introduction, it has been assumed by some, for example the Epicureans, that a life in the light of philosophical truth would make at least oneself more fulfilled than would any other sort of life. Even if they do not believe that philosophical truth will positively promote any satisfactionalist aim, many seem to assume that it is at least compatible with such an aim because our fundamental attitudes are 'error-proof', in the sense that they cannot be shown to be irrational by philosophical analysis. Philosophy "leaves everything as it is", to apply a saying of Wittgenstein's. This is the purport of what Mark Johnston calls "Minimalism" (1997), that our fundamental attitudes and practices cannot be shown to be rationally unjustified by being shown to rest upon faulty metaphysical pictures. Such sentiments seem to lie at the basis of much of 'common-sense' philosophy of the ethical intuitionism type. But it is a mistake to assume that truth must be immanent in our fundamental attitudes. It could transcend them, and I hope that it is now manifest that, though some of these attitudes are not exactly underpinned by wrong-headed metaphysical notions, they can be shown to be cognitively irrational, by springing from perception-distorted representations of the facts. Since these attitudes are so deep-seated and central to our psychology, rationalism is thrown into conflict with satisfactionalism. The magnitude of our para-cognitive irrationality is so great that the removal of it is at odds even with a fully rational satisfactionalist aim.

Although I have conducted this discussion in terms of a subjectivist theory of value and of practical reason, I do not want to suggest that these conflicts cannot arise on an objectivist ground. On the contrary, it would seem to be natural for objectivists to acknowledge both the value of living in the light of truth and reason and that of striving for fulfilment. Some might maintain that the conflict could assume an even more acute form here, since objective values must be taken more seriously. Indeed, the presumption is rather the opposite: that a dilemma between rationalism and satisfactionalism, especially in the prudentialist form, cannot arise within the conceptual space of subjectivism, since the latter vouchsafes the rationality of prudentialist satisfactionalism. Against this backdrop, I take my project of working out the shape of the dilemma on a subjectivist ground to be of interest not only to those who share this ground, but to anyone primarily concerned about the sort of dilemma investigated.

To summarize the overarching claims of this book:

(1) Pursuing the rationalist goal of having para-cognitive attitudes that are fully cognitively rational cannot in the end be reconciled with pursuing a satisfactionalist goal, even if the latter is rendered cognitively rational (by the imposition of requirements of temporal and personal neutrality and the removal of desert and rights from the conception of justice), owing to the depth and the breadth of the attitudes that are cognitively irrational.

(2) There is nothing (such as the truth of psychological hedonism or objective values) to make the rationalist goal (more or) less rational than a (fully rational) satisfactionalist goal, that is, idealism (e.g. of a rationalist sort) is rationally permissible.

(3) So, individualism reigns in prudence and morality: there is no kind of life, such as the life that contains most satisfaction that, regardless of one's personality, is the best life for all, and no goal—like everyone's leading lives that score as highly and as equally as regards fulfilment as possible—which is the moral goal for all.

It is also noteworthy that in the case of all the attitudes whose cognitive irrationality has been exposed, their causes are similar: they have to do with the dominance that the perceived exercises over thinking rather than with the irrationality of more abstract thinking. This explains both why these attitudes are widespread among conscious beings and why they are hard to get rid of. Their resilience is the reason for the conflict between rationalism and rationalized satisfactionalism stated in (1).

Broadly speaking, the perception-related sorts of facts to which the cognitive irrationality of our fundamental para-cognitive attitudes is largely due are these:

(a) we tend to represent much more vividly that which is present to our senses than that which is sensibly absent, and the formation of our para-cognitive attitudes is an upshot not directly of the propositions that are dispositionally stored in our minds, but of those that are episodically represented;

(b) how we perceive things is in some respects incompatible with how things are according to our best scientific theories, and having been with the human species for a long time, our most fundamental attitudes must have been formed by how we perceive things, and accordingly think of them, rather than by our much more recent scientific theories.

We can conceive of conscious beings of whom neither (a) nor (b) is true. We could, for instance, imagine conscious beings (a*) who spontaneously produced just as lively representations of things absent or whose para-cognitive attitudes were just as sensitive to abstract representations and (b*) whose perceptions, and associated ways of thinking, would be completely borne out by their most well-founded theories.

But (a*) is most unlikely to be true in a world in which there is a struggle for survival, and survival first and foremost depends on fending off perceptible threats. It is also of obvious survival value that, at the primitive stage at which we react only to what we perceive, we have some fixed attitudes that, perforce, are oriented towards the perceived. As for (b*), it is undeniable that the picture that science, for example physics, paints of the world radically contradicts the perceptible or 'manifest' image of it. Many philosophers endorse a *direct realism* according to which perception by unaided senses presents the world as it really is independently of observers. But, for my own part, I am inclined to believe that, independently of us, things are rather as science portrays them. Since this is an issue which, though it imposes no rational constraints on satisfactionalist aims, has a bearing on the topic in Part IV, I shall discuss it, but have placed the discussion in an appendix.

So the features that make our attitudes cognitively irrational are not of the kind likely to be otherwise. Since, for evolutionary reasons, it is to be expected that we are equipped with strong urges both to form our para-cognitive attitudes in the light of reason and to strive for happiness, we are destined for a dilemma between rationalism and satisfaction-alism. The wish that we could have it both ways—because the world supports the rationality of our central attitudes—is utterly futile. It may however be a consolation to some that the very impetus that makes us have this wish—to the point of indulging in wishful thinking—drives us to go on living just the same, irrespective of what irresolvable conflicts we encounter.

Appendix

ON BEING OUT OF TOUCH: THE ATTITUDINAL IMPACT OF INDIRECT REALISM

MANY have thought that, prior to philosophical reflection and scientific investigation, the universal belief about perception is a *direct realism*, that is, roughly, the doctrine that in normal perception the world presents itself to us as it is independently of our perception. Many have also thought that, when we begin to examine critically the phenomenon of perception, we shall be converted to the belief that reality *never* appears to us as it is independently of us: we perceive things as being continuously extended in space, as being coloured, hot or cold, where there are in reality arrangements of particles with none of these features. On this view, perception of the physical world is an *indirect* or *mediate* affair that consists in the world causing us to be in perceptual states the direct or internal objects of which fundamentally differ from the real, physical ones.

I shall refer to this doctrine as *indirect realism* and take it to be made up of two claims, one about the nature of perception and the other about the physical reality that exists independently of perception:

(1) perceiving a physical thing consists in being caused by it to be in a state of directly perceiving some (other) object, and

(2) the latter object, internal to the act of perception, differs radically from the physical thing which causes the perception.

Different forms of indirect realism differ on how radically these two objects differ. One may even conceive a version of indirect realism according to which the perceptual contents faithfully copy the physical realities causally responsible for them. But surely, whatever credibility accrues to the move of distinguishing an internal object of perception from the external object derives in large part from arguments to the effect that how things are independently of perception differ widely from how they are perceived to be. I think that the most plausible form of indirect realism is a so-called *scientific realism* on which the best description we have of physical objects, as they are independent of perception, is the one supplied by contemporary physics because it is in terms of such a description that we should in the end causally explain our perception. According to this form of indirect realism, the difference between appearance and reality will be very radical, indeed, for physical objects will lack secondary qualities and the primary qualities with which they are equipped will be very dissimilar from those of the objects of direct perception. Roughly, what to us appears to be solid things will in reality be swarms of particles.

In opposition to indirect realism, direct realism denies (1) and (2). If thoughtfully developed, it will not deny that perception of a physical object is essentially a causal process, for, intuitively, this is a very plausible claim. It must, however, reject the view that this causal process involves the direct perception of some objects distinct from the physical ones, since otherwise the perception of the latter will be indirect or mediate; in other words, it must affirm the directness of perception of physical things. As this duplication of perceptual objects is disallowed, the possibility of them being radically different naturally does not arise.

There are two options open to direct realists who want to hold on to the causal element. They can claim that (a) the state caused, though perceptual in nature, does not have an internal object— this is what, for example, the so-called adverbial analysis of perceptual experience is up to—or, more radically, they can assert that (b) this state is not a distinctively perceptual or sensory state, but one of thinking or believing. For if it is conceded that the state is *sui generis* perceptual and object-oriented then, since perceiving something physical comprises being causally affected by it, and since causes and effects must be entirely distinct and not overlap, such an object internal to the state cannot be identical to (the part of) the physical object that does the causing. Hence, it would follow that perceiving something physical must be an indirect relation that consists in the physical object causing this state with a distinct object—and this is the thesis of indirect realism. Therefore, direct realists must deny that perception of a physical object involves being caused by it to have *an object-directed perceptual experience*.

Direct realism is not only our pre-reflective belief; nowadays it is also the view of many philosophers. In fact, in many philosophical quarters indirect realism is considered outmoded, and either strategy (a) or (b) is endorsed. As I have made clear elsewhere (1985a), I believe both of these strategies to be untenable. Instead, my sympathy lies with a variant of the form of indirect realism just outlined, though this is not the place to argue the point. But let us assume that indirect realism has been established, and explore what attitudinal modifications a switch from direct realism to it would force upon rationalists. It is convenient to start by asking what attitudinal effects indirect realism harbours in virtue of the fact that it implies (2) (as specified by scientific realism) and then move on to what it harbours in virtue of the fact that it implies (1).

Indirect Realism and Replaceability

If it is brought home to us that, as entities existing independently of perception, we are swarms of elementary particles whose members are constantly renewed, I think we could more readily acknowledge the truth of two theses about our identity across time for which I have argued in Part IV. The first is that we are fuzzy beings whose diachronic identity is indeterminate. This strikes us as implausible as long as we trust everyday perception and proprioception which present us, that is, our bodies, as sharply delimited from our surroundings and as persisting relatively unchanged. But this air of implausibility vanishes if we come to accept that this is a mere appearance and that in reality we are configurations whose members incessantly change. It is natural to think that there is no sharp boundary between one such configuration and another, neighbouring one, and that the transtemporal identity of such a configuration, whose members are constantly renewed, is a vague matter. Against this background, it no longer seems far-fetched to compare us, as Parfit has done (1984: 213–14, 242–3) to macroscopic collectives like clubs and nations and to claim that our identity is just as loose and conventional as theirs.

The second thesis is that our identity is no more important than any other mechanism that equally reliably preserves resemblances in perceived respects valued, for example a foolproof decomposition–replication process. Intuitively, we are prone to invest greater trust and importance in identity as its appearance of qualitative continuity suggests some sort of solid immutability. Of course, this inclination will be extinguished if we take to heart the view that in reality we are swarms whose members change without interruption. The difference between these members being successively replaced and their being replaced at one go is less dramatic than the difference we feel between ordinary survival and decomposition with replication.

So far I have examined the attitudinal impact of a conversion to (a scientific version of) (2). By supporting these two claims about the indeterminacy of identity and about it being important only as a guarantee of similarity, the conversion helps undermine the doctrine that identity in itself is important. The intrinsic unimportance of identity is further underlined by a conversion to (1). I should like to put forward the hypothesis that the attachment to particular items—not just other conscious beings, but inanimate things, too—which makes us reluctant to have them replaced even by perfect replicas, is instinctively or spontaneously formed whenever, over a longer period of time, one takes oneself to be *directly* perceiving a thing and, in some manner, it serves one well. In other words, I take seeing and/or tactually feeling a material thing, as conceived by direct realism, as a necessary condition of becoming attached to it in a way which makes one tend to resist having it replaced.

One could become attached in this fashion to the most humble object, say, a radiator, if for years one sees and handles it, and it functions well. But if one experiences only the effects of a source of heat, as I experience the heating system of my flat, one would not mind if it were exchanged for a different one as long as the effect is qualitatively the same, as I would not mind the exchange of the heating system of my flat if my flat will be just as warm and the bill not higher. This indicates that forming an attachment to a particular thing presupposes that one assumes oneself to be directly perceiving the thing itself. Perceiving a mere effect of it is not any as good; if it makes one attached to anything, it is in the first instance only to the effect. (Having often heard a voice on the telephone, and having begun to like the sound of it, one may find, upon encountering its owner, how far this is from liking the appearance of the latter.)

In other words, what one instinctively becomes non-transferably attached to are objects of which one has frequently had direct experience. Consequently, if perceiving a material object is directly experiencing only an effect of it, as (1) maintains, what one grows immediately attached to, if anything, will be the effect. The attachment to the cause would be derivative from it: it would be attachment to the cause because it produces this kind of effect. Any relevantly similar cause that has this kind of effect would do; so, the numerical identity of the cause would be a matter of indifference.

It would be fallacious to argue that the cause must be identical because it is essential that the effect be numerically the same. For, on indirect realism, even when numerically the same material object is perceived on two occasions, what it causes in the way of experiential content would be numerically distinct, just as it would be if two numerically distinct, but indistinguishable, material objects had been perceived. Hence, if indirect realism were internalized, the mechanism that makes one grow non-transferably attached to a thing if it is directly perceived often enough would become virtually inoperative, since no individual thing is directly perceived 'often enough'. Under these conditions, the attachment generated by immediate perception would probably rather be to a *kind* of thing.

Note that I did not say that *any* cause that has the same type of perceptible effect will do; the qualification 'relevantly similar' is indispensable. Consider the following example: if indirect realism were true, would one be indifferent to whether one's perceptual experience was caused by the sort of entities physics posits or was produced by a team of skilful neurologists who have implanted electrodes in one's brain? As Peter Unger (1990: 298 ff.) has forcefully argued, in the ordinary frame of mind one would definitely prefer the former: facing a choice between being placed in an "experience inducer" which generates hallucinatory experiences and going on perceiving the world (as one believes one does), one would opt for the latter—even though the former stretch of experiences would be much more pleasant.

I do not think that this preference hinges on our propensity to be direct realists: even if perception of the physical world involves the mediation of sensory impressions the contents of which do not match their causes, there are still some points of resemblance—in respect of spatial arrangement— which would be absent were the impressions produced by the manipulation of the team of neurologists. In other words, these causes would not be similar to each other because one of them bears a greater resemblance to the effect, and this might be held to provide a reason for preferring the causation which brings along this resemblance. Also, the fact that causation in one case involves intentional agency might be seen as a relevant difference (for better or worse).

To summarize this argument about the effect of indirect realism on our attitudes to particulars other than ourselves: the main point I have attempted to make is that, to the extent that we adjust to the truth of (1), internalize the doctrine that what we directly perceive is not the physical object itself but something different from it, the instinctive repulsion we feel at the idea of transferring our attitudes to a perfect replica, or a relevantly similar thing, will be corroded, for it rests on our unreflective direct realism. But the argument can also be read as making a distinct though related point: it amplifies the case, laid out in Part IV, against the *cognitive rationality* of non-transferable attitudes to particulars other than oneself: if all that we directly perceive are effects of physical things, and these will be numerically distinct on different occasions of observation, irrespective of whether the physical cause is the same or just similar, the numerical identity of the cause will be unimportant from the point of view of cognitive rationality.

Loss of Contact and Loneliness

This is one attitudinal modification which conversion to (1) brings in its wake, but there are others. To facilitate a discussion of them, let us make, with respect to the five perceptual avenues we are ordinarily recognized to have to the external world, two distinctions that cut across each other. First, we divide them into those that provide us with what, pre-theoretically, we take to be percep-tions of *the material things themselves*—namely, the visual and tactile modalities—and those that supply us with perceptions of a class of phenomena that are *effects* of the former things, namely the auditory, olfactory, and gustatory modalities. For sounds, smells, and tastes are conceived as being caused by the operations of objects seen and tactually felt, and the latter alone are proper material things or bodies.

Secondly, as presaged in Chapter 2, we can divide the sensory avenues into, on the one hand, those along which we can perceive things *at a distance*, somewhere 'out there' in a perceptual space that extends outwards from our bodies, which we perceive from the inside and, on the other hand, those along which we necessarily perceive them as being *in contact with our bodies*. The visual and auditory modalities belong to the former category: I see a tree twenty yards away and hear the birdsong as coming from it. In contrast, what I tactually feel, I feel with some part of my body, on a surface of it, the smell I experience, I experience in my nostrils, the taste I experience, I experi-ence in my mouth. So the tactile, olfactory, and gustatory sense-modalities are of the latter kind.

Now, when one feels lonely and desires the presence of another, it offers some satisfaction and comfort to perceive an effect of the other—as when, after a period of separation, we again hear the voice of somebody dear and exclaim, 'How nice to hear your voice!' Generally, it would be more satisfactory to perceive the being itself, at least if it is pretty close, which the sense of sight permits one to do, but most satisfactory of all it would be also to perceive oneself as being in contact with it, and this is something that only the sense of touch can be thought to supply. If, however, indirect realism is true, not even the sense of touch allows one to be in perceptual contact with another being, to perceive an actual contact between two bodies, one's own and that of another, two bodies which exist independently of perception with the properties one perceives them to have. Like hearing (or tasting or smelling), the tactile sense, on the indirect construal, allows one to savour only *effects* of the other being. Consequently, the consolation that the sense of touch could really offer in moments of loneliness and isolation would rather be on a level with that lower degree which hearing signs of company is commonly thought to provide.

Next, consider the state of feeling love and affection for another and wanting to express it. These feelings can be expressed at distance, by producing an effect that the other will experience, for example verbally, by saying something nice. But again, it is more fulfilling to express it by seeing and being in tactile contact with that being, by embraces, caresses, etc. But if indirect realism is true, this more satisfactory expression is denied us: that which we pre-reflectively assume to be directly seeing and feeling contact with what is really (the surface of) the body of the other, in which its mind is embodied, is just experiencing effects of it (or the particles composing it). The closeness to another that we take ourselves to experience particularly in touching it, as long as we believe in direct realism, would be lost.

Certainly, even on indirect realism, there will be, if not proper contact, some closeness or mingling at the level of elementary particles, between the swarms of particles composing oneself and the other, respectively. It seems, however, clear that this form of nearness is inadequate because the entities involved are so far removed from what we take ourselves to be. What we desire is to see and, especially, to feel a contact with another body which is really as we perceive it to be (our own body also really being what it is perceived to be, of course). The following analogy might help to bring out the point: suppose that your body and the body of another are actually in touch, but that you do not see and feel this contact. Instead neurologists, who have implanted electrodes in your brains, feed you with tactile and visual impression of another type of contact with that being. When informed of the true state of affairs, you would not consider yourself to have been together in a fashion that breaks isolation or allows the expression of affection. Of course, the analogy is somewhat crude, but it demonstrates that actual physical closeness in conjunction with non-matching impressions of contact do not suffice to fulfil our need for bodily contact.

To sum up, by ruling out the direct perceptual contact with the body of another mind that the tactile sense-modality would provide if direct realism were true, and making its data analogous to those of the causal senses, like hearing, indirect realism allows one to escape the sense of isolation and to express affection only to the lesser degree that these senses permit. It puts an unbridgeable distance between oneself and others, by letting one directly perceive only effects of others, not these beings themselves. It so to speak confines one to the sphere of one's own sense-impressions, and this is detrimental both to one's desire to reach others and to one's desire to be reached by them.

To have a desire that one has discovered to be unsatisfiable causes one to feel constant frustration, unless one suppresses consciousness of the fact of its being unsatisfiable, which is something that rationalists cannot do. Consequently, to save themselves frustration, they must try to strip themselves of those desires for physical contact that are satisfiable only if direct realism is true.

These desires, however, will—like the instinctive repulsion towards replication—go away if they take to heart the truth of indirect realism.

Some may think that the surrendering of direct realism will have further attitudinal consequences. They might want to contend that, if direct realism is false, one could not entertain a well-founded belief that there *is* a world independent of one's perceptual experience, a world that causally sustains this experience. (The current popularity of direct realism probably stems to no small measure from such a view.) If indirect realism thus inexorably led to solipsism, the attitudinal consequences would, of course, be vast. But I believe solipsism to be avoidable, although this is a huge issue that will have to be left aside now.

Let us, however, suppose that the truth of indirect realism has been established. Then we should first notice that in contrast to the topics discussed in Parts III, IV, and V, this would not impose any rational requirement (like that of temporal or personal neutrality) on the satisfactionalist aim. (This is one reason why I have placed the discussion of this topic in an appendix.) Thus, we cannot oppose the attitudinal reform that indirect realism forces upon rationalists with the one it forces upon satisfactionalists whose aim is under a rationality constraint that it imposes. Rather, we have to take the satisfactionalist aim to be independently specified.

It is, however, clear that there is a conflict between the pursuit of satisfactionalism, in any of the ways it has been specified, and trying to be cognitively rational to the extent of having attitudes conforming to the truth of indirect realism. To attain this measure of rationality seems overwhelmingly difficult because of our exceedingly powerful tendency to assume that we directly perceive things as they are independently of us. (Again, this is not a positive belief, but a failure to think of what we immediately perceive as being caused by an independent reality.) If there is a clash between how perception represents physical things and how they are according to our best abstract reasons, the instinct to trust the former is sure to prevail. As we perceive ourselves and our environment as consisting of solid, relatively stable things that are definitely demarcated from, though in contact with, each other, we have a well-nigh ineradicable propensity to believe that this is how things really are, despite evidence to the contrary. It is this irresistible tendency, I have conjectured, which makes the desire for being in touch with others and our practically non-transferable attachment to them fundamental attitudes of ours. And this tendency alone is enough to make it virtually impossible for us to have those attitudes that would be cognitively rational on the assumption that direct realism must be rejected.

Some writers maintain that it is reasonable to have a presumption in favour of views received or accepted by common sense.[1] This presumption can be more or less strong. It may be merely to the effect that, if the evidence for and against a received view is equally strong, we should continue to believe in it and act upon it. Or it may be to the effect that we should stick to it until it is conclusively refuted. For such a reason, it may be contended that we should cling to direct realism because the evidence against it does not refute it and may not even make its falsity more likely than its truth. But why should we endorse this presumption in favour of received views? It seems to me that the strongest reason is the satisfactionalist one, that it is costly to give up well-entrenched frames of mind. This is, however, a reason which is not decisive for rationalists. They will follow the thrust of evidence.

Although this is not something I should like assert, I am inclined to believe that there are no further philosophical truths beyond those already reviewed that would put us in the retreat of reason sort of dilemma. Certainly, there are conceivable, sceptical answers to, say, the problem of

---

[1] For instance, Haksar (1991: e.g. ch. 4) argues that there is a presumption in favour of the substantial self because it is a presupposition of our practical life. This would seem to amount to a methodological principle of intuitionism.

other minds and of induction that could make attitudinal modifications on a grander scale rationally required. But, given that these answers were acceptable, it would not be relatively rational even for satisfactionalists (in contrast to rationalists) to suppress them, since these answers undercut their aims. (If it were not rational to believe in induction even prudentialism would be undercut, whereas the rationality of suspending belief in other minds would only undercut the aim to maximize the satisfaction of other beings than oneself.) This book may, then, have achieved a complete coverage of the philosophical truths that force us to face the dilemma of the retreat of reason, though in many aspects this coverage has been sketchy.

REFERENCES

ALSTON, WILLIAM P. (1967a): 'Emotion', in P. Edwards (1967).

—— (1967b): 'Pleasure', in P. Edwards (1967).

ANSCOMBE, G. E. M. (1957): *Intention*, Oxford: Blackwell.

—— (1981): 'Causality and Determination', in her *Metaphysics and the Philosophy of Mind*, Oxford: Blackwell.

ARMSTRONG, DAVID (1962): *Bodily Sensations*, London: Routledge & Kegan Paul.

ARNOLD, MAGDA B. (1960): *Emotion and Personality*, i, New York: Columbia UP.

AUDI, ROBERT (1979): 'Weakness of the Will and Practical Judgement', *Noûs* 13: 173–96.

—— (1989): *Practical Reasoning*, London and New York: Routledge.

—— (1997): *Moral Knowledge and Ethical Character*, New York: Oxford UP.

—— (2001): *The Architecture of Reason*, New York: Oxford UP.

AUSTIN, J. L. (1970): 'Ifs and Cans', in *Philosophical Papers*, 2nd edn., Oxford: Clarendon Press.

AYER, A. J. (1956): *The Problem of Knowledge*, Harmondsworth: Penguin.

—— (1980): 'Free-will and Responsibility', in van Straaten (1980).

AYERS, MICHAEL (1991): *Locke*, 2 vols. London and New York: Routledge, O'Shaugh Nessy(1980)

BAIER, KURT (1958): *The Moral Point of View*, Ithaca, NY, and London: Cornell UP.

BAKER, LYNNE RUDDER (2000): *Persons and Bodies*, Cambridge: Cambridge UP.

BENN, STANLEY (1988): *A Theory of Freedom*, Cambridge: Cambridge UP.

BENNETT, JONATHAN (1980): 'Accountability', in van Straaten (1980).

—— (1984): *A Study of Spinoza's Ethics*, Cambridge: Cambridge UP.

BEN-ZE'EV, AARON (2000): *The Subtlety of Emotions*, Cambridge, Mass.: MIT Press.

BERMÚDEZ, J. L. (1998): *The Paradox of Self-Consciousness*, Cambridge, Mass.: MIT Press.

—— MARCEL, A., and EILAN, N. (eds.) (1995): *The Body and the Self*, Cambridge, Mass.: MIT Press.

BEROFSKY, BERNARD (1987): *Freedom from Necessity*, London: Routledge & Kegan Paul.

BIGELOW, JOHN, DODDS, S., and PARGETTER, R. (1990): 'Temptation and the Will' *American Philosophical Quarterly*, 27: 39–49.

BISHOP, JOHN (1983): 'Agent-Causation', *Mind*, 92, 61–79.

—— (1989): *Natural Agency*, Cambridge: Cambridge UP.

BLACKBURN, SIMON (1988): 'Supervenience Revisited', reprinted in Sayre-McCord (1988a).

—— (1998): *Ruling Passions*, Oxford: Oxford UP.

BOK, HILARY (1998): *Freedom and Responsibility*, Princeton: Princeton UP.

BOND, E. J. (1983): *Reason and Value*, Cambridge: Cambridge UP.

BRANDT, R. B. (1979): *A Theory of the Good and the Right*, Oxford: Clarendon Press.

BRATMAN, MICHAEL (1987): *Intentions, Plans and Practical Reasoning*, Cambridge, Mass.: Harvard UP.

BRENNAN, ANDREW (1988): *Conditions of Identity*, Oxford: Clarendon Press.

BRINK, DAVID O. (1988): *Moral Realism and the Foundations of Ethics*, Cambridge: Cambridge UP.

—— (1997): 'Rational Egoism and Separateness of Persons', in Dancy (1997).

BROAD, C. D. (1952): *Ethics and the History of Philosophy*, London: Routledge & Kegan Paul.

BROOME, JOHN (1999): 'Normative Requirements', *Ratio*, 12: 398–419.

BROWN, ROBERT (1987): *Analyzing Love*, Cambridge: Cambridge UP.

CAMPBELL, C. A. (1957): *On Selfhood and Godhood*, London: Allen & Unwin.

CARTER, W. R. (1989): 'How to Change Your Mind', *Canadian Journal of Philosophy*, 19: 1–16.

CASSAM, QUASSIM (1993): 'Parfit on Persons', *Proceedings of the Aristotelian Society*, 93: 17–37.

——(1997): *Self and World*, Oxford: Oxford UP.

CHANG, RUTH (2004): 'Can Desires Provide Reasons for Action?', in R. J. Wallace, M. Smith, S. Scheffler, and P. Pettit, (eds.), *Reason and Value: Essays on the Moral Philosophy of Joseph Raz*, Oxford: Oxford UP.

CHISHOLM, RODERICK M. (1966): 'Freedom and Action', in K. Lehrer (ed.), *Freedom and Determinism*, New York: Random House.

——(1976): *Person and Object*, London: Allen & Unwin.

——(1982): ' "Self-Profile" and "Replies" ', in R. J. Bogdan (ed.), *Roderick M. Chisholm*, Dordrecht: Reidel.

——(1994): 'On the Observability of the Self', reprinted in Quassin Cassam (ed.), *Self-Knowledge*, Oxford: Oxford UP.

CLARKE, RANDOLPH (1995): 'Towards a Credible Agent-Causal Account of Free Will', in O'Connor (1995*a*).

COCKBURN, DAVID (1997): *Other Times*, Cambridge: Cambridge UP.

COTTINGHAM, JOHN (1998): *Philosophy and the Good Life*, Cambridge: Cambridge UP.

CULLITY, GARRETT, and GAUT, BERYS (eds.) (1997*a*): *Ethics and Practical Reason*, Oxford: Clarendon Press.

——(1997*b*): Introduction to Cullity and Gaut (1997*a*).

CUPIT, GEOFFREY (1996): *Justice as Fittingness*, Oxford: Clarendon Press.

DAMASIO, ANTONIO R. (1994): *Descartes' Error*, New York: Avon Books.

DANCY, JONATHAN (1981): 'On Moral Properties', *Mind*, 90: 367–85.

——(1993): *Moral Reasons*, Oxford: Blackwell.

——(ed.) (1997): *Reading Parfit*, Oxford: Blackwell.

——(2000): *Practical Reality*, Oxford: Oxford UP.

DARWALL, STEPHEN (1983): *Impartial Reason*, Ithaca & London: Cornell UP.

——(2002): *Welfare and Rational Care*, Princeton: Princeton UP.

DAVIDSON, DONALD (1980): *Essays on Actions and Events*, Oxford: Clarendon Press.

——(1982): 'Paradoxes of Irrationality', in R. Wollheim and J. Hopkins (eds.), *Philosophical Essays on Freud*, Cambridge: Cambridge UP.

——(1985*a*): 'Deception and Division', in E. LePore and B. McLaughlin (eds.), *Actions and Events*, Oxford: Clarendon Press.

——(1985*b*): 'Reply to Christopher Peacocke', in B. Vermazen and M. B. Hintikka (eds.), *Essays of Davidson*, Oxford: Clarendon Press.

DAVIS, WAYNE A. (1981): 'Pleasure and Happiness', *Philosophical Studies*, 39: 305–17.

——(1982): 'A Causal Theory of Enjoyment', *Mind*, 91: 240–56.

——(1986): 'Two Senses of Desire', in Marks (1986*a*).

——(1988): 'A Causal Theory of Experiential Fear', *Canadian Journal of Philosophy*, 18: 459–83.

DEIGH, JOHN (1994): 'Cognitivism in the Theory of Emotions', *Ethics*, 104: 824–54.

DENNETT, DANIEL C. (1978): *Brainstorms*, Montgomery, Vt.: Bradford Books.

——(1984): *Elbow Room*, Oxford: Clarendon Press.

DENT, N. J. H. (1984): *The Moral Psychology of the Virtues*, Cambridge: Cambridge UP.

de SOUSA, RONALD (1987): *The Rationality of Emotion*, Cambridge, Mass.: MIT Press.

DOUBLE, RICHARD (1991): *The Non-Reality of Free Will*, New York and Oxford: Oxford UP.

DUNN, ROBERT (1987): *The Possibility of Weakness of Will*, Indianapolis: Hackett.

EDGLEY, ROY (1969): *Reason in Theory and Practice*, London: Hutchinson.

EDWARDS, PAUL (ed.) (1967): *The Encyclopedia of Philosophy*, London and New York: Macmillan & Free Press.

EDWARDS, REM B. (1979): *Pleasures and Pains*, Ithaca, NY, and London: Cornell UP.

EKSTROM, LAURA WADDELL (2000): *Free Will: A Philosophical Study*, Boulder, Colo.: Westview Press.

ELSTER, JON (1999): *Alchemies of the Mind*, Cambridge: Cambridge UP.

EVANS, GARETH (1982): *The Varieties of Reference*, Oxford: Clarendon Press.

FARRELL, DANIEL M. (1980): 'Jealousy', *Philosophical Review*, 89: 527–59.

FEINBERG, JOEL (1970): 'Justice and Personal Desert', in his *Doing and Deserving*, Princeton: Princeton UP.

FELDMAN, FRED (1992): *Confrontations with the Reaper*, New York: Oxford UP.

—— (1997): 'On the Intrinsic Value of Pleasures', *Ethics*, 107: 448–66.

—— (1999): 'Desert: Reconsideration of Some Received Wisdom', reprinted in Pojman and McLeod (1999).

FISCHER, JOHN MARTIN (1994): *The Metaphysics of Free Will*, Oxford: Blackwell.

—— and RAVIZZA, MARK (1998): *Responsibility and Control*, Cambridge: Cambridge UP.

FLEMING, BRICE NOEL (1981): 'Autonomy of the Will', *Mind*, 90: 201–23.

FLEW, ANTHONY (1963): 'Tolstoi and the Meaning of Life', *Ethics*, 73: 110–188.

FOSTER, JOHN (1979): 'In *Self*-Defence', in G. F. McDonald (ed.), *Perception and Identity*, London and Basingstoke: Macmillan.

—— (1985): *A. J. Ayer*, London: Routledge & Kegan Paul.

—— (1991): *The Immaterial Self*, London and New York: Routledge.

FRANKFURT, HARRY (1988): *The Importance of What We Care About*, Cambridge: Cambridge UP.

FUCHS, ALAN E. (1974): 'The Production of Pleasure by Stimulation of the Brain: An Alleged Conflict between Science and Philosophy', *Philosophy and Phenomenological Research*, 34: 494–505.

FUMERTON, RICHARD (1990): *Reason and Morality*, Ithaca, NY, and London: Cornell UP.

GARRETT, BRIAN (1998): *Personal Identity and Self-Consciousness*, London: Routledge.

GAUS, GERALD (1990): *Value and Justification*, Cambridge: Cambridge UP.

GIBBARD, ALLAN (1990): *Wise Choices, Apt Feelings*, Oxford: Clarendon Press.

GINET, CARL (1990): *On Action*, Cambridge: Cambridge UP.

GLOVER, JONATHAN (1988): *I: The Philosophy and Psychology of Personal Identity*, Harmondsworth: Penguin.

GOLDIE, PETER (2000): *The Emotions*, Oxford: Clarendon Press.

GOLDSTEIN, IRWIN (1989): 'Pleasure and Pain: Unconditional, Intrinsic Value', *Philosophy and Phenomenological Research*, 50: 255–76.

GORDON, ROBERT M. (1986): 'The Circle of Desire', in Marks (1986a).

—— (1987): *The Structure of Emotion*, Cambridge: Cambridge UP.

GOSLING, J. C. B. (1969): *Pleasure and Desire*, Oxford: Clarendon Press.

GRICE, H. P. (1967): 'The Causal Theory of Perception', reprinted in G. J. Warnock (ed.), *The Philosophy of Perception*, Oxford: Oxford UP.

HAJI, ISHTIYAQUE (1998): *Moral Appraisability*, New York: Oxford UP.

HAKSAR, VINIT (1991): *Indivisible Selves and Moral Practice*, Edinburgh: Edinburgh UP.

HALL, RICHARD J. (1989): 'Are Pains Necessarily Unpleasant?', *Philosophy and Phenomenological Research*, 50: 643–59.

HAMPTON, JEAN (1998): *The Authority of Reason*, Cambridge: Cambridge UP.

HARE, R. M. (1963): *Freedom and Reason*, Oxford: Clarendon Press.

HARE, R. M. (1969): 'Pain and Evil', in J. Feinberg (ed.), *Moral Concepts*, Oxford: Oxford UP.

—— (1971): 'Wanting: Some Pitfalls', in R. Binkley, R. Bronaugh, and A. Marras (eds.), *Agent, Action, and Reason*, Oxford: Blackwell.

—— (1981): *Moral Thinking*, Oxford: Clarendon Press.

—— (1988): 'Comments', in D. Seanor and N. Fotion (1988).

—— (1989): 'Supervenience', reprinted in his *Essays in Ethical Theory*, Oxford: Clarendon Press.

HARRISON, ROSS (1981–2): 'Discounting the Future', *Proceedings of the Aristotelian Society*, 82.

HART, H. L. A. (1955): 'Are There any Natural Rights?', *Philosophical Review*, 64: 175–91.

HELM, BENNETT W. (2001): *Emotional Reason*, Cambridge: Cambridge UP.

HIRSCH, ELI (1982): *The Concept of Identity*, New York and Oxford: Oxford UP.

HOBART, R. E. (1934): 'Free Will as Involving Determination and Inconceivable without it', *Mind*, 43: 1–27.

HOLTON, RICHARD (1999): 'Intention and Weakness of Will', *Journal of Philosophy*, 96: 241–62.

HONDERICH, TED (1988): *A Theory of Determinism: The Mind, Neuroscience, and Life-Hopes*, Oxford: Clarendon Press.

HOSPERS, JOHN (1961): *Human Conduct*, New York: Harcourt Brace & World.

HUMBERSTONE, I. L. (1992): 'Direction of Fit', *Mind*, 101: 59–83.

HUME, DAVID (1739–40/1978): *A Treatise of Human Nature*, Oxford: Clarendon Press.

IBBERSON, JOHN (1986): *The Language of Decision*, London and Basingstoke: Macmillan.

VAN INWAGEN, PETER (1983): *An Essay on Free Will*, Oxford: Clarendon Press.

—— (1990): *Material Beings*, Ithaca, NY, London: Cornell UP.

IRANI, K. D., and MYERS, G. (eds.) (1983): *Emotion: Philosophical Studies*, New York: Haven.

JACKSON, FRANK (1984): 'Weakness of Will', *Mind*, 93: 1–18.

JAMES, WILLIAM (1890/1950): *The Principles of Psychology*, i, New York: Dover.

JOHNSTON, MARK (1987): 'Human Beings', *Journal of Philosophy*, 84: 59–83.

—— (1997): 'Human Concerns without Superlative Selves', in Dancy (1997).

KAGAN, SHELLY (1989): *The Limits of Morality*, Oxford: Clarendon Press.

KAMM, F. M. (1992): *Creation and Abortion*, New York: Oxford UP.

—— (1996): *Morality, Mortality*, ii, New York: Oxford UP.

KANE, ROBERT (1985): *Free Will and Values*, Albany, NY: SUNY Press.

—— (1989): 'Two Kinds of Compatibilism', *Philosophy and Phenomenological Research*, 50: 219–54.

—— (1996): *The Significance of Free Will*, New York: Oxford UP.

—— (1999): 'Responsibility, Luck, and Chance: Reflections on Free Will and Determinism', *Journal of Philosophy*, 96: 217–40.

KENNETT, JEANETTE (2001): *Agency and Responsibility*, Oxford: Clarendon Press.

KENNY, ANTHONY (1963): *Action, Emotion and Desire*, London: Routledge & Kegan Paul.

KIM, JAEGWON (1984): 'Epiphenomenal and Supervenient Causation', *Midwest Studies in Philosophy*, 9.

—— (1985): 'Concepts of Supervenience', *Philosophy and Phenomenological Research*, 45: 153–76.

KLEIN, MARTHA (1990): *Determinism, Blameworthiness and Deprivation*, Oxford: Clarendon Press.

KLEINIG, JOHN (1971): 'The Concept of Desert', *American Philosophical Quarterly*, 8: 71–8.

KORSGAARD, CHRISTINE, M. (1983): 'Two Distinctions in Goodness', *Philosophical Review*, 92: 169–95.

—— (1986): 'Skepticism about Practical Reason', *Journal of Philosophy*, 85: 5–25.

—— (1997): 'The Normativity of Instrumental Reason', in Cullity and Gaut (1997a).

—— (1998): 'Motivation, Metaphysics, and the Value of the Self', *Ethics*, 109: 49–66.

KRAUT, RICHARD (1972): 'The Rationality of Prudence', *Philosophical Review*, 81: 351–9.

KRAUT, ROBERT (1983): 'Objects of Affection', in Irani and Myers (1983).

—— (1986): 'Love *De Re*', *Midwest Studies in Philosophy*, 10.

KRIPKE, SAUL (1980): *Naming and Necessity*, Oxford: Blackwell.

—— 'Identity over Time', unpubl. lectures.

LEIGHTON, STEPHEN, R. (1985): 'A New View of Emotion', *American Philosophical Quarterly*, 22: 133–40.

LEWIS, DAVID (1976): 'Survival and Identity', in Rorty (1976).

—— (1981): 'Are We Free to Break the Laws?', *Theoria*, 47: 113–21.

LEWIS, HYWEL D. (1982): *The Elusive Self*, London and Basingstoke: Macmillan.

LOCKE, DON (1974): 'Reasons, Wants, and Causes', *American Philosophical Quarterly*, 11: 169–79.

—— (1975): 'Three Concepts of Free Action', *Proceedings of the Aristotelian Society*, Suppl. vol. 49.

LOCKE JOHN (1689/1975): *An Essay Concerning Human Understanding*, Oxford: Clarendon Press.

—— (1690/1990): *Two Treatises on Government*, London: J. M. Dent & Sons.

LOCKWOOD, MICHAEL (1985): 'When Does a Life Begin?', in M. Lockwood (ed.), *Moral Dilemmas in Modern Medicine*, Oxford: Oxford UP.

LONG, A. A., and SEDLEY, D. N. (1987): *The Hellenistic Philosophers*, i, Cambridge: Cambridge UP.

LOWE, E. J. (1989): *Kinds of Being*, Oxford: Blackwell.

—— (1996): *Subjects of Experience*, Cambridge: Cambridge UP.

LUCAS, J. R. (1993): *Responsibility*, Oxford: Clarendon Press.

LUCRETIUS (1975), *De Rerum natura*, Loeb Classical Library, Cambridge, Mass., Harvard UP.

LYONS, WILLIAM (1980): *Emotion*, Cambridge: Cambridge UP.

MACDONALD, SCOTT (1991): 'Ultimate Ends in Practical Reasoning: Aquinas's Aristotelian Moral Psychology and Anscombe's Fallacy', *Philosophical Review*, 100: 31–66.

MCDOWELL, JOHN (1978): 'Are Moral Requirements Hypothetical Imperatives?', *Proceedings of the Aristotelian Society*, Suppl. vol. 52.

—— (1981): 'Non-cognitivism and Rule-following', in S. H. Holtzman and C. M. Leich (eds.), *Wittgenstein: To Follow a Rule*, London: Routledge & Kegan Paul.

—— (1983): 'Aesthetic Value, Objectivity and the Fabric of the World', in E. Schaper (ed.), *Pleasure, Preference and Value*, Cambridge: Cambridge UP.

—— (1985): 'Values and Secondary Qualities', in T. Honderich (ed.), *Morality and Objectivity*, London: Routledge & Kegan Paul.

MACKIE, DAVID (1999): 'Personal Identity and Dead People', *Philosophical Studies*, 95: 219–42.

MACKIE, J. L. (1976): *Problems from Locke*, Oxford: Clarendon Press.

—— (1980): *Hume's Moral Theory*, London: Routledge & Kegan Paul.

MCLEOD, OWEN (1999): Introduction, in Pojman and McLeod (1999).

MCMAHAN, JEFF (2002): *The Ethics of Killing*, New York: Oxford UP.

MCNAUGHTON, DAVID (1988): *Moral Vision*, Oxford: Blackwell.

MADELL, GEOFFREY (1981): *The Identity of the Self*, Edinburgh: Edinburgh UP.

MARKS, JOEL (1982): 'A Theory of Emotion', *Philosophical Studies*, 42: 227–42.

—— (ed.) (1986a): *The Ways of Desire*, Chicago: Precedent Publ.

—— (1986b): 'The Desire Between Motivation and Desire', in Marks (1986a).

MARTIN, C. B., and DEUTSCHER, MAX (1966): 'Remembering', *Philosophical Review*, 75: 161–96.

MARTIN, RAYMOND (1998): *Self-Concern*, Cambridge: Cambridge UP.

MELE, ALFRED R. (1987): *Irrationality*, New York: Oxford UP.

—— (1992): *Springs of Action*, New York: Oxford UP.

—— (1995): *Autonomous Agents*, New York: Oxford UP.

MELE, ALFRED R. (2003): *Motivation and Agency*, New York: Oxford UP.

MELLOR, D. H. (1981): *Real Time*, Cambridge: Cambridge UP.

—— (1998): *Real Time II*, London: Routledge.

MELZACK, RONALD (1973): *The Puzzle of Pain*, Harmondsworth: Penguin.

MILGRAM, STANLEY (1974): *Obedience to Authority: An Experimental View*, New York: Harper & Row.

MILLER, ALEXANDER (2003): *An Introduction to Contemporary Metaethics*, Cambridge: Polity.

MILLER, DAVID (1999): 'Desert and Determination', reprinted in Pojman and McLeod (1999).

NAGEL, THOMAS (1970): *The Possibility of Altruism*, Oxford: Clarendon Press.

—— (1979): *Mortal Questions*, Cambridge: Cambridge UP.

—— (1986): *The View from Nowhere*, Oxford: Clarendon Press.

NEU, JEROME (1980): 'Jealous Thoughts', in A. Rorty (ed.), *Explaining Emotion*, Berkeley: University of California Press.

NIETZSCHE, FRIEDRICH (1886/1973): *Beyond Good and Evil*, Harmondsworth: Penguin.

NOONAN, HAROLD W. (1989): *Personal Identity*, London and New York: Routledge.

NOZICK, ROBERT (1974): *Anarchy, State and Utopia*, New York: Basic Books.

—— (1981): *Philosophical Explanations*, Oxford: Clarendon Press.

NUSSBAUM, MARTHA (1994): *The Therapy of Desire*, Princeton: Princeton UP.

O'CONNOR, TIMOTHY (1993): 'Indeterminism and Free Agency: Three Recent Views', *Philosophy and Phenomenological Research*, 53: 499–526.

—— (ed.) (1995a): *Agents, Causes and Events: Essays on Indeterminism and Free Will*, New York: Oxford UP.

—— (1995b): 'Agent Causation', in O'Connor (1995a).

—— (2000): *Persons and Causes*, Oxford: Oxford UP.

ODERBERG, DAVID, S. (1993): *The Metaphysics of Identity over Time*, London: Macmillan.

OLSON, ERIC, T. (1997): *The Human Animal*, New York: Oxford UP.

—— (1999): 'There is no Problem of the Self', *Journal of Consciousness Studies*, 6: 49–61.

ORTONY, A., CLORE, G., and COLLINS, A. (1988): *The Cognitive Structure of Emotions*, Cambridge: Cambridge UP.

O'SHAUGHNESSY, BRIAN (1980): *The Will*, 2 vols., Cambridge: Cambridge UP.

—— (1995): 'Proprioception and the Body Image', in Bermúdez et al. (1995).

PARFIT, DEREK (1984): *Reasons and Persons*, Oxford: Clarendon Press.

—— (1986): 'Overpopulation and the Quality of Life', in P. Singer (ed.), *Applied Ethics*, Oxford: Oxford UP.

—— (1997): 'Reasons and Motivation', *Proceedings of the Aristotelian Society*, Suppl. vol. 71.

—— (2001): 'Rationality and Reasons', in D. Egonsson, J. Josefsson, B. Petersson, and T. Rønnow-Rasmussen (eds.), *Exploring Practical Philosophy*, Aldershot: Ashgate.

PENNER, TERRY (1972): 'Thought and Desire in Plato', in G. Vlastos (ed.), *Plato: A Collection of Critical Essays*, ii, London and Basingstoke: Macmillan.

PEREBOOM, DERK (2001): *Living without Free Will*, Cambridge: Cambridge UP.

PERRY, DAVID (1967): *The Concept of Pleasure*, The Hague and Paris: Mouton.

PERRY, JOHN (ed.) (1975): *Personal Identity*, Berkeley, Los Angeles, and London: University of California Press.

—— (1976): 'The Importance of Being Identical', in Rorty (1976).

PERSSON, INGMAR (1981): *Reasons and Reason-Governed Actions*, Lund: Studentlitteratur.

—— (1985a): *The Primacy of Perception*, Lund: Gleerup.

—— (1985b): 'The Universal Basis of Egoism', *Theoria*, 51: 137–58.

—— (1988a): 'Review of Nagel: *The View from Nowhere*', *Theoria*, 54: 55–67.

—— (1988b): 'Rationality and Maximization of Satisfaction', *Noûs*, 22: 537–54.

—— (1989): 'Universalizability and the Summing of Preferences', *Theoria*, 55: 159–70.

—— (1990): 'Parfit on Neutrality', *Danish Yearbook of Philosophy*, 25: 61–72.

—— (1991): 'A Determinist Dilemma', *Ratio*, 4: 38–58.

—— (1992*a*): 'Sensational Beauty', in J. Emt and G. Hermerén: *Understanding the Arts*, Lund: Studentlitteratur.

—— (1992*b*): 'The Indeterminacy and Insignificance of Personal Identity', *Inquiry*, 35: 271–83.

—— (1993): 'Review of van Inwagen: *Material Beings*', *Noûs*, 27: 503–8.

—— (1994): 'The Groundlessness of Natural Rights', *Utilitas*, 6: 9–24.

—— (1997*a*): 'Hume—Not a "Humean" about Motivation', *History of Philosophy Quarterly*, 14: 189–206.

—— (1997*b*): 'The Involvement of Our Identity in Experiential Memory', *Canadian Journal of Philosophy*, 27: 447–65.

—— (1999*a*): 'Our Identity and the Separability of Persons and Organisms', *Dialogue*, 38: 519–33.

—— (1999*b*): 'Awareness of Our Bodies as Subject and Object', *Philosophical Explorations*, 2: 70–5.

—— (2001): 'Equality, Priority and Person-Affecting Value', *Ethical Theory and Moral Practice*, 4: 23–39.

—— (2003*a*): 'Two Claims about Potential Human Beings', *Bioethics*, 17: 503–16.

—— (2003*b*): 'The Badness of Unjust Inequality', *Theoria*, 69: 109–24.

—— (2004*a*): 'Two Act-Omission Paradoxes', *Proceedings of the Aristotelian Society*, 104, pt. 2.

—— (2004*b*): 'The Root of the Repugnant Conclusion and its Rebuttal', in J. Ryberg and T. Tännsjö (eds.), *The Repugnant Conclusion*, Dordrecht: Kluwer.

—— (2004*c*): 'A Defence of Extreme Egalitarianism', paper presented to a conference on equality, Copenhagen, autumn 2004.

—— (2005*a*): 'Double Effect Troubles', in Felix Larsson (ed.), *Kapten Mnemos Kolumbarium*, Web series, Dept. of Philosophy, Gothenburg University, http://phil.gu.se/skriftserier.html web

—— (2005*b*) 'The Act-Omission Doctrine and Negative Rights' (unpubl.).

PETTIT, PHILIP, and SMITH, MICHAEL (1990): 'Backgrounding Desire', *Philosophical Review*, 99: 565–92.

PINK, THOMAS (1996): *The Psychology of Freedom*, Cambridge: Cambridge UP.

PIPER, ADRIAN M. (1985): 'Two Conceptions of the Self', *Philosophical Studies*, 48: 173–97.

PLATTS, MARK (1979): *The Ways of Meaning*, London: Routledge & Kegan Paul.

—— (1980): 'Moral Reality and the End of Desire', in M. Platts (ed.), *Reference, Truth and Reality*, London: Routledge & Kegan Paul.

—— (1991): *Moral Realities*, London: Routledge & Kegan Paul.

POJMAN, LOUIS P., and McLEOD, OWEN (eds.) (1999): *What Do We Deserve?*, New York: Oxford UP.

PUGMIRE, DAVID (1998): *Rediscovering Emotion*, Edinburgh: Edinburgh UP.

QUINN, WARREN (1978): 'Moral and Other Realisms', in A. I. Goldman and J. Kim (eds.), *Values and Morals*, Dordrecht: Reidel.

—— (1993): *Morality and Action*, Cambridge: Cambridge UP.

RABINOWICZ, WLODEK, and RØNNOW-RASMUSSEN, TONI (1999): 'A Distinction in Value: Intrinsic and For its Own Sake', *Proceedings of the Aristotelian Society*, 99.

RAILTON, PETER (1986): 'Moral Realism', *Philosophical Review*, 95: 163–207.

RAWLS, JOHN (1971): *A Theory of Justice*, Cambridge, Mass.: Harvard UP.

RAZ, JOSEPH (1999): *Engaging Reason*, Oxford: Oxford UP.

RESCHER, NICHOLAS (1988): *Rationality*, Oxford: Clarendon Press.

RICHARDS, DAVID A. J. (1971): *A Theory of Reasons for Action*, Oxford: Clarendon Press.

RICHARDS, NORVIN (1986): 'Luck and Desert', *Mind*, 95: 198–209.

ROBERTS, ROBERT C. (1988): 'What an Emotion Is: A Sketch', *Philosophical Review*, 97: 183–209.

—— (2003): *Emotions*, Cambridge: Cambridge UP.

ROBINSON, JOHN (1988): 'Personal Identity and Survival', *Journal of Philosophy*, 85: 319–28.

RORTY, AMELIE (ed.) (1976): *The Identities of Persons*, Berkeley, Los Angeles, and London: University of California Press.

ROSATI, CONNIE S. (1996): 'Internalism and the Good for a Person', *Ethics*, 106: 297–326.

ROSENTHAL, DAVID M. (1983): 'Emotions and the Self', in Irani and Myers (1983).

RYLE, GILBERT (1949): *The Concept of Mind*, London: Hutchinson.

—— (1954): *Dilemmas*, Cambridge: Cambridge UP.

SACKS, OLIVER (1985): *The Man who Mistook his Wife for a Hat*, New York: Summit Books.

SAYRE-McCORD, GEOFFREY (ed.) (1988a): *Essays on Moral Realism*, Ithaca, NY, and London: Cornell UP.

—— (1988b): 'Introduction: The Many Moral Realisms', in Sayre-McCord (1988a).

SCANLON, T. M. (1998): *What We Owe to Each Other*, Cambridge, Mass.: Harvard UP.

SCHECHTMAN, MARYA (1990): 'Personhood and Personal Identity', *Journal of Philosophy*, 87: 71–92.

SCHEFFLER, SAMUEL (1982): *The Rejection of Consequentialism*, Oxford: Oxford UP.

SCHIFFER, STEPHEN (1976): 'A Paradox of Desire', *American Philosophical Quarterly*, 13: 195–203.

SCHMIDTZ, DAVID (1995): *Rational Choice and Moral Agency*, Princeton: Princeton UP.

SCHOPENHAUER, ARTHUR (1841/1995): *On the Basis of Morality*, Providence and Oxford: Berghahn Books.

SCHUELER, G. F. (1995): *Desire*, Cambridge, Mass.: MIT Press.

SEANOR, D., and FOTION, N. (eds.) (1988): *Hare and Critics*, Oxford: Clarendon Press.

SEARLE, JOHN R. (1983): *Intentionality*, Cambridge: Cambridge UP.

—— (2001): *Rationality in Action*, Cambridge Mass.: MIT Press.

SEN, AMARTYA (1979): 'Utilitarianism and Welfarism', *Journal of Philosophy*, 76: 463–89.

SHAFFER, JEROME (1983): 'An Assessment of Emotion', *American Philosophical Quarterly*, 20: 161–73.

SHATZ, DAVID (1986): 'Free Will and the Structure of Motivation', *Midwest Studies in Philosophy*, 10.

SHER, GEORGE (1987): *Desert*, Princeton: Princeton UP.

SHOEMAKER, SYDNEY (1970): 'Persons and their Past', *American Philosophical Quarterly*, 7: 269–85.

—— (1984): *Identity, Cause and Mind*, Cambridge: Cambridge UP.

—— and SWINBURNE, RICHARD (1984): *Personal Identity*, Oxford: Blackwell.

SIDGWICK, HENRY (1907/1981): *The Methods of Ethics*, 7th edn., Indianapolis and Cambridge: Hackett.

SINGER, PETER (1988): 'Reasoning towards Utilitarianism', in Seanor and Fotion (1988).

—— (1993): *Practical Ethics*, 2nd edn., Cambridge: Cambridge UP.

SIRCELLO, GUY (1989): *Love and Beauty*, Princeton: Princeton UP.

SLOTE, MICHAEL (1975): 'Existentialism and the Fear of Dying', *American Philosophical Quarterly*, 12: 17–28.

—— (1980): 'Understanding Free Will', *Journal of Philosophy*, 77: 136–51.

—— (1983): *Goodness and Virtues*, Oxford: Clarendon Press.

—— (1984): 'Morality and the Self-Other Asymmetry', *Journal of Philosophy*, 81: 179–92.

—— (1989): *Beyond Optimizing*, Cambridge, Mass.: Harvard UP.

SMILANSKY, SAUL (2000): *Free Will and Illusion*, Oxford: Oxford UP.

SMITH, MICHAEL (1987): 'The Humean Theory of Motivation', *Mind*, 96: 36–61.

—— (1994): *The Moral Problem*, Oxford: Blackwell.

SNOWDON, P. F. (1990): 'Persons, Animals, and Ourselves', in C. Gill (ed.), *The Person and the Human Mind*, Oxford: Clarendon Press.

——(1991): 'Brain Transplants and Personal Identity', in D. Cockburn (ed.), *Human Beings*, Cambridge: Cambridge UP.

SOLOMON, ROBERT C. (1976): *The Passions*, New York: Anchor Press/Doubleday.

SOSA, ERNEST (1990): 'Surviving Matters', *Noûs*, 24: 297–322.

SPINOZA, BARUCH (1675/1949): *Ethics*, New York & London: Hafner.

SPRIGGE, TIMOTHY (1988): *The Rational Foundations of Ethics*, London: Routledge & Kegan Paul.

STAMPE, DENNIS W. (1986): 'Defining Desire', in Marks (1986a).

——(1987): 'The Authority of Desire', *Philosophical Review*, 96: 335–81.

STAUDE, MITCHELL (1986): 'Wanting, Desiring, and Valuing: The Case Against Conativism', in Marks (1986a).

STEINER, HILLEL (1994): *An Essay on Rights*, Oxford: Blackwell.

STERN, LAWRENCE (1974): 'Freedom, Blame, and the Moral Community', *Journal of Philosophy*, 71: 72–84.

STOCKER, MICHAEL (1983): 'Psychic Feelings: Their Importance and Irreducibility', *Australasian Journal of Philosophy*, 61: 5–26.

——(1989): *Plural and Conflicting Values*, Oxford: Clarendon Press.

STONE, JIM (1988): 'Parfit and the Buddha: Why There Are No People', *Philosophy and Phenomenological Research*, 48: 519–32.

VAN STRAATEN, Z. (ed.) (1980): *Philosophical Subjects*, Oxford: Clarendon Press.

STRAWSON, GALEN (1986): *Freedom and Belief*, Oxford: Clarendon Press.

——(1994): *Mental Reality*, Cambridge, Mass.: MIT Press.

——(1997): ' "The Self" ', *Journal of Consciousness Studies*, 4: 405–28.

——(1999): 'The Impossibility of Moral Responsibility', reprinted in Pojman and McLeod (1999).

STRAWSON, P. F. (1959): *Individuals*, London: Methuen.

——(1974): *Freedom and Resentment and Other Essays*, London: Methuen.

——(1980): 'Reply to Ayer and Bennett', in van Straaten (1980).

SUMNER, L. W. (1987): *The Moral Foundation of Rights*, Oxford: Oxford UP.

——(1996): *Welfare, Happiness and Ethics*, Oxford: Oxford UP.

SWINBURNE, RICHARD (1985): 'Desire', *Philosophy*, 60: 429–45.

TAYLOR, GABRIELE (1985): *Pride, Shame and Guilt*, Oxford: Clarendon Press.

TAYLOR, RICHARD (1966): *Agent and Purpose*, Englewood Cliffs, NJ: Prentice-Hall.

——(1982): 'Agent and Patient', *Erkenntnis*, 18: 223–32.

TELFER, ELIZABETH (1980): *Happiness*, London and Basingstoke: Macmillan.

THOMSON, JUDITH JARVIS (1990): *The Realm of Rights*, Cambridge, Mass.: Harvard UP.

THORP, JOHN (1980): *Free Will*, London: Routledge & Kegan Paul.

TOLSTOY, LEO (1940): *A Confession*, World Classics, London and New York: Oxford UP.

TRIGG, ROGER (1970): *Pain and Emotion*, Oxford: Clarendon Press.

TYE, MICHAEL (2003): *Consciousness and Persons*, Cambridge, Mass.: MIT Press.

UNGER, PETER (1986): 'Consciousness and Self-Identity', *Midwest Studies in Philosophy*, 10.

——(1990): *Identity, Consciousness and Value*, Oxford: Clarendon Press.

VELLEMAN, J. DAVID (1988): 'Brandt's Definition of "Good" ', *Philosophical Review*, 97: 353–71.

——(1996a): 'Self to Self', *Philosophical Review*, 105: 39–76.

VELLEMAN, J. DAVID (1996b): 'The Possibility of Practical Reason', *Ethics*, 106: 694–726.

——(2000): *The Possibility of Practical Reason*, Oxford: Clarendon Press.

WACHSBERG, MILTON (1983): 'Personal Identity: The Nature of Persons and Ethical Theory', Ph.D. diss., Princeton University.

WALDRON, JEREMY (1988): The Right to Private Property, Oxford: Clarendon Press.

WALLACE, R. JAY (1994): Responsibility and the Moral Sentiments, Cambridge, Mass.: Harvard UP.

WARNER, RICHARD (1980): 'Enjoyment', Philosophical Review, 89: 507–26.

——(1987): Freedom, Enjoyment and Happiness, Ithaca, NY, and London: Cornell UP.

WATSON, GARY (1975): 'Free Agency', Journal of Philosophy, 72: 205–20.

——(1977): 'Skepticism about Weakness of Will', Philosophical Review, 84: 316–39.

——(1987): 'Free Action and Free Will', Mind, 96: 143–72.

WHITING, JENNIFER (1986): 'Friends and Future Selves', Philosophical Review, 95: 547–80.

WIGGINS, DAVID (1980): Sameness and Substance, Oxford: Blackwell.

WILKES, KATHLEEN (1988): Real People, Oxford: Clarendon Press.

WILLIAMS, BERNARD (1973): Problems of the Self, Cambridge: Cambridge UP.

——(1981): Moral Luck, Cambridge: Cambridge UP.

——(1993): Shame and Necessity, Berkeley: University of California Press.

WILSON, J. R. S. (1972): Emotion and Object, Cambridge: Cambridge UP.

WOLF, SUSAN (1981): 'The Importance of Free Will', Mind, 90: 386–405.

——(1982): 'Moral Saints', Journal of Philosophy, 79: 419–39.

——(1986): 'Self-Interest and Interest in Selves', Ethics, 96: 704–20.

——(1990): Freedom within Reason, Oxford: Clarendon Press.

WRIGHT, ROBERT (1994): The Moral Animal, New York: Pantheon Books.

YOUNG, P. T. (1961): Motivation and Emotion, New York and London: John Wiley & Sons.

ZEMACH, EDDY (1987): 'Looking Out for Number One', Philosophy and Phenomenological Research, 47: 209–33.

ZIMMERMAN, MICHAEL J. (1988): An Essay on Moral Responsibility, Totowa, NJ.: Rowman & Littlefield.

INDEX